Sociolinguistic Variation

Why does human language vary from one person, or one group, to another? In what ways does it vary? How do linguists go about studying variation in, say, the sound system or the sentence structure of a particular language? Why is the study of language variation important outside the academic world, in say education, the law, employment, or housing? This book provides an overview of these questions, bringing together a team of experts to survey key areas within the study of language variation and language change. Covering both the range of methods used to research variation in language, and the applications of such research to a variety of social contexts, it is essential reading for advanced students and researchers in sociolinguistics, communication, linguistic anthropology, and applied linguistics.

ROBERT BAYLEY is Professor in the Department of Linguistics at the University of California, Davis.

CEIL LUCAS is Professor in the Department of Linguistics at Gallaudet University.

Sociolinguistic Variation
Theories, Methods, and Applications

ROBERT BAYLEY

University of California, Davis

CEIL LUCAS

Gallaudet University

CAMBRIDGE
UNIVERSITY PRESS

CAMBRIDGE UNIVERSITY PRESS
Cambridge, New York, Melbourne, Madrid, Cape Town, Singapore, São Paulo, Delhi

Cambridge University Press
The Edinburgh Building, Cambridge CB2 8RU, UK

Published in the United States of America by Cambridge University Press, New York

www.cambridge.org
Information on this title: www.cambridge.org/9780521691819

First published 2007

Printed in the United Kingdom at the University Press, Cambridge

A catalogue record for this publication is available from the British Library

ISBN 978-0-521-87127-3 hardback
ISBN 978-0-521-69181-9 paperback

To Walt Wolfram

"And gladly wolde he lerne and gladly teche"

Contents

Figures

* Reproduced with permission from Gallaudet University Press.

Tables

Acknowledgments

The editors gratefully acknowledge the usual assistance of their institutions in providing appropriate homes for academic activity, even the editing of others' work. We thank especially Michael Montgomery, who approached us with the idea for a volume dedicated to Walt Wolfram, and Andrew Winnard of Cambridge University Press for his contributions to shaping a volume that would not only serve as a tribute to our friend and colleague, but that would be useful to the field as a whole. Jodie Barnes and Sarah Parker of Cambridge University Press assisted greatly with production and we thank them for their contributions. We also thank Adrian and Helen Stenton for expert copy editing. Thanks also to Marge Wolfram and Tyler Kendall for answering numerous queries.

The contributors to this volume constitute a distinguished roster of sociolinguists from several generations. We thank them all for their timely contributions and for the willingness and good-humor with which they responded to our requests. Finally, we thank Ann Robinson and Stephen Brown, who continue to support all our endeavors.

Chapter 13 is from A. F. Vaughn-Cooke. 1999. Lessons learned from the Ebonics controversy – Implications for language assessment. In C. T. Adger, D. Christian, and O. Taylor (eds.), *Making the connection: Language and academic achievement among African American students*. Washington, DC and McHenry, IL: Center for Applied Linguistics and Delta Systems. 137–168. Reprinted with permission.

Editors and contributors

ROBERT BAYLEY is Professor of Linguistics at the University of California, Davis. His publications include *Second Language Acquisition and Linguistic Variation* (ed. with Dennis Preston, 1996), *Sociolinguistic Variation in ASL* (with Ceil Lucas and Clayton Valli, 2001), *Language as Cultural Practice* (with Sandra R. Schecter, 2002), and *Language Socialization in Bilingual and Multilingual Societies* (ed. with Sandra R. Schecter, 2003).

CEIL LUCAS is Professor of Linguistics at Gallaudet University in Washington, DC. Her recent publications include *The Sociolinguistics of Sign Languages* (2001), *What's Your Sign For PIZZA? An Introduction to Variation in ASL* (with Robert Bayley and Clayton Valli, 2003), *Language and the Law in Deaf Communities* (2003), *The Linguistics of American Sign Language*, 4th ed. (with Clayton Valli and Kristin Mulrooney, 2005), and *Multilingualism and Sign Languages: From the Great Plains to Australia* (2006).

Contributors

CAROLYN TEMPLE ADGER directs the Language in Society Division at the Center for Applied Linguistics in Washington, DC, where she focuses on language diversity in educational settings. Her publications include *Kids Talk: Strategic Language Use in Later Childhood* (ed. with Susan Hoyle, 1998) and *Dialects in Schools and Communities* (with Walt Wolfram and Donna Christian,1999).

JOHN BAUGH is Margaret Bush Wilson Professor of Psychology and Director of African and African American Studies at Washington University in St. Louis. His publications include *Out of the Mouths of Slaves: African American Language and Educational Malpractice* (1999) and *Beyond Ebonics: Linguistic Pride and Racial Prejudice* (2000).

ALLAN BELL is Professor and Director of the Center for Communication Research at Auckland University of Technology (New Zealand). He is the author of *The Language of News Media* (1991) and the editor of *Approaches to Media Discourse* (with Peter Garrett, 1998) and *New Zealand English* (with Koenraad Kuiper, 1999).

RONALD R. BUTTERS is Professor of English and Cultural Anthropology at Duke University, where he has taught since 1967. He co-chairs (with Walt Wolfram of North Carolina State University) the inter-institutional doctoral program in sociolinguistics.

His current research interests are lexicography, American English, and language and law, especially trademarks.

DONNA CHRISTIAN is President of the Center for Applied Linguistics in Washington, DC. She has written on issues related to language in education, including co-authored or co-edited volumes on *Bilingual Education* (1997), *Dialects, Schools, and Communities* (with Carolyn Adger and Walt Wolfram, 1999), and *Educating English Language Learners: A Synthesis of Research Evidence* (2006).

RALPH W. FASOLD is Professor Emeritus of Linguistics at Georgetown University. He is an expert in formal and functional explanation in syntax, language policy, language maintenance and shift, syntax and sociolinguistics of Ebonics. His publications include *The Sociolinguistics of Society* (1987), *The Sociolinguistics of Language* (1990), and *An Introduction to Language and Linguistics* (2006).

LISA GREEN is Associate Professor of Linguistics at the University of Massachusetts. She teaches courses on syntax, syntactic variation, socio-syntactic approaches, linguistics and education, and English dialects. She is the author of *African American English: A Linguistic Introduction* (2002) and book chapters and journal articles on topics in syntax and dialects of English.

GREGORY R. GUY is Professor of Linguistics at New York University. He previously taught at Stanford, Cornell, Temple, Sydney, and York University. His publications include *Towards a Social Science of Language* (1998) and several papers in *Language Variation and Change* dealing with variation and phonological theory. He is also co-author of *Análise Quantitative em Sociolingüística* (2007).

KIRK HAZEN is Associate Professor of English at West Virginia University. He specializes in variationist sociolinguistics and his interests include Appalachian English, African American English, and varieties of Southern US English. His teaching goal, for both classes and the public, is to foster better understanding of language variation.

MICHAEL MONTGOMERY is Distinguished Professor Emeritus of Linguistics and English at the University of South Carolina. He has written widely on the history of American English in two general areas: (1) the American South and Appalachia; and (2) colonial American English and its transatlantic connections with Ireland and Scotland. His recent publications include *The Dictionary of Smoky Mountain English* (with Joseph S. Hall, 2004) and *From Ulster to America: The Scotch-Irish Heritage of American English* (2004).

DENNIS R. PRESTON is University Distinguished Professor of English at Michigan State University. His work focuses on sociolinguistics, dialectology, ethnography, and minority language and variety education. His most recent book-length publications are *Folk Linguistics* (with Nancy Niedzielski, 2000), *A Handbook of Perceptual Dialectology*, Vol. II (with Daniel Long, 2002), and *Needed Research in American Dialects* (2003).

ANGELA E. RICKFORD is Associate Professor of Education at San José State University. Her publications include *I Can Fly: Teaching Narratives and Reading Comprehension to African American and Other Ethnic Minority Students* (1999), and numerous articles, including "Techniques for Teaching Reading and Writing to Struggling Secondary Education Students," *Language Learner* (September/October 2006).

JOHN R. RICKFORD is Professor of Linguistics at Stanford University. His books include *Dimensions of a Creole Continuum* (1987), *African American Vernacular English* (1999), *Spoken Soul* (with Russell Rickford, 2000), *Style and Sociolinguistic Variation* (ed. with Penelope Eckert, 2001), and *Language in the USA: Themes for the 21st Century* (ed. with Ed Finegan, 2004).

NATALIE SCHILLING-ESTES is Associate Professor of Linguistics at Georgetown University. Her publications include *The Handbook of Language Variation and Change* (with J. K. Chambers and Peter Trudgill, 2002) and *American English: Dialects and Variation*, 2nd ed. (with Walt Wolfram, 2006).

ROGER W. SHUY is Distinguished Research Professor of Linguistics, Emeritus, at Georgetown University, where he created and headed the sociolinguistics program for thirty years. His recent books include *Language Crimes* (1996), *Bureaucratic Language in Government and Business* (1998), *The Language of Confession, Interrogation and Deception* (1998), *Linguistic Battles in Trademark Disputes* (2002), *Creating Language Crimes: How Law Enforcement Uses and Abuses Language* (2005), and *Linguistics in the Courtroom: A Practical Guide* (2006).

IDA J. STOCKMAN is Professor in the Colleges of Communication and Education at Michigan State University. Over the past twenty-five years, she has published research articles and book chapters related to African American children's spoken language and used their normative data to create least biased assessment procedures for identifying those with language disorders. Stockman is a Fellow of the American Speech-Language-Hearing Association and has received the Distinguished Faculty Award from Michigan State University.

SALI A. TAGLIAMONTE is Associate Professor of Linguistics at the University of Toronto. She is the author of *African American English in the Diaspora* (with Shana Poplack, 2001) and *Analysing Sociolinguistic Variation* (2006) as well as numerous articles on North American and British dialects in journals such as the *Journal of Sociolinguistics* and *Language Variation and Change*.

ERIK R. THOMAS is an Associate Professor in Linguistics at North Carolina State University. His works include *An Acoustic Analysis of Vowel Variation in New World English* (2001) and *The Development of African American English* (with Walt Wolfram, 2002). He has recently worked on recognition of African American speech and on Mexican American prosody.

A. FAY VAUGHN-COOKE is Professor at the University of Maryland Eastern Shore (UMES). She was the Vice President for Academic Affairs at UMES, Dean of the School of Graduate Studies and Research at Florida A&M University, and Chairperson of the Department of Languages and Communication Disorders at the University of the District of Columbia. She has received numerous grants from Federal agencies to support her research and projects in sociolinguistics, language acquisition, and language.

Introduction

ROBERT BAYLEY AND CEIL LUCAS

Beginning with the pioneering work of Labov, Shuy, Fasold, and Wolfram in the mid and late 1960s, the study of variation has formed one of the key areas, if not the key area, of sociolinguistics. Alone among the various sociolinguistic subfields, the study of variation has been enriched by two regular conferences – New Ways of Analyzing Variation (NWAV), now in its 36th year, and, beginning in 2001, the International Conference on Language Variation in Europe (ICLaVE) – as well as by its own journal, *Language Variation and Change*. In recent years, conferences on language variation have also been held in England (VIEW 1998, VIEW 2000), and a sociolinguistics laboratory dedicated to the study of linguistic variation has been established at Nanjing University in China. Moreover, although the study of variation began with a focus on varieties of English, French, and Spanish, variationist studies now encompass many languages ranging from Guyanese and Jamaican Creoles to Brazilian Portuguese to Chinese to American Sign Language and Australian Sign Language. Variationist approaches have also met with considerable success in studies of second language acquisition. However, despite the prominence of variationist studies in North American sociolinguistics and, increasingly, in other areas of the world, most widely used textbooks in sociolinguistics devote only a chapter or two to the study of variation. Only one textbook in sociolinguistics, Chambers (2002), is devoted primarily to variation.

This volume brings together a group of contributors widely recognized for their contributions to variationist sociolinguistics with the purpose of providing accessible overviews of the major areas of concern for students of linguistic variation. And while the chapters in this volume make it very clear that we have come a very long way in over forty years of variationist studies, they also demonstrate that three fundamental facts about variationist studies remain constant: that the variation observed in real language use is systematic and its analysis can directly inform a number of theoretical frameworks about human language use; that the development of the study of real language use has been accompanied by the development of sophisticated methods of data collection and analysis tailored to the requirements of the study of variation; and that variationist studies have very frequently received their impetus from real human situations in the areas of education, employment, and the law, and that the results of variationist studies have had very tangible and important applications in all of these areas.

In the section of the volume on theory, variation is described as it has been studied in the areas of phonology (Guy), syntax (Green, Fasold and Preston), and style (Bell). In addition, a historical perspective on the study of variation is provided (Hazen) and variation as it pertains to historical linguistics (Montgomery) and second language acquisition (Bayley) is also examined. Finally, the role of language modality in variation is considered, with a comparison of spoken and sign language studies (Lucas).

The chapters in the methods section provide clear and comprehensive introductions to fieldwork methods for the study of variation (Schilling-Estes), to methods of quantitative analysis (Tagliamonte), and to the study of sociophonetics (Thomas).

The chapters in the applications section provide a powerful demonstration of the kind of wide impact that variationist studies can have on education (Adger and Christian, Vaughn-Cooke, Rickford and Rickford), language acquisition (Stockman), the law (Butters), and linguistic profiling (Baugh). The volume concludes with an essay by Roger Shuy, one of the founding figures of sociolinguistics, on Walt Wolfram, a scholar who has contributed directly or indirectly to nearly all of the areas covered in this book.

The important connection in variationist studies between theory, methods, and applications reflected in this volume has consistently shaped and informed the work of Walt Wolfram, to whom the volume is dedicated. All of the contributors to this volume worked very enthusiastically to produce a fitting tribute to our excellent colleague, teacher, and friend.

PART 1

Theories

1 Variation and phonological theory

GREGORY R. GUY

Introduction

The study of linguistic variation is often perceived to be quintessentially engaged with phonological phenomena. This is a manifest misperception: variationist work on morphosyntactic issues began with the original foundational articles that launched the "variable rule" framework (Labov [1969] on the English copula, and Labov [1972d] on negative concord), and continues to be among the most active areas in the field. But it is instructive to consider *why* such a misperception persists. There are two factors that drive this view. First, there exists an almost prescriptive attitude that phonology is the only domain in which linguists *should* speak of variation, arising from an uneasy suspicion that any alternations found at other levels of linguistic structure might involve intentional differences in meaning. In Labov's informal definition, variation involves "different ways of saying the same thing," and for most linguists it is easy to conclude that *runnin'* and *running* are different versions of the "same thing," but rather worrisome to make the same claim about *Kyle got arrested* and *Kyle was arrested*. Hence the view that variationists tidily confine their labors to the vineyard of phonology alleviates this existential angst about the status of morphosyntactic variation.

But a second, more interesting, reason for this view is that it is indeed quite true that work on phonological variation has been deeply intertwined with phonological theory. Phonological variation in all languages is massively structured and orderly; there is a random component, such that the surface realization of a given utterance cannot be predicted categorically, but the patterns of realizations in particular contexts are probabilistically structured with great regularity – particular realizations are strongly favored by particular phonological contexts. Most of these patterns of contextual constraints on phonological variables find clear explanation in principles of phonological organization; in other words, phonological theory can (and should) explain the variable aspects of phonology along with the categorical facts. And this relationship, as with all scientific theories, is reciprocal and reinforcing: the evidence from phonological variation has been brought to bear on a variety of theoretical questions in phonology. This includes quantitative evidence and quantitative argumentation, approaches which were historically uncommon and unfamiliar in phonological theory, but which are becoming increasingly evident in recent years (cf. for example, the work of Anttila [1997] and Kiparsky [in press] on partial constraint rankings, and of Boersma and Hayes on Stochastic Optimality Theory [Boersma 2003, Boersma and Hayes 2001]). In this respect, work on phonological variation is comparable to the development of laboratory phonology, in that it provides new kinds of data to inform and illuminate the development of phonological theory.

This chapter explores the reciprocal, mutually illuminating relation between phonological variation and phonological theory. First, we will consider some examples of how theory contributes to explaining the data; in particular, we will see how the linguistic constraints evident in phonological variation are consistently interpretable in terms of the principles and mechanisms proposed in phonological theory. Second, we will examine some of the ways that variation data has contributed to clarifying or even resolving theoretical issues in phonology. Finally, we will discuss the general theoretical question of how to best construct a theory that models both the variable and invariant facts about the sound systems of human language, and hence explains how language can be both discrete and continuous in its organization.

Explaining the patterns: what phonological theory does for the study of variation

The fundamental observation of research on linguistic variation is that it displays, in the words of Weinreich, Labov, and Herzog (1968), "orderly heterogeneity"; in other words, the alternating variants occur in probabilistically regular patterns, not in a random distribution. These orderly patterns exhibit social regularities (e.g. higher status speakers always use more of the socially highly valued variants), which are discussed elsewhere in this volume. Our focus here is on the linguistic regularities that are also apparent. These take the form of contextual conditioning: certain linguistic contexts favor the occurrence of particular variants. Thus phonological reduction processes, if sensitive to stress, typically occur more often in unstressed syllables, assimilation processes typically occur more often word-internally than across word boundaries, and vocalization of sonorants occurs more often in coda positions than onsets. Such results are unsurprising. To a phonologist, none of the examples just cited contravenes any theoretical principle, while all of them resemble numerous cases involving categorical alternations. The central observation here is that variable processes display the same patterns of occurrence and non-occurrence that are found for categorical alternations, and hence are likely governed by the same principles and generated by the same processes of grammar. Since alternations are what phonological theories have classically been designed to account for, we can reasonably expect that extant theories incorporate explanatory principles and generalizations about linguistic structure that are relevant to variable alternations.

As an example, consider the patterns of alternation between occurrence and non-occurrence of word-final consonants. We find many cases of categorical alternation, such as French liaison, where a consonant is articulated at the ends of given words when the following word in the utterance begins with a vowel, but is absent when the next word begins with a consonant. Such cases are typically described in phonological theory as involving an underlying consonant that is suppressed under certain conditions that would be phonologically infelicitous – in this case, when it is in the coda – but retained in more favorable conditions, e.g. when it can be syllabified as an onset. In the terminology of Optimality Theory, a markedness constraint like *Coda outweighs considerations of faithfulness to the underlying form.

Parallel patterns showing the same kind of constraint but involving variable rather than categorical conditioning are also easy to find. English (also Dutch) has alternating presence and absence of final coronal stops, and this alternation is affected by whether a following word begins with a vowel or consonant, but the alternation is not categorical. That is, a word like *east* can occur as *eas'* in any following context, but the form with deletion is much more common when there is a following consonant. Thus the pattern is:

> frequent, preferred: *east end   eas' side*
> possible, but rarer: *eas' end   east side*

The generalization is that the language prefers retention before vowels and deletion before consonants. This is the same generalization that could be made about French liaison. The difference between the two cases is that in French, the dispreferred cases are absent, while in English coronal stop deletion they are not entirely absent, but simply occur less often.

This is an example of what has been described as the "stochastic generalization" relating variable and categorical observations in linguistics (Clark 2005:209, Bresnan, Dingare, and Manning 2001). Many of the principles and processes proposed in phonological theory to account for categorical facts are also evident in variable operations, in a probabilistic form. Some principle enunciated on the basis of the observation that in language A, structure X never occurs, turns out in language B to explain why structure X is very rare, although not categorically absent.

In the balance of this section, we consider some examples of how general phonological principles are reflected in the probabilistic distributions found for phonological variation. The exposition focuses on one variable which is typical of the kinds of patterns evident in variable phonology: the alternation in Brazilian Portuguese between presence and absence of word-final sibilants.

Final sibilant deletion in Brazilian Portuguese

In vernacular speech, Brazilian Portuguese shows great variation in the realization of word-final sibilants: words such as *menos* "less, minus" and *ônibus* "bus" are,

Table 1.1 *Constraints on final sibilant deletion in Brazilian Portuguese (Data from Guy 1981)*

Factor	N	% deleted	Factor weight
Word stress			
Stressed monosyllable	7504	6	.24
Stressed polysyllable	1375	10	.34
Unstressed	1392	53	.86
Following segment			
Vowel	3625	8	.40
Consonant	4876	16	.60
Voicing of following consonant			
−voice	2270	9	.42
+voice	2606	21	.58
Place of following consonant			
Labial	1600	14	.53
Alveolar	2240	21	.66
Velar	1036	6	.31
TOTAL	10271	13	−

for many speakers, more often realized as *meno*, *ônibu* without the final conso-nant. This variation is subject to a number of constraints, which are illustrated in Table 1.1.

These data raise basic linguistic questions: why do we find these patterns, and not others? Why do these contexts have the observed effects? These are the kinds of issues that phonological theory is intended to answer. Let us consider each constraint in turn.

Stress

Word stress is found to condition phonological operations and distribution in virtu-ally every language that has a stress contrast. The direction of effect observed here is that stressed syllables have greater retention (i.e. are more faithful to underlying form), while unstressed syllables are more congenial to deletion. This is consis-tent with theories of prosody, positional prominence, etc., and with categorical alternations in many languages. It is also consistent with diachronic principles: in language change, stressed positions are more resistant to lenition and deletion processes.

Following segment

Increased rates of deletion in preconsonantal contexts are widely observed in variation studies. The theoretical explanation for this lies in principles of syllable structure. A word-final consonant resides underlyingly in coda position, which is universally marked and disfavored. Theories of syllable structure state this in various ways; thus, CV phonology (Clements and Keyser 1983) treats CV as the universally unmarked syllable type, while Optimality Theory postulates NoCoda as part of the universal inventory of phonological constraints. So coda deletion is an expected repair, and a common diachronic change. However, a following vowel licenses the consonant as an onset, which is an optimal position for retention. Word-internally in Portuguese, as in many other languages, prevocalic consonants are obligatorily syllabified rightwards, as onsets. Across word boundaries, this is optional, and the outcomes are variable.

Voicing of following consonant

The data show appreciably more deletion before voiced than voiceless consonants. A theoretical explanation of this result requires one additional observation about Brazilian Portuguese. Voicing of sibilants is not phonemically distinctive in coda position; hence final sibilants assimilate obligatorily to the voicing of a following segment. The pattern shown here therefore reduces to the generalization that voiced fricatives are deleted more than voiceless ones, which has a ready explanation in markedness. Voiced fricatives are universally more marked than their voiceless counterparts; they are also typologically rarer, and raise aerodynamic problems in articulation, since the glottal impedance associated with voicing reduces the airflow required to generate the turbulence of frication.

Place of following consonant

The figures in the table indicate a robust effect of the place of a following consonant, with highest deletion rates before an alveolar, second highest before a labial, and least deletion before a velar. This is a clear example of the Obligatory Contour Principle (OCP), which states that adjacent identical elements are dispreferred. It was first proposed in phonological theory to account for the avoidance in tonal languages of sequences of adjacent identical tones, but it has been generalized to phonological processes that avoid adjacent identical segments and features (cf. Yip 1988).

As the name implies, the OCP was originally postulated to account for obligatory, categorical phenomena, but numerous gradient or variable phenomena also confirm a general preference for "contoured" sequences (where adjacent elements are dissimilar) over "level" sequences where adjacent elements are identical or similar. For example, Guy and Boberg (1997) found that English coronal stop deletion shows an OCP effect of the preceding consonant: there is more deletion after segments that are phonologically similar to the targeted /t,d/, i.e. those that share more features. Thus deletion is favored by preceding stops (e.g. *act, apt* – same in continuancy and obstruency) and alveolar fricatives (*last* – same in place and obstruency), but disfavored by preceding liquids (*cold, hard*) and labial fricatives (*left*), which share fewer features with the target.

The place data in Table 1.1 show essentially the same pattern. A conventional distinctive feature treatment of place contrasts velar, alveolar, and labial in terms of several features, as in the following matrix:

	[coronal]	[back]
labial	−	−
alveolar	+	−
velar	−	+

In this treatment, alveolar place shares one feature with labial place, but none with velar. Hence the deletion target, a coronal sibilant, is most similar in place to a following coronal consonant (like t,d,n), partially similar to labials (p,b,m), and most different from velars (k,g). The deletion facts in Table 1.1 follow this cline of similarity, implying that they are governed by a Contour Principle that is not obligatory, but probabilistic.

Constructing the theory: what variation does for phonological theory

The above examples illustrate the explanatory value of phonological theory for the analysis of variation. Now we turn to the utility of variation data for the evaluation and construction of phonological theory. As with any data, evidence of variation can be used in several ways: it can provide empirical tests of theoretical issues, it can confirm or deny the predictions of theoretical models, or it can provide facts that theory must account for. But the greatest theoretical significance of the study of phonological variation is that it has the potential to resolve theoretical issues that cannot be addressed by other means. Categorical alternations lack nuance: given a defining set of conditions, they abruptly select a single outcome. But the continuous frequency ranges of phonological variables, displaying sensitivity to a number of features of the context, offer a subtler analytical tool that can probe more finely into phonological structure. In this section I will offer an extended example of how variation data provide a unique empirical test of a theoretical issue in phonology: the treatment of lexical exceptions to phonological processes.

Phonological theory is centrally concerned with identifying generalizations about sound systems and hypothesizing mental grammatical structures that explain why and how those generalizations come about. Generative and post-generative models of phonology typically assume a bipartite architecture consisting of a phonological component, in which the generalizations are captured, and a lexicon, which lists the ungeneral, specific characteristics of individual words. For example, in the word *act*, the fact that the coda cluster /kt/ shows a constant value for the feature [−voice] throughout, and has the /k/ preceding, rather than following, the /t/, are general features of English phonology, but the fact that the vowel is /æ/ rather than /ey/ or /iy/ is one of the distinctive properties of this lexical item that distinguish it from *ached*, *eked*, and other words of English. The basic organizing principle is: general properties = phonology, specific properties = lexicon.

The problem that arises, however, is that there are many phonological generalizations that do not apply to the entire lexicon; rather, some lexical items are exceptional in certain respects when compared to most other words in the language. Thus English shows a vowel laxing alternation in *serene–serenity, obscene–obscenity*, but not in *obese–obesity*. Also, in Philadelphia English, the vowel /æ/ is tense before tautosyllabic anterior nasals and fricatives (hence tense *man, mansion, ham, hamster, half, after*, vs. lax *hang, hammer, planet, scaffold, have, that, sad, sack*, etc.); however, *mad, bad, glad* are tense despite the following /d/ (cf. lax *sad, Dad, had, fad*, etc.). How are such cases to be accounted for?

Although the theoretical literature on lexical exceptions has focused on categorical alternations, the same issue also arises in phonological variation. There it takes the form of lexical items that undergo certain processes at an exceptional rate, compared to other words of comparable structure. For example, the word *and* is produced without a final stop far more often than phonologically similar words like *hand* or *band*. So an adequate phonology of variation faces the same problems confronted by a categorical phonology.

Given the phonology-with-lexicon architecture, there are just two ways that lexical exceptions have been handled without dropping the generalization from the phonology. First, exception features can be attached to lexical items to co-index them with phonological processes; this is the mechanism suggested by Chomsky and Halle (1968). A lexical item that fails to undergo rule n can be annotated in the lexicon with a feature [−rule n]; similarly, a set of lexical items that undergo some rule m that other words do not can be annotated with a feature [+rule m]. Second, the exceptional outcomes can be directly represented in the underlying representation of the exceptional words, preempting the phonological processes that would otherwise apply or fail to apply.

These two approaches to lexical exceptionality have survived the theoretical shift in phonology from rules to constraint-based formalisms. Optimality-theoretic treatments of exceptionality use the same two strategies, relying either on preemptive structural marking of underlying representations or on lexically-specific constraints that apply only to co-indexed lexical items (cf. Pater and Coetzee 2005). It therefore appears that the roots of these approaches lie in the dichotomous architecture of phonology vs. lexicon – one repository for general facts, one for particular facts. The existence of exceptions implies that there are "generalizations" that are only partially true, i.e. partly general and partly specific. The dichotomy between phonology and lexicon therefore gives us two choices. We can focus on the supralexical generality of the pattern, thus retaining the phonological mechanisms that would capture it (whether they are rules, representations, or constraints), but delimiting their lexical scope by means of exception features; this is the "phonological" approach. Or, we can focus on the particularity of the exceptions by writing them directly into the lexical representations, thereby preempting the phonological mechanisms from accounting for them; this is the "lexical" approach.

The question for phonological theory is: which of these approaches is prefer-able, or in some sense "superior"? Chomsky and Halle had a formal algorithm for answering this question based on economy: write a rule whenever it saves more features than it costs. But it's not clear that language and mind work on so strict a parsimony principle. Empirical evidence is often unhelpful in deciding this issue, because the two analyses end up making the same predictions. Thus the Philadelphia /æ/ example could be treated either way: an exception-feature treatment would assign *mad*, *bad*, *glad* a diacritic to indicate that they undergo /æ/-tensing, and a lexical treatment would simply mark these words as tense in the lexicon. So the issue has remained undecided through four decades of theoretical development in phonology.

Happily, quantitative evidence from phonological variation offers the prospect of an empirical test of the two approaches. The examples discussed above are undecidable partly because of their lexically categorical nature: a given word either is or is not an exception to some phonological generalization, so there is no possibility of interaction with other conditions that might clarify the question. But variable processes, as we have seen, typically are strongly conditioned by features of the context. If these contextual conditions are equally present in exceptional and unexceptional words, this would suggest that all words are operated on by the phonology, hence an exception-feature analysis. If, however, the exceptional words show different conditioning from the non-exceptional, it would suggest that the exceptions are not undergoing the phonological processes in the same way as other words, hence favoring a lexical analysis in which the exceptions have distinct underlying representations.

Consequently, for certain cases of lexical exceptionality in variable processes, the two approaches make different quantitative predictions, which can be empir-ically tested in a suitable mathematical model. I will illustrate using the familiar variable rule (VR) framework (cf. Chapter 10 of this volume for an extended discussion), but other mathematical models should yield comparable results.

To see how this works, consider the case of English *and,* which is observed to have an exceptionally high rate of absence of the final coronal stop. In a phonological (exception-feature approach), *and* is indexed with a feature that tells the deletion process to raise the probability of affecting this word. This is easily represented in the VR model by associating the word with a factor weight that captures the effect of that particular word on the probability of occurrence of the variable. This lexically specific factor weight for *and* would have a value greater than .5, which in the variable rule model would boost the probability of deletion in this word above the rate experienced by words lacking such an exception feature.

In the lexical approach, however, the exceptionality of *and* is captured by an alternative underlying representation lacking the final -*d*: i.e. *an'*. I submit that this is what is implied by the common orthographic device of spelling *'n'* in phrases like *rock 'n' roll*, an orthographic recognition of this mental representation. In this approach, speakers have two mental representations for this word: when they select underlying *and*, it undergoes deletion at the same rate as other words, like *band* and *land*, yielding the expected proportions of full and deleted forms. But sometimes speakers will select the underlying form *an'*; in this case the deletion rule is irrelevant and the word will always surface without the final /d/. What we observe on the surface is thus the sum of two different pathways to /d/ absence, with the mathematical effect of boosting the observed cases of missing /-d/s in this word. If, for example, a speaker with a 30% coronal stop deletion rate also selected the exceptional *an'* representation half the time, they would have a surface rate of absent -*d* of 65% in this word, composed of the 50% of tokens derived from underlying *an'*, plus the usual 30% deletion of the other 50% of tokens derived from underlying *and* (30% of 50% equals an additional 15% of the corpus).

This is crucially relevant to deciding the theoretical issue at hand because the two analyses are *not* mathematically symmetrical! Rather, they make different predictions with respect to how they interact with other constraints on the variable process. The phonological or exception-feature approach predicts that other constraints on the process should be entirely independent of the status of lexical items, while the lexical approach predicts the other constraints should be attenuated or nullified in a set of observations. (Note that a variationist study of this problem must rely on a corpus rather than single cases. For any single utterance we cannot say whether it was selected from the lexicon or generated by the phonology. But in a quantitative analysis of optional processes, we can often find statistical regularities in a *corpus* of utterances that allow us to draw inferences about what is going on. This is the method that is relevant to the present example.)

The independence of linguistic constraints has been confirmed by most of the research in the variationist framework, so it is the default expectation for lexical exceptions. Independence in this sense means that the effect of one constraint is evident and proportionally constant regardless of what other constraints are operative in a given case. Thus the constraints on English coronal stop deletion mentioned above – the OCP effect (more deletion after a preceding coronal segment, and less after a non-coronal, hence, more deletion in *west* than *left*) – and the following segment effect (more deletion before a following word beginning with a consonant than a vowel) show this relationship: phrases with following consonants but differing OCP values like *west side* and *left side* both display more deletion, by proportionately the same amount, than phrases with following vowels like *west end* and *left end*, while at the same time, words like *west* (that reflect OCP avoidance of double-coronal sequences) have proportionately more deletion in all phrasal contexts, in comparison with words like *left* (with no OCP effect).

In a VR analysis, therefore, an exception feature should work just like any other contextual constraint. A word that came with such a feature, like *and*, would experience an independent adjustment in its probability of deletion in comparison with other words, *but the effect of other contextual features will continue to operate at the same magnitude!* Thus we would predict that *and* followed by a vowel should show the same reduction in deletion as *west, left,* or *land* followed by a vowel, vis-a-vis the same words followed by consonants. Hence, *ham and eggs* should have less deletion than *cheese and crackers*, in the same proportion as *second effort* compared with *second son*. In this approach, all other contextual effects should be constant across exceptional and non-exceptional words.

However, the lexical approach makes a quite different quantitative prediction. Under this hypothesis, whenever a speaker selects underlying *an'* without the final -*d*, such tokens never undergo deletion, and so show *no* effect of contextual constraints. Hence one should be just as likely to say *ham 'n' eggs* as *cheese 'n' crackers*. Intuitively, I feel that this is correct. Retaining the -d in *ham and eggs* sounds overly precise.

However, since speakers do occasionally pronounce a /d/ in *and*, even if rarely, they must still have an underlying representation that retains a final -d; when this form is selected, coronal stop deletion can still apply, in which case the contextual constraints on the process will still operate. Therefore, the surface corpus is actually a composite of two data sets produced by different derivational pathways; one in which contextual effects are evident and one in which they are not. The statistical effect of this conjunction will be to weaken the apparent contextual effects in the observed corpus, because they apply to only some of the words in the corpus, not all. Selection of -d-less allomorphs acts as statistical noise in the corpus, attenuating the statistical evidence for the external constraint effect.

Therefore, phonological variables with lexical exceptions offer straightforward empirical tests of the two approaches. If speakers' grammars use exception features, they should have the same magnitude of constraint effects for exceptional and unexceptional words, but if their mental grammars rely on alternative lexical entries for exceptional words, these should exhibit surface attenuation of the effects of contextual constraints.

Quantitative testing of phonological theory

As it happens, there are several phonological variables described in the literature that are known to have lexical exceptions and can provide testing sites for this theoretical problem. As a first example, we return to the case discussed above of final sibilant deletion in popular Brazilian Portuguese. The general alternation between presence and absence of -s is systematic across the lexicon: all words with final -s enter into it, and virtually all show the same contextual effects seen in Table 1.1. Hence, the straightforward analysis is to postulate the alternation as a general pattern belonging to the phonology. The relevant words appear in the lexicon with underlying final -s, while surface presence or absence of -s is governed by a phonological process. In a generative phonology this is a variable -s deletion rule; in an Optimality Theoretic approach, this is captured by a version of the NoCoda constraint, like *–S##, which is variably ordered with respect to an appropriate faithfulness constraint and the constraints that capture the contextual effects.

Table 1.2 *Final -s deletion in Brazilian Portuguese: Following context effects and lexical exceptionality (factor weights; data from five cities in VARSUL corpus)*

Features of following consonant		Non-exceptional words		Lexical exceptions (-*mos* forms)	
Voice/Manner	sonorant	.69		.49	
	voiced obstruent	.44		.58	
	voiceless obstruent	.36		.44	
Range			.33		.14
Place	labial	.32		.58	
	coronal	.61		.53	
	velar	.44		.39	
Range			.29		.19
N		5880		1225	
Log likelihood		− 704.8		− 791.5	

For present purposes, the most relevant contextual constraints are those that are external to the lexicon, the following context. We focus on two of them: the *place* and the *voicing/manner* of following consonants. The place effect is OCP-like, with *more* deletion of -s before another coronal consonant, less deletion when the following consonant has a different place. The voicing effect is presented here in more detail than in Table 1.1: the deletion-promoting voiced segments are here broken down into sonorants and obstruents, with the result that sonorants favor deletion more than voiced obstruents, with the least deletion occurring before voiceless obstruents.

Previous studies have demonstrated that these constraints affect the lexicon as a whole. But recent work on this variable, by myself and colleagues in the VARSUL consortium in southern Brazil, has revealed a significant lexical exception that was not adequately treated in earlier studies. This is the verbal morpheme -*mos*, which marks first person plural: *nós falamos, nós comemos* "we speak, we eat." In running speech in the VARSUL corpus (Zilles 2005), these typically occur without the final -s at a higher rate than other unexceptional final -s words, like *menos* and *ônibus*. So people say *falamo, comemo* more often, relatively speaking, than they say *meno*.

The overall figures on this point are quite striking. The deletion frequency in this corpus for -*mos* forms is 41%, versus only 10% for other unstressed non-inflectional -s (in words like *menos*) and just 2% for stressed -s (e.g. *demais, rapaz*). Accordingly, we ran separate analyses of the -*mos* forms vs. other words, and the results are shown in Table 1.2, organized according to place and manner of following consonant.

For non-exceptional words, the results confirm the findings seen in Table 1.1: for voicing/manner, more deletion before voiced segments, with peak deletion before sonorants, and for place, maximum deletion before other coronals. The magnitude of these effects can be measured by means of the range of values in the factor group from highest to lowest: strong effects should have large ranges, while weak effects have values clustered close to .5, with smaller ranges. In this case, both factor groups have substantial ranges: .33 for voicing/manner and .29 for place.

When we look at the same constraints on the -*mos* words, however, the picture is quite different. First, the generalizations about which contexts are most favorable are both lost. Sonorant is no longer the most favorable voicing category, and remarkably, coronal is not the most favorable place! This is striking, given the systematic evidence for OCP preferences in many phonological processes, both variable and invariant. This is strong evidence of a non-phonological process affecting these data. Now consider the ranges; in both factor groups the range of values has shrunk in the exceptional cases, by a factor of one-third for the place effect, from .29 to .19, and by more than half for the voicing effect, from .33 to .14. The phonological effects appear weakened in these data, suggesting a pre-phonological variable accounts for increased -s absence in -*mos* forms.

Another comparison of the exceptional and non-exceptional cases can be made with the log likelihood (l.l.) statistics – the goodness of fit measure incorporated in the VARBRUL procedure. This is a negative number whose absolute value increases with respect to two parameters: the number of tokens in the corpus, and the goodness of fit between model and data – a worse fit gives a bigger l.l. In these data, the non-exceptional corpus of 5900 words has a l.l. of −705. The lexical exceptions, with a corpus only one-fifth the size (1225 words), show a *larger* l.l., of −792! The fact that non-exceptional words have a smaller l.l., even with many more tokens in the analysis, means they fit the model much better than the exceptional items. The appropriate conclusion is that the exceptional items are not well predicted by purely phonological factors; something else is going on. That "something else," I suggest, is lexical: many verbal plurals lack a final -s in underlying representation, in the input to the phonology; therefore, the phonological context does *not* explain their absence very well.

A second empirical test of the treatment of lexical exceptions comes from Salvadoran Spanish, which also has a final -s deletion process. Hoffman (2004) finds exceptional behavior in several discourse markers that show exceptionally high rates of -s absence, namely *entonces, pues,* and *digamos.* When she analyzed these tokens separately, she found different results for the phonological constraints on the process. The results for two constraints, stress and following segment, are presented in Table 1.3.

The following segment effect parallels the Portuguese case: vowels and voice-less consonants disfavor deletion, but voiced consonants and sonorants favor. But the magnitude of the effect is smaller in lexical exceptions: the range of values is reduced from .42 to .25. The stress effect, in which unstressed tokens favor deletion, also shows a reduction in magnitude in exceptional words, by a factor of one-third. Remember, the exceptional cases show a higher rate of absence overall,

Table 1.3 -s *deletion in Salvadoran Spanish: Stress and following context effects and lexical exceptionality (factor weights; data from Hoffman 2004)*

Factor group	Factor	Non-exceptional words	Lexical exceptions (*entonces, digamos, pues*)
Following context	sononant	.60	.63
	voiced obstruent	.75	.55
	voiceless obstruent	.33	.38
	vowel	.36	.38
	pause	.44	.56
	range	.42	.25
Syllable stress	stressed	.38	.42
	unstressed	.62	.58
	range	.24	.16

so it is not simply the case that effects are attenuated by a lack of evidence. Rather, these results parallel the Portuguese case, suggesting that the increased absence of final segments in the exceptional cases is due to the inclusion of items that are not conditioned by context, because they do not have the final -s present in their underlying representation.

Finally, for a third example, let us return to the case of English *and*. Precisely because of the exceptionality of *and*, there are few published studies that deal with it. Since it was recognized in the earliest work on coronal stop deletion that *and* doesn't behave like other lexical items, the practice was adopted of excluding *and* from studies investigating the general process. But one published study that did look at *and* is Neu (1980). The data in Table 1.4 are drawn from Neu's work.

Since Neu presented her data in univariate frequency tables, no VARBRUL analysis is possible, and the figures in Table 1.4 represent percentages, not factor weights. Overall, Neu finds that *and* surfaces without a -d some 90% of the time – an extraordinarily high figure compared with an overall deletion rate of about 30% for other words. As noted above, English coronal stop deletion is strongly conditioned by following segment effects, and this shows up in Neu's results: non-exceptional words have 39% deletion when followed by consonants, vs. under 16% when followed by vowels, for a range of 23%. But what happens in the exceptional word *and*? In the percentage data, the figures are 95.7% deletion before consonants and 82.1% before vowels, for a range of 13.6%, which is only about half the range found for the non-exceptional words. So on these facts, the data support the lexical selection model: there is an additional lexical entry for *and*, without a final -d, which is selected some 70–80% of the time.

All of the examples we have considered support the same conclusion: exceptional lexical items in cases of variable phonological processes are best treated lexically, by means of alternative underlying representations, rather than by means

Table 1.4 *Coronal stop deletion in English: Following context effect and lexical exceptionality (% deleted; data from Neu 1980)*

	Non-exceptional words		Lexical exception (*and*)	
Following context	N	% deleted	N	% deleted
Obstruent consonant	572	39.3	441	95.7
Vowel	495	15.8	312	82.1
Range		23.5%		13.6%

of an exception-feature approach. If the exception-feature treatment were valid, at least some cases ought to show a constant effect of other phonological constraints across both exceptional and non-exceptional words, which would be the empirical manifestation of a model in which both kinds of words are subject to the same processes and constraints, albeit at different overall rates. But this is not the case. There is no evidence that exception features are operative in the mental grammars governing these cases of phonological variation.

These facts suggest a further prediction. In principle, the exception-feature approach permits both positive and negative exceptions – that is, there should be words that undergo phonological processes at both exceptionally high and exceptionally low rates. But the lexical approach, which encodes outcomes directly in the lexicon, does not permit exceptionally low rates of occurrence, at least in cases of deletion. There is no reasonable way to construct alternative entries for *and*, *-mos*, or *entonces* that will resist the deletion processes more than other words. Hence the lexical approach predicts that only words with exceptionally *high* rates of occurrence should be found. It is my impression that this prediction is consistent with the cases discussed in the literature.

Assuming this prediction is also confirmed, we will have strong quantitative evidence bearing on the theoretical issue at hand: all the data are consistent with the predictions of the lexical approach to exceptionality, and none are consistent with an exception-feature treatment. This is a potentially decisive resolution from phonological variation that has not been achieved in four decades of work on categorical processes.

Towards an adequate theory of phonology

Formal theories of phonology have, for the most part, been constructed to account for invariant facts. This is due to the dominant bias in structuralist and post-structuralist linguistics favoring categorical, invariant models and generalizations over probabilistic ones. Informally, this bias reflects an assumption of invariance; that only categorical generalizations are valid products of grammar. Hence a generalization that is not always true is of little value; encountering these, the linguist is trained to refine the statement of the generalization so as to exclude the variable bits, seeking an absolute definition that is always true within a certain domain. Outside of linguistics, of course, there is a general recognition of the validity and utility of probabilistic generalizations: men are taller than women, dark clouds bring rain, it's bad to drink and drive. None of these is categorically true, but all are useful principles for organizing one's observations of reality; they constitute valid generalizations that a "theory" of life would do well to incorporate.

In the domain of phonology, any careful observation of the way people talk reveals that there are both categorical and probabilistic patterns in the data. An adequate theory of phonology should be able to account for both. As we have seen, the same principles govern both categorical and variable patterns: for example, the OCP, which governs categorical alternations such as the realization of the -s and -ed suffixes in English (which always have an epenthetic vowel inserted whenever they are attached to a root ending in a like consonant, but not other-wise – *passes* vs. *puffs*, *raided* vs. *raked*), also governs the variable alternation between presence and absence of final coronal stops in English and of final sibi-lants in Portuguese. In the case of English -ed and -s, adjacent *identical* segments are categorically prohibited, while in the variable deletion examples in English and Portuguese, adjacent *similar* segments are probabilistically disfavored. But both observations reflect a common harmonic principle that has the status of a phonological universal: phonologies prefer contours – sequences of differing articulations – over non-contoured sequences involving repetition of the same articulatory gestures. A phonology that captures only the categorical generaliza-tion, while ignoring the probabilistic one or consigning it to be treated by a separate non-categorical principle, is self-defeating. Such an approach is either inadequate, because it leaves some of the facts unexplained, or logically unsound, because it violates Occam's razor by unnecessarily multiplying explanatory principles. A sound and adequate treatment, however, would see such cases as manifestations of a single principle governing outcomes with a range of probabilities: some-times the predicted probability is 1 (the categorical cases), sometimes it is less than 1 (the variable cases). But in all cases, the common prediction is made that non-contoured outputs are less favored than contoured ones.

Such stochastic generalizations of phonological principles are a central element of an adequate theory of phonology. Abandoning the assumption of invariance enables a broader range of facts to be brought under the explanatory scope of the grammar, including the quantitative patterns evident in variation.

It is important to note that accounting for variation does not, for the most part, demand or preclude any particular formal framework, once the assumption of invariance is suspended. Any framework that incorporates a representation of optionality can, in principle, be adapted to account for phonological variation. Theoretical treatments of variation have been proposed within most of the influ-ential phonological frameworks of the last half-century. Labov's early accounts of phonological variables such as (r) and (th) are couched in a structuralist ter-minology, in which units at one level of description (in this case the variable) subsume several realizations at another level, much as the structuralist phoneme comprises several contextually-selected allophones. The quantified, probabilistic model known as the "variable rule" (VR) model, developed by Labov (1969) and Cedergren and Sankoff (1974), was formulated in the terminology of generative phonology. In this model, each rule of grammar is assumed to be associated with a probability of application, which is 1 for categorical rules, and less than 1 for optional – i.e. variable – rules. Additionally, quantified constraint effects are represented in the VR model by attaching probabilities to particular features of the context of a rule.

Subsequent developments in formal phonology have also been adapted to treat variation. In non-linear phonologies, representational structures such as phonological tiers and feature geometries have been utilized to model variation by means of devices such as variable placement of association lines; for example, Guy (1991b) treats English coronal stop deletion as a variable attachment of the segmental tier to its licensing position in the CV tier, with deletion arising from a generalized process of stray erasure. This analysis explained the higher rates of retention in prevocalic position as a result of resyllabification – the coronal stops are relicensed as onsets of the following syllable – and it made the novel and unexpected prediction that following /l/-initial words would favor deletion more than /r/-initial words, because of the English prohibition on *tl-, *dl- onsets. This prediction has subsequently been empirically confirmed.

Morphophonological aspects of variability have also received a formal account within the framework of Lexical Phonology (LP). A well-known example of morphological conditioning of phonological variation is the contrasting rates of coronal stop deletion in various morphological classes of English words: deletion is highest in underived words (e.g. *past*, *pact*, *bold*), lowest in regular past tense forms (*passed*, *packed*, *tolled*), and intermediate in irregular past tense forms (*lost*, *kept*, *told*). Guy (1991a, 1991b), as well as Santa Ana (1992) and Bayley (1994a), explain this in terms of differing derivational histories in LP. The higher deletion rate in monomorphemic words is a consequence of multiple exposures of these words to a deletion process that iterates at each derivational level. By contrast, regular past tense verbs have lower rates of deletion because they only become candidates for deletion at the postlexical level.

This theoretical treatment also led to an unforeseen prediction which empirical research confirms: the relationship between retention rates in word classes with different derivational histories should be an exponential function. If x is the rate at which final coronal stops words are retained in words exposed to deletion only once (in this case, the regular verbs), then words exposed twice (irregular verbs, available for deletion both at one lexical level and again postlexically) have a retention rate of x^2, and words exposed three times (monomorphemic words, subject to deletion at one postlexical and two lexical levels) will have a retention rate of x^3. Several studies confirm this prediction: speakers who retain, say, 90% of coronal stops in regular past tense forms also retain about 81% (the square of .9) in irregular verbs, and about 72% (the cube of .9) in monomorphemic or underived words. This result offers an unparalleled confirmation of the vision of the overall architecture of phonology that LP incorporates.

Variation in Optimality Theory

The most far-reaching development in recent phonological theory has been the emergence of constraint-based approaches, in which general, possibly universal, principles expressing desirable phonological states do most of the work of accounting for phonological generalizations. In Optimality Theory, these principles are summarized in a ranked list of constraints, each of which will prevail unless in a given case it would cause a violation of a higher-ranked constraint. Alternative realizations of a word or utterance ("candidate forms") are evaluated by the grammar according to the number and severity of constraint violations that they incur; the evaluation metric selects the candidate that incurs the least severe (lowest ranked) violations as the optimal output.

This model was originally conceived as deterministic and categorical: only one optimal candidate should exist for any set of circumstances, and that form should occur categorically in the output. This is accomplished by means of a fixed and comprehensive rank-ordering of the constraints: if constraint A always outranks B, then for any candidate set where they conflict, a form that satisfies A will always be preferred over one that violates A but satisfies B. However, the model is straightforwardly adaptable to account for variation by means of variable or indeterminate rankings for some of the constraints. Where A and B conflict, and are variably ordered, then sometimes the candidate that satifies A will be selected, and sometimes the candidate that satisfies B.

A number of scholars have taken this step and postulated OT models that can account for both variable and invariant facts in the same grammar, by means of variable or partial constraint ranking. Particularly notable are the works of Kiparsky (in press) and Anttila (1997, 2002), and in a somewhat different vein, the Stochastic OT model of Boersma and Hayes (2001). The approach taken by Kiparsky and Anttila (cf. also similar work by others, e.g. Nagy and Reynolds [1997]), relies on the different selections made by different rankings to predict the frequencies of occurrence of competing forms. In the coronal stop deletion case, for example, if the only constraints implicated were a faithfulness constraint and a markedness constraint against complex codas, and these were freely ranked, then whenever the faithfulness constraint ranked higher, final -t,d would be retained, and whenever the markedness constraint prevailed, -t,d would be deleted. If these orderings were random, each should occur half the time, predicting a surface coronal stop deletion rate of 50%. However, more complicated cases generate different quantitative predictions. If a following vowel favors retention because of a constraint that prefers onsets, then we might postulate three variably-ranked constraints affecting cases like *east end*. Deletion would occur only when *ComplexCoda outranked both Onset and Faith. Among the six possible orders of these three constraints, this would occur in only two of them, or one-third of the time, predicting a deletion rate in such phrasal contexts of just 33%.

The jury is still out on the empirical adequacy of this model at predicting the actual frequencies of occurrence of phonological variables in differing contexts. Anttila (1997, Anttila and Cho 1998) has achieved remarkable quantitative accuracy with this approach, but Nagy and Reynolds (1997) were only partially successful. Guy (1997) has criticized this procedure because the frequencies end up being mere epiphenomena, a pure function of how many constraints are involved in the variable ordering – as we have seen, with just two constraints involved, the only possible frequency prediction is a 50–50 split between two outcomes, while with three, the only possible frequency predictions are 1/6, 1/3, 1/2, 2/3, or 5/6. A linguist who encountered some variable phenomenon with a robust 25% frequency rate would therefore have to conclude that at least four constraints were implicated, whether or not there was any theoretical or empirical evidence to support this conclusion.

Stochastic OT takes the variable ordering insight a step further, by distributing constraints as probability functions along a continuous linear scale rather than assigning them discrete ordinal rankings. Thus a constraint A centered at .9 on the scale would normally outrank a constraint B centered at .85, but in the production of actual utterances, both fluctuate over a range. In the evaluation of a particular candidate set, constraint A might on some occasion locate at the value .87, while B located at .88, with the result that a different candidate is considered optimal.

The crucial quantitative difference between this procedure and the variable ranking approach is that the distance between any two constraints in Stochastic OT can assume a range of values: two constraints can be very close together, or quite far apart. When they start out close together, their probability of overlapping will be high, but if their central distribution is far apart, they will rarely or never occur in an inverted order. Consequently, the likelihood of selecting particular candidates can be expressed as a function of the proximity of two constraints, rather than as a function of the number of constraints affecting an evaluation. In principle this should offer substantial improvement in the quantitative adequacy of the model for explaining the observed patterns of variation.

Conclusion

One of the promising trends in phonological theory in recent decades has been a widening of the data horizons, with more and more evidence from non-traditional sources being adduced in the construction and evaluation of theoretical models. Phonetic evidence, including experimental work in articulation and perception, child language data, data from language contact such as the treatment of loanwords, neurolinguistic and psycholinguistic evidence, statistical analyses of the phonotactics of lexical items – all of these have been brought to bear on theoretical questions in phonology. The patterns and probabilities of phonological variation are part of this expanding landscape. An adequate theory of phonology will offer explanations of the broadest range of sound patterns, including non-categorical, probabilistic patterns, and the study of variation will inform the construction of such a theory. The assumption of invariance, which has dominated linguistic theory since the Neogrammarians, has been useful in the history of linguistics as a debating strategem in certain theoretical arguments, and as a heuristic device for driving the research agenda, but it is not a design principle of human language. Phonological theory now has the tools in hand to replace it with more realistic models that can hope to achieve elementary observational and descriptive adequacy, in addition to pursuing the capacity to explain.

2   Syntactic variation

LISA GREEN

Introduction

This chapter considers the syntax of dialects of English from a view that incorporates issues in dialectal variation and syntactic theory. Variation in dialects of languages such as Italian, German, Dutch, and Flemish has been analyzed in a model of microparametric variation, which takes into consideration the distribution of syntactic variables in geographical areas and formal analyses of syntactic properties (Barbiers, Cornips, and van der Kleij 2002). On the other hand, research on dialects of American English has focused mainly on morphosyntactic, phonological, and, to some extent, syntactic variables in the context of social factors, linguistic constraints, and variation and change. The focus on questions about origins has led to comparative analysis of dialects and English in early periods. By and large, the topic of variation and change in American English dialects has been the domain of sociolinguistics.

Because one of the goals of sociolinguistics is to understand the correlation between social factors and linguistic variation and ordering of linguistic constraints with respect to variability of rules, variation theory is an integral part of the research paradigm. On the other hand, syntactic theory is not always incorporated in variation analyses, although it is clear that sociolinguists are concerned with theoretical notions of the scientific study of language. Along these same lines, there has not been a tradition of incorporating approaches to variation into syntactic theory (Wilson and Henry 1998).

There have been at least three types of approaches to syntactic variation. The variable rule approach accounts for variability by allowing variable rules to apply in different contexts at different probability levels. Another approach has been to determine the parameters that account for differences among languages and dialects of a single language (Henry 1995, Kayne 2000). In the multiple grammars/competing grammars approach, variability is due to the selection of different grammars (Adger and Smith 2005, Roeper 2006). Under this approach, the view is "that there is more than one system of grammatical knowledge in the head of the native speaker, and variation boils down to the decisions that the speaker makes about which grammatical output to choose" (Adger and Smith 2005:164). Under both the parametric variation and multiple grammars approaches, speakers make choices about particular constructions. On the other hand, the variable rule approach assumes that variability is part of a single grammatical system.

Studying syntactic variation presents a good opportunity to bring together syntactic theory and approaches in sociolinguistics to provide descriptive accounts of American English dialects – how they differ from each other, how they differ from the mainstream variety, and the type of variation that is allowed within them. In addition, child speakers learn the linguistic variation in their speech communities, so studying syntactic variation also provides an opportunity to consider acquisition paths for variable syntactic structures.

Incorporating variation in syntactic theory

The different goals of syntactic theory and sociolinguistics have led to different approaches to the study of language. For instance, questions have been raised in the sociolinguistics literature about the claim that linguistics should be concerned with the "ideal speaker-listener in a completely homogeneous speech-community" (Chomsky 1965:3), which seems to ignore the inherent variation associated with language. The difference is that syntactic theory has been concerned with the description of language as a property of the human brain and principles that can account for the grammatical constructions of a language in a homogeneous speech community. In this way, there has not been a long-standing tradition of the incorporation of variation in syntactic theory, so it is no surprise that only a limited amount of research on syntactic properties of dialects of American English has been in syntactic frameworks. However, more recently the theoretical frameworks of Optimality Theory (OT) and the Minimalist Program (MP) have been characterized as being well-suited for dealing with variation.

Sells, Rickford, and Wasow (1996) use OT to account for the alternation between negative inversion and non-inversion constructions in African American English (AAE) on the basis that the two structures have no differences in meaning or affect. Negative inversion constructions (1a) are declarative sentences which are characterized by an initial negated auxiliary (e.g. *don't*) followed by an indefinite noun phrase (NP) (e.g. *nobody*), and the corresponding non-inversion constructions (1b) begin with a negative indefinite NP followed by a negated auxiliary. Both sentences give rise to negative concord readings because the two negative elements (*don't, nobody*) are interpreted as a single negation, as indicated by the glosses.

(1) (a) Don't nobody want no tea.
         "Nobody wants tea" or "There isn't anybody who wants tea"
     (b) Nobody don't want no tea.
         "Nobody wants tea"

OT is a theory of generative linguistics, which proposes that languages have their own rankings for the set of violable universal constraints, and different rankings lead to different patterns which result in variable constructions. Given that the theory can accommodate variation such as the different order of the negated auxiliary and the negative indefinite NP (as in 1a, b), it can be naturally extended to accounts of dialectal variation. OT is argued to have advantages over other syntactic approaches because of the principled way in which it is able to account for the occurrence of both (1a) and (1b) – why it is possible for the negated auxiliary to be sentence initial and why there is also an option for the negative indefinite NP to occur at the beginning of the sentence in some contexts. It is possible to derive (1a) and (1b) by ranking constraints that will generate the negated auxiliary in the initial position or the indefinite negative subject at the beginning of the sentence, but the two constructions must be assumed to have the same semantic features.

The MP includes general syntactic operations, and variability is connected to features of lexical items. Adger and Smith (2005) explain that the MP also has a way of accounting for variation. They illustrate this with morphosyntactic variation in *was/were* alternation and *do* absence in negative declaratives in English in Buckie, Scotland. For instance, *was/were* alternate in environments in second person singular *you*, first person plural *we*, existential *there*, and NP plural constructions (2a, b), but not in third person plural pronoun *they* constructions (2c).

> (2) (a) Buckie boats were a' bonny graint.
> "Buckie boats were all nicely grained"
> (b) The mothers was roaring at ye comin' in.
> "The mothers were shouting at you to come"
> (c) They were still like partying hard.
> "They were still partying hard" (2005:156)

The claim is that the MP can account for *was/were* variation in the appropriate contexts as well as for the categorical occurrence of *were* in the environment of *they* subjects. Adger and Smith explain that the source of variation is in the features associated with the lexical items *was* and *were*. That is, *was* and *were* are specified for different morphological features, but they have the same semantic features; so they can be used interchangeably and the meaning remains constant. The morphological features are sensitive to the subject (pronoun or full NP), so the features of the subject interact with those of *was* and *were*. *Be* is spelled out as *was* or *were*, depending on the interaction between its features and those of the subject. This means that the features for *they* and the *be* forms are specified such that only the *be* form that is spelled out as *were* is compatible with *they*, and this accounts for the categorical occurrence of *were* with *they*. Only this *be* and *they* are compatible because the person features on *be* that are spelled out as *was* and the person features associated with *they* do not agree. Along these same lines, variable *was* and *were* will arise in instances in which a particular subject can combine with either *be*; that is, the subject will be compatible with the features of both *be*'s.

Given that in the OT approach the grammar is taken to be a set of ranked constraints, speakers of varieties in which sentences such as (1) are produced have access to different grammars that will generate such sentences. Along these same lines, the MP approach allows for options in the grammar because lexical items can have the same semantic features but different grammatical features. These theoretical syntactic models allow for different outputs that are semantically equivalent; however, unlike some sociolinguistic variation models, they do not incorporate probability and frequency of occurrence of variables into the framework.

Henry (1995) presents a model within syntactic theory that can account for variation within Belfast English (BE) and differences between that variety and Standard English. She explains that the differences within dialects of BE and Standard English are due to different parameter settings or choices between possible structures. For example, according to Henry, the parameters in BE are set such that the verb can occur in the position to the left or right of the subject in imperatives, and certain positions are available to the subject:

(3) (a) Go you away./You go away.
     (b) Read you that./You read that. (1995:45)

Henry reasons that the different parameter settings make possible a number of different grammars, and speakers have the task of selecting from the limited number of possible grammars made available by Universal Grammar that will accommodate the data for imperatives. Henry's approach, along with the OT analysis in Sells *et al.* (1996) and the MP analysis in Adger and Smith (2005), allows for options in the grammar. While the incorporation of variation in syntactic theory is a relatively new enterprise, some progress has been made, and this approach may be useful in answering questions and making predictions about the possible ways dialects can vary and the limitations for options in the grammar.

Dialectal variation and features: questions and negation

Questions and the Q feature

Subject–auxiliary inversion in yes-no and *wh*-questions occurs in Mainstream American English (MAE) as well as in non-standard varieties, and there is considerable variation in question inversion in these varieties. Hendrick (1982) discusses reduced yes-no and *wh*-questions in MAE. He reports the following types of examples of grammatical reduced yes-no questions (4b, 5b), which occur without auxiliaries:

(4) (a) Did you see Mary (yesterday)?
     (b) You see Mary (yesterday)? (1982:804)
(5) (a) Were you (ever) bit by a dead bee?
     (b) You (ever) bit by a dead bee? (1982:805)

Table 2.1 *Yes-No questions in AAE and MAE*

	Type 1 (aux+tns-subj-V)	Type 2 (∅ aux+tns-subj-V)	Type 3 (subj-V+tns)	Type 4 (subj-aux-V)
AAE	✓(6a)	✓(6b)	✓(6c)	✓(6d, e)
MAE	✓(4a, 5a)	✓(4b, 5b)	✗	✗

Hendrick argues that the process responsible for reduced yes-no questions in MAE is syntactic rather than phonological deletion. The process is sensitive to the tense structure and the recoverability condition, which states that the deleted material can be recovered from information remaining in the reduced question, so the initial auxiliary need not occur.

The type of reduced yes-no questions (4, 5) that Hendrick reports also occurs in non-standard varieties of American English, such as AAE (6b). In addition, there are two other types of yes-no questions in AAE, as in (6c, d):

(6) (a) Do you want to read this book?   (Type 1, aux+tense-subject-verb)
     (b) You want to read this book?   (Type 2, ∅ aux+tense-subject-verb)
     (c) You saw my book (yesterday)?   (Type 3, subject-verb+tense)
          "Did you see my book yesterday"
     (d) You can see my book?   (Type 4, subject-aux-verb)
          "Can you see my book?"
     (e) How she's doing?   (Type 4, subject-aux-verb)
          "How is she doing?"

As shown in (6a) and (6b), AAE allows subject–auxiliary inversion and reduced questions, respectively, in which the inverted tensed auxiliary (*do*) is omitted (i.e. zero (∅) auxiliary occurs). In addition, ∅ auxiliary questions are allowed in AAE in which tense is indicated on the main verb (6c, *saw*). The question in (6c) is a true yes-no question; it is not a rhetorical question. Finally, in AAE auxiliaries can occur in their original positions following the subject in questions (6d, e), giving rise to non-inversion. It should be noted that yes-no questions in AAE may also be produced with final level or falling contours (Foreman 1999, Green 1990), another property that might interact with inversion and the occurrence of auxiliaries. The question alternatives for these varieties are summarized in Table 2.1.

As Table 2.1 indicates, ∅ auxiliary (reduced) questions occur in AAE and MAE. The difference in question variation for the two varieties is not just one of frequency, such that more reduced questions are produced in AAE than in MAE, which may also be the case. A broader range of reduced yes-no questions occurs in AAE. Types 2 and 3 are represented as two separate types of questions, but one way to look at Type 3 (6c) is as a present perfect form in which the auxiliary *have* is deleted because the information can be recovered from the verb form, especially given the fact that AAE, like some other varieties of American English, does not distinguish morphologically between the past and participial verb forms. However, one reason to argue against deriving (6c) from *Have you saw my book*? is that given the adverbial *yesterday*, that question is simple past, not present perfect. The sentence *You saw my book before* may be derived from *Have you saw my book before?*, so it may be a Type 2 example.

In some syntactic analyses, a question feature (*Q*) is said to attract the auxiliary to the position preceding the subject in subject–auxiliary inversion exemplified in Type 1 questions. The *Q* feature can be used to characterize the similarity and difference between yes-no questions in AAE and MAE. In both AAE and MAE, *Q* can attract an auxiliary to the position preceding the subject (Type 1), and in both varieties this auxiliary can remain unpronounced (∅) under certain syntactic conditions (Type 2). The difference is that in AAE there is also the option in which *Q* does not attract an auxiliary (Types 3, 4). In these latter questions, *Q* can be construed as identifying the construction as a question that can be signaled by question intonation. It does not need to attract an auxiliary to it; that is, there is no requirement for subject–auxiliary inversion.

Wh-questions, which begin with *wh*-words *who, what, why, when, where,* and *how*, also share similarities in AAE and MAE. In characterizing reduced *wh*-questions in MAE, Hendrick (1982) notes that three restrictions are placed on them: (1) they seem to be unacceptable with deleted *will* or *do*; (2) they are unacceptable when the subject is first or third person singular; and (3) they are unacceptable when the main verb *be* is deleted. He argues that they are different from reduced yes-no questions in that reduced *wh*-questions are the result of phonological deletion of the auxiliary. The diagnostics he uses are based on Labov's (1969) observation that an auxiliary can delete wherever it can contract, and it cannot delete in environments where it cannot contract.[1] In effect, in all instances in which the auxiliary can delete in *wh*-questions in MAE, it can contract in those environments. Hendrick gives the following examples, in which (7a, b) have grammatical reduced *wh*-question counterparts (a′, b′):

(7) (a) Why're you sitting here?
     (a′) Why you sitting here?
     (b) Who've they been insulting tonight?
     (b′) Who they been insulting tonight?
     (c) Why's she sitting here?
     (c′) *Why she sitting here?
     (d) Who's he been insulting tonight?
     (d′) *Who he been insulting tonight? (1982:811)

---

[1] Labov made this observation in his account of the absence of the copula and auxiliary *be* in AAE.

Table 2.2 Wh-*questions in AAE and MAE*

	Type 1 (wh-aux+tns-subj-V)	Type 2 (wh-Ø aux+tns-subj-V)	Type 3 (wh-subj-aux+tns-V)	Type 4 (wh-subj-V+tns)
AAE	✓(8a)	✓(8b)	✓(8c)	✓(8d)
MAE	✓(What did you say?)	✓(with person, number restrictions (7b′))	✗	✗

The reduced *wh*-questions in (7a′, b′) are predicted to be grammatical because the auxiliary can contract and thus delete; (7c′, d′) are predicted to be ungrammatical because the subjects are third person singular.

The following examples from AAE show that there is some overlap in the inventory of *wh*-questions in AAE and MAE:

(8) (a) What did you say?   (Type 1, *wh*-aux+tense-subject-verb)
   (b) Who he/they been insulting tonight?
                      (Type 2, *wh*-Ø aux+tense-subject-verb)
   (c) How she was doing when you saw her?
                      (Type 3, *wh*-subject-aux+tense-verb)
        "How was she doing when you saw her?"
   (d) What he said yesterday?
                      (Type 4, *wh*-subject-verb+tense)
        "What did he say yesterday?"
   (e) What you ate yesterday?
        "What did you eat yesterday?"

Again, if we only looked at subject–auxiliary inversion (8a) and reduced questions (8b), then we might conclude that there is no substantial difference between the inventory of *wh*-questions in AAE and MAE, and that the only difference is that AAE has fewer restrictions on reduced *wh*-questions, so third person singular pronouns can also occur as subjects in reduced *wh*-questions. However, the example in (8c) shows that in *wh*-questions in AAE, the auxiliary can also remain in the position following the subject (subject–auxiliary inversion), and it can be omitted and tense can occur on the main verb (8d, e). The inventory of *wh*-questions in AAE and MAE is summarized in Table 2.2.

While it is possible to say that AAE also has a rule of phonological deletion of the auxiliary in *wh*-questions, not all questions can be accounted for by a phonological rule. For instance, the Type 3 *wh*-question cannot be generated by auxiliary deletion, so a syntactic analysis accounting for the auxiliary in its original position in *wh*-question structures is also necessary. The *Q* feature can also be used in the characterization of *wh*-questions. In both AAE and MAE, a

Q feature can attract an auxiliary to the position preceding the subject (Type 1), and the auxiliary can be deleted by a phonological rule (Type 2) (Hendrick's reduced *wh*-question analysis). Of course, in MAE phonological deletion must adhere to restrictions, which may not hold in AAE. As in yes-no questions in AAE, the *Q* feature does not obligatorily attract an auxiliary to it in *wh*-questions. The auxiliary may remain in its base position below the subject (Type 3), or tense may be expressed on the main verb in the absence of the auxiliary (Type 4).

Matrix yes-no questions and embedded questions in MAE have different requirements where subject–auxiliary inversion is concerned. It has been argued that there is no subject–auxiliary inversion in embedded clauses in MAE, but at least some MAE speakers produce subject–auxiliary inversion in embedded clauses in informal registers. Some speakers allow embedded subject–auxiliary inversion, a question introduced by the verb *wonder* in the following example in brackets (e.g. *She wondered* [*would he come back*]). The embedded inversion example, in which the auxiliary *would* is in the initial position (preceding the subject) in the embedded clause, may be used in what Emonds (1976) refers to as semi-indirect speech. Embedded inversion occurs freely in non-standard varieties of English in direct speech, in BE (Henry 1995), Hiberno English (HE) (McCloskey 1992), Appalachian English (AppE) (Wolfram and Christian 1976), and AAE (Green 2002). In these varieties, and in Mainstream English (ME), embedded questions can also be introduced by the complementizers *if* or *whether* (e.g. *She wondered* [*if he would come back*]). Some of these varieties place stronger restrictions on embedded subject–auxiliary inversion than others. For instance, in HE embedded inversion is introduced by certain types of predicates, but in BE a wider range of different predicates can introduce embedded inversion. While both varieties allow the sentence in (9a) with *ask* in the matrix clause, only BE allows the one in (9b), with *establish* in the matrix clause:

(9) (a) Ask your father [does he want dinner]. (✓BE, ✓HE)
     (b) The police couldn't establish [who had they beaten up].
          (McCloskey 1992) (✓BE, ✗HE)

Regardless of whether the varieties place constraints on the type of predicates that can introduce embedded auxiliary inversion, they all require either an auxiliary or the complementizer *whether* or *if* to introduce the embedded question. Henry gives the following examples for BE (1995:114, 117):

(10) (a) I asked if/whether they were leaving.
      (b) I asked were they leaving.
      (c) *I wondered if had they read the book.
      (d) *I asked they were leaving.

The sentences in (10a, b) are grammatical because in each case either a complementizer or auxiliary introduces the embedded clause. The sentence in (10c) is ruled out because the embedded clause *[*if had they read the book*] is introduced by two elements (*if*, *had*) in its initial position, when there is only room for one.

Table 2.3 *Summary of auxiliary to satisfy* Q *in AAE matrix and embedded questions*

	Matrix yes-no	Embedded yes-no	*Wh* (matrix and embedded)
Aux to satisfy *Q*	Optional (11)	Obligatory, unless *Q* is satisfied by a complementizer (13)	Optional (12, 14)

(10d) is ungrammatical because there is no complementizer or auxiliary at the beginning of the embedded clause. Instead of having inverted to the position before the subject (*they*), the auxiliary (*were*) is still in its original position following the subject. In descriptive terms using the *Q* feature, English varieties such as BE, HE, AppE, and AAE all require the *Q* feature that signals questions in embedded clauses to be satisfied either by an auxiliary or a complementizer. Satisfaction of this *Q* feature is also obligatory in embedded clauses in MAE; however, in MAE a complementizer introduces the clause. As a specific case in point, it has been shown that in AAE, auxiliary inversion is optional in matrix questions, but it is obligatory in embedded clauses if there is no initial complementizer.

Now compare matrix yes-no (11) and *wh*-questions (12) and embedded yes-no (13) and *wh*-questions (14) in AAE:

(11) (a) Did they bring my car in?
       (b) They brought my car in?
(12) (a) What did they bring in?
       (b) What they brought in?
(13) (a) Go over there and see [did they bring my car in]. (Green 2002:87)
       (b) Go over there and see [if they brought my car in].
       (c) *Go over there and see [they brought my car in].
(14) (a) Go over there and see [what did they bring in].
       (b) Go over there and see [what they brought in].

Subject–auxiliary inversion is optional in matrix yes-no and *wh*-questions and in embedded *wh*-questions; however, it is obligatory in embedded yes-no questions if there is no complementizer, which explains the ungrammaticality of (13c). These observations are summarized in Table 2.3.

Question data from different varieties of English help to show the extent of variation in subject–auxiliary inversion and the requirements that must be met in questions.

The *Q* feature can be used to describe the attraction of the auxiliary to the position preceding the subject. Because children grow up in communities in which there is variability in the way questions are formed, especially in the placement of the auxiliary, questions should also be considered from the perspective of child language development. Knowledge about variation must be part of what child speakers acquire in learning mechanisms that are necessary to produce grammatical questions that are in line with the variety of language they acquire. One of the major issues in the study of early questions in MAE concerns the stages during which child speakers produce subject–auxiliary inversion. It has been shown that MAE-speaking children begin to produce subject–auxiliary inversion once they acquire auxiliaries (Stromswold 1990, Guasti 2002). On the other hand, AAE-speaking children continue to use Ø auxiliary and non-inverted yes-no and *wh*-questions even after they have the competence to produce subject–auxiliary inversion. The following examples are from 3- to 5-year-old developing AAE-speaking children:[2]

(15) yes-no questions

    (a) I be saying, "Mama, can I bring my bike to you?" (R113, 5)
        "I always say, 'Mama, can I bring my bike to you?'"

    (b) Do this phone go down or up? (J025, 5)
        "Does this phone go down or up?"

    (c) You a pour me some juice? (J003, 3;8) (where *a* can be taken to be a reduced form of *will, will→'ll→a*)
        "Will you pour me some juice?"

    (d) You want to hear me spell my name? (R113, 5)
        "Do you want to hear me spell my name?"

    (e) Y'all BIN having y'all basketballs in? (J015, 4)
        "Have you (pl.) had your basketball in (the store) for a long time?"

(16) *wh*-questions

    (a) Now what is this? (D007, 3;11)

    (b) Int: Ask them the price of their cereal.
        L031: How much is the price of cereal? (L031, 5)
        "How much is cereal?"

    (c) And who this is? (Z091, 4;5)
        "And who is this?"

    (d) What they said on my phone? (R013, 4)
        "What did they say on my phone?"

    (e) How she broke her leg? (T127, 5;7)
        "How did she break her leg?"

    (f) Where her brother? (R093, 5;4)
        "Where is her brother?"

In the speech of 3- to 5-year-old developing AAE-speaking children, we find that some questions are produced with subject–auxiliary inversion (15a, b, 16b), and we find an overwhelming number of questions without auxiliaries (Ø auxiliary) (15d, e, 16d, e, f) and non-inversion (15c, 16c), where the auxiliary is present but it is not inverted (i.e. it is in the position following the subject, not preceding the

---

[2] These examples were produced in spontaneous speech and elicitation tasks in research supported by an NSF grant (BCS-0214388) to the author (2002–2005).

subject). (Note that the main verb (copula) *is* has auxiliary properties. Like the other auxiliaries in questions in AAE, it can invert (16b) or not (16c).) At first glance, the high rate of Ø auxiliary and non-inversion might suggest that developing AAE-speaking children stay in the question developmental stage much longer than their MAE-speaking peers. What is important to note about the child question data is that the AAE-speaking children develop canonical subject–auxiliary question inversion, and they must also develop the grammatical variation in forming questions, which also involves non-inversion and Ø auxiliary questions, that is an option in their language community. The AAE developmental stages are not simply paths to subject–auxiliary inversion, in which *Q* attracts an auxiliary; they must be paths to the range of options for forming questions in the variety.

Negation and the *NegFoc* feature

Features such as the *Q* feature can be useful in describing the requirements that must be met to derive variable structures in which the auxiliary is inverted or not, or in which it is present or not. In addition to the *Q* feature, a Negative Focus (*NegFoc*) feature may be used in a descriptive account of two types of negation structures that also occur in varieties of American English. The *NegFoc* feature is associated with negative inversion (NI) constructions that were introduced earlier in the discussion of Optimality Theory and syntactic variation. While these constructions occur in American English varieties AAE (Labov, Cohen, Robins, and Lewis 1968, Martin 1992, Sells *et al.* 1996, White 2006), Alabama English (AlE) (Feagin 1979), and AppE (Montgomery and Hall 2004, Wolfram and Christian 1976), they have not been reported for other varieties of English spoken outside of the US. For instance, Henry, Maclaren, Wilson, and Finlay (1997) note that NI does not occur in BE and Bristol English (BrE). As already noted, NI constructions begin with a negated auxiliary that is followed by a negative indefinite NP:

(17) (a) Can't nobody tell you it wasn't meant for you.
            "Nobody can tell you it wasn't meant for you"
            (Green 2002:78; AAE)
      (b) Didn't none of us ever learn that. (Feagin 1979:235; AlE)
            "None of us ever learned that"
      (c) Didn't nobody get hurt or nothin'. (Wolfram and Christian 1976:113; AppE)
            "Nobody got hurt or anything"
            [I have added the glosses for (17b, c.).]

There are different analyses of these constructions in the literature (in addition to Sells *et al.* 1996) that try to account for the order of the negated auxiliary and negative indefinite NP (subject), that is, the alternation between (17) the inversion structures and (18) the non-inversion structures, in which the negated subject precedes the negated auxiliary:

(18) (a) Nobody can't tell you is wasn't meant for you.
      (b) None of us didn't ever learn that.
      (c) Nobody didn't get hurt or nothin'.

Feagin (1979), Green (2002), Labov *et al.* (1968), and Wolfram and Christian (1976) consider the alternation between (17) and (18) to be one of a type of inversion, such that (17) is derived from (18) by a mechanism in which the negated auxiliary inverts to the position preceding the negative indefinite NP. This process is similar to auxiliary inversion in questions, but a *Q* feature does not trigger it. Both types of constructions (17, 18) are available, and they have the same truth conditions. That is to say that both (17a) and (18a) mean roughly "Nobody can tell you it wasn't meant for you." Labov *et al.* (1968) suggest that the sentences in (17) are affective; however, this issue has not been resolved. These sentences can certainly be affective, but it is not clear that the ones in (18) cannot, so it is not clear that affect is always the characteristic that distinguishes (17) and (18). Emphasis may play a role in distinguishing these two sentence types, but further research must be conducted on the types of pragmatic environments and situations in which they occur to determine whether they are used to highlight or convey meaning in ways that the sentences in (18) are not. While there is no general consensus about whether the negative inversion construction is more affective or emphatic than the non-inversion counterpart in (18) or whether they have different pragmatics, both constructions have the same general meaning and truth conditions. This is certainly the type of issue that is the topic of discussion in Romaine (1984), in which she raises the question about the extent to which techniques used in phonological variation can be extended to syntactic variation, especially given the necessity of taking into consideration semantic and pragmatic equality of the "syntactic variables." In effect, the truth conditions of the constructions must be the same, a point also addressed in Weiner and Labov (1982). That issue bears heavily on characterizing (17a, b, c) and (18a, b, c), respectively, as variants. Feagin (1979) suggests that sentences such as (17) and (18) can be used in the same contexts. She reports that one of her informants began to produce the inverted construction but self-corrected by restarting "his sentence with a negated subject followed by the negated auxiliary" (1979:236).

The sentences in (17) can be described as requiring a negated auxiliary in the initial position due to a *NegFoc* feature which attracts the negated auxiliary and is responsible for its being stressed. In this way, NI constructions may be emphatic. This feature would be sufficient to distinguish sentences in (17) from those in (18). While NI sentences (19a, b) have a *NegFoc* feature, the question (19c) has a *Q* feature which attracts the auxiliary:

(19) (a) *NegFoc*Didn't nobody come to your party.
      (b) *NegFoc*Didn't anybody come to your party.
      (c) *Q*Didn't anybody come to your party?

Table 2.4 *Negative inversion and related constructions in English varieties*

	AlE	AppE	AAE	BE	BrE
Neg concord	✓	✓	✓	✓	✓
Neg Inv	✓	✓	✓	✗	✗
Exp	✓	✓	✗	NA	NA

It is important to include (19b), in which the indefinite form *anybody* can also be used by some speakers in NI, as noted by Wolfram and Christian (1976). In the case of (19a, b), the auxiliary hosts the accent encoded in the *NegFoc* feature, so the auxiliary should be stressed. On the other hand, the *Q* feature encodes different types of information about the question force of the sentence. The sentences in (19b, c) are distinguished from each other by the type of feature that attracts the auxiliary. Studying NI and non-inverted negative sentences provides a good opportunity to consider variation in syntactic structure in American English dialects, and it also provides an opportunity to address the issue of whether a certain type of pragmatic meaning is associated with one related structure or the other.

American English varieties such as AlE and AppE differ from AAE in that they also allow an expletive to occur with NI constructions, such as the ones in (17).[3] The expletive in (20a, b) is *they* (argued to be a form of expletive *there*):

(20) (a) I mean, back in them days, *they didn' nobody* live up there. (Feagin 1979:238)
   (b) *They didn't none of us* ever get snakebit, but some of the work animals did. (Montgomery and Hall 2004:lxiv)

Given that a *NegFoc* feature occurs in structures in which the negated auxiliary is in sentence or clause initial position, the sentences in (20) would not be derived by a *NegFoc* feature attracting an auxiliary to it. Instead in these sentences the expletive *they* is in the initial position (subject position) of the clause (20a) or sentence (20b). Given the data, sentences such as (17), (18), and (20) are possible in varieties that allow multiple negative elements to indicate a single negation; however, varieties will differ in the extent to which they allow negative inversion constructions. If we consider AlE, AppE, AAE, BE, and BrE, we can make the following observations (as seen in Table 2.4).

All of the varieties allow negative concord (multiple negative elements construed as a single negation), but only the American English varieties, AlE, AppE,

---

[3] AAE also allows expletives to occur with negative constructions as long as there is some *be* form (e.g. *It wasn't nobody in the classroom*).

and AAE, allow negative inversion. AlE, AppE, and AAE can be characterized as having a *NegFoc* feature that attracts a negated auxiliary, but only AlE and AppE allow the subject position of these negative concord constructions to be filled by either a negative indefinite NP or an expletive. In AAE, the subject position of these negation constructions with auxiliaries other than some form of *be* (that is, *can't, didn't, shouldn't, wouldn't, haven't*) can only be filled by a negative indefinite NP, not an expletive. Neither BE nor BrE has a *NegFoc* feature that triggers inversion of a negated auxiliary in negative concord constructions such as (18).

It should be noted that a limited number of similar expletive negative constructions (such as those in (20)) have been identified in ex-slave narratives and in the work of early twentieth-century African American author Charles Chesnutt. These examples suggest that earlier varieties of AAE may have allowed expletives in these negative concord constructions, but more historical research must be conducted on recorded ex-slave narratives. Research may shed some light on language change and variation and the availability of this construction in some varieties but not in others and on the question about whether NI constructions (e.g. 17) are historically related to expletive constructions such as (20).

Variation in negative concord constructions raises important questions about the acquisition path for the development of NI and non-inversion constructions. Henry *et al.* (1997) explain that while children acquiring BE and BrE both acquire negative concord, the children acquiring BE develop it later than those who develop BrE negative concord. Developing AAE-speaking children also acquire negative concord, and they produce these constructions and comprehend them as having a single negative meaning (Green 2005):

(21) (a) They don't have no training wheels. (T085, 4;6)
           "They [those bikes] don't have training wheels"
      (b) I can't uh ride my bike without no training wheels. (D007, 5)
           "I can't ride my bike without training wheels"

However, there is no evidence that developing 3- to 5-year-old AAE-speaking children produce NI constructions. In conclusion, while NI constructions may be superficially similar to question inversion, they are not acquired as early as questions, nor is it clear whether or not they are acquired right at the period during which the child begins to develop negative concord. Syntactic theory cannot shed much light on the social factors that may contribute to the stages of acquisition of NI; however, syntactic theory may be useful in an account of the structure and may help to answer questions about why NI appears later in the developmental stage. If research supports the claim that the negative focus is linked to pragmatic or emphatic properties of NI, then the *NegFoc* feature could be used in descriptions and explanations of the development of variation in production of NI and non-inversion.

Syntactic variation and language development

Labov (1969) maintains that an approach to the study of language that encompasses variable rules and constraints on the application of rules could help to answer questions about the acquisition of rule systems and the way "norms of the speech community" are acquired (1969:760). Henry (2002), based on data from acquisition of BE, explains that children do not just acquire a single grammar, they acquire "variable forms at an early age" (2002:278), and they "have learned the statistical distribution of forms at an early age" (2002: 279).

Just as there is a division between syntactic theory and sociolinguistic models, which incorporate methods for determining variability and probability, there is also a divide between research on child language development and the acquisition of variation. That is to say that variation in child language has been considered from the sociolinguistic perspective, and this is especially due to the association of variation with social meaning and style. On the other hand, acquisition research that is concerned only with linguistic factors has focused on the development of categorical features. Given the focus on obligatory occurrence or categorical features and the development of the adult grammar, there has not been much consideration of the role variation plays in language development in research on general stages of acquisition. Also, as Roberts (2002) notes, one of the challenges of studying child language variation is that it is not easy to distinguish developmental variation from that which is socially motivated.

Here I would like to place the development of the copula and auxiliary *be* in AAE, a well-studied morphosyntactic feature, in the context of syntactic variation. The copula refers to forms of *be* preceding nouns, adjectives (e.g. *He is nice*), and prepositions, and the auxiliary *be* precedes verbs in the *-ing* form (e.g. *He is running*). To answer questions about the developmental stages, it is necessary to have specific information about the copula and auxiliary *be* patterns in AAE as well as general developmental patterns for children acquiring the copula and auxiliary *be* in other varieties such as MAE. It is commonly reported that in varieties of AAE in the US, the production of the copula and auxiliary *be* depends, in large part, on the preceding and following linguistic environments, which may effect phonological deletion. In adult and adolescent AAE, the *be* form is said to occur (near) categorically with the first person singular pronoun (*I'm*). It occurs with increasing frequency preceding *gonna*, V-*ing*, locative (as in prepositional phrases), adjective, and NP, with fewer overt occurrences preceding *gonna* and more preceding NPs.[4]

The research on *be* forms in the acquisition of MAE has considered different types of environments. For instance, in her work on the acquisition of the copula in MAE-speaking children, Becker (2000) notes that the copula occurs with varying frequency, depending on whether it occurs in the environment of a predicate that

---

[4] This description is simplified in that it does not discuss full and contracted *be* forms separately, and there are also questions about the extent to which *be* forms occur before locatives and adjectives.

indicates a permanent property (i.e. state that lasts permanently, such as the state of being a female) or a temporary property (i.e. event or state that is temporary, such as running or being angry). While the copula is omitted frequently in the environments preceding locatives (e.g. [*is*] *in the store*) and adjectives referring to temporary properties (e.g. [*is*] *hot*), it is retained more often in the environments following deictic *there* (e.g. *there is the milk*), *that* (e.g. *that is a book*), existential *there* (e.g. *there is a bird in the cage*), and nominal predicates (e.g. *she is a doctor*), or those indicating permanent properties (e.g. *is a girl*). According to Becker, *be* is obligatory in constructions with predicates indicating permanent properties due to the need for an overt tense marker because the constructions do not include any other temporal marker or feature. On the other hand, predicates indicating temporal properties "contain an intrinsic temporal feature, which provides temporal reference for the utterance" (2000:113–14), so there is no need for an overt tense marker, copula *be*.

Copula omission is common in the development of MAE, not just in the development of non-standard varieties such as AAE; it shows non-uniformity given its propensity to occur in certain environments but not in others. Because the overt copula is generally obligatory in adult MAE, children acquiring that variety are expected to produce Ø forms with a certain level of frequency in developmental stages but overt forms beyond that. On the other hand, children acquiring non-standard varieties of English (e.g. AAE) with Ø *be* forms are expected to produce Ø forms with a certain level of frequency in developmental stages and in the adult grammar. However, research on the acquisition path for the development of *be* in non-standard varieties of American English is limited.

Given the influence of Labov (1969), much of the subsequent research on the AAE copula and auxiliary *be* replicated that study. As a result, some of the research on child AAE approached developmental *be* patterns from the angle of adult AAE variable rules and raised questions about the extent to which adult models could be extended to the child language. Kovac (1980) and Kovac and Adamson (1981) looked at the occurrence of *be* and the preceding and following environments and constraint rankings reported in Labov (1969). Kovac (1980) concluded that developmental and sociodialectal processes are interconnected, so it may be impossible to separate them in descriptions of *be* patterns in child language. In addition, she noted that, based on the data in her study, it may not be possible to extend an adult model of contraction and Ø *be* forms to child language. Along these lines, Kovac noted that Ø *be* forms in child AAE may be a result of a syntactic process, rather than the phonological process, that has been posited for adult AAE. Kovac and Adamson (1981) concluded that not all *be* absence could be characterized as developmental; some must be due to deletion that is a result of the sociodialectal process. However, the diagnostics that Kovac and Adamson used to distinguish developmental Ø *be* from sociodialectal Ø *be* are not clear. Wyatt (1996) found that preschool AAE speakers also developed similar variable use of the copula to that associated with adult AAE; however, in broadening the contexts, she noticed that Ø copula was also governed by additional pragmatic constraints in early AAE. Previous research shows that developing AAE speakers systematically produce Ø *be* forms along with overt *be*, which is in line with the variable occurrence of the copula and auxiliary *be* in adult AAE. However, research on adult AAE has considered the process responsible for Ø *be* to be phonological, and there is limited discussion about the syntactic (but note Kovac's [1980] observation that Ø copula may be the result of a syntactic process in child AAE) and semantic constraints on the production of *be* that might be general developmental phenomena. Benedicto, Abdulkarim, Garrett, Johnson, and Seymour (1998) considered contexts beyond the preceding and following grammatical environments to account for the occurrence of the copula in child AAE. They found that the copula is (near) categorical in the past and in presentational sentences, which introduce some type of participant. In the following sentences from Benedicto *et al.*, *a girl* (22a) and *her shoes* (22b) are the participants that are introduced in the presentational sentences, and an overt copula (contracted *'s*) occurs in each sentence:

(22) (a) It's a girl.
      (b) Huh! Here's her shoes. (1998:52)

They argue that the copula occurs in presentational contexts because it is needed to host information about an event or situation. They also explain that the copula is required in past contexts (e.g. *He was a student*) to support a past tense feature in the syntactic structure. Of course, early variation studies noted that the copula was (near) categorical in past tense contexts, but there was no discussion about how the requirement was linked to syntactic structure. Given Benedicto *et al.*'s analysis, the copula is not required in predicational contexts, in which a predicate such as a noun or adjective follows the copula (e.g. *He a boy/mad*), because the predicate carries the necessary information. This analysis differs from the one proposed in Becker (2000) in that it does not distinguish between predicates that indicate temporary properties and those that denote permanent properties. Data from developmental AAE should be studied carefully to determine whether there is support for these types of syntactic (and semantic) analyses.

Consider the following summary of *be* constructions in a sample of speech from a developing AAE-speaking female at 3; 4 (A117). The sample is based on her narration of the picture book *Good Dog, Carl*.[5]

The *be* construction summary in Table 2.5 shows that A117 uses zero *be* categorically preceding V-*ing*, *gon/gonna* ("going to"), adjectives, and nouns. The number of adjectives and nouns is low in the sample, so it would be useful to consider these constructions in additional samples from A117. Also, there are no *be* + preposition sequences in the sample. On the other hand, *be* as a contracted form with *it*, *that*, and *what* is near categorical. What has generally been important in the sociolinguistic variation literature that is concerned with the distribution

---

[5] These examples are taken from data collected in connection with a project supported by an NSF grant (BCS-0214388) to the author.

Table 2.5 *Copula and auxiliary* be *summary (A117, 3;4 years)*

Construction	% Ø *be*	(N)	Example
*be+*V-*ing*	100%	(33)	1. He Ø running on the flo' [floor].
			2. The baby Ø laying down and he Ø not sleeping.
be+gon/gonna	100%	(5)	1. He Ø gon bite.
			2. And it's p – and it Ø gon burn his mouth.
*be+*Adj	100%	(1)	He Ø mad.
be+N	67%	(3)	1. He Ø a boy.
's (1) Ø (2)			2. He's a boy. [repetition of interviewer's line]
			3. And they Ø brothers.
it's (5) it Ø (1)	16.7%	(6)	1. Cause it's pepper!
			2. It's not a good dance.
			3. And it's p – and it Ø gon burn his mouth.
that's	0%	(6)	1. And that's not her dog.
			2. That's bleet. [i.e. bleeding or blood]
what's	0%	(3)	1. What's happening? [repetition of interviewer's line]
			2. What's that on your book?

of *be* is the type of preceding or following grammatical category; however, in order to compare the child AAE data with other child *be* data, it is necessary to look beyond the preceding and following grammatical and phonological environments. The copula and auxiliary *be* are categorically absent in the constructions in which the predicate indicates a temporary property (e.g. *running, mad*). This is an environment in which Ø *be* occurs at a high rate in Becker's child data. The following environment V-*ing* favors Ø *be* in adult AAE also; however, there is no separate discussion about the effect of adjectives denoting temporary properties on the occurrence of *be* in the copula literature on AAE. Ø *be* also occurs with nouns in A117's data, which indicate permanent properties. If a larger data set of *be* with nouns corroborated the trend here, the findings would be against Becker's claim about permanent properties and overt *be*. It would be useful to have more data in which there are tokens of nouns and adjectives indicating permanent properties to get a clearer view of the *be* patterns in A117's speech and the way they interact with predicates with different temporal properties.

Benedicto *et al.* can account for the finding with nouns in A117's sample because there is no distinction between permanent and temporary properties in their analysis; they predict that the copula can be absent in that environment as well as in the environment preceding predicates that indicate temporary properties. Overt contracted *be* in *it's* and *that's* has generally been accounted for in the AAE literature as resulting from a phonological process. If the cases of *it's* and *that's* in A117's speech are presentational, then they would be accounted for under Benedicto *et al.*'s analysis, and they can also be accounted for in Becker's analysis.

Table 2.6 *Copula and auxiliary* be *summary (Z091, 4;5 years)*

Construction	N	Ø	Overt	% Ø be	Example
be+V-*ing*	3	3	0	100%	That's where he sleeping tonight?
be+*gon*	2	2	0	100%	We gon fix it.
be+N	6	3	3	50%	1. He a bad boy.
					2. And this is his bed, too?
be+Adj	1	1	0	100%	My bike still broke.
presentational	1	0	1	0%	And there's a police car.
what's	3	0	3	0%	What's his name?
inversion	3	2	1	67%	1. This Bruce?
					2. Is this his bed?
I'm	1	0	1	0%	I'ma throw it away.
be+Prep/Adverb	2	2	0	100%	Bruce right there again.
it's	0			NA	
that's	1	0	1	0%	That's where he sleeping tonight?
past	5	0	5	5%	They was crying.
sentence final	3	0	3	3%	Who this is?

It is important to raise questions about the extent to which A117 is acquiring patterns in adult variation, but it is also necessary to consider her data in light of developmental AAE and general copula developmental patterns. Both Becker (2000) and Benedicto *et al.* (1998) are useful in pursing this line, which must also include issues about non-uniformity of development of *be* in different syntactic and semantic contexts and in different English varieties.

In Tables 2.6 and 2.7, we see additional patterns in *be* development in data from an older developing AAE speaker (Z091) at ages 4;5, 4;8, and 4;11.[6]

Z091's data resembles A117's in that there is categorical Ø *be* in certain contexts, but the difference is that in Z091's summary, there is also a range of variable *be* occurrence. In this summary, the categorical occurrences of *be* closely resemble those in adult AAE. For instance, it is well known that a *be* form is generally required to host past tense, and this is also in line with Benedicto *et al.*'s prediction. In research on adolescent and adult AAE, Ø *be* forms occur optionally before prepositions, and both Becker's and Benedicto *et al.*'s analyses would predict optional occurrence preceding prepositions. For Becker, optional occurrence would be due to the nature of the temporary predicate (which does not require *be*), and for Benedicto *et al.* it would be due to the claim that nothing requires there to be a *be* form in the syntactic structure. While Z091 has Ø *be* forms, he is also developing variable *be* in appropriate contexts. For instance, Z091's patterns fall

[6] Z091's sample is based on speech produced during spontaneous speech and interaction during two elicitation tasks. This research was supported by an NSF grant (BCS-0214388) to the author.

Table 2.7 *Copula and auxiliary* be *summary (Z091, 4;8 and 4;11 years)*

Construction	N	Ø	Overt	% Ø *be*	Example
be+V-*ing*	7	6	1	86%	1. He cooking.
					2. I'm making him talk.
be+*gon/gonna*	7	4	3	57%	1. We gon do another book?
					2. I'm gon swing on some trees.
be+N	7	4	3	57%	1. And he the ghost.
					2. My daddy is a cop.
be+Adj	7	4	3	57%	1. It look like he mean right there.
					2. You're smart.
presentational	5	2	3	40%	1. It's a radio right here.
					2. There's Jenny.
what's	0			NA	
inversion	4	3	1	75%	1. Who's Faye?
					2. You gon do another book?
I'm	5	1	4	20%	1. Ok, I'ma come on.
					2. I finna pass this test.
be+Prep/Adverb	2	1	1	50%	1. This where you put your hand.
					2. It's in my booksack.
it's	0			NA	
that's	2	0	2	0%	That's what we do?
past	16	0	16	100%	When I was twisting, I had did a flip.
sentence final	2	0	2	100%	I don't know what it is.
finna	1	1	0	100%	I finna pass this test.

in line with adult (near) categorical production in the case of *be* with first person singular (*I'm*), and the developmental account in Becker and Benedicto *et al.* can account for this finding. Note that based on the limited number of examples, Z091 takes the occurrence of *be* forms in presentational contexts to be variable. Because there is a limited number of presentational contexts in Z091's data, it is not clear whether *be* forms would be more likely to be overt in those environments or not. It would be interesting to determine whether or not Z091's presentational contexts become (near) categorical *be* contexts as development progresses. Such data is important in determining the extent of syntactic and semantic variation in the development of *be* constructions in child AAE. Acquisition data reveal trends in the development of variation in the distribution of the copula and auxiliary *be*, but it also makes clear the point that the questions we should ask cannot be limited to whether developing AAE speakers have patterns of adult variation in grammatical and phonological contexts. It is also important to address questions about syntactic (and semantic) constraints that may provide insight into developmental trends.

Conclusion

Variation in non-standard dialects of American English has received some attention in sociolinguistics, with emphasis on the social factors, linguistic constraints, and language change that play a role in variable structures. In addition, in sociolinguistic variation theory, variable structures in these varieties may also be characterized by a probability index, which may be argued to be part of the grammar. Syntactic variation is also beginning to be addressed in theoretical frameworks, such as Optimality Theory and the Minimalist Program, which raise questions about whether speakers have multiple grammars and choose from among them. The integration of variation in syntactic theory could contribute to our understanding the range of possible intradialectal and interdialectal variation in various constructions such as negation and questions.

Consideration of variation in theoretical syntactic models would also help to broaden research on the acquisition of variation and the developmental paths children take as they learn their community grammars. The copula and auxiliary *be* have received considerable attention in linguistic research, and given the variable occurrence of the *be* forms in child language, more data and research in this area would be useful in providing information about developmental patterns in child language, especially in child AAE, which is often compared to adult AAE without much focus on the properties of stages of acquisition.

3 The psycholinguistic unity of inherent variability: old Occam whips out his razor[1]

RALPH W. FASOLD AND DENNIS R. PRESTON

Introduction

Sociolinguists and generativists seem to have incompatible views of the psycholinguistic or cognitive status of variation. The sociolinguistic notion of *inherent variability* points to a single mental construct (i.e. a *grammar*) in which alternative realizations are possible. Generativists suggest that variation results only from the choice of different *structures*, an understanding that would imply different grammars, leaving only *grammar switching* as an alternative to inherent variability. Only some very recent contributions (e.g. Cornips and Corrigan 2005) attempt to deal with these apparently opposing views, and, in fact, historical attention to the problem has been minimal (but see Butters [1990], Fasold [1991], Preston [1991a, b, 1996a, b, 2000b, 2001b, 2002, 2004], and Wolfram [1991] for earlier attempts to deal with the psycholinguistic validity of the notion *variable rule*). To approach this problem, we propose at least three kinds of variationist sociolinguistics, although we might more properly speak here of levels rather than kinds.[2]

Level I

Some few variationist studies have concerned themselves only with the correlation of linguistic and social facts, and the outcomes from such Level I studies do not seem to lead to ready psycholinguistic interpretations. This does not mean that such studies have no theoretical interest; such interest, however, seems to lie principally in the area of social theory or in the interaction of social forces and linguistic forms (see note 2). For example, in a study of doctor–patient interaction (Marsh 1981), the occurrence of definite article versus pronominal in such

---

[1] Parts of this paper have appeared in Preston 2000b, 2002, and 2004.
[2] We approach this problem only from the point of view of variationist (or "Labovian") sociolinguistics. We are aware that such sociolinguists as Dell Hymes have noted that a full grammar of a language must have a component of "communicative competence" as well as the Chomskyan notion of "(grammatical) competence," but that requirement does not figure in our considerations here. Both authors believe that speakers indeed have such abilities as those Hymes speaks of, but both also believe that they interact with the rules of linguistic competence rather than constitute a part of them.

Table 3.1 *Percentage of appearance of the definite article (Marsh 1981:548)*

Patient class	New patients		Long-term patients	
	Patient	Physician	Patient	Physician
Upper middle	52%	53%	12%	44%
Lower middle	32%	38%	14%	28%
Upper working	32%	29%	16%	27%
Lower working	32%	25%	20%	25%
Average	37%	36%	16%	31%

sentences as *How's the pain in the/your hand?* is investigated. Table 3.1 shows how this choice is distributed for patients and physicians, patient social status, and long-term versus short-term physician–patient relationships.

This study has nothing to say about the grammatical shape of determiners versus pronominals. What it has a great deal to say about is the use of one linguistic form or another to symbolize power, solidarity, register – a whole host of sociocultural facts. It's not surprising that it has little to say about determiners and pronominals. If one is a doctor or patient, lower or higher class, in a long- or short-term relationship, one cannot say either just *hand* (*Hello doctor. *I'd like to have you take a look at hand*) or article+pronominal+hand (*Hello Walt. *I'd like to have a look at the your hand*). Those are facts of English (although not Polish and Italian, respectively), and one may study the structure of such constructions with no reference whatsoever to sociocultural facts. It is only if one wants to study the *distribution* of determiners versus pronominals that one is lost without sociocultural facts. Somebody may be going around saying that one cannot study grammatical facts at all without reference to sociocultural facts, but we suspect that it is not a sociolinguist from the variationist tradition.

In fact, it is possible to examine the structure of possessives in English, and even to compare the results with a language like Italian. If we assume a *D(eterminer) P(hrase)* analysis of substantives, for languages that include English (and also Italian), then a reasonable way to understand possessives in English would be that the possessive suffix *'s* actually *is* a determiner, as in Figure 3.1a (Radford 1997). That is, we have a determiner, *'s*, which selects an *NP* complement, as determiners typically do, and the complement *NP* expresses the possessed entity. When *'s* is the determiner, the *DP* must also have a *Specifier*, which expresses the possessor. On the other hand, if *the* is selected as the determiner, a *Specifier* is not required (and perhaps not possible), as we see in Figure 3.1b. If this analysis is correct, then the variation between *my hand* and *the hand* is a matter of which determiner a speaker selects. The fact that English does not allow *the your hand* is a consequence of the fact that there is only one determiner position, and if it is occupied by *the*, it cannot be occupied by *'s*. The facts for Italian are apparently

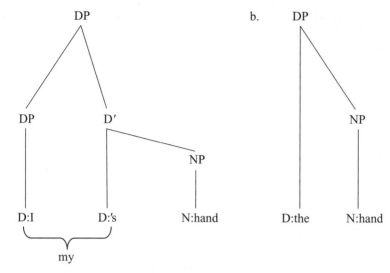

Figure 3.1 *Structure of* my hand *and* the hand *in English*

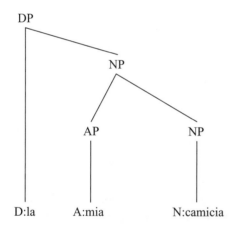

Figure 3.2 *Structure of* la mia camicia *"my shirt" in Italian*

different. It seems that possessive pronouns in Italian can occupy an Adjective (or other attributive) position within the *NP*, and this position is independent of the *DP*. This analysis is illustrated in Figure 3.2. Since the possessive pronoun *mia* does not occupy the head position of *DP*, there is nothing to prevent a determiner and a possessive pronoun from appearing in the same construction, so *la mia camicia* "my shirt," literally "the my shirt," is possible.[3]

In a Level I variationist approach, sociocultural facts and linguistic ones are put in touch with one another. If one chooses to call that connection a psycholinguistic

---

[3] According to instructional grammars, body parts take the article only, so *la mano* "my hand" (literally "the hand"), rather than *la mia mano, mia mano,* or *mano mia.* Deciding whether this is a matter of conventions of usage or a matter of syntactic analysis would take us much too far afield here.

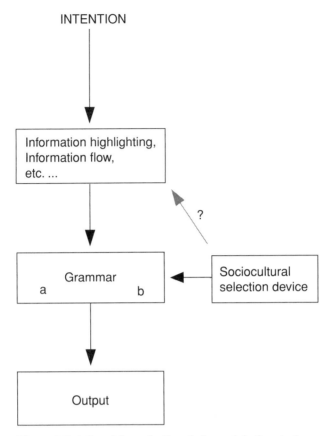

Figure 3.3 *A Level I psycholinguistic model of variation*

one, that is taking a broad view of psycholinguistics, and we are not opposed to it, but we want to be clear, however, about the separateness (or *modularity*) of the devices that are at stake here. Figure 3.3 (borrowing heavily from Levelt [1989]) shows what we have in mind.

After you know what you want to say and have "contextualized" it according to information status (including knowledge of your interlocutor's information state, causing the hedge between the *information* and *sociocultural* components), you go to your *grammar* to choose those things that reveal your intention (and information organization). When it comes to talking about *hands*, you may choose either *the* as the determiner, resulting in "the hand" (Figure 3.1b), or *'s* with the first person pronoun in the *Specifier* position, resulting in "my hand" (Figure 3.1a). Either choice is fully grammatical in English. In short, there are two forms (which are not internally incompatible, no matter what view of syntax you take) available in the competence of at least the English speakers Marsh is talking about. In Level I variationist studies, the choice between one or another of these forms is based on the sociocultural selection shown in Figure 3.3.

From a more sophisticated sociocultural perspective, that device should be related to more general socio-cognitive principles. Why do patients pay so much attention to length of relationship and doctors so much more to social status of patient? Answers to such questions depend on our ability to characterize social relations and the sorts of social-psychological forces (e.g. power, identity) which underlie them. What linguistic forms we choose to symbolize such social facts may, in some cases, be relatively transparent (e.g. honorifics) and in other cases more subtle (e.g. the greater politeness of preterite [e.g. *would*] rather than present [e.g. *will*] modals). Even an elaborate theory of why some linguistic items are selected (e.g. the relationship between politeness and indirectness suggested in Brown and Levinson [1987]) tells us only that the connection between the socio-cultural selector and the grammar is not a completely unpredictable one; it does not suggest that sociocultural facts are the same as grammatical ones. (Note that the subtitle of Brown and Levinson's work is, in fact, "Some universals in language *usage*" [italics ours].)

In Marsh's examples, it is not hard to see how the alternatives fit into power and identity considerations. Referring to body parts, one's own or someone else's, can be seen as something of an assumption of intimacy. There are languages – Italian is one (cf. footnote 3), German is another – in which speakers generally use the "the hand" strategy to refer to their own body parts. Using this option linguistically places distance between the speaker and addressee and the body part. This idea would be consistent with Marsh's discovery that both doctors and patients use less of the article form (meaning more of the possessive pronoun form) when the relationship between doctors and patients is long-term rather than new. The increased use of the pronoun reflects the increased intimacy that has developed. It is possible that people who are measured at lower social statuses are from social groups who value interpersonal closeness over respectful distance, and that this value is more consistent with the use of the pronoun form. To put this in Brown and Levinson's terms, they might prefer positive-face politeness over negative-face politeness. There might even be an explanation for the fact that there is little or no difference between the two forms as used by doctors depending on length of the relationship when the patient is from the lowest social statuses. It may be that the doctors see the lower-status patients as not being the sort of people that can expect respectful distance. Alternatively, it may be that some of the doctors can see that lower-status patients are more comfortable with a more intimate ambiance.

Let's make sure we are not begging the question. What sort of linguistic competence does Figure 3.3 suggest? We believe it accurately displays a linguistic (and we mean a strictly grammatical) competence, which licenses two constructions in English, those yielding "my/your hand" or "the hand." That licensing (or generating) imposes no internal contradictions on the grammar. If by "inherent variability" one means that two (or more) forms which can fulfill the same communicative task (or, as in Figure 3.3, realize the same intention) exist in a single linguistic competence, then this model of Level I variation displays

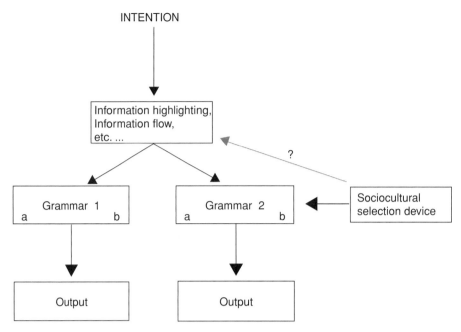

Figure 3.4 *A Level I psycholinguistic model of interlanguage variation*

such inherent variability, and we cannot think of any theoretical objections to it. Figure 3.3 can, in fact, be modified to take care of slightly more complex selection. Figure 3.4 shows a sociocultural selection device that has more than one grammar to select from. This has to be true, or fluent speakers of two languages would not know how to use sociocultural facts in determining the appropriateness of one language or the other. Unfortunately, there has been some apparently rather dubious speculation about where different grammars are necessary.

> . . . every human being speaks a variety of languages. We sometimes call them different styles or different dialects, but they are really different languages, and somehow we know when to use them, one in one place and another in another place. Now each of these languages involves a different switch setting. In the case of [different languages] it is a rather dramatically different switch setting, more so than in the case of the different styles of [one language] . . . (Chomsky 1988:188)

It appears that Chomsky asserts here that there is necessarily a different grammar every time there is a stylistic shift. Intuitively, there often seems not to be such a requirement, as in cases like the physician–patient data. No different switch settings – whatever they are – even of the less dramatic sort seem to be required for the variation observed there; it is all derived from one grammar of English, one in which its inherent options were made use of by the sociocultural selection device.

Let's take a closer look at what Chomsky means by *different language*. For Chomsky, *language* tends to be equated with the grammar of that language. It would follow that, since Chomsky is committed to *Universal Grammar*, there is a sense in which there is really only one human language. The various instances of what are commonly called languages arise, in a formal theory which includes Universal Grammar, from different settings of *parameters*. Parameters are on–off switches that are supposed to determine, for example, whether or not you have a null-subject language (Spanish or Italian) or an obligatory-subject language (English or French), or whether you have a polysynthetic language (Algonquin), or a more analytic language (most of the best-known European or Asian languages, cf. Baker [1996]). This is theoretically the only device available to distinguish languages, dialects, or even styles: the difference being the magnitude of the effect of switching a parameter on or off; in this theory, a rather trivial difference. Hence, Chomsky can say with a straight face, "every human being speaks a variety of languages."[4]

There is one more sophistication needed in Level I psycholinguistic representations. A selection device might be seen as one that peers into a grammar and chooses between one form or another. Table 3.1 shows, however, that not one of the social characteristics selected for that study had a categorical selection effect. The patient's social class, for example, (perhaps for distance versus intimacy reasons mentioned above) caused physicians to select *the/your hand* at different rates, while length of relationship caused patients to radically alter their behavior, but never at one hundred percent or zero percent. That probabilistic influence has caused Bickerton (1971), for example, to argue that such behavior requires a speaker to keep a tally of occurrences so that he or she may modify selection up or down to keep the proportion right over the long haul. He imagines a scenario in which, say, a lower-middle-class patient in a short-term relationship with his or her physician is about to make a *hand* reference and reasons as follows: "Let's see; I'm lower-middle-class and I've only seen this doctor once before. The last two times I said *hand*, I said *my*. If I'm going to turn in my thirty-two percent *the* performance, I'd better get one in now." Even if this is a representation of non-conscious mechanisms at work (and surely it is), Bickerton imagines much too difficult a task. In a number of places (e.g. Preston 1989, 1991a, 1991b, 1991c, 1996a, 1996b) a model has been suggested that variation ought to be considered from the point of view of a psycholinguistic model (i.e. from the point of view of the individual) as well as that of a sociolinguistic one (i.e. from the point of view

---

[4] Chomsky (1995:131) also mentions with favor the possibility that "there is only one human language, apart from the lexicon, and language acquisition is in essence a matter of determining lexical idiosyncrasies." Chomsky can say both "every human being speaks a variety of languages" and "there is only one human language" without feeling the slightest twinge of contradiction, because the notion "languages" plays no real role in his thinking. It will not be possible here to explicate the attractive idea that languages might be distinguished only by lexical idiosyncrasies, but suffice it to say such lexicons would include functional elements whose properties trigger various syntactic configurations.

Table 3.2 *Hypothetical contribution of social factors in the selection of* the *(derived from Marsh 1981)*

Factor	Probability
Non-physician	.40
Short-term relationship	.28
Lower middle-class status	.30
Combined influences	.32

of the speech community). The model proposed involves a probabilistic device, revised in the several versions cited above.

For a two-way variable, a speaker (and we will operate on a speaker- rather than hearer-focused model) is equipped with a coin, the two sides of which represent the options for that variable; it is flipped before the product appears. In Marsh's study above, a two-sided coin (with *my/your* on one side and *the* on the other) is prepared.

Since normal coins are fair, the one proposed here is as likely to turn up heads as tails (i.e. the two sides are in "free variation"), but, when we were kids we believed that unfair coins could be made. We thought that if you added weight to the tails side of a coin and flipped it, it was more likely to come up heads (and vice versa); the more weight you added to one side, the greater the probability it would come up on the other side. Although this theory may be physically suspect, we believed it as kids (and suspected kids who won a lot of money of knowing how to do it); let's also naively believe here that it is true so that we may make this coin responsive to various influences, some relatively permanent (e.g. social status), some fleeting (the phonetic environment).

Marsh has shown that social and professional status and length of relationship all influence the probability of article versus pronoun realization – the result of unfair coin tosses. For the purposes of this illustration, let's select the lower-middle-class patient in a short-term relationship with his or her physician mentioned just above, and let's further imagine that we have done some more sophisticated statistical work in which we have shown the precise contribution of each factor (status, profession, relationship) to the probability for *the* (Table 3.2).

If our fictional respondent uttered one hundred mentions of his or her hand (admittedly unlikely in such a short-term relationship), there would be approximately thirty-two instances of *the* and sixty-eight of *my*. In short, such a model is psycholinguistically plausible; it shows how Bickerton's objection to variability is not an issue. When respondents issue twenty, forty, or sixty percent of one form of a variable, they are not monitoring their overall performance with some sort of tallying device. They are evidencing the influence of a set of probabilistic weights that come to bear on each occurrence, a cognitively plausible (rather simple) operation. Since this is Bickerton's principal psychostatistical objection to the notion of variation, we may put it aside. Note that so far the model proposed is also compatible with the claim that variation is the result of moving back and forth between alternative grammars (or "lects") but that Bickerton regards such fluctuation as due to unstudiable social factors. As Marsh has shown, however, the influence of such social factors as status, profession, and length of relationship are not unstudiable at all.

A second objection to such modeling came from those who suggested that figures of groups or speech communities did not reflect the even more variable performance of individuals (e.g. Petyt 1980:188–90), although we are not sure what psycholinguistic claim was being made about the individual in this objection (except to somehow suggest that the variability is so idiosyncratic that it is not worth studying). The first (and most conclusive) answer to this claim was provided by Macaulay (1978), who showed that the actual performance of individuals reveals that such statistical modeling is accurate. In short, the community- or group-derived norms reflect individual (i.e. psycholinguistic) facts.

From another perspective, it is perhaps true that sociolinguists have not been as preoccupied with the underlying cognitive foundations of the social categories used in Level I studies as theoretical linguists have been with the cognitive founda-tions of human language. But sociolinguists are still linguists, and, even at Level I, seek correlations of social facts with linguistic form. It is the correlation which interests them, and they look to others (e.g. cognitive anthropologists) to pro-vide evidence for the cognitive foundations of social identities and relationships. Perhaps such foundations will turn out to be as simple as X-bar relations. For example, perhaps they will be reducible to such characteristic animal behaviors as territoriality and display, and their correlation with variant linguistic features will, therefore, be no more than different superficial manifestations of relatively straightforward (perhaps innate and not even uniquely human) biological man-dates. You might want to reanalyze Brown and Levinson's "faces" and their correlation with linguistic indirectness in just that way. Anyone who watches the same animal channels we do will not take long to come up with the idea that the use of some linguistic forms might be thought of as submissive displays. But we are wandering (although not perhaps too wildly, as Jakendoff [1994, espe-cially Chapter 15], suggests). In summary, Level I sociolinguistics links socio-cultural factors (however deeply rooted in even biological forces) with linguistic forms (all enfranchised by a grammar or several grammars, themselves all rooted in some sort of species linguistic mandate). That linking is probabilistic, not categorical.

Level II

In Level II sociolinguistic studies, variationists tease out the influence of one linguistic factor on another. Table 3.3 shows the results of a recent example of such a study.

Table 3.3 *Factors influencing subject doubling in Ontario French (adapted from Nadasdi 1995)*

Factors	Factor weight	Tokens	%
1. Noun Type			
1st and 2nd person pronoun	KO		100
3rd person pronoun	.861	145/195	74
Proper noun	.681	51/118	43
Common noun	.462	496/2187	23
Indefinite pronoun	.261	14/115	12
2. Subject NP			
Transitive/unergative	.607	477/1306	37
Unaccusative	.414	215/1160	19
Passive	.251	14/149	9

In Ontario French, as in several non-standard varieties of English, one may produce double subjects such as the following:

Mes parents *ils* étaient partis.
"My parents *they* left."

Just as in Level I studies, the choice of alternatives here (double subject/no double subject) is related to certain factors. As Table 3.3 shows, the specificity of the subject and the grammatical type of the subject promote (and demote) the occurrence of double subjects. Level II studies seek reasons for such linguistic influences just as Level I studies try to provide sociocultural explanations for why certain identities and relationships distinguish themselves linguistically. In this case, Nadasdi (1995) suggests that the clitic personal pronouns which realize the subject doubling should share features with the subject which they duplicate (as in the Matching Hypothesis suggested by Suñer [1988]). Since these pronouns are +specific, they are more likely to be realized if the degree of specificity of the subject is high (as it is in first and second person pronouns) and much less likely to be realized if the subject is less specific (as is the case with indefinite pronoun subjects). This specificity continuum has been independently suggested by, for example, Comrie (1981), Chesterman (1991), and Quirk, Greenbaum, Leech, and Svartvik (1972).

   Doubling is also more likely to occur when the subject is a typical agent-like subject of a transitive (e.g. *touch*) or unergative (e.g. *speak, sleep*) verb. Doubling is much less likely when the subject is one of an unaccusative verb, in which the subject is patient-like (e.g. *break*, as in *The vase broke*), and double subjects are extremely unlikely when the subject is one of a passive. Nadasdi points out that again there is a feature mismatch, this time between the subjects of unaccusatives and passives and the clitics which duplicate them. The clitics have a +subject feature, but, although the subjects of unaccusatives and passives surface as subjects, their deeper patient or object role does not match up well with the +subject feature of the clitics.

This search for influencing factors among (not outside) the components of a grammar characterizes Level II sociolinguistic research, and Level II work is not unusual; it is, in fact, common among sociolinguists. For example, the leading journal in our enterprise, *Language Variation and Change*, Volume 9 (1997), contained fifteen articles in all; two were Level I only studies; six were Level II only; the remainder combined Level I and II observations. That is not surprising to us, for we believe linguistic (not sociocultural) motives for variation are strongest. In an extensive review of the literature (Preston 1991a, b), it was found that linguistic influences were so much stronger than sociocultural ones that this relationship was formulated as the *Status Axiom* (by analogy with Bell's [1984] *Style Axiom*). This observation suggests that such variability as that in Nadasdi's study, determined as it is by linguistic forces, is available to lower-level sociocultural (or status) variability (so that it surfaces in Level I studies) but that such linguistic influences are nearly always probabilistically heavier than sociocultural influences. In some ways, we think this observation, although it was based on a large number of careful statistical studies, may have been almost too obvious. When some part of the sociocultural world (whether one which reflects identity or relationship) wants to symbolize itself linguistically, it most subtly does so by asserting a preference for one form or another. Where will it find alternative modes of expression? The sociocultural world itself is not prepared to provide the sort of variation described in Nadasdi's study, for the sociocultural world is not made up of such things as passive versus unaccusative subjects. If there are options in the grammar, however, based primarily on accompanying linguistic forces, they may be reweighted by sociocultural ones to carry part of the burden of the presentation of identity and the manipulation of interactional stances.

What sort of psycholinguistic device have we made for ourselves now? Figure 3.5 shows us two possibilities, both of which we suspect may have some truth to them. In the first possibility, shown entirely inside Grammar 1, a fact "c" (e.g. transitive subjects in Ottawa French) has an influence on the selection of "a" (double subject clitic pronouns) on the basis of the underlying and superficial matching feature +subject. One feature of the grammar selects another. A second possibility is that the occurrence of one feature in the grammar, in this case "c" (third person pronoun subject in Ottawa French) refers to an extragrammatical feature "d" (degree of specificity, taken from the discoursal or information structure realm). This continuum, then, exerts an influence on the choice of double subjects, in this case, one which makes the occurrence more likely "a" since there is a more highly specified subject.

We might seek even further and suggest that the position of a double subject clitic pronoun in I of I′ (as Nadasdi suggests, Figure 3.6) is precisely in the place where agreement is checked by subjects. If Ottawa French no longer recognizes the typically phonetically reduced verbal morphology which realizes agreement

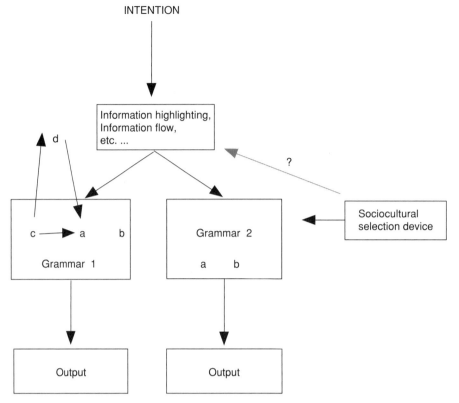

Figure 3.5 *A Level II psycholinguistic model*

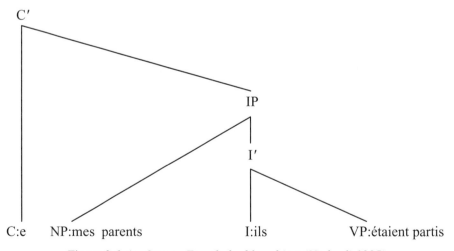

Figure 3.6 *An Ottawa French double subject (Nadasdi 1995)*

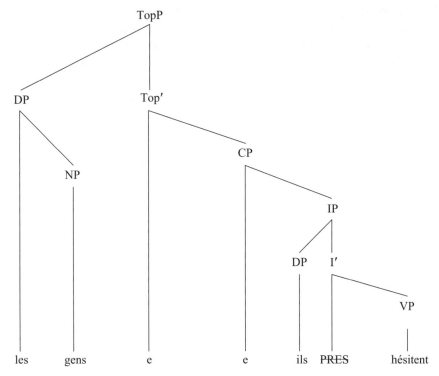

Figure 3.7 *Topicalized structure for* (En Ontario) les gens ils hésitent

features on verbs, the presence of the "extra" clitic subject pronoun is motivated by the subject's need to check off an agreement feature and the verb's inability to satisfy it. In such a case, the clitic pronoun no longer has the status of pronoun (since it would require the same theta-role as the subject) and has simply become an agreement feature.

Since the site (I) is there in French grammar in general, the variability has only to do with what sort of material fills it. Again, we see no need to suggest that a different grammar is required when the I is filled by a double subject clitic pronoun (perhaps only an "overt agreement feature") and when it is not. When variationists seek to explain such internal grammatical variability in Level II studies, they seek the same sorts of explanatory evidence general linguists do. They are, admittedly, less likely (perhaps like old Occam and his razor, even reluctant) to believe that every such piece of variation requires a new grammar, suspecting, instead, that inherent variability exists where grammatical systems permit it and that different grammars (perhaps especially for the same speaker in the same language) are rather radical requirements.

It will be useful to examine just how Level II variation phenomena can be incorporated into a contemporary Minimalist Program theory, if they can be at all. It is not clear to us that Nadasdi's clitics-as-agreement analysis is to be pre-ferred over a topicalization or left-dislocation analysis (e.g. Figure 3.7) (despite the fact that Nadasdi gives arguments against topicalization). But if Nadasdi's interpretation turns out to be right, it would still be possible that the double subject constructions are derived historically from topicalization. In other words, we might be looking at a historical syntactic change, where a later generation reanalyzes what for their parents was topicalization, as double subjects in some cases. The choice available to the generation of speakers with the new syntax, between verbal inflections that are not phonetically realized and those that are realized as clitics, still might do some of the same discourse work that topicalization did for their parents, though perhaps not as much so (since topicalization is still available to the younger speakers). In other words, double subjects might serve discourse needs as a kind of "topicalization light." In any case, we would expect that where there is a choice in syntax, it will be exploited pragmatically to make discourse distinctions.

In any case, the independent syntactic variables that Nadasdi finds to favor double subjects – definiteness, specificity, and provenience of the subject – would not be part of a variable syntactic process, but the effect of pragmatic influences on the choice of one structural configuration rather than another. In other words, they would be selected in a general discourse context in which "light topicalization" is also likely to be selected. These variables would no more causally "favor" double subjects than owning a Lexus causally "disfavors" suffering from hunger. As long as we assume an autonomous syntax, all there is in syntax is a set of possible constructions, which may or may not be chosen. Whether or not they are chosen in a particular utterance does not affect their syntactic analysis one wit.

But suppose that view is not correct, and there are grammar-internal factors that directly affect the choice of variants of a variable. If so, we should consider what sort of modifications would be required of generative syntax to accommodate a model that allowed for the direct and variable influence of purely syntactic features on some resulting construction. First of all, if we interpret variation as it is normally interpreted in variationist sociolinguistics – as an attempt to account for the distribution of elements in records of observed speech – then expecting generative syntax to account for that would require a philosophical sea change in generative syntax as it has always been practiced. Generative syntax has always been about *sentences,* that is, about what constructions are and are not permitted under the constraints of Universal Grammar and its allowable parameters. Variation analysis, in practice at least, has implicitly been about *utterances,* that is, about accounting for what we find in records of observed speech. To be sure, variationists take what is observed to be evidence of what is possible, but the practice is about the analysis of utterances. That is, the validity of a variable rule statistical analysis is judged by how well it predicts what is found in the data. But there is no reason why both approaches could not agree that variation is, at least in part, a measure of *degree of grammaticality*. Constructions that are more likely to show up in records of utterances and/or are judged more acceptable could be taken as more grammatical than others, though other instances might also be taken as having some lesser degree of grammaticality.

In Nadasdi's analysis, we might allow NPs that are candidates for the initial subject in double-subject constructions to bear variable values for specificity and definiteness, rather than plus or minus. A definite NP like *les gars* "the guys" might have a value of, say, [.69 definite], while *un homme* "a man" might get [.31 definite]. These values would contribute to the ability of these NPs to satisfactorily match the [+definite] value that the clitic, now interpreted as the head of inflection, has. When all the variable values contributed by the definiteness, specificity, etc. of the NP are computed, we end up with a value that measures how grammatical the resulting construction is, if the clitic inflection is used. This idea would be hard to implement, since it is far from clear how individual NPs would get their definiteness values assigned within an autonomous syntax. It would be more feasible, perhaps, to resurrect the old-fashioned variable-rule format of Labov (1969). Instead of particular probabilities, we could assign Greek letter values to a feature like [specific] in place of plus or minus. This results in a ranking of the variable contribution of these features, rather than a particular numerical value. Nadasdi's Table 3.1 (1995:7) is exactly the kind of display that would have led to the assignment of α to [specific] ([α specific]) and β to [definite] ([β definite]) in the old variable rule system. This could be taken to predict that if the initial subject is [+specific] and [+definite], the selection of the double subject results in the most thoroughly grammatical construction; if it is [+specific] and [−definite] it is next most grammatical, with [−specific] and [+definite], then [−specific] and [−definite], predicting successively lower levels of grammaticality.[5] Such a theory would not predict the likelihood of the occurrence of a double subject under any of these conditions, but that could be estimated from a set of observed speech data, as is presently done using statistical methods such as VARBRUL.[6]

Either of these implementations would be a radical departure from anything we are aware of as having been proposed in variation analysis, or, even less likely, in Minimalist syntactic analysis. But it seems that if we want a way of making precise what inherent syntactic variability means, something of the sort would be required.[7] Furthermore, merely assigning probability or Greek-letter values to

---

[5] With the concomitant assumption that more grammatical constructions appear more often in observed language use than less grammatical constructions do.

[6] Notice that we are assuming here, contrary to what we said earlier and to what Nadasdi says, that features like [definite] and [specific] are binary. This is true even when we speak of [.69 definite] or [±definite]. These notations refer only to the inclination to select the double-subject construction if the binary feature has a + value. The reality seems to be that these features are not binary at all, but take on a degree of definiteness or specificity based on the discourse context, and that there is a sliding correlation between degree of definiteness, say, and the tendency toward double subjects. It is possible that a theory that allows this sort of case to be expressed in its syntax module is desirable, but the resulting theory would not be a version of generative syntax. Generative syntax is about sentences, not utterances, and its computations can refer only to features that elements bring with them from the lexicon, not what they may gain when used in context. We obviously cannot try to develop such a theory here; to develop one with the degree of precision of existing formal theories would take many years of work.

[7] In any case, this modification of syntax, even though it would not require accepting a syntactic theory of utterances, would still require the acceptance of a syntactic theory that assigned degrees of grammaticality. In the judgment of one author (Fasold), it would be far more reasonable to

features like [specific] and [definite] would obscure the level of explanation we can get by associating these features with the discourse functions of topicalization, perhaps as the historical source of the present-day double-subject phenomenon.

In fact, the desire to limit the number of grammars in individuals (especially in monolinguals) seems to us to go along with one of the very best traditions of the generative movement – the desire for economy and simplicity. Current models of syntax suggest that lexical items bring their grammatical demands with them. Items which have considerable categorical similarity may, in fact, bring very different syntactic demands, imposing natural variation on any human language. Let's look at just one simple English example. English has verbs such as *be*, *have*, *walk*. When verbs are used in question sentences, they trigger different kinds of syntactic behavior.

Bill is in the other room. Is Bill in the other room?
Bill walks to school. Does Bill walk to school?

Why no *Does Bill be in the other room?* (in most dialects) nor *Walks Bill to school?* (in Modern English)? The answer is easy: *be* verbs and non-*be* verbs bring different syntactic instructions along with them when they come from the lexicon. How about this?

Bill has a dollar. Does Bill have a dollar?
Has Bill a dollar?

Most people will recognize that most Americans cannot say "Has Bill a dollar?" but that many speakers of other Englishes can. It might be tempting to say that these are two different grammars (and that a person who can use both has two different grammars). We would not like to say that. At least, we would not like to say that there are two grammars in a speaker's mind on the basis of two settings for a verb like *have* when both of those settings correspond to ones for such other items as *be* and *walk*. If you can say "Does have Bill a dollar?" or "Has a dollar Bill," we will concede a different grammar, but we are not prepared to grant different grammars to individuals who have some lexical items set to different characteristics when those very characteristics are the same as those for many other well-established items. To be precise, if *have* can behave like a *be* verb and a *walk* verb in some varieties, we take that to be a double classification in the lexicon with no repercussions whatsoever on what syntactic configurations are allowed and disallowed in English. As suggested before, once both forms are there, either sociocultural (Level I) or other linguistic (Level II) items may (in fact, almost certainly will) exert probabilistic influences on their selection.

The various linguistic features which have an influence on one another might belong to different modules of linguistic competence, but we know of no serious

keep grammar and usage separate. The theory of syntax would then remain a theory of what is possible in the syntax of natural language. The results of variation analysis would be taken as a measure of the influence of discoursal, identity, and "style" factors on the usage of these possible constructions.

theoretical proposal which suggests that these modules are not in communication with one another. In short, that we have not yet arrived at a more definitive theoretical proposal concerning the exact shape of linguistic competence (and its relation to modules outside it) will not hurt the model proposed here, and we hope it will not damage any egos to suggest that theoretical work in variationist linguistics is simply a little ahead of some other subfields. That will be true almost by definition, for we have not had the luxury of "ideal native-speaker hearers," a reasonable fiction which has allowed a productive head start in many areas of linguistic concern but will probably not do the job of providing a full account of linguistic competence as regards real people.

Finally, perhaps it is important to note that sociolinguists who till Level II fields are not necessarily functionalists. Nadasdi's work on the preference for subject doubling is based on syntactic features, and work by Scherre and Naro (1991) shows that subject–verb agreement marking in Brazilian Portuguese depends most crucially on whether or not a previous item was marked, not on any desire to disambiguate.

Level III

Finally we come to whatever it is sociolinguists could be doing at Level III. Surely we must have covered the territory! Not at all; sociolinguists are particularly concerned with ongoing linguistic change, and they seek to relate patterns of linguistic change to both the sociocultural forces studied in Level I and the linguistic forces of Level II. Let's look at one such data set. Tagliamonte (1998) studies a number of standard and non-standard realizations of *was/were* in Yorkshire English. One context she looks at in detail is the occurrence of non-standard *was* in existential constructions (e.g. *There was no apples in the barrel*). Table 3.4 shows the results.

This is pretty clearly Level I work since, surprisingly, women outstrip men in non-standard performance (.56 to.40), and, predictably, better-educated speakers use the non-standard form less (.36 to.55). It is also obviously Level II work since such grammatical features as polarity and such other features as adjacency proved to be significant. (The latter tells us whether the verb is next to or removed from the NP with which it should agree, e.g. *There was three men here* versus *There was as recently as last Friday three men here*, respectively.)

Tagliamonte adds, however, as have many variationists, the category "Generation." It is important to distinguish age as a social category from age as an attempt to look at emerging (and receding) linguistic practices (and, presumably, the grammars which underlie those practices). Of course, age may be simply a "social category." Teenagers use slang items which they will not use when they become adults; they are, therefore, not indicators of cutting-edge forms in the language. They are, instead, generationally distributed features, ones which indicate a speaker's age by virtue of his or her use but do not point us in the

Table 3.4 *Factor weights and percentages for influences on non-standard* was *in existential constructions (Tagliamonte 1998:181)*

Factor group	Weight	%	N
1. Polarity			
affirmative	.54	66	287
negative	.11	17	23
2. Adjacency			
non-adjacent	.55	67	239
adjacent	.33	45	69
3. Sex			
female	.56	67	191
male	.40	55	119
4. Generation			
20–30	.70	77	57
30–50	.50	55	44
50–70	.50	67	81
over 70	.41	57	125
5. Education			
to 16 years	.55	64	232
beyond 16 years	.36	59	76

direction of the future of the language. It is often difficult to tell the difference between such age-related performance and actual change, but variationists have developed a number of tests which make the distinction less difficult to make. For example, in many cases, the younger and older members of a speech community agree in being the most frequent users of a non-standard feature, for they are the groups least influenced by the daily pressure of the linguistic marketplace to conform to more overt community norms (e.g. Chambers and Trudgill [1998:78–9], who show such a distribution for a number of features, including *-in* versus *-ing* variation in English). That is clearly not the case in Table 3.4. The youngest speakers are the principal users of non-standard *was* in existential constructions, and the oldest use it least, with the generations between balanced at exactly .50. If, as Tagliamonte suspects, this is an indication of linguistic change in progress (that is, that non-standard *was* is emerging as a new norm), then the unusual pattern of sex and education can be explained. Since women most often are more inclined to use more overtly prestigious forms (i.e. those promulgated by schools, usage authorities, and the like), it was noted above that women's preference for the non-standard *was* form was surprising. Since younger speakers also prefer non-standard *was*, however, and there is no surprising interaction between sex and age, young women are the most frequent users of this non-standard form. This relationship between sex and age allows us to conclude, tentatively if you like, that non-standard *was* is an emerging norm in this speech community, for young women are leaders (though usually not inventors) in implementing linguistic change. That is, as soon as a new form is relatively well established in the speech community, younger women are among the first to adopt it and promote its use. In this case, although conservative forces have kept the new norm slightly behind on the educational dimension, the relationship between the categories age and sex make us fairly certain that a new norm is emerging.

Of course, all the work done in Level I and Level II studies should be done in such studies as well as the "historical" interpretation (and its relation to the Level I and Level II factors, only one part of which has been done here). For example, although many sociolinguists would agree that women are both conservative (in their adherence to overt linguistic norms) and leaders (in being early promoters of incipient norms), why that is so is difficult indeed (e.g. as the exchange between Eckert [1989] and Labov [1990] shows). But we will assume that it is understood that it should be done and that grammatical or other cognitive interpretations of the effects of polarity and adjacency are also a part of the variationist's obligation in such a study. If you grant that, on the basis of such suggestions given above, we will move on.

What has Level III work done to the psycholinguistic model? We're afraid it will introduce an element not to everybody's liking. Figure 3.8 shows a shaded area in the Grammar 1 and a completely shaded Grammar 2. We leave it open for the purposes of this paper whether the clear and shaded areas in Grammar 1 represent sets of choices within one grammar or a choice between two grammars. Those shadings represent weaker areas of the grammar (or a weaker grammar). What is the source of grammatical weakness?

Native speakers typically learn a "vernacular" – the first-learned form of their language. Needless to say, it comes from interaction with parents, siblings, and other children in contexts which are relatively free from formal constructions. Whatever else we learn (whether native or non-native) is *postvernacular*, and it will, no matter how good we get at it, not have the deeply embedded status of our vernacular. We will not be as fluent in our postvernacular. Consider the following:

(a)   If I had more money, I'd buy a BMW.
(b)   Had I more money, I'd buy a BMW.

In the case of both authors, (a) belongs to the vernacular. If we want to express the idea contained in (a) and (b) (which we take to be the same), we will with the greatest of ease go to our vernacularly-embedded choice – namely (a). We don't know when we learned (b); certainly not while one author (Preston) was playing hoops in Southern Indiana ("Quick! Had I the ball, I'd score!"), but we eventually learned it, first, no doubt to process it and later to produce it, although we are fairly certain that our production is still "imitative" in some sense rather than productive. That is, we cannot imagine any circumstance in which we would use it (spoken or written) except to imitate (probably sarcastically) a high-falutin' style (or, more likely, to mock such a speaker). We also have no doubt that there

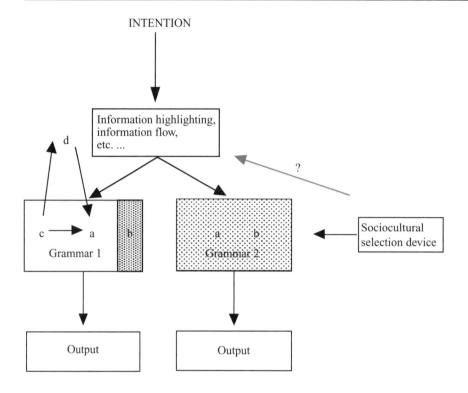

Figure 3.8 *A Level III psycholinguistic model*

are weaknesses in our grammaticality judgments of sentences constructed along the lines of (b) above but that we are rock-solid in the (a) territory.

This outrageous claim means, of course, that any real speaker who could hope to pretend to be an ideal native-speaker/hearer (with the sorts of judgments we would want to elicit when we attempt to confirm claims about competence) would have to be one questioned about the linguistic competence of his or her pre-postvernacular period. The further afield any postvernacular constructions are from the grammatical settings of the vernacular, the weaker the grammar at those points and the less reliable respondent judgments about that territory will be. It follows that performance in that area as well is less likely to be an accurate reflection of competence.

When we refer to adult grammars, therefore, we refer inevitably to grammars which look like those of Grammar 1 in Figure 3.8 – ones which have postvernacular areas in which the constructions are less well embedded in competence or "weaker." In short, adult learners of their own language encounter syntactic (and other) characteristics which they learn in no substantially different a way than the way second or foreign language learners learn things (as in Grammar 2 in Figure 3.8), and we have no reason to assume that they end up embedded in the underlying grammars in any significantly different way.

The idea of postvernaculars corresponds to recent very sophisticated work in historical linguistics, which has shown that the statistical robustness of input is crucial to the establishment of parameters. Lightfoot (1999) reckons it to be somewhere between seventeen and thirty percent in his account of the loss of V2 ("verb second") in English (1999:436). DeGraff (1999) summarizes what Lightfoot concludes:

> One of *David Lightfoot's* cardinal pleas is that models for syntax acquisition and for syntactic change be sensitive to factors outside of syntax . . . Assuming that UG . . . is genetically wired and remains constant, one reason why parameter values would shift through acquisition is that factors *external* to syntax and/or to language itself indirectly effect changes in certain aspects of the triggering experience – for example in the frequency of occurrence of particular construction types that "cue" the learner to the values of certain parameters [italics in original].   (1999:33)

First, if this is so, and Lightfoot reviews a great deal of careful quantitative historical work which suggests it is, at the very least one would want to know the quantitative product of variation studies in the search for parametric-setting cues, which are based, as he suggests, on their frequency in input. We hope it is clear that this statement is somewhat different from earlier representations of frequency in language use as having no relevance to the study of language competence whatsoever.

Second, however, we find even Lightfoot's welcome representation of the importance of performance frequency to competence settings not radical enough. Lightfoot's discussion refers to external language phenomena to be found in observed speech ("E-language"), which he contrasts with the internal principles and parameters of the presumed biological language endowment ("I-language"). He seems to assume a sort of facile bidialectalism in all speakers who evidence both forms, but he fails to demonstrate that factors predicted by V2 and non-V2 grammars co-occur exclusively when a speaker is using one dialect or the other. In short, he does not convince us that the non-V2 setting was not "weakly" estab-lished in some individual grammars (as shown in Figure 3.8) and became the dominant pattern over the years. We do not doubt that south of England vari-eties of English at that time had the growing prestige which allowed the eventual crucial input figure to drive out the competing V2, but we do doubt that all speak-ers who used V2 and non-V2 constructions were fluent bidialectals, employing "properly" all the attendant constructions which would depend on those settings "downstream" from their occurrences. More likely, many had weak grammars of one setting or the other, so weak, for example, that the attendant characteristics of that setting could be suppressed or might emerge only in conjunction with certain lexical items, spreading to the entire grammar as it strengthened.

At a different level of representation, the notions of strength outlined above seem to relate to the mysterious factor which lurks behind what has been called "style" in general throughout the history of quantitative sociolinguistics. Perhaps

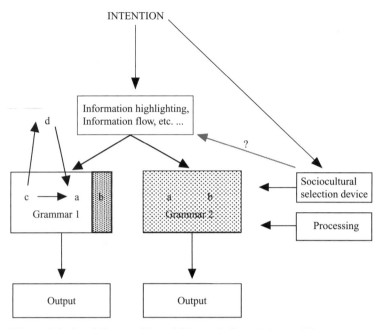

Figure 3.9 *An elaborated Level III psycholinguistic model*

the major psycholinguistic upshot of such factors is, as Labov has suggested (e.g. 1972g), "monitoring" or "attention to speech." Although "style" is, we suspect, a cover term for a much larger number of sociocultural functions which need to be teased out in greater detail, the psycholinguistic upshot of some items being sought by more careful monitoring may be conveniently related to the notion of the postvernacular outlined above. One must look more carefully for items not so well embedded, and even that will not insure that they are retrieved (or retrieved "correctly"). That fact suggests that the model provided so far, although based on "internal" and "external" factors which are required for a general psycholinguistic account of competence and performance, overlooks the component which contains the abilities most often addressed in psycholinguistic accounts – memory, accessibility, processing, and the like. We are aware that such factors play an important role and may be associated directly with the "weakness" of the Grammar we characterize above. Figure 3.9 repairs that oversight, without detail (and mentions another important connection which we discuss only briefly below).

Although we agree with Lightfoot that changes are very often the result of misparsings, misunderstandings, mishearings, and the like, which the historical account of any language is rich with, we are much more likely than him to suggest that those which ought to imply far-reaching parametric resetting consequences may not immediately do so (if ever). That they do not, is another source of variable competence.

What might the grammar of a speaker with a weak postvernacular innovation look like? One suggestion is that speakers have a genuinely new grammatical feature, one that has inevitable downstream consequences, but are too unsure of the new thing to actually *use* the new feature except in contexts in which they heard it. Here's what we mean. Suppose that *do*-support developed when English was a V2 language, from the use of *do* that meant "cause," as some historical linguists speculate (cf. Kroch 1989a, 1989b). That would mean that one could say things that in modern English words and spelling would sound like:

She did him sit and rest and comforted him.
"She made him sit and rest and comforted him."

If one were to question the first conjunct of this example according to the grammar of the time, the first verb would be moved to the second position:

Did she him sit and rest?

On the other hand, the second conjunct would come out:

Comforted she him?

Cases like this, where the complement clause of *did* contains an overt subject (here *him*), make it clear that the causative meaning is intended. But there are other cases where the complement clause subject is PRO, so that one might hear:

A castle he did [PRO raise].
"He had a castle built."

The question form of this would be:

A castle did he [PRO raise]?

When verbs in the English lexicon began to lose their strong agreement feature – the feature that forces the movement to the second position – *do* took on a kind of semantically empty meaning, simply supporting the agreement features left stranded by the new verb property that prevented non-auxiliary verbs from moving to second position.

Now suppose early adopters of the new, weak-agreement-verb grammar had both kinds of verbs in their mental lexicon. More accurately, suppose that the lexical feature that designates verbs comes in two versions, one that implies strong agreement, and one that does not. It could even be the case, and perhaps it is likely that it was, that at first only some verbs came in these two versions, while the rest all had strong agreement. To a person with the new weak-agreement grammar a sentence like

Did he raise a castle?

would be ambiguous. It could have either of the structures below.

Did he [PRO raise a castle]?
Did he raise a castle?

It could mean either "Did he have somebody build a castle?" (the first structure above) or "Did he build a castle?" (the second structure), while for a speaker

without the innovation, it could only mean the former. Since the difference in
the two readings is pretty subtle, the two kinds of speaker could communicate
without much danger of serious misunderstanding. If speakers with the innovation
limited their use of the new *do*-support *do* to contexts in which the ambiguity was
possible, there would be no apparent "downstream" consequences. If one were
to ask such speakers, "Can you say: 'Did he wash his hands?'", i.e. in a context
where the causative meaning is unlikely, they might well say, "I don't know, it
sounds odd. It would be better to say 'Washed he his hands?',", despite the fact
that their grammars have the option to produce the *do*-support version (assuming
that *wash* is one of the verbs that comes in both strong- and weak-agreement
flavors). The grammar is there, but only weakly there, hence the reluctance to
use, or even endorse the use of, the new feature in contexts beyond those where
it began to develop.

Since sociolinguists have theirs ears to the ground, they are most likely to
catch those emerging performances, whether they have far-reaching effects on
the language or not. It is clear to anyone who has spent a great deal of time
listening to current US English that something is up with auxiliaries. We bet
almost anyone can give the interrogative form of *He should not have left so soon.*
Speakers who say *Should he not have left so soon?* or *Shouldn't he've left so soon?*
are ones pretty much like us. Somewhat younger speakers might be able to say
Shouldn't've he left so soon? or even the, to us, amazing *Shouldn't've he've left so
soon?* We are absolutely certain that these new patterns are tied to a reanalysis of
the underlying form of *have*, one which goes far beyond its occurrence as stressed
of, regarded by some as a trivial (misunderstood) phonological (or only written)
alternative to *have*. Although we are interested in the new encliticization (which
the current grammar can handle), we are also interested in the repercussions of
such reanalysis on the arrangement of items in the grammars of real, emerging
Englishes.

As suggested earlier, even if the radical proposal that individual grammars
contain not only alternatives but even competing alternatives (in the sense that they
imply but do not deliver different constructions in related parts of the grammar)
is not acceptable, recall that even Lightfoot endorses the idea that performance
criteria (e.g. frequency), themselves based on such non-linguistic features as
prestige and geography, are essential in determining linguistic change. Of course,
there is much left undone here. We have not really outlined a careful representation
of how these weak grammars are to be fully represented. We have only stated
rather than shown that psycholinguistic processes such as retrieval, accessibility,
memory, and the like are the areas at stake in the concept of weaker grammars (or
parts of grammars). Moreover, the probabilistic model we have drawn here does
not fully determine the output of grammars since the "intention" of a speaker may
interact with his or her sociocultural identity. That is, one may choose to "perform"
(or perform to a greater or lesser extent) an available sociocultural identity, and
such choices must play a role in the activation of the selection determined by
sociocultural selection. That proviso, however, makes this program more difficult,

not inconceivable. We have also ignored the operation of probabilistic or variable rules in the framework of phonology and morphophonology, the areas most often exploited in variationist research. We do this in part because we believe it is much less controversial to suggest that internal factors (e.g. natural phonetic processes) have an obvious influence on the realization of other (internal) phonetic facts.

In conclusion, however, we hope our readers are convinced of (or at least are agnostic about) the possibility of the sort of variable competence outlined here. Those readers who are will join those of the most theoretically oriented persuasion who see the importance of quantity in the development of new grammars (and the modification of old ones), and they will certainly join with variationists whose modularity is, we hope to have shown, beyond suspicion.

4 The study of variation in historical perspective

KIRK HAZEN

Variationist linguistic analysis

As Milroy and Gordon (2003:5) document in their introduction to sociolinguistics, variationist methodology is often considered a subfield of sociolinguistics. Chambers maintains a similar view: "The social significance of language variation is only one aspect of the discipline of sociolinguistics, broadly conceived" (2002b:1). The current chapter focuses primarily on developments within sociolinguistic variation research but also notes that other traditionally non-sociolinguistic fields have also employed variationist methodology. For a superb comparison of variationist and formal linguistic scholarly roots, see Chambers' (2002b) *Correlations* which details why the *axiom of categoricity* is a postulate language scholars must either adopt or reject (2002b:15). Here, this chapter is intended to provide a hint as to why so many scholars, including many outside of sociolinguistics proper, have chosen to reject it.[1]

Preston describes the quantitative sociolinguistic paradigm as one where language variation is not random: "The frequency of their [variable elements] occurrences is predicted (a) by the shape and identity of the element itself and its linguistic context; (b) by the stylistic level of the interactions; and (c) by the social identities a [*sic*] relationships of the interlocutors" (2001:691). The emphasis is on how language variation works; variationist scholars reject models where variation is an aberrant state between two seemingly stable states, instead following the concept of inherent variability first propagated by Weinreich, Labov, and Herzog (1968).

Although a wide variety of arguments are made in variationist work, they generally adhere to some basic tenets. Jones and Tagliamonte enumerate these "lines of evidence: (1) Which of the following factors is statistically significant? (2) What is the relative contributions of the linguistic features selected? Is it strong or weak? (3) What is the constraint ranking of the categories within each factor? (4) Finally,

---

[1] A note on the coverage of scholarly works in this chapter: as Chambers, Trudgill, and Schilling-Estes (2002:2) point out, "Until sometime in the 1980s, it was possible for an enterprising graduate student facing comprehensive examinations to read virtually everything in the field of sociolinguistics." This situation is no longer possible as even the subfield of variationist sociolinguistics has expanded voluminously since the mid-1980s.

does this order reflect the direction reported in the literature?" (2004:110). This approach incorporates the essence of variationist language analysis: quantitative empirical elucidation contributing towards a descriptive and explanatory analysis. Most often social and linguistic factors are considered, in line with variationists' sociolinguistic roots.

The scholarly genealogy for this methodology in variationist sociolinguistics is not as clearly demarcated as one might hope. Koerner (1991) argues that the broad and diverse field of sociolinguistics was not new in the 1960s but developed naturally from earlier dialectology (both European and American), historical linguistics, and multilingualism studies. For example, the social and historical examination of language was combined regarding sound change as motivated by class structure in Kloeke's (1927) study of Holland's dialect geography which Bloomfield (1933) exemplified for a discussion of isoglosses. Although scholars from these earlier fields made it possible to develop variationist analysis, by framing lexical and phonological variation, it is difficult to see where these earlier scholars innovated variationist analysis in a field-wide manner. To be sure, McDavid's (1948) analysis of post-vocalic /-r/ in South Carolina and Georgia is an early sociolinguistic study: he surmises that, "A social analysis proved necessary for this particular linguistic feature, because the data proved too complicated to be explained by merely a geographical statement or a statement of settlement history." Yet its careful sociohistorical background and empirical foundation beg for variationist analysis;[2] however, any influence it had on others' methodology has rarely been cited (cf. Shuy 1990). As Chambers (2002a:6) perceptively remarks, "The relationship between traditional dialectology and sociolinguistics is oblique rather than direct, but both in the broadest sense are dialectologies (studies of language variation). In terms of intellectual history it is plausible to view sociolinguistics as a refocusing of traditional dialectology." From dialectology, the conceptual field was fertile for the growth of the linguistic variable and its methodology; yet with variationist methodology, the focus of study became detached from only *regional dialects*. At times variationist sociolinguistics has focused on social dialects, at times on language variation patterns associated with dialects.

As linguists, variationists work from the findings of cognitive science to construct explanations for language variation both in the speech community and in the mind. The extraordinary trait of variationists-cum-linguists is the inclusion of social factors as well as linguistic factors in the explanations of language variation. Variationist linguistics is one of the newest linguistic approaches, but scholars have noted language variation since the ancient Greeks.

---

[2] To be fair, McDavid does divide counties/areas of South Carolina and Georgia into those with or without constriction and thus approximates a variationist analysis. But given the high quality of the article, and the fascinating footnotes, a modern reader expects to see a statistical analysis somewhere in the article.

Historical precedents

In 360 BCE, Plato wrote the dialogue *Cratylus* (Jowett 1937) where Socrates asks a simple question: Are names inherent to their objects or are they conventionally associated? Socrates argues for a natural connection and decries that "the present generation care for euphony more than truth." This complaint is one of the earliest extant complaints of language variation in western civilization. Many people have grumbled about language variation since Socrates, although few have systematically studied it.

Plato's *Cratylus* appears not to have fostered any schools for the study of language, apart from the already active study of *grammar* "the art of writing." Chambers (2002a:6) also recognizes the Roman Varro (116–127 BCE), who noted language variation and connected it to vernacular language use. Chambers proposes Varro's maxim, *consuetudo loquendi est in motu*, for the motto of sociolinguistics: "The vernacular is always in motion."[3]

In the modern era, Hermann Paul (1891) argued for the role of the individual for the focus of language study. He was reacting to the *Völkerpsychologie* which took up an ethos of community to be the controlling entity for social action. Paul intended for individuals, and their individual language decisions, to become the bounded scope for language analysis. He reasoned that only in individual decisions did language choices get made.[4] Although pricking the conceptual conscious of the other *Junggrammatiker*, he must not have envisioned the lengths to which the individual focus of language analysis would be taken. Weinreich, Labov, and Herzog (1968) identify this dichotomy as the fundamental problem of twentieth-century language-change paradoxes.

At the turn of the twentieth century, the study of language change incorporated only the examination of external language forms from large-scale communities of greatly different time periods. The linguistic *Gestalt* switch from the study of language change to internal language systems was based on the role of the individual.

In contrast to the *Junggrammatiker*, Saussure ([1916]1972) de-emphasized diachronic analysis in favor of synchronic analysis, but he retained to a small extent the concept of the individual as the locus of language: "The performance of language is never made by the group; it is always the individual, and the individual is always the master"[5] (1916[1972]:30). The scholarly study of an individual's grammar eventually found a stable home in the term *idiolect*.[6]

---

[3] Chambers employs this maxim as the epigraph to his book, *Sociolinguistic theory* (2002b).

[4] Paul also promoted a *psychischer Organismus*: a psychologically internalized grammar which generates the utterance of speakers (1891:105).

[5] "l'exécution n'est jamais faite par la masse; elle est toujours individuelle, et l'individu en est toujours le maître" [translation by the author]. In the very next paragraph, Saussure defines the term "la langue" as only perfectly existing in the collectivity.

[6] Saussure (1916[1972]:141) does use the prefix *idio* when discussing the focus of synchronic linguistics: "L'objet de la linguistique synchronique générale est d'établir le principes fondamentaux de tout système idiosynchronique ("the object of general synchronic linguistic

Weinreich, Labov, and Herzog (1968) essentially banished the term *idiolect* from sociolinguistics when they strongly opposed the nested view of language whereby an aggregate of idiolects compose a dialect. Instead, they argued that only the grammar of the speech community had consistent patterns and that individuals acquired their patterns from the speech community grammar. Thus within sociolinguistics, language variation patterns of individuals were not often studied except when aggregated to approximate and reveal the language variation patterns of the speech community.

The modern period

In 1963, William Labov's "The social motivation of a sound change" was published in *Word*, and in connection to its historical linguistic disposition, the context for the study may not have appeared as the most obvious choice. Up until that point, historical linguistics had only been concerned with languages of vastly diachronic situations. As a scholar, Labov was reacting to Saussure (1916[1972]) and Bloomfield (1933): specifically, he challenged their assessments of how language changes yet serves the community. Labov engaged Sturtevant's (1947) contribution where sound change starts in a few words and may then spread by analogy to others of the same class. The change may progress slowly and only end up appearing as a regular process.

In his study of Martha's Vineyard, Labov found that /ay/ and /aw/ had raised and centralized variants, [əy] and [əw]. Labov knew about the history of these vowels and other features of the area from the *Linguistic atlas of New England* (LANE, Kurath *et al.* 1941) and a previous study of some families on the island. For this island, the rapidly changing social scene allowed social divisions to drive differentiation of sociolinguistic variants. The native up-islanders resented the outsiders for overshadowing the traditional industry of fishing, in contrast to the down-islanders who supported the tourists. Labov implemented the apparent-time construct, assessing the percentage of raised, centralized variants against age groups.

Labov found that centralization corresponded with certain age groups. As importantly, he found that orientation towards Martha's Vineyard corresponded strongly with centralization. The import from this study was at least two fold: first, Labov demonstrated that sound change, long assumed to be either cataclysmic or glacially slow, was observable in synchronic variation; second, sound changes were connected to the social forces in a community. These were conceptual turning points in the scientific study of language.

study is to establish fundamental principles of all idiosynchronic systems" [translation by the author]). But the first use of the term *idiolect* is by Bernard Bloch (1948:7) in revising a set of postulates by Leonard Bloomfield: "The totality of possible utterances of one speaker at one time in using a language to interact with one other speaker is an *idiolect*." Bloch coined the term in order to establish a locus for language inside the larger abstractions of speech community and language.

In 1968, Uriel Weinreich, William Labov, and Marvin Herzog wrote the manifesto for variationist studies ("Empirical foundations for a theory of language change"). Historically speaking, its publication in the same year as Chomsky and Halle's *Sound pattern of English* (1968) is a poignant insight into the contrast of linguistic theories at the time. Weinreich *et al.* (1968) was an argument for the empirical examination of language. They also had to argue for the unification of synchronic and diachronic study in contrast to Saussure (1916[1972]) and Chomsky (1957).

For Paul, Saussure, and Chomsky, the legitimate object of study had been the language (system) of the individual, and thus homogeneity was a prerequisite for analysis. Weinreich *et al.* (1968) proposed that a focus on the heterogeneity of the speech community leads to better description of competence. Here they do not discard the goal of describing language knowledge in the mind but do offer up different methodologies for its description. In regards to diachronic variation, Weinreich *et al.* (1968) postulate a strong form and weak form for theories of language change: the strong form would be a theory that supports predictions;[7] the weak form assumes that a language is in continual change and scholars formulate constraints on that change (the theory might then predict what changes will not take place).

Weinreich *et al.* (1968:125) also were reacting to Chomsky's propagation of the *homogenous speech-community*[8] and the corresponding theoretical irrelevance of diversity. They (1968:150) instead offer a different view of change, where variation and regularity are both an integral part of language change. One major mechanism for encoding this theory for language variation and change was the concept of the linguistic variable[9] and the variable rule.[10]

One important finding, articulated in both Weinreich *et al.* (1968:180) and Labov (1966), demonstrated that stylistic variation is systematic, and the social class leaders of language change were not the upper class.

Labov (1966) is an innovative work on many levels for variationist studies. It was the first work to study on a large scale dialect patterns in an urban area. This study of New York City developed methods of previous sociological work in order to explore the interaction of language variation and social class. This urban focus was a major switch from the rural studies of dialectologist work, yet rural studies have continued in variationist work (Hazen 2000a, McNair 2005, Schilling-Estes 2002, Thomas 2001, Wolfram, Adger, and Christian 1999).

Expanding from Labov's work and Wolfram's own urban sociolinguistic work in Detroit, Wolfram (1973) focuses on the theoretical possibilities for variable rules, exploring the premises for the acceptance of such a concept. In early

---

[7] Perhaps this strong form is more conceivable today with the larger databases and more enhanced computational power under our control.

[8] See Patrick (2002) for an modern version of this debate.

[9] Later, primarily considered as a *sociolinguistic variable*.

[10] Linguists of today must realize the importance and dominance of mental rules in all varieties of linguistic theories of the time to understand the rhetorical draw of this concept.

variationist work such as this, the scholarly contextual forces are palpable: variationists were attempting to justify and develop their methodologies in the larger field of linguistics. Wolfram (1973) examines the substance of *inherent variability*, *replicable regularity*, and *language specificity*. Inherent variability, now a common assumption, is the position that the observed variation comes from a unitary system, rather than code-switching or borrowing. It may be hard for contemporary scholars to imagine anyone questioning the regular patterns of language variation, but it required defending in the early 1970s. Language specificity is also a topic most contemporary linguists would not consider defending: the contested concept was whether constraints on variation were universal or not; if they were, then they could not be included in a specific language's grammar.[11] Instead, modern scholars would be arguing the inverse (e.g. Chambers 2002a), that certain qualities are part of the Universal Grammar.

(Socio)linguistic variables and variable rules

Variable rules were first introduced in Labov (1969). In this original variable rule proposal, social factors did not play a role but were placed outside the variable rule. They could still affect the relative frequencies produced, but they did not play a direct role in the variable rule itself. Fasold (1991) argues that this theoretical choice is the most fruitful manner for analyzing linguistic variation. He elegantly reasons that since linguistic constraints rarely interact with each other, but social constraints do, the nature of these constraints (or rules) are different.

Labov (1969)[12] examines the copula, specifically *is*, in the Black English of New York to assess whether the grammar of that speech community had transformational grammar rules for the copula as did other dialects or whether it lacked those rules (1969:718). Publishing within *Language* may have prompted this purview. The results were that Labov foregrounded formal rules, brought to bear empirical observation of language behavior, and provided variable rules. As Labov (1969:715) writes in the abstract: "a model is presented for the decisive solution of abstract questions of rule form and rule relations, based upon the direct study of linguistic behavior." Specifically, Labov (1969:738) adds φ (phi) to the formal rule structure which "denotes the proportion of cases in which the rule applies as a part of the rule structure itself." In doing so, and establishing $\varphi = 1 - k_o$ where k_o is the variable input to the rule, Labov postulates that the factors influencing variable production are restraining categorical application of the rule rather than prompting production from the non-application of the rule.

---

[11] Apparently, the universal qualities were not considered to be part of a specific language's grammar. In more modern times, universal traits are built into speakers' mental grammars (and thus are part of a specific language's grammar also).

[12] The arguments about data and the variationist enterprise in Labov (1969a) are still relevant today and may still be the most direct and persuasive available in the variationist literature. Labov (1969a) should be required reading for any future sociolinguistic variationist.

Another important derivative of Labov (1969) was the principle of accountability. Labov (1969:fn.20, 1972b:72) states (small capitals removed): "that any variable form (a member of a set of alternative ways of 'saying the same thing') should be reported with the proportion of cases in which the form did occur in the relevant environment, compared to the total number of cases in which it might have occurred." This principle is a basic, and unquestioned, part of variationist methodology today, but at the time Labov was guarding against scholars picking and choosing data to conveniently (retro)fit their theories.

The variationists techniques of that time have been developed into generally accepted tenets today. Bayley (2002:118) discusses the principles of multiple causes and the principle of quantitative modeling. The first is the assumption/expectation that language variation is rarely the result of a single factor, be it linguistic or social; the second is the assertion that "we are able to make statements about the likelihood of co-occurrence of a variable form and any one of the contextual features in which we are interested." These two principles are required in order to entertain the traditional variationist idea of variable rules, but the demise of variable rules does not render these principles obsolete.

The same maintenance of underlying variationist concepts applies to Guy's (1991b) two principles of language variation patterns (as cited in Bayley 2002): (1) "Individual speakers may differ in their basic rate of use of a variable rule, that is, in their input probability for the rule"; (2) "Individuals should be similar or identical in the factor values assigned to constraints on the rule." For the first one, the rate for the language variation pattern is separate from a variable rule concept; the same separation applies to the second in that weighted values in VARBRUL can apply to constraints in a grammar as easily as to factors in a rule.

The observation of independence or interaction remains important for variationists today. In analyzing both linguistic and social factors, variationists shoulder the responsibility for understanding the nature of these factors on language variation. The primary mathematical tool for variationists, the VARBRUL program (see Tagliamonte this volume and 2006) assumes there is no interaction between the factor groups (cf. Hazen 2002). However, as Fasold (1991:8) writes, "The assumption of independence is a computational expedient, not a theoretical principle."

In comparing linguistic environments to assess the relative frequency effects, cross-product displays were used. The cross-product display presented an organized set of rule outputs when considering different combinations of factors. As Fasold (1991:5) notes, cross-product displays suffered from two problems: first, the factors in the variable rule are best presented when binary; second, some cross-products may be linguistically impossible (and hence blank). The VARBRUL software program alleviates these two problems by extending the variable rule concept to weighted statistical analysis (Cedergren and Sankoff 1974).

There remained the problem that variable rules documented frequencies for phonological variation, but these rules did not explain any phonological or social motivations for those frequencies. As Fasold (1991:15) writes, "the internal variable constraints demand more of an explanation than the straightforward assignment of weightings in a variable rule provides." For example, Sanchez (1986) presented a study of *of* reduction in Black English by employing variable rules and found that the preceding phonological environment greatly influenced *of* reduction, but in and of itself, an empirical description is not a phonological explanation.

For the variable rule itself, Fasold (1991:17) writes: "In current work in variation analysis, the variable rule as part of linguistic theory has been quietly abandoned, perhaps because of an implicit understanding of the problems of explanation and the different requirements of theories of structure and the theories of use." Fasold reasons that "nothing terribly crucial is lost" when abandoning the variable rule, as long as the quantitative assessment of synchronic and diachronic language variation continues. This practice appears to be commonplace in the post-variable-rule era.

The concept of variable rules was debated from the outset. Some argued that variable rules were unnecessary (Bickerton 1971) because mental grammars with different rules (or different constraints on the same rules) could produce the same results. Others argued that variable rules would require a "variable rule speech community" where the same variable rules would be in the minds of each speaker (Fasold 1991). The uniform, homogenous casting of a variable rule speech community is over-extended in its application of the idea of variable rules; however, given the primary tenet of Weinreich, Labov, and Herzog (1968), the casting of an aggregated set of "variable rules" for the speech community would appear to be unavoidable as they allow no individual grammars which are not informed from the community grammar (cf. Sankoff and Labov 1979).

Variationist analysis in action

Wolfram (1991:22) surmises that, regardless of the theoretical tradition, all descriptive branches of linguistics which handle fluctuating language forms "operate with some notion of the LINGUISTIC VARIABLE," including traditional dialect studies (e.g. Kurath and McDavid 1961). He further argues that the linguistic variable is a device crafted as part of the methodological toolkit, rather than as a construct within a proposed mental grammar: "A survey of the literature on language variation suggests that the notion of the linguistic variable is typically used as a convenient construct employed to unite a class of fluctuating variants within some specified language set." He reviews the different types of linguistic variable – such as *allo-forms of a structural category*, *co-occurrence relationships*, and *lexical items* – and deduces that "the operational definition of a linguistic variable in variation studies includes a fairly wide range of linguistically based units and relationships." Wolfram states that the original, and most useful, definition of the linguistic variable could mix both EMIC and ETIC units within the variants of a linguistic variable. Wolfram's (1991:25) motivation for this argument is that "[t]he linguistic variable in early variation studies was obviously motivated by the desire to reveal the most clear-cut pattern of social and linguistic covariation."

Wolfram (1991:26) contrasts the original variationist concept of the linguistic variable with that of the variable rule. The important difference between the two is that the variable rule had as its foundation a linguistic rule made optional, conditioned stochastically by social factors. For example, the (ING) variable began as a generally defined variable of co-occurrence (e.g. Fischer 1958), noted for centuries due to its social significance; not until the 1980s (e.g. Houston 1985) did the linguistic variable come to be seen as linguistically motivated (as an echo of variation between verbal and nominal suffixes). Even within the factors affecting variants of the same variable, the forms do not have to be linguistically related in an organic manner: for copula absence, originally conceived of as a deletion rule feeding off of contraction (Labov 1969), the following grammatical environment played a significant role in most studies; yet in this environment the most prevalent form for copula absence *gonna* has become a grammaticalized future (and a single lexical) whereas the next most prevalent category is any progressively marked verb in English.

For a successful analysis, the linguistic variable should be the one which provides the best descriptive account and theoretical motivation for the language variation. However, Wolfram (1991:30) cautions that "[m]ethodologically and descriptively, it appears that the notion of a systematic variability in fluctuating forms should not be confused with a variable linguistic rule – as has apparently happened in much current variation analysis."

Perhaps the most intensive quantitative utilization of the linguistic variable was that of Cedergren (1973), who examined approximately 22,000 tokens of syllable-final /s/ in the Spanish of Panama City. Her work clearly details the nature of the statistical foundation for variable rules. This casting of the linguistic variable in a phonological guise was the normal mode at the time and even today (see Guy, this volume); however, numerous scholars heeded the call for the study of variation within other language components. In working with Montréal French and Tok Pisin of Papau New Guinea, G. Sankoff (1973:45) argues to justify the variationist enterprise and to extend it beyond phonological variation: "There is, in my view, mounting evidence that such semantic, discourse, or cultural constraints will be no more (or less) categorical than the type of linguistic constraints now agreed to be allowable." Scholars undertaking variationist analysis have regularly been willing to apply such methods to new realms.

One such realm is the divide between the speech community and the individual speaker, which Wolfram (1973:5) questions: "In the light of data such as these, it is difficult to understand why some variationists have maintained that the speech of the social group is much more regular than the speech of an individual speaker." Robson (1973) also engages the issue of variation and the individual by examining changes in adult Jamaican English. In the same vein, Kypriotaki (1973) also argues for the differing rules which may result in the same global patterns for the Philadelphia African American English (AAE) speakers examined.

Developing different angles, either in analysis or in the object of study, from previous work has been a normal mode of operation for variationists. For example, Clarke (1987) conducted a sociolinguistic study of a village of Montagnais speakers (an Algonquian dialect) in order to reveal how variation is manifested in communities which are not overtly stratified along several spectra, such as Detroit (Wolfram 1969), where ethnicity and class were marked axes for sociolinguistic variation.

From a wider linguistic angle, Preston (1991:52) argues convincingly that in most sociolinguistic circumstances, the range of possible linguistic variation is wider than possible status variation,[13] which is in turn wider than possible style variation. From this perspective, linguistic factors produce possible linguistic forms, social status factors organize those language possibilities according to identity groups, and individual style ranges derive from community knowledge of differential status forms. This relationship between the language variation of status and style was previously noted in Bell's (1984) STYLE AXIOM. For the relationship between the range of language variation and status, Preston (1991:37) reviews a considerable number of variationist studies and maintains that for a sociolinguistic variable, at least one linguistic factor group will display a greater range of variation, between favoring and non-favoring conditions, than that of status factors: "This relationship obtains in a very large number of VARBRUL studies which report on both linguistic and status characteristics." The primary exceptions to these statistically ranging tendencies are grammatical and lexical variables which demonstrate "sharp" stratification: for example the use of *socé* in Brazilian Portuguese (Silva 1981) where the VARBRUL weightings for the relative age between the interlocutor and the speaker ranges between .73 and .21 but those for the linguistic factors of subject and object range between .66 and .34.

African American Vernacular English and variationist scholarship

From the 1960s through the contemporary period, the study of African American Vernacular English (AAVE) has played an important part of sociolinguistic variationist study (see Green 2002, Rickford 1999). The large, urban studies providing the bedrock of variationist methodology – such as Labov, Cohen, Robins, and Lewis (1968), Wolfram (1969), Fasold (1972) – focused on AAVE. Other vernacular varieties were also investigated, for example Wolfram's (1974) study of Puerto Rican Spanish in New York, but AAVE captured the minds and hearts of variationists inside sociolinguistics (e.g. Baugh 1988).

The investigation of AAVE shifted from description to dialectological explanation with NWAVE-12 (Sankoff 1986), when the divergence debate came to full

---

[13] Status such as social class, education, neighborhood.

life with the papers of Labov, Harris, Myhill, Graff, and Ash. These papers appear to be directed both at the academic variationist community and at a wider audience interested in Black–White speech relations. These included both perception and production studies of grammatical and phonological features.

Butters (1987) re-examines the divergence debate by employing data from Wilmington, NC (Nix 1980). In problematizing the divergence issue, Butters finds that several of the features noted for African Americans in northern cities such as Detroit are shared by European Americans in Wilmington. This kind of cross-regional discussion about AAVE is far from settled (Rickford 2006). Recent works by Poplack (2000) and Wolfram and Thomas (2002) bring to the debate exemplary variationist statistical analysis and data handling from different communities (Canadian and southern US respectively). Their work ensures that the AAVE origins debate should see no quick resolution as the complexity of the issue has grown with these new results.

Variable methodologies

Variationist scholarship focusing on the AAVE origins debate is fairly close to its dialectological roots, but variationist methodology has successfully stretched beyond the traditional boundaries. The bridge between quantitative variationist study and the examination of social meaning has been most successfully built by Eckert (2000). Whereas many previous and subsequent studies focus on a single variable to elicit social meaning out of a community, Eckert (2000:213) argues that "While the individual variables available in a dialect may correlate with various aspects of social membership and practice, most of them take on interpretable social meaning only in the context of the broader linguistic styles to which they contribute, including both the inventory of variables and their use. When we view each variable in isolation, thinking of speakers as leading or lagging in the use of advanced variants, we miss the overall effect of speaker's choices." Social meaning from this perspective is a result of the creative process of style from all speakers and not a static entity attached to any one (or set of) variables (see also Coupland 2001).

In the anthropological approach, the question is how meaning, including identity of individuals, is composed and negotiated by different social groups; in the dialectologist approach, the focus is on the dialect as separate from the holders of the dialect and how language changes alter the reified object (the dialect); in the generative and perhaps diachronic approaches, the concern is the language and the linguistic factors which influence its operation (production or perception). All of these approaches to language study have used variationist methodology to advance their academic ends; however, their goals are not the same and the emphasis of the variationist analysis is most likely not the same.

Variationist methodology has also been successfully employed by other distinctly separate fields. Variationist approaches have met with considerable success in studies of second language acquisition where social and linguistic factors have been considered to be coinfluential (e.g. Bayley and Preston 1996, Bayley and Regan 2004, Preston 1989). The study of narrative has also been a part of variationist work. Johnstone (1988) examines how narrative styles vary regionally. Within narratives from Indiana, she specifically explains *extra-thematic orientation*, where more contextually orienting material is provided than is necessary. Wolfram and Wolfram (1977) investigated a discourse construct when traditional norms were violated. Their results indicated different recovery strategies depending on the age (and social experience) of the informant.

The same success of variationist methodology can be seen within the burgeoning linguistic study of sign languages. With the linguistic components of sign language, such as phonology, variability has been found to operate much as it does with spoken languages. Lucas, Bayley, and Valli (2001:110) found that for signs involving the 1 handshape, the produced variants vary systematically according to the grammatical category of the sign, the features of the preceding and following sign segments, and the age, social class, and regional affiliation of the speaker. Their findings also show how social factors interact with linguistic factors in the production (and perception) of sign languages as well as spoken languages. In Lucas (2001:90), a correspondence is established between the linguistic variable in spoken languages and a corresponding variable in signed languages: for example, with syllable deletion, spoken languages may have syncope but signed languages have the first or second element of a compound deleted.

Lastly, corpus studies have become increasingly important in linguistics overall and their quantitative availability have allowed analytical procedures on increasingly larger sets of data. In connecting variationist scholarship to corpus studies, Bauer (2002:109) notes, "All variationist studies are corpus-based, but most of the corpora have not been public ones." Several different kinds of corpus studies have incorporated the analysis of variation. Biber (1987) made a textual comparison of British and American writing with attention to grammatical differences between the varieties. As an example of a diachronic study, Nevalainen (2000) demonstrates differences in the advancement of language change with men leading in replacing multiple negation with single negation and women leading in replacing -*th* with -*s* and the use of *you* in subject position. Nevalainen is also part of a group[14] which has established a series of corpora to study diachronic variation in language.

Variationists and outreach

The pervasive question of the language-education debates center around what role non-standard language should play in institutional education: should vernacular language be encouraged, allowed, or discouraged in the classroom? Should

---

[14] Research Unit for Variation and Change in English: www.eng.helsinki.fi/varieng/index.htm

beginning writers and readers work with spelling and language which may reflect their most familiar variety, whether it be vernacular or not? Through the 1960s and 1970s, sociolinguists sided with two different approaches to language variation and education. The first is a dialect rights position, proposed in 1974 formally by a subdivision of the National Council of Teachers of English (NCTE) (see Wolfram, Adger, and Christian 1999:115), where students have a right to their own language. The implications for an English curriculum have never been fully explored from this position. The second approach has been implemented in so-called additive dialect methods, where standard language features are supposedly taught to vernacular speakers (rarely ever are vernacular features taught to non-vernacular speakers). The difficulty with this approach is that it often conflates language variation with writing and other academic conventions: hence, successful students in such programs should be able to control different registers and genres (including numerous conventions not associated with language). From a variationist perspective, humans do not have the ability to develop two separate language variation systems (Hazen 2001, Labov 1998), but certainly all humans have different styles which may reflect different ethnic and social sources (Schilling-Estes 2002, Eckert and Rickford 2001). The other criticism of the additive method attacks the acquiescence to institutionalized prejudice: variationists know that vernacular features are labeled as such because of prejudice against the social groups who use the forms (e.g. using *knowed* instead of *knew* does not result from a hatred of <-ed> preterite forms). Given this basic premise, how do variationists endorse such prejudice by legitimating that some forms are better? Both Lippi-Green (1997: Ch. 6) and Sledd (1969) present this argument as a critique of the lack of recognition of the underlying prejudice in "choice" of standard language forms.

In a study with such educational implications, Berdan (1977) provides analysis of comprehension for African Americans and European Americans which strongly indicates that grammatical differences influence the interpretation of ambiguous phrases. He directly links the importance of these findings to language and education where it had been previously claimed that language differences did not affect comprehension. For example, sentences such as *Everyday the teacher put up new pictures* were interpreted as always past tense by fifty percent of the European-American respondents but as not past tense by nearly fifty percent of the African American respondents.

Perhaps the most widely known text from this early period of variationist study is Labov's "The logic of nonstandard English" (Ch. 5 of Labov 1972b), which has both educational and social implications. In concord with that article, Labov (1982:172–3) later promotes the *principle of error correction* and the *principle of debt incurred* from which several educational goals arise. Variationists should teach about how language variation works, especially for vernacular speaking communities whose language may be misunderstood and slandered by institutional forces. During the 1960s, sociolinguists were at the forefront of language scholars in arguing that vernacular dialects, especially AAVE, were different yet legitimate varieties of English. Such a claim is often seen as ludicrous by the general public, but for variationist approaches to be effective, this argument must be faced directly.

The efforts of variationists continued on with occasional recognition by educational communities up until 1979, when a legal case became widely publicized. This case involved the education of elementary students in Ann Arbor, MI, who were being unjustly categorized (and educated) on the basis of their language variation patterns (AAVE). The ruling predominantly enforced the school's obligation to accommodate the language variation. Smitherman (1981) has a detailed discussion of these issues which still retains relevance and importance for ongoing debates (see also Smitherman 2000:154). As part of that work, in an overview of AAVE in Detroit, Edwards emphasizes the need to recognize variation in the local community while emphasizing the social need for more standard forms in some contexts. He also (1981:407) proposes a multi-point plan for teachers including the advice to not approach the teaching of English in a way that might cause AAVE speakers "to feel that their natural speech habits are diseased."

Variationist interactions with formal fields

Milroy and Gordon (2003:4) discuss several differences between traditional formal approaches to language study, a *generative* approach in their view, and variationist work. These differences include the nature of "appropriate" data and the use of non-linguistic factors in scholarly analysis. Milroy and Gordon (2003:5) and Chambers (2002b:17) also argue that the concept of the linguistic variable, as a theoretical tool for analysis, has reified some of the divide between these branches of language scholarship.[15] This view of the linguistic variable is possible because of scholars' desires to make the linguistic variable useful: as Fasold (1991:12) remarks: "Sociolinguistic variation analysis is concerned with choices speakers make among the alternatives available to them regardless of the structural provenience of those choices."

From the early NWAV proceedings, it is clear the variationist enterprise was a call for all linguists interested in variation to come together around a common approach to empirical data, and not necessarily a common area of linguistics. These linguists were semanticians, syntacticians, phonologists, creolists, and dialectologists. A separate linguistic profession of "variationist" does not appear to have been a goal, although it was a term from the outset.

In addressing the tendency for traditional generative phonologists to only examine categorical competence, Anttila (2002:210) argues, "There seems to be no reason to limit the scope of phonological theory in such ways." Pierrehumbert

---

[15] An equally important divide is not discussed in this chapter: the difference between sociolinguists primarily concerned with speakers' motivations and social interactions with language and those primarily concerned with the language as a system. See Milroy and Gordon (2003:8) and Johnstone (2000) for a discussion of this important and continually reverberating division.

(1994) provides a clear overview of the approaches to handling phonological intralanguage variation.

As Guy (this volume) remarks, variationists are often viewed as focusing predominantly on English phonology, but a review of variationist work reveals a wide diversity of interests. In *Variation omnibus* (Sankoff and Cedergren 1981), the novel feature was a delineated section on New World Romance languages. Similarly, in Puerto Rican Spanish, Poplack (1980a) focuses on two syllable-final consonants, (s) and (n), with a role to play in inflectional morphology. Her study reveals that phonological constraints interact with semantic and morphosyntactic constraints. Variationists and diachronic scholars have often directed their attention to word-final material: for example, Joseph and Wallace (1992) explained the variation and urbanization of Latin final -*s* deletion in ancient Rome.

Even within the studies which involve English phonology, the focus is often not simply a description of that phonological system. For example, Foulkes, Docherty, and Watts (2005) examined the phonetic realizations of the linguistic variable (t) in child-directed speech (CDS) from a corpus drawn from thirty-nine mothers living in Tyneside, England. They found that variant usage in CDS differed markedly from that of inter-adult speech and that CDS to girls contained more standard variants than CDS to boys. Their study is an important and illustrative crossover between phonetics, child-language acquisition, and variationist sociolinguistics.

The direction within variationist phonology does follow in the trends of mainstream generative phonology and the innovations of formal phonology can prove highly beneficial: Guy and Boberg employ the Obligatory Contour Principle to offer an "integrated account of the preceding segment effect on English coronal stop deletion" (1997:162). In his overview of language variation and phonological theory, Anttila states in relation to the upsurge of interest in language variation connected to phonological theory: "The initial empirical success of Optimality Theory gives one hope that generative phonology is beginning to answer some of the empirical questions raised by variationist linguists" (2002:236) (e.g. see Zubritskaya 1997). The nature of Optimality Theory, accounting for variation among languages with violable and orderable constraints on well-formedness, allowed for a productive integration with quantitative variationist knowledge. Guy (1997) disputed, however, not the potential for OT, but the novelty of it, considering the range of variable phonological constraints sociolinguistic variationists had been working with for thirty years.

As with many areas of linguistics, the insights and observations have utility far beyond their immediate purposes. For a larger history of linguistics, and especially Optimality Theory, scholars should consider the discussion of constraints offered by the works in Bailey and Shuy (1973). Fasold (1973) examines implicational arrays of variables, detailing the possibilities, including how they model variation knowledge in a speaker's competence. Fasold cleverly integrates variationist results within mainstream linguistic contexts and provides a compelling argument for the variationist paradigm.

In the phonetics–phonology interface, but outside variationist sociolinguistics, numerous studies have not only chosen to focus on language variation but incorporated an account of variation in their theoretical models. Pierrehumbert (2003) and Beckman, Munson, and Edwards (in press) assert that children make generalizations of variation over words and sounds in order to learn more categorical phonological structures of language. Their arguments contrast with previous models of language acquisition, which hypothesized that children ignore variability unrelated to contrastive semantic distinctions when learning phonology.

From an employment perspective, in the last half of the 1990s until the present, few linguistic positions were advertised for just a phonologist or just a phonetician.[16] By 2006, most of these kinds of positions are advertised as phonetician/phonologist. Whereas the non-discrete nature of phonetics did not previously impinge on formal phonology (at least directly following Chomsky and Halle [1968]), the nature of phonological study is also shifting. In writing against formal phonology, Port and Leary (2005:929) argue that "Classic generative phonology is built on two basic assumptions: that language is a kind of knowledge and that linguistic knowledge is formal . . . The symbolic-knowledge assumption is taken to permit exploitation of all capabilities of discrete mathematics to model linguistic knowledge." Their argument falls directly in line with variationist methodology and Chambers' (2002b) overt reinvention of the axiom of categoricity as a postulate. Part of Port and Leary's argument is against foundational discreteness of sound units in human language and part of it is for the inclusion of real-time observation of language behavior. They write (2005:957): "The descriptions [of phonological patterns] should be supported both by traditional distributional data of phonological research and by experimental results that clarify the category structure at issue. There is much to learn about phonological systems: about the physical and neural equipment that supports them as well as how they are shaped through time both in children and in language-learning adults." Port and Leary's approach interfaces tightly with the synchronic and diachronic goals of variationist sociolinguistics.[17] It is exactly this type of time-related, non-discrete approach which Hay and Sudbury (2005) employ in providing empirical evidence on the diachronic relationship between the decline of rhoticity and the emergence of /r/-sandhi in New Zealand English.

Within the work of syntax is a basic examination of *variation*. As Fasold (1991:12) notes: "Analysis of variation in syntactic structure, even when VARBRUL is used, is nonetheless not about 'rules' at all, at least not in the ordinary sense. Rather, it seems to be about the social and discourse consequences of making certain choices within language." What is understood as variation is not always on the same scale with sociolinguistic variationists: for formal syntacticians, the variation implies variation in competence for mutually unintelligible languages, in other words, variation of parameters in the Universal Grammar.

---

[16] I thank William Idsardi for this observation.

[17] Echoing variationist sociolinguistic thoughts, Port and Leary (2005:956) also write: "Language will never be understood by insisting on the distinction between Competence and Performance."

Wilson and Henry (1998) consider parameter theory itself as a constrained and formalized casting of language variation. Yet this casting of variation is expanding. Within a traditional approach, the *Linguistic variation yearbook* (e.g. Pica and Rooryck 2001) explicitly focuses on "the study of the nature and scope of linguistic variation from the point of view of a Minimalist Program." From an extension of European studies of non-standard dialect syntax, Tortora, Bernstein, Zanuttini, and den Dikken[18] are conducting a study of microparametric variation on the syntax of subjects within Appalachian English in the United States; specifically, they focus on subject-contact relatives (e.g. *I got some kin people lived up there*) and the Scots-Irish influenced subject–verb concord (e.g. *Me and my sister gets in a fight sometimes*).

Echoing the debates of earlier decades, in arguing against a "competing grammars" theory of syntactic variation, Henry (2002:272) disputes Kroch's (1994) conclusions about the possibilities for acquiring (or not) periphrastic *do* into the mental grammar. Henry argues that Kroch's approach does not allow for syntactic variation over long periods of time. In addition, her own syntactic research (Henry 1995) highlights variability in a range of syntactic structures synchronically, although not evenly distributed throughout the speech community. This debate, about the locus of variation, is unresolved and full of potential. It reoccurs throughout the NWAV proceedings: for example, Singler (1988) explores the question of "where in the grammar do variable constraints operate upon plural marking, and how are these constraints to be represented" for Kru Pidgin English. In his argument, Singler does not make an overt distinction between a community grammar and an individual mental grammar.

Adamson (1988) draws comparisons and conclusions from cross-products and VARBRUL for morphological variation, at the edges of syntax and semantics. Adamson's work dovetails with the Bybee research program investigating the prototypical structures which lexically support morphological categories (e.g. Bybee 2001, 2002). Adamson (1988) argues that such syntactic concepts as construction grammar constructs greatly resemble variable rules (minus the ranking of factors) and that variationist methods could be used to assess their relative strength.

Even within traditional realms, such as clitic placement, variationist methodologies have been successfully employed. Pappas (2004) developed a variation analysis of the placement of weak "clitic" pronouns in Medieval Greek by employing VARBRUL. His primary focuses were the factors inducing this variation, and how it came to be resolved in later (Modern) Greek.

Also in a traditional research realm, Dawson (2005) dissected, in the Vedic Sanskrit of the *Rigveda*, variation between -a: and -au as suffixes. In this quantitative study, she accounts for the wide range of factors that lead to the attested variation including phonological effects, poetic effects, lexical idiosyncrasies, and grammatical categories. She concludes that (2005): "The variation found in the

---

[18] http://163.238.8.180/~tortora/AppalachianSyntax.htm

Rigveda is reflective of variation and change taking place in the living language at the time of composition."

Within a different end of syntactic assessment, Martin and Wolfram (1998) provide a typology/description of African American English sentences. Green, who specializes in syntax and child language acquisition, provides (2002: Chs. 2 and 3) a detailed descriptive account of verbal markers and morphosyntactic properties in African American English. These kinds of descriptions are not quantitative themselves, but quantitative accounts are not possible without these thorough explanations of the semantic, morphophonological, and syntactic patterns of AAE.

Even language variation patterns in sociolinguistic variationist research are now being examined from psycholinguistic and other linguistic perspectives. The Northern Concord rule has drawn interest from several fields (e.g. "All of our brothers and sisters *lives* here"; Hazen 2000b, Tagliamonte 1998, Tagliamonte and Smith 1997, Wolfram and Christian 1976). Bock, Butterfield, Cutler, Cutting, Eberhard, and Humphreys (2006) argue for a psycholinguistic theory that explains verb and pronoun agreement differences between British and American English sentence subjects which have collective head nouns within a parallel architecture of lexical and syntactic formulation.

Following argumentation from a traditional semantic quandary, Ariel (2004) examines scalar quantifiers, predominantly English *most*, in order to assess its lexical meaning. The key difference for Ariel's scholarship, and bellwether of a methodological shift in formal linguistics, is that Ariel's analysis and conclusions are based on empirical data and not intuitions.

Perhaps the most sweeping nonsociolinguistic approach to variation is the research program by Bybee (2001, 2002). Although a proper description of the complexities of Bybee's model of language is beyond the purview of this paper, it incorporates usage frequencies, for example of lexical items, to build exemplars in the mental grammar from which patterns emerge. The connections to variationist research in general are clear and important for an accurate assessment of human cognition in that probabilities are an inherent part of grammar. In examining the classic variable of /t,d/ deletion from this new approach, Gahl and Garnsey (2004) employ this model to provide evidence that the probabilities of syntactic structures affect pronunciation variation and thus "knowledge of probabilities forms an integral part of grammatical knowledge" (2004:769).

An exposition of variationist means and ways and the future of variationist analysis

So has variationist analysis revolutionized linguistics? In some ways variationist methodology has produced important changes in linguistic practice. It is more common today for claims about languages to be supported by empirical evidence;

in addition claims of more and less now require statistical support. Yet from a different perspective, variationist methodology has not unified sociolinguistics or merged previously separate fields such as dialectology and linguistic anthropology. Linguists focused on anthropological and sociological concerns attend and publish in those venues most germane to their purposes (e.g. Eckert and McConell-Ginet 1992). The same is true for dialectology (e.g. Kautzsch 2002, Labov, Ash, and Boberg 2006). The innovative spur of academia which employs variationist methodology are the sociolinguists who focus on explaining linguistic patterns under the influence of social and linguistic constraints (Labov 1994, 2001).

As for regular practice of variationist methodology, the overlap between the dialectological variationists and the sociolinguistic variationists is considerable. Numerous studies, for example Hazen (2000a), have attempted to combine a narrow dialectological focus and a linguistically-leaning sociolinguistic analysis. The crossroads where the most productive discussions about the variable nature of language have taken place is within the topic of African American Vernacular English. For example, the continuing debate about the origins of AAVE have prompted an entire subfield of variationist research (e.g. Butters 1989, Poplack 2000, Poplack and Tagliamonte 2001, Wolfram 2003, Wolfram and Thomas 2002).

Early on in the variationist enterprise, a wide range of voices in and out of sociolinguistics argued for the careful study of quantitative language patterns (e.g. Napoli 1974, Ross 1973, Sag 1973). Although sociolinguists and dialectologists were the predominant advocates and innovators of variationist methodology, they were not the sole purveyors of the trade.

Early advocates of variationist study argued for several interconnected methodological choices: to use data from speakers; to examine quantitative patterns; to avoid claims without data. On all these counts, the early advocates have won. Variationist methodology has diffused to many different fields.

The short history of variationist studies has passed through several stages. In the beginning, an overt focus on developing variationist methodology was the norm along with the establishment of the credibility of variationist work. After the validity of variationist methods was established, the sociolinguists and dialectologists returned to the core work on which those methods had been built: assessing how societal factors influence language production and perception[19] and documenting the current and past states of dialect variation. Basic tenets of variationist methodology are now employed in many fields of linguistics, including those fields previously unwilling to consider such constraints. To a great extent, polemical variationist goals have been accomplished. The field of linguistics is primarily an empirical field today, even though different levels of abstraction remain necessary for modeling, and within the empirical study of language, accounting for

---

[19] Determining how language influences society is much more germane to the realm of the sociology of language.

variation in language is a regular task for many subfields. This shift from the 1960s and 1970s necessitates a name change: previously, the term *variationist* may have been understood to mean "one who works with language variation" and thus consequently refer to a *sociolinguistic variationist*; more recently, a wide variety of scholars work with language variation.[20] An appraisal of the recent sociolinguistic variationist dissertations reveals sophisticated high-quality work with a range of language topics: for example, Charity (2005) investigates AAVE in the educational context; Reaser (2006) examines dialect awareness programs and their effects on teachers' and students' attitudes about language variation; Childs (2005) examines the dialectological and linguistic relations of a small Appalachian community; while Mallinson (2006) takes up the sociological relations of the language variation in the same community.

The variationist community faces at least two challenges in the future: first, scholars must assess and document language variation of every type from a wider range of languages; second, scholars must integrate theoretical explanations of language variation in the mental grammar with explanations of language variation in society (perhaps with the aid of the concept of *emergence*). If variation is a natural and inherent part of human language, only the full range of human language experience should suffice for evidence.

A historical overview of this type suffers by being both incomplete in scope and inadequate in explanation. Yet it is clear even from this limited view that the nature of language requires variationist explanation. As Sapir (1921:38), one of the early leaders of empirical linguistic observation, wrote, "Unfortunately or luckily, no language is tyrannically consistent. All grammars leak." Variationists of all stripes have convincingly argued for the fortunate interpretation.

---

[20] Even formal syntacticians within popular literature embrace the concept of variation among languages (Baker 2002).

5 Style in dialogue: Bakhtin and sociolinguistic theory[1]

ALLAN BELL

Introduction: style in sociolinguistics

Issues of "style" have been addressed in variationist sociolinguistics since the earliest work of William Labov. In his pioneering New York City study (1966) Labov operated with two dimensions of linguistic variation: the "social," that is, the range of variation for particular sociolinguistic variables across the different speakers that he recorded; and the "stylistic" dimension, the range of variation produced by individual speakers within their own speech. This approach was adopted in the urban US studies which followed close upon Labov, notably in Detroit (Wolfram 1969).

In this tradition, style was tightly defined on both the linguistic and social dimensions. The language features examined in Labov's initial work were micro aspects of linguistic structure – two or more specific sounds which can alternate as variants of one linguistic "variable." Typical is the choice between whether to pronounce an /r/ after a vowel or not in words such as *car* or *card*. As studied by Labov in New York City (1966) and Wolfram and associates in Detroit (Shuy, Wolfram, and Riley 1968a), the choice is treated as different ways of saying the same thing. Pronouncing the /r/ is prestigious in these communities and throughout most of North America, omitting it is not prestigious (although the opposite is true in some other speech communities, for example in England). Counting the relative frequencies of such alternative pronunciations has shown how they vary depending on who the speaker is, the linguistic context, and the social context, including the situation he or she is in.

[1] An earlier draft of this chapter was presented as the Closing Plenary Address to the European Sociolinguistics Symposium, Bristol, UK, April 2000. A briefer version was given at the NWAV Conference, East Lansing, Michigan, in October that year. On that occasion, as so often, I was encouraged by feedback from Walt Wolfram on the value of this enterprise. His early joint book on *The study of social dialects in American English* (Wolfram and Fasold 1974) served as a crucial methodological text for my doctoral work, conducted on the other side of the world. In 1981 when I came to Washington, DC, as a "freelance academic nomad" (his terms), Wolfram's mentoring as Research Director at the Center for Applied Linguistics when I was a Visiting Research Associate, was pivotal in turning me from a student into a scholar. Nearly two decades later, when Nikolas Coupland and I came to launch the *Journal of Sociolinguistics*, I was pleased to receive a submission from Wolfram *et al.*, which was reviewed and accepted as the first paper of the first issue of the new journal (Wolfram, Hazen, and Tamburro 1997). *Kia ora*, Walt.

Labov devised means for eliciting different styles of speech from people within the compass of a single interview. As well as seeking answers to questions, the interviewer has informants carry out several language tasks, designed to focus increasing amounts of their attention on how they are speaking. When a speaker discussed topics in which they were particularly involved, they were likely to be paying the least attention to their speech, and this was considered "casual" style. When answering questions in typical interview fashion, speakers would be paying rather more attention to their speech and therefore producing "careful" style. And so on, with increasing levels of attention, through reading a brief story, a list of words and finally "a list of minimal pairs" (words which differ by only one sound), where the speaker was held to be paying the maximum amount of attention.

Such an approach to style was for fifteen years the "received wisdom" in sociolinguistics (Wolfram, personal communication), but in the 1980s it was challenged on a number of grounds. Labov's explanation of "style shift" as caused by speakers paying differing amounts of attention to their speech was critiqued by me among others (Bell 1984) for its mechanistic approach. The concept of style from the beginning of variationist sociolinguistics tended to the parsimonious, in the interests of establishing tight correlations between linguistic and social factors. In another area of the growing field, however, Hymes (e.g. 1972a) was at the same time advocating a much richer smorgasbord of contextual influences on a speaker's linguistic choices, although at the cost of far less analytical precision.

A second ground for critique is more fundamental in its implications for the variationist enterprise. This challenges the notion that style can be equated with "style shift" which is evidenced in quantitative changes in single sociolinguistic variables. A great deal has been learned from isolating particular vowels, consonants, and morphosyntactic variables and quantifying their occurrence and correlation with linguistic and extralinguistic factors. However, for an understanding of how speakers position themselves through the use of linguistic resources, this now seems too limited an approach. What happens when a speaker talks in any social situation involves many linguistic features almost simultaneously, at all levels of language, all contributing to the mosaic of the sociolinguistic presentation of self in everyday life. And these features occur in any given interaction too rarely for variationist quantification to be practicable as the main means of analysis.

The result has been on the one hand an opening to the investigation of the social context of linguistic self-presentation, in particular to examine the particularities of specific interactions. And on the other hand, there has come examination of linguistic phenomena on-line as they occur and co-occur in stretches of speech; something much less tractable to a taut definition of constrained linguistic variation and more open to the inherent messiness of actually occurring data. Thus instead of being sidelined as a subsidiary dimension of language variation, "style" finds a place at the center of our study. It treats the variety of voices which speakers use as a central aspect of sociolinguistics, requiring a fundamental reappraisal of how we approach method, data, analysis, theory, and even the nature of language itself. Here the individual speaker becomes a focus of study in their daily language usage and linguistic personas.

This kind of approach is well illustrated in some of the work of Wolfram and associates on isolated dialects such as Ocracoke English (e.g. Schilling-Estes 1998, Wolfram, Hazen, and Tamburro 1997). Here, building on studies in the community, the focus turns to how individuals position themselves through their linguistic usage. A particular individual may align with more than one variety and group, such as the African American Ocracoker studied by Wolfram *et al.* (1997), who aligns partially with African American vernacular, and partially with the Ocracoke variety. Or speakers may actively perform varying degrees of local dialect at different times, largely dependent on how they view themselves in relation to the people around them, which frequently differs from situation to situation. Particularly in Schilling-Estes's work on performance speech, ways and degrees of identifying with a particular place or group are shown to be crucial to how language is actually used.

Putting the vagaries and unpredictability of the individual's language variation and performance – style, if you will – at the heart of research has required sociolinguists to look around for approaches and theories which are capable of coping with such rich and fluid data. In this enterprise of understanding the variety of individual language, the work of Mikhail Bakhtin has become increasingly foundational for sociolinguistic thought (and is so applied by Schilling-Estes). The approach of this Russian theorist – most of whose works were written decades before the founding of North American sociolinguistics by Hymes, Labov, and their contemporaries – gives a basis for addressing the profuse variety of language and its production by speakers. I believe Bakhtin's thought points to a principled and realistic way forward in the understanding of style. An examination of his work, its development and some of its principal strands yields both an opportunity and a challenge for sociolinguistic theory and practice.

Approaching Bakhtin

A fraught life

The shape of Mikhail Bakhtin's life and his oscillating academic career is essential context to understanding his thought. His story should come with a Government Health Warning specifically targeted at authors. Bakhtin was a committed chain-smoker – although he did live to nearly eighty years of age. However not all his works lived with him. In the spartan years of World War II in the Soviet Union, Bakhtin ran out of cigarette papers. The only suitable paper he could find was his copy of one of his own manuscripts, and this he used page by page to roll his cigarettes. The book had been accepted for publication, but the publisher's copy disappeared in the destruction wreaked by the German invasion. There was no third copy of the manuscript, and so the book – on the eighteenth-century German form of the novel, the *Erziehungsroman* – was lost utterly, smoked away by its own author.

That incident (recounted in Holquist 1981) exemplifies Bakhtin's rocky road to publication and recognition – not to mention academic employment – throughout his career. He was born in 1895, and his foundational work was done in the 1920s but much of it did not see the light of day even in the Soviet Union until forty years later. Bakhtin had trouble getting an academic job, although particularly in the 1920s he was surrounded by groups of like-minded intellectuals who tend to now be labelled "the Bakhtin circle."

He was arrested in 1929 during a Stalinist purge and exiled for six years in Kazakhstan working as a financial bookkeeper. But he survived through World War II, writing much but publishing little between 1930 and 1960. He submitted his Ph.D. thesis on Rabelais for examination in 1940 – it was controversial, the degree was not awarded, and the thesis was eventually accepted only for a lesser degree twelve years later. It was published in 1965, another thirteen years later.

But Bakhtin's story is also an encouragement to scholars who may feel their voice is not being heard. In 1960 at the age of 65 he was rediscovered by a younger generation of scholars who had come across his work but thought he was dead. They – literally – rescued him from obscurity, and began to bring his work into publication and Bakhtin himself into more comfortable living circumstances in the last years of his life.[2]

This led on to Bakhtin's eventual discovery by the Western academy in the 1970s and 1980s. He has since been celebrated among literary theorists, sociocultural philosophers, religious thinkers, anthropologists, discourse analysts, ethnographers of communication, and those many post-modern scholars who have "turned" to language over the past two decades. Although Bakhtin can arguably be best classed as a philosopher of language, he is virtually unknown in general theoretical linguistics – particularly in its hegemonic, North American-originated forms – despite his core concern with the nature of language. While regarded as a patron by discourse analysts, he has had much less impact on variationist, micro-level sociolinguistics, even though his approach to language is quintessentially a social one. But Bakhtin has much to offer not just to discourse analysts but also to sociolinguists.

Caveats

My approach to Bakhtin comes with several health warnings of its own. First is the complication that what is regarded as his principal work on language (*Marxism and the philosophy of language*) was published in someone else's name (Voloshinov 1929). Voloshinov was a member of the so-called "Bakhtin circle"

---

[2] Our knowledge of Bakhtin's life is hampered by a sheer lack of information, and I am indebted to Clark and Holquist's biography (1984) for the content of this outline. Their biography remains seminal to an understanding of Bakhtin and his context, despite its being critiqued for filling gaps with assumptions (Titunik 1986), e.g. that his positions and activities necessarily align with aspects of this context.

in the 1920s, when he, Bakhtin, and colleagues met regularly in Leningrad and elsewhere to smoke, debate, and drink strong tea. It is quite unclear – and hotly debated – to what extent the work is or is not Bakhtin's own. Bakhtin's biographer and main editor in English – Michael Holquist – maintains that most of this text published in the name of Voloshinov is by Bakhtin (Holquist 1981). Others strongly disagree (e.g. Titunik 1984).

I am not in a position to add to this debate, although I will observe that in its orderliness and expositional style *Marxism and the philosophy of language* reads rather differently to the rest of the Bakhtin I have read. I will reference the English version as Voloshinov (1929[1973]) but treat it for the purposes of this discussion as part of Bakhtin's oeuvre.[3] It is of course a nice – and perhaps not accidental – irony that someone such as Bakhtin – who was absorbed in the nature of the author and wrote much about taking our words from the mouths of others – should have his work so embroiled in apparently insoluble authorship issues.

Second, some pleas of personal ignorance. I do not read Russian, and have therefore been reliant on translations, whose quality I have no way of judging. What I do know is that the English of most of these works is difficult to read, and they are prefaced by translator comments that Bakhtin's Russian is itself difficult. Probably in common with most readers, I do not have a background in much of the philosophy and literature which forms the backdrop to and often the substance of Bakhtin's writing. Nor am I current with much of the vast secondary Western literature that has developed from Bakhtin in the past twenty years across a wide spectrum of disciplines. I welcome correction and dialogue from those readers who know the work better than I do.

Third, Bakhtin did not believe in finished products. He stressed the Unfinishedness of things, especially in thought, in systems, in theory (e.g. 1935[1981]:346). My encounter with Bakhtin is also very much a work in progress rather than a finished product. My reading of Bakhtin is – literally – unfinished. I have managed to strand twice on one of his major works dealing with language ("Discourse in the novel," 1935[1981]). This increasingly appears to me to be not just excuse or ineptitude or idleness. It is brought about by the nature of Bakhtin's own thought and writing, which through the decades circles repeatedly around the same issues. To at least that extent, this chapter is itself not a finished product.

Lastly, in this chapter, to use Bakhtin's own concept, I will speak double-voiced. That is, I will incorporate Bakhtin's words with my own and will not always attempt to identify when I am direct-quoting and when I am not, or to separate what are Bakhtin's words and what are mine. In truth, I doubt whether I could pick apart my words from Bakhtin's in some sections. I will identify and source in separate *italicized* paragraphs longer quotations which I know to be taken direct from Bakhtin, but it is entirely in the spirit of Bakhtin that words or phrases lifted from him should be incorporated dialogically and without flagging into my

---

[3] Given the lapse of time between their appearance in Russian and publication of English translations, referencing Bakhtin's works is tricky. I will use the original dates, but necessarily dual-reference the works with the date and page numbers of the English versions from which quotations are taken, i.e. Voloshinov 1929[1973], and Bakhtin 1935[1981], 1953[1986a], and 1970[1986b].

own text. This is not just sophistry. Bakhtin may be difficult to read, but he is even harder to paraphrase and not easy to excerpt effectively. The source material is quite intractable, and seems to require this kind of dialogue appropriately of those who would understand it.

Thus this chapter represents a sociolinguist looking from inside his own discipline at the work of Bakhtin, using largely Bakhtin's own words rather than secondary sources, drawing parallels with the history of Western sociolinguistics, and seeking insights to illuminate and challenge the principles and practice of contemporary sociolinguistics. While I note his biographers' caveat that Western scholars tend to pick from Bakhtin the cherries that suit their tastes (Clark and Holquist 1984:3), my approach to Bakhtin is as a sociolinguist, and I view him through that lens. I hope not just to reinvent him in my own image, for example in his approach to the significance of the audience in language (cf. Bell 1984), nor to reinvent him in our own image, that of early twenty-first-century Western sociolinguistics. I hope rather to be stimulated, challenged, changed, even revolutionized, by his thought.

A forerunner of sociolinguistics

I believe Bakhtin can reasonably be claimed as a forerunner of contemporary sociolinguistics – perhaps not a sociolinguist as such, but at least a foreshadowing theorizer of social language. In the 1920s and 1930s he engaged in advocacy for a social linguistics which pre-echoed the kind of polemics put forward by Hymes and Labov in the 1960s.

This is less surprising in a historical-disciplinary context than it might seem. Much of Bakhtin's linguistic theorizing was explicitly against Saussure; against structuralism, which was well known in the Soviet Union in the 1920s (Clark and Holquist 1984). As Bakhtin's work in the 1950s shows, he was also well acquainted with American structuralist linguistics. His 1953 essay on "The problem of speech genres" (published in English 1986) is basically an explicit piece of linguistic and sociolinguistic theorizing. Here he in effect propounded and defined communicative competence (1953[1986a]:78) in contrast with structuralist grammatical "competence" a decade or more before Hymes did. The co-incidence was not coincidental, of course, since Hymes and Labov were also reacting against the structuralist hegemony of the 1960s, in their case transformational-generative grammar. I will recognize here three areas where early sociolinguistic theorizing is foreshadowed in Bakhtin.

On the data of linguistics

In his 1972 book *Language in the inner city*, Labov wrote about the theoretical linguist as social "lame," criticizing the transformational, introspectionist approach to data – that is, "my dialect" linguistics:

> To refine the intricate structure of one's own thoughts, to ask oneself what
> one would say in an imaginary world where one's own dialect is the only
> reality, to dispute only with those few colleagues who share the greatest part
> of this private world – these academic pleasures will not easily be abandoned
> by those who were early detached from the secular life. The student of his
> own intuitions, producing both data and theory in a language abstracted from
> every social context, is the ultimate lame.   (Labov 1972c:292)

A trenchant critique, and one which we find foreshadowed by Bakhtin's characterization of the database of structuralist linguistics (emphasis throughout as in
original):

> *Dead, written alien language* is the true description of the language with
> which linguistic thought has been concerned. The *isolated, finished, mono-
> logic utterance,* divorced from its verbal and actual context and standing open
> not to any possible sort of active response but to passive understanding on
> the part of a philologist – that is the ultimate "donnee" and the starting point
> of linguistic thought.   (Voloshinov 1929[1973]:73)

Core to both these criticisms is the use of "language abstracted from every social
context" as the central data of the linguistic study of language. The artificiality of
the data linguistics has used is characterized by Bakhtin as "dead," in particular
because it is language that is produced without the actuality of response from an
audience. We will see later that the monologic quality of such language renders
it deeply unauthentic to Bakhtin and inimical to his concerns and theorizing.[4]

On context

The quotation from Bakhtin above stressed the need to treat language in context.
So what is "context?" Sociolinguists are accustomed to beginning such discussions with a rubric such as Fishman's "Who speaks what language to whom and
when?" (Fishman 1965). Or we turn to Dell Hymes' more detailed SPEAKING
mnemonic (e.g. 1972a) and the taxonomies it summarizes, e.g. speaker, listeners,
genre, topic, key, purposes, etc. Bakhtin is there first:

> In order to assess and divine the real meaning of others' words in everyday life,
> the following are surely of decisive significance: *who* precisely is speaking,
> and under *what* concrete circumstances? . . . The entire speaking situation is
> very important: who is present during it, with what expression or mimicry is
> it uttered, with what shades of intonation?   (1935[1981]:340)

Here Bakhtin specifies (at least) the speaker, the audience, the situation, and the
"key" or tone of an instance of speech as needing to be taken into account in any
analysis.

---

[4] These strictures most aptly characterize structuralist theoretical linguistics, generally in their North
American guises. European-based theoretical linguistics has always maintained more contact with
language as it is used, and its frequent functionalist emphasis (e.g. Halliday 1973) has had more
engagement with language in its social context.

On the nature of sociolinguistics

In the late 1960s and early 1970s, Dell Hymes engaged in advocacy for a social linguistics. As well as being explicitly in opposition to the reductionism of the transformational-generative grammar of the period, Hymes' approach was much broader and deeper in its conception than that practiced by William Labov in the same period. This is well summarized in Hymes (1972b), the text of his closing plenary to that year's Georgetown University Round Table on "Sociolinguistics: current trends and prospects," one of the foundational conferences of North American sociolinguistics:

> A "socially constituted" linguistics is concerned with social as well as referential meaning, and with language as part of communicative conduct and social action. Its task is the thoroughgoing critique of received notions and practices, from the standpoint of social meaning . . . Such a conception reverses the structuralist tendency of most of the twentieth century.   (Hymes 1972b:316)

Nowadays, Hymes' polemic reads more like a manifesto from Critical Discourse Analysis. But compare it with Bakhtin in 1929:

> The actual reality of language-speech is not the abstract system of linguistic forms, not the isolated monologic utterance, and not the psychophysiological act of its implementation, but the social event of verbal interaction implemented in an utterance or utterances. Thus, verbal interaction is the basic reality of language.   (Voloshinov 1929[1973]:94)

Four decades before sociolinguistics was established as a field in North America, separated in time and place from the sources of the modern discipline, and working on the other side of the great political–ideological divide of the twentieth century, the thinking of Bakhtin is remarkably cognate with that of the founding sociolinguists: language can only be studied and understood from within the active social and communicative situation in which it is embedded.

Part of Bakhtin's interest for the sociolinguist is, therefore, that he foreshadowed positions which were later to be taken up by the North American founders of sociolinguistics. But there remain differences between his approach and theirs, and it is at these points of difference that Bakhtin's inflection of the issues can illuminate and challenge the more familiar approaches and formulations of Western sociolinguistics.

Bakhtin and the field of sociolinguistics

Bakhtin now holds an accepted place within the conduct of ethnographic sociolinguistics and discourse analysis, especially in European contexts (e.g. Coupland 2001, Tsitsipis 2004) but also in North America (e.g. Bucholtz 1999b, Hill and Hill 1986). Yet he has received much less attention in variationist approaches. There are some practical and principled reasons for this neglect:

(1) Bakhtin is difficult to read. His syntax is tortuous, his argument is not structured or ordered in the way Western academics are accustomed to, and he creates a terminology rife with cumbersome and opaque neologisms (apparently in Russian as well as in English translation). Among these neologisms see for example the following, whose meanings are by no means always clear in the texts which introduce and explicate them, and whose pronunciations can be difficult even for native speakers to be sure of:

> multilanguagedness
> internally persuasive discourse
> internally dialogized interillumination.

(2) Bakhtin appears to be a literary theorist and philosopher, not a socio/linguist. The titles of the three most pertinent works – "Discourse in the novel" (1935[1981]), *Marxism and the philosophy of language* (Voloshinov 1929[1973]), and "The problem of speech genres" (1953[1986a]) – are not the first place a sociolinguist, let alone a structuralist linguist, would go looking for a theory of language.

(3) Bakhtin mainly expounds and philosophizes, offering few examples and little analysis, and – paradoxically enough – most of that analysis is of literary texts rather than actual speech. There are no specific conversational data excerpts of his own in what I have read, although there is a little from general observations such as "the kind of thing you hear in the street." On the other hand, there is of course a practical reason for the absence of such direct vernacular data – Bakhtin was mostly writing before the age of the tape recorder (that said, one cannot imagine that Bakhtin would have set about the systematic recording of spoken data even if he had had the technological means).

(4) Bakhtin was in the wrong place at the wrong time, as far as the Western academy goes. Fortunately he was re/discovered, first within the Soviet Union and then in the West – but it was a close-run thing. As his editor observes in the dedication to *The dialogic imagination*, "There is nothing more fragile than the word, and Bakhtin's was almost lost" (Holquist 1981:vii).

Bakhtin's theory

Bakhtin as a forerunner of contemporary sociolinguistics is of much more than just historical or comparative interest. His thought is important in its own right for the insight he brings about the nature of language as a social linguistics should conceive of it. This represents a much more radical re-forming of our views of language and its study than has often been accepted in current sociolinguistics. Here I want to pick up just three of Bakhtin's foundational – and related – concepts, which are all aspects of what he calls "dialogism" (of which more below). Here as well as expounding Bakhtin's concepts and citing his examples, I will intersperse cognate analyses from my own work. These three concepts are:

(1) centripetal and centrifugal language forces
(2) heteroglossia and multiple voicing
(3) addressivity and response.

Centripetal and centrifugal forces

Bakhtin maintains that in society, language is a site of struggle between the dynamic centrifugal forces which whirl it apart into diversity, difference, and creativity, and the centripetal forces which strive to normalize, standardize, and prescribe the way language should be, often from the top of society. He acknowledges standardization as a force but celebrates the centrifugal – the divergence, individuality, creativity, even the chaos of language variety. He is neither structuralist nor social constructivist – or perhaps he is both, because he recognizes both the normative and creative in language.

> Alongside the centripetal forces, the centrifugal forces of language carry on their uninterrupted work; alongside verbal-ideological centralization and unification, the uninterrupted processes of decentralization and disunification go forward. Every concrete utterance of a speaking subject serves as a point where centrifugal as well as centripetal forces are brought to bear. The processes of centralization and decentralization, of unification and disunification, intersect in the utterance.   (1935[1981]:272)

Bahktin was therefore aware – not surprisingly in the Soviet Union – of the structure and agency paradox: that we are simultaneously both free-acting individual agents and constrained by our situations, e.g. of the sociopolitical system in which we are brought up. The centrifugal and centripetal forces operate at both social and individual levels. Bakhtin saw this struggle as basic to language, discourse, and communication, or even as a crusade for the centrifugal. He was not neutral in response to these forces, but celebrated language as kaleidoscope:

> What is involved here is a very important, in fact a radical revolution in the destinies of human discourse: the fundamental liberation of cultural-semantic and emotional intentions from the hegemony of a single and unitary language.   (1935[1981]:367)

We can exemplify this in a thousand local sociolinguistic contexts. In a globalizing world New Zealand English, for example, is – contrary to expectation – becoming more itself, more distinctive rather than more American, more British, or more media-oriented (e.g. Bell 1997). And it is diversifying locally as immigrant ethnic groups establish their own recognizable varieties of the language. Where variety is lost on the one hand, it tends to be gained on another. Language loss often leads to dialect gain. A minority may give up its language, but simultaneously it is creating a new variety of the majority language which will serve its identity and communicative purposes. Thus we have here not just variety but process, not just the linguistic but the social, not just the social but the political, and not just description but advocacy.

Such a view of linguistic variety is home territory for sociolinguistics, but with unusual and enlightening inflections. Sociolinguists are on the side of the centrifugal. We who are students of language variety should also be the advocates of variety rather than of standardization – as we have often been historically in support for endangered or denigrated languages or dialects.

Heteroglossia and multiple voicing

The fruit of the centrifugal forces in language is heteroglossia, Bakhtin's best-known term among sociolinguists and discourse analysts. Although the idea and term are familiar for example in Critical Discourse Analysis, Bakhtin tends to apply the concept more at the micro-linguistic level than to discourse. Usually his examples come from below the level of the sentence, often with lexical material, although sometimes also suprasegmentals.Two of Bakhtin's definitions of heteroglossia set the scene:

> The internal stratification of any single national language into social dialects, characteristic group behavior, professional jargons, generic languages, languages of generations and age groups, tendentious languages, languages of the authorities, of various circles and of passing fashions, languages that serve the specific sociopolitical purposes of the day, even of the hour (each day has its own slogan, its own vocabulary, its own emphases) – this internal stratification [is] present in every language at any given moment of its historical existence.   (1935[1981]:262)

> At any given moment of its historical existence, language is heteroglot from top to bottom: it represents the co-existence of socio-ideological contradictions between the present and the past, between differing epochs of the past, between different socio-ideological groups in the present, between tendencies, schools, circles and so forth, all given a bodily form.   (1935 [1981]:291)

Variety, therefore, is endemic to language, native to it, innate. It is also multi-dimensional. The kind of variety that Bakhtin depicts above does not coincide with any one obvious parameter such as the demographics of a speaker in a Western urban context. Rather he offers many cross-cutting social and social-psychological phenomena – groups, purposes, ideologies, registers.

To illustrate heteroglossia in action, here is an example from Billy T. James, New Zealand's best known comedian of the late twentieth century, who died quite young in 1991. Several years later there was screened a retrospective television tribute, which juxtaposed two of Billy's performance voices. Here is the first voice, an anecdote concerning the formidable Maori entertainer Prince Tui Teka, who predeceased Billy:

Prince Tui Teka and the takeaway bar

We drove into this takeaway bar, eh.   1
Geez, I was laughing.
We pulled up.
Tui wound the window down,
looked up at the girl behind the counter –   5
you know, typical Australian,
smokes Rothmans, chews PK,
got a fountain pen mark over here, you know,
where she's been putting it in:
"Yeah, what do you want?"   10
Tui goes:
"Ah – gi' us – ah – gi' us –
three double eggburgers
ah – three whole chickens
and ah – four litres of diet coke."   15
And we went:
"Hah – Tui's shouting the boys."
And he turned around and said:
"You fellas want anything?"
And that's a true story   20
and I'll always remember that eh
about my bro Tui.

GLOSSES:
shout – buy food or drink for someone
bro – brother or mate

This excerpt is shot through with New Zealand vernacular, and more particularly, with Maori Vernacular English (cf. Bell 2000). Some of the markers:

- The discourse particle EH is used in lines 1 and 21 – the most stereotypical marker of Maori Vernacular English (Bell 2000, Meyerhoff
  1994).
- As well as general New Zealand vernacular lexicon such as *shout*, the
  word *bro* is marked as used only between Maori or other Polynesian
  New Zealanders (particularly male and young), meaning "mate."
- In the phonology, there is devoicing of final /z/, as in *eggburgers*,
  chickens, *litres*, and *boys* in lines 13–17. Studied by Holmes (1997)
  and Bell (2000), this is especially marked in these plurals. It is not
  accidental that all these tokens occur when Billy is quoting his characters.
- Affrication of /dh/ (Bell 2000, Holmes 1997) in *the* (line 17) and *that*
  (21).
- Centralization of the DRESS vowel before /l/ in line 19, leading to
  dialect-orthographic representation as "fullas."

- Raising and fronting of the KIT vowel. As found in Bell (1997), some Maori sometimes pronounce the short /ɪ/ with a close front realization, here used in *chickens* (14, and the second syllable of *anything*, 19). This realization is much more like an RP or even Australian representation than the usual New Zealand centralized schwa.
- In prosody, many of these ethnically distinctive forms are closely linked with a rhythm of speech that distinguishes Maori from non-Maori New Zealand English, being mora-timed rather than syllable timed. Billy uses this in some lines (e.g. 5, 19), yielding full vowels rather than the expected schwa on unstressed syllables.

So we have here a stylization in the terms of Coupland (2001) and Rampton (1999). Billy T. James was the public incarnation of stylized Maori Vernacular English, the icon of this New Zealand stereotype (which sometimes led to criticism among his fellow Maori). Visually for this sketch he appears on stage in the guise of a naughty Maori boy, dressed in shorts and a black singlet.

The second excerpt which the retrospective programme juxtaposed to the above is at the other end of the New Zealand stylistic spectrum, visually as well as dialectally. In a television variety series called *Radio times*, made in the early 1980s, Billy plays the host of a fictional 1930s radio show. His dress is in absolute social contrast to his young Maori vernacular persona – bow tie and tails. In keeping with stereotypes of the New Zealand broadcast accent of the times, when most radio announcers were British-born, Billy produces an RP approximation, especially in his diphthongs (most noticeably the GOAT vowel, but also KIT). This is also a stylization, of course. It is distant in time from the era in which it is set, by about fifty years, and distant in place from the variety which it is intended to echo, British Received Pronunciation. It is, as Bakhtin says of the centripetal, a very obvious example of a frozen form.

Hosting *Radio Times*

Good evening, good evening, listeners.
And let me assure you
that there is no cause for feeling bad tonight
because everything on Radio Times is looking good.
This is your host Dexter Fitzgibbons
welcoming you to another fun-filled fascinating fifty minutes,
with the Southern Hemisphere's greatest dance band,
the Radio Times Orchestra,
Bunny le Veau, Guy Bosanquet,
Tommy Blackhouse, the High Spots,
and the gentlemen of the Radio Theatre.

This is centripetal English, internationally recognizable and comprehensible. No transcript or glossing is necessary for non-local listeners to understand the audio track of this excerpt, whereas these are both required for non-New Zealand audiences to follow the soundtrack of the Prince Tui Teka excerpt. The need for interpretation nicely encapsulates the contrasting footings of the standard and the vernacular, the international and the local, the centripetal and the centrifugal. As Bakhtin writes:

> The authoritative word is located in a distanced zone, organically connected with a past that is felt to be hierarchically higher. It is, so to speak, the word of the fathers. Its authority was already *acknowledged* in the past. It is a *prior* discourse . . . Its language is a special (as it were, hieratic) language. It can be profaned. It is akin to taboo.   (1935[1981]:342)

The standard, then, looks back and away. The standard for the *Radio times* show was both geographically and temporally distant from the New Zealand of the 1980s. If this sounds familiar to a sociolinguist, it is probably because such distancing is also one of the defining characteristics of diglossia, particularly in the classical original sense of Ferguson (1959). There the High language was defined as domiciled either in the past, or in a geographically distant place, or both. It is also, as Ferguson noted and Bakhtin implies, often identified with a sacred text (such as the Koran for Arabic). It represents the past era versus the present reality. It is socially charged – an accent that in contemporary New Zealand stands for the outsider and the former. Heteroglossia, by contrast, looks forward and close by.

> It is necessary that heteroglossia wash over a culture's awareness of itself and its language, penetrate to its core, relativize the primary language system underlying its ideology and literature and deprive it of its naïve absence of conflict . . . The entire dialectological makeup of a given national language, must have the sense that it is surrounded by an ocean of heteroglossia.   (1935[1981]:368)

As we have already seen in the mixing of Maori vernacular among more general New Zealand features by Billy T., heteroglossia is not just a macro-level concept, operating at the level of different societies or different social groups. Bakhtin sees heteroglossia as present at the micro level of language where variationist sociolinguistics does its work, individual features within single utterances:

> As a result of the work done by all these stratifying forces in language, there are no "neutral" words and forms – words and forms that can belong to "no one"; language has been completely taken over, shot through with intentions and accents . . . All words have the "taste" of a profession, a genre, a tendency, a party, a particular work, a particular person, a generation, an age group, the day and hour. Each word tastes of the context and contexts in which it has lived its socially charged life; all words and forms are populated by intentions.   (1935[1981]:293)

Bakhtin's claim is that a mix of past voices is echoed when the words of a language are spoken. He also sees this mixing operating in the syntactic structure of sentences:

> What we are calling a hybrid construction is an utterance that belongs, by
> its grammatical (syntactic) and compositional markers, to a single speaker,
> but that actually contains mixed within it two utterances, two speech man-
> ners, two styles, two "languages," two semantic and axiological belief sys-
> tems . . . The division of voices and languages takes place within the limits
> of a single syntactic whole, often within the limits of a simple sentence. It
> frequently happens that even one and the same word will belong simulta-
> neously to two languages, two belief systems that intersect in a hybrid con-
> struction – and consequently, the word has two contradictory meanings, two
> accents.   (1935[1981]:304)

In one of his relatively rare structural analyses of a piece of actual language,
Bakhtin chooses an excerpt from Charles Dickens' *Little Dorrit*:

> That illustrious man and great national ornament, Mr. Merdle, continued his
> shining course. It began to be widely understood that one who had done
> society the admirable service *of making so much money out of it*, could not be
> suffered to remain a commoner. A baronetcy was spoken of with confidence;
> a peerage was frequently mentioned.   (cited in Bakhtin 1935[1981]:306
> – his italics)

Bakhtin comments that the beginning and end of this excerpt represent "general opinion" – that is, they contain the kind of things that might have been
written in a newspaper or spoken among people at gatherings, including descrip-
tors such as *illustrious man* and *great national ornament*, and the foreshadowing
of a baronetcy or peerage. But embedded in the second sentence is another voice,
that of the author himself, with a comment that does not fit the tone of the other
voice: the service Merdle has rendered society is that *of making so much money
out of it*. This is a subversive voice, which Bakhtin identifies as that of the author,
and it certainly represents authorial gloss on Merdle's achievements. But, I may
add, it may also reflect another, underground social discourse which complains
that Merdle's main contribution has been to make himself rich, and questions why
he should be honored for that.

Bakhtin observes that the hybrid construction here is typical in its structure,
with the main clause remaining in someone else's speech (in this case, the general
public) while the subordinate clause contains direct authorial speech. So we can
see also in Billy T. James's first excerpt above a mixing of several voices – general
authorial, authorial Maori, Maori character (Tui Teka), Maori group ("the boys"),
Australian (food worker). It is noticeable that the vernacular features appear most
where Billy is quoting his characters, but they also appear when he is speaking in
his own, narrator's voice. This calls to mind Bakhtin's point that a direct quotation
may often infect the voice around it with its own voice.

Similarly, what a particular linguistic realization means socially may depend
on other aspects of the linguistic (or non-linguistic) context. This is shown nicely
in the counterpointed characters of Billy T. James in the analysis above. In
New Zealand English, a close front realization of the KIT vowel may mean

"Maori," as it does in Billy's first persona above. Or it may be an RP pronunciation, meaning "elite British." This is its meaning for Billy's second persona, taking its dialectal orientation, so to speak, from the clustering of other RP features around it. Thirdly, it could also mean Australian – but (regrettably) no K I T vowels happen to occur in Billy's one-line representation of the Australian food worker.

Addressivity and response

Central to Bakhtin's approach to language are the mutually dependent characteristics of addressing and responding to another person. Bakhtin writes:

> An essential (constitutive) marker of the utterance is its quality of being directed to someone, its *addressivity*. As distinct from the signifying units of a language – words and sentences – that are impersonal, belonging to nobody and addressed to nobody, the utterance has both an author . . . and an addressee. This addressee can be an immediate participant-interlocutor in an everyday dialogue . . . And it can also be an indefinite, unconcretized *other* . . . Both the composition and, particularly, the style of the utterance depend on those to whom the utterance is addressed, how the speaker (or writer) senses and imagines his addressees, and the force of their effect on the utterance . . . The addressee of the utterance can, so to speak, coincide *personally* with the one (or ones) to whom the utterance responds. This personal coincidence is typical in everyday dialogue or in an exchange of letters.   (1953[1986a]:95)

Some of these points will be familiar to those acquainted with the Audience Design framework put forward in Bell (1984) and developed in Bell (2001). The indefinite or imagined addressee corresponds to the "Referee Design" of that framework. Audience Design was an early attempt from within sociolinguistics to develop an approach to language in which hearers matter as well as speakers. The reciprocity of speaker and hearer in creating an utterance is of paramount significance for Bakhtin, who expresses it as shared territory – a common enough concept for sociolinguistics. More strikingly, he images language as a bridge thrown across the divide between speaker and listener, depending on both for its efficacy:

> Orientation of the word toward the addressee has an extremely high significance. In point of fact, *word is a two-sided act*. It is determined equally by *whose* word it is and *for whom* it is meant. As word, it is precisely *the product of the reciprocal relationship between speaker and listener, addresser and addressee*. Each and every word expresses the "one" in relation to the "other." I give myself verbal shape from another's point of view, ultimately, from the point of view of the community to which I belong. A word is a bridge thrown between myself and another. If one end of the bridge depends on me, then the other depends on my addressee. A word is territory shared by both addresser and addressee, by the speaker and his interlocutor.   (Voloshinov 1929[1973]:86)

This sense of the significance of the listener for the shape and meaning of any utterance takes Bakhtin a step further to consider response as the prime component of the speaking situation:

> In the actual life of speech, every concrete act of understanding is active . . .
> To some extent, primacy belongs to the response, as the activating principle:
> it creates the ground for understanding, it prepares the ground for an active
> and engaged understanding. Understanding comes to fruition only in the
> response . . .   (1935[1981]:282)

Bakhtin stresses the activeness of response, an emphasis again which Audience Design shares (e.g. Bell [1984:184] – although I was unaware of Bakhtin or his work at the time of writing that paper). Audience Design originated in a reaction to the mechanistic views of "style" that were predominant in early variationist sociolinguistics. It was subsequently itself critiqued for being too passive and reactive, although I do not regard responsiveness as passivity, and nor does Bakhtin. He sees hearers as active, co-creators of social meaning in language. However, acknowledging force in these objections, the "initiative" dimension of the Audience Design was later further developed (Bell 2001) as part of an approach which takes more account of the centrifugal as well as the centripetal forces in language.

A concrete instance imaging the primacy of the audience occurs in a series of television advertisements for New Zealand on Air, the publicly funded body which supports local content on New Zealand television. These took the format and genre of the awards ceremony but instead of presenting awards to performers and producers, presented them to viewers:

New Zealand on Air advertisement
Scene: Television awards ceremony, two presenters at the podium.

A: Our stories help to define us as New Zealanders
     so NZ on Air makes sure they get made
     and can be watched.
B: Here to prove it
     Best Viewer of a Locally Made Drama
     [opens envelope]
     Mrs. S. Wilson.
     [switch to shot of elderly lady in concentrated attention]
A: And for Best Viewer in a Supporting Role
B: Mr. Wilson
     [enters with two dinners on plates]
     Also watching New Zealand drama.
     [applause]

These advertisements take a recognizable television genre and re-voice it for another purpose. They subvert our expectations and point up the place of the audience in even mass-mediated content. In so doing they challenge our stereotypes of how communication operates. When someone is described as "a good communicator," it is invariably their speaking or presentation skills which are being praised. But cannot someone who listens well be as justifiably termed a "good communicator?" Bakhtin's argument above leads us in that direction, and he unpacks the complex process of listener responsiveness in some detail:

> The person to whom I respond is my addressee, from whom I, in turn expect a response (or in any case an active responsive understanding). But in such cases of personal coincidence one individual plays two different roles, and the difference between the roles is precisely what matters here. After all, the utterance of the person to whom I am responding (I agree, I object, I execute, I take under advisement, and so forth) is already at hand, but his response (or responsive understanding) is still forthcoming. When constructing my utterance, I try actively to determine this response. Moreover, I try to act in accordance with the response I anticipate, so this anticipated response, in turn, exerts an active influence on my utterance (I parry objections that I foresee, I make all kinds of provisos, and so forth). When speaking I always take into account the apperceptive background of the addressee's perception of my speech . . . These considerations also determine my choice of a genre for my utterance, my choice of compositional devices, and, finally, my choice of language vehicles, that is, the **style** of my utterance.   (1953[1986a]:95)

This attempt to unpack the blow-by-blow complexities of accommodating to one's audience pre-echoed the schemata proposed by Coupland, Coupland, and Giles (1988) within the frame of Communication Accommodation Theory. Above all, Bakhtin emphasizes, the nature of the word is to always want to be heard: "for the word (and, consequently, for a human being) there is nothing more terrible than a *lack of response*" (1970[1986b]:127).

Conclusion: style and a dialogical theory of language

These then are facets of what Bakhtin calls dialogism. Dialogism is that kind of approach to language which sees dialogue as the basic instantiation of language, which regards the addressee as being as important as the speaker, which treats response as being as active and essential to communication as is initiative, which places "style" at the center of linguistic variety, and which proposes a dialogical theory of language to encompass these. Firstly, then, Bakhtin's own summary of his conclusions (emphasis in original):

> Let us conclude the argument with an attempt to formulate our own point of view in the following set of propositions:
>
> 1. *Language as a stable system of normatively identical forms is merely a scientific abstraction,* productive only in connection with certain particular practical and theoretical goals. This abstraction is not adequate to the concrete reality of language.

2. *Language is a continuous generative process implemented in the social-verbal interaction of speakers.*

3. *The laws of the generative process of language are not at all the laws of individual psychology, but neither can they be divorced from the activity of speakers.* The laws of language generation are *sociological laws.*

4. *Linguistic creativity does not coincide with artistic creativity nor with any other type of specialized ideological creativity . . .*

5. *The structure of the utterance is a purely sociological structure.* The utterance, as such, obtains between speakers.   (Voloshinov 1929[1973]:98)

Second, all sociolinguists would probably agree with Bakhtin's judgment of structuralist linguistics outlined earlier, and we have seen that it runs parallel to early sociolinguistic critiques. The logic of that evaluation could also however be applied to some aspects of sociolinguistics itself, and I suspect that Bakhtin would be equally hard on some approaches. Classical Conversation Analysis, for example, has a commendable and skilled apparatus to unpack the detail of dialogues. However, in its purest orthodoxy, its refusal to take into account the social and ideological dimensions of language behavior would fall under the same critique that Bakhtin offered to structuralist linguistics or formalist approaches to literature. Again, any practice of sociolinguistics that deals solely in quantification abstracted from the actual, qualitative usage of individual linguistic features in conversations would, I believe, be seen by Bakhtin as too distant from the actual living utterances to be a rounded representation of real language. The best work in sociolinguistics has always known and followed this path, and it is no accident that some of the most exciting contemporary sociolinguistic research combines skilled quantitative analysis with a solid presentation of qualitative text.

Third, Bakhtin also emphasizes the crucial fact that one of the main subjects and contents of speech is language itself – that is, the re-presentation of what others have said. Sociolinguists know this and study this, of course – the great variety of ways in which our speech quotes the speech of others, which is one of our chief resources for stylistic differentiation and alignment. But Bakhtin goes further and makes a very bold and specific quantitative claim about quoted language:

> We need only keep our ears open to the speech sounding everywhere around us to reach such a conclusion: in the everyday speech of any person living in society, no less than half (on the average) of all the words uttered by him will be someone else's words (consciously someone else's).   (1935[1981]:339)

This is not a passing idea, because Bakhtin repeats it. He did not of course do any quantification to prove that half of our words are conscious quotes from others, but he may be right. Some discourse studies have shown the extent to which conversationalists may embed the voices of others into their talk. I suspect Bakhtin's "half" is an exaggeration – but perhaps not by much.

Fourth, Bakhtin does not talk about speakers but rather about "the speaking person." This is salutary. Sociolinguists can become inured to the term "speaker," and speakers can ironically become too easy to depersonalize, to treat as subjects, informants, eventually objects. But the speaking person is foremost a *person,* and this emphasis accords with Bakhtin's stress on addressivity and response, and on language as something that occurs between people. This also closes the circle to the study of style, which is first and foremost the variety of ways that individual speaking persons use language in dialogue with others.

Finally, what might a dialogical theory of language and style look like? Bakhtin's theorizing on language begins where most other theories – even sociolinguistic ones – leave off. Bakhtin's whole approach to language is built around irony, parody, quotation, hybrid utterances, double voicing, and the like – the sort of phenomena that make strong linguists blanche and turn elsewhere but that are essentially stylistic. However, just because he places these intractable characteristics at the heart of his theory, if it works it is an enormously powerful tool for approaching the complex and multiple ways in which speaking persons style their language for a variety of ends.

General theoretical linguistics shows no more sign of encompassing sociolinguistics now than it ever has, still less of adopting it as the best way to do linguistics. To my mind what distinguishes sociolinguistics from linguistics is the former's interest in hearers, in the audience. Theoretical linguistics has no place for hearers. Chomsky's ideal speaker/hearer is in fact only a speaker. S/he never listens. I believe with Bakhtin that we should no more conceive of language without hearers than of a language that has no speakers. To acknowledge only – or even primarily – the speaker is to inevitably practice a-social linguistics. A dialogical theory of language is the foundation of a rounded sociolinguistic theory, placing stylistic variety at the heart of our enquiry, and asserting with Bakhtin the centrality of language to our humanness.

6 Variation and historical linguistics

MICHAEL MONTGOMERY

Introduction

When Ferdinand de Saussure outlined his celebrated distinction between synchrony and diachrony in what became his *Cours de linguistique générale*, he stated that "the opposition between the two viewpoints . . . is absolute and allows no compromise. A few facts show what the difference is and why it is irreducible" (1916[1959]:83). Nearly a century later, linguistic scholarship has considerably united the two perspectives on language and resolved, one must hope, Saussure's quandary about how the linguistic present and the linguistic past inform one another. Because it is socially situated and motivated, variation is intrinsic to natural language and is always potentially unstable. It follows then that by comparing variation between two or more points one can detect and measure change. Historical linguistics and the study of language change have been inconceivable without an awareness of language variation.

Today those who explore the evolution of language through tracking variation have far more diverse tools than ever before. Traditional philological methods for assessing and interpreting written texts have a rich tradition for analyzing pronunciation and grammar from which many trained in modern speech-based linguistics can learn. Over the past forty years sociolinguistic concepts and quantitative methods have been applied to language change and variation, producing increasingly sophisticated explorations. Cross-generational analysis of change in progress, based on the construct of "apparent time" (Bailey 2002), posits that historical change is observable by comparing contemporary age cohorts, that in essence synchrony can be converted to diachrony. The scholarship of social historians (e.g. on migration) has made possible better informed study of the ecological scenarios in which linguistic variation and change take place.

This chapter shows how the different approaches cited can be married in sociohistorical methodologies enriched by all of them. It outlines ways in which a corpus of linguistic material, an important, necessary precursor, can be constructed for sociohistorical investigations to deepen understanding of the roles different social groups have played in language evolution. Particular attention is given to how letters of semiliterate commoners can help reconstruct non-standard varieties of English of eighteenth- and nineteenth-century American Southerners, Black and White, and explore how English was transplanted from the British Isles to

North America. One major resource for the first emphasis is the Southern Plantation Overseers Corpus (SPOC), a compilation of 537 letters (155,000 words) from fifty White plantation overseers in the antebellum South (Schneider and Montgomery 2001).[1] Another source is Ulster emigrant letters, written back to family members in Ireland. Emigrant letters are the most informal and numerous extant documents for studying the language of foundational colonial periods (Montgomery 1995).

Preliminaries

A wide range of written and spoken texts form the arsenal of text-types for reconstructing the linguistic past and often for inferring the linguistic past from the linguistic present. Written ones include literature (novels, poetry, plays), legal documents, sermons, textbooks, memoranda, newspaper advertisements, cookbooks, etc., and the commentary and observations of contemporary travelers and language specialists (grammarians, orthoepists, lexicographers, spelling reformers, etc.); see Montgomery (2001a: 96–104) for a typology and discussion. Spoken ones include any record of speech converted to a permanent form, from recorded interviews to transcriptions of items rare in interviews or written texts, such as single-word responses to a survey, observed examples noted and logged (as for multiple modal verbs; Mishoe and Montgomery 1994), or even grammaticality judgments (Montgomery 2006).

Spoken records have many advantages over written ones, whose relationship to speech is often uncertain. More data, both linguistic and social, from more diverse individuals can usually be obtained through speech samples, making it more easily categorized, coded, quantified, and compared. Linguists have therefore often privileged spoken texts without knowing how closely they approximate their usual object of study (the vernacular) and have sometimes used twentieth-century records alone to reconstruct the speech of many generations ago. The exclusion of written data from consideration has even led Myhill (1995) to argue a negative, that from their absence in the Works Progress Administration's (WPA) recordings of African American ex-slaves (Bailey, Maynor, and Cukor-Avila 1991), some linguistic features did not exist in nineteenth-century African American Vernacular English (AAVE).[2]

While indispensable for investigating linguistic developments over the past two centuries, especially in comparing generations of speakers in apparent time

---

[1] The letters in SPOC were written between 1794 and 1876 (mainly in the 1830s–50s) by working-class White men who ran a plantation in the absence of its owner, who lived in another county or state of the South. Typically they deal with the progress of sowing, harvesting, and marketing crops, the weather, diseases among slaves, and similar matters. This informal text-type was produced by speakers who often had little education and relatively low status.

[2] The Library of Congress holds many collections with hundreds of stories, sermons, interviews, and other texts recorded from both Blacks and Whites in the 1930s yet to be consulted by linguists. See Montgomery (2003) for further information.

(Wolfram and Thomas 2002) when rapid change has been taking place, speech records can extend only so far. Positing linguistic connections between varieties before 1850 using twentieth-century data alone pursues comparison before reconstructing earlier stages, compromising a basic tenet of historical linguistics. Internal reconstruction establishes prior or proto-forms without reference to other languages (or varieties). The intermediate stages it provides constitute a historical baseline for and validates comparative reconstruction for both relatively shallow and relatively great time-depths (e.g. Indo-European consonants, whereby these are reconstructed in individual Germanic languages before being compared to other branches of proto-Germanic and then proto-Indo-European). Internal reconstruction is also crucial for regional and social varieties whose recent development has been very dynamic. Without it, the linguist can often not distinguish with certainty what is retained from an older period from what may have been borrowed or developed through language contact.

Researchers like Biber and his colleagues (e.g. Biber and Finegan 1989) have often compared different written genres diachronically, but most historical linguists seek material as close to actual speech as possible, only in written form. The only records of language beyond a century and a half ago are written ones. However valuable the work of earlier language specialists such as John Walker's *Critical pronouncing dictionary and expository of the English language* (1791), it lacked a standard system of transcription and the transparency of later speech records. Along with commentary from other observers and representations of speech in plays and fiction, it can be employed to reconstruct specific forms, but rarely displays the conditioned variation of speech justifying quantitative or comparative analysis.[3]

In considering the closeness of written texts to actual speech events, Schneider (2002:72–81) proposes a continuum of five distances between an event and its written record, based on the reality of the event, the relationship between the speaker and the writer, and the temporal distance between the event and its written record: (1) texts recorded on the spot (interview transcripts, trial records of witness testimony); (2) texts recalled or written down from notes or memory (ex-slave narratives produced by the WPA in the 1930s; Rawick 1972/1977/1979, Schneider 1989); (3) imagined texts, ones potential or conceived due to the non-presence of a writer's addressee (letters, diaries); (4) texts observed, containing utterances of others a writer considers to be typical of their speech (commentaries by grammarians, etc.); and (5) invented texts having imagined speech considered typical of others with whom the writer is familiar (literary dialect).

Schneider's categories help researchers gauge how speech-based a range of written records are, but they can mislead those who interpret them as having graduated degrees of validity for revealing speech patterns. Sitting a bit awkwardly amid the others is Schneider's third category, the only one not representing actual speech utterances. It has many advantages over the others, in including first-person, authentic records from known and datable, but less-experienced

---

[3] But see Ellis (1994) for an exception to this generalization.

individuals whose writing, in contexts of widespread illiteracy, reveals much about the linguistic masses. These semiliterate writers "could render words with letters but for whom writing was a difficult, unusual task, not a daily habit" (Schneider and Montgomery 2001:389). They wrote naively, with little self-consciousness, influence from formal education, or awareness of prescriptive rules, language authorities, social norms, or models. Their letters are private documents having no amanuensis (depositions and trial records have the latter) and, having no expectation of wider readership, less constraint on formality. The limited literacy of such writers led speech to intrude into their written language and to the retention of linguistic variability. For many features it brings researchers reasonably close to earlier non-standard varieties.

Semiliterate letters present their own range of interpretative issues and some types of language (e.g. pidgins and creoles) rarely show up written in them at all. Despite obvious limitations compared to speech records (e.g. less substantial demographic or biographical information on authors), these are offset by greater time-depth. The argument is untenable that the effects of standard spelling and grammar inevitably obscure speech patterns and make semiliterate writing too problematic to analyze. Manuscript documents are in a fundamental way speech-based, in that less-literate writers compose and spell by ear rather than by written model. Given the difficulty of identifying any data on eighteenth- or nineteenth-century AAVE or other non-standard varieties, researchers should utilize such documents, while understanding their limitations. They involve fewer uncertainties than literary portrayals, often used routinely and uncritically to document and reconstruct antebellum AAVE (Stewart 1968, Dillard 1972, inter alia). Unlike literary texts, semiliterate documents do not face problems of reliability, so long as linguists either employ manuscript originals or vet transcriptions (or a sampling thereof) made by others against manuscript originals. African American correspondence has been compiled or consulted in this regard for the eighteenth (Montgomery 1999) and nineteenth century (Montgomery, Fuller, and DeMarse 1993, Van Herk and Poplack 2003).

Collectively semiliterate letters enable researchers to detail many aspects of pre-1850 vernaculars of American English and afford internal reconstruction that can often confirm or disconfirm relationships reached by cross-variety comparisons alone. Ignoring them, even for features having a putative common ancestor of only two or three centuries ago, can unwittingly lead the comparative linguist astray. A case in point is the verb *be* when expressing habitual activities (*they be working there every night*). Its remarkably similar patterning in twentieth-century African American English and Irish English led two decades of linguists to argue eighteenth-century input from Ireland, through indentured servants and other plantation laborers (Dillard, Sledd, Hamp, and Hill 1979, Rickford 1986b).[4] However, the feature is likely an innovation on both sides of the Atlantic

[4] The situation is far more complex than indicated here, in that today habitual *be* is the prevalent form in Ulster and *do/does be* elsewhere in Ireland. If the same geographical pattern prevailed in the seventeenth and eighteenth centuries, *do/does be* would likely have been brought to the

because there is no sign of it in emigrant letters,[5] fictional dialogue, or other written records in Ireland before the mid-nineteenth century (Montgomery and Kirk 1996). There it apparently arose and spread rapidly in the early nineteenth century through large-scale shift from Irish to English. Though plantations overseers often had ancestry from Ireland (especially Ulster),[6] SPOC has no instance of finite *be* in any sense. Moreover, cross-generational research has found that habitual *be* in AAVE is largely a twentieth-century development (Bailey and Maynor 1985). In the final analysis, the absence of evidence for a feature in written documents never constitutes irrefutably its absence from speech, but from wide-ranging eighteenth- and nineteenth-century evidence the failure of internal reconstruction to find it on either side of the Atlantic argues strongly that habitual *be* was not a prevalent feature in the American Colonial era and was probably not brought from Ireland.

Methodological approaches

We can start with no better place than Labov's dictum that "the more that is known about a language [or language variety], the more we can find out about it" (1972h:98). Using multiple analytical approaches and types of sources provides complementary evidence to reconstruct the evolution of non-standard varieties (e.g. Kautzsch [2002] employs analogous written and spoken evidence for nineteenth-century AAVE). Quantitative analysis has brought deeper insights and prompted linguists to develop more explicit, accountable methodologies for assessing the validity of their data. Such issues come sharply into focus in preparing a historical corpus, because the researcher often has so little control over the texts available.

Philology

Written texts consist of orthographic forms that can be subjected to linguistic interpretation. Until codification into a formal written "standard" (a process which for living western European languages began in the fifteenth century), all writing more closely approximates speech than thereafter. Though writing was highly variable in every sense, no one's writing simply mirrored their speech. Thus, variant spellings make earlier stages of the Great Vowel Shift in English more discernible and datable (Dobson 1968). For later ones, historical linguists must examine post-1600 writings of less-educated, less-privileged individuals and

Caribbean (where neither it nor *be* is found today) and *be* to the American South. Some scholars (e.g. Rickford 1986b) have recognized the quandary this situation presents.

[5] According to Boling (1994), an extensive compilation of features from Irish emigrant letters. The author is grateful to him for making this document available.

[6] From his study of working-class White communities in the antebellum South, Scarborough (p.c. 1994) presumes that most overseers were emigrants from Ulster or descendants of such emigrants, people traditionally called the "Scotch–Irish" in the United States.

regional varieties (as those found in northern England and Ireland) that are peripheral to the metropolitan centers where standards most frequently have developed and been influential.

To examine how the basic philological method applies to the interpretation of pronunciation from spelling evidence, consider an 1854 letter from a plantation overseer:[7]

> we ar all well I have not hawled up any wheat yet have a fine crop of whe the Rust ingerd about one hundred bushels Sum little the wheat that was cuverd by cake frum the fresh making it Rather late, I have the Rise of Eight twen hundred Stackes, my oat crop will be Short on a ccount of the drouth, Last wednsday and thirs day two weakes a go we had a Rain on Each day that wet the Land a bout one inch is all the Rain we have had Since you ware up, un till yes tar day yes tar day we had a fine Rain that wet the land affecturdly, the wind was very Rapid blowing nearly all of my whet down I have ges finished Sit ing it up, will commence hawling it to geather tus day, my oats that I had not cut was blown down Level with the grown tha ware not very Ripe and Seames to be Rising very well So that I think I will be able to Save them very well, I ware about halfth dun cutting when the Storm came, I have two day plowing in my corn yet only the middles the corn is So blone dawn if it dont Rise, Sum potion I cant plow, whare the corn is largest, my corn Loks well, and has Stwod the drouth much better than I Ex pect ed it could have dun, my to bacco Stands very well Ex cept the branch barn Lot and Se cand years ground I Replanted them twoo pieces yes tar day, I have not Sint of my tobacca yet, Mr john Brodnax Ses he will Send a boat fo the tobacco as Soon as he can, taby and Charlot has boath had their Children and are well, I had six twen hodgs head of to bacco finished prising Last Saturday
>
> youre frend
>
> Alexander Carter

Writers like Carter handle the written code and likely the physical act of writing with difficulty. Their many misspellings, which result when a writer "suffers from imperfect recollection of the visual image of the word in its conventional spelling, but tries to spell it from memory rather than by any phonetic or analogical principles" (Stephenson 1967:38), make their writing initially appear erratic and unsystematic, with so many aberrant forms and the lack of punctuation that speech patterns are obscured and orderly variation not detectible. This presumption is tantamount to saying that such documents, however valuable to other scholarly fields, should be dismissed by linguists because variable patterns reflecting speech cannot always be distinguished from difficulty with writing, in particular the inability to follow conventions of written English.

Not all variable structures prevalent in speech even occur in semiliterate letters (e.g. contracted forms like *he's* and *won't*, with or without an apostrophe). Because no written document is a direct transcript of speech, having passed

---

[7] Alexander Carter to Judge Thomas Ruffin, 8 July 1854, from Thomas Ruffin Papers, Southern Historical Collection #641, University of North Carolina at Chapel Hill.

through a "filter" of one or more "layers" (Schneider 2002:68), one cannot predict which features will turn up in a person's writing. However, one can often infer that what appears in writing reflects speech, if not always in a simple, straightforward way, and analyze it for its regularity and approximation to evidence from other sources, such as contemporary linguistic commentary and earlier and later records. The conformity of many misspellings to known pronunciations and the systematic patterning of grammatical features argue that the language of such documents is far from random and haphazard and can fill gaps in the history of the language.[8] While misspellings do indicate a struggling writer, normally his/her speech is brought constantly to bear in this process, producing "systematic attempts by writers to utilise what orthographic knowledge they possess in a rule governed way to express their phonological and phonetic intuitions" (Jones 1991:83). Unconventional spellings are frequently phonetic in whole or in part, though most represent the common pronunciation of all English speakers.

To analyze pronunciation through written texts, one must distinguish meaningful variation from non-meaningful variation through interpreting "occasional spellings," which are unconscious "departure[s] from the conventional spelling of a word" (Stephenson 1967:37). Excluding accidental miswritings that give no information about pronunciation, potentially meaningful occasional spellings (those giving clues to underlying pronunciation) are of two kinds, phonetic and inverse. A phonetic spelling is "one in which the writer has substituted for the conventional spelling a spelling based on some familiar correspondence of symbol to sound" (1967:39), e.g. *ginneral* for *general*. An inverse spelling is "one in which the writer has substituted for the conventional spelling of a word a spelling based on the analogy of some other word containing an orthographic fossil, perhaps etymologically justified but no longer symbolizing a sound in the writer's dialect . . . The imitative introduction of an orthographic fossil into the spelling of a word where it is not traditional usually means that the writer has created or employed an unhistorical spelling, although the fossil may be historical in the model the writer is imitating" (1967:40), e.g. *kneed* for *need*. Examples in the latter category may also be characterized as orthographic hypercorrections.

Which occasional spellings give the most useful clues to pronunciation? Scholars analyzing Middle English texts endeavor to distinguish scribal convention (what writers have inherited from reading) from scribal practice (what writers spell according to their own perceived pronunciation). The brief answer to the foregoing question is those spellings which: (1) display a structural pattern in a particular spoken language variety (the phonetic spellings *fo* and *potion* in the letter above, as well as inverse spellings *gorn* "gone" and *Surpose* "suppose" in others by Carter, suggest /r/-lessness) and do not merely reflect a case of

---

[8] For example, Carter's letter and many others shows evidence of the "northern present-tense rule" of verbal concord (Ihalainen 1994:221–2; Montgomery 1994), whereby a verb form in the present tense takes an -*s* suffix (or by analogy is *is* or *has* and sometimes *was*) unless its subject is a single adjacent personal pronoun. Thus, we find *taby and Charlot has*.

graphemic reversal (non-meaningful spellings that may be either phonetic (*dun, frum*) or inverse (*twoo*)); (2) occur among more than one writer (preferably at some distance in time or space from one another); and (3) provide plausible corroboration of pronunciation from other sources and other varieties.

Although we customarily associate scribal practices with such venues as monastic scriptoriums of centuries past, all writers exhibit them, and they involve more than orthographic habits. Those who are less literate produce occasional spellings with some frequency, whether first-grade students or working-class writers like plantation overseers, and these merit linguistic attention. Among the meaningful phonetic spellings in SPOC that evidence one feature, the merger of the front lax vowels /ɛ/ and /ɪ/ before /n/ or /m/ in stressed environments, are *agin, attintion, aginst, entinded,*[9] *fince, frind, ginerl* "general," *ginerly, intered, Sinate, sind, sint,* and *thin* "then." Meaningful inverse spellings include *cence, contenue, hem, menut, Prence, sence* "since," and *tember.*[10] Equally important to note is the lack of occasional spellings in stressed non-prenasal environments, where SPOC has only *git* and its derivatives *gits, giting,* etc. These forms, from overseers in the Carolinas and Alabama, reveal a pattern of pronunciation two or more generations earlier than that argued as becoming prevalent by Brown (1991) and Bailey (1997) using linguistic atlas and other evidence. Interestingly, one finds in the overseer letters a conspicuous absence of occasional spellings for *them, men,* and *ten* (*hem* "him" does occur once), possibly because even barely literate writers could spell extremely common words. By comparison with evidence from nineteenth-century overseers, documents from eighteenth-century North Carolina exhibit more than eighty different forms (*frish, nixt,* etc.) with occasional spellings in stressed non-nasal environments. This contrast provides some evidence that fluctuation between /ɛ/ and /ɪ/ was well on its way to a conditioned merger by the early nineteenth century. At the same time, spellings like *Seames* "seems" and *Grean* "green" in eighteenth-century Ulster emigrant letters indicate that a late stage of the Great Vowel Shift (the raising of /e/ to /i/, meaning that *meat* and *mate* were both still /met/) had not yet taken place in Ireland and was brought to America (Montgomery 2005:348–9).

The foregoing examples show the usefulness of the philological approach in revealing and dating sound change, including the actuation of environmental constraints. They permit the researcher to examine manuscript documents on a principled basis for selected features, especially pronunciation. For many reasons (e.g. the widely different spelling habits of individuals otherwise socially similar), this approach is used largely to identify, rather than quantify, conditioned patterns of speech. One cannot say as much for literary attestations, which are by nature archetypal rather than variable and often over-used to distinguish or dramatize characters.

---

[9] Examples are limited to vowels in stressed syllables because spellings such as *imployed* and *entend* may reflect the tendency for vowels to neutralize typical of all native English speech.

[10] For further discussion of the history of this sound change, see Montgomery and Eble (2004).

Sociolinguistics

According to Weinreich, Labov, and Herzog (1968:100), a speech community's language (Saussure's *parole*) forms a system of "orderly heterogeneity," which implies that variation is omnipresent and non-random, constrained by multiple linguistic and social factors. From this precept two generations of researchers have examined, most often through multivariate or other quantitative analysis, how functionally equivalent variants correlate with social groupings based on extralinguistic factors (gender, age, social class, level of educational attainment, etc.; see Bayley 2002). This research was pioneered by Labov (1963) on Martha's Vineyard and exemplified in studies by him, Wolfram (1969), and Trudgill (1974), among others, and has shown that quantitative distributions of variants within synchronic data sets often indicate change in progress (even when not proceeding to completion) and tell us much about how language change is embedded in social structures, i.e. the social mechanisms, motivations, and constraints on it. In understanding how non-linguistic factors affect a speaker's choices between alternative expressions, this approach has sought more broadly to "construct an integrated vision of language, within which its past and present-day appearances can be accounted for" (Kytö and Rissanen 1997:10).

Comparing originally the speech of different age groups in apparent time, the cross-generational model of quantitative sociolinguistics has more recently been applied to written records. Both cases require the researcher to formulate social categories that are culturally sensitive and applicable consistently and insightfully to all speakers/writers. "Culturally sensitive" means categories that reflect the internal organization of a speech community. Valid categories for historical communities are challenging to identify and manipulate, but without them a researcher may obscure rather than elucidate. For example, extralinguistic factors can be fluid even within two or three generations (e.g. a 10th-grade education in the United States in 1910 was probably equivalent to four years of college in 1990 and was certainly less common), and urban-based social class categories (type of housing or occupation) cannot be applied appropriately to rural communities. As in all social sciences, researchers must guard against reifying categories (e.g. Is race a dichotomy between "Black" and "White," and do this and other dichotomies obscure the complexity of small rural communities?). And, as in all sciences, equating correlations with causation or even "conditioning factors" should be approached conservatively and with thorough argumentation.

A recent criticism of quantitative sociolinguistics is that social categories such as gender and class are not fixed, but sometimes situationally constructed (as in types of interaction, performance, telling family stories, etc.) and locally situated. Tagliamonte (2002:730) counters that using standard categories ensures comparability and gives the researcher more ability to tease out fine-grained, variable patterns from complex linguistic systems. However true it is that quantitative sociolinguistics makes sophisticated analysis possible, it has employed narrowly circumscribed sets of social categories and variable features, in part because large amounts of data are usually needed to examine contextual conditioning.

Cross-generational research is less achievable with written documents because the selection of ones that have survived is heavily biased toward standard or near-standard language. Those who worked as plantation overseers drew from across much of the social scale. They were sometimes members of the gentry or even the sons of landed families learning plantation management; those whose letters comprise SPOC can be classified as working class mainly because their letters lack the written conventions that indicate access to education (punctuation, capitalization, spelling, etc.).

In contrast to recorded interviews, audience factors come forcibly into play when analyzing an individual's letters, which may be addressed to parents or children, royalty or servants, men or women, etc. An innovative project taking these factors into account and designed to explore how sociolinguistic methods apply to historical language data is the Corpus of Early English Correspondence (CEEC), comprising 2.5 million words (4,845 letters from 640 authors) between 1420, when the first extant private letters were written, and 1681 (Nevalainen and Raumolin-Brunberg 1996, Raumolin-Brunberg 1997). It also codes letters to a comprehensive set of social parameters, among which are author's rank, father's rank, social mobility, place of birth, location of main domicile, education, and religion. By rank, the CEEC means social stratification relevant to the period (e.g. "gentry," "clergy," etc.) and qualifies these designations as upwardly mobile (e.g. a priest who rose to become a bishop) or not. The coding for audience factors enables analysis of stylistic and pragmatic variation both synchronically and diachronically.

In contrast to cross-generational comparison, the cross-variety approach dates back more than a century. Using data from two or more speech communities, it seeks or presumes a common historical ancestor. Cross-variety comparison has been used as a short cut for internal reconstruction when earlier, usually written, data is deemed impossible to find, too scarce to be informative or to use (as for multiple modal verbs; see Montgomery and Nagle 1994), or for some other reason. It typically uses survey data from older, less-educated, less-mobile speakers to capture details of variation, rarely comparing generations. Cross-variety comparisons may be either inventorial, classifying speakers, communities, or varieties on whether or not a given feature or form occurs in them, or quantitative, computing for different groups of speakers percentages of occurrence by linguistic context. Anglophone creolists have routinely pursued such comparisons to posit a common creole or pidgin ancestor of three or four centuries ago in the Caribbean or West Africa (as Hancock 1987). More recently (as Rickford and Handler [1994] for Barbadian Creole), they have mined the documentary record for earlier evidence, though this rarely pre-dates the nineteenth century or comes from speakers themselves. Another qualitative paradigm of cross-variety research is that of linguistic atlases to research spatial and social differences in American English vocabulary and pronunciation. From data collected by the Linguistic Atlas of the United States and Canada in the 1930s and the 1940s for speakers born well back in the nineteenth century, Kurath (1949) and Kurath and McDavid (1961) sought to establish a historical baseline from which to infer British input patterns from the seventeenth and eighteenth centuries, outline transatlantic connections, and map American dialect areas. American atlas surveys are valuable tools because fieldworkers have collected so much social information about the speakers surveyed and their family histories and because of their large samples (more than a thousand speakers each for the Linguistic Atlas of the Middle and South Atlantic States and the Linguistic Atlas of the Gulf States).

For morphological features quantitative cross-variety comparison has been pursued more recently by sociolinguists, as in the research of Poplack (2000b) and Poplack and Tagliamonte (2001) on African American English; they have compared two late-twentieth-century descendants of diaspora varieties in the Dominican Republic and Nova Scotia, both originally taken abroad two centuries ago, with the transcripts of ex-slave narratives in Bailey *et al.* (1991). Tagliamonte and Smith (1998, 2000, 2002) have extended this approach across the Atlantic (see below), with Tagliamonte (1999) arguing that "isolated British communities" retain "relic varieties [that] provide the critical time-depth" for comparison and reconstruction.

Quantitative analysis and corpus formation

As already suggested, the type of data available constrains whether qualitative or quantitative analysis is appropriate. Most quantitative analysis of linguistic variation, and thus of historical variation and change, is predicated upon a corpus of texts or text-samples and is possible only with large amounts of data. In constructing a corpus, the researcher identifies, describes, and selects texts or text-samples and the people who produced them. We can define a corpus as "a principled compilation of texts or text-samples upon which linguistic analysis can be conducted." "Principled" means that the researcher identifies and justifies the criteria for selecting what the corpus includes and excludes (Kytö and Rissanen 1997, Meyer 2002).[11]

For examining historical variation, corpora of both written and spoken texts are valuable. Many issues of historical development can be addressed fruitfully only with a written corpus of some kind. One of the most widely used electronic corpora for cross-genre and cross-stylistic studies within and across time periods is the Helsinki Corpus of English Texts (HCET; Kytö 1996) of 1.5 million words dating from the eighth to the eighteenth centuries, compiled between 1984 and 1991 at Helsinki University's Research Unit for Variation, Contacts, and Change. Each of its texts and text-samples is coded for twenty-five parameters that are textual (date of the original, text-type), social (age of author, social rank of author), pragmatic (audience description, participant relation), etc.

---

[11] Meyer has an excellent presentation on criteria relating to genre, size, length of samples, number of texts, range and social profiles of speakers/writers, timeframe, and so on.

As happened in English-language lexicography after the famous call for period dictionaries following the completion of the *Oxford English dictionary* (Craigie 1936), period and genre corpora have proliferated following the HCET.[12] Others produced at Helsinki University include the Corpus of Early English Correspondence (based on printed editions) and the Helsinki Corpus of Older Scots (Meurman-Solin 1995), based on printed editions and on manuscripts where possible. Sizable corpora developed from manuscripts require many years of patient composition. From the identification, copying, transcription, and several rounds of proofing to final editing of letters the SPOC required eight years. Three gateways to linguistic corpora of machine-readable texts are the International Computer Archive of Modern and Medieval English (ICAME) (http://icame.uib.no), the Linguistic Data Consortium (www.ldc.upenn.edu), and the Oxford Text Archive (http://ota.ahds.ac.uk).

In corpus construction, texts are selected using accountable, transparent principles, e.g. they are the earliest or the most reliable edition of a printed work, or they form equal-sized text-samples chosen by time period, genre, type of author/speaker, locale, mode of language, etc. Validity and representativeness are multi-dimensional, ever-present issues in corpus construction regardless of the provenance or authorship/source of texts. Cooley's statement that as much "sociocultural, historical, and ethnographic information about a text or genre [as possible] is necessary before accepting its use in linguistic history as being appropriate" (1997: 58) also pertains to their authors. Among the dimensions and questions that must be considered in corpus construction are the following:

(1) *Textual dimensions.* What type of text is it? How close to speech is it? What is its register and style? Written documents differ widely in their circumstances of production and their relationship to spoken language (cf. Schneider's continuum outlined earlier). Texts purporting to represent speech (plays, fictional dialogue, etc.) are composed for public consumption, present perceived and often exaggerated variation, and exploit stereotypes. Their relation to real-life models is thus uncertain. Their accessibility (indeed scanability) makes literary documents, with representations of speech very attractive to corpus-builders often to the exclusion of more-valuable semiliterate manuscript documents (Bliss 1979, Hickey 2003), which are much more difficult to amass. True, literary documents alone can and often do attest non-standard features or varieties of a given place or time period. Eighteenth-century North American ethnic varieties of English cannot be studied without such material, which is extensive for Irish, German, Scottish, African American, Amerindian, Yiddish, and other character types (Cooley 1995). However, when it first appeared in American colonies in the mid-1700s, literary dialect already drew on

---

[12] For a report on those completed or in progress only five years after the appearance of the HCET, see Kytö and Rissanen (1997).

comic stereotypes not native to America, as the social background of an author can sometimes reveal. For example, Cooley (1997) shows that the African American dialect in the 1768 play/comic opera *The padlock* was based on a Caribbean, not an American, model.

(2) *Temporal dimensions.* When was the text produced? What period of the language does it represent? As language and literary historians know, many texts existed in oral form for an indeterminate time before being written down, and many written texts have varying, derivative forms, which require reconstruction of an *Ur*-version. These realities mean that the first question above often has a hypothetical answer, but one necessary before addressing the second question. Among simple advantages that letters, private or public, possess is that they indicate a date and a place of origin. The date associated with literary and many other texts is that of publication, which may occur years after a text was written, which could have occurred years after an author observed the speech portrayed. For letters, that the age and thus the exact time of an author's acquisition of language are sometimes known raises the possibility, assuming apparent time, of observing change in progress in the letters of extended higher echelon families such as the Celys (Hanham 1975), Pastons (Davis 2004), or Montgomerys (Montgomery 2004). These three family collections date from the fifteenth or sixteenth centuries, before the completion of standardization; indeed, they are primary documents in which that process can be seen taking place. Beyond their name, nothing is known for certain about the plantation overseers in SPOC than the dates and places of their letter(s). Their language represents that of two, and possibly three, generations earlier than any extant speech records from the same rank of society. Ultimately the age of some overseers may be ascertained from the 1850 census, the first detailed one conducted in the United States.

(3) *Social dimensions.* By whom was the text produced? What do we know about that person? Whose language does the text represent? For published texts more than one hand has often been involved, with the identity and the social profile of the intermediary (secretary, editor, printer, etc.) unknown. Thus, in relating language patterns to social factors, private manuscript documents have a distinct advantage. Clerks wrote depositions, trial proceedings, and other court transactions, but did these amanuenses faithfully record the language of those who testified? The former were usually anonymous, the latter not. Even if they do have the "feel" of speech, can we know to what extent such documents reflect the language of clerks?

To be sure, this issue must be considered for private letters as well. Royalty have no doubt long had secretaries, but what about the gentry? Even semiliterate documents could have been written by or dictated to someone else. Evidence on authorship must be marshaled and assessed for each set of documents, often for individual documents, and this often requires patiently consulting archivists and social historians. The latter use protocols to evaluate the authorship of manuscripts and often indicate their judgments in published documentary editions. Linguists also must consider both internal and external evidence before deciding whether the signatories of documents were the authors. For working-class writers, the composition of their immediate community is crucial in assessing authenticity. For the SPOC, there is little reason to believe the overseers were not the authors. In the owner's absence, he was the highest-status person on the plantation, the one most likely with the highest level of education (however scant), and frequently the only one with any command of reading and writing. He was often the only White person there, except perhaps for his wife and children.

A similar issue arises for nineteenth-century letters apparently by African Americans. The antebellum abolitionist literature has count-less cases of White teachers, clergymen, reporters, and others assisting ex-slaves, transcribing (and nearly always standardizing) or ghost-writing narratives of slavery, escape, and liberation for publication. This hardly implies that we can never be reasonably sure that a doc-ument from a semiliterate writer came from an American of African descent, because historical research can support a presumption that no Whites lived or worked in the same community (Van Herk and Poplack 2003 for Liberia, Montgomery 1999 for Sierra Leone).

(4) *Spatial dimensions*. From where does the text originate? What is the author's nationality or regional origin? Is the text (hence its variety of language) localizable? Here letters of the gentry and upper classes would seem to have an advantage because these groups more likely kept records and had civil or religious institutions preserve records on them. More information can be unearthed about authors from more elite classes, though there is a trade-off because they rarely used non-standard language. We know the locale from which each letter in the SPOC was written, but the writers were transient, usually employed on annual contracts. We do not know where they were even born or even if this was in the United States (here too the 1850 census may help). Letters from British and Irish emigrants give us far more certainty. These were normally addressed by an adult member of a family to others remaining in or near the author's native community (Erickson 1972, Montgomery 1995).

One must still be careful in ascribing a person to the geographic locale in which his/her family lived and consult family history and local records if possible before inferring their regional origins. For example, Bailey, Maynor, and Cukor-Avila (1989) argue that the "NP/Pro constraint"[13] occurred generally in late-fifteenth-century England from its appearance in letters of the Cely merchant family,

---

[13] See note 7.

natives of London. However, only one family member, Richard Cely the Younger, actually manifested the feature more than marginally in non-existential contexts (where it has long occurred super-regionally). Since this son was the only writer reared outside London (in York-shire), it is not surprising that he followed the constraint, the historical pattern in northern Britain (Montgomery 1997a:137). Likewise, can we know that prisoners and vagrants transported to American colonies in the early seventeenth century and whose speech was reported in depositions from Bridewell Court Minute Books (Wright 2001) were natives of London, given the internal migration from the countryside into the metropolis in the sixteenth century?

(5) *Representativeness dimensions.* From how many individuals do the documents come? Of what portion of society are they typical? How generalizable are the language patterns they evidence? These questions are usually answered by the haphazard survival of documents. "The great art of the historical linguist is," according to (Labov 1972h:100), "to make the best of this bad data – 'bad' in the sense that it may be fragmentary, corrupted, or many times removed from the actual productions of actual speech." This dimension is intimately bound up in the four preceding ones.

The value of any data, both apparent-time and real-time, "is in large part a function of the size and representativeness of the sample from which it is taken" (Bailey 2002:329), but researchers into historical variation cannot define a sample like modern-day sociolinguists. For any corpus of written texts, including ones of semiliterate letters like in the SPOC, that their producers could write introduces a biased selection, because only a minority of people until recent generations were literate. One might then suppose that the SPOC does not represent the spoken language of a broad segment of antebellum White working-class southerners, even though mitigating circumstances sometimes prompted barely literate people to write, and this produced a wider representation of writers (see below). However, to ask whether overseers represent entirely typical colloquial speakers is a flawed, premature question. The nineteenth-century American South was quite a diverse region socially, and we should expect to discern this in the linguistic varieties among overseers. As Schneider and Montgomery (2001) show, overseers could differ radically from one another, as in variation between *was* and *were*. Thus, for the historical linguist the issue is not whether one has a "representative" sample so much as it is to profile scrupulously the sample at hand for what inferences may be drawn from it.

Finally, in documenting the sociolinguistic circumstances and identity of an author, the researcher must remember that even one whose sociogeographic profile and background are known may have had contact with other varieties or languages. One manifestation of this is their access, however limited, to the written word.

Given the difficulties in locating semiliterate letters, can sociohistorical linguists trust as reliable the transcriptions in documentary editions that social historians have produced? Van Herk and Poplack answer emphatically no. In considering printings of nineteenth-century correspondence by African Americans who emigrated to Liberia, they cast alleged lapses in one letter transcribed in Wiley (1980) as typical of the historical profession at large, stating that "Historians tend to tidy up non-standard punctuation, spelling, and grammar in order to make letters more readable" (2003:247). This assessment is at best poorly informed and misleading, and it flies in the face of two generations of documentary editors who draw no distinction between content and form and who are usually religious about form because their reputations rely on the accuracy of their transcriptions, including such details as word endings, unconventional spellings, and non-standard forms. Textual editors typically discuss their transcription practices and editorial methods explicitly. In not doing so, Wiley is the very rare exception.[14]

The importance of using original, unaltered manuscripts for linguistic research cannot be overstated. To ascertain their reliability, printed transcriptions (or a sample thereof) should be compared to manuscript originals whenever possible.[15] No sociohistorical study that relies on published transcriptions alone should fail to state this. The same caveat pertains to speech records on which transcriptions are based. Recent documentary editions of African American correspondence (Miller 1978, Berlin, Ready, and Rowland 1982) and other less-skilled writers are generally excellent and have many distinct merits. Their editors are practitioners of what Labov lauds as a practice of critical scholarship: "*reference* – the act of making the original texts available for the inspection of others who may have other biases and prejudices" (1972h:100). They provide general and personal background on those whose writing is transcribed and cite the location of the manuscripts they publish. Finally, historians are usually better, less-fallible transcribers than linguists because of serving apprenticeships in the craft and becoming seasoned paleographers familiar with earlier handwriting practices.[16]

---

[14] One can contrast this to a much more typical statement of method from the work of another historian who edited letters from Liberia: "In order to preserve the integrity and flavor of the letters and to capture any distinct Afro-American dialect, the letters are printed as found in the originals, with the few minor exceptions described below. End-mark dashes have been rendered as periods when this seemed to be the writer's intention. When no end mark exists but the sentence is complete, the sentences are separated by extra space. Otherwise, punctuation and spacing follow the practice in the original. Capitalization conforms to the writer's style" (Miller 1978:14–15).

[15] The CEEC drew its texts from published versions but compared a sample of these against manuscript originals to ensure reliability. Because this corpus has not been prepared for the study of pronunciation, the reliability of its transcription does not loom as large an issue as otherwise. In any case, establishing the reliability of published transcriptions by comparing a sample to manuscript originals gives the researcher confidence in trusting the remainder.

[16] The experience of historians gives them other advantages over trained linguists in transcribing semiliterate documents, e.g. their familiarity with subject matter such as agriculture. For the SPOC

Social history

As suggested with respect to the Corpus of Early English Correspondence, western societies were in earlier times organized quite differently from modern-day ones, and this must be taken into account when coding and interpreting variation in historical data. More broadly, this reality implies that researchers should: (1) understand from the inside the society or community whose language they are exploring; and (2) detail the ecology of the language or language variety they are studying. By absorbing the social history of their sites they give their work a valid foundation, avoid misconceptions and fallacies, and designate the varieties, peoples, and areas under study appropriately. Too often linguistic studies present simplistic characterizations of communities or consult the work of historians only to locate a convenient quotation or summary to frame or justify their arguments. Too rarely do they collaborate with social historians, who usually understand very well that each type of evidence has its problems and what those problems are (but see Rickford and Handler 1994).

The first requirement above is essentially a bottom-up, anthropological one: to ask questions like how the society/community would have seen itself and what roles were played by those whose language is being studied. The second is a top-down, demographic and geographic one that considers the larger conditions surrounding a language or variety, including the size of the community, its economic and social relations with others, migration and settlement history, and so on, at each relevant period. Because population movement is almost always at play, language and dialect contact must be accounted for (Mufwene 2001). Population ratios, especially in formative colonial periods, can be crucial, as can the frequency and nature of linguistic features in the varieties spoken by the dominant founder population; such features "often have selective advantage" (Mufwene 1996:123). An account of linguistic ecology not grounded in social history may impose inappropriate modern categories, perceptions, and distinctions on historical data.

One great strength of linguistic geography, for example, has been its practitioners' willingness to learn from geographers and historians in comparing settlement and migration to linguistic usage. Linguistic pictures outlined by Kurath (1949) for the Eastern United States and Pederson *et al.* (1986–92) for the American South, based on primary, secondary, and tertiary settlement patterns, rarely conform to either state boundaries or perceived regions, yet linguists have frequently preferred both to the cultural or physiographic regions that much better reflect population distribution. Rickford (1997) compares the proportion of slaves to Whites in the thirteen Atlantic colonies from New Hampshire to Georgia c1750 to estimate the relative contact between them in each. More revealing

---

Schneider and Montgomery (2001) employed historians and documentary editors to check their transcriptions against manuscript originals, to decipher handwriting, and to interpret readings (e.g. of abbreviations) unclear to the corpus editors. After exhaustive review, the number of remaining doubtful passages in the SPOC was infinitesimal.

(and providing more support for his arguments) would have been a comparison of the coastal South with the interior South (i.e. the eastern halves of Virginia and the Carolinas with their western halves). Other researchers into regional differences in earlier African American English have grouped states into sub-regions (e.g. Walker and Van Herk [2005] into the Deep South and the nebulous "non-Deep South"). In contrast, Schneider (1989:229–31) based his regional comparisons on patterns of settlement and land use, a less convenient but more valid approach.

As challenging as the use of appropriate spatial demarcations might be, this is a macro-issue for which the basic research has already been done by other fields. More complex are issues of language and dialect contact, which usually must be dealt with on a micro-level. The letters in the SPOC reveal patterns of antebellum White speech that would have formed models for many African Americans acquiring English on southern plantations (of course, the linguistic influence could have gone in either direction). According to Scarborough (1966:xi), "no figure occupied a position of greater importance in the managerial hierarchy of the southern plantation system than did the overseer . . . To the overseer were entrusted the welfare and supervision of the [slaves]; the care of the land, stock, and farm implements; the planting, cultivation, and harvesting of both staple and subsistence crops; and many other responsibilities associated with the management of a commercial agricultural enterprise." Their responsibilities to others off the plantation, whether it was large or small, counterbalanced their authority on the plantation. The contact between them and African American slaves no doubt varied depending on the size of plantation, and not infrequently letters indicate that overseers worked alongside slaves in the field. The SPOC is thus a compilation that invites many case studies using the rich plantation family collections from which the letters are drawn.

One common way to bypass issues of social heterogeneity and dialect contact is to study the speech of communities argued to be "isolated," "enclaves," "peripheral," "insular," or "relic areas." Sometimes even large regions are described in such blanket terms (for example, Appalachia, which, depending on its definition, comprises parts of from eight to thirteen states and twenty million people). Such labels usually reflect the perception of outsiders far more than insiders or a proper assessment of a community's historical access to markets, frequency of contact with other communities, psychological orientation toward the outside world, and many other conditions (Montgomery 2000). What appears isolated today may have formerly been considerably less so. For example, take Buckie, a fishing village in northeastern Scotland studied by Tagliamonte and Smith, who describe it as a "relic area [having] peripheral geographical isolation" and "isolated social and/or political circumstances" and emphasize its stable, endogamous population (2000:141). But was Buckie so "peripheral" in the past? For centuries it must have been much less so than nearby inland (indeed most landlocked) communities and its ecology on the North Sea littoral more complex. Its access to the sea, the only highway before relatively recent times, gave it maritime contacts with other communities along the Scottish coast and farther afield. Men joined those from other villages in fleets fishing as far away as Donegal in northwestern Ireland (Bell 1991), and unmarried women from fishing villages in northern Scotland worked as far down the coast as northern England in the seasonal fish-gutting industry. Using Linguistic Survey of Scotland data, Mather (1966, 1972) found lexical and phonological evidence that fishing villages from the English/Scottish border all the way to the Moray Firth beyond Buckie shared items not found in their own hinterlands. From a landward point of view Buckie may appear remote or "isolated" to twentieth-century eyes, but maritime history indicates that fishing villages like it have been locales par excellence of cultural contact in times past, however endogamous their own populations. That the speech of seemingly peripheral communities has not necessarily been the most conservative is illustrated by research on the Outer Banks of North Carolina and the Chesapeake Bay Islands of Virginia and Maryland, where on islands three hundred miles apart *was* has been regularized to affirmative contexts and *were* to negative ones, regardless of the number of their subject (thus, *he was*, but *he weren't*; Wolfram and Schilling-Estes 2004).[17]

Tagliamonte and Smith (2000) and Tagliamonte (2002) also investigate variation between *was* and *were* in sketching the transplantation and maintenance of constraints on the form of their subject(s), processes encompassing more than two centuries and thus requiring a large, carefully researched backdrop. According to them, "in broad terms, settlement of the American colonies was actually highly circumscribed in the seventeenth and eighteenth centuries. British southerners went to the northern US and British 'northerners' went to the southern US" (2000:149). With this dichotomous scenario (misattributed to Fischer 1989[18]) and finding similarities in *was/were* variation between communities in late-twentieth-century Scotland and Nova Scotia, they argue that: (1) the language of older natives in modern-day Buckie typifies that brought to southern American colonies in the early- to mid-eighteenth century from "North Britain" (which they define, following Fischer [1989], as a culturally homogeneous territory that includes Scotland, much of Ireland, and England north of the River Humber);[19] (2) this "North British" speech served as the superstratal model for African American slaves in southern colonies, who subsequently were liberated by British forces during the American Revolution and migrated to Nova Scotia in the 1780s or went there in the 1810s; (3) the language of modern-day Afro-Nova Scotian communities descends from that earlier Nova Scotian variety and preserves the historic "North British" pattern of *was/were* variation; and thus (4) this preservation can be traced to contact between Whites and Blacks in the eighteenth-century American South.

[17] Quite likely this feature manifested in common indicates a shared earlier history but whether it resulted from eighteenth-century maritime contact or from the British Isles has not yet been explored (Montgomery 2005:349–50).

[18] Fischer sketches migratory patterns that originated in four different parts of the British Isles and settled largely in four sections of North America.

[19] Few people emigrated from northeastern Scotland to North America, but Tagliamonte and Smith do not claim that many did. The largest group of "North British" emigrants was from Ulster.

Many difficulties confront the emigration and settlement history of British North America underlying this ambitious sketch, not the least being that: (1) in the seventeenth century it was British southerners, not northerners, who were the main group of Europeans to found and populate southern American colonies (Virginia and the Carolinas; see Bridenbaugh 1963, Fischer 1989); and (2) British northerners arrived mainly at ports of the Delaware Bay and were the primary settlers of interior Pennsylvania and, starting only around 1740, spread from there into the interior or "back country" of the southern colonies of Virginia and the Carolinas. According to Tagliamonte, "the original input settlers to [the Afro-Nova Scotian communities] can be traced back to the southern states" (2002:747), but the colonial South was far from uniform, having at least three distinct cultural regions in the eighteenth century: in the Chesapeake, the Carolina/Georgia Low Country (whose rice and other plantations had the highest concentrations of Africans to Whites on the continent), and the later-settled interior, where comparatively few slaves were to be found. It was not the interior, but the coastal South (whose British founder population was mainly from southern England) from which freed African Americans derived, a point supported by Huber (2004). In examining a sample of the Afro-Nova Scotians who emigrated to Sierra Leone in the 1790s, he finds that the largest segments of freed Africans came from the narrow Gullah-speaking coast of South Carolina and Georgia or from the Chesapeake Bay area and only one or two came from the Interior South. Thus, Tagliamonte and Smith's contention that "crucially, for our purposes, the geographic regions in which the African populations were most numerous were precisely the same geographic regions in which the immigrants from the north British 'Borderlands' were most numerous" (2000:149–50) cannot be sustained. In ignoring a distinction in cultural geography crucial in the eighteenth century (as well as today), they have apparently read the present into the past, as a result underestimating the complexity of the language contact situation.[20] However conservative late-twentieth-century varieties may be, they can hardly be taken to represent earlier ones without confirmatory evidence from written records, and the latter reveal a much more complex picture of eighteenth-century *was/were* variation in both "North Britain" and South Carolina (Montgomery 2001b, in press). How far back and how well one might reasonably extrapolate from late-twentieth-century evidence alone is an important issue of continuing debate (Clarke 1997, Montgomery 1989, Tagliamonte 2002). Modern Buckie speech may in some sense be a common descendant of Afro-Nova Scotian English, but it is anachronistic to call the former a "likely Northern British source dialect" (Poplack 2000b:22)

---

[20] For a more detailed discussion of Tagliamonte and Smith (2000), see Montgomery (2001b). Using eighteenth-century documents the latter study shows that variation between *was* and *were* in "north Britain" was far from homogeneous in the eighteenth century, indicating that modern variation in Buckie is unlikely to reflect a large, earlier region in a straightforward way. *Was/were* variation among eighteenth-/early-nineteenth-century White South Carolinians was also quite diverse, with at least three distinct patterns. This means that the superstrate model of English for African Americans, and thus the linguistic ecology, was far more complex than Tagliamonte and Smith presume (Montgomery, in press).

of the latter, even if both had not experienced extensive contact over the past two hundred plus years.

Applications

Existing historical corpora remain heavily skewed to texts from more educated social strata because researchers of pre-twentieth-century non-standard varieties confront four paradoxes in locating valid written records. First, they are much more difficult to locate than spoken records collected in the twentieth century from even the oldest, most insular, most traditional speakers, yet inferences from the latter can easily produce overstated, possibly inaccurate scholarship. Second, those from lower social stations whose non-standard speech intruded more directly into their writing wrote less frequently and less likely had it preserved. Documents survive least from those whose language we most want to know about. Third, more can be discovered about authors from established classes, but they rarely if ever use non-standard language. Fourth, the sociohistorical linguist wrestles with a version of the well-known observer's paradox: "to obtain the data most important for linguistic theory, we have to observe how people speak when they are not being observed" (Labov 1972h:113).

How does one deal with these paradoxes and not be misled in analyzing the writing that has survived? Plantation overseers, Ulster emigrants, and many other semiliterate English-speaking commoners in the eighteenth and nineteenth centuries typically began letters with standard conventions like "I now seize this opportunity to take pen in hand to write a few lines hoping that you are well as I am thanks be to God." From this one might thus suspect that they are presenting an artificial variety of English from which we cannot determine speech, much less variation in speech. However, these writers are normally following not a manual of some kind, but oral formulas memorized from hearing letters read aloud, a fact often strikingly revealed by the absence of punctuation and capitalization and by phonetic or semiphonetic spellings (e.g. "i now seiz the opertunity to writ a fiew lins hopeing that you ar well thanks be to god"). Such rhetorical devices support the argument that semiliterate writers were relying on an oral rather than a written model.

How then do sociohistorical linguists locate the documents least skewed toward formality? Why did semiliterate individuals write at all? The answer to the first question is often simple: consult social historians of the period, because they work with such documents every day. To address the aforementioned paradoxes and locate appropriate documents, one must identify persons of little education having a compelling reason to write and who might have had their letters preserved, whether in a larger collection of official or estate papers or as family keepsakes. These writers were of at least three kinds: "desperadoes" (those in a situation of injustice or need), "lonelyhearts" (those separated from loved ones, such as emigrants or soldiers off at war), or "functionaries" (those required by their occupation to submit periodic reports that might, like those of overseers, provide little information about the writers themselves); see Montgomery (1997b, 2005) for further discussion of these types. Such writers usually did not anticipate a readership beyond the addressee and would have been less constrained by formality. More importantly, want, separation, and obligation prompted people to write who would never otherwise have put words to paper and to overcome inhibitions, regardless of their limited literacy or whether they were writing to one in authority. Consequently, the written version of the observer's paradox is mitigated and researchers of a later day are provided the least monitored language likely to be found from earlier periods.

After potential documents are found, the next logical step is assembling a corpus using principled criteria. Schneider (1989:53–61) based his selection of WPA ex-slave narratives on whether they had internal variation. He also diversified, stratified, and randomized his sample. For semiliterate documents considering the process of selection has only begun. Van Herk and Poplack use both external and internal criteria for their Ottawa Repository of Early African American Correspondence. They exclude correspondents who wrote more than three letters (because they were considered the most literate) and letters by "officials and friends of the [American Colonization Society]" or letters if they "showed such evidence of full literacy as punctuation, sentence-initial capitalization, and fully standard spelling" (Van Herk 2002:35, Van Herk and Poplack 2003:249). The SPOC includes letters that have at least two occasional spellings and generally lack punctuation and capitalization. Since they were business reports, there was no reason to exclude letters from overseers who wrote frequently (Alexander Carter, whose letter was reproduced earlier, had ninety-six survive), there being in any case no discernible difference in the quality of writing between those who frequently had their letters preserved and those who did not. In a study using Ulster emigrant letters, Montgomery (1995:34) chose letters that were unambiguously from Ulster and that attested at least one grammatical form that would be considered non-standard today, but the danger of circularity in analyzing documents selected on the basis of linguistic phenomena that are the subject of the investigation proper must be acknowledged.

Conclusions

A quarter century after Romaine coined the term "socio-historical linguistics," it remains the case that "there are a great many methodological and theoretical problems arising from the nexus of sociolinguistics and historical linguistics" (1982:x). This is in part due to the territory that lay ahead being so little charted, in part to the problems which could be foreseen but which arise from the challenge of developing social categories and constructs meaningful for time periods and cultures about which much had to be learned. If its goal is to understand language diachrony thoroughly through the interplay of people and their social groups and networks, sociohistorical linguistic research will always be an ongoing process, because one can never know too much about individuals and their times.

Achieving a coherent, comprehensive picture of the life of a language begins with assembling all of the relevant kinds of sources available, because "the scarcity of useful sources recommends a broad strategy of analysing and comparing as many different sources as possible, with results from different text categories supplementing each other and contributing to a mutual evaluation" (Schneider 2002:80–81). Among these are the letters of semiliterate writers from earlier periods, whose non-standard language brings us closer to the everyday life of a language and assists the study of linguistic diffusion, evolution, and general principles governing natural language change. Linguists will make limited further progress in understanding the circumstances in which non-standard varieties have evolved without fuller sociohistorical contextualizations and sociolinguistic interpretations for the sources they use, and these objectives are not possible without interdisciplinary research. Collaboration between linguists and researchers in other disciplines should be the life blood of sociohistorical linguistics.

The reconstruction of regional and social varieties of American English, especially with respect to their antecedents in the British Isles, requires a daunting amount of work, like most other sociohistorical issues. Comparing varieties across oceans and centuries is possible only after patient reconstruction of individual features, always with a careful eye for history, the use of historical data whenever possible, and appreciation of the complexities involved. Only then can researchers truly make sense of the variation and change they find and have a response that might satisfy Saussure.

7 Second language acquisition: a variationist perspective[1]

ROBERT BAYLEY

Introduction

The late 1960s and early 1970s witnessed the development of two subfields of linguistics: the quantitative study of linguistic variation pioneered by Labov (1966, 1969), Shuy (Shuy, Wolfram, and Riley 1968a), Wolfram (1969), and Fasold (1972), the focus of this volume, and the systematic investigation of second language acquisition (SLA), exemplified by studies such as Cazden, Cancino, Rosansky, and Schumann (1975) and Hakuta (1976). These two areas of research were motivated by a common concern to understand the underlying systems of language varieties, often socially stigmatized varieties in the case of quantitative sociolinguistics, and learner language in the case of SLA. Moreover, since its emergence as a distinct paradigm, variationism has been concerned with confronting the linguistic stereotypes of non-standard varieties by serious scientific study. Sankoff (1988a), for example, dates the development of variationism as a paradigm distinct from dialectology, ethnolinguistics, and traditional pidgin and creole studies from 1969, with the appearance of Labov's first major publication on the African American Vernacular English (AAVE) copula, rather than from 1963, the publication date of his study of Martha's Vineyard, or 1966, the publication date of his earlier work on New York City. The variationist paradigm was very quickly extended to speakers of other socially stigmatized language varieties, including American Sign Language (Woodward 1973), working-class British English (Trudgill 1974), Puerto Rican Spanish (Poplack 1980a), and Guyanese Creole (Rickford 1987), to name just a few.

Just as in variationist sociolinguistics, several early studies of second language acquisition focused on socially marginalized speakers, often working-class immigrants from the developing to the developed world. "Alberto," the subject of Schumann's (1978) influential study, *The pidginization process*, is a case in point, as is "Ge," a Hmong immigrant to Hawaii whose untutored acquisition of English was documented by Huebner (1983). The guest workers whose acquisition of German was studied by researchers in the Heidelberg project (Heidelberger Forschungsprojekt "Pidgin-Deutsch" 1978) and the Vietnamese refugees studied by Wolfram and Hatfield (1984, Wolfram 1985) provide additional examples.

[1] An earlier version of this chapter appeared as Bayley (2005).

And, even in cases where SLA researchers focused on relatively privileged speakers, as in Dickerson's (1975) pioneering study of the acquisition of English by Japanese university students in the United States, the concern was with discovering the underlying systematicity of variable learner production. Indeed, the concern with the systematicity that underlies variable production was a logical outgrowth of Selinker's (1972) concept of interlanguage as a learner's "approximate system," which shared features of the learner's first language and the target language but was fully explainable by neither. Somewhat later, Noyau elaborated the idea of interlanguage and described the task of the SLA researcher as being "to describe . . . learner languages, which are to be considered as unknown languages of which the learner is the unique speaker" (1990:144–5). If learner varieties are characterized as "unknown languages," it follows that, like all human languages, they must also be characterized by "orderly heterogeneity" (Weinreich, Labov, and Herzog 1968). That is, the variability that is clearly evident to even a casual observer is likely to be probabilistically constrained by features of the linguistic and social environments as well as by characteristics of the speaker.

Despite the apparent convergence of interest in understanding variability in language and in the speech of socially marginalized groups and individuals, until relatively recently research on sociolinguistic variation had little influence on SLA research. To be sure, a number of studies conducted in the 1970s and early 1980s employed established methods of variationist analysis. For example, Dickerson (1975) examined the effects of different phonological environments on the pronunciation of /l/ and /r/ by Japanese learners of English and argued that interlanguage consisted of a system of variable rules. To take another example from the same period, Adamson and Kovac (Lucas) (1981) used VARBRUL (Sankoff 1988b, Tagliamonte 2006, this volume), to reanalyze Schumann's (1978) data on the acquisition of English negation by an adult L1 Spanish speaker. In addition, Wolfram (1985) examined the effect of a range of phonetic factors on the past tense marking by Vietnamese speakers of English living in northern Virginia. However, until the late 1980s variationist studies were relatively rare in SLA. Preston (1996a) attributed the relative neglect in SLA research of the insights to be gained from variationist linguistics to three main factors: (1) the dominance of formal models in SLA, as in other areas of linguistics; (2) the reduction of the aims of sociolinguistics to what Preston has referred to as "socially sensitive pragmatics" (1996a:25); (3) misunderstandings by SLA researchers of basic concepts and methods of variationist linguistics. These issues are treated at length by Preston (1996a). However, because misunderstandings of variationist methods and aims persist, I shall briefly treat the third area.

Misunderstandings of variationist research

For some time, the misunderstanding of basic concepts in variationist linguistics, often by leading scholars in SLA, posed one of the most persistent challenges facing researchers in second language variation. For example, Ellis, in a widely used textbook on SLA, defined a variable rule as follows:

> If it is accepted that learners perform differently in different situations, but that it is possible to predict how they will behave in specific situations, then the systematicity of their behavior can be captured by means of variable rules. These are "if . . . then" rules. They state that if x conditions apply then y language forms will occur.   (1985:9)

As Preston (1996a) pointed out, Ellis's definition, which he has since revised, is simply wrong. Rather than a variable rule, Ellis defined a context-sensitive categorical rule.

According to Young and Bayley (1996), another problem affecting studies of interlanguage variation has been the tendency of many researchers to explain the variation found in learners' language by reference to a single co-occurring contextual factor. Frequently cited studies by Beebe (1977), Ellis (1987), Selinker and Douglas (1985), and Tarone (1985) provide convenient examples. Beebe attributed the variation that she observed in the spoken Thai of Chinese–Thai bilinguals to the ethnicity of their interlocutor. Ellis attributed variation in the use of the past tense by intermediate learners of English from a variety of backgrounds to the amount of time available to them for discourse planning. Selinker and Douglas found that the variation in discourse organization by a Mexican learner of English could be attributed to the discourse topic, while Tarone sought to explain variation by borrowing Labov's concept of "attention to speech." Remarkably, each of these studies found evidence from interlanguage variation in support of the researchers' theoretical positions: speech accommodation for Beebe, the distinction between planned and unplanned discourse for Ellis, discourse domain for Selinker and Douglas, and attention to speech for Tarone. When we take a step back from these studies and compare them, the question of which is the real cause of variation presents itself. Is it speech accommodation, planning time, discourse domain, attention to speech, or perhaps some other factor that has not been examined? Or do these factors affect different groups of learners differently?

Research in the variationist approach, in contrast to research that seeks a single overarching explanation, assumes that interlanguage variation, like variation in any language, is likely to be subject to the influence of not one but multiple contextual influences. That is, variationist research, whether on native or non-native languages, adopts what Young and Bayley (1996) have referred to as the principle of multiple causes. The question for the researcher is thus not which single factor is associated with variation, but what the relative strength of the different factors associated with variation is. In order to assess the effects of the multiple factors that may be reasonably hypothesized to condition second language use, SLA researchers, as Tarone (1979) pointed out, must report in detail the nature of the task, the interlocutors, the physical surroundings, and the topic of discussion. All these features of the social and physical context, as well as the features of the linguistic context of the variable form, should be reported and either controlled in a conventional manner or excluded from the model of variation. To attempt to explain interlanguage variation as a result of a single factor is to ignore the complexities of SLA as well as to ignore the benefits to be derived from using tools developed in an allied discipline. Of course, since variationist studies are normally based on production data, students of SLA who choose to work within a variationist paradigm must accept the principle that learner production (as opposed to learner performance on grammaticality judgment tasks) is a reasonable reflection of at least some of the developing interlanguage. Such acceptance is hardly universal (see e.g. Gregg 1990); however, it is becoming increasingly widespread.

Contributions of variationist linguistics to second language acquisition research

Variationist methods offer a number of advantages for SLA research. Here, I shall deal with four potential contributions:

(1) Variationist linguistics offers a clear way to study the effects of language transfer. As long as the speakers' first languages are included as a factor in the statistical model of variation, the detailed study of linguistic variation provides a way to test empirically the effect of the first language on speaker performance on a wide range of variables.

(2) The detailed analyses of variable forms produced by quantitative sociolinguists in speech communities around the world provide a much more realistic view of how target languages function than do traditional grammars. Empirical studies conducted in the target language community are important for understanding transfer as well as for understanding acquisition, particularly in communities where learners receive much of their input from speakers of non-standard varieties.

(3) Variationist analysis provides a means of testing whether SLA involves a process of repeated restructuring, as Huebner (1983) and others have suggested, or whether it proceeds gradually along a multidimensional continuum.

(4) A relatively new strand of research that examines the acquisition of target language patterns of variability offers insights into the process by which learners may move (or fail to move) beyond the formal style that characterizes most classroom instruction.

Language transfer

The potential utility of variationist methods in accounting for language transfer has been treated extensively by Preston (1996a). In conducting multivariate analysis, whether with VARBRUL (Sankoff 1988b) or commercially available software for performing logistic regression such as SPSS, it is a relatively simple matter to include a factor group for first language in the statistical model. (For details on the use of the VARBRUL programs see Paolillo [2002], Tagliamonte [2006, this volume], Young and Bayley [1996].) Provided that other potential sources of inter-learner variability are conventionally controlled or accounted for, one may then perform several analyses, with groups of learners representing different first languages combined, and with learners separated by first language to determine if indeed the same factors affect speakers of different first languages in the same way. If speakers of different languages pattern in different ways, and if the difference reflects a linguistic difference in their first languages, we might reasonably conclude that the difference is attributable to the effects of the first language.

Accurate descriptions of the target language

The potential contributions of variationist linguistics to our understanding of language transfer are not limited to such common-sense tests as those described in the previous section. Thanks to sociolinguistic studies conducted in many languages around the world, we now have a much clearer idea of the target languages that learners are seeking to acquire. Such understanding can be crucial to judging what constitutes transfer and what does not, as a study by Ghafarsamar (2000) makes clear. Previous studies of the acquisition of English by native speakers of Persian had attributed the presence of resumptive relative pronouns in Persian–English interlanguage to "transfer" from Persian, in which, according to traditional grammars of Persian, the resumptive pronoun is underlyingly present under certain circumstances. However, in an empirical variationist study of relative pronoun use by Persian L1 learners of English, Ghafarsamar showed that the influence of the speakers' L1 played only a trivial role. Rather, most of the variation could be explained by factors that had been observed in studies of relative pronoun choice by native speakers of English.

In addition to providing a basis for distinguishing interlanguage features that may be attributed to transfer from those that may not, variationist studies can also provide a basis for determining what constitutes acquisition. For example, English coronal stop deletion, or -t,d deletion, is one of the most extensively studied variables in sociolinguistics (see e.g. Bayley 1994a, Guy 1980, 1991, Labov 1989, Santa Ana 1992). Numerous studies of a wide range of native-speaker dialects have shown that final -t,d may be missing from regular verbs such as *miss/t/,* although at a lower rate than from monomorphemic words such as *mist.* Thus, if we wish to determine whether learners of English have acquired regular past-tense marking, we must examine not only the extent to which past tense *-ed* is present in their spoken production, but also the extent to which -t,d consonant clusters of all types are reduced. That is, we need to determine whether the absent past-tense endings are absent as a result of a phonological process that operates on all -t,d clusters (although at a different rate for words of different

Table 7.1 *-t,d absence in Chinese–English interlanguage: Grammatical category by social network*

Social network	Monomorpheme		Semiweak verb		Participle		Preterite	
	%	VARBRUL weight	%	VARBRUL weight	%	VARBRUL weight	%	VARBRUL weight
Mixed	41	.54	11	ns	43	.57	64	.69
Chinese	26	.53	4	ns	23	.53	60	.83

NOTES: For Mixed network, $n = 1909$; for Chinese network, $n = 1261$.
Source: Bayley 1996:113.

morphological classes) or the result of learners' failure to supply an obligatory inflectional morpheme.

Variationist methods provide one way of deciding which of the explanations is correct. In one study (Bayley 1996), for example, I reported on the intersection of variable processes in the speech of twenty Chinese adult learners of English. Results show that inflectional -t,d is more likely to be absent in the speech of more advanced speakers who participate in social networks that include native-speakers of English than in the speech of less advanced speakers whose social networks consist exclusively of other Chinese. That is, the speakers who we would expect to use more native-like inflectional morphology appear to be using less. An examination of the extent to which all clusters are reduced, however, resolves the apparent paradox of more advanced speakers using fewer native-like inflectional forms. Not only was inflectional -t,d absent more frequently in the speech of the learners who interacted frequently with native speakers of English; -t,d was also absent more frequently from monomorphemic words as well. The learners with greater native-speaker input had begun to reduce final consonant clusters in a manner similar to native speakers. However, they had not yet acquired a constraint to inhibit cluster reduction when final -t,d functioned as an inflectional morpheme. Table 7.1 shows the results from the study for morphological class and social network.

The case of third person singular -s provides another example of how a clearer understanding of variation in the target language can help us to understand second language acquisition. It is well known that third person singular -s is highly variable in African American Vernacular English (AAVE) and other non-standard varieties of English (Fasold 1972, Godfrey and Tagliamonte 1999, Poplack and Tagliamonte 1989). Moreover, research on the acquisition of English dating back to the morpheme studies of the early 1970s has shown that verbal -s tends to be acquired very late (Cazden *et al.* 1975). SLA researchers have tended to judge acquisition by the percentage of target language forms in obligatory contexts as defined according to the standard language. However, the acquisition criterion of near categorical use in obligatory contexts is inappropriate if the primary native-speaker input learners receive comes from speakers of a variety in which the form under investigation is used variably. In New York City, for example, many Spanish-speaking Puerto Ricans acquiring English receive a great deal of their native-speaker input from speakers of AAVE. Moreover, as shown by Zentella (1997), some migrants from Puerto Rico identify more closely with African Americans than with middle-class speakers of Standard English. For such speakers, we cannot assume that the absence of third person singular -*s* represents a failure to acquire an obligatory feature of the target language. Rather, it may well reflect acquisition of a feature of the dialect that the second language user has chosen as the target. That is, absence of an inflectional morpheme that is obligatory in the standard language but variable in vernacular dialects may represent a second language speaker's sociolinguistic competence rather than linguistic incompetence. To assess acquisition adequately, we must compare the pattern of variation in learner speech with the pattern of variation in the vernacular dialects with which learners are in contact and which they may select as the target.

Understanding the nature of SLA processes

The methods of quantitative sociolinguistics have the potential to provide evidence to enable us to choose between two different models of SLA. I focus on two theoretical assumptions about the relationship between variation in performance and grammatical competence and about the nature of speech communities that are especially relevant to SLA:

(1) individual speakers may differ in the basic rate of the use of a variable rule, i.e. in their "input probability";

(2) individuals [who are members of the same speech community] should be similar or identical in the factor values assigned to linguistic constraints on the rule (Guy 1991b).

Evidence that linguistic factors have different effects on speaker performance, then, indicates that speakers have different internal grammars. For example, Guy (1980) found that a following pause has a different effect on the likelihood of -t,d deletion in the speech of New Yorkers and Philadelphians. He argued that the different factor weights for the two groups represented a dialect difference between the two groups of speakers.

Guy, among many others (see Labov [1989] for a review), also showed in fine detail that linguistic constraints operated in the same way for all speakers of the same variety, regardless of the extent to which they used a particular variant. For example, regardless of their overall rate of -t,d deletion, all speakers were more likely to delete the final consonant from a monomopheme such as *past* than from a past-tense form such as *passed*. Hoffman (2004), in a study of /s/ aspiration and deletion by Salvadorean immigrants in Toronto, also found that individual patterns replicated the group pattern. Turning to adult second language learners,

Table 7.2 *Past tense marking in Chinese–English interlanguage by aspectual category and proficiency level*

	Lower proficiency			Higher proficiency			Combined		
	VARBRUL weight	%	N	VARBRUL weight	%	N	VARBRUL weight	%	N
Perfective	.67	42	856	.69	73	1,406	.68	61	2,262
Imperfective	.33	15	964	.31	38	1,691	.32	30	2,655

Source: Bayley 1994:175.

Bayley and Langman (2004) examined the acquisition of verbal morphology by Chinese learners of English and Hungarian. Again, the constraint rankings for individuals were identical or highly similar to the group pattern, although the speakers in their study varied greatly in the extent to which they used target language forms.

The principle that speakers who possess substantially identical internal grammars may vary in their frequency of use of a variant, but not in constraint ordering, provides a means to test empirically whether SLA involves repeated restructuring of the grammar or whether it proceeds gradually along a multi-dimensional continuum. If SLA is characterized by restructuring, the results of multivariate analysis of longitudinal data or of synchronic data from speakers of different levels of L2 proficiency should show that different factors constrain speakers' choices of variants or that the same factors have substantially different effects on the production of learners at different stages of acquisition. On the other hand, if acquisition proceeds gradually along a multi-dimensional continuum, with each factor group representing a single dimension, then once a rule has entered the grammar (e.g. English past-tense marking or /s/-plural marking), both factor groups and individual factors within groups should have very similar effects on the performance of speakers, regardless of their stage of acquisition.

As it turns out, the literature on interlanguage variation offers examples in support of both models. My own work on past-tense marking by adult Chinese learners of English (Bayley 1994) showed that one factor, whether a verb was perfective or imperfective, had very similar effects on learners of widely varying degrees of proficiency. Table 7.2 shows the results of VARBRUL analysis for this factor. Proficiency levels are based on scores in the Test of English as a Foreign Language (TOEFL).

As Table 7.2 shows, even though higher proficiency learners marked many more past reference verbs for tense than did lower proficiency learners, the factor values remained unchanged. That is, Chinese learners of English, regardless of their level of proficiency, are far more likely to mark perfective than imperfective past reference verbs. Moreover, as shown in detail in Bayley and Langman

Table 7.3 */s/-plural marking in Chinese–English interlanguage by animacy and proficiency level*

	Low proficiency			High proficiency			Combined		
	VARBRUL weight	%	N	VARBRUL weight	%	N	VARBRUL weight	%	N
Animate	.36	34	105	.61	75	243	ns	63	348
Inanimate	.53	59	442	.47	70	772	ns	68	1,174

Source: Young 1991:140, 142.

(2004), the results for individual learners conform to the group patterns shown in table 7.2. The strong effect of perfectivity may be explained by the fact that perfectives are prototypically past (Dahl 1985), as well as by the fact that in Chinese, the perfective is the marked member of the perfective–imperfective opposition (Ramsey 1987).

The preceding example shows that some factors are common to learners at different stages of acquisition. With respect to the effect of perfectivity on past-tense marking, learners do not restructure their grammars as acquisition proceeds, at least not until they have fully acquired the system under investigation. At that point, in the case of obligatory target language forms, we should expect to see a gradual end to variation. Other studies, however, do provide evidence that some factors have different effects on learners at different stages of acquisition and thus provide support for a model that views SLA as involving a series of restructurings. Young's (1991) study of /s/-plural marking by Chinese learners of English provides a convenient example of how the same factors may have different effects on low- and high-proficiency learners. Along with many other factors, including the preceding and following phonological environment and the ethnicity of the interlocutor, Young tested the effect of animacy on adult Chinese learners' use of /s/-plural marking in obligatory contexts. As in the previous example, the division into proficiency levels was based on participants' TOEFL scores. The results by proficiency level are shown in Table 7.3.

Young's results show that for low-proficiency learners, animate NPs disfavored /s/-plural marking. For high-proficiency learners, they had the opposite effect. When data from the two groups were combined, the results of the low- and high-proficiency learners neutralized one another and animacy failed to reach statistical significance.

Although studies such as Bayley (1994) and Young (1991) are limited to the acquisition of English by speakers of a single language, the results can provide some guidance as to what types of factors are likely to influence all language learners in the same way, and thus be candidates for universals, and what types are likely to be confined to speakers of a particular language at specific stages of acquisition. Moreover, the differences shown in the effect on learners of different proficiency levels of perfectivity on English past-tense marking and animacy on /s/-plural marking suggest that the acquisition of different types of interlanguage features proceeds in different ways. The results for the effect of perfectivity suggest that learner performance at all levels of proficiency is strongly constrained by prototypical aspectual categories such as perfectivity. Young's results for animacy of the NP, on the other hand, indicate that with respect to some factors learners appear to restructure their grammars as they progress from invariant non-usage of the target language form to variable usage and finally to categorical usage in obligatory contexts.

Acquiring sociolinguistic competence

The work discussed thus far has dealt with the acquisition of features that are usually considered categorical in the target language, e.g. past-tense and plural marking in English. However, another strand of research has emerged in recent years, one that is perhaps more relevant to the interests of those who work in quantitative sociolinguistics: the acquisition of target language patterns of variability.

Successful communication, whether within a culture or between persons of different cultures, requires an understanding of the meaning of speech acts within a community as well as the ability to interpret the meaning of speakers' uses of different linguistic forms, many of which are variable. Within sociolinguistics generally, a substantial amount of recent work has focused on the ways that speakers use variation to perform specific identities and to index certain stances. Kiesling (1998), for example, studied interactions among US college fraternity men and showed in fine detail how the alveolarization of /ŋ/ was related to the type of speech event that the participants were engaged in as well as to the image of themselves that speakers wished to present. In another recent study, Benor (2004) showed how newly orthodox Jews made use of a variety of linguistic features to index their orthodox identity.

Second language studies that focus on the acquisition of target language patterns of variation, or what Mougeon and others refer to as Type II variation (Mougeon, Rehner, and Nadasdi 2004), have begun to examine how learners use variable features to mark aspects of their identities or to create a new L2 identity. In an early study, Adamson and Regan (1991), for example, examined the use of the (ING) variable in words like *workin'/working* by Southeast Asian immigrants to the United States. They found that in contrast to native speakers of English, men increased their use of the informal variant, which is associated with masculinity, in more formal styles that required increased attention to speech. In a study of university L2 learners of English, Major (2004) recently reported similar findings. For the English L2 speakers studied by Adamson and Regan and by Major, the effect of gender appeared to be more important than the effect of style.

The relationship between individual style and use of variable forms is highlighted in a recent study of Hispanic English in North Carolina, the state with the most rapid percentage increase in the Hispanic population during the 1990s (Wolfram, Moriello, and Carter 2004). Wolfram *et al.* discuss the different patterns of language use of an 11-year-old girl and her 13-year-old brother whose parents are immigrants from Mexico. The boy identifies strongly with the local athletic culture. Unlike the majority of speakers discussed by Wolfram *et al.*, he has adopted monopthongal /ai/ and other salient features of Southern US English. His sister, on the other hand, is strongly oriented to mainstream institutional values and shows little evidence of accommodating to the Southern vowel system.

Much of the most interesting work on the acquisition of the variable target language features that speakers use to construct their identities has focused on French as a target language, both in Europe and in Canada. Overall, this work has emphasized the crucial role of contact with native speakers in a variety of situations. Regan (1996), for example, studied the acquisition of the deletion of *ne*, the first particle of negation, by Irish learners before and after a year's study in France. Learners approached native speaker colloquial usage after their time abroad. Howard, Lemeé, and Regan (2006) reported similar gains in the acquisition of a phonological variable, /l/ deletion, by Irish learners of French after study in France. Recently, Nagy, Blondeau, and Auger (2003) examined subject-doubling in the French of young Anglophone Montrealers. They found that young people who interacted regularly with their francophone counterparts were far more native-like in their use of this variable than those who had few such contacts. In an extensive series of studies, Raymond Mougeon and his colleagues have studied the (non)-acquisition of native-like patterns of variation by students in French immersion classes in Toronto (Mougeon and Rehner 2001, Mougeon, Rehner, and Nadasdi 2004, Rehner, Mougeon, and Nadasdi 2003, Uritescu, Mougeon, Rehner, and Nadasdi 2004). On the basis of an analysis of thirteen variables, Mougeon and his colleagues found that, unlike native speakers of Ontario French, the immersion students rarely or never used most marked vernacular variants. The students did, however, make some use of mildly marked variants. Such use was more common among students who had spent time in Quebec. Finally, as might be expected from language learners who have little exposure to the target language outside of the classroom, the immersion students over-used formal variants.

Mougeon and Dewaele (2004) note that studies of the acquisition of target language patterns of variation have practical as well as theoretical interest because even after years of study, instructed learners often have great difficulty in developing a range of styles and alternating appropriately between them. As Tarone and Swain (1995) observe of Canadian students in French immersion classes, in the typical language classroom students learn a superordinate style that is "fundamentally institutional discourse. The student is not just talking to the teacher; the student is talking to the teacher about institutional and academic business" (1995: 168). To acquire full sociolinguistic competence, however, speakers need more than "institutional discourse." Sometimes, as mentioned by one of the students discussed in Tarone and Swain (1995), they need to be able to say "'Well, come on guys, let's go get some burgers' and stuff like that" (1995:172). To interpret this utterance, at the very least learners need to understand that the invitation is casual and, in vernacular US and Canadian English, "guys" may include both males and females.

Conclusion

The examples discussed above illustrate only some of the ways that SLA and sociolinguistics may contribute to one another. As Bayley and Regan (2004) suggest, several other areas of investigation are particularly promising. Within mainstream sociolinguistics, scholars such as Eckert (2000) and Zhang (2001) have combined ethnographic and variationist methods to examine the relationships among language change and the ways that speakers construct multifaceted identities. Second language studies that combine variationist and ethnographic methods have the potential to provide a better understanding of the development of learner competence over time. Moreover, to the extent that such studies focus on different contexts of use, they have the potential to document how L2 speakers come to acquire the stylistic resources necessary to function effectively in a variety of social situations with both native and non-native speakers of the second language. Another promising strand of inquiry concerns the role of gender in SLA. Do L2 learners replicate native-speaker patterns of gendered target language use as Adamson and Regan (1991) and Major (2004) suggest? How do L2 speakers deploy the sometimes limited target language resources at their command to enact gendered identities and how does this affect learning? How do the gendered identities that target language societies present to L2 learners, and L2 learners' acceptance or rejection of those identities, impact on acquisition? Sociolinguistic research on the acquisition of languages other than English, French, and German also has the potential to broaden our understanding of SLA generally and to inform us about what processes are common to all learners, regardless of the target language or the learner's L1, and which are specific to learners of particular languages or L1s. Finally, research that examines how speakers acquire and learn to deploy their linguistic resources, including the use of variable linguistic forms, across a range of social situations, will expand our understanding of both second language acquisition and sociolinguistics.

8 Variation and modality[1]

CEIL LUCAS

Introduction

As can be seen from the other chapters in this volume, spoken languages have been the focus of most studies of sociolinguistic variation, but work has also been done on sociolinguistic variation in sign languages and a basic theoretical question arises: "In what way, if any, is modality reflected in variation?" That is, does sociolinguistic variation in sign languages exactly parallel what has been described for spoken languages or is the fact that sign languages are produced with the hands, face, and body as opposed to with the vocal apparatus borne out in the sociolinguistic variation that sign languages exhibit? Do visual sign languages and oral–aural spoken languages differ in fundamental ways when it comes to sociolinguistic variation? And what of the constraints, both linguistic and social, on this variation? This chapter will review the history of the study of sociolinguistic variation in sign languages, with a focus on American Sign Language (ASL), describe the ways in which sign language variation parallels spoken language variation, and discuss some ways in which modality differences may show up in variation.

Signs have parts

The title heading for this section is also the title of a 1980 chapter by Robbin Battison in which he reviews William C. Stokoe's ideas about the structure of sign languages. For the purposes of the present chapter, it is important for the reader to grasp a basic concept about the structure of the signs in any sign language, namely that signs are not at all indivisible wholes; rather, they have parts analogous to the parts of spoken words. Signs are composed of one or more handshapes, the palm orientation of which may also be contrastive, one or more locations either on the other hand or on the body or in the space around the signer, movement of various kinds, and facial expressions. As will be discussed in more detail below, each of these parts is subject to variation.

---

[1] Portions of this chapter are adapted from Lucas, Bayley, and Valli (2001), Lucas, Bayley, Rose, and Wulf (2002), and Lucas and Bayley (2005).

Perspectives on variation in sign languages

Early perspectives on sign language variation

The formal education of the deaf in the United States began in 1817 with the establishment of the American School for the Deaf (ASD; originally called the American Asylum for the Deaf and Dumb) in Hartford, Connecticut. Classes were taught through signing. The first teacher at the school was a young deaf Frenchman by the name of Laurent Clerc who had been recruited by Thomas Hopkins Gallaudet. Clerc used "manual French adapted to English" (Lane, Hoffmeister, and Bahan 1996:56) along with the so-called "methodical signs," signs invented to represent the morphemes of spoken French or English that did not have counterparts in signing. (The use of these methodical signs was abandoned fairly early on.) Lane *et al.* state that Clerc instructed the school's hearing teachers in the use of this manual French adapted to English and also gave private lessons "to nearly a dozen hearing teachers from as many eastern cities" (1996:56). In addition, some of the students brought their own sign systems to the school, such as the one used by both hearing and deaf people on Martha's Vineyard. The signing used at the school was not yet referred to as ASL, rather as "the language of signs" (ASD 1818).

Central to a discussion of sociolinguistic variation is that the establishment of ASD was followed very quickly by the establishment of residential schools for deaf children in a number of states and that most of these schools were established by teachers and graduates of ASD. Lane *et al.* state:

> In America, as in France, the mother school sent its teachers and Deaf graduates throughout the country to teach in various Deaf[2] schools and to found new ones. *As early as 1834, a single signed dialect was recognized in the schools for Deaf students in the U.S.* [emphasis added]. By the time of Clerc's death in 1869, over fifteen hundred pupils had graduated from the Hartford school, and there were some thirty residential schools in the United States with 3,246 pupils and 187 teachers, 42 percent of them Deaf. Most such pupils and teachers married other Deaf persons and had children. This, too, helped to disseminate ASL.   (1996:58)

So the establishment of the residential schools – which, it should be noted, have been until fairly recently the powerful crucibles of Deaf culture and language use in the United States – led to a de facto standardization in ASL. But the establishment of these schools in the vast geography of nineteenth-century America also led fairly quickly to regional variation that was noticed by educators of the deaf. For example, in the proceedings of the fourth Convention of American Instructors

---

[2] Upper-case *D* is used to denote communities and language users who are culturally deaf, that is, who share values, beliefs, and behaviors about deafness. Lower-case *d* is used to denote audiological deafness, that is, the physiological condition of not being able to hear. Individuals who are deaf may not necessarily be Deaf.

of the Deaf held at the Staunton, Virginia, school in 1856, J. R. Keep describes how "teachers of the Deaf and Dumb" should acquire knowledge of signing:

> It is answered in this inquiry that there is a language of signs; a language having its own peculiar laws, and like other languages, natural and native to those who know no other . . . *There may be different signs or motions for the same objects* [emphasis added], yet all are intelligible and legitimate, provided they serve to recall those objects to the mind of the person with whom we are communicating. As a matter of fact, however, although the Deaf and Dumb, when they come to our public Institutions, use signs differing in many respects from those in use in the Institutions, yet they soon drop their peculiarities, and we have the spectacle of an entire community recalling objects by the same motions.   (1857:133)

In response to Keep's remarks, Dunlap (in Keep) compares the signs used at the Indiana School for the Deaf with those used at the Ohio and Virginia schools and states that there is a need for uniformity "not only in Institutions widely separated but among teachers in the same Institution" (1857:138). In another response to Keep's remarks, Peet (in Keep) refers to Deaf signers as "those to whom the language is *vernacular*" [emphasis added] and in a discussion of a class of signs described in current theory as classifier predicates or depicting verbs, states "Here is room for difference of dialects. One Deaf Mute may fall upon one sign and another upon another sign, for the same object, both natural" (1857:144–6).

These writings provide a clear indication of early awareness of sign structure and variation, even though formal research in these areas did not begin until the 1960s.

Variation in the *DASL*

A dictionary of American Sign Language on linguistic principles (known as the *DASL*), written in 1965 by William Stokoe, Dorothy Casterline, and Carl Croneberg, was the first comprehensive attempt (after Stokoe's [1960] paper on the structure of sign languages) to describe ASL signs from the standpoint of sign language structure. The signs appear in the dictionary not in the alphabetical order of the English words to which they correspond, but in order of the handshapes, locations, and movements from which the signs are constructed. A comprehensive list of possible handshapes, locations, and movements is provided along with a notation system for transcribing signs. The notion that the language used by Deaf people was a "real language," analyzable in the same way that spoken languages are analyzed, was of course groundbreaking and even controversial for both hearing and deaf people. The notion was controversial because, after the 1817–1880 period that some have referred to as the "Golden Age of ASL" (www.asd-1817.org/history/history-deafed.html), over eighty years of severe and harsh oralism followed during which the use of sign language as the medium of instruction for deaf education was forbidden (Baynton 1996). ASL and other sign languages had of course endured in Deaf communities around the world but their status as real languages on the par with spoken languages was seriously damaged, in the case of ones that had been allowed to emerge, such as ASL, and totally unrecognized in the case of tens of others.

And not only did the *DASL* claim that ASL was a real language. It also included two appendices written by Carl Croneberg entitled "The Linguistic Community" (Appendix C) and "Sign Language Dialects" (Appendix D) that provide an introduction to the use of ASL. Appendix C describes the cultural and social aspects of the Deaf community and discusses the issues of economic status, patterns of social contact, and the factors that contribute to group cohesion. These factors include the extensive networks of both a personal and organizational nature that ensure frequent contact even among people who live on opposite sides of the country. Croneberg stated in 1965 that "there are close ties also between deaf individuals or groups of individuals as far apart as California and New York. Deaf people from New York on vacation in California stop and visit deaf friends there or at least make it a practice to visit the club for the deaf in San Francisco or Los Angeles . . . The deaf as a group have social ties with each other that extend farther across the nation than similar ties of perhaps any other American minority group" (1965:310). And these ties of a personal nature are reinforced by membership in national organizations such as the National Association of the Deaf (NAD), the National Fraternal Society of the Deaf (NFSD), and the National Congress of Jewish Deaf (NCJD).

In Appendix D, Croneberg deals with the issue of sociolinguistic variation as it pertains to the preparation of a dictionary. While the terms he chooses are not precisely the ones that linguists working on spoken languages were choosing at that time, the constructs he refers to are analogous. He states that, "One of the problems that early confronts the lexicographers is dialect, and this problem is particularly acute when the language has never before been written. They must try to determine whether an item in the language is *standard* [italics in the original], that is, used by the majority of a given population, or *dialect,* that is, used by a particular section of the population" (1965:313). He outlines the difference between what he terms *horizontal* variation (regional variation) and *vertical* variation (variation that occurs as a result of social stratification) and states that ASL exhibits both. He then describes the results of a study of lexical variation based on a 134-item sign vocabulary list that he undertook in North Carolina, Virginia, Maine, New Hampshire, and Vermont. He finds that for ASL, the state boundaries between North Carolina and Virginia also constitute dialect boundaries, in that North Carolina signs are not found in Virginia and vice versa. He finds the three New England states to be less internally standardized (that is, people within each of the three states exhibit a wide range of variants for each item) and the state boundaries in New England to be much less important, with a lot of overlap in lexical choice observed between the three states. He points out the key role of the residential schools in the dissemination of dialects, stating, "At such a school, the young deaf learn ASL in the particular variety characteristic of each local region. The school is also a source of local innovations, for each school generation comes up with some new signs or modifications of old ones" (1965:314). Finally, in the discussion of vertical variation but without much detail, he mentions age, ethnicity, gender, religion, and social status as factors in variation. The latter is related to economic level, occupation, educational background, and relative leadership within the deaf community. Croneberg's focus is on lexical variation and no explicit mention is made of the possible role of modality in the variation observed.

It is important to consider Croneberg's appendices within the context of other variation research being undertaken at the same time. The years between 1958 (the year Fischer's pioneering study of sociolinguistic variation was published) and 1977 were very busy for spoken languages and sign languages alike. Labov's study of vowel centralization on Martha's Vineyard was published in 1963 and his pivotal study of New York City speech followed in 1966. Shuy, Wolfram, and Riley completed their study of sociolinguistic variation in Detroit in 1968 and Wolfram's dissertation appeared in 1969. It was in this context that Georgetown University's doctoral program in sociolinguistics was established in 1971 and James Woodward was one of the first students in that program. Woodward had worked with Stokoe and his 1973 dissertation was the first to explore variation in a sign language. As Woodward states in the abstract, "This study attempts to utilize recent developments in variation theory in linguistics to analyze variation that occurs on the deaf diglossic continuum between American Sign Language and Signed English." His committee included Roger Shuy, Ralph Fasold, and William Stokoe and his analysis of morphosyntactic variation in ASL was done within the framework of implicational scales developed by C. J. Bailey (1970, 1971).

After the *DASL*

The years following the publication of the *DASL* witnessed a number of studies of variation in ASL. In addition to Woodward's dissertation, phonological variation in the form of thumb extension was explored by Battison, Markowicz, and Woodward (1975). Woodward, Erting, and Oliver (1976) looked at signs that are produced variably on the face or the hands, and Woodward and DeSantis (1977) examined signs that are variably one-handed or two-handed. DeSantis (1977) looked at location variation, in signs variably signed at the elbow or on the hands, and while called a historical study, Frishberg (1975) looked at processes such as centralization still seen in ASL today, i.e. signs usually produced at high locations (such as the face) or low locations (below the waist) being produced in the more central space in front of the signer. Morphological and syntactic variation have also been explored, as has lexical variation. (For a full review of variation in ASL, see Lucas, Bayley, Valli, Rose, and Wulf [2001].)

All of the early studies of phonological variation in ASL explore both linguistic (internal) and social (external) constraints on the variation. Of particular relevance to the discussion here is that all of the linguistic constraints on the phonological variables are what Wolfram (personal communication, 1993) would call *compositional*, that is, features of the signs themselves that may be playing a role in the variation. For example, Battison, Markowicz, and Woodward (1975) identified six internal constraints on thumb extension. Signs such as FUNNY or CUTE[3] are produced in citation (dictionary) form with the index and middle fingers extended and all other fingers including the thumb closed, but the thumb may be variably extended. The six constraints identified were: (1) indexicality (i.e. is the sign produced contiguous to its referent, as in a pronoun or determiner); (2) bending of fingers (i.e. do the other fingers involved in the sign bend, as in FUNNY); (3) middle finger extension (i.e is the middle finger extended as part of the sign); (4) twisting movement (i.e. does the hand twist during the production of the sign, as in BORING); (5) whether the sign is produced on the face, as in BLACK or FUNNY; and (6) whether the sign is made in the center of one of the four major areas of the body. These studies had studies of spoken language variation as models and naturally looked for the same kinds of linguistic constraints that had been identified as operating in spoken language variation.

Variation in signed and spoken languages

In fact, as can be seen in Table 8.1, the same kinds of variation found in spoken languages can also be found in sign languages. Specifically, the features of individual segments of signs can vary, individual segments and whole syllables can be deleted or added, and parts of segments or syllables can be rearranged. There can be variation in word-sized morphemes (i.e. lexical variation) or in combinations of word-sized morphemes (i.e. syntactic variation). Finally, there can be variation in discourse units.

Two kinds of variation in sign languages, however, seem to be artifacts of a language produced with two identical articulators (i.e. two hands as opposed to one tongue). That is, sign languages allow the deletion, addition, or substitution of one of the two articulators. Two-handed signs become one-handed (CAT, COW), one-handed signs become two-handed (DIE), and a table, chair arm, or the signer's thigh may be substituted for the base hand in a two-handed sign with identical handshapes (RIGHT, SCHOOL). In addition, one-handed signs that the signer usually produces with the dominant hand (i.e the right hand, if the signer is right-handed) can be signed with the non-dominant hand. Variation is also allowed in the relationship between articulators, as in HELP, produced with an A handshape placed in the upward-turned palm of the base hand. Both hands can move forward as a unit, or the base hand can lightly tap the bottom of the A handshape hand.

---

[3] It is customary for the English glosses of ASL signs to be represented with upper-case letters.

Table 8.1 *Variability in spoken and sign languages*

Variable unit	Example	
	Spoken languages	Sign languages
Features of individual segments	Final consonant devoicing, vowel nasalization, vowel raising and lowering	Change in location, movement, orientation, handshape in one or more segments of a sign
Individual segments deleted or added	*-t,d* deletion, *-s* deletion, epenthetic vowels and consonants	Hold deletion, movement epenthesis, hold epenthesis
Syllables (i.e. groups of segments) added or deleted	Aphesis, apocope, syncope	First or second element of a compound deleted
Part of segment, segments, or syllables rearranged	Metathesis	Metathesis
Variation in word-sized morphemes or combinations of word-sized morphemes (i.e. syntactic variation)	Copula deletion, negative concord, *avoir/être* alternation, lexical variation	Null pronoun variation, lexical variation
Variation in discourse units	Text types, lists	Repetition, expectancy chains, deaf/blind discourse,turn taking, back channeling, questions

Reprinted with permission from Lucas, Bayley, and Valli (2001:25).

Probably more important to the examination of possible modality differences in sign language variation are the internal constraints that operate on variation. Table 8.2 provides a comparison of such constraints in spoken and sign variation.

As mentioned, earlier studies of variation in ASL focused on compositional constraints, that is, the variation was seen to be conditioned by some feature of the variable sign itself. Sequential constraints are those that have to do with the immediate linguistic environment surrounding the variable, such as the hand-shape, location, or palm orientation of the sign immediately preceding or following the variable sign. Functional constraints pertain to the role that the sign's grammatical category plays in the variation, while the constraint of structural incorporation has to do with the preceding or following syntactic environment surrounding the variable. Finally, pragmatic features such as emphasis may help explain the variation observed.

Analyses of variation in sign languages subsequent to those undertaken in the 1970s clearly continued to look to spoken language analyses for models of how to account for the variation. And they look to explanations in which sequential constraints are the focus of the explanations. Liddell and Johnson, for example, explain variation in two forms of the sign DEAF (ear to chin and chin to ear) as a process governed solely by phonological constraints: "A number of signs

Table 8.2 *Internal constraints on variable units*

	Example	
Constraint	Spoken	Signed
Compositional	Phonetic features in nasal absence in child language	Other parts of sign in question (e.g. handshape, location, orientation)
Sequential	Following consonant, vowel, or feature thereof	Preceding or following sign or feature thereof
Functional	Morphological status of -s in Spanish -s deletion	Function of sign as noun, predicate, or adjective
Structural incorporation	Preceding or following syntactic environment for copula deletion	Syntactic environment for pronoun variation
Pragmatic	Emphasis	Emphasis (e.g. pinky extension)

Reprinted with permission from Lucas, Bayley, and Valli (2001:29).

exchange an initial sequence of segments with a sequence of final segments in certain contexts that appear to be purely phonological. The sign DEAF is typical of such metathesizing signs" (1989:244). They also describe the central role of the location of the preceding sign, such that the first location of the sign DEAF in the phrase FATHER DEAF would be produced at the ear, close to the forehead location of the sign FATHER, while in MOTHER DEAF, the first location of DEAF would be produced at the chin, the same location as the sign MOTHER (1989:245).

Liddell and Johnson also comment on the variable lowering of signs (e.g. KNOW) that are produced at the level of the forehead in citation form: "[T]he phonological processes that originally must have moved them are still active in contemporary ASL. The rules which account for [these signs] appear to be variably selected in casual signing, and like the vowel reduction rules in spoken languages, have the effect of neutralizing contrasts of location" (1989:253). They also attribute variation in signs produced with a 1 handshape (index finger extended, all other fingers and thumb closed) to phonological processes, again with a focus on constraints of a sequential nature: "There are numerous instances of assimilation in ASL. For example, the hand configuration of the sign ME (= PRO.1) typically assimilates to that of a contiguous predicate in the same clause" (1989:250).

Variation in ASL reconsidered

In 1994, Lucas, Bayley, and Valli (2001) undertook a study of variation in ASL with large-scale spoken language studies as models. The overall goal of the study was a description of the phonological, morphosyntactic, and lexical variation in

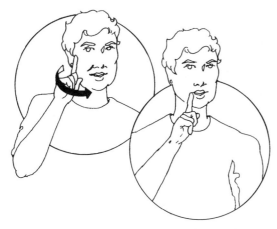

Figure 8.1a DEAF, *citation form (ear-to-chin)*

Figure 8.1b DEAF, *non-citation form (chin-to-ear)*

ASL, and the correlation of variation with external constraints such as region, age, gender, ethnicity, socioeconomic status, and also factors pertaining specifically to the Deaf community such as school language policies and language use in the home. The data collection methodology and the findings of the study have been widely reported and will not be reviewed here. The part of the study that will be focused on is the behavior of specific linguistic constraints and what their behavior might reveal about modality differences between spoken language and sign language variation.

The constraints in question are those related to the three phonological variables analyzed in the study: the sign DEAF, the location of a class of signs represented by the verb KNOW, and signs made with a 1 handshape. DEAF has three main variants, which are shown in Figures 8.1a, b, and c.[4]

[4] Thanks to Robert Walker for providing the illustrations of signs used in this chapter and to M. J. Bienvenu for serving as the sign model.

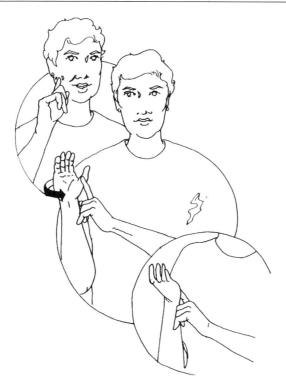

Figure 8.1c DEAF, *non-citation form (contact cheek* + CULTURE*)*

In the citation form, DEAF is signed from ear to chin. DEAF may also be signed from chin to ear or reduced to a contact of the index finger on the cheek. Signs represented by the sign KNOW are produced in citation form at the level of the forehead but can be produced at the level of the cheek, jaw, or even in the space in front of the signer. 1 handshape signs exhibit a wide range of variation, from thumb open to all fingers and thumb open and variants between these two. Lucas *et al.* examined 1,618 tokens of DEAF, 2,594 of signs in the KNOW class, and 5,195 1 handshape signs. And following both spoken language studies and earlier analyses of variation in ASL, the linguistic constraints included in the analysis pertained to the linguistic environment immediately surrounding the variable sign. For DEAF, this meant the location of the preceding and following sign, as in the example discussed earlier – FATHER produced on the forehead as opposed to MOTHER produced on the chin; for signs like KNOW, since the focus is on variability in location, this meant the location of the preceding and following signs and also whether or not the preceding or following sign had contact with the head or the body; for 1 handshape signs, this meant the handshape of the preceding and following sign. Other linguistic constraints were also concluded and the motivation for their inclusion requires some historical background.

The summer of 1993

The LSA Summer Institute in 1993 was held at the Ohio State University and included a two-week course on VARBRUL taught by Gregory Guy. Since I knew that I would want to use VARBRUL for the sociolinguistic variation in ASL project (Lucas *et al.* 2001), I signed up for the course and collected 489 tokens of DEAF to take with me to Columbus. The first surprise came during the data collection: I was expecting to only find examples of two variants, the citation ear to chin form and the chin to ear variant, a variant which results from location metathesis, i.e. the sign starts at the chin location as opposed to the ear location. In the course of watching videotapes, I began to notice and could not ignore the numerous instances of DEAF produced as a simple contact of the tip of the index finger on the cheek. I included them in the pool of tokens. I then coded my tokens in anticipation of using the VARBRUL program and in addition to coding for the location of the preceding and following sign, I also (and somewhat serendipitously) coded for the grammatical category of the sign DEAF itself. The sign DEAF of course functions as a "regular" adjective, as in the phrases DEAF CAT or DEAF MAN. However, it can also function as a noun, as in the sentence DEAF UNDERSTAND ("The deaf understand") and as a predicate adjective, as in the sentence PRO.1 DEAF ("I am deaf"). In addition, it occurs in a number of compound forms such as DEAF^PEOPLE, DEAF^WORLD, DEAF^WAY, and DEAF^INSTITUTION (meaning residential school for the deaf). I also coded for the relative informality or formality of the context. And even though I coded for the grammatical category of the sign DEAF, I fully expected the VARBRUL results to fully confirm earlier claims that the metathesis was due to the location of the preceding or following sign. So the results of the VARBRUL analysis (reported in Lucas 1995) were quite surprising: the phonological factors – location of the preceding and following signs – were thrown out as not significant, as was formality or lack thereof. What was significant was grammatical category, whether the sign was an adjective, a noun or predicate adjective, or part of a compound (what I referred to at that time as a "fixed phrase"). Thinking that this might be the result of a small number of tokens, I planned to redo the analysis with data from the larger study. But the statistically significant finding that the key factor in explaining the variation was grammatical category and the fact that the phonological factors had simply been thrown out was intriguing, to say the least.

The reconsideration continues

Based on the 1993 results, all three phonological variables examined in the large-scale study – DEAF, signs like KNOW, and 1 handshape signs – were coded for grammatical category and once again, grammatical category emerged as the most significant factor, confirming the 1993 results. Table 8.3 shows that compound forms with the sign DEAF favor a non-citation form, predicate adjectives disfavor

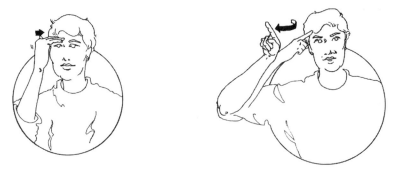

Figure 8.2 *Citation forms of* KNOW *and* FOR

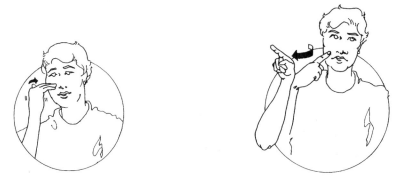

Figure 8.3 *Non-citation forms of* KNOW *and* FOR

non-citation forms, and nouns and adjectives constitute a nearly neutral reference point. The other significant factor, discourse genre, shows that non-citation forms tend to occur more in narratives than in conversation. (It should be noted that when the two non-citation forms of DEAF – chin to ear and contact cheek – are compared, the location of the following sign – i.e. a phonological factor – is significant.)

The VARBRUL results for location variation in signs like KNOW, illustrated in Figures 8.2 and 8.3, are seen in Table 8.4.

Once again, while the phonological factors preceding location and following contact are significant, grammatical category emerges as the most significant factor, with preposition and interrogative signs favoring lowered forms, and nouns, verbs, and adjectives disfavoring them. Table 8.5 summarizes the rankings of the linguistic constraints for all three variables and shows that grammatical category is the most powerful factor for all three.

The influence on variation of factors other than features of the preceding and following signs discussed here has also been found in other studies of ASL. In a small-scale study, Hoopes (1998), for example, looked at signs such as THINK, WONDER, and TOLERATE, all signed in citation form with the pinky closed but variably produced with the pinky extended. While we might expect pinky

Table 8.3 *Variation in the form of* DEAF: *+cf vs. −cf (application value: −cf)*

Factor group	Factor	Weight	Percentage	n
Grammatical category	Noun, adjective	.515	71	1063
	Predicate	.370	58	361
	Compound	.660	81	194
Discourse genre	Conversation	.489	69	1489
	Narrative	.628	74	129
Total	Input p_0	.743	69	1618

Notes: χ^2/cell = 1.2952; all factor groups significant at $p < .05$. Reprinted with permission from Lucas and Bayley (2005:56).

Table 8.4 *Variation in the location of signs represented by* KNOW: *Linguistic factors (application value: −cf)*

Factor group	Factor	Weight	Percentage	n
Grammatical category	Preposition, interrogative	.581	59	485
	Noun, verb	.486	52	2052
	Adjective	.316	35	57
Preceding location	Body	.503	53	1648
	Head	.452	48	614
Following contact	No contact	.525	55	1323
	Contact	.466	48	991
Input (*p sub 0*)	Total	.518	53	259

Notes: χ^2/cell = 1.1702; all factor groups are significant at $p < .05$; results for preceding location and following contact do not include pauses, which were tested in separate factor groups that proved not to be significant.
Reprinted with permission from Lucas and Bayley (2005:56).

extension to be governed by the handshape of the preceding or following sign, based on earlier claims, pinky extension appears to be a prosodic feature of ASL that adds emphasis or focus to the sign with which it co-occurs. In another study, Mulrooney (2002) investigated variation in fingerspelling with the goal of determining what governs the production of non-citation forms of the individual signs that make up a fingerspelled word. Again, one might expect the immediate phonological environment to play some role, specifically the handshape of the immediately preceding or immediately following sign. However, neither of these turned out to have a significant effect. The immediately preceding and following locations had modest influence, but once again the strongest role was played by the category of the fingerspelled word in which the target form occurred,

Table 8.5 *Summary of linguistic constraints on phonological variation in ASL*

Variable	Analysis	Constraint Ranking
DEAF	+cf vs. −cf	Grammatical category > discourse genre
	Chin-to-ear vs. contact-cheek	Grammatical category > location of following segment (assimilation)
Location of KNOW, etc.	+cf vs. −cf	Grammatical category > contact with body of following sign > location of preceding sign
1 handshape	+cf vs. −cf	Grammatical category > features of preceding and following handshapes (assimilation)
	L handshape vs. all others	Features of preceding and following handshapes (assimilation) > grammatical category
	Open hand vs. all others	Grammatical category > features of preceding and following handshapes (assimilation)</>

Reprinted with permission from Lucas and Bayley (2005:61).

with proper nouns favoring citation forms, common nouns being neutral, and verbs favoring non-citation forms. Finally, the influence of grammatical category on phonological variation has also been observed in Australian Sign Language (Auslan) (Schembri, Johnshon, and Goswell 2006), so this is a phenomenon evidently not limited to ASL.

Is modality a factor?

So the main question is why grammatical and prosodic constraints have a more important role than the features of the preceding and following signs in conditioning phonological variation in ASL. The first answer is simply that, as in spoken languages, phonological variation in ASL is not constrained only by phonological factors, at least if these are restricted to the features of the preceding and following signs. The focus heretofore may have been on features of the preceding and following signs, but large data-based quantitative studies such as the one undertaken by Lucas *et al.* show that grammatical factors must also be considered.

A second answer concerns differences between spoken and sign languages. Having established that sign languages are indeed "real" languages, research on all aspects of sign language structure has begun to show some fundamental and most likely modality-related differences between spoken and sign languages. Of most relevance to the present discussion are the basic differences in how morphology functions and how the differences manifest themselves in variation. In many of the spoken languages in which phonological variation has been extensively explored, morphology is a "boundary phenomenon." That is, meaningful segments are added to the beginning or end of other units in the language in the form of plural markers, person and tense markers, derivational affixes, and so forth. These units are essentially added to an existing phonological environment. It stands to reason that when variation occurs, a good place to look for the cause of this variation is the immediate environment to which units have been added (i.e. the preceding and following segments). In fact, many studies of spoken language variation have demonstrated the key role of the immediate phonological environment in governing variation.

However, morphology in sign languages is by and large not a boundary phenomenon, at least not to a great extent. There exist very few affixes. Morphological distinctions are accomplished by altering one or more features in the articulatory bundle that makes up a segment or by altering the movement path of the sign. For example, segments are not usually added to other segments to provide information about person or aspect. Rather, the location feature of a segment (e.g. near or away from the signer) indicates person, and movement between locations indicates the subject and object of the verb in question. Similarly, a particular movement path indicates continuative or inceptive aspect. As Emmorey states with specific regard to aspect marking in ASL:

> In many spoken languages, morphologically complex words are formed by adding prefixes or suffixes to a word stem. In ASL and other signed languages, complex forms are most often created by nesting a sign stem within dynamic movement contours and planes in space . . . ASL has many verbal inflections that convey temporal information about the action denoted by the verb, for example, whether the action was habitual, iterative, continual. Generally, these distinctions are marked by different movement patterns over-laid onto a sign stem. This type of morphological encoding contrasts with the primarily linear affixation found in spoken languages. For spoken languages, simultaneous affixation processes such as template morphology (e.g in Semitic languages), infixation, or reduplication are relatively rare. Signed languages, by contrast, prefer nonconcatenative processes such as reduplication; and prefixation and suffixation are rare. Sign languages' preference for simultaneously producing affixes and stems may have its origins in the visual-manual modality.   (1999:173)

The results of the Lucas *et al.* analyses indicate that these fundamental differences manifest themselves in the variable components of the language. That is, the immediate phonological environment turns out not to play the major role in governing phonological variables, in part because the variables themselves are not affixes. The grammatical category to which the variable in question belongs is consistently the first-order linguistic constraint.

This finding has important implications for our understanding of variation between spoken and signed languages. As the modality differences between spoken and signed languages manifest themselves in the basic phonological, morphological, and syntactic components of the language, so they also seem to appear in the patterns of linguistic variation. As the phonological and morphological processes go, so apparently goes variation.

The question arises as to the parallels between ASL and spoken languages (e.g. Chinese) that, like ASL, do not use affixes to any great extent. The gist of the question is whether the variation in these spoken languages resembles that in ASL, specifically with respect to the prominent role of grammatical factors in governing the variation. In the absence of a substantial number of studies of sociolinguistic variation in Chinese and other languages that have no or only minimal inflectional morphology (see, for example, Bourgerie 1990), we cannot rule out modality differences as a contributing factor to the patterns reported here. At this point, the role of grammatical factors in conditioning phonological variation in ASL seems to be best described as a *matter of degree*. There clearly are grammatical constraints on spoken language phonological variation, and features of the preceding and following signs obviously influence variation in sign languages.

What the analyses of Lucas *et al.* suggest is that modality differences may account for a difference in the relative importance of the constraints. In the phonological variation observed thus far in sign languages, grammatical constraints are consistently more important than phonological ones. Ironically, it may be the visual nature of sign languages that reinforces the impressions and hypotheses that phonological variation in sign languages is governed by constraints having to do with the features of the preceding and/or following segments. That is, we can actually *see* the lower and higher locations that precede and follow DEAF and signs such as KNOW; we can *see* the handshapes that precede and follow 1 handshape signs. Being able to see the phonological environment surrounding the variation easily leads to hypotheses about this environment accounting fully for the variation, but these hypotheses are simply not supported by the data. However, as stated earlier, it may be a *matter of degree*. In a project completed in a course on variation analysis, Goeke (2006) examined two-handed signs which can become one-handed, such as DEER, WANT, and SURPRISE. She coded 611 tokens for presence of internal movement in the target sign, contact of the target sign with the body (or not), grammatical category of the target sign, handshape of the target sign (unmarked or marked), and handedness of the preceding and following sign (two-handed or one-handed). Only contact and handedness of the preceding and following sign were found to be significant. To wit, two-handed signs were favored by a lack of contact with the body and by two-handed signs preceding and following the target. The relevant factors were purely phonological, as grammatical category of the target sign was not found to be significant. Even though this study looked only at female signers and needs to be expanded, the results are important. More investigation is warranted into why grammatical category was not at all a factor in explaining this variation as well as research on variation and the constraints upon it in a wide range of sign languages.

What remains, of course, is research on variation and the constraints upon it in a wide range of sign languages, research that we can look forward to. Should such research consistently reveal the prominent role of grammatical category as a constraint on phonological variation, this will allow us to build an ever-clearer picture of how variation works in sign languages and what role modality plays in that variation.

PART 2

Methods

9   Sociolinguistic fieldwork

NATALIE SCHILLING-ESTES

Introduction

Conducting fieldwork to obtain data for sociolinguistic study is at the same time one of the most challenging and most rewarding aspects of sociolinguistic investigation. Among the challenges that immediately come to mind are: (1) How do I decide who to get data from? (2) How do I get people to talk to me and let me record them, and can I get them to talk in a fairly relaxed way? (3) How do I explain to people why I'm recording them, and how much detail should I go into? (4) How do I make good-quality recordings, especially out in the "field" vs. in a quiet laboratory? and (5) How involved should I get with my research participants and in what ways? This last question connects directly to what is perhaps the biggest reward associated with gathering linguistic data from "real" people out in the "real" world – getting the chance to meet, talk with, befriend, and perhaps help all sorts of interesting people who may have just as much to teach the researcher about different ways of looking at life as about different ways of speaking.

In the sections that follow, the above questions are addressed, along with others that arise in the course of designing and conducting field research for sociolinguistics. Though researchers may have initially believed (or hoped) that it was possible to develop a set of universal guidelines for conducting sociolinguistic fieldwork, experience has demonstrated that there is no one "right" answer to any of the questions above. Rather, each community and each interaction is unique, and sometimes researchers must adapt tried-and-true techniques to suit the specifics of their situations, devise innovations of their own, or improvise on the spot. Nonetheless, experience has led sociolinguists to develop guiding principles and a large body of advice that can help the beginning researcher through any fieldwork experience. Some of these basic guidelines are presented below, though necessarily with caveats, disclaimers, and "blanks" where each individual researcher must make their own research-related decision.

Designing the field study

The first step in conducting sociolinguistic fieldwork is of course designing the study. In large part, the study design will be based on the researcher's interests and goals. For example, one sociolinguist may be interested in how language change diffuses across large geographic areas and through large social groups such as socioeconomic class groups. Another may be more interested in how social meanings, groups, and relationships are manifested, negotiated, and altered through the creative use of linguistic variation. No matter what the main research questions, research begins with selecting a population for study and determining an appropriate subset of the population from which to obtain data. As part of this latter step, the researcher may need to divide the sample population according to particular social categories. Finally, research planning ends with the submission of an application for approval of the study to the appropriate Institutional Review Board (IRB) at the researcher's university or other institution. Such Boards exist to ensure that the research conducted will not adversely affect human subjects. Researchers who fail to apply for and receive IRB approval prior to data collection will probably not be allowed to use their data in any academic venue, with the possible exception of practice research in the classroom setting. Because IRB requirements vary from university to university, they will not be discussed here; however, the topic of fieldwork ethics is recurrent throughout the chapter.

Selecting the population for study

Again, the type of community chosen for study will depend on the researcher's particular interests; however, there are some general questions that can help guide one's choice of population. First, and not necessarily very obviously, is the question of what actually "counts" as a community in the first place. Because sociolinguistics is situated at the intersection of language and society, it has long been an issue whether sociolinguists should define the community of study primarily on the basis of language, including not only how people speak but their evaluations of different types of speech,[1] or on the basis of social matters, including frequency and types of social interaction and shared values. For example, as a new student of sociolinguistics under the mentorship of Walt Wolfram, I became involved in a series of studies of Outer Banks English, the distinctive variety spoken in the historically isolated Outer Banks islands off the coast of North Carolina, USA (e.g. Wolfram, Hazen, and Schilling-Estes 1999, Wolfram and Schilling-Estes 1996a). In this case, the community was chiefly linguistically defined, since our interest was in obtaining data on a particular language variety, not on the range of varieties (and languages) of residents of the Outer Banks. Conversely, in a study located on a rather larger "island," in Sydney, Australia, Barbara Horvath (1985) decided that she wasn't so much interested in one particular language variety (i.e. the speech of native speakers of English, of English descent, who had been born and raised in Sydney) but rather how language

---

[1] Throughout this chapter, "speech" and related terms are used to refer to both spoken and signed linguistic usage, unless referring to a specific study of one type of language or the other.

variation patterned in the Sydney community, including among non-native immigrants to the city and their descendents.

The issue of whether to base community studies on linguistic or social factors is encapsulated in different researchers' definitions of what constitutes the proper object of sociolinguistic study, or what has often been called the "speech community." For example, Peter Patrick defines the speech community as "a socially-based unit of linguistic analysis" (2002:577), taking a very language-centered approach; while on the opposite end of the spectrum, Mary Bucholtz defines the speech community as "a language-based unit of social analysis" (1999:203; quoted in Patrick 2002:577). For decades, many sociolinguists were guided by William Labov's classic definition of the speech community as a group of people with shared norms and common evaluation of linguistic variables (e.g. 1966). In this view, while members of a speech community typically do have a common core of shared linguistic features, it is *not* expected that they all talk exactly the same way, only that they orient toward the same speech norms (e.g. they all have the same understanding of what "correct speech" is like). Other researchers have questioned whether there might be a bit more room for conflict within the speech community, whether linguistic or social. For example, whereas in some populations people in different sub-groups may indeed share common norms (e.g. members of different social class groups agree that upward mobility is a good thing), in other cases there may be more internal conflict – for example, members of lower social class groups may position themselves in opposition to upper-class groups rather than aspire to reach their status (e.g. Rickford 1986a).

Further questions relate to scale: for example, can an entire country be considered a speech community? Can two people be a speech community? Others relate to geographic contiguity. In other words, is geographic area (e.g. Outer Banks Islands; Sydney, Australia; the Lower East Side of New York City [Labov 1966]) the primary defining criterion for "community," or can one also consider discontinuous communities such as an Internet group who holds regular chat sessions pertaining to a common area of interest? Researchers who are interested in smaller groups and their interactional patterns often steer clear of the term "speech community," referring instead to "social network"-based analyses. Still others prefer to work within the "community of practice" framework, in which the focus is not only on patterns of interaction but on *why* people come together in the first place – i.e. what practices they engage in and how these practices shape, and are shaped by, their linguistic usages (e.g. Eckert 2000). Finally, there is the question of whether the researcher can fully delimit a speech community before beginning the study, or whether what constitutes the community will have to emerge as one learns more about the people being studied.

Despite the complexity of the above questions, again, there is no one "best" type of community to study, and researchers have benefited greatly from studying all kinds of communities, sometimes within a single geographic area. Thus, for example, Labov's pioneering investigation of language variation in the speech community of White, native English speakers in New York City's Lower East Side has provided invaluable grounding for subsequent studies of the role of social class and speech style in patterns of language variation and change. At the same time, his up-close investigation of language use in the social networks/communities of practice of African American youth groups in inner city Harlem were crucial in demonstrating such important concepts as the effect of the strength of one's network ties on one's vernacular language usage, as well as the artistry and logical complexity of speech that has long been considered "substandard" (1970, 1972a).

Sampling

Random sampling

Unless one chooses a very small community for study (e.g. a teenage friendship group with twenty or so members), the next step in designing the field research project is selecting a subset or "sample" of community members for recording and analysis. There are several different ways of sampling a community. In many social sciences, researchers employ random sampling, in which, as the name suggests, study participants are chosen randomly (usually by computer) from a comprehensive list of community members, for example a telephone directory or electoral register. Genuinely random sampling of a large enough subset of the population ensures that the sample will be statistically representative – in other words, that the patterns observed in the sample can be generalized to the population as a whole.

Unfortunately, obtaining a truly random sample in sociolinguistic study is problematic for several reasons. For one, even the most seemingly complete list of community members is likely to be biased in some way – for example, a telephone directory will not include community members without telephone service (e.g. lower-income residents) or those with only mobile phones (e.g. younger residents). In addition, it is highly unlikely that every person on a computer-generated list will agree to participate in the study, and so the researcher must decide how to replace people in a way that ensures that randomness is preserved. Further, in most cases, sociolinguists are interested in the relation between patterns of language variation and particular social characteristics (e.g. age, gender, ethnicity, membership in locally important social groups). There is no guarantee that a truly random sample will include members of every group of interest, or that each group will be represented equally. Another problem with achieving genuine statistical representativeness is obtaining a large enough sample size. While the statistical requirements are complex, Neuman (1997:222; quoted in Milroy and Gordon 2003:28) suggests that a good rule of thumb is that for small populations (under 1,000), a sample size of 300 is appropriate, while for large populations (over 150,000), a sample size of at least 1,500 is necessary. Given that the chief method of obtaining data for quantitative sociolinguistic study is conducting informal interviews with each participant of at least an hour's length (see below), one can immediately see that getting a large enough sample for statistical representativeness would be extremely time-consuming in even a small community. And even with limitless energy (and time and funding), the practical difficulties increase exponentially when one begins the analysis phase; indeed, even transcribing alone takes at least ten hours per hour of recorded speech! However, it has been noted that linguistic usage is typically more homogenous than other behaviors that may be studied via survey methods (e.g. purchasing preferences), so it is probably not necessary to obtain a truly representative sample in order to conduct a meaningful sociolinguistic study (e.g. Labov 1966:180–81, Milroy and Gordon 2003:28–9, Sankoff 1980:51–2).

Judgment sampling

For these practical and theoretical reasons, most sociolinguists do not rely on random samples but instead use a technique called judgment sampling. This method involves using one's judgment to decide in advance what types of speakers to include in the study and then obtaining data from a certain number of each type of speaker. Deciding what types of speakers to include can be a complicated issue. Categories may be based on researcher interests, including comparability with previous studies of the same or other populations, on what appears to be important/relevant to community members, or on a combination of both. For example, in her studies of language variation in a high school in the Detroit suburbs (2000), Penelope Eckert grouped speakers according to categories that have been shown to influence patterns of language variation in numerous other sociolinguistic studies (e.g. gender, socioeconomic class). However, because she conducted extended ethnographic (i.e. participant-observation) study of the high-school community, she was also able to group students into locally relevant groups (jocks and burnouts), as well as examine patterns of variation according to particular practices in which the students participated (e.g. varsity sports, academic clubs, hanging out with non-high schoolers in neighborhood parks or in Detroit).

Of course, as Milroy and Gordon point out (2003:24–8), using a judgment rather than random sample is only appropriate if one is at least fairly familiar with the basic characteristics of the population (e.g. the basic socioeconomic and ethnic make-up of the community); otherwise, important segments of the population may be overlooked – for example, members of an ethnic group of whose existence the researcher is unaware. However, in most cases judgment samples do indeed reveal interesting and important patterns of co-variation between linguistic and social factors, especially if one is careful to design the sample based on "objectively defensible criteria" such as "specifiable sociological and demographic criteria" (Milroy and Gordon 2003:31), or on categories uncovered in the course of careful ethnographic study.

Stratifying the sample

As noted above, because sociolinguists are interested in the interrelation between linguistic variation and people's social characteristics, interactional patterns, and attitudes, researchers often divide their sample populations into various social categories. Traditionally, variationists have relied on seemingly "objective" demographic categories such as age, sex, social class, and race. However, researchers have increasingly questioned whether such categories are indeed objective, or if objective measures should take precedence over community members' subjective perceptions. For example, one's position in the socioeconomic hierarchy based on economic measures (e.g. income, type of housing) may or may not bear a direct relation to one's social status in a given community, or one's own sense of one's position in the local social order (e.g. Milroy and Gordon 2003:40–7). And usually the latter two factors correlate more closely with one's linguistic usages and other behaviors than objective measures of economic worth. For example, in studies I and my colleagues conducted in Ocracoke Island, in the North Carolina Outer Banks, we found that one of the wealthiest men on the island was also one of the most vernacular, most likely because he did not hold himself above others in the community and, like others in his core friendship group, took pride in his islander identity and his "down to earth" persona which included dressing very casually, engaging in "working-class" activities such as fishing, boating, and poker playing, and speaking with a heavy local accent.

Further, as noted above, the researcher may not be able to determine prior to study what the important social categories in the population will be, and so as the study unfolds they may need to re-classify participants or even go back and interview new types of speakers. In addition, the researcher may be interested not only in how language patterns according to group membership but also such factors as the type of interactional ties that characterize one's social relationships (i.e. what type of social network(s) one is a member of) or what types of practices one engages in, with members of various groups. If one takes a social network or community of practice-based approach, then one's research population and its subdivisions will look rather different from the population, sample, and social categories that emerge when investigating a larger group of speakers who may or may not interact on a regular basis. Regardless of the type of population studied, one will most likely find linguistic variation that correlates with social differences. For example, social network-based studies have shown that speakers in close-knit networks usually show stronger maintenance of localized vernacular ways of speaking than those with looser network ties (e.g. Milroy 1987). Similarly, a peripheral member of a particular community of practice (e.g. a community of girls who self-identify as "nerds" in a California high school; Bucholtz 1999a) will show different linguistic usages than a core member of this group; in addition, she may even show different patterns in different interactions or portions of an interaction, depending on her and other participants' goals, understandings, and other highly localized social factors.

In sum, then, as one designs a field study, it should be borne in mind that there is no one "best" type of community, sampling method, or way of categorizing speakers. Instead, research design will be guided by one's interests and goals and is likely to change as the study begins and the researcher learns more about the community under study. More and more, variationists are realizing that the best studies are not fully planned in advance but rather that one achieves the fullest understanding of the interrelation between linguistic and social meanings if one keeps an open mind and allows the particularities of each different community, as well as community members' own perspectives, to inform studies as they progress. In other words, variationists increasingly are seeking to use ethnographic methods involving careful, long-term participation in and observation of the communities they study rather than relying solely on pre-determined, "objective" social factors, whether the population under study is a small community of practice that may not be immediately evident to outsiders (e.g. a group of teenage "nerds" in a particular high school) or a large city like Sydney, Australia.

Data collection techniques

Once the researcher has chosen a community of study and the types of people from whom to try to get data, the next step is determining how to get these data, including both linguistic and social data. As noted above, variationists increasingly are using ethnographic methods to learn about locally important linguistic and social meanings, but this does not mean that one can simply live in and observe a community for an extended period of time and then come away with the data needed for quantitative sociolinguistic study. For one, ethnography itself involves careful, systematic observation of social and linguistic practices, as well as taking careful field notes and regularly reviewing and reflecting on one's observations (among many other procedures; see e.g. Duranti [1997: Ch. 4] for an overview). Secondly, because variationists need large amounts of language data they can closely analyze, perhaps over and over again, they need to obtain audio (and perhaps video) recordings of extended stretches of language rather than simply taking qualitative notes on observed usages. Thus, the systematic collection of recorded data from interviews or other conversational interactions is typically at the heart of variationist sociolinguistic studies. In particular, variationist studies have long been grounded in, and continue to be based on, a particular type of interview known as the sociolinguistic interview.

The sociolinguistic interview

Originally conceptualized by Labov (e.g. 1972g, 1984, Wolfram and Fasold 1974a), the sociolinguistic interview is basically an interview designed to approximate as closely as possible a casual conversation. Questions are grouped into topical areas (modules) which can be arranged and rearranged so that they flow fairly naturally into one another; in addition, they are based on topics that will most likely be of interest in the community under study, topics believed to be of general interest, and topics designed to minimize people's attention to the fact that they are being recorded as part of a linguistic study. Most of the questions are open-ended (as opposed to yes-no), and interviewees are encouraged to talk on any subject that catches their interest, whether or not it is included in the original interview questionnaire (often called a "schedule" because of its relatively looser design). The main goal is to obtain a large quantity of speech that approximates people's everyday speech as closely as possible. In addition, though, researchers need to obtain basic demographic and other social information from participants (including, for example, information on interactional networks and attitudes about language and other matters), and so more pointed questions will be included as well.

Labov's emphasis on obtaining speech which is as casual and unselfconscious as possible is based on his Vernacular Principle, which holds that "the style of speech which is most regular in its structure and in its relation to the evolution of the language is the vernacular, in which the minimum attention is paid to speech" (1972g:112). Of course, when someone knows their speech is being recorded or otherwise observed, they are likely to start becoming self-conscious about their language use; thus, linguistic researchers are faced with what Labov calls the Observer's Paradox: "To obtain the data most important for linguistic theory, we have to observe how people speak when they are not being observed" (1972g: 113). Thus, Labov maintains, sociolinguists need a data collection instrument like the sociolinguistic interview, in which the interviewees' attention to speech is minimized by getting them involved in the topics they're talking about.

A couple of questions regarding the efficacy of the sociolinguistic interview may come to mind. For a start, if one needs to obtain speech that is as casual and unselfconscious as possible, why would one conduct interviews at all, rather than simply recording spontaneous conversations? In addition, if ideally one needs data on how people speak when they're not being observed, why don't researchers simply record them secretly? Hopefully, the answer to the second question is obvious: in many cases, it is illegal to surreptitiously tape-record people, and sociolinguists are generally of the consensus that such behavior is always unethical. In addition, the sociolinguistic interview has a number of advantages over recording other types of conversational interactions. First, the sociolinguistic interview allows the researcher to collect a large amount of speech in a relatively short amount of time, whereas people engaged in everyday interaction may or many not produce large quantities of talk. For example, one may not obtain very much speech if one records a family looking through old photo albums or a group of older men at the community store playing checkers. Secondly, the sociolinguistic interview allows the researcher to obtain recordings of high quality in which all participants can be easily identified, since they typically involve one researcher and one interviewee, and the researcher can arrange to conduct the interview in as quiet a place as possible, with microphone(s) and/or video cameras placed as advantageously as possible. While some variationists do record spontaneous conversations, such conversations can take place just about anywhere and involve quite a few participants and much overlapping talk, making it difficult to get good quality recordings and then later tell the various speakers apart. Further, it can be difficult to launch into spontaneous conversation with a study participant one has just met, and it can be invaluable in getting conversation flowing to have a pre-planned interview schedule to refer to, if only occasionally, during the recording session.

Despite the advantages of the sociolinguistic interview, a number of criticisms remain. While any type of interview might be considered to be less "natural" or at least more formal than a spontaneous conversation, the sociolinguistic interview has been criticized as being *less* rather than *more* natural than more typical types of interviews (e.g. Wolfson 1976). Many people are familiar with interviews that follow a fairly straightforward question-and-answer format (e.g. television interviews of various sorts); however, they typically have no conception of what a conversational interview, or "spontaneous interview," is supposed to be like. Thus, they may resist interviewers' attempts to get them to talk at length about whatever topics they like, instead seeking to provide succinct or even "correct" answers to questions, and they may prod researchers to stop listening to them talk and "ask the next question." In addition, although those conducting sociolinguistic interviews are indeed urged to allow interviewees to control the conversation, in reality interviewers typically do control things, since they ask most of the questions, decide which questions are asked and in what order, and are usually responsible for initiating and terminating the interaction. Further, it has been noted that the direct questions that characterize interviews are not typical of everyday casual conversations and may even be considered impolite or inappropriate in some cultural groups. And even if direct questions are perfectly appropriate, even the best-designed questions sometimes fall flat. For example, Labov's best-known question for eliciting highly vernacular speech, usually in the form of animated narratives, is his famous "danger of death" question, in which the researcher asks the interviewee, "Have you ever been in a situation where you were in serious danger of being killed, where you thought to yourself, *This is it*? . . ." (Labov 1972g:113). While Labov seems to have enjoyed great success with this question in communities such as New York City in the 1960s, my colleagues and I typically received a simple "no" in our studies of Outer Banks English. In addition, Milroy and Gordon note that in Lesley Milroy and James Milroy's studies of Belfast, Northern Ireland, in the mid 1970s and early 1980s, an area then characterized by much violence, people were so accustomed to being in danger of death that the topic did not produce excitement or animation but simply "matter-of-fact accounts" (2003:65–6).

Finally, researchers have criticized not only the Labovian interview but variationists' persistent focus on vernacular, unselfconscious speech. This focus is a bit limiting for a number of reasons. For example, it is by no means certain that each speaker can be said to have a single, "genuine" vernacular style unaffected by situational and speaker-internal factors such as who they're talking to and how much attention they're paying to their speech. Instead, people may have a range of quite casual, unselfconscious styles they use with various people in different circumstances (e.g. Eckert 2000:78–82, Hindle 1979, Milroy and Gordon 2003:49–51; Schilling-Estes 2001). For example, the styles one uses with one's parents vs. one's child vs. one's pets may all be quite "casual" yet quite different. In addition, variationists increasingly are recognizing that people's everyday speech repertoires include a range of unselfconscious and more self-conscious varieties and that self-conscious speech can lend valuable insight into "real-life" patterns of language variation and change, as well as people's perceptions of particular linguistic variants. For example, people may show exaggerated production of linguistic innovations in highly self-conscious, perhaps overtly performative styles (e.g. Arnold *et al.* 1993, Eckert 2000:182–4), while speakers' self-conscious performances of their own or others' dialects may point to which features are most salient in a given language variety (e.g. Preston 1992, 1996c, Schilling-Estes 1998).

Despite its limitations, the sociolinguistic interview nonetheless remains a key tool in conducting variationist fieldwork and is likely to remain so for some time to come, especially if researchers are sensitive to community and individual norms and preferences for social interaction, are aware that speech is always shaped by a range of contextual factors, and realize that they can gain valuable knowledge from a range of speech styles, even the most self-conscious. Further, it is possible to move a bit beyond the basic sociolinguistic interview while still retaining the advantages of obtaining a large quantity of high quality data in a relatively short amount of time.

Modifications to the sociolinguistic interview

Researchers, including Labov, have been modifying the basic sociolinguistic interview since its inception. For example, some of Labov's earliest studies involved interviewing groups of friends rather than one research participant at a time (e.g. Labov, Cohen, Robins, and Lewis 1968), and researchers continue to this day to capitalize on the increased informality and decreased focus on the researcher that the group interview format provides. As noted above, though, it can be difficult to separate speakers in an audio-recording of multi-party conversation, especially if there is a lot of overlapping speech; thus, it is best if each participant in a group interview is recorded with a separate microphone (e.g. a lavaliere or clip-on mike). Similarly, a researcher conducting a video-recorded interview with a group of participants using signed language will have difficultly obtaining an adequate view of each participant's communications and responses if only one camera is used (Lucas, Bayley, Valli, Rose, and Wulf 2001). Other researchers have based their studies on spontaneous conversations rather than interviews with any sort of pre-designed schedule, no matter how loosely structured. For example, recording spontaneous conversations was the preferred method of Lesley Milroy and James Milroy in their community studies of Belfast, and of Becky Childs and Christine Mallinson in their studies of a small community of African Americans in the North Carolina mountains (e.g. Childs and Mallinson 2004, Mallinson and Childs forthcoming). In these cases, the researchers' knowledge of the community, gained through extended participant-observation, enabled them to readily come up with topics of conversation, even when they hadn't met participants prior to recording. Still others have had success with using pairs of interviewers (including natural pairs like husband–wife teams) to circumvent the formality of the one-on-one interview, including, for example, Walt Wolfram and his research team in Ocracoke. In addition to contributing to a less "interview-like" feel, the presence of an additional interviewer made it easier for the researchers to monitor both recording quality and the interviewee's talk, and to come up with new topics of discussion when one faded away or simply didn't work.

It is even possible to record conversations and other everyday interactions with no interviewer present, although the researcher cannot then monitor recording quality as the interaction unfolds (unless it can be done remotely). In addition, it can be difficult to ensure that all participants are fully aware that they are being tape-recorded, since participants may come and go. An ingenious compromise between the one-on-one interview format and group recordings made in the researchers' absence was achieved by Jane Stuart-Smith (1999) and Ronald Macaulay (2002) in their studies of language variation and change in Glasgow. These researchers arranged for pairs of friends to engage in conversation in a quiet setting with high-quality recording equipment set up and running but no researcher present. The data thus obtained was for the most part extremely relaxed and casual, especially from adolescents, who can often be quite reticent to talk to adult researchers, and yielded data on a number of forms, including various discourse markers such as *y'know* and *well*, that are often difficult to capture, or capture accurately, in more structured interviews.

Other data-collection techniques

In addition to recording casual interviews and conversations, variationists have employed other data-gathering techniques, including "rapid and anonymous observation" (Labov 1972g:117, 1972e) and large-scale surveys of usage or reported usage in which speech data may or may not be tape-recorded.

Rapid and anonymous observations

The rapid and anonymous observation technique was made famous by Labov, in his study of *r*-pronunciation vs. *r*-lessness among employees in three New York City department stores that catered to clientele of different socioeconomic classes (1972g). To conduct this study, Labov kept his identity as a researcher anonymous. Rather than interviewing a selection of employees in each store, he instead interacted with his subjects in a very natural way: he asked employees where in the store a certain item was located, to which he already knew the answer would be "fourth floor," a response which of course provides two potential environments for *r*-lessness. Further, in order to elicit a more careful speech style, he asked each employee twice, pretending he didn't quite hear the answer the first time. Because the employees did not know they were being studied, Labov could not tape-record their responses. Instead, he wrote down each subject's responses as soon as possible after hearing them, once he was out of sight of the employee. His findings mirrored those obtained via interview data: people used higher levels of *r*-pronunciation in higher socioeconomic classes (or, in the case of the stores, in settings where they come into more contact with members of higher-class groups) and in addition showed more *r*-pronunciation in careful vs. casual speech.

The advantages of rapid and anonymous observation are evident in its name: one can conduct a rapid and anonymous survey extremely quickly (as compared with interviewing participants for at least an hour each), and in addition the Observer's Paradox is completely surmounted, since subjects have no idea that their speech is being studied. The disadvantages, though, should be clear as well. One can only obtain a very limited amount of linguistic data using such a technique, since it is difficult to accurately perceive and note down more than one or two linguistic features following each encounter. In addition, obtaining accurate and complete social information on each speaker is even harder, since one can only observe the most basic demographic characteristics, and even then one's observations may not be complete or accurate (e.g. one can only guess participants' approximate ages). Despite these limitations, rapid and anonymous observations can be a valuable research technique, especially if used as a supplement to more in-depth interview-based study or perhaps part of a pilot for a more in-depth study.

Large-scale surveys

In many cases, variationist studies are conducted by recording large quantities of data from a relatively small number of people. In some instances, though, researchers are interested in obtaining a general picture of the patterning of variation in a very large population, perhaps covering a large geographic area (e.g. a US state, North America). In such cases, researchers typically do not rely on extended sociolinguistic interviews but instead use survey questionnaires, typically consisting of fill-in-the-blank and short-answer questions, in which they obtain a more limited amount of social and linguistic information from a greater number of participants. Such surveys are often administered over the telephone and are audio-recorded; in some cases, though, surveys are administered by mail, and the researcher must rely on participants' written responses. In addition, researchers are making increasingly frequent use of Internet-based surveys.

While some large-scale surveys seek information on participants' actual linguistic usages (e.g. via telephone interviews covering various non-linguistic topics), others are based on participants' self-reports of their linguistic usages and/or perceptions. For example, in conducting their surveys of Texas speech in the late 1980s, Guy Bailey and his colleagues (e.g. Bailey, Wikle, and Tillery 1997) used data from a telephone survey of a random sample of Texas residents who, as part of a larger sociological survey, answered a number of questions about their knowledge and use of various lexical items and grammatical constructions. A typical question might take the form: "Have you heard the term *snap beans* used for the beans that you break in half to cook?" "How often would you use the term: all of the time, some of the time, not very often, or never?" In a somewhat different vein, Bartłomiej Plichta, Dennis Preston, and Brad Rakerd (2005) conducted an

Internet survey of people's perceptions of vowels associated with the Northern Cities Vowel Shift (currently taking place in much of the Inland Northern US), in which participants from both within and outside the Northern Cities region listened to computer-synthesized words with various degrees of vowel shift (e.g. words ranging along the continuum from *sock* to *sack*) in several different phrases and then selected whether they had heard, for example, *sock* or *sack*.

Clearly, such survey techniques are not without their disadvantages: in order to obtain wide breadth of coverage, one necessarily must sacrifice depth. In addition, caution must be used in interpreting self-report data, since speakers can easily over- or underreport their usage of particular linguistic forms. Nonetheless, survey questionnaires are a useful tool for variationists, especially when they are interested in obtaining information from a very large population and/or geographic area and simply cannot obtain lengthy audio recordings from every participant.

Out in the field

Entering the community

Once the researcher has completed at least some preliminary research and planning, it is time to enter the community of study in order to refine the study design and begin pilot data collection, and finally launch into the study in earnest. Though some researchers choose to study communities of which they are already a member, many enter a new community as complete strangers. In what follows, the focus is on the more typical case of the outsider as researcher; however, since outsiders can very quickly become insiders (at least in some sense, since they are necessarily accorded *some* social role in the community), issues and problems that arise for insider researchers are addressed as well.

Presenting oneself and one's project

When researchers enter and begin engaging with an unfamiliar community, they very often find themselves having to explain what they are doing there. Nearly all applications for IRB approval of sociolinguistic research projects include an Informed Consent Form which outlines the project in greater or lesser detail, according to the requirements of the institution. It is not necessary to produce this document when first introducing oneself to potential participants or other community members. In fact, people will probably be disconcerted if one produces an official-looking form immediately upon greeting them. However, successful researchers are usually prepared with an informal description of who they are and what the research project will entail. This description need not include a great deal of linguistic detail. In fact, such detail, while exciting to the linguist, may bore potential participants, or cause them to view the researcher as someone who thinks they're smarter than the people they're studying, and so may serve to discourage rather than recruit potential participants. Further, providing too much detail on exactly what one wishes to study may heighten the Observer's Paradox. For example, if a researcher states at the outset that the focus of study is *r*-lessness, this may cause people to become overly self-conscious about pronouncing their *r*'s. Even stating that one is interested in studying a particular "dialect" may have negative consequences, since the term dialect often carries connotations of "incorrect" or "broken" speech. Thus, it is usually best to describe the study in very general terms, using phases such as "I'm interested in studying the community and its language" or "I'm interested in learning more about how different types of people talk around here."

Researchers may even find it awkward to introduce themselves, especially in a community where people may have less education than the researcher and may think that highly educated people consider themselves to be superior. In general, researchers do not need to provide too much detail regarding their academic credentials (unless asked, of course), and in addition they can highlight aspects of themselves that do not directly relate to their role as researcher. For example, when I first entered the community of Smith Island, Maryland, in the late 1990s (in hopes of conducting a follow-up to a study conducted by Rebecca Setliff in the mid-1980s), I didn't lie about my status as a professor at a nearby university; however, I stressed that I was interested in the island because I grew up near there (which was true). In addition, I happened to find out that a former high-school classmate now resided on the island, so I was able to highlight that aspect of my connection to the community as well.

Once the researcher has been in the community for awhile, especially if it's a smaller community, they may gradually be able to dispense with describing themselves and their project each time they meet someone new; however, they must still to be prepared to face this potentially awkward situation any number of times, and to realize that no matter how long they research or reside in the community, they may always be regarded as something of an outsider. It is better to accept this outsider status than effect full membership in the community, since most people will tolerate a friendly stranger far more readily than someone who pretends to be "one of them."

Making initial contacts

As researchers begin making their way into a community, they of course must decide who to approach first. If they are interested in obtaining data from highly vernacular speakers, they will probably avoid the initial temptation to go to community leaders or institutional authorities (e.g. teachers, preachers) as their first contacts, since such people are likely to lead them to who they perceive to be the "best" representatives of their community, most of whom will be more standard-speaking than may be ideal for the study. However, community leaders are often the easiest to approach, since they are typically used to dealing with outsiders, or acting as "brokers" between the community and outsiders. Further, in some communities, if researchers do not first approach the appropriate local leaders, they may not be able to make any inroads into the community at all. For example, when Setliff first entered the Smith Island community in the mid-1980s, all "brokering" with outsiders was done through the island pastor, and so she had to introduce herself and her study to the pastor before she was permitted access to anyone else. Luckily, she was able to obtain quite vernacular data despite her entry through "official" channels, partly because the island community was so small (and is in fact even smaller today, with only about 350 residents), and most residents are quite vernacular, no matter what their standing in the community. Interestingly, in the late 1990s when I went back to Smith Island, the pastor played a much smaller role, and I and my research team were free to approach people on our own, ranging from the unofficial (but generally acknowledged) island historian to cashiers in island stores and restaurants. Finally, as discussed in more detail below, it is often very useful to try to find some sort of contact through whom one can enter the community, rather than simply going in without knowing any-one. My research colleagues and I have often found such contacts through fellow members of the university community – for example, perhaps a fellow student has family in the community of study. And sometimes one may get lucky and find a connection after entering the field site, as happened to me when I came upon my old classmate in Smith Island.

Finding participants

The "friend of a friend" method

One of the most helpful types of contacts to find in the community of study is a "friend of a friend" – that is, a community member with whom the researcher shares a common friend or acquaintance (Milroy 1987, Milroy and Gordon 2003:32–3). And even if the researcher doesn't initially know anyone in the com-munity, once they have befriended one person, it is then often possible to enter that person's friendship network and be introduced in subsequent interactions as "a friend of Mr. X's" rather than "a student at the university" who is a complete stranger. In other words, if one enters enter the community through a friend of a friend, or soon befriends a community member, this friend can then guide the researcher to his or her friends, who can then steer the researcher toward their friends, and so on. Even if the research plan involves a judgment sample that isn't based on social networks per se (e.g. the plan may involve interviewing equal numbers of males and females in each of three generational groups, regardless of whether the participants are friends or not), researchers still often find that the friend of a friend method, or "snowball" technique (Milroy and Gordon 2003:32) is an excellent way of finding participants who fit the needed categories. Fur-ther, because the friend of a friend is a readily recognized social role, it easily supersedes that of "linguistic researcher" and enables researchers to record more naturalistic speech than if they are viewed chiefly as a researcher.

However, there are a few problems and issues associated with the friend of a friend method that should be borne in mind. For one, it is not possible to obtain a statistically representative sample via this method, and it is also likely that one will obtain a less than adequately representative judgment sample if one works strictly within a single social network. In addition, once the researcher has been accepted into a particular social network, it may be difficult to widen contacts beyond this network, since the researcher is no longer simply an outsider to the community but rather part of one particular sub-segment, one which may or may not have cordial relations with other sub-groups. Further, because the role of "researcher" so readily takes a back seat to that of a "friend of a friend," the researcher needs to take extra care to ensure that participants do not entirely forget about the "researcher" role, or the fact that recordings are being made. For example, in Lesley Milroy and James Milroy's Belfast research, they found that participants sometimes were so relaxed that they conversed freely on controversial topics, seemingly having forgotten about the existence of the tape-recorder. To the researchers' credit, rather than simply making off with this very unself-conscious speech data, they checked at the end of each recording session to see if participants wanted any portions of the tape erased (e.g. Milroy and Gordon 2003:83).

Finally, being a friend of a friend entails not only privileges but also obligations. As a friend of a friend, a researcher cannot simply collect data and go home; rather they are expected to participate in the network's "mesh of exchange and obligation relationships" (Milroy 1987:97). In other words, if one capitalizes on people's friendships, it is typically expected (and considered good form) that one will give something back in return. Researchers' involvement in their communities of study is covered in more detail below.

Beyond the "friend of a friend"

Unless the researcher is conducting a study of only one social network, they must aim to move beyond a single network in their search for study participants. One very good way of achieving this is exemplified in Eckert's study of the Detroit-area high school. Prior to entering the school, Eckert constructed a random sample of the high-school population. Once she entered the community, she very quickly began finding participants through the snowball technique – so many, in fact, that she knew she would never be able to actually analyze all the data she was collecting. Nonetheless, despite the large amounts of data she was getting and the relative comfort of going through friends of friends to set up her next interviews, she returned periodically to her random list and made the effort to get to know (and subsequently record) people on the list she had not yet encountered through the snowball method, thus ensuring that no major friendship groups were left out, as well as that a few loners found their way into the sample as well (Eckert 2000:69–84).

Researchers have also had success with other methods besides the friend of a friend technique, for example through simply hanging out in neighborhood streets or even making "cold calls" on doorsteps. However, the snowball technique seems to be the current method of choice for finding study participants, with the very good reason that it works so well and is far less intimidating and unnatural than simply walking up to people one doesn't know.

The researcher's role in the sociolinguistic interview

In addition to thinking about one's role in the community (insider, outsider, friend of a friend), the researcher also needs to give careful thought to their role in the sociolinguistic interview (or other recorded interactions). Labov (e.g. 1984) and others stress that in conducting the interview, the researcher should strive to lessen the power (whether perceived or real) of the interviewer over the interviewee, both in order to obtain speech that is as relaxed as possible and out of respect for study participants. After all, though sociolinguistic researchers sometimes have more formal education than research participants and almost certainly know more about linguistics, members of the research population have a lot to teach outsiders about their community, and their ways of looking at the world and at language. Highlighting one's role as a learner and the role of participants as experts on their community can go a long way toward obtaining casual speech and building good relations. Other fairly simple ways of minimizing dominance in the interview situation and maximizing casualness include dressing casually (if appropriate in the community and interview setting), using recording equipment that is an unobtrusive as possible, avoiding relying too heavily on a written interview schedule (perhaps using it only as an occasional reminder of questions that can be asked), and even carrying equipment in a casual-looking bag rather than a formal-looking briefcase or equipment case.

Some critics of the sociolinguistic interview have argued that attempting to reverse roles so that the interviewee becomes the authority will not work, since there is too great an expectation that the interviewer will be in charge of the speech event (e.g. Wolfson 1976). In particular, it may be difficult to get people who are in subordinate positions in their community (e.g. younger people, women) to take charge of the interview event. However, I and others have found that role relationships are readily altered in the sociolinguistic interview and indeed may change any number of times during the course of a single interview. Thus, for example, a participant may initially view the interviewer as the authority figure and provide only short, succinct answers to their questions; however, as the interview progresses, the interviewee may warm up to the researcher and begin producing long stretches of talk and animated stories. Further, when they feel really comfortable, interviewees often start questioning the interviewer, perhaps asking them about their schooling, personal interest, etc.

In addition to minimizing one's authority, Labov (e.g. 1984) and others have also urged researchers to minimize the amount of talk they themselves produce in the interview (e.g. by keeping questions as short as possible), allowing the interviewee maximal talking time. However, others such as L. Milroy stress that, like other conversational interactions, the interview is an exchange, and researchers will most likely get better results if they allow themselves to talk fairly freely, too, though of course they should be careful not to dominate the interaction (Milroy 1987:47–9).

The researcher's role in the community

Finally, in thinking about what sorts of roles researchers should adopt in the community and during recording sessions, it is also important to think about aspects of one's identity that cannot be readily changed and how they affect interactions with community members. Despite society's best efforts to eliminate prejudices and discrimination based on factors such as sex, ethnicity, and age, people will form certain opinions about researchers and perhaps limit their access to community groups and interactions based on such factors. In addition, it can be important to think about such factors in setting up and conducting interviews. For example, researchers may get more vernacular speech if they ensure that interviewees are interviewed by researchers of the same ethnicity (e.g. Rickford and McNair-Knox 1994); further, in some communities it may not even be possible to conduct interviews if the researcher is not similar demographically to the interviewee or possesses characteristics the interviewee judges negatively. For example, in the mid-1990s, I participated in a sociolinguistic study of the rural, tri-ethnic community of Robeson County, NC, comprised of approximately equal numbers of African Americans, Lumbee Native Americans, and Whites (e.g. Wolfram and Dannenberg 1999). At the time, the county was highly racially segregated, and it was much more difficult for African American than White interviewers to interview Lumbee Indians. Similarly, ethnicity and audiological status of the interviewer have been shown to affect the success of sociolinguistic interviews with Deaf participants (Lucas and Valli 1992). In addition, being a woman may limit one's access to certain traditionally male activities in a community, though sometimes a community outsider can circumvent sanctions that apply to insiders. Further, I and others have found that in many cases women are perceived as less threatening than men, and so they may actually be more rather than less welcome in a wider range of communities and interactional settings.

The matter of community members' beliefs regarding different types of people and behaviors also raises the issue of whether and to what extent researchers should effect pretenses in order to win community members' favor. For example, if the researcher is a teetotaler conducting research in an island community where many residents engage in heavy drinking of alcoholic beverages, should the researcher have a few drinks, or maybe effect drunkenness, during a wild party to win friends in the community? Or if the researcher is an atheist, should they attend church in the community if invited? There are no easy answers to such questions, though I my colleagues and I have found that maintaining a degree of subtle, respectful distance from beliefs and behaviors that are not one's "own" is perhaps a better course of action than either pretending to embrace such behaviors or roundly denouncing them. For example, a non-drinker could attend a community party and interact in a friendly way with everyone without drinking or pretending to drink. Similarly, a non-religious researcher could attend a religious service if invited, but if asked direct questions about religious beliefs, they could respond by saying that they prefer to keep their views private. Again, it is important to keep in mind that one enters a community as a researcher in order to learn from the community, not to pre-judge them or seek to become one of them. In addition, personal and demographic differences between researchers and study participants are not insurmountable. Entering the community with an open mind and a friendly, humble demeanor can go a long way toward breaking down barriers and bridging differences, and researchers should never (or at least only rarely) presume that they will not be welcome in a particular community or sub-community because of who they are and what beliefs they hold.

Recording and record-keeping

Recording

After the researcher has gone through all the hard work involved in designing the study and data collection instrument, establishing themselves in the community, and conducting interviews that feel friendly and relaxed, there is nothing worse than returning home only to realize that the recordings are of such poor quality that they are barely usable. It is well beyond the scope of this chapter to go into the intricacies of the physics of speech sound and of audio- and video-recording. It is also not possible here to recommend particular products or even the general type of recording equipment one should use (e.g. cassette tape, solid state digital recorder), since new products and technologies are constantly being innovated. It is possible, however, to offer a general set of guidelines for obtaining high-quality recordings and for balancing recording needs with the equally important need to hold good-quality conversations and maintain good relations with community members.

Audio-recordings

Since portable tape-recorders first became fairly readily available, sociolinguists researchers have relied on audio-recordings of interviews and other speech events as a primary source of data. Since the inception of Labovian sociolinguistics, researchers have gone from using reel-to-reel tape-recorders to cassette tapes to digital recorders with or without removable storage media (e.g. Digital Audio Tapes, mini-CDs). Presumably, the beginning researcher will want to use current technologies, but choosing from among the multitude of products available at any given time can be a daunting task, and one should bear in mind that not all "cutting-edge" technologies are capable of producing recordings of high enough quality for fine-grained linguistic analysis, especially acoustic phonetic analysis, a key component of many variationist studies. To help guard against the accidental purchase of trendy yet poor quality recording devices, it is highly recommended that one consult phoneticians, phonologists, and experienced sociolinguistic field researchers, as well as helpful web sites such as that of sociophonetician Bartłomiej Plichta, http://bartus.org/akustyk/. It is also useful to consult with professional audio technicians or sound engineers, if possible. In addition, introductory acoustic phonetics texts can be helpful, for example Keith Johnson's *Acoustic and auditory phonetics* (2003).

In addition to a high-quality audio-recorder, a high-quality external microphone is essential, even if the recorder has a built-in mike, since the external mike will generally be of better quality and enable the mike to be positioned more freely. Many sociolinguistic researchers use clip-on or lavaliere mikes, since these can be placed very close to speaker's mouths and are much less obtrusive (after the first few minutes of wear) than handheld or stand-mounted mikes. In addition, one must consider whether one's recording needs will be best met by an omnidirectional mike (which picks up sound in all directions) or a unidirectional mike, which mostly picks up sounds coming from the front (and a bit to the sides). In one-on-one sociolinguistic interviews, a unidirectional mike is typically preferred, since it picks up the speaker's voice clearly with a minimum of ambient noise. For group recordings, if it is not possible for each participant to have their own mike, then an omnidirectional mike may be used, though the researcher should be aware that the omnidirectional mike will pick up background noise in addition to participants' conversational contributions.

Finally, the researcher should bear in mind that in addition to meeting certain technological requirements, the equipment must also be rugged enough for field use, and sometimes one will have to sacrifice optimal quality for a bit more durability.

Video-recordings

Some sociolinguistic researchers interested in spoken-language use are now gathering data via video-recording in addition to audio. Clearly, video data can add much valuable information to sociolinguistic accounts of interactions or communities, including, for example, information on people's relative positions, eye gaze, gestures, facial expressions, and so on. Further, video-recordings are necessary if one's research involves signed language (Lucas *et al.* 2001). However, just as audio-only recordings are limited in that they do not capture any visual information, video recordings do not portray a full, accurate picture of the recording event either. After all, cameras have to be positioned somewhere (even if the person working the camera moves around while recording), and where one chooses to place the camera or how and when they move it will affect watchers' perceptions of the recorded event. In addition, whereas people can sometimes become rather performative when being audio-recorded, they can really "ham it up" in front of video-recorders. And while there is nothing wrong with studying self-conscious linguistic performances, the researcher should not mistake such data as representative of everyday, "unselfconscious" communicative interaction.

Where to record

Once the researcher has chosen recording equipment and lined up study participants, they must then decide where to conduct recordings. Ideally, for recordings
of spoken-language interaction they should seek a fairly quiet place where rever-
berations will be limited, for example a quiet outdoor location or an indoor room
with few flat, hard surfaces. In addition, background noise should be avoided,
including the noises emanating from the many electrical devices that are now
so pervasive that they are barely noticed. For example, computers and fluores-
cent lights are particularly noisy on tape, though people barely hear them in a
non-recording situation. Further, if video-recording is being used, then considerations of lighting and positioning of camera(s) and participants, must be taken
into account as well.

Of course, because researchers rely on community members' cooperation, they
often need to make compromises between optimal sound quality and participants'
comfort. Thus, for example, even though the kitchen is one of the worst rooms in
the house for recording, it is one of the best for socializing, and participants often
insist on holding recording sessions in this room. In addition, while a researcher
may be able to politely ask an elderly participant to turn their television off "so I
can pay attention to what you have to tell me," they may not be able to ask them to
turn off their window air-conditioning unit in the middle of summer. Sometimes,
researchers simply have to endure recording sessions which they know will result
in data of rather poor recording quality, so as not to sacrifice good relations with
participants or the community. And while such "extraneous" interviews are indeed
time-consuming, one may glean valuable information from their content and in
addition may be able to set up additional recording sessions in better locations
once the interviewee's trust is gained.

Record-keeping

Also well beyond the scope of this chapter is a full treatment of how to keep track
of data once one begins to amass it. There are a number of database applications
for non-experts which can be customized to meet particular needs; in addition,
increasing numbers of sociolinguists are building custom databases and creating
computer-searchable corpora of their field data. However, if one follows a few
basic guidelines, one need not resort to high-tech solutions to keep track of tapes
or digitized audio or video data, participant and community information, and
other research-related material such as field notes.

Even a very small project can quickly become an organizational nightmare
if one does not start out by keeping good field notes in which one notes general
impressions of the community, details of specific interactions with community
members, and contact information for any potential participants to which one is
referred.

Once the researcher begins audio- or video-recording, it is vital that every tape
or file is clearly labeled as soon as possible after recording, and that backup copies

are made soon thereafter. In addition, it is essential to keep track of all participants and their general characteristics, possibly in a database, though spreadsheets or clearly labeled text documents will suffice as well. Further, shortly after each interview, researchers often write a brief report (or fill out a brief form designed ahead of time) outlining the general characteristics of the interview (e.g. descriptions of participants and setting, impressions of the sound or visual quality, quality of the conversation, etc). In this report, researchers may also note sections of the recording that struck them as noteworthy, for ease of reference in later analysis. All records (audio, database, text documents, etc.) should be stored in multiple formats and locations, for example hard drive, flash drive, CD, hard copy (for text documents), and perhaps a shared drive or secure Internet location as well.

Finally, good researchers make it a habit to check the quality of each recording as soon as possible. Many people do a short test with the participant prior to the start of each interview; in addition, though, the researcher should listen to or watch various portions of the recording once the interview is over to make sure nothing went wrong. If one does have a recording disaster (and everybody does!), the problem needs to be corrected right away, not after conducing four or five more interviews. In addition, if a particular recording does not work out well, it may be possible to get the interviewee to agree to be recorded again while the researcher is still on site, but it may be much more difficult days, weeks, or months after the initial interview.

Preserving confidentiality

While it is essential to keep careful records of all recordings and participant information, it is also necessary to keep a careful eye on these records, since, in most cases, sociolinguists have agreed with study participants to preserve participants' confidentiality. To ensure confidentiality, researchers must store data and present findings in such a way that participants' names and other identifying information are not readily available to people outside the research team. One simple expedient is to label copies of recordings and associated records with pseudonyms or initials or codes (e.g. SI #42, M52, for Smith Island interview #42, male, age 52), preserving original, fully labeled data in a secure location. The coded information is then used in all analyses, presentations, and publications. In addition, it is a good idea (and may be required under the terms of one's IRB protocol) to use digital audio-editing techniques to obscure community members' names on sound files, as well as video-editing techniques to obscure the faces of participants in video-recordings.

Special care must be taken if one chooses to store data or portions of it on a shared drive or the Internet. Clearly, raw data housed on an Internet site must be password-protected; but one must also be careful in posting even data excerpts on non-protected sites, especially if the community is small and and members could identify one another on the basis of even very short clips. If one does post excerpts (perhaps for illustrative purposes), they should be kept fairly short and should not contain any material that may be potentially harmful to the participant or the community. Of course, what counts as "harmful" may be very different in different communities, so it is safest to check with participants before posting even a portion of their data on the Internet, a largely public venue which many people are often lulled into thinking is fairly private.

Community involvement

This chapter has already touched on a number of issues involving fieldwork ethics, including how involved the researcher should be in the community and it what ways. Issues of community involvement are here discussed in a bit more detail.

The basics: ethical treatment and IRB guidelines

There is general agreement among sociolinguistic researchers (and other social scientists) that if nothing else, researchers have the obligation to follow basic codes of ethics – i.e. preserving participants' anonymity where promised and compensating participants for any inconvenience or uneasiness associated with the study (perhaps monetarily, perhaps through assistance of another sort). When researchers submit their IRB applications, they are required to describe the steps they will take to ensure that research participants will be treated ethically. They must then abide by the terms of the IRB protocol throughout the duration of the research project (and beyond, in matters such as preserving confidentiality). In addition, any changes researchers wish to make to their study design, Informed Consent Form, or measures for ensuring ethical treatment must be approved by their IRB prior to implementing those changes.

Beyond the basics: community involvement

Some researchers argue that community involvement should not go far beyond ensuring basic ethical treatment, believing that researchers should maintain their distance in order to preserve objectivity. Many, however, feel that, since social scientists are people conducting research on people, they cannot help but affect the people they study is some way, and therefore, they should work to ensure that their involvement has positive effects. Once committed to this general belief, researchers can then become involved on any of several different levels.

First, if one's research reveals that commonly held beliefs about language, and practices associated with those beliefs, are wrong, one can work to right these wrongs. This position is encapsulated in Labov's Principle of Error Correction:

> A scientist who becomes aware of a widespread idea or social practice with important consequences that is invalidated by his [*sic*] own data is obligated to bring this error to the attention of the widest possible audience. (Labov 1982:172)

Beyond seeking to correct generally held misperceptions, sociolinguists may wish to use their linguistic knowledge to help community members themselves. This notion is captured in Labov's Principle of the Debt Incurred:

> An investigator who has obtained linguistic data from members of a speech community has an obligation to use the knowledge based on that data for the benefit of the community, when it has need of it.   (Labov 1982:173)

There are a number of instances where sociolinguists have worked to correct public misconceptions about language variation, and this work has often been of direct benefit to particular communities, including those characterized by non-standard dialects. For example, sociolinguistic testimony on the regular patterning of vernacular dialects, including African American Vernacular English, was crucial in effecting an important legal ruling (the Ann Arbor Decision, 1979) stating that educators and officials in the Ann Arbor educational system were guilty of discrimination against African American children, in part because the educators had not taken adequate measures to overcome language barriers.

Finally, some researchers argue that one should not wait until a community asks for help, or for a need to become obvious, but rather should proactively seek ways of benefiting the community through one's linguistic knowledge. This belief is captured in Wolfram's Principle of Linguistic Gratuity:

> Investigators who have obtained linguistic data from members of a speech community should actively pursue positive ways in which they can return linguistic favors to the community.   (1993:227)

To this end, Wolfram and his research associates have worked in various communities over the past decades, not only to correct general misperceptions and right wrongs, but to increase community members' understanding of their own and other language varieties. For example, Wolfram and his colleagues have designed and taught dialect awareness units in middle-school classrooms in communities ranging from Baltimore, MD, to Ocracoke, NC; in addition, Wolfram has pioneered the development of educational materials designed to be accessible and entertaining to adults. For example, he and his colleagues have built museum displays on dialect variation and produced a number of documentaries on various North Carolina communities and language varieties, including *Voices of North Carolina* (Hutcheson 2005, Reaser and Wolfram 2006a, 2006b), an encompassing look at language variation across the entire state. Wolfram's efforts have been extremely well received, and little by little, he and dedicated researchers like him are chipping away at harmful misconceptions about language variation, especially the all-too-common belief that non-standard varieties and their speakers are incorrect, sloppy, or even "stupid."

Of course, not all researchers will have the time, energy, creativity, and confidence (not to mention funding!) it takes to develop and produce such a wide range of dialect awareness materials. Further, it is not necessary for researchers to focus their community involvement on linguistic favors. Instead, there are a number of ways to give back to the community, including such seemingly simple but greatly appreciated efforts as providing transportation (e.g. Milroy 1987:55–6), helping someone with a home improvement project (as one researcher did in Robeson County), or simply being a good listener, perhaps even a friend. And it is the friendships that one forms with community members, and the understandings one gains from them, more so than the academic results achieved, that truly make sociolinguistic fieldwork worth the time, energy, and emotional commitment it entails.

10 Quantitative analysis[1]

SALI A. TAGLIAMONTE

Modeling language variation

Quantitative analysis involves an examination of individual instances of linguistic forms in the context of the grammar from which they come. Thus, quantitative analysis is not so much interested in individual occurrences of linguistic features (i.e. tokens), but the recurrent choices an individual makes in the course of linguistic performance (i.e. patterns of occurrence) (Poplack and Tagliamonte 2001:89). These choices are taken to represent the (underlying) variable grammar of the speaker as well as the speech community to which she belongs.

In this chapter I will demonstrate quantitative analysis by using a well-known (and popular) linguistic feature as a case study – the use of quotative "be like," as in (1a–c).

(1) (a) 'Cause then they were talking about Krispy Kreme and then Tita Laura *was like*, "Oh, I've never been there, do they sell coffee there?" And Tito Emilio *was like*, "No, I don't think so. It's just doughnuts." And **I**'*m like*, "No, they sell coffee too." And she'*s like*, "Oh yeah?" And then he'*s like*, "Oh yeah?" And I *was like*, "Yeah." (CF/16/02)

(b) So then, she *was like*, "Oh, it's okay. Just remember to count to five and everything's okay." And I *was like*, "Oh, that's, that's okay." So then um, today she *asked* me again, "How are you juggling everything. I hope everything's going okay." And I *said*, "Well not really this week. This week is really stressful." (CF/17/03)

(c) I just *said*, "Hello" and then, *Ø* "I'm trying to set up my webcam," and just generally that I'm doing okay. And then I *was like*, "It's not very long." But then he *was like*, "Oh it's okay, I just wanted to hear your voice." (CF/18/03)

[1] I am indebted to Jonille and Larissa Clemente for their co-commitment to this mini panel study. I thank David Sankoff, as ever, for answers to my perpetual questions on method.

The data come from a series of sociolinguistic interviews conducted with Clara Felipe.[2] These materials represent approximately six hours of data from a single individual – a mini-corpus that could represent a typical data set collected by a novice analyst embarking on a quantitative analysis of linguistic variation.

Quantitative analysis asks the question: how can Clara's use of *be like*, as in (1), be explained? It aims to provide an "accountable" investigation of language use and structure. Accountability means that Clara's utterances must be contextualized, both linguistically as well as socially. In this case, Clara was born and raised in the city of Toronto, the largest city in Canada. Thus, the broad social context is an urban variety of Canadian English spoken at the turn of the twenty-first-century among teenagers. It is also important to know that Clara comes from a middle-class family and lives in a suburban neighborhood.

The analyst will have devised appropriate data collection techniques as a means to gain access to Clara's vernacular, the style of speaking which most closely approximates "everyday speech" (Gillian Sankoff 1974:54) or "real language" (Milroy 1992:66). This is considered the ideal target for quantitative analysis. In this case, I have about an hour and a half of conversational materials from four different interviews conducted in September between 2002 and 2005.

From these data, I aim to "tap into" Clara's use of quotatives as she converses. Being "accountable" linguistically means that one must determine the precise nature of quotatives generally, and then the contexts within that sub-system of grammar where the choice of one variant over another is possible. In other words, does Clara use *be like* all the time or some of the time? Is *be like* restricted to one type of context or can it occur in several? The only way to find out is to turn directly to the data itself.

The linguistic variable

The key to quantitative approaches to language variation is the observation that language is inherently variable. Speakers make choices when they speak. These choices are potential "linguistic variables." A linguistic variable in its most basic definition is "two or more ways of saying the same thing." In other words, the choices are viewed as alternatives with the same referential value (meaning) in running discourse (D. Sankoff 1988a:14–43). Although variants may differ subtly in meaning and distribution, they are viewed as members of the same structured set in the grammar (Wolfram 1993:195). The choice of one variant or the other varies in a systematic way. Once an adequate number of choices has been taken into account, the selection of one variant or another can be modeled statistically (Cedergren and Sankoff 1974, Labov 1969). This is where the quantitative approach differentiates itself from many other methods – counting. One must

---

[2] Excerpts of Clara's speech are referenced by her initials, (CF), her age at the time of the interview (16, 17, 18, 19), and the year of data collection (2002, 2003, 2004, 2005).

Table 10.1 *Number of tokens per year*

Interview date	2002 [16 years old]	2003 [17 years old]	2004 [18 years old]	2005 [19 years old]
	191	81	203	92

tabulate every time Clara used a quotative verb and which particular form she used each time.

Frequency

Quantitative methods necessarily involve counting, but the question is what does one count? If one were to tally the tokens of *be like* in its quotative function in Clara's speech, the numbers in Table 10.1 would be the result.

What do these numbers demonstrate? It looks like Clara's use of *be like* falls, rises, falls, and rises over the four-year period. In fact, bare numbers such as this actually reveal little about Clara's use of *be like* or, indeed, her use of quotative verbs in general. This is because bare numbers such as this do not take into account the *proportion* these *be like* tokens represent out of all the relevant contexts where such a form *might have been used* in the data.

Principle of accountability

A foundational concept in the quantitative approach is the "principle of accountability" (Labov 1972g:72). This principle stipulates that it is necessary to count the number of occurrences of all the relevant forms in the sub-system of grammar that have been targeted for investigation, not simply the variant of interest. In this case, while I may be interested in the use of *be like* in particular, I cannot gain access to how it functions in the grammar without considering it in the context of the quotative system as a whole. In other words, Clara's use of *be like* must be reported as a proportion of the total number of relevant constructions, i.e. the total number of times she used quotative verbs more generally (Wolfram 1993: 206).

If one were to count the tokens of *be like* in the data as a proportion of all the quotative verbs Clara uses in each interview, the outcome would be the numbers shown in Table 10.2.

It is now evident why the number of *be like* tokens rises and falls. It is simply the result of the total number of quotative verbs in each interview!

Moreover, the results in Table 10.2 now reveal that while Clara's predominate quotative verb is *be like*, further examples from the data reveal quite a few others, including the more standard variants *tell/told* and *said/say*, as in (2a–e).

Table 10.2 *Proportion of* be like *tokens out of total number of quotative verbs by year*

Interview date	2002 [16 years]	2003 [17 years]	2004 [18 years]	2005 [19 years]
Proportion	65.4%	66.7%	78.8%	73.9%
Number of tokens of *be like*	125	54	160	68
Total quotatives	191	81	203	92

(2) (a) Yeah, and I was talking about the double cohorts. And they *were saying* like, "Oh yeah, I think they're going to raise the standard-." ... She *said*, "Yeah, they're going to raise ... the number of people they're going to accept for each programme. It'*s like*, "Oh-my-God!" (CF/16/02)

   (b) And she *told* me like, "Oh, you have a lot of close guy friends." And I'*m like,* "Not really." (CF/16/02)

   (c) I'*m not just going to be like,* "Euh! You suck, I'm going to ditch you." (CF/16/02)

   (d) He'*s just going* like, "Shut-up! Blah-blah-blah!" Like, it's so real like to Diego. And that's why he's like making all these faces and it's like so funny. 'Cause Diego *was just like,* "Oh, I wasn't the one who was like being aggressive." And then Nick *was like*, "Shut-up!" (CF/16/02)

   (e) Not really good as in, "Whoa, he's hot!"
       But like good as in *like*, "Whoa, that's the like– that's like the way it should be." (CF/16/02)

One might think that the use of *like* in (2e) is a separate type of quotative verb due to its location just before the quoted material. However these tokens must be put in context with Clara's use of *like* elsewhere in her grammar. In fact, she is a copious user of discourse *like*, as in (3a–b).

(3) (a) ... But it was okay. It was kind of whatever *like* not really boring, but just *like*, "Okay. So when you guys going-to leave?" (CF/16/02)

   (b) I'm just *like* that annoying, that I just barge in here *like*, "So Manang?" (CF/16/02)

Are these tokens quotative *like* or discourse *like*? It is impossible to tell. Chances are they are discourse *like* and if so they should be treated as zero quotative contexts. What evidence could support this interpretation? Table 10.3 shows the distribution of this use in time.

Table 10.3 *Proportion of like* ALONE *tokens out of total number of quotative verbs by year*

Interview date	2002 [16 years]	2003 [17 years]	2004 [18 years]	2005 [19 years]
Proportion	19.4	9.9	7.9	7.6
Number of tokens of *like* ALONE	37	8	16	7
Total quotatives	191	81	203	92

$N = 567$.

Table 10.3 reveals that the use of these constructions declines markedly after age 16. This is consistent with earlier research which suggests that discourse *like* is an age-graded phenomenon in Toronto that peaks in adolescence (Tagliamonte 2005). Thus, from this point onwards, such tokens will be treated as instances of discourse *like* making these constructions instances of zero quotative verbs.

The latter point emphasizes how important it is to circumscribe the variable context to quotative verbs only. In other words, one must be very wary of the function of the tokens included in the analysis. According to the principle of accountability, the data must be circumscribed to only those contexts that are functionally comparable as well as variable.[3]

In sum, a fundamental component of the quantitative method is to know the overall distribution of forms in the data. However, this counting enterprise must be tempered by meticulous attention to: (1) where variation is possible; (2) where variation is not possible; and (3) inclusions of only those tokens where the targeted function is consistent throughout and more generally, as Wolfram (1993:218) argues "a good dose of common sense." This is the starting point for studying the underlying system under investigation (i.e. the variable context). In this case, the system is quotative verbs.

Data such as in (1) and (2) which are replete with non-standard forms may make it appear that Clara's use of quotatives is not simply non-standard but also haphazard, even random. But is it? The next question becomes: under what conditions does *be like* occur?

Distributional analysis

The essential goal of quantitative analysis of variation is to view the behavior of the dependent variable (in this case choice of quotative verbs) as these distribute across a series of cross-cutting independent factors, whether external (social)

---

[3] Good practice dictates that such tokens be coded separately so that they can be viewed independently as you have just seen.

Table 10.4 *Overall distribution of quotatives*

	be like	zero	say	go	tell	other	be	think	be all	ask
%	71.8	16.4	6.3	1.2	1.2	0.5	0.4	0.9	0.2	1.1
N	407	93	36	7	7	3	2	5	1	6

N = 567.

Table 10.5 *Overall distribution of main quotatives*

	be like	zero	say	other
%	71.8	16.4	6.3	5.5
N	407	93	36	31

N = 567.

or internal (grammatical). To gain access to this information, it is necessary to determine how the choice of, for example, *be like* is influenced by different aspects of the contexts in which it occurs (D. Sankoff 1988b:985).

The first question to ask is: what is the full inventory of Clara's quotative verbs? This overall distribution is shown in Table 10.4.

Table 10.4 shows that *be like* is the most frequent variant by far representing 71.8% of Clara's quotative verbs (407/567). However, what verbs are represented in the remainder of the system now becomes clear. The zero variant ranks second at 16.4% (93/567), and the standard variant *say* ranks third at 6.3% (36/567). The remaining quotative variants are spread across a number of different types, including *go, think, tell, ask*, and a number of idiosyncratic others, as in (4a–d).

(4) (a) So then um, today she **asked** me again, "How are you juggling everything?" (CF/17/03)
     (b) And they just **re-cap**, "Oh this is when you're having tests." (CF/19/05)
     (c) I **tell** them, "Alright." (CF/19/05)
     (d) And she **goes**, "I don't know. When are you free?" (CF/18/04)

The very small numbers of variants, often seven tokens or under, across a broad range of types makes it difficult to discern underlying trends. Standard practice in a quantitative approach is to group the data so as to more felicitously view the major variants. Therefore, I will now collapse together all the minor variants and retain the major forms: *be like*, zero and *say*. The new distribution is shown in Table 10.5.[4]

---

[4] The condition file that reconfigured the original coding schema for the dependent variable is shown in Appendix A.

Table 10.6 *Overall distribution of major variants by age*

Age	be like		zero		say		other	
	%	N	%	N	%	N	%	N
16	65.4	125	24.1	46	5.2	10	5.2	10
17	66.7	54	16.0	13	6.2	5	11.1	9
18	78.8	160	10.8	22	7.9	16	2.5	5
19	73.9	68	13.0	12	5.4	5	7.6	7
Total N		407		93		36		31

Notice that the number and proportion of *be like*, zero, and *say* stay the same, but now there is a fourth category, a new combined "other" grouping, which now represents the sum of all the stragglers (31/567).

Factor by factor analysis

The next step is to determine the cross-cutting factors that may influence where *be like* can occur. A comparison of marginals analysis (Rand and Sankoff 1990:4) refers to the relative frequencies and percentages of the variant forms of the dependent variable in the data, either alone (an overall distribution of forms), or with the independent variables that condition or constrain it (a factor by factor analysis). Standard practice is to focus on external factors first (Tagliamonte 2006:96).

External factors

Recall that this particular data set has been constructed specifically so as to view potential changes in the quotative system in real time. Table 10.6 shows the distribution of major variants according to Clara's age at the time of the interview.

This view of the quotative system by year reveals some important patterns. As we saw earlier, use of *be like* is high (65.4%) from the time Clara was 16, increasingly incrementally to 66.7% at age 17, then jumping to 78.8% when she was 18. By the time of the last interview at 19 years of age, however, the overall rate of *be like* drops back somewhat to 73.9%. Similarly, *say* increases over the first three periods, and declines in the fourth. In contrast, the zero quotative, which is the second most frequent variant for every interview, decreases, from 24.1% when she was 16 years old, to 16% in 2003 when she was 17 years old, with a slight resurgence at 19 years of age. Contrasting with all of these is the "other" category, which is highest when Clara was 17 years of age. Without further information, it is difficult to interpret these trends.

Table 10.7 *Overall distribution of existential*
it *subjects*

	be like	zero	*say*	other	TOTAL
%	**95.0**	0.0	0.0	5.0	8.5
N	38	0	0	2	40

Internal factors

At this point, one should turn to the internal linguistic factors. For this, it is necessary to refer to the literature. Who has studied this feature before? What have they found? The data must be coded in such a way as to test these factors in a coding system that is "linguistically principled" (Wolfram 1991:216). A comprehensive review of the research on quotatives in contemporary English reveals that there are a number of internal factors which are widely held to constrain quotative use: grammatical person, content of the quote, and tense/temporal reference.[5]

Grammatical person

The grammatical person of the subject is one of the most pervasive grammatical influences on the use of quotative verbs. Some subject types exhibit little or no variation. For example, *be like* is virtually the only quotative that can occur with existential *it*, as in (5a–d).

(5) (a) It'*s like*, "Hello! It's a nutcracker!" (CF/16/02)
    (b) So it *was like*, "Um, whose house is this?" (CF/17/03)
    (c) But then it'*s like*, "What did you do?" (CF/18/04)
    (d) It'*s like* "First of all, your bra is bad." (CF/19/05)

Traditional quotatives cannot occur with existential subjects, although some forms other than *be like* are possible here, as in (6).

(6) I don't know it just jokes *like*, "Oh so I'll see you later!" (CF/17/03)

The distribution of quotative verbs with referential *it* subjects in Clara's speech is shown in Table 10.7.

Guy (1988) argues that any context over 95% or under 5% should be removed from a variable rule analysis. Why? They simply aren't variable. Thus, from this point forward the 40 tokens of existential *it* are excluded.[6]

Considering the remaining grammatical subjects, *be like* tends to occur with first person, as in (7a–e).

---

[5] The coding schema for this analysis of quotative verbs replicates that of Tagliamonte and Hudson (1999) and Tagliamonte and D'Arcy (2004, 2007). It is shown in Appendix B.

[6] Notice that the method requires you to remove all the contexts of existential *it*, not simply the tokens that occur with *be like*. The condition file recode for this revision is shown in Appendix C.

Table 10.8 *Distribution of* be like *across grammatical person*

	be like	
	%	N
First person singular	88.5	165
Other	61.6	362
Total *N*		527

(7) (a) And I *was like*, "Whoa, that's cool." (CF/16/02)
    (b) I'd just *be like*, "You're so old Sandy!" (CF/17/03)
    (c) I'*m like*, "What are you talking about?" (CF/18/04)
    (d) So I *was like*, "Ah." (CF/19/05)
    (e) I *was like*, "That was nice." (CF/19/05)

The consistency of this effect across studies (Blyth, Recktenwald, and Wang 1990, Cukor-Avila 2002, Ferrara and Bell 1995, Tagliamonte and D'Arcy 2004:509, Tagliamonte and Hudson 1999) suggests that it is a defining characteristic of *be like*. Is it a characteristic of Clara's grammar too?

Table 10.8 shows the distribution of *be like* according to whether the subject is first person or not.

The table shows a marked difference between first person singular subjects, which are encoded with *be like* 88.5% of the time, compared with other types of subjects at 61.6%. Clara replicates the expected pattern.

Note two methodological points. First, the total *N* in this table equals 527 because the 40 tokens of existential *it* were removed. Second, for this reconfiguration of the data all the non-first person singular subjects have been grouped together.[7]

Content of the quote

The content of the quoted material exerts an influence on the use of different quotative verbs. *Be like* appears to have originated to introduce non-lexicalized sounds (8a–c) or gestures (8d) (Butters 1982, Tannen 1986).

(8) (a) So then everybody *was like*, "Boo!" (CF/16/02)
    (b) And I *was like*, "Aww." (CF/18/04)
    (c) And I *was like*, "Ew!" (CF/19/05)
    (d) And everybody *was like*, << slow clapping >> (CF/16/02)

Robust use of *be like* is also associated with the internal thoughts of narrators, as in (9a–c) and (10a–e).

---

[7] The condition file recode is shown in Appendix D.

(9)   (a)   And I *was like*, "I don't feel well."
      (b)   I *was like*, "If I get up now I won't make it to the washroom."
      (c)   But then I *was like*, "If I close my eyes then I might pass out!"
            (CF/19/05)

(10) (a)   ... And then he's *like*, "Don't you change for anybody."
      (b)   So I *was like*, "Ah."
      (c)   I *was like*, "That was nice."
      (d)   so he's *like*, "Well maybe when I become."
      (e)   ... So I *was like*, "Okay." (CF/19/05)

Inner thought may occur juxtaposed with spoken dialogue, as in (11b) and (11d), where Clara is recounting an interaction with her aunt.

(11) (a)   She calls me Lara. "So how's school, Lara." (CF/16/02)
      (b)   I'*m like*, "Oh man!" (CF/16/02)
      (c)   But like, she's called me that so many times that I can't turn back
            and *be like*, "It's Clara." (CF/16/02)
      (d)   Cause I *was-just like*, "Euh, whatever Tita." (CF/16/02)

Use of *be like* for the inner thoughts of protagonists in the speaker's stories is also possible, as in (12c). In this case Clara is recounting a story about one of her teachers.

(12) (a)   He had like, a band-aid on his finger, but it kept coming off.
      (b)   So he put like a condom on it. [1] Oh-my- [01] To keep it in place.
      (c)   And everybody *was like*, "What the hell? Sir?"
      (d)   I dunno, he's so weird like that. (CF/16/02)

To be consistent with the hypotheses in the literature, Clara's use of *be like* should be most frequent with non-lexicalized sounds and gestures, next frequent for inner thought, and least frequent for spoken dialogue.

Table 10.9 shows the distribution of *be like* according to the content of the quote.[8]

Contrary to expectation, the most frequent use of *be like* is with spoken dialogue at 71.4%, followed closely by internal thought at 66.4% and non-lexicalized sound and gesture at 64.7%. For this factor, there appears to be little to distinguish these categories. Content of the quote apparently does not influence the choice of quotative for Clara.

Tense

The tense of the quotative verb also influences the choice of variant. From the earliest research on *be like* it has been found to occur more often in the present

---

[8] The condition file that reconfigured the original coding schema for content of the quote and tense/temporal reference is shown in Appendix E. Note that the Total *N* of 524 reflects the fact that three tokens of quotes of written material were removed from consideration.

Table 10.9 *Overall distribution of* be like *across content of the quote*

	be like %	be like N
Spoken dialogue	71.4	388
Internal thought	66.4	119
Non-lexical sound/gesture	64.7	17
Total *N*		524

tense than in the past tense (Blyth *et al.* 1990, Romaine and Lange 1991, J. V. Singler 1991:272–3). However, occurrences of the present tense are often historic present (HP). The HP is a stylistic device used in story-telling in which events in the past are encoded with present tense morphology for dramatic effect (see Schiffrin 1981, Wolfson 1979, 1981), as in (13a–f).

(13) (a) Because she*'s like*, "Oh, do you guys, ah, like working?"
    (b) And they*'re like*, "No!"
    (c) So then like, "Do you want like civies days or something?"
    (d) So we*'re like*, "Yeah."
    (e) She*'s like*, "Yeah!"
    (f) So then, it*'s like*, "Alright! So, let's get this party started!" (CF/16/02)

The present tense may also be used to recount timeless or habitual events, as in (14a–d).

(14) (a) He*'s* always so *like*, "Oh, okay I gotta remember that." (CF/18/04)
    (b) Most of the time, I*'m like*, "No." (CF/17/03)
    (c) She*'s* always, "Oh, I ran this far in cross-country." (CF/17/03)
    (d) I guess anyone he just sees, he*'s like*, "Hey!" (CF/18/04)

Both of these types must be distinguished, and kept separate from contexts in which past events are recounted with past tense morphology (see Tagliamonte and D'Arcy 2007), as in (15a–d).

(15) (a) Cause Diego *was-just like*, "Oh, I wasn't the one who was like, being aggressive." (CF/16/02)
    (b) . . . And then Nick *was like*, "Shut-up!" (CF/16/02)
    (c) He *was* um, *like*, "So how did they meet?" (CF17/03)
    (d) And I *was like*, "I don't know." (CF/17/03)

In addition, other verbal constructions may also occur, including conditional modals and future as in (16a–e). For now, I will group these types together.

Table 10.10 *Overall distribution of* be like *across tense/aspect*

	%	N
Other	90.5	42
Historic present	89.6	163
Past	75.4	207
Present	67.4	43
		455

(16) (a) It's not like you *can be like*, "Stop the ride!" (CF/16/02)

(b) Man, I'*d be like*, "What the heck? I'll buy you more nuts mom!" (CF/16/02)

(c) I don't want *to be like*, "Oh you have a pouch it looks bad." (CF/19/05)

(d) So, I'm not just *going to be like*, "Euh! You suck, I'm going-to ditch you." (CF/16/02)

(e) I'*ll be like*, "I think you'll fit a nine-ten". So at least if you don't like it, just be like, understanding. (CF/19/05)

Table 10.10 shows the distribution of *be like* according to the tense and temporal reference of the verb phrase.

The analysis of this factor shows that Clara's foremost context for use of *be like* is the "other" tense/aspect constructions at 90.5%. However, these represent a relatively small proportion of the data overall (only 42 tokens, 9.2% of the data) and a diverse range of types. The historic present ranks closely after these at 89.6%. Somewhat lower are past tense constructions at 75.4% and present tense is the most conservative rate at 67.4%. Although the rates of use of *be like* are relatively high across the board, the distinction between historic present contexts in contrast with present and past suggests that this factor constrains the use of *be like* in Clara's grammar.

In sum, the factor by factor distributions in Tables 10.6–10.10 have shown the tendency of the dependent variable (quotative verb) to occur in different contexts (real time, grammatical person, content of the quote, and tense/temporal reference).

Another methodological point is important here. Sometimes in the literature, linguistic forms may be presented according to their *distribution* across factors instead of how they are *influenced* by those different factors. Consider the results in Table 10.11.

The table shows that every quotative verb occurs with spoken dialogue more than any other context. It also shows that speech represents the bulk of the quoted material overall (74%). While this information is interesting, it says

Table 10.11 *Distribution of quotative verbs across content of the quote types*

	Spoken dialogue	Internal thought	Sound/gesture	N
be like	75.5	21.5	3	367
zero	59.8	37	3.3	92
say	97.2	2.8	0.0	36
other	72.4	17.2	10.3	29
Total	388	119	17	524
	74%	*22.7%*	*3.2%*	

nothing about how the different content of the quote types constrain the appearance of variant forms! Compare Table 10.9 and 10.11 to view the difference. Table 10.9 shows that *be like* occurs with internal thought 66.4% of the time, only slightly less than spoken dialogue at 71.4%, whereas Table 10.11 makes it look like *be like* occurs with spoken dialogue 75.5% and with internal thought considerably less, only 21.5% of the time. (But, of course, this would be reading Table 10.11 incorrectly!)

Multivariate analysis

The next step in a quantitative analysis is to ask whether or not any of the factors considered to this point exert a genuine effect or are due to chance. In other words are they statistically significant or not? In order to answer such a question statistical methods are required. One of the most versatile tools for the quantitative analysis of naturally occurring linguistic data is the variable rule program (D. Sankoff 1988b:6). The variable rule program is a statistical tool for modelling the effect of multiple factors (D. Sankoff 1988b:2). This is why it is also referred to as "multivariate analysis." It enables the analyst "to separate, quantify, and test the significance of the effects of environmental factors on a linguistic variable" (Guy 1993:237). The variable rule program can be downloaded for free from various sites on the Internet.[9] Standard descriptions of the variable rule program can be found in the following references: Cedergren and Sankoff 1974, D. Sankoff 1988b, D. Sankoff and Labov 1979, D. Sankoff and Rousseau 1979; and perhaps most clearly in the following digests: Guy 1988, 1993, Young and Bayley 1996, Bayley 2002, Tagliamonte 2006. Paolillo (2002) is perhaps the most detailed with a focus on statistical terms and explanations.

[9] *Goldvarb 2.1*, a system 9 application for Macintosh, can be downloaded at: www.crm.umontreal.ca/~sankoff/GoldVarb_Eng.html *Goldvarb 2001*, an application for Windows, can be downloaded at: www.york.ac.uk/depts/lang/webstuff/goldvarb/ *Goldvarb X*, an application for either Macintosh or Windows, can be downloaded at: http://individual.utoronto.ca/tagliamonte/Goldvarb/GV_index.htm

In order for variable rule analysis to be appropriate the analyst must perceive that there is "a choice between two or more specified sounds, words or structures during performance." The choice must be seemingly haphazard based on known parameters. Finally, the choice must recur repeatedly in discourse. Given these conditions statistical inference can be invoked (D. Sankoff 1988b:2). Variable rules are actually "the probabilistic modelling and the statistical treatment of discrete choices and their conditioning" (D. Sankoff 1988b:2).

Three types of evidence

There are three types of evidence that can, and should, be used to interpret a variable rule analysis. They are: (1) statistical significance; (2) constraint ranking; and (3) relative strength (Poplack and Tagliamonte 2001:92, Tagliamonte 2002:731).

Statistical significance

The variable rule program assesses which factors are statistically significant (at the .05 level) and which are not. Significant factors as well as non-significant factors are important for interpreting the results. Significance of one or a set of specific factor groups may lead to one interpretation. Significance of another factor group (or set) may lead to another.

Constraint ranking

The program also assigns factor weights or probabilities to each category of the factor groups included in the analysis. Constraint ranking is the hierarchy from more to less of the factor weights of categories within a factor group. In essence this is the "grammar" underlying the variable surface manifestations (Poplack and Tagliamonte 2001:94).

Relative strength

An interpretation of the relative strength of each factor group can be assessed by considering: (1) the "range" in each factor group; and (2) the order of selection of factors in the regression analysis. While these are not always meaningful, they are generally helpful to interpretation, especially when there is little interaction in the factor effects. The "range" is determined by subtracting the lowest factor weight from the highest factor weight in the factor group. When these numbers are compared for each of the factor groups in an analysis, the one with highest number (i.e. range) typically identifies the strongest constraint. The lowest number identifies the weakest constraint, and so forth. The order of selection of factors can be found by looking at the progress of the multiple regression, which tells which factor group is selected first, second, and so forth. The order of selection of factor groups typically mirrors the order of strength of factors as assessed by the range. However, this may not always be the case. For example, it is possible that within a factor group a particular environment, represented by a very small number of tokens, might have a near-categorical effect, while the other environments, represented by much larger numbers of tokens, might be much closer. In this case, the range for that factor group might be greater than it would be for another factor group which actually has more effect. This means that if there is conflict between the range and the order of selection of factor groups, it will be necessary to seek other evidence in order to argue for which factor group is actually the strongest.

In sum, the three lines of evidence must be used together in order to arrive at an interpretation, especially if there are conflicting indications. The key to interpreting the results is to make use of the entire analysis.

Table 10.12 shows a variable rule analysis of factors contributing to the probability of *be like* in Clara's speech. It provides all the necessary information for interpreting the quantitative results. The INPUT indicates the overall tendency of the dependent variable (in this case the be like quotative) to surface in the data. The TOTAL N records the total number of contexts treated in the analysis. The *N* records the number of tokens per cell.[10] Each of the factor groups that have been considered in the analysis is listed with the results for each factor. Point-form numbers are FACTOR WEIGHTS. These indicate the probability of the dependent variable to occur in that context. The closer these numbers are to 1, the more highly favoring the effect is; the closer they are to zero the more disfavoring the effect is. The RANGE provides a non-statistical measure of the relative strength of the factor. The higher this number is, the greater the contribution of that factor to the probability of the form. For further discussion of how to use the variable rule program, consult e.g. Tagliamonte (2006: Ch. 7), Young and Bayley (1996), Paolillo (2002).

Let's now put the "lines of evidence" to work. First, all the constraints are statistically significant, except for content of the quote. Second, the direction of effects for each factor group are as predicted in the literature: (1) within the tense/temporal reference factor group, the HP is the most favorable environment for use of *be like* and there is a clear distinction between it and other present tense contexts which pattern similarly to past tense; (2) first person subjects favor *be like* while third persons disfavor; and (3) internal thought favors *be like* over direct speech but this effect is so marginal it is not significant. Third, the range values indicate that the tense/temporal reference of the verb is the strongest factor, followed closely by the grammatical person constraint. Examination of the order of selection of factor groups in the regression shows that grammatical person is selected first. We may conclude that tense/temporal reference of the verb and grammatical person are the most important influences for the use of *be*

---

[10] Note that this value is the denominator, not the numerator. For example, there are 163 tokens of historic present of which 146 are *be like*. 146/163 = 89.6%.

Table 10.12 *Variable rule analysis of contributing factors to the probability of* be like *in Clara's speech*

Input: 0.826			
Overall proportion: 70.0			
Total $N = 527$			
	Factor Weight	%	N
Tense/Temporal reference			
Historic present	**.72**	89.6	163
Past	**.37**	67.4	43
Present	**.30**	75.4	207
Range 38			
Grammatical person			
First person singular	**.74**	88.5	165
Other	**.38**	61.6	362
Range 34			
Content of quote			
Internal thought	[.52]	66.4	119
Spoken dialogue	[.49]	71.4	388
Age			
19	**.56**	73	89
18	**.57**	78.1	196
17	**.39**	63.9	72
16	**.43**	61.8	170
Range 13			

like. Finally, the moderate effect of speaker age shows that the frequency of *be like* is shifting significantly in real time. Late adolescence is the prime time for *be like*.

Comparison

An important facet of variation analysis is its utility for making comparisons. In sociolinguistics, the comparative method involves comparing data sets contrasting age groups in a single community, different speakers interviewed at different points in time, different dialects or communities, etc. Further, the focus of the comparison is on the patterning of linguistic variables. Information arising from the lines of evidence from variation analysis is the key to determining similarities

Table 10.13 *Variable rule analyses of contributing factors to the realization of* be like *in Clara's speech across age*

	Age					
	16–17			18–19		
Overall proportion:	62.4			76.5		
Input	0.77			0.87		
	FW	%	N	FW	%	N
Grammatical person						
First person singular	**.84**	89.8	59	**.67**	87.7	106
Other	**.37**	53.6	183	**.40**	69.8	179
Range	47			27		
Tense/Temporal reference						
Historic present	**.67**	84.1	82	**.78**	**95.1**	**81**
Past	**.37**	68.8	77	**.35**	79.2	130
Present	**.30**	57.9	19	**.31**	75.0	**24**
Range	37			47		
Content of quote						
Internal thought	[.56]	61.8	68	[.47]	72.5	51
Spoken dialogue	[.48]	63.8	160	[.51]	76.8	228

NOTE: Factors not selected as significant in square brackets.

and/or differences (Poplack and Tagliamonte 2001). Let us now determine what such comparisons can tell us.

Clara at different ages

First, I have the possibility to compare Clara's quotative system at different points in real time as she moves from early to late adolescence. Does she maintain the same variable grammar? Recall that previous research has suggested that first person subjects and internal thought favor *be like*, but that as *be like* use continues to rise in frequency, the latter constraint is falling away. Clara, who was 16 years of age in 2002 and whose incidence of *be like* rises until age 17, may well be on the forefront of this development.

Table 10.13 shows two independent variable rule analyses of factors contributing to the realization of *be like* at 16–17 years of age and 18–19 years of age.[11]

Despite the marked increase in frequency of use of *be like* from one time period to the other Clara's variable grammar in these two time periods is remarkably stable. The same factors (grammatical person, tense/ temporal reference) are

---

[11] Recall that these ages patterned together in the analysis in Table 10.12.

Table 10.14 *Variable rule analyses of contributing factors to the realization of* be like *in Clara's speech and other Torontonian teenagers of the same approximate age (17–19)*

	Clara 16–19 [2002–2005]	Torontonian teenagers 17–19 [2002–2004]
Input	.83	.82
Total *N*	527	1992
Tense/Temporal reference		
Historic present	**.72**	**.67**
Past	**.37**↑	**.32**↓
Present	**.31**	**.44**
Range	*41*	*35*
Grammatical person		
First person singular	**.75**	**.55**
Other	**.38**	**.45**
Range	*37*	*10*
Content of quote		
Internal thought	[.52]	**.54**
Spoken dialogue	[.49]	**.49**
Range		*5*

N O T E : Factors not selected as significant in square brackets.

statistically significant and the same factor (content of the quote) is not significant. Further, the ranking of constraints is parallel within each factor group. The one difference is that the relative strength of factors shifts. Grammatical person is the first ranked constraint at age 16–17. However, it is usurped by tense/temporal reference at 18–19. This development appears to be the result of ongoing specialization of *be like* for historic present.

The individual and the group

Next, let us compare Clara's variable grammar for *be like* with that of the rest of her age cohort by making a comparison with the results from large-scale analysis of the same community (Tagliamonte and D'Arcy 2007: Table 2), as in Table 10.14.

The parallels between the two analyses are remarkable. The same constraints are statistically significant with the exception of content of the quote. For Clara, however, even here the direction of effects runs parallel. There is also a small deviation in constraint ranking in the tense/temporal reference factor group in the contrast between past and present tense. For the larger cohort of teenagers, present tense ranks slightly higher than past, whereas for Clara this is the other way round. However, for both data sets, past and present ranks low in comparison to historic present. Finally, relative strength of factors is exactly the same for both

Clara and the other Toronto cohort, with content of the quote lowest of all and the bulk of the explanation is the strong conditioning by tense/temporal reference and grammatical person.

In early studies of *be like* the pragmatic coloring of content of the quote was found to be the strongest constraint on the use of *be like* (e.g. Cukor-Avila 2002, Tagliamonte and Hudson 1999). Research on the wider community in Toronto suggested that this effect is weakening (Tagliamonte and D'Arcy 2004:507).

With all this in mind, the data from Clara must be put in context. She was a member of the age sector of the speech community who was most likely to be advancing change. She was young, female, middle class, upwardly mobile, and, by age 19, in university. Her data is also the most recent material on *be like*, circa 2002–2005. The findings from the analysis, with its strong conditioning by tense/temporal reference, maintenance of the grammatical person constraint, and a defunct pragmatic condition, reveal that Clara was on the forefront of change. The question is, what will happen as she gets older, finishes university and enters the workforce? Only time will tell.

Apparent time/Real time

I also have the possibility of comparing Clara's individual grammar in real time (a panel study) with the same age groups of the population of Toronto in apparent time (a trend study) (Tagliamonte and D'Arcy 2007). This type of comparison would enable us to assess whether Clara, as an individual, is patterning similarly with other members of her age group. Let us consider a simple comparison of frequency levels of *be like* in Figure 10.1.

Figure 10.1 gives us a unique view of the use of *be like* in Toronto. Notice that Clara patterns a little ahead of the mean. Yet her frequency of use of *be like* as well as her trajectory of increasing frequency is parallel with the apparent time results. The other important observation is that in the last period, the point in time when both Clara and the rest of the Toronto teenagers were 19, their rates of *be like* merge. Interestingly, this is considered the age of stabilization of the vernacular (Labov 2001:447). Thus, this coalescence may represent the height of *be like* usage for this generation in Toronto.

Ethnicities

Another dimension to contemporary urban speech communities is the increasing diversity of populations with respect to ethnicity. According to some research, there are dramatic differences in the way different ethnic populations participate in ongoing linguistic change (Fought 2002). Since *be like* is a feature that is undergoing recent and rapid change and is also associated with mainstream, middle-class speakers, it may enable us to "tap in" to such differences. Although Clara was a typical Canadian teenager, she was also a member of a particular

Table 10.15 *Overall distribution of* be like *across ethnic group by content of the quote*

	Jewish		Asian		Anglo-Saxon		Eastern European		Italian	
	%	N	%	N	%	N	%	N	%	N
Content of quote										
Internal thought	67	18	**66**	208	72	82	93	30	97	38
Spoken dialogue	43	70	**76**	890	59	305	89	140	76	141
Total *N*		88		1098		387		170		179

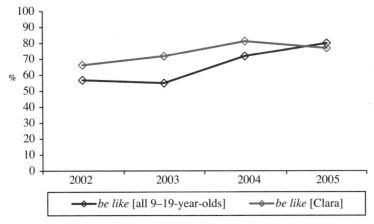

Figure 10.1 *Overall distribution of quotatives in 9–19-year-olds in Toronto English in real time and in Clara Felipe in real time*

ethnic group. Her background, both maternal and paternal, was Filipino. Does this make a difference in her use of *be like*? Given the diverse ethnic mix of our Toronto English corpus, I can now compare Clara's variable grammar for *be like* with other members of her age cohort (17–19-year-olds), now separated by the major ethnic groups in our corpora.

Table 10.15 shows most ethnic groups with the exception of Asian teenagers use *be like* more often for internal thought than spoken dialogue. So does Clara. Her frequency of *be like* was 71% for first person and 66% for "other."

Table 10.16 shows that every ethnic group uses *be like* more often with first person subjects than any other. So does Clara. Her frequency of *be like* was 89% for first person and 62% for "other."

Table 10.17 shows that for most ethnic groups, with the exception of Jewish teenagers aged 17–19, *be like* occurs more often with historic present than present

Table 10.16 *Overall distribution of* be like *across ethnic group by grammatical person*

	Jewish		Asian		Anglo-Saxon		Eastern European		Italian	
	%	N	%	N	%	N	%	N	%	N
Grammatical person										
First person singular	**85**	26	**88**	401	**73**	156	**96**	81	**88**	69
Other	32	68	64	799	53	273	80	113	74	116
Total *N*		94		1200		429		194		185

Table 10.17 *Overall distribution of* be like *across ethnic group by tense/temporal reference*

	Jewish		Asian		Anglo-Saxon		Eastern European		Italian	
	%	N	%	N	%	N	%	N	%	N
Tense/temporal reference										
Historical Present	**76**	9	**94**	128	**100**	33	**100**	16	**84**	138
Past	67	37	77	163	86	36	25	4	64	88
Present	76	10	76	94	81	37	80	5	76	42
Total *N*		56		385		106		25		268

tense or past tense.[12] So does Clara. Her frequency of *be like* was 90% for historic present, 75% for past, and 67% for present.

In sum, the comparison of constraints by ethnicity reveals that in virtually every case the direction of effects runs parallel across the board. There is no evidence here to pursue an interpretation of ethnic differentiation. Indeed, the parallelism among these diverse populations suggests that the diffusion of *be like* in Toronto has no ethnic boundaries.

Future research

The English quotative system offers sociolinguists and other analysts of language an exciting topic for study. The change toward *be like* happened recently and quickly and this feature is still spreading in contemporary varieties of English. As language change progresses the grammar shifts gradually as new forms jostle for

[12] The small numbers for Jewish Torontonians means you cannot place much interpretation into this result.

position in the evolving system. This means that there are new variants coming to the fore. Reports of usages such as *be all* and *be* alone are beginning to be reported (e.g. John Victor Singler 2001) and Clara does evidence rare instances of these, as in (17).

(17) (a) 'Cause on the tread-mill you'd ***be all***, <<panting>> (CF/17/03)
     (b) it*'s just*, "Okay! I'm turning my eyes away." (CF/16/02)
     (c) And then he*'s*, "Good." (CF/16/02)

There is also potential ongoing development in the operation of internal (grammatical) constraints on the use of forms. For example, third person pronouns may be distinct from third person noun phrases in the diffusion of *be like* in the grammar, as in (18a–c).

(18) (a) People ***were like***, "Oh, pacers, pacers!" (CF/18/04)
     (b) Everybody*'s **like***, "Yeah!" (CF/16/02)
     (c) And then Katherine*'s **like***, "Stop, stop!" (CF/18/03)

The separate behavior of noun phrase subjects is typically invisible in contemporary studies because these categories are typically grouped together as third person.

Another development is the spread of *be like* into a variety of tense/aspect constructions, including conditionals, futures, and modals, as shown earlier in (16), as well as in (19a–d).

(19) (a) I *have to **be like***, "Can I help you get a size?" (CF/19/2005)
     (b) In the future I*'d **be like***, "You know what?" (CF/16/2002)
     (c) People *have been **like***, "Oh my God are you kidding me?" (CF/19/2005)
     (d) It's not like you *can **be like***, "Stop the ride!" (CF/16/02)

Recall that these are highly propitious for use with *be like* (see Table 10.10).

Yet another trend is the proliferation of additional specification along with *be like*, particularly the use of adverbial *just,* as in (20a–c).

(20) (a) And I*'m just **like***, "Whatever." (CF/16/02)
     (b) And she ***was just like***, "Yeah, she's really smart." (CF/18/04)
     (c) I ***was just like***, "Can you just kill it?" (CF/19/05)

Precisely how these factors pattern remain to be discovered. They can easily be operationalized by including new factor groups in the analyses.

As time goes on, and the English language moves ever forward on its developmental path, more developments will unfold. It will be exciting to track these changes into the future.

Appendix A: recode for the dependent variable

```
(2
;like
   (l (col 2 l))
;zero
   (0 (col 2 0))
   (0 (col 2 L))
;say
   (s (col 2 s))
;other
   (- (col 2 a))
   (- (col 2 o))
   (- (col 2 b))
   (- (col 2 A))
   (- (col 2 t))
   (- (col 2 T))
   (- (col 2 g))
)
```

Appendix B: coding schema

```
;FG 1: AGE
; 6 = 16
; 7 = 17
; 8 = 18
; 9 = 19
;
;FG 2: DEPENDENT VARIABLE
; l = be like
; L = like alone
; 0 = zero
; s = say
; g = go
; t = tell
; a = ask
; b = be
; A = be all
; T = think
; o = other
;
;FG 3: PERSON
```

; 0 = null subject
; 1 = first pers. sing.
; 2 = second pers. sing.
; 3 = third pers. sing.
; N = singular NP
; 4 = first pers. pl.
; 5 = second pers. pl.
; 6 = third pers. pl.
; P = plural NP
; e = everyone, everybody
; s = someone, somebody
; n = no-one, nobody
; y = impersonal "you", "one"
; i = existential 'it'
; I = referential 'it'
;
;FG 4: TENSE
; 0 = no overt tense
; p = past
; P = present
; h = hist. present
; x = present perfect
; c = conditional
; F = future
; G = going to
; m = modal
; i = imperative
; I = infinitive
; h = habitual
;
;FG 5: ASPECT
; s = simple
; c = continuous
; 0 = no overt tense
;
;FG 6: CONTENT OF QUOTE
; s = speech
; t = thought
; w = writing
; n = non-lexical sound
; g = gesture

Appendix C: remove existential *it* tokens

```
(2
;existential 'it' removed from factor group 3
   (NIL (col 3 i))
)
```

Appendix D: recode grammatical person

```
;grammatical person factor group recoded into
;first person vs. other
(3
   (1 (col 3 1))
   (- (col 3 4))
   (- (col 3 2))
   (- (col 3 3))
   (- (col 3 5))
   (- (col 3 6))
   (- (col 3 n))
   (- (col 3 0))
   (- (col 3 N))
)
```

Appendix E: recode for content of the quote and tense/temporal reference

```
;content of the quote
(6
   (s (col 6 s))
   (t (col 6 t))
   (/ (elsewhere))
)
```

```
;tense/temporal reference
(4
   (P (col 4 P))
   (p (col 4 p))
   (h (col 4 h))
   (/ (elsewhere))
)
```

11 Sociophonetics

ERIK R. THOMAS

What is sociophonetics?

The term *sociophonetics* has been in currency, according to Foulkes and Docherty (in press), at least since Deschaies-Lafontaine (1974) used the term for a study of Québec French. In the span of time since then, it has come to be used in slightly different ways by experimental phoneticians and by sociolinguists. To phoneticians, it generally means any kind of phonetic research that incorporates dialectal variation, as sessions at recent meetings of the Acoustical Society of America and the International Conference on Spoken Language Processing attest. To sociolinguists, however, it has taken on a somewhat narrower meaning. Sociolinguists generally use the term to refer to variationist studies that incorporate methods borrowed from modern phonetics. As a result, sociolinguistic studies that employ only impressionistic, IPA-style phonetic transcription are usually not thought of as "sociophonetics." However, studies that use a variety of techniques used by contemporary phoneticians, ranging from acoustic analysis to perception experiments, certainly are.

The split between phonetic and sociolinguistic notions of what constitutes sociophonetics goes further. Phoneticians tend to use the term for studies that address issues of interest primarily to phoneticians, such as differences in the phasing of articulatory gestures (e.g. Fourakis and Port 1986), differences in the cues used for phonological distinctions (e.g. Kingston and Diehl 1994), or ways that listeners understand the speech of speakers with differing mouth sizes (e.g. Strand 1999). Sociolinguists, on the other hand, usually use the term for studies that address issues of sociolinguistic interest, such as constraints on sound changes (e.g. Labov 1994), ways that dialectal differences can be manifested (e.g. Docherty and Foulkes 1999), or the ability of listeners to recognize identity features of different groups (e.g. Thomas and Reaser 2004). It might be better to reserve the term *sociophonetics* for the more phonetically-oriented kinds of studies and to refer to more sociolinguistically-oriented studies as *phonetic sociolinguistics*, though the name *sociophonetics* is becoming increasingly entrenched among sociolinguists.

Sociolinguists often view sociophonetics (in their definition of the term) as primarily methodological in nature. While a large part of phonetic sociolinguistics does involve adopting techniques developed by phoneticians, it is a mistake, in

215

my opinion, to view sociophonetics as essentially methodological. In fact, socio-phonetics is concerned with addressing some quite basic theoretical issues in lin-guistics, foremost of which is how language is processed cognitively. Although sociolinguists have found phonetic methods useful for studying issues such as mechanisms of sound change and the realization of identity, those methods offer sociolinguistics a means of becoming better incorporated into the rest of linguis-tics because they allow sociolinguistics to address theoretical issues that concern other branches of linguistics. The utility of language variation for such issues and sociolinguists' familiarity with language variation may make sociolinguists better equipped in many cases to address those issues than phoneticians are.

Sociolinguistics has always had an uneasy relationship with the rest of the field because of differences in both methods and theoretical aims. It is no acci-dent that a large fraction of sociolinguists are housed in non-linguistics depart-ments. Sociological approaches have always been part of sociolinguistics, of course. Such approaches, particularly the ethnography of speaking movement led by Dell Hymes, John Gumperz, Charles Ferguson, and others, can legitimately claim to be the oldest forms of sociolinguistics (Murray 1998). The influence they wield over sociolinguistics, however, is a primary reason for the isolation of soci-olinguistics within linguistics. The older generation of quantitative sociolinguists provided a counterbalance with their emphasis on linguistic structure and various attempts to situate sociolinguistics within linguistic theory, such as the variable rule movement (see Fasold 1991) or Labov's efforts to formulate a phonological basis for vowel shifting tendencies (Labov 1991, 1994). In recent years, though, a strong movement toward sociological issues such as power and identity has materialized within sociolinguistics, especially among younger sociolinguists. The sociological focus dominates some topics, such as language and gender, especially thoroughly, as recent collections (e.g. Coates 1998, Hall and Bucholtz 1995) attest. While these issues are unquestionably important from a sociologi-cal standpoint, their influence will inevitably draw sociolinguistics farther from other branches of linguistics. Sociolinguistics thus faces the same sort of threat that led to the demise of dialect geography in North America, in that dialect geography became increasingly concerned with cultural geography issues – especially the relationship between settlement history and lexical variation – during the mid-twentieth century and lost sight of its role as a means of testing linguistic theories (see Pickford [1956], though ironically Pickford was mainly criticizing the utility of dialect geography for sociology). Sociophonetics – or phonetic sociolinguistics – represents a path into the mainstream of linguistics. Whether sociolinguistics will exploit or squander this opening remains to be seen.

History of sociophonetics

Sociophonetics in the sociolinguistic sense appears to begin with Labov, Yaeger, and Steiner (1972), who introduced the acoustic analysis of vowel formants to sociolinguistics. Before that, impressionistic phonetic transcription had been used extensively by students of dialectal variation, including both dialect geographers (most notably Gilliéron and Edmont 1902–10, Jaberg and Jud 1928–43, Kurath and McDavid 1961, Orton, Sanderson, and Widdowson 1978) and sociolinguists (e.g. Labov 1966). Although impressionistic analysis continued to hold sway among sociolinguists (e.g. Milroy and Milroy 1978, Trudgill 1974), vowel formant analysis gradually grew more popular in the field. William Labov provided the impetus for most of this work (e.g. Labov 1980, 1991, 1994) and until the mid-1990s most formant analyses of dialectal variation were conducted by him and/or his students (e.g. Ash 1988, Hindle 1979, Veatch 1991), with infrequent exceptions (e.g. Godinez 1984, Habick 1980, Maclagan 1982). Since 1990, vowel formant analysis has blossomed among scholars without a direct connection to Labov (e.g. Esling and Warkentyne 1993, Fridland 2000, Ito and Preston 1998, Thomas 2001, Thomas and Bailey 1992, Wolfram, Hazen, and Schilling-Estes 1999). Nevertheless, vowel formant analysis has remained far more popular in North America than anywhere else, with only occasional use of it for dialectal analysis elsewhere (e.g. Cox 1999, Maclagan 1982, McClure 1995) and very little outside of English (e.g. Heuven, Edelman, and Bezooijen 2002).

Sociolinguists have had a more difficult time adopting phonetic techniques besides vowel formant analysis. In large part, this slowness has been due to the absence of anyone to fill the pathfinder role that William Labov played for formant analysis. Perception experiments have appeared sporadically and, once again, Labov has played a leading role. Acoustic work on consonantal variation has been meager (Docherty and Foulkes 1999), though Docherty and Foulkes themselves have provided some impetus for further work. Acoustic analyses of prosodic variation have commenced, with most of the work so far focusing on certain features of intonation or on the degree of syllable timing vs. stress timing. Other aspects of prosody remain to be examined. Voice quality variation has attracted almost no scrutiny. These realms of language will be examined in turn in succeeding sections.

Sociophonetic studies by phoneticians have been more diffuse, without the leadership of a single influential figure. As might be expected, phoneticians are interested in different research questions than sociolinguists. Although, as Foulkes and Docherty (1999:22) state, phoneticians have often been "treating variation as a nuisance," they have at times found it useful for their own inquiries. Two exemplary studies are Fourakis and Port (1986) and Munro, Derwing, and Flege (1999). Fourakis and Port compared the speech of Americans and South Africans and found that Americans inserted an epenthetic [t] between the /n/ and /s/ of words such as *dense*, making *dense* homophonous or nearly so with *dents*, while South Africans did not do so. They attributed the difference to differences in "phasing rules," that is, rules governing the relative timing of articulatory gestures. Munro *et al.* had listeners from Canada and Alabama rate Alabamian speakers, Canadians who had always lived in Canada, and Canadians who had moved to Alabama for how Canadian or Alabamian they sounded. Both groups of listeners rated the

Canadians who had moved to Alabama as intermediate between the other two speaker types, suggesting that the mobile Canadians had somehow undergone dialectal accommodation after moving. A further examination of those speakers' vowels and rate of speech revealed some shifting of diphthong quality, but not of rate of speech.

Applications of sociophonetics

Variation and shifting in vowel quality

Vowel formant analysis, as noted above, has become quite popular in North America since Labov *et al.* (1972) introduced it as a sociolinguistic analysis technique. The method is to measure vowel formants, nearly always including F_1 and F_2 (the first and second formants) and often F_3 or even F_4, at a temporal position relevant to the research issues being addressed. Most often, that measurement will be obtained at a position where a formant reaches a maximum or minimum, e.g. where F_1 reaches a maximum, or it will be obtained at the center of the vowel. If the vowel is a diphthong, measurements may be obtained near the onset and offset in order to represent both the nucleus and the glide. A far less commonly used technique is to take measurements at intervals, e.g. one measurement every 10 ms or measurements one-fourth, one-half, and three-fourths through the vowel. In the earlier days of vowel formant analysis, readings were obtained by physically measuring the centers of formants in wideband spectrograms or by estimating formant values from the harmonic peaks in narrowband spectrograms. Today, formant measurements are nearly always obtained by means of a linear predictive coding (LPC) program. LPC estimates formant peaks mathematically. Most acoustic programs have default LPC settings that are appropriate for adult male speech, and researchers may have to adjust the number of poles, or LPC coefficients, if the program gives inappropriate formant readings. For example, the number of poles may need to be lowered for children and some women, and it may need to be raised for nasal vowels.

William Labov has dominated work in vowel formant analysis of dialectal variation. In his most important publications on the subject (Labov 1991, 1994, 2001, Labov, Ash, and Boberg 2006, Labov *et al.* 1972) he has had two related aims: delineating the most important shifting patterns in English and determining a set of principles that describe the recurrent patterns of vowel shifting in the world's languages. His work has focused on vowel nuclei. An important assumption of Labov is that vowels can be divided into a "peripheral" set and a "non-peripheral" set. Peripheral vowels are located along the edge of the vowel envelope in F_1/F_2 space, while non-peripheral vowels are located to the inside, and long or "tense" vowels are usually (but not always) peripheral while short or "lax" vowels are ordinarily non-peripheral.

His solution to determining the predominant vowel shifts of English was to propose that English has three basic shifting patterns. As depicted in Figure 11.1, he named them the Northern Cities Shift, the Southern Shift, and the Third, or Merger, Dialect. The Northern Cities Shift is found in the Great Lakes region of the United States and consists of a rotation of six vowels, the TRAP, LOT, THOUGHT, STRUT, DRESS, and KIT classes (using the names invented by Wells [1982]). Labov (1991, 1994) argued that some Scottish dialects show a similar set of shifts. The Southern Shift occurs in the South of the United States, in southern England, and in Southern Hemisphere English. It consists of peripheralization of the nuclei of KIT and DRESS and concomitant non-peripheralization and lowering of the nuclei of FACE and FLEECE; fronting of GOOSE, GOAT, and perhaps FOOT; nuclear backing or monophthongization of PRICE; and raising or diphthongization of THOUGHT. The shifts off FLEECE, FACE, and PRICE (along with raising of CHOICE) were already known to British linguists as the "diphthong shift" (Wells 1982). In the Third Dialect, the LOT and THOUGHT classes are merged. Labov limited the Third Dialect to Canada and parts of the United States, particularly the West, though the same merger also occurs in parts of Scotland (McClure 1995, Stuart-Smith 1999). He stated that the Third Dialect does not show wholesale vowel shifting like the other two shifting systems, though he conceded that fronting of GOOSE and GOAT had been found in the Third Dialect, and Labov *et al.* (2006) corroborated that fact. He noted that certain dialects not included in one of the major shifting systems, such as those of New York City and Philadelphia, were either mixtures of Northern Cities and Southern Shift features or were changing from one to the other.

The principles of vowel shifting that Labov proposes have undergone several modifications. As laid out in Labov (1994:116ff.), they state that:

Principle I. In chain shifts, long vowels rise.

Principle II. In chain shifts, short vowels fall.

Principle IIa. In chain shifts, the nuclei of upgliding diphthongs fall.

Principle III. In chain shifts, back vowels move to the front. This principle is also stated as "In chain shifts, tense vowels move to the front along peripheral paths, and lax vowels move to the back along non-peripheral paths."

Principle IV, called "the lower exit principle." In chain shifting, low non-peripheral vowels become peripheral.

Principle V, called "the upper exit principle." In chain shifting, the first of two high morae may change peripherality, and the second may become non-peripheral.

Principle VI, called "the mid exit principle." In chain shifts, peripheral vowels rising from mid to high position develop inglides.

Principle VII, called "the redefinition principle." Peripherality is defined relative to the vowel system as a whole.

Principle VIII, called "the unmarking principle." In chain shifts, elements of the marked system are unmarked.

The Northern Cities Shift

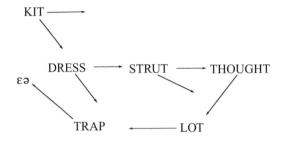

The Southern Shift

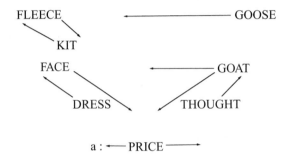

Shifting in the Third Dialect: The Canadian Shift

Figure 11.1 *The three major vowel shifting systems of English*

Among the most noticeable modifications of these rules is the restatement of Principles I and II from Labov (1991), where they were presented, respectively, as "Peripheral nuclei rise" and "Non-peripheral nuclei fall." This change had to do with the behavior of nuclei that are long but non-peripheral. One example of the shifting patterns that Labov (1994:126) provides and which illustrates three of the Principles occurred in North Frisian. In that language, the long vowel /æː/

rose (Principle I) and broke (principle VI) to [iə] and the long /aː/ rose (Principle I) to [æː] while the short /i/ fell (Principle II) to [a].

Few authors have challenged Labov's theories of vowel shifting. Cox (1999) criticized his principles on the grounds that the short LOT set was being raised in Australian English, but this shift would not be problematic in Labov's earlier (1991) formulation because LOT is clearly peripheral in Cox's plots. In Thomas (2003), I offered a different kind of critique, pointing out that shifts attributed to peripherality must have some other, underlying cause(s). For the most part, Labov's ideas have been accepted by North American sociolinguists, and although there has been little research testing his principles of vowel shifting, his demarcation of major shifting patterns has set off a great deal of work. Various researchers have investigated details of the Northern Cities Shift (e.g. Eckert 1989, Gordon 2001, Ito and Preston 1998), the Southern Shift (e.g. Fridland 2000, 2003), and the merger dialect (e.g. Boberg 2005, Clarke, Elms, and Youssef 1995). Clarke *et al.* (1995), in fact, showed that the LOT/THOUGHT merger set off its own chain shift, with lowering of TRAP, DRESS, and KIT, which they called the "Canadian Shift." Subsequent studies have followed up on their discovery. Vowel configurations of African American English and Mexican American English have begun to attract some attention (Fought 1999, Fridland 2003, Thomas 2001, Bailey and Thomas 1998).

One issue that often plays a role in studies of vowel quality is vowel normalization. Vowel normalization techniques have been developed because different speakers have different mouth sizes, which in turn causes their formant resonances to differ. Scholars have proposed numerous normalization formulas. Two useful reviews of normalization formulas are Disner (1980) and Adank, Smits, and van Hout (2004). These two reviews disagree on which techniques are best; Disner favors normalization techniques that rely on vowel-intrinsic information because they yielded better results in cross-linguistic comparisons that she performed, while Adank *et al.* favored techniques that compare a range of vowels because they matched transcriptions by trained impressionistic phoneticians better. Phoneticians often frown on normalization techniques because they tend to see the aim of normalization as modeling human vowel perception and no normalization technique seems to model human auditory processing perfectly – in fact, there is now evidence that human vowel perception does not even employ normalization (Pisoni 1997). Linguists studying dialectal variation in vowels need normalization for a completely different reason, however. To study variation, it is necessary to filter out variation caused by physiology (i.e. differences in mouth size) in order to isolate dialectal variation. Thus, for many types of studies in which vowel quality of different speakers is compared, normalization is crucial.

Other vowel characteristics

Quality, which is reflected in differences in formant values, is the most often studied attribute of vowels. Other attributes have received scant attention. Some work has occurred on dialectal variation in phonation of vowels – see below – but far more is needed. One vowel attribute that is well-known, if seldom studied acoustically, is length. Vowel length can be examined fairly easily by measuring duration in spectrograms if vowel-intrinsic and contextual factors, such as vowel height, overall rate of speech, and position within an utterance, are accounted for (Myers 2005). Relatively few acoustic studies (e.g. McClure 1995) have examined dialectal differences in length, at least in English. Various issues, such as whether dialects or sociolects differ in having a length distinction at all, whether the magnitude of difference between short and long vowels differs, dialectal variation in how length is affected by prosodic factors, and the interaction – as through trading relations – of length with other phonetic cues (such as degree and direction of gliding, phonation, and quality), all warrant attention.

Another factor that can affect vowels is undershoot. Undershoot – the tendency of vowels to show a more schwa-like quality, more coarticulation with neighboring segments, or, for diphthongs, truncation – is often thought of as simply an automatic consequence of durational shortening or weakening of stress. However, as discussed in Thomas (2002a:179–81), it exhibits interspeaker variation in its magnitude and could easily act as a sociolinguistic variable. Moreton and Thomas (in press) show how a dialectal variation in undershoot was one factor that led to the development of "Canadian raising" of /ai/, in which /ai/ nuclei are higher before voiceless consonants than before voiced consonants, in the Cleveland, Ohio, area.

Consonantal variation

Sociolinguistic studies of consonantal variation are common. Among the best-known variables in English are simplification of final consonant clusters, absence of coda /r/ (called "*r*-lessness" or "non-rhoticity"), mutations of /θ/ and /ð/ to other sounds, and deletion of /h/; in Spanish, shift of final /s/ to [h], lenition of /tʃ/ to [ʃ], "ceceo" (in which /θ/, as in *caza* "hunt," remains distinct from /s/, as in *casa* "house") vs. "seseo" (in which /θ/ is merged with /s/), and assibilation of /rr/; in Arabic, reflexes of Classical Arabic /q/ in different forms of Modern Colloquial Arabic. Far less common are acoustic studies of consonantal variation, the consequences of which are bemoaned by e.g. Docherty and Foulkes (1999) and Purnell, Salmons, and Tepeli (2005). The widespread assumption among sociolinguists is that impressionistic transcription of consonantal variation is sufficiently accurate and far more practicable than acoustic analysis. However, acoustic analysis can reveal details that impressionistic transcription overlooks (Docherty and Foulkes 1999) and in some cases impressionistic transcription can lead to mislabeling, as when "deleted" consonants in clusters are present but masked by other consonants (Browman and Goldstein 1990; see Thomas 2002b:116 for further discussion).

Instrumental techniques could be applied to a wide range of consonantal variables. For example, some approximant variables are readily studied acoustically and/or articulatorily. Van de Velde and van Hout (2001) is a collection of studies, mostly impressionistic, on variation in /r/ in several western European languages. However, two of its included papers, Demolin on [ʀ] in Belgian French and Docherty and Foulkes on variation between [ɹ] and [ʋ] in English syllable onsets, include acoustic analyses, and Demolin even shows an x-ray. Another /r/ issue that is important in English, the variation between the "bunched-tongue" [ɹ] (which actually shows pharyngeal, dorsal, and, in syllable onsets, labial constrictions) and the retroflex [ɻ] (which may also show a pharyngeal constriction) is probably best studied through instrumental articulatory analyses because the two sounds are more or less identical acoustically (Mielke, Baker, and Archangeli 2006).

Consonants besides approximants can be studied instrumentally as well. Docherty and Foulkes (1999) and Foulkes and Docherty (in press) examined medial and final voiceless stops in the vernacular speech of two cities in northern England, Newcastle upon Tyne and Derby. They found that medial stops in Newcastle showed two variants. One, which had previously been described impressionistically as [ʔ], turned out to occur frequently as a period of creaky voicing with no stop gap at all. The other variant, previously described as a glottalized stop, such as [ʔt], also proved to lack stop gaps much of the time, though it included a burst. Newcastle also featured distinctive variants for final stops. Continuation of voicing well into the "voiceless" stop was common, and frication or "preaspiration" of the final stop was frequent and increasing. These variants were rare or absent in Derby. Foulkes and Docherty's findings give some indication of how fruitful acoustic analysis of consonantal variation could be on a wider scale. Other consonantal variants, such as the taps that occur as positional variants of coronal stops in American and Australian English, could easily be studied acoustically.

A different type of consonantal variation is variation in the cues that signal consonantal contrasts. Voice Onset Time, or VOT, describes the interval of time between a stop burst and the onset of vocal fold vibration. It is widely recognized in phonetics as a factor that distinguishes voiced and voiceless stops in syllable onsets, yet it varies from language to language. For example, in Spanish, voiced stops show vocal fold vibration well before the burst, while voiceless stops show a short interval between the burst and subsequent vocal fold vibration; in English, voiced stops often show little vocal fold vibration before the burst, but voiceless stops, because they are aspirated, show a long lag between the burst and the onset of vibration. Not surprisingly, dialectal variation has been observed in VOT. Syrdal (1996) found variation among American dialects in VOT of word-initial /p/ and /b/, with Westerners showing the greatest differentiation between /p/ and /b/ and New Yorkers the least. VOT is especially prone to dialectal variation in language contact situations. Heselwood and McChrystal (1999) found that British speakers with a Punjabi substrate showed different VOT patterns than cohorts without a substrate language. VOT is not the only cue that can vary dialectally, however. Purnell, Salmons, and Tepeli (2005) examined coda consonants in the speech of German-substrate natives of one Wisconsin town. German does not contrast voicing for coda consonants. They found that their speakers failed to produce two cues used by non-substrate speakers, the F_0 and F_1 contours preceding the consonant, and hypercorrected a third cue, the presence or absence of vocal fold vibration. In a related study, Purnell, Tepeli, Salmons, and Mercer (2005), analyzing speakers from across southeastern Wisconsin, found a diachronic shift in cues to consonant voicing. The oldest speakers showed little differentiation of preceding vowel length between voiced and voiceless obstruents but considerable glottal pulsing during voiced obstruents; the youngest speakers showed substantial differentiation of preceding vowel length but less glottal pulsing during voiced obstruents. In Thomas (2000), I found that the height of a preceding /ai/ glide could serve as a cue to the voicing of a following consonant and that the magnitude of this cue was much greater for non-substrate speakers of American English than for speakers with a Spanish substrate, both in production and in perception. The same study found cross-dialectal differences in the frequency of realization of stop releases, suggesting another consonantal variable that could be studied.

Intonation, tone, and tone-accent

Instrumental studies of intonation, tone, and tone-accents – the last characterizing languages such as Swedish, Japanese, and Serbo-Croatian in which some, but not all, words show distinctive tones – generally rely on pitch tracks, normally produced through the autocorrelation method. Current autocorrelation techniques work well for modal phonation, but poorly for breathy voicing and especially poorly for creaky voicing. In such cases, the best alternative may be simply to measure F_0 from narrowband spectrograms, though this method is exceedingly time-consuming if many time points are needed. Because breathiness grades into voicelessness, at some point F_0 will become unmeasurable if the voicing becomes breathy enough.

Studies of intonation that employ pitch tracking usually relate what the pitch tracks show to some transcription system. In recent years, the most popular transcription system – and the one used in most studies of dialectal variation in intonation – has been the Tone and Break Index, or ToBI, system (Beckman and Hirschberg 1994). This system, though originally designed for standard varieties of English, has been adapted for various other languages. ToBI transcription is ordinarily accomplished through a combination of impressionistic listening and examination of pitch tracks. Level tones, falling and rising contours, resetting of the pitch after major intonational breaks, and pauses that are transcribed can all be identified in the pitch tracks. In addition to features of F_0, variations in amplitude are also utilized, especially in the identification of IP and ip breaks. ToBI recognizes several levels of intonational categories, the most important of which are intonational phrases (IP), which involve a resetting of pitch at their beginning, and intermediate phrases (ip), which do not show a complete reset but consist of a pause or hesitancy. As with other intonational transcription systems, prominent tones are called pitch accents. ToBI includes two basic pitch accent tones, high (H*) and low (L*), which may be augmented by rises or falls, and two boundary tones, high (H%) and low (L%), which are marked at the end and uncommonly at the beginning of IPs. Downstepping of pitch accents is also marked. ToBI transcriptions have separate tiers for marking of tones and for marking of what level an intonational break represents.

Dialectal or stylistic studies of intonational variation are noticeably more common in Europe than in North America. Among the most prominent students of intonational variation are Esther Grabe in England (e.g. Grabe, Post, Nolan, and Farrar 2000); Peter Auer, Margret Seltung, and their colleagues in Germany (e.g. Seltung 2003); and Carlos Gussenhoven in the Netherlands (e.g. Gussenhoven and van der Vliet 1999). An excellent sampling of European work on dialectal variation in intonation is Gilles and Peters (2004), which contains papers on intonation of varieties of German, Italian, Greek, and British English, as well as one on German/Portuguese bilinguals in Brazil. In the Western Hemisphere, there has been relatively little work on non-English languages (see Willis [2003], who compares dialects of Spanish, and Kaminskaia and Poire [2004], who compare Québec French with European French).

Within English, a few selected intonation features have attracted variationist attention. Perhaps the best known is "high rising terminals," or "uptalk," in which intonational phrases show a high final boundary tone instead of the usual low tone. This feature shows correlations with social class, gender, and style. It appears to be quite prevalent in New Zealand (Britain 1992, Warren 2005) but also occurs elsewhere in the English-speaking world (e.g. Guy, Horvath, Vonweiler, Daisley, and Rogers 1986, McLemore 1991). Another dialectal feature that has been studied is whether a dialect exhibits compression or truncation of F_0 contours when the intonational phrase is short. Grabe *et al.* (2000) and Grabe (2004) note that dialects in the British Isles show considerable variation in this regard, and work on it is needed in other English-speaking countries. The British Isles also offer plenty of other intonational variation, as articles such as Pellowe and Jones (1978) and Douglas-Cowie, Cowie, and Rahilly (1995) indicate. Within the United States, a large fraction of the meager research conducted on dialectal intonation has focused on minority dialects. African American English is known to show distinctive intonational patters (Loman 1975, Tarone 1973), though instrumental work has been limited (Cole, Thomas, Britt, and Coggshall 2005, Jun and Foreman 1996). Mexican American English is also reported to show distinctive intonation (Penfield and Ornstein-Galicia 1985:47–52), but work on it has been even more limited.

Studies of tone and tone-accent are not as frequent or are less accessible in the West. Both can be studied using the same techniques. For example, Bauer, Cheung, and Cheung (2003) examined a possible merger of tones in Hong Kong Cantonese using F_0 measurements at designated points through the course of vowels. Their use of these designated sampling points, along with a normalization procedure for F_0, allowed for inter-speaker comparisons. They were able to show that the two tones were distinct for some speakers but apparently merged for others.

Rhythm

By far the largest fraction of linguistic work on rhythm has concerned the opposition of syllable timing versus stress timing. In syllable-timed languages, each syllable is supposed to have approximately the same length, regardless of stress. In stress-timed languages, each foot is supposed to have approximately the same length, with stressed syllables significantly longer than unstressed syllables and stressed syllables in monosyllabic feet longer than stressed syllables in polysyllabic feet. In the past, the emphasis was placed on inter-linguistic differences; for example, Germanic languages were regarded as stress-timed, while Romance languages and Greek were regarded as syllable-timed (Abercrombie 1967, Pike 1945). Subsequently, however, it was shown that the reputed distinctions do not hold: syllable-timed and stress-timed languages do not differ significantly in inter-stress duration, and syllable durations may vary widely in syllable-timed languages (Borzone de Manrique and Signorini 1983, Dauer 1983, Roach 1982, Wenk and Wiolland 1982). Furthermore, research suggested that syllable timing and stress timing represented a continuum instead of an absolute difference (Miller 1984, Ramus, Nespor, and Mehler 1999:268–9). Dauer (1983) and Ramus *et al.* (1999) asserted that stress and syllable timing were simply functions of the phonological structures of languages – to wit, whether they exhibit vowel reduction in unstressed syllables and whether they allow consonant clusters and coda consonants. Not all researchers agree that rhythm is entirely an artifact of phonological structure, though. Gut, Urua, Adouakou, and Gibbon (2002) presented evidence from west African languages that it is not.

Simultaneously, researchers have developed mathematical formulas to gauge stress timing/syllable timing. Ramus *et al.* (1999) developed a formula based on phonological structure. Low and Grabe (1995) and Low, Grabe, and Nolan (2000) created a different formula, which they dubbed the Pairwise Variability Index (PVI), that is calculated based on the relative durations of vowels in adjacent syllables. Deterding (2001) developed his own formula, the Variability Index (VI), which is based on durations of entire syllables, not just the vowels.

These formulas, especially the PVI formula, have proved useful for intralinguistic comparisons. Most such studies thus far have examined varieties of English with influence from one or more syllable-timed substrate languages. Low and Grabe (1995), Low *et al.* (2000), and Deterding (2001) all compared Singapore English, which is spoken as a second language by the majority of its speakers, with standard British English. All three studies arrived at the result that Singapore English is clearly more syllable-timed than British English. Gut (2002) and Udofot (2003) found that at least some speakers of Nigerian English, which is also a second language for most of its speakers, are more syllable-timed than

British English speakers. Fought and Fought (2002) and Carter (in press) both found evidence that Mexican American English is more syllable-timed than Anglo-American English. Thomas and Carter (2006), using the PVI method, compared several groups of speakers from the US South, mostly from North Carolina. They found that European Americans and contemporary African Americans were both quite stress-timed, that Spanish produced by Mexican Americans was strongly stress-timed, and that Mexican American English and Jamaican English were intermediate. The latter two varieties show incontrovertible substrate influences. When they examined recordings of African Americans born before 1865, they found that these speakers showed intermediate rhythm characteristics as well, suggesting that substrate influence may have affected earlier African American English.

Although this opposition of syllable timing to stress timing has received nearly all the scholarly attention directed toward rhythm, other rhythmic differences are also possible. For example, two varieties that appear alike on the stress timing/syllable timing continuum could still lengthen or shorten different elements within phrases. Such differences could easily be interconnected with features of intonation. Detailed work is needed to tease out possible rhythmic differences of this sort.

Voice quality

Sociolinguists have seldom ventured into work on voice quality. For that matter, experimental phoneticians have devoted far less attention to it than to other topics. Most work on voice quality continues to be conducted by speech pathologists. As a whole, sociolinguists have tended to write off voice quality as a physiological factor, a trait of individual voices, and have not recognized the potential for voice quality to serve as a group identity marker. Henton and Bladon (1985) note a danger in this attitude: speech pathologists are liable to view deviations in voice quality as abnormalities that require therapy, and without sociolinguists to counterbalance them, they can easily misdiagnose what are actually sociolinguistic differences.

Of the few sociophonetic studies of voice quality that have been published, a number focus on phonation – i.e. the continuum between creaky voicing and breathy voicing – especially on breathy voicing. Henton and Bladon (1985) compared the speech of male and female speakers of two dialects of British English and found that females were typically breathier than males. They argued that this difference was sociolinguistic, not physiological. Di Paolo and Faber (1990), Di Paolo (1992), Faber (1992), and Faber and Di Paolo (1995) presented evidence that, in Utah English, vocalic distinctions that are no longer realized through formant differences may be preserved as phonation differences. These studies all relied on spectral decay to gauge breathiness. That is, in breathy voicing, the fundamental frequency shows a greater amplitude, relative to higher harmonics, than it does for modal or creaky voicing, and thus phonation can be measured by comparing the relative amplitudes of F_0 and other harmonics. Another way to determine breathiness is the Cepstral Peak Prominence (CPP) method described by Hillenbrand, Cleveland, and Erickson (1994). Instead of spectral decay, it measures overall spectral tilt. Considerable high-frequency aperiodic noise characterizes breathy voicing, and the CPP formula captures the degree of this noise that is present. Shrivastav and Sapienza (2003) evaluate various methods of measuring breathiness and rate the CPP method as most accurate. However, the CPP method is more difficult to use.

Breathiness is certainly not the only feature of voice quality that may be sociolinguistically relevant. Creakiness may also characterize some dialects or speech styles. It is commonly measured either by taking an F_0 value, which will be especially low for creaky voicing, or by measuring the amplitudes of the lowest harmonics. With creakiness, F_0 shows a lower amplitude than the second (or sometimes the third) harmonic.

Nasality is often popularly associated with certain dialects, but it has attracted little attention from sociophoneticians. One possible reason is that popular descriptions of dialects as "drawling," "clipped," "twang," "brogue," or "nasal" are often meaningless. Nonetheless, some individuals show extra nasality because of incomplete closure of the velum, and it stands to reason that dialects could differ in their overall degree of nasality. Generally, when extra nasality is described, it is associated with vowels. One means of measuring nasality is to search for nasal antiformants. Antiformants often appear clearly on power spectra, but they can be isolated more easily by creating power spectra after inverse filtering of the signal. Another method, suggested by Chen (1995) and refined by Plichta (2006), involves comparing the amplitudes of oral and nasal formants; Plichta recommends computing the difference between the amplitudes of the first oral and the second nasal formant. A quite different method is to use a device that measures a speaker's oral and nasal airflow. Plichta (2002, 2006) used both the method that compares oral and nasal formants and an airflow-measuring device and found that a greater degree of overall nasality was correlated with presence of the Northern Cities Shift.

Beyond phonation and nasality, a wide variety of other voice quality features are also distinguished. Some dialects may exhibit a lower overall F_0 than others, as Hudson and Holbrook (1981) and Walton and Orlikoff (1994) reported for African American English. Analyses of harmonics-to-noise ratio, jitter (local F_0 perturbation), and shimmer (local amplitude perturbation) can be performed, as Walton and Orlikoff (1994) and Purnell, Idsardi, and Baugh (1999) did in comparisons of African American English with other ethnic varieties. These measures, however, subsume numerous other voice quality factors. Unfortuately, there are no widely followed acoustic techniques for measuring most of the specific factors that speech pathologists examine. As a result, these features are ordinarily measured impressionistically using specially trained judges. In addition to phonation and nasality, they rate lip protrusion; whether the jaw is open, close, or protruded; pharyngealization and faucalization; tendency for the tongue body and tongue tip to show non-modal placement; overall height of the larynx; and laryngeal tension. Two detailed examples of this method are Esling (1978), who examined voice quality in Edinburgh English, and Stuart-Smith (1999), who analyzed voice quality in Glasgow English. Both studies found correlations between voice quality and social class, and Stuart-Smith also found a correlation with gender. These findings suggest that, in shying away from voice quality analyses, sociolinguists are overlooking a whole family of variables that could be important markers of virtually any dialect and of speech styles as well.

Perception

The preceding components of phonetics have been discussed in terms of speech production. However, they should all be thought of in terms of perception as well. Perception studies of variation have not been quite as extensive as production studies. Nevertheless, the importance of perception should not be underestimated. At the same time, the potential for perceptual research is virtually limitless. Fortunately, interest in perception has been increasing among sociolinguists.

Researchers have generally focused on particular issues in perception instead of on the various components of phonetics. In Thomas (2002b), I divided the various socio-perceptual studies into five groups, according to the basic issues they addressed. The first of these issues is the ability of listeners to distinguish groups of speakers. This issue encompasses a number of related questions, including whether listeners can identify or distinguish the groups in question, what phonetic cues they use to do so, whether and why some listeners are better at the task than others, and whether some speakers are easier than others to identify. This general issue, or set of related questions, has been quite fertile. Perhaps the most popular demographic constituency for speech identification experiments has been African Americans. As reviewed in Thomas and Reaser (2004), at least thirty studies have involved experiments on the discriminability of African Americans and European Americans, beginning with Dickens and Sawyer (1952), and among them they have addressed all the questions noted above. This work can have social and legal applications, as Purnell *et al.* (1999) and Baugh (this volume) note. Elsewhere, Renée van Bezooijen and her colleagues have been actively engaged in investigations of dialect distinguishability and intelligibility, mainly in Dutch (Bezooijen and Berg 1999, Bezooijen and Gooskens 1999, Bezooijen and Ytsma 1999). They have been successful at determining how able listeners are at identifying and understanding regional dialects and at pinpointing particular cues. Quite recently, Clopper and Pisoni (2004a, 2000b) have taken a similar approach, testing how well subjects can identify American English dialects by ear and determining the cues they use but also determining the similarity of those dialects based on subjects' responses by means of cluster analysis.

The second issue is whether listeners' preconceived notions affect their perception. Work in this area is limited, but it has shown that preconceptions about speakers can affect perception. Strand (1999) demonstrated that listeners shift their segmental perceptual boundaries depending on what sex they think a speaker is. Niedzielski (1999) showed that listeners can do the same depending on where they think a speaker is from.

The third issue is how dialectally varying mergers and splits are perceived. Perhaps the most prominent studies of this type are Janson and Schulman (1983) and Labov, Karen, and Miller (1991). Janson and Schulman presented evidence that speakers of the Lycksele Swedish dialect could not perceive a distinction that they produced in their speech. Labov *et al.* objected to the experimental technique that Janson and Schulman employed, which involved having listeners identify synthetic words presented in isolation, and devised a more elaborate experiment that tested whether Philadelphians could perceive in a context a contrast that was nearly merged in their speech. Results showed that their ability to do so was impaired, but that control listeners did not show the impairment.

The fourth type of issue is whether speakers of different dialects categorize sounds differently. Janson (1983) examined the perceptual boundary between /aː/ and /oː/ in Stockholm Swedish, where /aː/ has been shifting toward /oː/. He found that the perceptual boundary differed for older and younger Stockholmers, reflecting the shift in production, but that the perceptual shift was not as fast as the production shift. Labov and Ash (1997) investigated the degree to which natives of Philadelphia, Chicago, and Birmingham, Alabama, could understand each other's vowels. They played excised words and words in context uttered by speakers of each urban dialect to listeners from each city. A surprising result was that listeners had difficulty with some vowels from their own dialect, but they were still more accurate at identifying them than speakers from the other two dialects.

The final kind of issue is investigation of stereotypical attitudes about particular groups, often called subjective reaction experiments. The classic study in this category is Lambert, Hodgsen, Gardner, and Fillenbaum (1960), which popularized the "matched guise" design in which the same individuals speak in two different languages or dialects. Lambert *et al.* found that both Anglo-Canadian and French Canadian listeners rated speakers more highly on various traits, such as intelligence, when they were speaking English than when they were speaking French. Most subjective reaction experiments have been carried out by social psychologists (see Giles and Powesland [1975] for a review of earlier work), but sociolinguists have occasionally conducted them with dialectal differences (e.g. Bezooijen 2002, Frazer 1987).

Cognitive processing of language

Sociophonetics can allow sociolinguists to address a number of issues related to the cognitive processing of language, such as how particular sounds are processed, how language acquisition takes place, or even how it is possible for sound changes to diffuse among speakers who are past the "critical period" of language acquisition. I discussed some aspects of the processing of particular sounds in Thomas (2002a). The examples discussed there involved low-level phonetic processes that are not contrastive but which still vary from dialect to dialect. These low-level processes range from the differences in phasing of articulatory gestures described by Fourakis and Port (1986) to differences in what cues are used to signal distinctions, as discussed by Purnell, Salmons, and Tepeli (2005), to differences in the degree to which undershoot processes affect one's speech, as discussed above. Dialectal differences in these low-level processes demonstrate that they are not automatic consequences of articulation but, instead, are cognitively encoded. Evidence from language variation has thus shown that cognitive encoding goes beyond the feature specifications that constitute what has traditionally been thought of as phonology. Further work is needed to define the scope of cognitive encoding on low-level phonetics, however, and information about dialectal variation is most likely the best tool for filling this picture out.

Probably the most promising theoretical area for which sociophonetics can contribute handsomely in the future is in testing exemplar theory. Exemplar theory is a new approach to phonology with a strong phonetic bent, and its main premise is that people construct their phonologies based on a bank of stored memories of words and phrases that they have heard other people utter (Hawkins 2003, Johnson 1997, in press, Pierrehumbert 2003, Pisoni 1997; see also Coleman 2002). It differs from older approaches to phonology in several important respects. One key difference is that the lexical and indexical aspects of language are seen as interconnected, not as separate modules. Foulkes and Docherty (2006) note that this feature of exemplar theory fits well with sociolinguistic findings that, for example, speakers are adept at using appropriate variants in different speaking styles. Sociolinguists could provide valuable data on speakers' command of styles and their ability to recognize dialectal variants that could be used to test the link between lexical and indexical meanings.

Another notable difference from older approaches is that, as Johnson (1997:146) states, "no abstract category prototypes [i.e., phonemes] are posited." Instead, sound categories are loosely delimited perceptual entities that can be seen as probability distributions of tokens that listeners experience hearing. Positing uncertain boundaries for sound classes could be useful to variationists because it can account for the difficulty that many speakers have, for example, in identifying whether the vowels of *sing* and *fear* belong to the same class as *beet* or *bit* or in identifying the vowels of *tore* and *toll* with any other vowel class (Guenter 2000). The more traditional alternative to exemplar theory, prototype theory, holds that individuals have norms with targets for each sound class. Among the stronger evidence for prototype theory is the "perceptual magnet effect" (Kuhl 1991), a tendency for listeners to perceive sounds as closer to the sounds of their own speech than they really are. Experiments involving language variation are the most obvious way to discriminate between exemplar theory and prototype theory.

Exemplar theory was first applied to speech normalization (Coleman 2002, Johnson 1997, Pisoni 1997). Previous attempts to explain how listeners are able to understand a variety of voices had all failed because different voices are not scaled the same way: for example, male and female voices are not scaled alike (Fant 1966). Evidence that speech perception improved as a listener grew more familiar with a speaker's voice was also poorly explained by traditional normalization theories. It was demonstrated that people have a surprisingly detailed memory of the voices of different speakers, eliminating the need for a normalization process because available storage space in the brain does not limit phonological knowledge to abstract categories. Of course, two consequences of such detailed memory are that listeners can learn to recognize numerous dialects and that their aptitude at understanding a dialect should increase with experience, which sociolinguists could readily test.

Language acquisition has also provided evidence for exemplar theory. Pierrehumbert (2003:185) noted that acquisition of phonological categories is gradual, not sudden, and is not identical to adult speech even by age twelve. Foulkes and Docherty (2006) discuss the potential for sociolinguistic use of exemplar theory with examples from child acquisition of local variants of /p/, /θ/, and /k/ in Newcastle upon Tyne, England. They note that the gradualness of acquisition of the different variants is correlated with their frequency and with what groups within the community use them more often. Observations from various other sociolinguistic studies that phonetic variables remain malleable throughout adolescence provide key evidence for the gradualness of acquisition (e.g. Eckert 1989, Labov 2001). One difference between the conventional sociolinguistic approach and the exemplar approach, however, is that the former assumes that adolescent acquisition of new variants is deliberate and conscious at some level, while the latter permits unintentional and completely subconscious acquisition. This difference has important consequences for explanation of the diffusion of linguistic changes and for the exact relationship between prestige and diffusion. That is, prestige could affect language in terms of whom a speaker associates with and pays attention to – thus gaining more exemplars from those people – more than from a deliberate focus on particular linguistic variants. Sociolinguists can certainly test this possibility.

Prospects

Sociophonetics, or phonetic sociolinguistics, has always depended on technological innovations. The increase in speed of spectrographic analysis since Labov *et al.* (1972) first introduced acoustic techniques to sociolinguistics and the shift from spectrographs to spectrographic computer software have aided the development of sociophonetics. So have improvements in speech synthesis, which have facilitated research on perception. Sociophoneticians could take greater advantage of other technology, such as electropalatography and x-ray microbeams. The future will bring further innovations. One of the most promising is development in brain scanning technology. This technology could ignite work on how neurons react in, say, different sociolectal situations, which, in turn, could address cognitive processing of language directly. Sociolinguists constantly need to remind other linguists about why sociolinguistic considerations are relevant to theoretical questions that concern the rest of linguistics. This kind of engagement will provide sociolinguists with a means of becoming better integrated with other branches of linguistics – if sociolinguists choose to follow this path.

PART 3

Applications

12 Sociolinguistic variation and education

CAROLYN TEMPLE ADGER AND
DONNA CHRISTIAN

Introduction

Improved understanding of, and sensible approaches to, linguistic and cultural diversity in society are increasingly critical to promote equity and respect, particularly in schools and workplaces, for members of all groups in our society. Language is a core element, both in real differences and in the symbolic proxy it provides for other social parameters, such as ethnicity. Headlines in recent years on hot issues such as Ebonics and bilingual education demonstrate the widespread misunderstanding of the underpinnings of those educational issues and of language in general. While scholars understand many of the linguistic principles underlying variation in language and multilingualism in society, the many educational and social issues that arise in connection with diversity remain significant challenges.

Better information and understanding of how language works and how people learn languages is sorely needed. Myths and misconceptions about language pervade public discourse and underlie policy decisions at all levels, and those knowledgeable about language need to be involved in those conversations. These issues were underscored by a panel convened by the National Science Foundation to consider the development of human capital, identifying research questions for the future and potential areas for contributions from linguistics (Wolfram and Schilling-Estes 1996b). The panel set its premise as follows:

> Given the cognitive basis of the human language faculty and the sociocultural context in which language use is embedded, linguistic investigation has played and should continue to play a central role in advancing our basic understanding of the effective utilization of human capital.   (1996b:1)

The group found strong links between linguistic research and potential contributions to issues that are basic to building human capital, on such themes as "educating for the future" (1996b:6); "employing a productive workforce" (1996b:8); and "reducing disadvantage in a diverse society" (1996b:9). The results of sociolinguistic inquiry are an important component of the response to this call for action since the relationship between linguistic and social phenomena is at the core of the work. Sociolinguistics has a strong tradition of interpreting and applying research for practical social benefit. It is in the very nature of the field that social consciousness runs high, since many of the questions addressed intersect with real-world issues. The study of vernacular dialects presents interesting theoretical questions about how to account for language differences linguistically or how to map the relationship between linguistic and social factors. At the same time, study of vernacular dialects is likely to bring the researcher face to face with consequences of the use of vernaculars in social contexts like schools and workplaces. As a result, sociolinguists have traditionally reached out to apply their knowledge to attempt to improve the world in which they live.

As researchers have attempted to extend their influence, they have begun to articulate a rationale for applying sociolinguistic research in the form of a set of principles pointing to the researcher's social obligations beyond the research community:

(1) *The Principle of Error Correction:* "A scientist who becomes aware of a widespread idea or social practice with important consequences that is invalidated by his own data is obligated to bring this error to the attention of the widest possible audience" (Labov 1982:172).

(2) *The Principle of the Debt Incurred:* "An investigator who has obtained linguistic data from members of a speech community has an obligation to use the knowledge based on that data for the benefit of the community, when it has need of it" (Labov 1982:173).

(3) *The Principle of Linguistic Gratuity:* Investigators who have obtained linguistic data from members of a speech community should actively pursue positive ways in which they can return linguistic favors to the community (Wolfram 1993:227).

From the early days of sociolinguistics, researchers have observed these principles in connecting their work to social endeavors. Sociolinguistic inquiry is rooted in a desire to explore linguistic phenomena in real contexts and to address social issues using the results of that research. The field of education has been a prime locus for applying sociolinguistic insights because of the central, but often hidden, role that language plays in many aspects of schooling. This is especially true for research on vernacular dialects, which have been and continue to be stigmatized in school, as they are in other social domains, but perhaps more so there because of the decidedly middle-class values that schools have preserved. The message for educators has always been lodged in the sociolinguistic understanding that systematic variation is a natural and normal linguistic phenomenon, rather than evidence of language breakdown. From a scientific perspective, no dialect is better or worse than another, and social systems that routinely privilege some dialects as standard, as schools do, do so on the basis of tradition, not science. Information on regular contrasts among language varieties can be used in various ways at school.

Despite the history of the connections between sociolinguistics and education, these views have not had the profound effect on practice that sociolinguists have hoped for. As an example, the Standards of Learning spelled out by the Virginia Board of Education indicate for every grade level that students will use "grammatically correct language" in speaking and adhere to Standard English conventions in writing (www.doe.virginia.gov/VDOE/Superintendent/Sols/2002/EnglishK-12.doc [last-accessed May 26, 2007]). The standards do not mention that students need understanding of language variation and of dialects in which these rules apply variably. Nor do they allow for or encourage interpretations of the standards that are sensitive to the dialects that students learn in their home communities. This chapter provides an overview of iconic links in the sociolinguistic variation/education connection and speculates about why its impact on curriculum, teachers, and students in United States schools is still rather limited.

Sociolinguistics and education: early connections

The relevance of sociolinguistic research to education began to be discussed in the 1960s by way of articles such as Labov's (1970) "The logic of non-standard English," which have turned out to be foundational in educational linguistics. Following the Principle of Error Correction, Labov attacked the concept of verbal deprivation that was current at the time in psychological testing – the notion that poor children tended to lack the amount and type of linguistic stimulation required for cognitive development, because their families did not talk to them enough. Labov pointed out that the assumptions about the nature of poor children's language that underlie both psychological tests and the testing situation were at odds with the findings of his research team that African American children were growing up with a high level of verbal stimulation and well-formed language. The schools, he said, did not encourage the kinds of speech activities in which children demonstrated their verbal expertise in the communities he was studying. The mismatch between the linguistic environment in the community and that in the school put them at disadvantage. Far from being the objective reflections of children's language abilities that they were considered to be, the tests and the situations in which they are administered reflect the generally middle-class assumptions about language that thread through the educational enterprise – for example, that displaying known or obvious information is valuable and that linguistic expertise can be measured by a testing task in which the child describes an object that is in full view of the adult who is administering the test.

At about the same time, Wolfram began to contribute sociolinguistic findings (e.g. Wolfram 1969) to another field that tests students' language – speech/language pathology (Wolfram 1970). Researchers and practitioners in that field who were aware of ongoing sociolinguistic research had recognized the need for evidence that could begin to erode the unwarranted assumptions about vernacular dialect and language development underlying diagnosis and placement in speech/language services (e.g. Taylor 1969). The tests being used to assess children's linguistic development assumed that normal development was marked by Standard English features and that deviation from that norm represented developmental delay. These tests, like those used in psychological assessments, were administered to children who had been referred by their classroom teachers as possibly demonstrating delayed development. Thus educational practice that was not informed by sociolinguistic understandings was likely to be compounded, with lasting consequences for students' school biographies.

Other early applications of linguistic and sociolinguistic research occurred in the area of reading instruction (Baratz and Shuy 1969, Laffey and Shuy 1973). Given research in bilingual education showing that children who learn to read in their dominant language are more successful, sociolinguists theorized that young speakers of vernacular dialects might benefit from early reading instruction in their own dialect. Thus a speaker of African American English might more easily read Version 2 below than Version 1.

> Version 1: *Standard English*
> "Look down here," said Suzy.
> "I can see a girl in here.
> The girl looks like me.
> Come here and look, David.
> Can you see that girl?"
>
> Version 2: *Vernacular Black English*
> Susan say, "Hey you-all, look down here!
> I can see a girl in here.
> The girl, she look like me.
> Come here and look, David!
> Could you see the girl?"
>   (Wolfram and Fasold 1969:52)

Texts incorporating vernacular features, called *dialect readers*, were developed for use in helping children build basic reading skills. They would later move on to reading texts in which vernacular and standard dialect versions of a passage appeared side by side and then to Standard English texts. Eventually, *Bridge: A cross-cultural reading program* (Simpkins, Holt, and Simpkins 1977) was developed and field-tested with older children who were not reading at grade level. After four months, all students took the Iowa Test of Basic Skills in Reading Comprehension. The average gain in the grade equivalent scores of students taught with dialect readers was 6.2 months for four months of instruction, whereas the control group averaged 1.6 months of gain (reported in Rickford and Rickford [1995]). Despite the apparent promise of this approach to improving reading for speakers of vernacular dialects and calls for more research, dialect readers were abandoned in the wake of negative reactions from linguists and community members who found the approach patronizing.

Sociolinguistic activism in educational domains

Common to the early efforts to inform and influence language-related educational practices is adherence to one or more of the principles of sociolinguistic obligation and a concern for equity across social groups. Sociolinguists provided evidence that institutionalized bias in favor of a standard dialect was placing speakers of vernacular dialects at a disadvantage in high stakes educational endeavors such as testing and literacy learning. A well-known example of linguistic activism is the case of *Martin Luther King Junior Elementary School Children, et al. v. Ann Arbor School District Board* (decided in 1979), which concerned a small group of African American children whose language was not being taken into account in classroom instruction. Predictable vernacular features in their speech led to children's classification as learning disabled. From its inception, preparation for this case was informed by sociolinguists, and sociolinguists provided expert testimony at the trial. At its conclusion, the judge decided for the children, finding that the school board had failed

> to recognize the existence of the language system used by the children in their home community and to use that knowledge as a way of helping the children learn to read standard English. . . . No matter how well intentioned the teachers are, they are not likely to be successful in overcoming the language barrier caused by their failure to take into account the home language system, unless they are helped . . . to recognize the existence of the language system used by the children in their home community.   (cited in Smitherman 2000:155)

This case did not end as the linguists had hoped, with sociolinguistic training being provided for all teachers in the school district that could counter the deficit perspective entrenched in schools. However, it undoubtedly raised the general public's awareness of dialect prejudice as the story was taken up, debated, and discussed in the national media (Smitherman 2000). And it made its mark in the field of sociolinguistics and linguistics broadly as the crucial relevance of dialect research to correcting educational belief and practice was upheld in courts.

By the time of the resurgence of popular attention to these issues as a result of the Ebonics affair some twenty years later, linguists packed the annual business meeting of the Linguistic Society of America (LSA) in 1997 to vote unanimously in support of a Resolution on the Oakland "Ebonics" Issue. The unusual presence of TV cameras and reporters at such a meeting allowed the LSA members to demonstrate their commitment to the social relevance of their field. The Resolution that passed outlines facts about African American English and other dialects that were being overlooked in media accounts and editorials on Ebonics: that African American English is systematic and rule-governed, that the distinction between language and dialect is made often enough on the basis of social and political factors as on linguistic facts, that there are individual and group benefits to maintaining vernacular varieties just as there are to acquiring standard varieties, and that using children's proficiency in the vernacular to teach the standard makes good sense pedagogically and linguistically. (The full resolution can be found on the LSA Web site, at www.lsadc.org.) As in past eruptions of this issue, the headlines faded, but the discussion will, it is to be hoped, have a lasting (if incremental) effect on the understanding of dialects and education. At a minimum, research was stimulated in the sociolinguistic community that should improve the education of vernacular dialect speakers in the future (Meier 1999).

Sociolinguistics and education: current trends and innovations

Some of the early efforts to bring the study of sociolinguistic variation to bear on education policy and practice have borne fruit. In the field of speech/language pathology, there is now wider recognition in some circles of sociolinguistic perspectives and of the contributions to research and practice by sociolinguists and scholars of speech/language pathology who were trained in sociolinguistics (e.g. Craig and Washington 2006, Lucas, Bayley, and Kelly 2005). Recently, the American Speech-Language-Hearing Association (ASHA) produced a CD-ROM (Adger and Schilling-Estes 2003) for training speech/language pathologists to recognize elements of the structure and use of African American English that researchers have described so as to avoid misdiagnosis of African American English speakers as language disabled. This product grew out of an application of sociolinguistic scholarship focused on designing a means to ensure the equitable assessment of African American English speakers' language development. That project involved fieldwork with speech/language practitioners in Baltimore, MD, aimed at local validation of a structural description of that dialect (Adger, Wolfram, and Detwyler 1993). The ASHA product has the potential to alter the current state of affairs in speech/language pathology, where a sociolinguistic model of clinical practice has found acceptance at some level but is not always evident in daily practice (Supple 1993, cited in Wolfram 2005b).

Some of the same sociolinguists who contributed to the Ann Arbor trial on the education of African American children had been active in promoting sociolinguistics in the field of English language arts education, working through its professional organization, the National Council of Teachers of English (NCTE), and its affiliates to shape the organization's policies, committee work, and publications. An early notable effort based on sociolinguistic findings related to language variation was a resolution by the NCTE affiliate Conference on College Composition and Communication (CCCC) (CCC 1974) on students' right to their own languages and dialects and an accompanying review citing sociolinguistic research. This resolution was followed by a similar one from NCTE. Recently, NCTE reaffirmed their resolution as an important principle for language arts education, and NCTE's Commission on Language is focusing on how to create the conditions required so that students have that right.

NCTE's national standards for what students should know and be able to do in language arts call for knowledge about language variation: "Students [should] develop an understanding of and respect for diversity in language use, patterns, and dialects across cultures, ethnic groups, geographic regions, and social roles" (NCTE/IRA 1996:3), in addition to being able to speak and/or write Standard English. Furthermore, the NCTE/NCATE (National Council for Accreditation of Teacher Education) standards for English language arts teacher preparation programs include explicit guidelines and expectations for teachers' performance related to language diversity. The goal is that teachers

> Show extensive knowledge of how and why language varies and changes in different regions, across different cultural groups, and across different time periods and incorporate that knowledge into classroom instruction and assessment that acknowledge and show respect for language diversity; [and] create opportunities for students to analyze how social context affects language and to monitor their own language use and behavior in terms of demonstrating respect for individual differences of ethnicity, race, language, culture, gender, and ability.   (NCTE/NCATE Program Standards 2003:7, 13)

But just as ASHA's leadership in training speech/language pathologists in sociolinguistic particulars appears not to be widely reflected in practice, the perspective of NCTE and NCATE has not trickled down to the state standards for student learning. There the traditional prescriptive focus on Standard English prevails in some states, as in the Virginia Standards of Learning cited above. The Maryland State Department of Education's four core learning goals for English language arts include controlling language ("The student will demonstrate the ability to control language by applying the conventions of Standard English in writing and speaking"), but as with the Virginia standards, there is nothing about other dialects.

Negative attitudes and erroneous assumptions about vernacular dialects and their speakers that have been criticized by sociolinguists over the years (e.g. Baratz and Shuy 1969) have not disappeared from schools, but there are now some instructional approaches that use these dialects in teaching and learning instead of seeking to obliterate them. One of these is Standard English instruction based on Contrastive Analysis with a vernacular variety (Wheeler and Swords 2006). This approach uses children's proficiency in the first dialect and thus implicitly acknowledges its regularity. The book lays out the sociolinguistic background knowledge that teachers must have if they are to use the Contrastive Analysis approach to Standard English instruction. It assumes that teachers may have no background in linguistics and that they view vernacular dialects as broken English. It goes on to give very detailed advice on how to teach children to code-switch from African American English to Standard English on some of the more stigmatized structures, such as possessive marker deletion, plural marker deletion, subject–verb agreement, past marker deletion, and habitual *be*. By acknowledging the value of the native dialect as a resource to build on, this approach has a more positive orientation than models that aim to replace it.

At the same time that the cognitive value of children's vernacular dialects is being recognized and used, the social value is beginning to be recognized elsewhere in the curriculum. In composition classes, vernacular-speaking students may be invited to write in their own dialect for rhetorical purposes and to protect vernacular features through the editing process, just as well-known authors such as Alice Walker and Lee Smith use vernacular features as one way of accomplishing voice. Offering this option to students who are proficient in a vernacular helps to make the point that vernacular varieties serve communicative functions and that writers suit language style to genre (Bean *et al.* 2003).

Another venue for vernacular dialects in schools is in the literature that teachers read to young children and that older students read themselves. Increasingly, schools are using authentic literature (as opposed to textbooks written for pedagogical purposes), some of which includes vernacular speech. Trade books are being used extensively in early childhood education to promote the development of pre-reading skills. Throughout elementary school, high-quality children's literature is available in classrooms and through the school library for children to read in literacy activities and independent reading. Efforts to improve school performance for students from lower socioeconomic status backgrounds have included an emphasis on making the curriculum culturally responsive – that is, selecting books with characters, settings, and plots that children recognize, including books whose characters use vernacular structures such as *The snowy day* by Ezra Jack Keats, for young children, and *The House on Mango Street* by Sandra Cisneros, for older children. But these books appear in schools in middle-class communities too, and other classics featuring vernacular dialect have gained prominence, including poems by Langston Hughes (*Do nothin till you hear from me*), essays by James Baldwin (*Go tell it on the mountain*), and plays by Lorraine Hansberry (*Raisin in the sun*). There is no way of knowing how teachers handle the fact that authors use vernacular structures to present believable characters by creating authentic voice, but the presence of books such as these in schools and their use in the curriculum suggests that the strict prohibition against vernacular at school is eroding. The National Council of Teachers of English has published a number of books and articles emphasizing the value of such texts.

These current approaches and possibilities represent progressive developments in educational practices. Some of them are far more enlightened linguistically than their predecessors. For example, Standard English instruction based on Contrastive Analysis uses precise sociolinguistic descriptions of vernacular features, rather than the generalized descriptions that are found in other Standard English programs (and incorporate some inaccuracies, such as no contextual constraints on final stop devoicing). As teachers learn to use this approach and children gain skills in the standard dialect, they are also learning something about sociolinguistics.

A dialect awareness curriculum

In another departure from established practice, explicit instruction in the disciplinary knowledge and perspectives of sociolinguistics is being extended into schools. There is no developmental reason to confine sociolinguistics to university linguistics and English departments: children can learn basic information about language variation from a very young age, for instance by focusing on the language in texts like those mentioned above. Because dialects are generally fascinating, it should not be difficult to direct children's attention to their details and expand students' knowledge about sociolinguistics throughout the school years, as happens with other sciences such as chemistry and physics.

One deterrent to introducing sociolinguistics at earlier ages has been the lack of linguistically informed methods and materials for teaching children about language variation. Because teachers are likely to have had very limited exposure to this discipline and thus lack the background knowledge needed to teach it, teaching and learning materials become all the more essential. But the few instructional materials that do exist typically focus on regional differences in vocabulary, if they treat dialects at all, and do not address systematic phonological and grammatical differences in any detail.

Over the past fifteen years, Walt Wolfram and his students and colleagues have been addressing this void by developing and trying out a dialect awareness curriculum composed of five lessons that introduce fundamental sociolinguistic concepts. This curriculum represents a robust and very promising model for broadening the audience for language variation scholarship to include students in grades four on up through high school. Early versions of the curriculum were taught by the developers as a means of pilot testing the materials and accommodating the fact that teachers are unlikely to have had substantial sociolinguistic training, but recent research investigated the feasibility of having teachers use the curriculum, with guidance from a teacher's manual (Reaser 2006).

The need for sociolinguistic education

The rationale for developing dialect awareness curricula for schools is related to all three of the sociolinguistic obligations principles. In terms of the Principle of Error Correction,

> The most persistent challenge in educating the American public about linguistic diversity continues to be the widespread application of the principle of linguistic subordination: interpreting the dialects of socially subordinate groups as unworthy, illegitimate versions of the socially dominant language variety. . . . The educational misrepresentation of the linguistic nature of language differences perpetuates one of the great scientific myths of modern society. Mitigating the effects of the dominant ideology involves long-term

formal and informal re-education on both a local and global level. (Wolfram, Reaser, and Adger 2005)

As for the Principle of Debt Incurred, Wolfram's and his colleagues' study of various vernacular dialects is of potential benefit to education, but

> there is no established tradition for promoting language awareness in American society. Although the NCTE standards specify that students are to "develop an understanding of and respect for diversity in language use, patterns, and dialects across cultures, ethnic groups, geographic regions, and social roles," devoting substantial attention to this standard does not fit within current paradigms of instructional planning. The initial challenge is thus establishing the need for information about language differences. This needs to be followed by the development of appropriate curricular materials for education about language differences.   (Wolfram, Reaser, and Adger 2005)

In line with the Principle of Linguistic Gratuity, the researchers have not only used the knowledge derived from data collected in the community for the benefit of the community (e.g. Wolfram, Hazen, and Schilling-Estes 1999), but they have actively pursued ways of returning the favor to the community by developing educational materials for use in and out of schools.

Curriculum content

Dialect awareness curricula are designed to confront the general stereotypes and misconceptions about dialects that students and their teachers can be presumed to have. In an early lesson for middle or high school classes, students view all or parts of of the documentary on dialects in the US called *American tongues* (Alvarez and Kolker 1987). This makes for a potent introduction to the language prejudice that is endemic but that children may not have really noticed. Although the film is somewhat dated, it makes its point with children, who are likely to have strong instincts about fairness.

After viewing the film, discussing it, and writing about it, students engage in a lesson or a series of lessons on the naturalness of variation. They listen to recordings of representative speech samples of regional, class, and ethnic varieties. They learn that Standard English is not monolithic by hearing Standard English speakers in different regions, and they learn that there are standard and vernacular varieties within regions.

An early lesson in the curriculum helps students learn that language is simultaneously organized on several levels, and that this perspective is essential to studying language variation. Lesson activities help them recognize these levels. The following items come from a worksheet in which students indicate whether the contrast between sentences in each pair is a matter of grammar, pronunciation, or vocabulary:

1. __ That **feller** sure was tall
   That **fellow** sure was tall
2. __ That road sure is **sigogglin**
   That road sure is **crooked**
3. __ They usually **be doing** their homework
   They usually **do** their homework
4. __ I was hanging out with my **peeps**
   I was hanging out with my **friends**   (Reaser and Wolfram 2006b)

As they discuss the contrasts, students learn that they exemplify not only different levels of language but also language differences associated with regional, social, and age groups.

The lessons are designed to demonstrate that dialects are patterned. Students are guided to develop hypotheses about the patterning of language features and to check them against language use, in activities that are analogous to those they have experienced in their science study. Students listen to a recording of speakers demonstrating the vowel merger in *pin* and *pen*, and examine a list of other words that exhibit the merger:

(1) *tin* and *ten*
(2) *kin* and *Ken*
(3) *Lin* and *Len*
(4) *windy* and *Wendy*
(5) *sinned* and *send*

Then they see a list of words in which the vowels are not merged:

(1) *lit* and *let*
(2) *pick* and *peck*
(3) *pig* and *peg*
(4) *rip* and *rep*
(5) *litter* and *letter*

The next step is to develop hypotheses for vowel merger, based on the evidence, and then to predict whether merger would occur in the following list:

(1) *bit* and *bet*
(2) *pit* and *pet*
(3) *bin* and *Ben*
(4) *Nick* and *neck*
(5) *din* and *den*   (Reaser 2006)

Students form hypotheses about grammatical structures too, again using carefully assembled data sets. The first task involves deciding which sentence in each of several pairs such as the following could correctly use the *a*-prefix:

(a) __ Building is hard work.
(b) __ She was building a house.

Students discuss their choices, comparing their intuitions about where *a-building* sounds better. Following consideration of a number of such choices, they generate hypotheses for where *a*-prefix can occur and where it cannot, based on grammatical considerations.

The next data set extends their understanding: *a*-prefixing cannot occur in prepositional phrases.

(a) __ They make money by building houses.
(b) __ They make money building houses.

The last data set shows that word stress also plays a role in *a*-prefixing:

(a) __ She was discóvering a trail.
(b) __ She was fóllowing a trail.

Following the scientific method, students formulate their findings in writing and then predict *a*-prefixing occurrence in another set of sentences.

Exercises such as these help students discover that dialects are patterned, and they also demonstrate what linguists do to find the patterns. This emergent understanding might lead to an interest in further exploration of dialect patterning. Under the guidance of a skilled teacher with some background in sociolinguistic fieldwork, students might go on to investigate aspects of the dialects in their own community.

Finally, to establish that language standards are flexible and that language change is inevitable, the curriculum includes examples of change in English over time. Students consider change currently under way and find out how to look at data from the language they hear and see around them.

This approach to dialect awareness has been well received and successful in the communities where Wolfram and colleagues have worked. Teachers and students alike testify to the eye-opening nature of the discoveries that they make, and they typically profess a greater appreciation of their own community's language as a result.

Sociolinguistic obligation

Contemporary applications of sociolinguistic research to education are intended to change educational practices in testing and in the curriculum that research has called into question. All of them derive from a robust research base, and all of them have face validity: they represent apparently sensible uses of that research in the service of error correction, satisfying debts incurred, and returning linguistic favors. Sociolinguists would probably agree that there is by now significant understanding of the dimensions in which standard and vernacular varieties contrast. The literature also contains many particulars for African American English, if fewer for other dialects. There may not be full agreement in the field about whether that knowledge could or should be used in building competence in the standard dialect. McWhorter (2001) has argued, for example, against teaching Standard English to African American children because they are likely to know these contrasts already but not to use standard features in certain circumstances for valid sociolinguistic reasons. Bidialectalism may be a matter of degree and preference. So, for example, miscues in reading may be attributed to dialect differences (where a child understands what is written on the page but pronounces it in the vernacular), and so there is no need to teach the standard form. But in his research on reading by vernacular dialect speaking children, Labov concluded that some of the discrepancies in children's oral reading of passages was likely to be a matter of not knowing certain Standard English features, such as possessive -s, rather than merely a matter of dialect interference (2003, www.ling.upenn.edu/~wlabov/Papers/WRE.html [last accessed May 26, 2007]). At any rate, it seems clear that sociolinguistic knowledge is relevant and useful to education, however the details of application are worked out.

Impact

Despite the fifty-year history of sociolinguistic applications in educational domains, disciplinary perspectives and research findings seem not to have been as fully embraced and integrated into educational processes as the authors of the applications have hoped. If there is some understanding that dialect discrimination harms students, there is still limited knowledge of the particulars of language variation that teachers and speech/language pathologists need in order to accommodate predictable differences. And clearly the public has not learned its dialect lesson, as indicated by the hysteria of the Ebonics affair in the late 1990s. This is not to say that there has been no influence or that sociolinguistic knowledge is routinely resisted by educators and education research. In some circles, it is respected and sought after. Rather, it seems to us that the impact of sociolinguistics is limited. In this section, we speculate on why that may be and on some ways in which application efforts might have more profound effect.

Situating linguistic expertise

One reason that sociolinguistic contributions to education have not been more influential may be a matter of where in the educational enterprise they are sited. Here we consider several domains.

Sociolinguistics in the school curriculum

The dialect awareness curriculum has gained a foothold in the North Carolina schools, with the researchers providing instruction for students directly, and there is strong interest in continuing to make it available. The delay in handover of the curriculum from linguists to teachers came not from any desire on the part of the developers to protect it, but from the fact that the teachers in whose classrooms the curriculum has been implemented were not prepared to teach it themselves. But a recent successful experiment involving middle school teachers teaching the curriculum with coaching from one of the developers found that instruction produced consistent, desirable effects on a post-implementation survey of students' knowledge and attitudes (Reaser 2006): 98.4% of the students reported learning something surprising about dialects that would change the way they thought about language, and 87.6% thought that the information they had studied was important. The Contrastive Analysis approach to teaching Standard English developed by Wheeler has had limited influence so far because development has not involved large numbers of teachers, but the fact that NCTE has published the materials for teachers to use in their classrooms (Wheeler and Swords 2006) suggests that the approach will spread.

These two cases of sociolinguistics in the school curriculum are similar in some ways. Both use sociolinguistic variation studies to update teaching and learning in domains where language prejudice has been prevalent. Both cases involve introducing findings from the scientific study of language variation to students and teachers who can be expected to subscribe to widely held myths about the superiority of Standard English. Both confront the related challenges of the lack of substantial language training for teachers and students' limited knowledge about language structure by providing substantial introductory background information for them.

The cases contrast in the way that they relate to the school curriculum and thus where educational ownership might be expected. The Standard English instruction program fits well with the traditional English language arts curriculum, which has always had a Standard English learning focus. Early experimentation with the dialect awareness curriculum was situated there too, because those lessons address the content standards (learning goals) related to knowledge about language structure discussed above. Later, the developers modified the curriculum so that it addressed the standards for social studies and began to teach it in social studies classes. For example, the lessons align with several competencies of the North Carolina Standard Course of Study (NCSCS) Social Studies Goals:

- The learner will access the influence of geography on the economic, social, and political development of North Carolina.
- The learner will evaluate the effects of earlier contacts between various European nations and Native Americans.
- The learner will judge the continuing significance of social, economic, and political changes since 1945 and draw conclusions about their effect on contemporary life.

The curriculum explicitly addresses these goals in the examination of the history of dialects and current changes in post-insular dialect areas. Shifting the dialect curriculum from English language arts to social studies may have political benefits. The perspective on dialects that the experimental curriculum introduces is at odds with the strong, traditional stance in English language arts that there is one standard variety that all students need to control and any deviations are errors. There is less wide acceptance of the newer position reflected in the NCTE standards that students should learn the linguistic facts of variation. Because the responsibility for reinforcing Standard English learning is typically sited in English language arts and because the Standard English versus language variation conflict is not resolved, it is probably much more expedient to take the dialect curriculum to another content area, at least for the time being.

Another difference between the dialect awareness curriculum case and the Standard English instruction case lies in their alignment with what schools are already doing. The dialect curriculum represents an addition to the curriculum, one that fits the standards, whereas the Contrastive Analysis intervention replaces the traditional way of teaching Standard English. A new approach to an accepted curriculum focus – and one in which students will be tested – seems more likely to be entertained and even to find favor, despite the fact that it embodies a perspective on language variation that teachers might not fully appreciate. Moreover, the approach is being brought to national attention through a book written for an audience of teachers, co-authored by a sociolinguist and a teacher who has used the approach, and published by the well-respected and influential National Council of Teachers of English.

In pointing to differences between these two current applications, we do not mean to suggest that one is more valuable than another or more likely to influence education, but rather to explore factors in the sociocultural context that may affect the impact of sociolinguistic research that is applied in the domain of education.

Whose need?

Taking action on the principles for applying sociolinguistic research can be risky: venturing into other disciplines, uninvited, to correct their errors and address their needs can be viewed as presumptuous (and may well be!). The rationale for doing so inevitably involves judgments about assumptions and conditions in the other discipline, and sociolinguists may not have the understandings they need to situate their advice appropriately. However, there are some strategies for crafting sociolinguistic applications that may improve their chances of being accepted by educational stakeholders rather than rebuffed or simply ignored.

An important tactic is to meet a need identified by educators. Sociolinguists with a mission have gained entry to fields of education that they want to influence by responding to the insiders' need for sociolinguistic information or by working to create awareness there of a need that the sociolinguists have identified. It takes time to establish the reputation and the connections with insiders that are essential to making impact, and sociolinguists who have succeeded in influencing educational practice have spent years working with education stakeholders at various levels. In the case of the dialect curriculum in North Carolina, when the developers were ready to broaden the audience, they made a visit to the North Carolina Department of Public Instruction to learn how decisions about curriculum are made at the state level. Having determined, based on years of experience in schools with the dialect curriculum, that social studies was the more hospitable content area, they knew how the curriculum was relevant to the state's social studies standards. Thus they were able to present themselves as knowledgeable outsiders asking for advice on how to work with the Department of Public Instruction. The answer they got was that the key to state adoption of the curriculum was to get teachers to advocate for it. Teachers need to argue that the topic of dialects is important to social studies, that they lack resources for teaching the required course on history and culture of North Carolina, and that the dialect awareness curriculum materials are usable and effective (J. Reaser, personal communication, June 16, 2006). An insider, grass-roots appeal to the state, buttressed by data showing that the curriculum produces a desirable effect on students, would be most effective. The developers followed up with the study of teacher-led use of the curriculum and with presentations at professional association meetings that teachers attend, all the while continuing to teach the curriculum themselves in schools around the state – thus expanding the cadre of teachers who can take their needs to the state.

Linguists working in the field of education need to be well aware of the goals and needs of educators and to tailor their applications to the existing educational framework. Educators at all levels – teachers, gatekeepers in state departments of education and credentialing organizations, teacher educators, education researchers, professional organizations for educators – must be convinced to be partners and allies early in the process of building new applications.

Moving on

To protect the gains that have been made in integrating insights about language variation into educational policy and practice, there is need for more collaboration between sociolinguists and educators. One important domain is teacher education, at both the undergraduate and graduate levels. As discussed above, the collaboration should build on goals and needs recognized by educators. The teacher certification program is packed with requirements stemming from state and national standards for teacher performance, and any changes to it must be approved outside the university. Although educational linguists would recommend training for teachers on topics like language variation, first and second language acquisition, and reading skills development, adding courses to the program is impossible, and changing existing courses involves negotiating with competing priorities. But the alternative, boosting teachers' knowledge once they are practicing, is no easy path because many topics compete for very limited time set aside for teachers' professional development and for attention from teachers who are already overloaded with responsibilities (Adger, Snow, and Christian 2002). As a result, information about variation and other insights from sociolinguistics cannot be infused into education through a self-contained add-on in teacher preparation. Introducing sociolinguistic knowledge into teacher education requires working with teacher educators on their agenda, which means getting to know the agenda and the individuals involved. Sociolinguists who already work in schools of education and those who are active in the National Council of Teachers of English are obvious mentors for others who desire to influence teacher education. Other natural allies are the researchers and teacher educators in education and English departments who may not identify themselves as members of the linguistics community but who have strong backgrounds in sociolinguistics.

Given these constraints, how can sociolinguists influence what teachers and their students learn about language? One important contribution is to develop learning materials that are linguistically accurate, that reflect various conventions of education (such as content area assumptions and knowledge bases), and that provide extensive background information for instructors whose training in linguistics is scant or lacking altogether. The dialect awareness curriculum and the Contrastive Analysis approach to teaching Standard English discussed here provide examples. Materials for teaching and learning provide the props for instructors who would like to include linguistics in their courses but who lack the time and knowledge to develop learning activities on their own. Getting involved in teacher education is another useful way to infuse sociolinguistic insights into educational policy and practice.

In the area of education, the principles of sociolinguistic obligation to the society remain as relevant today as when they were offered, but a postscript is needed, which perhaps should be formulated as a fourth principle: sociolinguists with information to contribute must work with partners within the field of education who can help determine how best to represent that mission to others in the field and who can verify or correct their perceptions of what educators need to know.

13 Lessons learned from the Ebonics controversy: implications for language assessment

A. FAY VAUGHN-COOKE

Introduction

For a brief period at the end of 1996 and the beginning of 1997, an unprecedented number of people in the United States engaged in an impassioned and often acrimonious debate about a specific variety of English – Ebonics. The intense and sometimes heated discussions attracted nearly everyone: the young, the old, Whites, Blacks, teachers, preachers, poets, politicians, leaders, followers, and, predictably, language professionals – linguists and speech/language pathologists (SLPs). The debate provided an important opportunity for SLPs to refocus on a long-standing professional challenge: providing valid language assessments for speakers of Ebonics, or African American Vernacular English (AAVE).

Given the knowledge about Ebonics from several decades of impressive, convincing linguistic research, it is safe to say that practitioners have more than enough information to provide an adequate assessment of the language of African American children. We already know a lot about their phonological, syntactic, semantic, and pragmatic systems (although we can always learn more). In other words, we already know enough to determine whether an African American child's language is normal.

Why, then, are so many invalid assessments still being made and used to place African American children in special education and related services? During the Ebonics debate the Oakland Unified School District reported that a staggering 71% of the students enrolled in special education were African American. This figure suggests that professionals did not learn anything from the Black English trial that focused on eleven Ebonics-speaking children at the Martin Luther King Junior Elementary School in Ann Arbor, Michigan (Smitherman 1981, Rickford and Rickford 2000), where the children were placed in special education classes after language assessments failed to take into account their linguistic heritage. Judge Joiner ordered the Ann Arbor School District Board to take linguistic differences into account when teaching academic subjects like reading and language arts.

While valid assessment for Ebonics speakers is still a major challenge for speech/language pathology, an even more formidable challenge facing the profession and the educational system is the *American people's assessment* of the language of Ebonics speakers. The Ebonics debate revealed that a linguistically naive public considers that Ebonics is inferior and unfit for classroom use, and that the children who speak it have limited intelligence. When we consider that regular and special education teachers and other professionals who provide basic services for Ebonics speakers come from the ranks of the American people who share this general perspective, we should not be surprised that so many African Americans are placed in special education and related services.

A first step toward solving the problems caused by the public's overwhelmingly contemptuous assessment of Ebonics is to study critically some of the lessons learned from the debate. They reveal that our 30-year-old strategy of simply restating the well-researched linguistic facts about the dialect needs to be abandoned, because it has not worked. I propose a new strategy, one that includes a national language policy supported by legislation (Baugh 1998). I will first discuss the lessons learned from the Ebonics debate, then my proposed strategy.

Lessons learned

Lesson #1 – The majority of people in the United States do not believe that all languages are equal

In spite of the fact the linguists have provided substantial evidence that all languages are equal in their capacity to serve as communication systems, we learned during the debate that the ill-founded belief that some languages are better than others is deeply entrenched in the minds of millions of Americans. People do not believe that rating some languages as good and others as bad is completely arbitrary, as Stanford linguist Merritt Ruhlen demonstrates with a hypothetical reversal of the historical record:

> If history had gone differently and Africans had come over and founded America and raided Europe and brought white slaves over, and this country ended up with a 10 percent white minority that was kept in ghettos and spoke white English, you'd find the same problems in reverse. . . . People would be saying, "Why can't the whites learn good black English?" We spend all our time in school learning "good" and "bad" grammar and can't see that it's an historical accident that white English is called the best.   (Weiss 1997:A10)

Irrational beliefs about the quality of languages cannot be changed by energetic presentations of linguistic facts. Language professionals and others who are committed to helping Ebonics speakers resist the social, educational, and economic subordination caused by irrational views about the quality of their language should develop new strategies that focus on changing national language policies (particularly those related to education) and not the minds of the majority.

Lesson #2 – The majority of people believe that Ebonics and other non-standard varieties of English are deficient

While language professionals, particularly SLPs and linguists, have argued for decades that Ebonics is *different* from Standard English, but not deficient, the debate taught us that the majority of people in the United States believe that Ebonics is inferior. This was evidenced by a proliferation of derogatory terms used to characterize the dialect. "You can call it Ebonics, but we call it junk" (Bowman 1997:C5) said Patricia Chase, chairman of the English Department at Roosevelt Senior High School in Washington, DC. Mary McGrory, a *Washington Post* columnist, maintained that the Oakland School Board was "legitimizing gibberish" (McGrory 1996). Other writers used a disease metaphor as titles of their articles: a column in the *Economist* was entitled "The Ebonics Virus"; the *Wall Street Journal* published a column called "The Ebonic Plague" (Rich 1997); *San Francisco Examiner*'s Rob Morse (1997) entitled his column "1996: E. coli, Odwalla, ebola, ebonics." Finally, Herb Boyd (1997) in his *Black Scholar* article "Been dere, done dat!" said, "The Ebonics debate swept the nation like a verbal ebola plague."

The linguistic facts about Ebonics have been resoundingly rejected by some of the most respected leaders and politically astute members of the larger African American community. If the American people are listening to linguists on this point, they are certainly not agreeing with them.

Lesson #3 – Many people believe that Ebonics is only slang

"The Clinton administration declared that . . . 'black English' is a form of slang that does not belong in the classroom," reported John E. Harris (1996a), a staff writer for the *Washington Post*. The administration presumably made this claim without consulting the language professionals who have been awarded millions of federal dollars to conduct research that proves that Ebonics is not slang. Slang, according to Smitherman, "refers to forms of speech that are highly transitory and limited to specific subgroups, e.g. today's Hip Hoppers" (1997:29). Ebonics and all other dialects of English, including Standard English (SE), have slang words and phrases; these usually constitute only a fraction of the linguistic knowledge required to speak and comprehend a language. The claim that Ebonics speakers use only slang is blatantly false.

The view that Ebonics is slang was supported by the syndicated columnist Carl Rowan (1996), who said, "Telling youngsters that a slang called black English (dressed up as 'Ebonics') is good enough for them . . . is guaranteeing failure for all youngsters who swallow this copout from hard work and study." The *New York*

Times also disseminated the slang falsehood. An editorial stated that "the school board in Oakland . . . blundered badly . . . when it declared that black slang is a distinct language that warrants a place of respect in the classroom" ("Linguistic Confusion" 1996).

The relegation of Ebonics to the linguistically trivial category of slang, without consulting any of the language experts, provides evidence that the American people, including the most powerful leaders in the country, have no intention of changing their negative assessment of Ebonics.

Lesson #4 – Many people believe that Ebonics is street language

"After years of dumbing down the curriculum . . . are we about to rule that street slang is a distinct language deserving of respect?" asked Mona Charen (1997:A7) in the *Detroit News*. Columnist George F. Will called Ebonics "the patois of America's meanest streets" (1997:B12), and a *New York Times* editorial noted that "the new policy is intended to help teach standard English and other subjects by building on the street language actually used by many inner-city children and their parents" ("Linguistic Confusion" 1996:A10). Eldridge Cleaver summed up his position about Ebonics this way: "The only place for Ebonics is the streets. We don't need it in the classroom" (1997:A36).

Cast aside here is the linguistic insight that no dialect, or variety of language is spoken only in the street. The journalist Mumia Abu-Jamal emphasizes that Ebonics, "for millions of us in the inner cities, and in the projects, is not street language – but home language, where we communicate our deepest feelings, fears, views and insights" (1997:27). Ebonics is spoken in homes where it is often the preferred dialect; it is spoken in many churches and numerous other places, including schools all over the United States. Indeed, it was the use of Ebonics in the Oakland schools that motivated the Board to draft the resolution that sparked the debate. The controversy revealed that many children in the United States are made to feel ashamed of the way that they speak every day, because their English is reviled as street language.

Lesson #5 – Many people believe that Ebonics speakers have limited intelligence

The intelligence of Ebonics speakers was frequently maligned during the debate; this was especially evident in some of the vicious material on the Internet. The example below is illustrative.

> Subject: Ebonics 101
> Leroy Washington is an [*sic*] 19 year old third grader in the city of Oakland who is becoming increasingly disillusioned with the public school system. One day Leroy got an easy homework assignment. All he had to do was put each of the following words in a sentence. This is what Leroy did.

HOTEL – I gave my girlfriend da crabs and the HOTEL everybody.
DISAPPOINTMENT – My parole officer tol me if I miss DISAPPOINT-
MENT they gonna send me back to the big house.
UNDERMINE – They is a fine lookin' hoe livin' in the apartment UNDER-
MINE.   (cited in Ronkin and Karn 1999)

These are three of the fifteen sentences created by someone with an exceptionally high level of metalinguistic awareness. The fact that the person chose to use
his or her special skills to launch such a blatant and cruel attack on the intelligence
and moral character of students in the Oakland school system is chilling.

Jokes about the supposed low intelligence of Ebonics speakers were common
during the debate. These jokes proliferated despite the fact that Bill Cosby and
many others who ridiculed Ebonics probably know numerous intelligent people
who speak the dialect. For example, the civil rights activist, brilliant strategist,
and organizer Fannie Lou Hamer spoke Ebonics, and she was not ashamed of her
dialect. In 1964, Ms. Hamer led sixty-eight delegates of the Mississippi Freedom
Democrats, a party that she helped to organize, to the Democratic National Convention in Atlantic City. The following is an excerpt from the speech she gave
there.

> Senator Humphrey, I ain't no stranger to struggle. . . . It was a struggle to
> get 68 of us here as delegates from the cotton fields of Mississippi . . . to the
> National Democrat convention, but we kept a struggling and we made it here.
> And we is asking you to help . . . Senator Humphrey, you can help us in this
> struggle if you want to; you just got to get up your nerve and go in there and
> do it!   (Young 1991:525)

The following portion of Ms. Hamer's speech was directed to Roy Wilkins, then
head of the NAACP.

> Mr. Wilkins, I know that you is a good spokesperson for the Negro peoples,
> and for the NAACP: I'm is not a sophisticated politician as you. And I know
> that you can speak clearer than me . . . sometimes. But you know Mr. Wilkins, I
> ain't never seed you in my community in Mississippi, and them is the people
> I represents, them is the people I speaks for. And they done already told
> me that we didn't come all this'a way for no two seats, since all a' us is
> tired.   (Young 1991:525)

Ms. Hamer's extraordinary level of intelligence was acknowledged by a number
of institutions of higher learning, as evidenced in an acceptance speech she made
at Morehouse College.

> To the president of Morehouse College . . . I want to thank you for inviting
> me here. I have just left Tougaloo College where this morning I received
> a honorary Doctorate of Humane Letters; and I am on my way to Howard
> University where I expect to receive another honorary Doctorate of Humane
> Letters. And I wants to thank you Morehouse, for this Plaque.   (Young
> 1991:526)

To make fun of the way the Fannie Lou Hamers of the world speak is a conscious and cruel tactic employed to make Ebonics speakers feel intellectually inferior and ashamed of the way they speak. Labov (1972a) spoke out against such tactics more than twenty-five years ago.

> Teachers are now being told to ignore the language of Black children as unworthy of attention and useless for learning. They are being taught to hear every natural utterance of the child as evidence of his mental inferiority. As linguists we are unanimous in condemning this view as bad observation, bad theory, and bad practice.   (1972a:67)

The stunning insensitivity of many of the views expressed during the Ebonics debate demonstrates that Labov's words went largely unheeded.

Lesson #6 – Many people believe that listeners cannot understand Ebonics

"I think it's tragic. . . . These are kids [who] have gotten themselves into this trap of speaking this language – this slang, really – that people can't understand. Now we are going to legitimize it" (Sneider 1996:1). Thus Ward Connerly, an African American businessman and University of California regent, summed up his reaction to the Oakland resolution. Like many other Americans, Connerly claims that Ebonics is difficult to understand. This myth was perpetuated by Bill Cosby (1997) in his parody of Ebonics that appeared in the *Wall Street Journal.*

> The first thing people ask when they are pulled over [by a policeman] is: "Why did you stop me officer?" Imagine an Ebonics-speaking Oakland teenager being stopped on the freeway by a non-Ebonics speaking California Highway Patrol officer. The teenager, posing that same question Ebonically, would begin by saying: "Lemme ax you . . ." The patrolman, fearing he is about to be hacked to death, could charge the kid with threatening a police officer. Thus, to avoid misunderstandings, notices would have to be added to drivers' licenses warning: "This driver speaks Ebonics only."

But Patricia J. Williams, who is not a linguist, made a further point about the comprehensibility of Ebonics.

> Perhaps the real argument is not about whether ebonics is a language or not. Rather, the tension is revealed in the contradiction of black speech being simultaneously understood yet not understood. Why is it so overwhelmingly, even colorfully comprehensible in some contexts, particularly in sports and entertainment, yet deemed so utterly incapable of effective communication when it comes to finding a job as a construction worker?   (1996: section 4:9)

As Williams suggests, the real issue is not the listener's ability to understand Ebonics, but the listener's objection to persons speaking Ebonics. Exceptions are always made, however, for certain words and phrases that exemplify the coveted linguistic creativity of Ebonics speakers. These are of course quickly appropriated by the mainstream. Consider the following verse from a poem used by Nike in a *Black Enterprise Magazine* advertisement (September 1997) featuring golfer Tiger Woods:

> You the Man, Mr. Rhodes.
> You the Man, Mr. Sifford.
> You the Man, Mr. Elder.
> I won't forget.

The familiar Nike logo appeared in bold relief at the end of the poem.

"You the man" is a distinct creation of Ebonics speakers; it means something like "you are the person with the power and I respect you." Note the absence of the copula verb *are*, a common syntactic pattern in Ebonics. The moguls at Nike had no difficulty understanding "You the man."

Another Ebonics expression that has been appropriated by the mainstream is "You go, girl," a phrase used to refer to a female who has completed an act of triumph, or who is about to engage in an act that is expected to end triumphantly. The February 23, 1998 cover of *People Magazine* featured the White American skaters Tara Lipinski and Nicole Bobeck and the Asian American Michele Kwan just before their Olympic competitions. Juxtaposed to the pictures, in big, bold letters, was Ebonics: "You go, girls!" Comprehension was not a problem for *People Magazine* or its readers.

During the Ebonics debate, a number of linguistically astute writers commented on the appropriation phenomenon. One was the African American columnist Michael Datcher. He said, "If the millions of white Americans who buy hip hop music teach us anything, it is that white people love the way we turn a phrase" (1997:15). This phenomenon is never acknowledged by the mainstream, as Dr. Mahmoud El-Kati, a history professor at Macalester College in Minnesota, pointed out in his analysis of the Ebonics controversy:

> There is a darker side to . . . this appropriation . . . that has to do with power and the ability to wield it. . . . In a sense, black English is elevated when it is incorporated in the wider culture . . . but when it comes out of black people's mouths it is associated with degradation or stupidity.   (DeWitt 1996: section 4:3)

In sum, Fannie Lou Hamer's speeches (she made many of them all over the country) and examples of appropriation by non-Ebonics speakers debunk the tired old myth that Ebonics is incomprehensible. There is abundant evidence that mainstream speakers not only understand Ebonics, they often borrow words and phrases from it, especially when these borrowings are economically and socially beneficial. However, many mainstream speakers need to justify their rejection and denigration of Ebonics; they do this by claiming that the dialect is incomprehensible. Arguing linguistic facts with such people is futile.

Lesson #7 – The evidence that Ebonics is systematic and rule-governed is often rejected or ignored

During the Ebonics debate, a simple but fundamental fact about Ebonics – that it is systematic and rule-governed like all languages of the world – was repeated on national and local television and on radio shows and in the print media by some of the most respected linguistic scholars and language specialists in the world. Yet a startling number of highly educated, intelligent, and talented people with a high level of awareness about language refused to accept this fact. The syndicated columnist William Raspberry was one of them. In a satirical column on Ebonics entitled, "To Throw in a Lot of 'Bes,' or Not? A Conversation on Ebonics," one of Raspberry's characters, a cab driver, concluded that it was not necessary for Ebonics speakers to follow linguistic rules:

> "Just out of curiosity, who corrects your Ebonics?"
> "That's the beautiful part," the cabbie said. "Ebonics gives you a whole range of options. You can say 'she wish' or 'they goes', and it's all perfectly fine. But you can also say 'they go,' and that's all right, too. I don't think you can say 'I does.' I'll have to check on that, but my brother-in-law tells me *you can say pretty much what you please, as long as you're careful to throw in a lot of 'bes' and leave off final consonants.*"   [emphasis added] (Raspberry 1996:A27)

The cab driver's conclusion, in italics above, is patently false. There is no language in the world in which speakers can say "pretty much" what they please: the absence of rules would make it impossible for speakers to communicate with each other. The use of "be" in Ebonics is governed by a set of semantic-syntactic rules that must be followed in order to use the form correctly. However, Raspberry seems to believe that Ebonics speakers are incapable of linguistic complexity. Perhaps that is why some of his examples of the use of habitual "be" were incorrect; for example, the last sentence in the column – "'Yo!' I said. 'Maybe you be onto somethin' dere, my bruvah" – exhibits an incorrect use of habitual "be." The form is never used to refer to the present; it is used to refer only to actions that occur habitually over time, for example, "Ricky be playing in the yard." This sentence expresses the concept that Ricky usually engages in playing in the yard. Raspberry's character should have said, "Maybe you onto somethin' dere, my bruvah"; the inflected form of "be" ("are") can be absent in this sentence.

Geoffrey Pullum, a professor of linguistics at the University of California, Santa Cruz, wrote a long and detailed letter to Raspberry, pointing out where the language of the characters in his column violated the linguistic rules of Ebonics. He ended his letter by saying this:

> Every time I saw another black columnist come out and join the ridicule chorus, as you did . . . it grieved me. The folks your alter ego accurately calls "the unlettered black masses" suffer so much, and take so much undeserved

contempt and abuse. It is just not appropriate to add insult to this injury by showering ridicule, contempt and abuse on the structurally interesting dialect they happen to speak. I was really sorry that virtually every columnist in the USA chose nonetheless to do just that.   (Pullum, personal communication, January 1997)

Raspberry never replied. Pullum's explanations and examples were clear and easy to understand. A person capable of thinking rationally about language diversity ought to have accepted them and corrected his erroneous representation of the linguistic abilities of a large segment of the African American population. The problem, however, is that Raspberry, an African American himself, and many other Americans do not think rationally about Ebonics. That is why the statement and re-statement of clear, well-developed arguments, supported with salient examples and presented by experts, are rejected by so many intelligent people.

Lesson #8 – Many people believe that it is acceptable to ridicule and to make jokes about Ebonics and other non-standard varieties of English

Courtland Milloy (1996) of the *Washington Post* wrote an enlightened article during the debate entitled, "Nothing's Funny About Ebonics." Given the outpouring of jokes that ridiculed and mocked the dialect and its speakers, Milloy must be one of the few people in this country other than language professionals who believes this. The hostile, vicious jokes that were boldly told about Ebonics provided the most powerful evidence that the strategy of disseminating well-researched facts was not working. The facts were drowned out by laughter. Bill Cosby (1997) coined a derisive new name, "Igno-Ebonics." Another well-known African American, Willie Brown, the mayor of San Francisco, incited laughter when he quipped, "I had dinner last night with the mayor of Oakland and had to bring a translator along" (Branson 1996:2).

Before the debate was over, however, the jokes and mocking assaults, led unfortunately by African Americans, turned painfully cruel for Ebonics speakers (Scott 1998). Exploiting the climate of permission to say anything about Ebonics, some jokers shifted the focus from the language to the people (Ronkin and Karn 1999). Consider the following event list from the "Ebonic Olympic Games" which appeared on the Internet:

> Ebonic Olympic Games Event List
> Opening Ceremonies
> The Torching of Olympic City
> Gang Colors Parade
> Track and Field
> Rob, Shoot and Run
> 9MM Pistol Toss

Molotov Cocktail Throw
Barbed Wire Roll
Chain Link Fence Climb
Peoplechase
Monkey Bar Race
100 Yard-Dog Dash (While Being Chased by Police Dogs)
200 Yard Trash Can Hurdles
500 Yard Stolen Car Battery Run
1000 Meter Courtroom Relay (Team of 4 Passing Murder Weapon)
1500 Meter Television Set Relay
1 Mile Memorial Richard Pryor Burning Ether Run
5 Mile High Speed Automobile Chase
Bitch Slapping (Bruises inflicted on wife/girlfriend in three 1 minute rounds)
Ebo-Marathon (26 Mile Ling Distance Run While Evading Bloodhounds)
(cited in Ronkin and Karn 1999)

This ruthless parody reeks with undisguised contempt and unbridled racism. The denigration of the people who speak Ebonics is deliberate. The joker's message is clear: Ebonics speakers not only have a bad language, they are bad people – vicious criminals who are comfortable engaging in heinous crimes. It is abundantly clear that presenting research to people like those who created this parody would only squander precious time.

Passionate appeals from distinguished linguistic researchers to end the cruel mockery of the language of Ebonics speakers, many of whom are young children, fell on deaf ears. Walt Wolfram, former president of the American Dialect Society and distinguished professor of linguistics at North Carolina State University, who has conducted research on Ebonics for nearly forty years, appealed to Bill Cosby to end his mockery in a letter to the *Wall Street Journal*. Wolfram wrote:

> As a dialect expert, Bill Cosby is a great comedian. Unfortunately, the minstrel-like parody of African American Vernacular Speech, or Ebonics, as "Igno-Ebonics" reinforces the most severe racist and classist stereotypes of what linguists know to be a highly intricate, patterned language system. As a public figure, Bill Cosby has a national forum for his opinion. That ought to be taken seriously rather than abused with misinformed, stereotypical caricature which ironically violates the systematic integrity of the dialect he mocks derisively – and the stated goals of the Oakland program. . . . I challenge Mr. Cosby to be responsible to his public stature and talk to the language scientists in the linguistics department at his alma mater, the University of Massachusetts, about what he obviously missed in Linguistics 101. I predict that he will follow the lead of Jesse Jackson, who withdrew his sharp criticism of the Oakland resolution after meeting with genuine language scientists.   (1997:1)

The *Wall Street Journal* never published Professor Wolfram's letter.

Lesson #9 – Many people think that the differences between Ebonics and Standard English are minimal and can be learned without formal instruction

Many people seem to think that Ebonics speakers can learn Standard English without the benefit of formal instruction. Among them is John McWhorter, a former professor of linguistics at the University of California at Berkeley. In the first of *The Black Scholar*'s two issues devoted to Ebonics, McWhorter claimed: "It is a fact that Black English is not different enough from standard English to pose any significant obstacle to speaking, reading, or writing it" (1997a:9). In *The Black Scholar*'s second issue on Ebonics, McWhorter restated his position more emphatically: "To suppose that black children cannot negotiate the one-inch gap between their home dialect and standard English . . . insults their intelligence" (1997b:2). The evidence is abundant, however, that thousands of intelligent students do not learn to close that gap. One of them is Michael Lampkins, who was a high school senior and student director on the Oakland School Board at the time of the debate. Commenting on the Oakland resolution in his Senate testimony, he noted:

> When a student doesn't understand the teacher and the teacher does not understand the student, learning does not take place. . . . We do have teachers who have went into the classrooms not having the capability to understand those students and have classified those students as special education.   (*Ebonics* 1997:1)

This accomplished and highly regarded student used a non-standard verb phrase, *have went*, that is common among speakers of Ebonics. Formal instruction on the rules that govern the irregular verbs of Standard English would be very useful for him.

Another student who has not learned to close the gap is Maurice White, a sophomore at Oakland Technical High School at the time of the debate. Responding to a fellow student's recommendation to give the Ebonics proposal a chance to be implemented, Mr. White said this:

> Ebonics should not exist. . . . Aside from teachers teaching standard English, them just talking about Ebonics means the slang will start coming out the teacher's mouth just 'cause they trying to help kids get it right.   (Evans 1997:A17)

Perceiving and learning the differences between the syntactic, semantic, and phonological features that distinguish Ebonics from Standard English (SE) are not easy tasks for some speakers. This is the reason that so many never succeed in learning SE as a second dialect. To minimize and trivialize the many differences between SE and Ebonics, even though both dialects share the same basic vocabulary, is misleading and unfair to Ebonics speakers. This trivialization impedes progress toward recognizing and accepting the fact that many need formal instruction in order to learn SE.

The Afrocentric scholar and founder of Kwanzaa, Dr. Maulana Karenga ("Dr. Karenga speaks" 1997), also commented on the problems that Ebonics speakers face when there is no formal instruction in SE.

> When a child is in a math class you don't interrupt him to tell him, "Say 'are' instead of 'is,' or 'is' instead of 'are.'" Can you imagine interrupting a chemistry class to stop an Asian for saying "valy" instead of "vary" because "l" and "r" are transposed in the language? What is the purpose of that? A linguistic discussion in the midst of chemistry class? They are not doing it to educate us, they are doing it to devalue us . . . they are not only devaluing our speech, they are devaluing our people and our culture.

Karenga highlights the urgent need to provide formal instruction in Standard English for Ebonics speakers.

Lesson #10 – Many people believe that federal and state funds should not be used to pay for Standard English instruction for Ebonics speakers

Almost everyone believes that all students who speak Ebonics should be required to learn SE. However, an important revelation during the debate was that no one wants to pay for their instruction. A disturbing number of politicians acted swiftly to introduce legislation what would prohibit the use of tax dollars for providing SE classes for Ebonics speakers. Leading the legislative prohibition was North Carolina Senator Lauch Faircloth, who said "Ebonics is absurd" and "Ebonics is just one more foolish plan by educators who should know better. It's political correctness that has gone out of control" ("Senate mulls" 1997). New York Representative Peter King (R-Seaford), a staunch supporter of making Standard English the federal government's official language, was another politician who introduced legislation that would bar the use of federal funds to help Ebonics speakers learn SE. He revealed his ignorance and contempt for the variety when he claimed that "Ebonics is a verbal stew of inner-city street slang and bad grammar – it is not a language" (Evans 1997:A17). Others who introduced legislation were California State Senator Ray Haynes (R-Murieta), Virginia delegate L. Preston Bryant, Jr. (R-Lynchburg), and lawmakers in Georgia and South Carolina.

Although no official request had been made for money, Secretary of Education Richard Riley announced that school districts that recognize Ebonics in their teaching cannot do so with federal funds targeted for bilingual education. This position was maintained even after the Oakland School Board clarified its position and stated that it did not intend to apply for federal money to fund programs that teach SE. Secretary Riley refused to listen to the language professionals who could have helped him make an informed decision about what is required to teach

SE to Ebonics speakers. This, unfortunately, provides another example of the failure of spreading accurate information.

Lesson #11 – Many people ignore and even ridicule language experts when they present the facts about Ebonics

Like many other linguistic scholars, I was invited to appear on a number of television and radio shows during the Ebonics debate. Their producers stressed that the purpose was to provide linguistic expertise and clarity for the public. I was stunned by the responses of many talk show hosts and members of the audience to my carefully selected linguistic examples that provided incontrovertible evidence that Ebonics is a systematic and rule-governed language. Most people flatly rejected the evidence. Some, like Bob Novak, one of the hosts on CNN's "Crossfire," which is shown all over the world, rejected my evidence and ridiculed it. After a rather heated discussion on Ebonics with Oakland School Board member Toni Cook and me, Novak said this to his cohost, Bill Press:

> Bill, for the first time that we have been together-agreeing [*sic*]. I'm terribly depressed and I'm depressed to find two well educated women giving this *gobbledygook* [emphasis added] and not saying that they can teach these kids what is proper English so they can get along in this very tough economy and tough environment they're going into. . . . And the depressing thing is . . . we have spent money all over the country on this pseudo language, pseudo dialect when we're so short of money to teach these kids things they really need for survival in a tough society and in a tough economy.   (Cable News Network January 3, 1997)

Bill Press closed the show with these remarks.

> And by the way, tell them they're wrong when they're wrong and it's not going to hurt their feelings and if it does, hey, that's part of growing up, Bob. From the left, I be Bill Press. Good night for Crossfire.   (Cable News Network January 3, 1997)

I was dumbfounded! The linguistic ignorance, the power to spread that ignorance, and the arrogance of these two men were breathtaking.

Other people's reactions to the linguistic experts were similarly dismissive. For example, African American sociologist Julia Hare and I appeared as guests on Geraldo Rivera's Ebonics show (March 4, 1997), also watched by millions of people. During the show, I attempted to support my position for the Oakland Board's revised resolution by indicating that the Linguistic Society of America had passed a resolution approving the Board's proposal. Ms. Hare looked at me squarely and said, "Oh, they are nothing but a bunch of linguistic missionaries."

At least one person, Jesse Jackson (he may have been the only one), did listen to the experts and dramatically changed his position about Ebonics and the Oakland Board's resolution. At the beginning of the debate, Reverend Jackson had criticized harshly the resolution by saying, "I understand the attempt to reach out to these children, but this is an unacceptable surrender, borderlining on disgrace. . . . It's teaching down to our children" (Lewis 1996). Jackson's criticism indicates that he, like many people, thought the Board had proposed to *teach* Ebonics. However, after a meeting with Oakland school officials and advisors that clarified the intent of the Board's proposal, Jackson changed his position and endorsed Oakland's plan. He pointed out that "they're not trying to teach black English as a standard language . . . They're looking for tools to teach children standard English so they might be competitive" (Davidson 1996:A6).

It was disturbing that Reverend Jackson was actually criticized for changing his position after meeting with Oakland officials. A number of columnists commented negatively on the leader's reversal. Rob Morse sneered, "For a few days it was fun listening to Jesse Jackson do 180s on the subject" (1997:A3) of Ebonics; and Louis Menand, writing in the *New Yorker*, said Jackson "has a knack for entering as a conciliator in controversies he himself helped stir up" (1997:4). To my knowledge, Jackson received no praise for acknowledging his misinterpretation of the issues and his subsequent decision to change his position after meeting with the experts. My impression is that most people were far more comfortable with Jackson's original position, which denigrated Ebonics, than they were with his later, more enlightened position.

It was disheartening to observe that many people who denigrated Ebonics were granted the status of experts during the debate. This was the case for Armstrong Williams, a conservative, nationally syndicated columnist and television talk show host. Mr. Williams was one of only a dozen people who were invited to testify at the Senate hearings on Ebonics. Here is an excerpt from his testimony.

> The controversy and the tumult surrounding Oakland School Board's proposal to use "Ebonics" as a means of teaching standard English deeply troubles me . . . [b]ut even more troubling to me is what I think is a misguided approach to education in this country. . . . I have with me here my editorial assistant . . . who was born and raised a short distance from here in Southeast Washington – I remember him telling me that when he attended Ketchum Elementary School in Anacostia, his mother constantly corrected his broken English, not allowing him or his brother to make a habit out of speaking his neighborhood slang.   (*Ebonics* 1997)

Armstrong Williams was *invited* to testify, in spite of the fact that he probably has never taken even an elementary course in linguistics. How did he qualify to provide testimony along with distinguished linguistic experts like Dr. Orlando Taylor, Professor and Dean of the Graduate School of Arts and Sciences at Howard University; Dr. William Labov, Professor of Linguistics at the University of Pennsylvania; and Dr. Robert Williams, Professor Emeritus of Psychology at Washington University and the scholar who coined the term *Ebonics*? Clearly someone with the power to select witnesses liked what Armstrong Williams had to say about Ebonics, in spite of the fact that his message was uninformed. When

I called Senator Specter's office and asked to be a witness, I was told that all of the witnesses had been selected. The distinguished Stanford University linguistic researcher John Rickford was also rejected as a witness; he had to submit his testimony in the form of a support letter. The witness selection process for the Ebonics hearings provides another telling example that we need to do so much more than publicize research findings to surmount the obstacles facing Ebonics speakers.

Lesson #12 – The intricate relationships between language and power in the United States are hidden from most people

The only way that we can explain many of the reactions to Ebonics is to consider the complex relationships between language and power, and the standard language ideology in this country. In his masterful discussion of these relationships, the British linguist Norman Fairclough noted that language is "being increasingly caught up in domination and oppression" (1989:4). For speakers of Ebonics and their ancestors, this was the case right from the beginning. The domination and oppression started during slavery and continues to this very day, although not to the same degree. Slave owners, the dominant group, used language as a calculated tool of oppression when they separated slaves who spoke the same language. The obvious goal of this ruthless act of language planning was to prevent communication among the slaves that might result in a successful insurrection and the end of domination by the slave masters. John Baugh's (1998) analysis is correct: Ebonics is indeed "the linguistic consequence of the slave trade."

Another powerful domination tactic during slavery was the strict prohibition against teaching slaves to read and write. In their comprehensive discussion of slave codes during the colonial period, Frankin and Moss noted:

> For major offenses . . . slaves were to receive sixty lashes and be placed in the pillory, where their ears were to be cut off. For petty offences, such as insolence and associating with whites and free blacks, they were to be whipped, branded, or maimed . . . Under no conditions were [slaves] to be taught to read and write.   (1994:58, 62)

For slaves and their descendants, the impact of the prohibition against formal instruction in reading and writing, which lasted nearly 200 years in some states, was inestimable. It supported the evolution and development of the linguistic rules that speakers use to generate modern-day Ebonics. There is no evidence of a group of illiterate people anywhere in the world who succeeded in learning a standard language before they had the opportunity to learn to read and write.

As the slave codes indicate, the dominant group exercised power over the slaves and their language through the use of coercion, including physical violence. Today this subordination tactic is prohibited, but the dominant group maintains linguistic power by employing the less transparent tactic of manufacturing consent (Fairclough 1989). This involves convincing the subordinate group to accept the standard language ideology, which Lippi-Green defines as "a bias toward an abstracted, idealized, homogeneous spoken language which is imposed from above, and which takes as its model the written language. The most salient feature is the goal of suppression of variation of all kinds" (1994:166).

The standard language ideology is pervasive and deeply entrenched in the United States. The dominant group has succeeded in achieving almost unanimous consent that Ebonics is bad and should be rejected, and that Standard English is good and should be the only acceptable variety. Discussion of the other lessons has indicated that subordination tactics are employed to suppress the use of Ebonics and other non-standard varieties of English. Chief among these during the debate were mockery, ridicule, and derogatory labeling.

Now we can explain why Bill Cosby, a person who is deeply committed to the empowerment of African Americans, would parody Ebonics. He has accepted the standard language ideology. While Mr. Cosby's support of African American causes and institutions has been unfailing, he, like almost everyone else in this country, is unable to see the extent to which his assumptions about SE and Ebonics have been shaped by relations of power between the dominant group and the subordinate one. Other African Americans – some prominent, like Maya Angelou, Kweisi Mfume, Jesse Jackson, and some not so prominent – could not see these relations either. (It is important to note again that Jesse Jackson changed his position regarding Ebonics.) Perhaps that is why everyone was laughing so uproariously at Ebonics jokes when there is nothing funny about using a group's language as a tool to degrade and deride them, to malign their intelligence and their moral character, and to continue their oppression.

Acceptance of the standard language ideology by well-educated African Americans should not be entirely puzzling. Conforming to the standards (for language and many other behaviors) set by the dominant group has been a requirement for survival, literally. Conformity was a requirement during slavery, with its strict, brutal, and coercive codes, and it is a requirement today, although the codes related to language rely more on consent than coercion. Comments during the debate about the need to speak Standard English in order to get a job elucidate this point.

> Black English may suffice on the streets of Oakland and other big cities. But don't expect it to get you into college or land you a well-paying job. For that only standard English will do. ("A pitiless hoax" 1996:B6)

This position was articulated in a *San Diego Union-Tribune* editorial and was supported by Albert Shanker (1997), president of the 900,000-member American Federation of Teachers, who noted that the Oakland Board members

> recognized that people who want to be successful in American society must be proficient in mainstream English. Many of Oakland's African-American students are not, and they are at a disadvantage when they try to get jobs or further education.

In her article "Ebonics is Black-on-Black Crime," Karen Hunter criticized leaders for not stressing the importance of the relationship between getting a good job and speaking Standard English.

> The Oakland school board, and the handful of New York leaders who jumped on the Ebonics bandwagon . . . claim to be concerned with making poor black children "feel better" . . . but how good will that kid feel when the only job he can hold down is at McDonald's? "Would you like fries with that?"   (1997:41)

Finally, Bill Cosby (Groer and Gerhart 1997) used another parody to express his views on the need to speak Standard English in order to get a job.

> I was at a fund-raiser for Morehouse College. . . . Some speakers called it Mo'house and some said Morehouse. Being the smart aleck that I am, I got up and said I wish someone would please explain for me, please, the difference. The school president explained . . . "The difference between Morehouse and Mo'house is that the ones that already have a job say Mo'house."   (1997:C3)

In spite of the possibility of an empty promise, Ebonics speakers and their descendants have waged a valiant struggle to conform to the standard language patterns. Failure to conform could indeed cost them a job, and if there is no job, there is no food, no shelter, and possibly no life. We should not be surprised then that so many African Americans embrace and cling to the standard language ideology. They are convinced that it is necessary for their survival. The poet June Jordan's warning captures this explicitly.

> The powerful don't play; they mean to keep that power, and those who are the powerless (you and me) better shape up/mimic/ape/suck-in the very image of the powerful, or the powerful will destroy you – you and our children.   (1985:138)

Lesson #13 – A relatively small but persistent chorus of voices has resisted the subordination of Ebonics for more than thirty years, and they continued this resistance during the debate

The coining of the term Ebonics twenty-five years ago was a bold act of resistance initiated by the Black psychologist Robert Williams (1975) at a conference he convened on cognitive and language development in the Black child. During the conference, attended by both Black and White scholars, Williams met separately with the Black scholars, who were frustrated and angry about the fact that White scholars dominated the research on Black English. It was then that the term *Ebonics* was coined. Williams reported:

> I coined the term ebonics. . . . I had grown sick and tired of White linguists writing about the language of African Americans. Their descriptions of our

> language were "substandard speech," "restrictive speech," "deviant speech,"
> "deficient speech," "nonstandard English," and so on in this negative fash-
> ion . . . My language is me. It is an extension of my being, my essence. It is
> a reflection and badge of my culture. Criticism of my language is essentially
> a direct attack on my self-esteem and cultural identity.   (1997:209)

I am not aware of any evidence that shows that White linguists used the terms
"deviant" and "deficient" to describe Ebonics, but many non-linguists certainly
did. Williams' anger stemmed from the fact that others had control over describing his language and deciding what to call it. Thus the naming process for the
psychologist and his colleagues represented a conscious and determined act of
resistance to the dominant group's power to name another group's language.
Williams noted:

> The African American scholars and I decided that we needed to become self-
> determined and take over this issue and name our language. We must name
> and define our reality rather than let others do that for us.   (1997:209–210)

Many people believe that the selection of the new name was a glib act, as evidenced by the jokes about it and by Margo Jefferson's claim that it is pretentious:

> Let's call it Black English instead of ebonics. Americans can never resist
> inventing pretentious names for new schools of thought, new religions or
> aspiring new disciplines: euthenics, Dianetics, ebonics.   (1997:C11)

The invention of the name Ebonics was overtly and highly political. It represented a deliberate rejection of all of the names designated by scholars from the
dominant group. Apparently Margo Jefferson was totally unaware of the complex race and class issues that provided the motivation for renaming the language
variety spoken by many African Americans.

The Oakland Board's resolution, which sparked the debate, represents another
act of resistance to the subordination of Ebonics. In spite of the fact that the
first version contained language that was confusing and misleading, the Board's
proposal to teach African American students Standard English without devaluing
Ebonics, the language that many speak at home, is revolutionary. The content
of the proposal indicates that the Oakland Board rejected the standard language
ideology propagated so successfully in this country; the Board members refused
to consent to the notion that Ebonics is bad and thus has no place in the classroom.

Other examples of resistance include the tireless efforts of language professionals, specifically the many linguists and speech/language pathologists who
have been disseminating the facts about Ebonics through publications, conference presentations, and workshops for more than three decades. At the height
of the debate, the 6,000-member Linguistic Society of America (LSA) issued a
resolution that supported the Oakland School Board's proposal. Drafters of the
resolution articulated in clear and convincing language a restatement of facts
about Ebonics.

> The variety known as "Ebonics," "African American Vernacular English" (AAVE), and "Vernacular Black English" and by other names is systematic and rule-governed like all natural speech varieties. In fact, all human linguistic systems – spoken, signed, and written – are fundamentally regular. The systematic and expressive nature of the grammar and pronunciation patterns of the African American vernacular has been established by numerous scientific studies over the past thirty years. Characterizations of Ebonics as "slang," "mutant," "lazy," "defective," "ungrammatical," or "broken English" are incorrect and demeaning.   (Linguistic Society of America 1997)

The LSA's resolution was followed by another resolution disseminated by the 90,000-member American Speech-Language-Hearing Association (ASHA):

> The current debate over whether Black English is a dialect or a second language is not new to . . . ASHA . . . which addressed the controversy 13 years ago and formally recognized Black English, or "Ebonics," as a separate social dialect with systematic and highly regular linguistic features . . . ASHA . . . recognizes Ebonics as one of many linguistic varieties including standard English, Appalachian English, southern English, New York dialect, and Spanish influenced English. ASHA . . . also contends that no dialectal variety of English is a disorder or a pathological form of speech or language and that each variety serves a communication function as well as a social solidarity function.

Finally, one scholar in the African American intellectual community, linguist Geneva Smitherman, has engaged in an extraordinary effort to resist the subordination of Ebonics. Dr. Smitherman uses Ebonics to write portions of her books and articles for academic journals. In a recent article entitled "Black language and the education of Black children: one mo once," Smitherman wrote:

> When the Oakland School Board tapped into the Ebonics framework, they were seeking an alternative pedagogical paradigm to redress the non-education of black youth in their school district. We should applaud their refusal to continue doing more of the same that has not worked in the past. *Speaking of which, how come ain none of dese black so-call "leaders" raise no sand bout the lack of literacy among black youth? Seem to me dat's where they ought to be puttin they energy instead of doggin those Oakland school folk!*   [emphasis added] (1997:29)

The last two sentences are replete with phonological and syntactic features characteristic of Ebonics: the use of the double negative *ain none*; the use of *bout* that exhibits the absence of the unstressed initial syllable *a*; the use of *dese* and *dat's*, which exhibits the *d* sound instead of the *th* sound; the use of *in* instead of *ing* in *puttin* and *doggin*, and the use of the regularized form of the possessive pronoun *they* instead of *their*.

In many publications, including her first book on Ebonics, *Talkin and testifyin: the language of Black America*, Smitherman (1986) writes in both SE and Ebonics, boldly rejecting all of the appropriacy arguments (Fairclough 1992, Lippi-Green 1997) put forth by proponents of the standard language ideology. Dr. Smitherman has the courage to practice what she preaches: Ebonics is just as good as SE, and it can be used for the same purposes as SE. Smitherman is in a class by herself; I know of no other linguist or SLP who has this kind of professional courage. Many of us have accepted the appropriacy arguments; thus we would not be comfortable writing academic documents in Ebonics, and most important, we are too afraid that our work might not get published if we wrote in that dialect. As Lippi-Green noted, the threats are real.

The need for a new strategy

The lessons learned from the Ebonics debate – and there are many – have revealed with disturbing consistency the colossal failure of the research dissemination strategy. Repeating, for more than three decades, the well-researched facts about Ebonics in distinguished, scholarly, impassioned, and energetic voices has not changed the American people's assessment of the dialect. The lessons learned provide overwhelming evidence that the majority of the people in the United States still believe that Ebonics is a pseudo-language, street language, slang, junk, gibberish, verbal stew, broken English, a joke, or just plain old bad English that needs to be corrected. It is futile to continue repeating the facts about Ebonics. We are already hoarse from continually screaming a linguistic message that almost no one wants to hear, let alone accept. Michele Foster pointed out

> that most pundits had already decided what they believed; they were saying, "Don't confuse me with the facts, I've already made up my mind." And they wouldn't change their minds even if they were presented with the linguistic facts, because the controversy over Ebonics is about more than language; it is about politics.   (1997:7)

Another strategy is urgently needed to help Ebonics speakers overcome the long-standing and crippling educational, social, and economic problems caused by the public's erroneous and contemptuous assessment of their language. We, the language professionals – linguists and speech/language pathologists in particular – have a responsibility to develop and implement a new, successful strategy. We owe this to Ebonics speakers. These speakers have given us so much; we have used their language to build our professional careers. The time is ripe for us to give something back – something substantial, as Rickford (1997b) articulated so persuasively in his splendid but guilt-provoking article "Unequal partnership: Sociolinguistics and the African American speech community."

The task of developing and implementing a viable new strategy has been made less daunting for everyone because John Baugh has already completed some of the groundwork. Baugh presents a compelling argument for a bold new strategy that would involve classifying Ebonics speakers as language minority speakers.

This would make them eligible for federal funds that could be used to pay for formal instruction in Standard English. Baugh (1998) argued:

> The term "language minority" is too narrowly defined under current regulations, and . . . a revised definition is needed in support of reforms that seek to provide high academic standards for all students; indeed, this need has been accentuated by the Ebonics controversy . . . We need language policies that will ensure that students who are *not-native speakers of standard English* [emphasis added] will not fail due to linguistic neglect. The status quo is one that favors students who arrive at school speaking standard American English . . . Unless systemic reforms take adequate account of the dynamics of linguistic diversity among students we are unlikely to meet our desired goal to combine high academic standards with greater educational equity for all.

Baugh also argued that classifying Ebonics speakers, who are non-native speakers of Standard English, as language minority students is justified because of their unique linguistic history:

> Slave descendants have a unique linguistic history . . . when compared to every other group that has migrated to the U.S. As forced immigrants . . . slaves did not have the linguistic luxury of a gradual transition to English. Whereas the typical European immigrant came to the U.S. with fellow speakers of their native language, slaves were linguistically isolated upon capture; that is, whenever possible. Whereas the typical European immigrant was able to maintain a family, slaves had no such right; as chattel they were subject to immediate sale; a practice that destroyed many black families. Whereas the typical European immigrant was able to attend public schools, slaves were denied education by law, and after emancipation, were subject to inferior education under strict policies of educational apartheid.

No one likes to talk about slavery; it was such a brutal, painful, dehumanizing, and sad chapter in our history. But Baugh is correct; it is essential that we take this history into full consideration, especially the language and education part of it, when searching for strategies to surmount the linguistic barriers that Ebonics speakers face. The time is long overdue for this country to acknowledge that it created the circumstances that gave rise to and sustained Ebonics. The United States has a responsibility to help Ebonics speakers add Standard English to their repertoires. This country owes these speakers formal instruction in Standard English, and yes, federal funds should be used to pay for it, contrary to the opinion of racist legislators. Americans cannot feign innocence and pretend that Ebonics speakers talk the way they do because they are "too lazy" to speak "correctly." This may be an expedient excuse to further suppress Ebonics speakers, but it is another blatant falsehood. Baugh has already proposed a new, well-motivated classification system that is based on the necessary and sufficient evidence for categorizing Ebonics speakers as a language minority group. His reformed categorization scheme highlights and justifies the need for federal funds. In Orlando Taylor's testimony during the Senate hearings on Ebonics, he also stressed the need for federal support for Ebonics speakers. He told Senator Specter that the federal government should

> provide funds and incentives for local school boards to upgrade the skills of the current teacher force to teach standard English to culturally and linguistically diverse learners [and] [p]rovide funds to support research and dissemination on "best practices" to teach standard English to African American and other children that do not speak standard English as their primary language system.   (*Ebonics* 1997)

If Americans are serious about the linguistic empowerment of Ebonics speakers, they will have to pay for them to learn Standard English. It is imperative that the people in this country recognize this essential fact. Language professionals have a key role to play, for we must provide the leadership required to change the educational policies so that they reflect an expanded definition of language minority students. Baugh has argued convincingly that the new definition should include all non-native speakers of Standard English. The enormous task of changing the relevant educational policies will not be easy or accomplished quickly. However, if we do not commit ourselves to completing this task and solving the oppressive language-related problems that Ebonics speakers have endured for so long, we will have no defense, as language professionals, when we are placed in the shameful category of imprudent, short-sighted Americans described by Randall Robinson:

> American decision makers, who walk the power corridors of media, government, industry, and academia, are characterized by a blissful and self-serving forgetfulness. When the great global and domestic problems that beset our society are divorced from their derivation or history, public policymakers do not feel constrained to attend to such problems before or beyond the predictable intermittent flare-up. Like impressive dreams that cannot be recalled moments after waking, Americans quickly forget about the crises whose evolution they never studied to begin with. The [Ebonics controversies], the Somalias, the South Central L.A.'s, the Three Mile Islands – with the loss of media interest these dissolve quickly from all public memory. Policymakers then without solving much of anything, move on to the next lighted stage.   (1998:125)

The Ebonics controversy was, indeed, a lighted stage, but some of us will not move on. We are committed to solving the problems that were illuminated, once again, by the debate. The lessons learned were first published nearly a decade ago; however, they are still relevant today for they offer critical insights that can be utilized to help solve the long-standing challenge of providing appropriate language assessments for Ebonics speakers.

14 Variation, versatility, and Contrastive Analysis in the classroom[1]

ANGELA E. RICKFORD AND
JOHN R. RICKFORD

Introduction

A fundamental principle of variation theory, from its inception more than forty years ago, is that linguistic variation is the norm rather than the exception in human language use. Indeed, it was the weakness of the standard tools for analyzing such variation in *linguistics* (free variation and categorical conditioning), pitted against the strength and ubiquity of variation in *language*, that led to the development of modern sociolinguistics, with its concepts of inherent variability, quantitative and variable rule analysis, attentiveness to the social and stylistic dimensions of language use, and so on.[2]

In American and other schools around the world, however, teachers have often sought to *limit* the linguistic variation of their students, deeming non-standard or vernacular varieties unacceptable for classroom (sometimes even playground) use, and eschewing literary materials or pedagogical approaches that refer to or use such varieties. The motivation for this is understandable: teachers and parents alike usually want to ensure that students acquire the standard variety associated with academic success and upward socioeconomic mobility. But the approach is ironic since some of the most successful authors and poets – Chinua Achebe, Robert Burns, James Joyce, V. S. Naipaul, Raja Rao, and Alice Walker, to name half a dozen who write in English – draw creatively on both their standard and vernacular varieties. Moreover, the experimental evidence we have on this point (see below) suggests that outlawing or ignoring the vernacular is LESS effective at helping students acquire the standard variety than recognizing it and studying its similarities to and differences from the standard via Contrastive Analysis (CA) and other methods.

In this paper, we suggest that instead of linguistic uniformity, teachers seek to develop linguistic *versatility* in their students, and we propose they do so through a revised Contrastive Analysis approach that builds creatively on literature and

---

[1] This is a considerably revised version of a paper given at NWAV-31, the thirty-first annual conference on New Ways of Analyzing Variation in language, held at Stanford University in 2002. It is a pleasure to include it in a volume dedicated to our friend and colleague, Walt Wolfram.

[2] See J. Fischer (1958), Labov (1972h), J. Rickford (1979).

music rather than the boring drills associated with CA in earlier times. The word *versatile* is defined as "capable of doing many things competently" (*American heritage dictionary of the English language* 2000:1912). Linguistic versatility, as we conceive it, is the applied counterpart of the orderly linguistic variation whose structure and meaning are studied by sociolinguists and variationists. To some extent, we want students and teachers to become variationists themselves, discovering anew the systematic patterning in variable language data, as students in Baltimore and Ocracoke did in the language awareness classroom exercises discussed by Wolfram, Adger, and Christian (1999). But we also want them to value linguistic versatility as an asset – one exemplified by the best writers and singers and rappers and comedians and preachers and pray-ers and actors and actresses from their own and other communities – and one that they should develop and learn to deploy strategically in their own speech and writing. While most of our examples will be drawn from the African American and Caribbean communities and literatures we know best, the approach can be adopted more widely, especially where mainstream and vernacular varieties are in contact.

Why should variationists care about classrooms?

In response to the question some might ask, about why variationists should be concerned about classrooms anyway, the answer is that we have an ethical responsibility to give back something to the people "whose data fuel out theories and descriptions" and careers (Rickford 1997:186). Unlike linguists working in some other subfields, variationists generally base their analyses on corpora of recorded speech from real people in real communities, and the time and cooperation they extend to us creates what Labov calls the "Principle of the Debt Incurred":

> (1)   An investigator who has obtained linguistic data from members of a speech
>   community has an obligation to use the knowledge based on that data for the
>   benefit of the community, when it has need of it.   (1982:173)

Walt Wolfram, the sociolinguist to whom this volume is dedicated, is one of the best exemplars of this principle, having shared the fruits of his sociolinguistic research on local varieties in North Carolina and elsewhere with community members through accessible books, videos, and library displays (e.g. Wolfram and Schilling-Estes 1997, Wolfram, Dannenberg, Knick, and Oxendine 2002, and the videos *The Ocracoke brogue* and *Indian by birth*), and through lifelong contributions to the study of African American and other vernaculars in education (e.g. Wolfram 1969, Wolfram and Adger, 1993, Wolfram, Adger, and Christian 1999).

In the case of African American and Caribbean speakers – so often the focus of variationist study – community needs are particularly acute in the classroom. Le Page (1968) first urged language specialists to help train teachers to use Contrastive Analysis and other linguistically informed methods in Caribbean schools after reviewing evidence that only 10.7% to 23.1% of the students in Barbados,

Table 14.1 *National Assessment of Educational Progress (NAEP)*
average reading scores for White and Black students in national
public schools, grades 4 and 8 for 2002, 2003, 2005

	White	Black	Gap
2002 (grade 4)	227.08 (0.334)	197.81 (0.555)	29.27
2003 (grade 4)	227.10 (0.245)	197.25 (0.426)	29.85
2005 (grade 4)	227.64 (0.19)	198.89 (0.337)	28.75
2002 (grade 8)	271.06 (0.473)	244.41 (0.760)	26.65
2003 (grade 8)	270.44 (0.225)	243.6 (0.507)	26.84
2005 (grade 8)	269.42 (0.172)	242.03 (0.441)	27.39

NOTE: Numbers in parentheses indicate standard errors.

Guyana, Jamaica, and Trinidad who took the English Language General Certificate of Education exam in 1962 had passed it. Craig (1999) reported similarly negative results. Within the US, the persistent Black–White achievement gap in the language arts and other subjects continues to be a source of great concern to educators and policymakers alike (Singham 2003). Recent data from the National Assessment of Educational Progress, shown in Table 14.1,[3] indicate that reading achievement scores for Black students in public schools nationwide lag behind those of White students by about 29 points at grade 4 and about 27 points at grade 8. Similar results obtain for writing; for instance, NAEP data for writing show that White eighth graders scored an average of 159.25 in 2002, while Black eighth graders scored 24.91 points less (134.31).

Contrastive Analysis

Given the long-standing belief and recent evidence (Charity, Scarborough, and Griffin 2003) that vernacular speaking students who are more competent in Standard English (SE) do better on measures of reading and writing, educators and sociolinguists interested in improving the proficiency of African American Vernacular English (AAVE) and Caribbean English Creole (CEC) speakers in SE have long advocated that teachers employ a version of Contrastive Analysis. Contrastive Analysis, initially developed five decades ago (Lado 1957) involves a comparison of the speaker's native language and target language to draw the attention of students and teachers to areas in which their systems differ, and to predict and help students avoid errors in the acquisition of the target language resulting from interference or transfer.

In the case of inner-city African American speakers, Contrastive Analysis involves comparisons between AAVE and SE, and a series of exercises to help

---

[3] Source: US Department of Education, Institute of Education Sciences, National Center for Education Statistics, National Assessment of Educational Progress data for each year, as made available at: http://nces.ed.gov/nationsreportcard/nde [last accessed 4 June 2007].

them recognize the differences and translate from AAVE to SE (Feigenbaum 1970). The massive handbook of the Standard English Program (SEP handbook, n.d.) in California, written by Orlando Taylor and others in the early 1980s to facilitate "proficiency in Standard English for Speakers of Black English," and reportedly used in 300 schools, including Oakland, was built around Contrastive Analysis, as the following quotation emphasizes:

> (2) The approaches used in this study are drills which are variations of the contrastive analysis and the comparative analysis [techniques] in teaching Black children to use Standard English. . . . By comparing the Standard English structure to be taught and the equivalent or close nonstandard structure, the student can see how they differ. Many students have partial knowledge of Standard English; that is, they can recognize and produce it but without accurate control. . . . For many students, this sorting out is the beginning of a series of steps from passive recognition to active production.

The extract from the SEP handbook in Table 14.2 illustrates a sample lesson on possessive -s, pursuing its objective of teaching the contrast between "non-standard" (AAVE) and "standard" (SE) through discrimination, identification, and translation drills.

The older but less well known "TalkAcross" program, designed by Crowell, Kolbar, Stewart, and Johnson (1974), is similar, featuring Contrastive Analysis between "Black English" (BE) and Standard English (SE) in a teacher's manual and activity book. As the authors note:

> (3) This . . . mixture of similarities and differences can create complex problems for both student and teacher when the student is a speaker of BE and the teacher a speaker of SE only. The student knows that what he speaks is different from SE, but he doesn't know how to articulate these differences. The teacher only hears mistakes, without being able to place the structures used by the student in a consistent framework. Both student and teacher need to learn something about the grammar – the system – of the other's dialect. And the best way to learn this is by **contrasting** the other's dialect with his own.   (Crowell *et al.* 1974:3)

The most recent exemplar of the Contrastive Analysis approach is Wheeler and Swords (2006). In this book, a sociolinguist and an elementary school teacher team up to develop a series of lessons to help students switch from Informal to Formal English – essentially AAVE to SE. One contrast with earlier work and one similarity with our own and more recent work (e.g. Sweetland 2006) is that the authors advocate less use of drills and they also make more use of literature:

> (4) Once you have located stories that contain the grammatical patterns most often used by your students, you can use the literature to enhance your lessons in contrastive analysis. When you are using a work of literature to emphasize a specific pattern, highlight this pattern by writing examples from the book on chart paper and discussing them before reading the story aloud.   (Wheeler and Swords 2006:146)

Table 14.2 *Extracts from a Contrastive Analysis exercise in the Proficiency in Standard English for Speakers of Black Language handbook (SEP, n.d.)*

Instructional Focus: Possessives (Morpheme /s/ with nouns)
Objective: Given structured drill and practice contrasting the use of possessive nouns, the students will be able to differentiate between standard and nonstandard usage and to formulate sentences using the standard form in response to statements or questions. . . .

1. In order to assess the students' ability in auditory discrimination, the teacher will lead the students in the following drill. Students will respond by displaying a <u>same</u> or <u>different</u> response card.

DISCRIMINATION DRILL

Teacher Stimulus	Student Response
This is Joe car	
This is Joe's car	Different
[Other examples] . . .	

2. Teacher will explain and model the standard form and have students repeat several examples, giving additional help where needed.
3. Teacher will lead the students in the following drill. Students will respond by displaying standard or nonstandard response cards.

IDENTIFICATION DRILL

Teacher Stimulus	Student Response
Mary brother is little	Nonstandard . . .
Tom's truck is red	Standard
[Other examples] . . .	

4. To check for understanding, the teacher will call on individual students to respond to questions and statements similar to those in the following drill. Students will respond in complete sentences using the standard form . . .

TRANSLATION DRILL

Teacher Stimulus	Student Response
Jesse truck is red	Jesses's truck is red . . .
Brian mother is ill	Brian's mother is ill . . .

There are several advantages to using Contrastive Analysis to help vernacular speakers acquire the standard variety, including the fact that it appears to have worked everywhere it was tried and evaluated, at least more so than alternative approaches that ignore or disparage the vernacular. For instance, in a study conducted at Aurora University (Taylor 1990), African American students from Chicago inner-city areas were divided into two groups. The experimental group was taught the differences between Black English and Standard English through Contrastive Analysis. The control group was taught composition through conventional techniques, with no specific reference to the vernacular. After eleven weeks, Taylor's experimental group showed a dramatic DECREASE (−59%) in the use of ten targeted Black English features in their Standard English writing,

Table 14.3 *Mean scores and gains for experimental and control writing groups, Los Angeles Unified School District (Source: Maddahian and Sandamela 2000)*

GROUP TEST	Mean pre-test score	Mean post-test score	GAIN
Experimental writing	10.80	13.30	2.5
Control writing	9.06	10.74	1.68

Table 14.4 *Reading composite scores for bidialectal and control groups, DeKalb County, Georgia, on Iowa Test of Basic Skills (Source: Rickford 2002; see also Harris-Wright 1999)*

Group	1994–95	1995–96	1996–97
Bidialectal post-test	42.39	41.16	34.26
Bidialectal pre-test	39.71	38.48	30.37
GAIN by bidialectal students	+2.68	+2.68	+3.89
Control post-test	40.65	43.15	49.00
Control pre-test	41.02	41.15	49.05
GAIN by control students	−0.37	+2.0	−0.05

while the control group showed a slight INCREASE (+8.5%) in their use of such features.

Data from two other programs are shown in Tables 14.3 and 14.4. Table 14.3 shows data from the Academic English Mastery Program (AEMP) in the Los Angeles Unified School District (formerly the "Language Development Program for African American Children" – see LeMoine and LAUSD 1999).[4] Students in the experimental group – the one that explicitly compares and contrasts African American language and mainstream American English – show greater gains on writing tests taken in 1998–99 than students in the control group. Similar results obtain for the reading and language components of the SAT-9 test.[5] Of course, it should be added that Contrastive Analysis is a central but not the only element in this program. Similar to this are results from Kelli Harris-Wright's bidialectal/Contrastive Analysis program in DeKalb County, Georgia, shown in Table 14.4. Note that the students in the bidialectal group, who were taught using Contrastive Analysis, made *bigger relative reading composite gains*

---

[4] The AEMP involves more than Contrastive Analysis, including language experience approaches, whole language, and an Afrocentric curriculum. But at the heart of it is respect for student's home language and comparison of African American language and Standard American English structures. For more information, see LeMoine (2001).

[5] For instance, at the 109th Street school, African American students in the experimental AEMP ($n = 12$) had mean scores of 21 and 24 on the reading and language components of the SAT-9, while a comparison group of African American students who were not in the AEMP ($n = 104$) had lower mean scores, of 16 and 20 respectively.

Table 14.5 *Mean performance of Northeastern African American third and fourth graders on sentence "correction" from AAVE to SE tests as a function of training condition (Source: Fogel and Ehri 2000:221)*

Training condition	Pre-test	Post-test	Gain
ESP	4.17	6.52	2.35
ES	3.69	3.43	−0.26
E	3.48	3.72	0.24

NOTES: ESP = Exposure to SE text; Strategy Instruction in SE rules, and Practice in converting AAVE to SE [essentially Contrastive Analysis]; ES = Exposure to SE text, plus Strategy Instruction in SE rules; E = Exposure to SE text only.

every year than students in the control group, who did not receive Contrastive Analysis.[6]

Similar to this is a report by Fogel and Ehri who describe experiments with eighty-nine third and fourth grade African American students in two Northeastern schools where the writing achievement levels were low. The children selected for the study used AAVE features in their writing. They were trained to use SE through one of the following three techniques (2000:212): "(1) exposure to SE features in stories [E]; (2) story exposure plus explanation of SE rules [ES]; and (3) story exposure, SE rule instruction and guided practice transforming sentences from BEV to SE features [ESP]." Although the authors do not refer to the third method as Contrastive Analysis, it is clear from their description that ESP is essentially Contrastive Analysis. And from the results in Table 14.5, it is equally clear that ESP/Contrastive Analysis is far more effective than the other methods in helping students translate AAVE syntax into SE, as measured by the gain between pre-tests and post-tests (2000:222): "Tukey pair-wise comparisons showed that students in the ESP condition made significantly greater gains from pretest to posttest ($p \leq .001$) than students in the ES and E conditions, which did not differ from each other ($p \geq .05$)."

The most recent experimental work on the effectiveness of Contrastive Analysis is that of Sweetland (2006). As Tables 14.6a and 14.6b show, fourth to sixth graders in Cincinnati, Ohio, who were taught by the "Sociolinguistic Approach" (which includes Contrastive Analysis as a central component) performed better than students in the Writing Process and No Treatment approaches, which were not

---

[6] Students in the bidialectal group generally had lower absolute scores (particularly in the 1996–97 year) than students in the control group, although it is striking that the bidialectal group was able to surpass the control group in their post-test performance in 1995.

Table 14.6a *Mean scores of students taught by different approaches for ten weeks, on a test of their ability to revise written vernacular text toward Standard English in elementary schools in Cincinnati, Ohio (Source: Sweetland 2006:197–8)*

Approach	Score
Sociolinguistic approach (CA)	68.9%
Writing process (No CA)	64.4%
No treatment (No CA or WP)	60.4%

Table 14.6b *Mean evaluations of elementary students' writing (by outside raters) on a "Conventions" trait rubric, in Cincinnati, Ohio (Source: Sweetland 2006:223)*

	Pre-test	Post-test	Gain	SIG?($p<$)
Sociolinguistic approach	2.79	3.09	0.30	YES .00001
Writing process	3.03	3.11	[0.08]	NO 37
No treatment	2.68	2.88	0.20	Yes .016

exposed to Contrastive Analysis, on tests involving revisions from the vernacular to the standard and adherence to English writing conventions.[7]

Despite this body of experimental evidence in its favor, traditional Contrastive Analysis programs do have weaknesses too. There are repeated critiques of its association with behaviorism and structuralism, and of its empirical weakness as a predictive model of learner's errors (see Wardhaugh 1970, Bialystok and Hakuta 1994). These may have been exaggerated (see Thomas 2002) and there is good reason to believe that the resilient utility of Contrastive Analysis in the classroom may have been under-estimated (Danesi and DiPietro 1991), especially for second *dialect* learning and teaching (Kenji Hakuta, personal communication).

But another difficulty is that Contrastive Analysis exercises often involve translation only from the vernacular to the standard, not in both directions. Recall the example of possessive -*s* from the SEP handbook (Table 14.2). This undermines proponents' claims about the integrity and validity of the vernacular, and it runs counter to the underlying ideology of bidialectalism. Traditional Contrastive Analysis is also too dependent on boring ("drill and kill") pattern practice

[7] According to Sweetland (2006:197–8), none of the adjacent score differences (68.9% vs. 64.4%, 64.4% vs 60.4%) was statistically significant, as measured by a pairwise *t*-test, but the difference between the mean score of the Sociolinguistic Approach (68.9%) and that of the No Treatment approach (60.4%) was statistically significant ($p \leq 0.04$). It should be added that Sweetland's training exercises also made creative use of literature – indeed we would recommend her lesson plans as a model to those contemplating CA in the vernacular speaking classroom.

exercises, and it focuses too narrowly and myopically on language forms, as though effective and successful language use involves nothing more than pronouncing the first consonant in *them* with a voiced *th* rather than a *d*, and having an *-s* on the end of your third person present tense verb (*He walks*, not *He walk*).

Updating Contrastive Analysis through the use of literature and music

A fundamental goal of the updated Contrastive Analysis we advocate is the development of linguistic *versatility*, so it could just as well be called the *Versatility Approach*, to emphasize what is new and to put some distance between us and the behaviorist orientations and drill-and-kill methods associated with Contrastive Analysis. Although the versatility approach we advocate would focus on switching from vernacular to mainstream English and vice versa, it could also include the versatility of using other languages (Spanish, Swahili),[8] and variant words, rhyme schemes, poetic forms, and narrative styles, allowing it to mesh smoothly with existing English and language arts curricula. As far as possible, the samples of writing or song that we use with students should be accompanied by brief bios of their exemplars and their accomplishments, and their own accounts of their experiences (sometimes struggles) with vernacular and mainstream usage. By this means we hope to increase the ability of students to identify with and take pride in these models (their forebears) and their linguistic versatility. The idea is to have a program that affirms and builds up students, rather than putting them down, as the cycle of one-way vernacular to standard correction in traditional Contrastive Analysis appears to do.

We'll discuss several examples, beginning with African American writers and singers and then turning to examples from the Caribbean, which could be used there as well as in US schools (e.g. in New York or Chicago – cf. Fischer 1992, Irish 1995, Nero 2006) with AAVE and Creole speakers.

US examples, featuring African American writers and singers

In relation to the use of AAVE in the classroom, we already have some evidence that African American adolescents struggling through language and identity issues in the critical late elementary and middle school years view the acknowledgment of their own language as an important element in their education and cognitive growth. As the quotations below show, African American middle schoolers in East Palo, California, enjoy and value the use of AAVE in narrative texts:

---

[8] Roberta Flack's breathtaking rendition of "Angelitos Negros" on her *First Take* album (1969) could be used to demonstrate the versatility of a distinguished African American balladeer in Spanish and English.

(5) "I like it because dialect makes the story more interesting,"
"it puts excitement in it," and "helps the story by making it enjoyable."
"I like it because it helps the story sound like real people are talking."
"I like it because it is like I am in the story. It helps the story a lot because it makes the story younik [unique] in its own way; people have to hear there own way of talking."
"I like the dialect because it was my kind of talk. I enjoy reading dialect stories and also I think it help the story."
"I like the dialect because it puts a lot of feelings in it (= the story)."
"I like it because it gives people who aren't that culture and know nothing about it a chance to see how other people are." (Rickford 1999:135–6)

Although we could draw examples equally from poetry or prose (see Holton 1984, Rickford and Rickford 2000:22–38, Green 2002:164–99), we'll represent the use of AAVE in literature in this paper from poetry alone. The presence of rhyme in the poetry, already a pervasive part of Black vernacular culture (see Lee 2002) would complement the emphasis on phonemic awareness (see Adams, Foorman, Lurdberg, and Beeler 1998) in the modern curriculum, especially in the lower grades.

We'll begin with James Weldon Johnson, whose life spanned the late nineteenth and early twentieth century. He is known to many African Americans as the co-creator of the "Black national anthem" – "Lift every voice and sing." We will first consider his poem, "Sence you went away." Written in 1900, it was rendered, as he would put it, in "Negro dialect":

(6) *Sence you went away* (James Weldon Johnson)
Seems lak to me de stars don't shine so bright,
Seems lak to me de sun done loss his light,
Seems lak to me der's nothin' goin' right,
Sence you went away.
Seems lak to me de sky ain't half so blue, 5
Seems lak to me dat ev'thing wants you,
Seems lak to me I don't know what to do,
Sence you went away.
Seems lak to me dat ev'ything is wrong,
Seems lak to me de day's jes twice as long, 10
Seems lak to me de bird's forgot his song,
Sence you went away.
Seems lak to me I jes can't he'p but sigh,
Seems lak to me ma th'oat keeps gittin' dry,
Seems lak to me a tear stays in my eye, 15
Sence you went away.

Except for *done* (line 2), and *ain't* (line 5), the dialect is represented almost entirely through *phonology* – the monophthongization of *lak* "like," the word-final alveolar instead of velar nasals in *nothin'*, *goin'*, and *gittin'*, the simplification of postvocalic same-voice clusters (*loss*, line 2, *jes*, line 10) but their retention in mixed voice clusters (*went*, line 4), and so on. Students, in analyzing Weldon's depiction of dialect phonology, might notice (or be led to notice) that it is VARIABLE. Sometimes the variation is governed by neat linguistic constraints – for instance, voiced *th* or "edh" is always represented as *d*, as in *de sun* (line 2), or *der's* (line 3), but voiceless *th* or "theta" is NEVER represented as *t*, for instance *nothin* (line 3) and *th'oat* (line 14). One finds this pattern in other writers (like Dunbar). And it has an analog in the synchronic reality of vernacular speech reported in Labov, Cohen, Robbins, and Lewis (1968:94–5) and McGuire (2002), who note that interdental fricative realizations of voiceless *th* (theta) are far more common than interdental fricative realizations of voiced *th* (edh), both in Harlem and in Ohio. Indeed, Green (2002:119) suggests that word-initial *th* is never simplified in the African American vernacular.

The poem's rhyme scheme – aaab – is also worth noting. The absence of a rhyme in the final line reinforces the contrast between it and the ten-syllable iambic pentameter structure of the first three lines in each verse; the reduced length (five syllables) of the final line mirrors the reduced circumstances of the poet's life since his loved one's departure.

Johnson's Standard English poem, "The glory of the day was in her face" (see (7) below), is written in iambic pentameter throughout, and follows a different rhyme scheme (abab, cdcd, etc.). A teacher could use it to demonstrate the poet's linguistic versatility, and perhaps he/she could ask students to attempt to render it in the vernacular, much as we might have them translate "Sence you went away" into SE or even deeper vernacular.

(7)   *The glory of the day was in her face* (James Weldon Johnson)
        The glory of the day was in her face,
        The beauty of the night was in her eyes.
        And over all her loveliness, the grace
        Of Morning blushing in the early skies.

        And in her voice, the calling of the dove;   5
        Like music of a sweet, melodious part.
        And in her smile, the breaking light of love;
        And all the gentle virtues in her heart.

        And now the glorious day, the beauteous night,
        The birds that signal to their mates at dawn,   10
        To my dull ears, to my tear-blinded sight
        Are one with all the dead, since she is gone.

More interesting, particularly for older students, would be to discuss Johnson's turning away from dialect poetry in later years, and his decision to represent the seven Black folk sermons in *God's trombones* (Johnson 1927) in Standard English rather than dialect because he came to regard the latter as a medium with only two stops, pathos and humor. Another fruitful subject for discussion with students would be the debates he had with his friend Paul Laurence Dunbar about the use of dialect in poetry, reported in Johnson's (1933) autobiography, *Along this way*.

It would be difficult N O T to discuss Dunbar (1872–1906) in any "versatility" curriculum, not only because "he wrote extensively in both black dialect and standard English," but also because he "is one of the two or three greatest poets in the African American tradition and one of the greatest American poets" (Harper and Walton 2000:72). Here is a brief extract (the first six lines) from "The party":

(8) *The party* (Paul Laurence Dunbar)
    DEY had a gread big pahty down to Tom's de othah night;
    Was I dah? You bet! I neveh in my life see sich a sight;
    All de folks f'om fou' plantations was invited, an' dey come,
    Dey come troopin' thick ez chillun when dey hyeahs a fife an' drum.
    Evahbody dressed deir fines' – Heish yo' mouf an' git away,   5
    Ain't seen no sich fancy dressin' sence las' quah'tly meetin' day; . . .

We include this extract in part to show that Dunbar followed the same pattern as Johnson did, of representing voiced *th* (edh) as *d*, but voiceless *th* (theta) as *th* (contrast *Dey* and *othah*, line 1). But note also the labiodental realization of theta in line 5 (*mouf*). We could and should draw students' attention to this last feature, inviting them to discover from their own intuitions and from spoken and other written data that labiodental realizations are possible for both theta and edh in word-final positions (*mouf, smoove*), and for edh in medial positions as well (*bruvver*).

The next Dunbar poem we'd like to discuss is "A negro love song," one of Dunbar's best known and most anthologized dialect poems. We reprint the first verse:

(9) *A negro love song* (Paul Laurence Dunbar)
    Seen my lady home las' night,
    Jump back, honey, jump back.
    Hel' huh han' an' sque'z it tight,
    Jump back, honey, jump back.
    Hyeahd huh sigh a little sigh,   5
    Seen a light gleam f'om huh eye,
    An' a smile go flittin' by –
    Jump back, honey, jump back. . . .

We can't recount here all the features of this poem we would want to draw to the attention of students. But we would want them to note that Dunbar's representation of AAVE phonology is even more extensive than Johnson's (postvocalic *r*-deletion is included, for example: *huh, Hyeahd*, line 5, in addition to most of the phonological features represented in (6) above). At the same time, Dunbar adheres as faithfully as Johnson did to a strict metrical structure (here seven syllables a line, except for the six-syllabled refrain, "Jump back, honey, jump back") and a very regular rhyme scheme (here: ababcccb). The colloquial nature of the refrain comes through remarkably despite the passage of more than a hundred years, finding its near parallels, as students might note, in modern forms like "You GO, girl!" and "Step back, honey, step back!" The conversational ring of this refrain, like the choice of vernacular for the entire poem, is consonant with the audience – here a young man bragging to his friend or friends about a romantic encounter.

By contrast, the third Dunbar poem we'll discuss, "We wear the mask," is written in Standard English throughout, with lexical items from a relatively exalted register (*guile, myriad subtleties*):

(10) *We wear the mask* (Paul Laurence Dunbar)
　　 We wear the mask that grins and lies,
　　 It hides our cheeks and shades our eyes –
　　 This debt we pay to human guile;
　　 With torn and bleeding hearts we smile
　　 And mouth with myriad subtleties.　　　　　　　　　　　5

　　 Why should the world be over-wise,
　　 In counting all our tears and sighs?
　　 Nay, let them only see us while
　　 We wear the mask.

　　 We smile, but oh great Christ, our cries　　　　　　　　10
　　 To Thee from tortured souls arise.
　　 We sing, but oh the clay is vile
　　 Beneath our feet, and long the mile;
　　 But let the world dream otherwise,
　　 We wear the mask!　　　　　　　　　　　　　　　　15

Here, in terms of Hymes' (1972a) components of speech, the message content, the scene, the purposes, the audience, and the key are all quite different from their equivalents in "Step Back Honey" – as the poet complains to his brethren and sisteren, and at one point, to God, about the twin faces that Black people have to assume to survive suffering and injustice. Without assuming that serious subjects would always require Standard English (playwright August Wilson and poet Gwendolyn Brooks could be used to demonstrate otherwise), these two poems could lead into a fruitful discussion about appropriate occasions for the deployment of mainstream and vernacular varieties.

The final Dunbar poem that we think should be included in any "Versatility" curriculum would be his authobiographical poem, "The poet":

(11) *The poet* (Paul Laurence Dunbar)
　　 He sang of life, serenely sweet,
　　 With, now and then, a deeper note.
　　 From some high peak, nigh yet remote,
　　 He voiced the world's absorbing beat.
　　 He sang of love when earth was young,　　　　　　　　5
　　 And Love, itself, was in his lays.
　　 But, ah, the world, it turned to praise
　　 A jingle in a broken tongue.

This poem should be included as part of a larger discussion of how society's constraints and expectations can hinder one's expressiveness. For in it, the greatest American dialect poet, as many call him, reflects morosely on the fact that the contemporary world (led by influential critic William Dean Howells) recognized and praised ONLY his dialect poetry ("a jingle in a broken tongue") and NOT the Standard English poems in which he sought to address some of his deepest concerns. It was not until much later that SE poems of his like "I know why the caged bird sings" would become standard pieces for African American and other students in elocution contests. Usually, when linguistically versatile African American and Caribbean poets are limited by what publishes and sells, it is their work in the vernacular that is disparaged and discouraged. Dunbar is a striking example of the reverse.

Moving forward in time, let us next consider two songs from the repertoire of the late great Nina Simone (1933–2003). The first one, "To be young, gifted and Black," is in Standard English (e.g. plural -*s*, *is*, and *are* copulas are all "intact," see lines 6, 7, 8, 12):

(12) *To be young, gifted and Black* (Nina Simone and Weldon Irvine, Jr.)
    To be young, gifted and black,
    Oh what a lovely precious dream
    To be young, gifted and black,
    Open your heart to what I mean.
    In the whole world you know   5
    There's a billion boys and girls
    Who are young, gifted and black,
    And that's a fact!

    Young, gifted and black
    We must begin to tell our young   10
    There's a world waiting for you
    This is a quest that's just begun.

    When you feel really low
    Yeah, there's a great truth you should know
    When you're young, gifted and black   15
    Your soul's intact.

    Young, gifted and black
    How I long to know the truth
    There are times when I look back
    And I am haunted by my youth.   20

    Oh but my joy of today
    Is that we can all be proud to say
    To be young, gifted and black
    Is where it's at.

This is a beautifully crafted (and rendered) song, written in 1968–69 in homage to Simone's long-time friend Lorraine Hansberry, whose vernacular-studded play

A raisin in the sun ran for 538 performances on Broadway and won accolades and awards when it made its debut in 1959. For maximum effect, the song should be played in the classroom. One could go on to discuss Hansberry's work in turn,[9] or the differences between Simone's soulful rendering of her very Black-affirming and uplifting song, and its subsequent renditions by Donny Hathaway, Dionne Warwick, and reggae stars Bob and Marcia, among others. (See David Nathan's liner notes for her CD *Sugar in my* bowl.)

One could discuss Simone's words, likely to provide needed inspiration to many an African American student, and contrast the style and language of her "Ain't no use" song, also on ***her *Misunderstood* CD. The first two verses are reproduced here:

> (13) *Ain't no use* (Nina Simone)
> Ain't no use, baby,
> I'm leavin' the scene.
> Ain't no use, baby,
> You too doggone mean.
>
> Yes, I'm tired of payin' the dues   5
> Havin' the blues,
> Gettin' bad news,
> Ain't no use, baby. . . .

Among the grammatical features this short extract illustrates are negative concord (*Ain't no use*, line 1) and copula absence, permitted with second person and plural *are* (*You Ø too doggone mean*, l. 4) but not first person *am*, which contracts instead (*I'm leaving the scene*). In taking students through the contrasts between AAVE and SE via literature and song, rather than a series of lessons and drills, one would have to be sure to keep selecting samples that together span the range of the crucial set of differences so systematically covered in some of the older Contrastive Analysis literature, like Crowell *et al.* (1974).[10]

In the AAVE canon, let us turn to Sonia Sanchez (1934–), still a vital presence on the African American artistic scene. We'll start with two poems in the haiku format (seventeen syllables in three lines: five in the first and final lines, seven in the middle). The first is in Standard English:

> (14) *My father's eyes* (Sonia Sanchez)[11]
> i have looked into
>   my father's eyes and seen an
>   african sunset.

---

[9] See Rickford and Rickford (2000:28) for commentary on some of the vernacular elements in *A raisin in the sun*.

[10] Although Baugh (1999b) does not deal with Contrastive Analysis per se, it does propose creative use of "lyric shuffle" and other games for literacy instruction with African American kids, building on their fondness for rhyme, poetry, and music.

[11] Sanchez' haiku tribute to her father is in Steptoe (1997).

This brief but powerful evocation of her African ancestry illustrates two SE features which AAVE speakers often lack in their SE speech and writing as a result of transfer from their vernacular: possessive *s* (*father's eyes*) and the present perfect (*have looked*, *[have] seen*). The second haiku evokes the colloquial tongue of the African diaspora domestics with whom she empathizes:

> (15) *Haiku (for domestic workers in the African diaspora)* (Sonia Sanchez)[12]
>   i works hard but treated
>   bad   man. i'se telling you de
>   truth   i full of it.

One linguistic feature of note is the apparent violation of the haiku five-syllable requirement in the first line, which, as written, has six syllables. A likely explanation is that *treated* is to be reduced to one syllable when spoken [*tree'd*], much as *I is* is reduced to *i'se* in the second line, on the pattern of colloquial speech in the Caribbean and elsewhere. The absence of first person *am* in the first line – generally impermissible in AAVE – could also be fruitfully discussed. One might think that this is also absent to meet the five-syllable requirements of the initial line in a haiku; but a more likely explanation is that this is not intended to be AAVE, but the speech of an African diaspora worker in or from the Caribbean, where absence of first person *am* is permitted.[13]

We cannot resist leaving Sistah Sanchez without a taste of the first verse of the following poignant poem:

> (16) *Song no. 3 (for 2nd and 3rd grade sisters)* (Sonia Sanchez)
>   cain't nobody tell me any different
>   i'm ugly and you know it too
>   you just smiling to make me feel better
>   but I see how you start when nobody's watching you . . .

Here, in addition to examples of deleted (*you [Ø are] just smiling*) and nondeletable (*i'm ugly*) tokens of the copula, we find a striking example of negative inversion (*cain't nobody*). This could be used to help students discover the restrictions on such inversion in the vernacular (including the fact that the subject NP must be a negative indefinite – see Sells, Rickford, and Wasow [1996]) and to introduce the contrasting system in SE.

Given the popularity of rap and hip hop, and the emergence of book-length studies of it by sociolinguists in recent years (e.g. Alim 2006), it might seem like a natural source of materials for the Contrastive Analysis classroom.[14] But

---

[12] This poem and the next one are both in Sanchez (1987:52–3).

[13] The fact that Sanchez has another haiku (two pages earlier – p. 50 – in Sanchez [1987] that refers explicitly to Guyana – "Haiku (walking in the rain in Guyana)" – increases the likelihood that this is the correct analysis.

[14] Two websites of potential interest to readers are the website of the HipHop Educational Literacy Program (www.edlyrics.com/), which includes classroom-useable lyrics from music by Kanye West, 50 cent, Common and Nas, and the Hiphop Lx website of Marcy Morgan's Hiphop Archive at Stanford (http://worldhiphop.net/lx/), which includes Hiphop vocabulary and grammar from various geographic zones in the US.

finding lyrics that illustrate alternation between AAVE and SE while being appropriate in subject matter and language for the classroom can be a challenge. One likely example is the "Where do we go?" track on Talib Kweli's *Quality* album. Except for a single token of *nothin*, the chorus by Res (Shareese Renèe Ballard) is in SE, but the main stanzas by university-educated Talib Kweli contain AAVE phonological and grammatical elements, including zero copula (*they Ø a pearl*, *they Ø growin*, *they Ø livin*) and unmarked third singular -*s* (*the sun still – rise*). In discussing this, as with most of our examples, one could ask why the artistes chose to frame their message as they did, how the song would sound if framed more standardly/more vernacularly, and with what effect:[15]

(17) *Where do we go?* (Talib Kweli)
[Chorus: Res – repeat 2X]
Where do we go? What do we say? What do we do?
Nowhere to turn, nowhere to run and there's nothin new
Where do we go for inspiration?
It's like pain is our only inspiration.

[Talib Kweli]
Yea, I see a place where little boys and girls
Are shells in the oceans not knowin they a pearl
No one to hold 'em while they growin
They livin' moment to moment without a care in the whole world
Now, if I could help it I tell it just like it is
And I may say some things that you don't like to hear
I know this: that people lie, people kneel
People die, people heal, people steal, and people shed tears
What's real, blood spills, gun kill, the sun still – rise
Above me, trust me, it must be, morning – time . . .

Caribbean examples, with alternation between creole and Standard English

Turning to the Caribbean, we begin with two poems from Jamaican poet Valerie Bloom (1956–) that are suitable for younger students. Her first poem, "Who dat girl" forms a nice parallel to Sonia Sanchez' "Song no. 3" because it deals similarly with a young Black girl musing about herself and her looks, but with more of the positive note that Sonia begins to sound in her final verse.

(18) *Who dat girl*?? (Valerie Bloom, Jamaica)[16]
Who dat wide-eye likkle girl
Staring out at me?
Wid her hair in beads an' braids
An' skin like ebony?

[15] From Talib Kweli's *Quality* (2002) album; we are grateful to Neale Clunie for this example.
[16] This poem and the next one are from Agard and Nichols (1994), pp. 18 and 14 respectively.

Who dat girl, her eye dem bright   5
Like night-time peeny-wallie?
Wid granny chain dem circle roun'
Her ankle, neck, and knee?

Who dat girl in Mummy's shoes
Waist tie with Dad's hankie?   10
Who dat girl wid teeth like pearl
Who grinning out at me?

Who dat girl/ Who dat girl?
Pretty as poetry?
Who dat girl in de lookin'-glass?   15
Yuh mean dat girl is me?

The poem would allow a teacher and class to talk about distinctive Jamaican phonology (*likkle* for "little", line 1) and lexicon (*peeny-wallie*, line 6, "large click beetle . . . having two luminous spots on its head, often taken to be its eyes . . . [or] firefly" – Cassidy and Le Page [1980:344]; see also Allsopp [1996:435]), as well as syntax (*NP dem* for plural marking, as in *her eye dem*, line 5). One could also note the variation between the creole and English systems in the plural (plural -*s* in line 3 and elsewhere) and possessive (zero marking in *grannyØ chain*, line 7, but possessive -*s* in *Mummy's shoes*, line 9, and *Dad's hankie*, line 10). This poem could be fruitfully turned into more basilectal or deep creole as well as a variety closer to standard English. By contrast, Bloom's Standard English poem "Water everywhere" is one of several by her that could be translated into creole ("Watuh deh pon de ceilin, Watuh deh pon de wall . . ."), with fruitful discussion of the resultant differences in language and voice:

(19) *Water everywhere* (Valerie Bloom)
  There's water on the ceiling
  And water on the wall.
  There's water in the bedroom,
  And water in the hall.
  There's water on the landing,   5
  And water on the stair.
  Whenever Daddy takes a bath
  There's water everywhere.

Finally, we'll consider the Jamaican poet Dennis Scott (1939–1990), winner of the Commonwealth Poetry Prize and someone who strikes us as deserving of even greater recognition in international poetry circles than he has received to date. We'll begin with his poem "Uncle time," written in mesolectal Jamaican Creole.[17]

---

[17] This poem and the next are both from Scott (1973). They can also be found in Burnett (1986) and other anthologies of Caribbean English poetry. Note that the elliptical points in lines 1, 6, and 20 of the "Uncle Time" poem are from the original, and do not represent omitted material, as they do in other extracts in this paper.

(20) *Uncle time* (Dennis Scott)

       Uncle Time is a ole, ole man . . .
       All year long im wash im foot in de sea,
       long lazy years on de wet san'
       an shake de coconut tree dem
       quiet-like wid im sea-win laughter,   5
       scrapin' away de lan' . . .
       Uncle Time is a spider-man, cunnin an cool,
       im tell yu: watch de hill an yu si mi.
       Huhn! Fe yu yiye no quick enough fe si
       how im move like mongoose; man, yu tink im fool?   10

       Me Uncle Time smile black as sorrow;
       im voice is sof as bamboo leaf
       but Laard, me Uncle cruel.
       When im play in de street
       wid yu woman – watch im! By tomorrow   15
       she dry as cane fire, bitter as cassava;
       an when in teach yu son, long after
       yu walk wid stranger, and yu bread is grief.
       Watch how im spin web roun yu house, an creep
       inside; an when im touch yu, weep . . .   20

Scott's poem exemplifies several of the vernacular features we've discussed already, and others, including the AAVE-like use of *a* rather than *an* before vowels (*a ole ole man*, not *an ole ole man*), as discussed by Ash and Myhill (1986). At the same time it includes creole features not found in AAVE, like the use of *im* as third singular subject and possessive (*im tell yu*, line 8, *im voice*, line 12) and the use of post-nominal *dem* as pluralizer (*de coconut tree dem*, line 4). These might themselves be made the focus of a Contrastive Analysis discussion, with SE, AAVE, and creole as foci, but more than anything else a versatility teacher might introduce this poem as an expressive work perfectly in harmony with its culture and environment – from the local island images (*wash im foot in de sea*, line 2, *dry as cane fire*, line 16, and the Anansi-like *spider man* metaphor in line 7) to its exploitation of creole features for poetic effect. Note, in line 1, for instance, how the absence of the final stop in *ole* allows us to prolong the syllable almost interminably, iconically recapitulating the age of Uncle Time (*looool ooool maan/*). And note also how the absence of third singular -*s* on the verb *creep* (line 19) facilitates the rhyme and the symbolic linkage with the chilling imperative (*weep*) with which the poem ends. Changing those last lines to Standard English, in this case, would destroy the rhyme and undermine the drama: "Watch how he spins a web around your house, and creeps/inside, and when he touches you, weep." This poem sends the message that the vernacular is not a weak alternative to the standard, but, as it is in many everyday contexts, a resource with its own inimitable strengths.

Equally remarkable, but in a quite different way, is Scott's stunning poem "Epitaph." It is as Black and revolutionary as ever, while couched in the most standard of Englishes.

> (21) *Epitaph* (Dennis Scott)
> They hanged him on a clement morning, swung
> between the falling sunlight and the women's
> breathing, like a black apostrophe to pain.
> All morning while the children hushed
> their hopscotch joy and the cane kept growing   5
> he hung there sweet and low.
>   At least that's how
> they tell it. It was long ago
> and what can we recall of a dead slave or two
> except that when we punctuate our island tale   10
> they swing like sighs across the brutal
> sentences, and anger pauses
> till they pass away.

What we'd want to discuss with students here is not the banalities of traditional CA ("look, the writer used past tense -*ed*"!), but how the poet exploits unusual lexicon and imagery and sound to express the intrusive, painful memories of Black ancestors. Note his ironic use of *clement* ("merciful," although we're more familiar with the noun *clemency* or the adjectival *inclement*, of weather) for a morning that was far from merciful except insofar as it brought relief from oppression to a hanged slave. And note the variation between *hanged* in line 1, the past tense form reserved for the execution sense of *hang*, and *hung* in line 6 (the past tense of *hang* in its more general sense). The poet's reference to the victim as a *black apostrophe to pain* in line 3 mediates both meanings of the word *apostrophe*, as a punctuation mark (the black ink apostrophe between two letters as in *it's* iconically depicting a hanging) and the lesser known use of the word for "the direct address of an absent or imaginary person" (*American heritage dictionary of the English language*, 2000:85). Note too the crucifixion-recalling images of the body "swung between the falling sunlight and the women's breathing" (lines 1–3) and the way the sibilants in lines 12–13 slow us down to pay homage to the slaves who *swing like sighs across the brutal sentences*. From the point of view of a teacher trying to develop linguistic versatility and a conscious reflexivity about language, this poem is hard to beat, the more so because it weaves metalinguistic references into the poem's imagery itself (*punctuate, brutal sentences*). The issue is not just whether one uses a standard or a vernacular variety, but whether, in using either, one can marshall and exploit its resources with power, creativity, effectiveness, and poise. That's what Scott, like many of our greatest writers and singers and wordsmiths, can teach our students, our teachers, and us.

Conclusion

In this paper we have argued for the involvement of variationists in the design and implementation of English and language arts curricula as part of the debt we owe to the communities whose language we record and study in developing our theories and careers. The educational needs are especially acute in African American and Caribbean communities, and we have argued that in these and other communities variationists could use a revised, energized variety of Contrastive Analysis that uses literature and music (rather than traditional drills) to help students and teachers alike appreciate and develop linguistic versatility. Versatility, in the sense that we propose, is the applied counterpart of the theoretical and descriptive study of variation in language, and properly applied, it could improve the performance of vernacular speakers in the classroom and on the job front, without the damage to their identities and psyches that current vernacular-eschewing strategies often involve.

While we have drawn the examples in this paper from African America and the Anglophone Caribbean, the versatility approach we advocate can be extended to a wide variety of ethnic groups, dialect and language situations, and grade levels. Almost anywhere that variationists gather their data, they can take the extra step of giving back to the community by becoming familiar with its literature and music and drawing on their understanding of the community's variation in speech to design classroom lessons that teachers and students can use to develop linguistic and expressive versatility.

15 Social-political influences on research practices: examining language acquisition by African American children[1]

IDA J. STOCKMAN

Introduction

Spoken language is a complex human process involving biological, mental, and social sub-systems. It ought not be surprising that language is acquired over time, its social-pragmatic aspects extending across the human life span. Age-dependent patterns of typical language use are important to the professional practices of applied fields such as communication disorders and education. They guide the diagnosis and treatment of communication disorders. They also guide the pedagogical practices, e.g. curricular planning and evaluation of student readiness to participate in school programs. Aside from professional practices, implicit norms of behavior, inclusive of spoken communication, guide the rules of social engagement and participation in the cultural institutions of religion, work, play, and the rituals of daily living. Even the staunchest defenders of nativist views of language acquisition concede that social factors influence language learning. Compromised language development in feral children (Curtiss 1977) is prima facie evidence that human social interaction is critical. However, what has been debatable is whether all social groups learn a language and/or engage in socialization practices that enable their adequate development. A case in point is the native-born group of African Americans in the United States (US), who are the focus of this chapter. It is the second largest racial minority group in this country (2000 Census). Many of its thirty million African American citizens acquire a non-prestige dialect of English as their first language, which is referred to here as African American Vernacular English (AAVE).

The perception that African Americans are culturally and linguistically inferior is likely to stem from their social-political history in the US. This history is unique relative to other minority racial groups in two respects. First, African Americans are the only racial group to have been legally enslaved. Social segregation and discrimination in various negative forms have continued even during the 150 years

---

[1] Portions of this chapter were included in a lecture, The social-political construction of science: evidence from language research on African American children, which was given at the City University of New York as a W. E. B. Dubois Distinguished Visiting Lecture.

since slavery was abolished. The dehumanizing face of slavery has the effect of marginalizing the culture and language of any enslaved group.

Second, the English dialect spoken by many African Americans has not been traced to a specific ancestral, non-English language. In contrast, the English dialect differences of other US minority racial groups can be traced to Indo-European (e.g. Spanish), Asian, Arabic, and Native American languages. Denied opportunity during captivity to transition gradually to English like other non-English minority speakers in the US (Baugh 1999a), African Americans developed an oral language whose contemporary patterns reflect pidgin-creole, African, and Anglican origins (Rickford 1999, Wolfram 2003). The absence of an ancestral language to account for AAVE has most likely contributed to the view that it is simply a poorly learned copy of Standard English (SE). This view could be justified, given the similarities and differences between the two dialects and the vestigial perception of former slaves as inferior in learning ability. The notion that AAVE speakers exhibit a language deficit was nourished further by research, which has repeatedly shown their lower performance relative to SE speakers of Caucasian and Anglo-European ancestry on a variety of language and cognitive tasks. It also is a reality that African Americans have not thrived on a variety of quality of life indicators (economic stability, health, and education), thereby reinforcing the impression that their culture and lifestyle do not lead to empowerment and well being.

The deficit view of AAVE and its speakers meant that even their typical or normal patterns of language use had to be fixed. Consequently, in the past, whole classes at school could be enrolled for speech therapy to eliminate common sound substitutions in the dialect's pronunciation of words, e.g. /f/ for /θ/ (cf. *bath* and *baf*). Ordinarily such demand for clinical service would be guided by speech and language development norms on the speakers. But this was not the case for AAVE speakers. Instead it seemed to be implicitly assumed that no norms were needed for a dialect recognized as neither a legitimate nor adequate linguistic system for its speakers. In effect, a normal speech and language difference was not distinguished from a real clinical or educational learning pathology or deficit. The expectation that even the typical AAVE speakers were incompetent language users created a socially constructed language disability in the sense that scholars have articulated the concept in special education (Manion and Berisani 1987).

The general lack of information about the normal language development of African American children motivated the research which Fay Vaughn-Cooke and I began in 1980. Instead of just describing the research in this chapter, I have taken on a more difficult task of discussing the social-political context that has shaped the kind of language research done on African American children. The premise is that inadequate language norms for African American children resulted partly from social-political influences on research practices, and in particular the paradigms used to study AAVE speakers. Exposing the social-political face of research practices ought to be instructive for two reasons.

First, there is increasing opportunity to offer clinical and special education services in countries where none has existed before. Language research on other social minority groups in a society can profit from the lessons learned from inappropriately applying the language norms of one group to another group, as was done in the US with African American speakers.

Second, a focus on social-political factors in science ought to inform the continuing dialogue about the epistemological status of the social sciences. For example, Hitchcock (2004) considers whether scientific knowledge in the social sciences is governed by laws in the same sense that they have been articulated for the natural sciences. Sociolinguistics is among the recently emerged social sciences that challenge a rigid traditional view of science. Unlike some of the social science disciplines, sociolinguistics "emerged partially in response to a number of well-articulated and compelling social issues" (Paulston and Tucker 2003:2). Its evolution was energized by the US movement for social justice on behalf of African Americans and other racial minorities. The scholarly goal was to describe not only the nature of minority languages and dialects, but also to actually participate in the crafting and testing of solutions to the practical problems created by their use in the society. Walt Wolfram's prolific scholarly productivity literally created *applied* sociolinguistics as a sub-discipline. His work has centered on cross-language/dialect issues that affect professional practices in speech/language pathology (Wolfram 1983, 1989, 2005b), and in education (Wolfram and Christian 1989). This work has been a direct response to the social factors that affect language learning and use. In the face of such evidence, some scholars, in the extreme, would argue that science is nothing but a social-political construction; others insist on the relative autonomy of science and social influences, as achieved most easily in the natural sciences (Brown 2001). Fortunately, there are moderating views between these two extremes. They seek to identify the specific ways that science is and is not immune to social-political influences (Brown 2001, Haack 2003, Leonard 2002). This chapter informs the debate by offering a glaring example of how social-political factors have influenced the research practices and outcomes related to the language development of a minority social group like African Americans.

Goals and structure of the chapter

In some respects, it is easy to take on the task of showing how the claims to science as objective and value-free knowledge are tempered by the social-political context of investigating African American children's language. In a skin-color conscious society, few people would deny the social-political reality of doing research on a racial minority group. In fact, some scholars may view such research as only "social-political fluff" – a fly in the ointment of otherwise normal science uncontaminated by a social-political reality. Therefore, it is first necessary to point out how all research is the product of a social-political context, as is done in the first section of this chapter. Then I interpret how the language research on African American children has been influenced by social-political context.

Broad social-political aspects of science

Science deified

Science refers here to both the process and product of producing knowledge from research (adapted from Medawar 1984). Chalmers (1982) pointed out that science is highly "esteemed" in modern times. When advertisements assert that a product has been *scientifically* shown to be better than a rival product, they imply that their claims are well founded and beyond dispute. It is widely believed that there is something about its method of acquiring knowledge that gives science more insight into how the world works than do intuition, voodoo, extrasensory perception, astrology, mythology, religion, and the haphazard hypothesis testing of our everyday experiences.

Historically, it has been assumed that the scientific method works because it yields *objective* knowledge (Kolakowski 1993) in the sense that its outcomes are: (1) verifiable by observation or what can be physically sensed as overt, quantifiable events; and (2) unbiased or value free – reflecting the researcher's detachment from the subject of inquiry. This traditional positivist view portrays science as a source of knowledge that transcends the human condition, and, by implication, its social-political context. An exalted view of science is understandably difficult to reconcile with the claim that science is a social-political construction. This is because the term *social-political* implies bias. In the narrow sense, bias projects images of deception designed to sway opinion or action for personal gain. But the term *social-political* is used here in the broadest sense to refer to inherent conditions (i.e. pre-imposed social, cultural, and historical ones) which define the social status of people and social institutions in ways that shape human action. The word *construction* is intended to remind us that science is not the result of mysterious or supernatural forces, but creative human work. In a broad sense, all human activity occurs in a social-political context whether we like it or not (Hammersley 1995).

Science and the social sciences

Fortunately, one need not probe deeply into contemporary philosophy of science to find agreement that social factors play more than a trivial role in research practices. Science obviously is a human enterprise (Slaate 1981), and it cannot be understood in isolation of what is involved in the human capacity to observe, reason, act, and so on. Moreover, the study of people is important to understanding what is in the world and how it works. Yet it is study of the non-human physical world which frames the expectation that knowledge can be pursued with dispassionate, value-free objectivity in which scientists are distanced from their subjects of inquiry. Social scientists have resisted this kind of traditional bias with good reason. There are fundamental differences between human and non-human phenomena, some of which are created by the very existence of a social-political reality (Hammersley 1995). Searle reminded us that people are "free, conscious, mindful, rational agents in a world that science tells us consists of entirely mindless, meaningless particles" (1984:13). Rocks and trees do not have intentionality; nor do they talk back to you. But people do. Their language, social habits, and beliefs are social-political constructions of the most obvious kind. They can create categories of observed reality that do not correspond neatly with physical states. For example, racial categories such as Black, White, and Brown exist as a social-political reality (Cashmore 1996, Webster 1992), whereas race as a biological concept is not definable by discrete boundaries (Millard 1994). Thus, social-political factors, historically regarded as peripheral to the natural sciences, must be a constitutive part of the social sciences if human behavior is the nature to be understood.

Researchers cannot investigate any topic they want to. Studies with predictably threatening or onerous human consequences are either discouraged or disallowed (Renzetti and Lee 1993). The sensitivity of a research topic has to do with its relationship to social context. For example, the focus on racial differences counts as sensitive research, particularly when it favors biological rather than social explanations of behavioral differences, as is the case for genetic determinants of racial intelligence. Some scholars avoid sensitive race-related research topics while others proceed under suspicion and strong opposition from within and outside of the research community (Tucker 1994).

Researchers in the human social sciences also are not free to observe anybody they want to, the topic issue aside. Human subjects' review boards monitor whether people willingly consent to participate in research studies under conditions that: (1) protect their rights to privacy and safety; and (2) reward their efforts either directly or indirectly (Tucker 1994, Harris 1996b). Such guidelines for human participation are not motivated by what is required to justify scientific truth. They arise from shared social values about human exploitation, civility, and fair play. Up to now, different values have applied to the sacrificial use of human and non-human animals. What ultimately comes to be known will be constrained by the social-political context for using people as research participants.

Even when it is acknowledged that social factors may play a peripheral role in the research process, it has been debatable whether they are central (e.g. Feyerabend 1975) or peripheral (e.g. Chalmers 1990) to what ultimately constitutes scientific knowledge. The following discussion identifies the social-political influences on research practices that go beyond research topics that can arise from peripheral or external social issues and the core research activity of selecting human subjects, as discussed already. Instead the discussion focuses on the core research activities of: (1) making and interpreting observations; and (2) selecting the procedures for justifying whether they count as scientific knowledge.

Social-cultural relativity and empirical observation

Making research observations

Scientific knowledge is presumed to be "objectively proven" because it is based on verifiable observation or data, i.e. what can be externally seen, heard, touched, and so on. In the positivist tradition, the insistence on observation-dependent facts aimed to put knowledge on a more secure footing by delivering it from the subjectivity of human introspection, personal bias, and opinion. However, a "naive inductivist" view of science (after Chalmers 1982) assumes that: (1) sensory experience gives us *direct* and *stable* access to the properties of the external world; and that (2) observations, as the starting point of knowledge, are free of presupposition. Both assumptions can be challenged partly because of the social-political context of human experience.

Culture, as habits of mind and action, creates mental categories that shape the perception of reality during a socialization process to which all researchers and their human participants are subjected. Collective cultural histories are powerful enough to alter the observations of different groups of people when witnessing the same event. For example, Mann *et al.* (1992) showed that mental health professionals from China and Indonesia were more likely to rate the behaviors of eight-year-old boys as hyperactive-disruptive than were those from Japan and the US when observing the same four video scenes. What is observed, therefore, is not determined solely by the physical registration of sensory stimuli. Rather, "Valuations are necessarily involved already at the stage when we observe facts and carry on theoretical analysis" (Myrdal 1969, as cited in Kaplan 1984).

Observer-dependent bias is the reason that instrumental measurements have been so valuable to scientific advancement. It frees some observations from the voluntary perceptual judgments of research participants. Even so, we do not escape the special training and skill that a researcher needs to do instrument-aided observation, as Chalmers (1990) pointed out. To the untrained eye, the tympanogram or electrocardiogram can look like meaningless stray marks on paper. The very goal of expert training is to build up expectancies or biases about what to observe and how to interpret the outcomes of instrumental measurement.

Interpreting research observations

Social-political context may influence not only what is observed but also how observations are *interpreted*. It is the interpretation of observations as generalization or theory that ultimately surfaces as knowledge anyway and not the discrete observations made as data in the laboratory or field. Scientific empiricism at its best demands theory-driven observations. This means that observations at the outset are expected to be *biased* by a theoretical paradigm. A paradigm defines the assumptions made about the world and the methods for testing their fit to reality. Kuhn (1970) argued that paradigms predispose scientists to see the world in particular ways –so much so that those working within rival paradigms may view the world in different and possibly irreconcilable ways. For example, earlier geologists believed that the earth's crust did not shift (permanence theory) while others believed that it did (continental drift theory) (Oreskes 1999). Any interpretation necessarily involves a subjective element, which is checked in science only by the requirement that theory fits with nature. In the social and behavioral sciences, *nature* is the reality of social structure, beliefs, and attitudes as shaped by historical context. Theoretical interpretations will reflect what is observed in addition to what makes sense in terms of culturally conditioned beliefs about what is possible or impossible. Perhaps it was the need to make observations fit a certain social reality that the behavior of African Americans has been interpreted as a deficit regardless of their performances relative to other groups. Empirical observations, which showed them to have a faster reaction time than Caucasians, were interpreted as evidence for their inferior intellect as were observations that showed a slower reaction time (Tucker 1994).

Social-cultural relativity and research procedures

Origin of proof procedures and practices

Justification of knowledge arguably can be achieved independently of social-political factors by applying acceptable proof procedures. They require research to be consistent with logical reasoning, known facts, and established standards for reliability, validity, controlled observation, and so on. Where do these proof procedures come from? Answering this question cannot entirely dismiss the role of social-political factors. Researchers make judgments about all sorts of things that constrain the conditions under which facts become known. They choose the type of participants, observation conditions, probability levels for evaluating statistical outcomes, and so on. Such judgments are likely to reflect a research community's methodological and/or theoretical biases at the time in addition to an investigator's own intuition, common sense, resources at hand, and personal biases.

For example, participant preferences in human research have been biased against the use of people with less favored social status in a society. This seems to be the case despite the broad scientific goal of revealing the universal laws of nature. In earlier times, scientific experiments were performed only before witnesses of "high social rank, gentlemen, or better" (Barnes 1989:52). Contemporary research practices exemplify the same kind of bias by excluding women and racial/ethnic minority participants from biomedical research. The latter type of participant selection bias has been so common in US research practices that the

National Institutes of Health now requires federally funded research to include these populations or justify their exclusion.

Social-political factors surely are at work whenever researchers cater to the biases of a scientific community solely to gain recognition for their work at the expense of what the problem space requires or what is entailed in serving the aims of science. Here reference is made to the deeply rooted preference for experimental and quantitative research over observational and qualitative research (Hammersley and Atkinson 1995). This is the case even though both types play complementary roles in the production of new knowledge (Henwood and Pidgeon 1993). As a result some questions are ignored because the preferred experimental research methods are not required to answer them. Other questions may be poorly answered because experimental research is inappropriately used to answer them.

Nevertheless, researchers cannot afford to ignore research community biases. Scientific research is a value that is carefully woven into the institutional fabric of modern society – expressing itself in the requirements for university degrees and tenure, professional merit as well as funding, publication, and peer recognition. The "bread and butter" consequences for not respecting community biases extend beyond the opportunity to be heard by fellow researchers.

Modifying proof procedures and practices

Regardless of their origin, new research procedures become the preferred standard for judging the worthiness of investigative outcomes only *after* they are tried out and found to be useful for producing new knowledge. However, it is the process of getting a new idea *tried out* and accepted that social-political factors within a research community become particularly evident. If established paradigms and practices are the standards for judging scientific worth, then resistance can be expected when a new precedent is set. Contentious relationships among peers arise because scientific knowledge has not evolved from a single standard about what sort of evidence justifies "real" knowledge.

Oreskes' (1999) analysis of the rejection of continental drift theory is instructive. Although the idea that the earth crust moves is now taken for granted, not all scientists took Alfred Wegener seriously when he proposed the idea at the turn of the twentieth century. The homologous geological evidence (e.g. similarities and differences among continental land masses in boundary configuration and type of rocks, plants, and fauna) was enough to convince British scientists of the worthiness of Wegener's theory. But US American scientists remained unconvinced until instrumental geophysical measurements of earth crust shifts were possible with the emergence of Plate Tectonics theory in the 1960s. The Americans in the US rejected the drift theory because Wegener's evidence for it was not rigorous enough. It did not help his case that a prominent US scientist, James Dana, had a competing "permanence theory." Yet Wegener's observations and predictions, however unobjective and vaguely defined by US standards, led to the same fundamental geological insight that was later corroborated by instrumental measurements.

Evidently then, judgments about the same evidence can vary across research communities. The choice between competing approaches may be understood not only in terms of the rules of scientific evidence, but also in terms of sociological and psychological factors (Kuhn 1970). Innovations in science are inevitable though because existing practices and knowledge only can be provisional. Facts always become known and accepted under a particular set of tried conditions. The art of persuasion, with all that is entailed in human social-political relations, plays a necessary role in resolving disputes between the researcher, as producer of knowledge, and the peers who are entrusted to judge whose research should be believed, funded, published, and so on. Clearly "who said so" matters when peripheral factors such as a researcher's credentials, personality, and professional reputation become issues in evaluating research credibility. Unknown researchers in particular must "expect some difficulty in gaining a hearing, and must often seek the ear of established and better known figures to champion their cause" (Barnes 1989:56). We cannot assume that researchers are always capable of being objective when evaluating research that contradicts their own viewpoint. The social-political process of gaining peer acceptance for new ideas influences at least the timeliness with which new knowledge is infused in the stream of scientific thinking, if not the scope of what we ultimately come to know.

A social-political perspective on a developmental study of AAVE

So far, it has been argued that science is practiced in a social-political context. The goal here is to illustrate how social-political factors influenced a language development study on African American children. An overview of the general goals and methodology of this study is followed by an analysis of the social-political factors that influenced it. This analysis exposes the blurred distinction between external and internal social-political influences on research practices in some studies of human behavior.

Overview of the research project

In 1980, Fay Vaughn-Cooke and I began to study the language development of African American children with two-year grant support from the US National Institutes of Education (NIE). The goal was to answer basic questions about the language of typically developing preschoolers who acquire AAVE as a first or native language. We wanted to know about the kind of meaning their words coded and in what developmental order over time. We also wanted to know about the kind of grammatical and pronunciation patterns used ordinarily to code meaning at different age-related developmental stages. Thus, this study had a descriptive focus. The broad goal was to create a methodological framework and database from which large-scale normative studies of this population could be launched later on.

Research goals

This study's goals were guided by three basic assumptions about African American children: (1) they acquire a spoken language for social communication that is rule governed and functionally adequate for social communication within their own linguistic community; (2) they acquire the spoken language of their communities without formal instruction unless a pathological condition prevents them from doing so; and (3) an adequate description of their language use requires a description of AAVE patterns that are like SE varieties in addition to those that are not.

General methodology

The cross-sequential design involved longitudinal sampling of language from twelve children, four at each of three age cross-sections: 18, 36, and 54 months. Thus, four children were 18 months when observation began, and they were at or close to 36 months when data collection ended. Those at 36 and 54 months were 54 and 72 months, respectively. Each age cross-section included equal numbers of male and female participants. The children were recruited from African American families whose income level qualified them for participation in Head Start programs in Washington, DC. The children and their caregivers were monolingual, native US English speakers. All except three of the children were first born to single mothers, half of whom were still teens living at home with their own mothers. All participants resided in neighborhoods of Washington, DC, that were predominantly African American where AAVE was used routinely for social communication. The habitual speech patterns of the children's familial caretakers included common AAVE features, e.g. variable absence of final consonants, copula, and inflectional verbs.

The children's ordinary use of oral language was observed in their homes every four to six weeks. Although a common set of activities, books and toys (a doll house, doll family, ball, car, truck, and blocks) was used for all the children at each age cross-section, the communicative interactions also catered to the talking routines and preferred activities in their homes. Audio-visual recordings were made of the two-hour, sampling sessions. The eighteen months of data collection yielded a database of more than 430 hours of language samples and at least 100,000 utterances for analysis. It spanned the entire period of early language acquisition from first word combinations at 17 to 18 months up to 6 years, the age at which children typically enter first grade. The audio-visual tapes were orthographically, and in some cases phonetically, transcribed independently by two or more persons. A transcript represented not only what a child said but also the speech preceding and following each utterance plus aspects of the non-verbal contexts that provided evidence for pragmatic intention and the meaning coded by the words. Observations were subjected to reliability checks and described in simple quantitative and qualitative terms.

The data analysis did not focus first on the children's grammatical and phonological forms, as earlier studies of African Americans had done. This study was tuned to the current language acquisition research at the time, which stressed the primacy of meaning and use relative to the forms of language. Therefore, we tried to figure out first what the words meant by paying attention to the contexts of talk in the tradition of rich interpretative analysis introduced by Lois Bloom (e.g. Bloom 1970, Bloom, Lightbown, and Hood 1975). Then we focused on the distribution of forms used, taking care to describe how talk was both similar to and different from SE. We searched for patterns of convergence across different children at a given age and divergence of patterns for the same child across age. In this way, we began to weave a developmental story that could frame testable hypotheses about the language of African American children and its acquisition.

The research in social-political perspective

The focus and methodological approach of this language acquisition project hardly seem controversial in the current climate of investigating African American children's communication patterns. In fact, the orientation of this project was, as intended, consistent with, if not a replication of, some studies of SE acquisition at the time. Nonetheless, social-political factors outside and inside the research community had shaped both the focus and framework of the research. As pointed out already, research in the human sciences is particularly vulnerable to social-political influences. Research on language, a uniquely human attribute, is no exception.

External social-political factors

The social-political climate external to the research community provided the impetus for our study on many fronts. First, the rich scholarly history of language research in the US makes clear that society values language as a communicative tool. Failure to acquire an adequate linguistic system has negative functional consequences for educational and vocational opportunity. Given this value bias in the culture, it is not surprising that minority language groups in the US won major legal concessions during the Civil Rights movement between 1960 and 1980. This language-focused, political fight, and the Civil Rights movement in general, were really about legitimizing social groups that had been historically marginalized in the society. In the main, speakers of non-English languages protested that their right to due process and equal protection under the law were denied when schools, in particular, disregarded the kind of native language they spoke.

The funding of our research proposal by the NIE in 1980 followed closely on the heels of a 1979 legal precedent, commonly known as the *King* decision. The case was the *Martin Luther King Junior Elementary School Children, et al. v. the Ann Arbor School District Board* (Civil Action No. 7–71861). This legal suit on behalf of eleven African American children alleged that they spoke a home language that prevented their equal participation in instructional programs, and that the school board had not taken action to overcome this barrier. Federal Judge Charles W. Joiner agreed. In a decision rendered on 12 July 1979, he concluded that there was no evidence from the four-week trial that

> the School Board had taken steps (1) to help the teachers understand the problem; (2) to help provide them with knowledge about the children's use of a "Black English language system"; and (3) to suggest ways and means of using that knowledge in teaching the students to read.   (Smitherman 1981:351)

The School Board was required to submit a plan for addressing these issues within thirty days.

Whereas previous rulings had affected speakers of non-English minority languages, the *King* decision was the first to apply the same legal status to an English dialect learned as a native language. The Joiner ruling generated much national discussion and debate. There was reason for the NIE to give funding priority to a project that focused on African American child use of AAVE. Access to such knowledge seemed key to meeting the requirements of the Joiner legal ruling. Although the legal decision could be based on sociolinguistic research that legitimized AAVE as a linguistic system for mature speakers at the time (e.g. Labov 1970, 1972b, Wolfram 1969), little was known about young children's use or acquisition of the dialect. The social-political context had provided a clear mandate to study the normal development of African American children. It also helped that concurrent shifts toward a sociocultural perspective in linguistic and psycholinguistic theory were attuned to a new social reality. Here reference is made to the emergence of sub-disciplines of inquiry that included sociolinguists (in the tradition of William Labov, Roger Shuy, Walt Wolfram, John Rickford, John Baugh, Lisa Green, and others), ethnolinguistics (in the tradition of Shirley Brice-Heath, John Gumperz, Dell Hymes, Muriel Saville-Troike, and others), and pragmatics (in the tradition of Elizabeth Bates, Lois Bloom, John Dore, Sue Ervin-Tripp, and others).

Why was so little known about the normal development of African American children in the first place, given the long US history of language research, and in particular the explosive expansion of child language acquisition research beginning in the 1960s? To answer this question, we must look within the research community to the biases in scientific practices that were shaped by social-political context.

Internal social-political factors ▓▓▓▓▓▓▓▓▓▓▓▓▓▓▓▓▓▓▓▓▓▓▓▓▓▓▓▓▓▓

The politics of exclusion

Given the external social-political impetus for our research, it is understandable why its sole focus on African American children could be viewed as politically motivated and concerned with narrow rather than basic issues of scientific inquiry. In fact, our research seemed to be distinguished primarily by its acknowledged focus on a particular population, as reflected in the titles of some papers, e.g. "Semantic categories in the language of working class Black children" (Stockman and Vaughn-Cooke 1982b). In contrast, the titles of most language development research studies do not typically identify the population studied. In not doing so, they give the impression of being concerned with basic developmental issues that have nothing to do with the cultural experiences of the particular group of participants observed. However, Graham (1992) concluded from a survey of child development journals that the participants in most developmental research represent the "invisible" culture of children who are Caucasian and middle class. Lerner (1990) lamented that too many researchers fail to even provide information about participants' cultural backgrounds. The decontextualized study of children gives the false impression that there is a "generic" child who can provide an absolute reference point for writing the developmental story.

At the time Fay Vaughn-Cooke and I began our research, little language development data existed on African American children because, quite simply, they had been excluded from the research aimed at establishing normative language behavior. Our perceived narrow research focus on African American children responded to the politics of exclusion in research practices. This exclusion appeared to reflect a value bias in research practices that was conditioned by the social status of people in the society. Those with favored social status in the society are included in research whereas those without it are excluded and treated as a variation from the norm. This point was echoed by Lois Bloom in her summary of the symposium on "Racism in developmental research," which she chaired at a meeting of the American Psychological Association's Division 7:

> The development of non-mainstream children is seen as "variation," "a confound," "noise" – in short, what Dubois called "a problem" – in the data because we have looked for the so-called "norms" of development only among those infants, children, and adolescents who swim in the mainstream.   (1992:2)

Yet developmental norms on African American children were needed because existing research, although presumably of a "basic" nature, was not always useful when evaluating them for educational and clinical purposes.

Of course, the exclusion of African American children also could be defended on practical grounds, namely, the lack of access to minority participants, and better yet, on scientific grounds, namely, that generalizations from data are likely to have a closer fit to reality when based on a culturally homogeneous participant pool. The latter reason to exclude racial minority participants implicitly recognizes different cultural experiences as control variables. In this view, the existing database on a single type of participant would be considered incomplete without similar studies on other populations who were judged as different. Replication studies on different populations should be critical to accomplishing science's broad aim of revealing universal laws of nature in the human social sciences. Cross-cultural studies could show whether a given truth prevailed despite cultural differences.

But the scientific goal of achieving the broadest generality of truth was not enough to engage research on the normal language development of African American children, the largest US racial minority group until the turn of the twenty-first century. Participant preferences in normal developmental research can be viewed as a validity issue of who can provide suitable normative data. This validity issue was resolved by a social-political context imposed on research practices, which viewed some people as more normal than others in the society. This point becomes more clearly supported below when considering the type of research which had been done on African American children prior to our research. See summaries in Stockman (1986b) and in Stockman and Vaughn-Cooke (1982a, 1989).

Paradigms and prejudice

The lack of adequate normative data on the language of young African American children clearly was not due to a participant access problem, given that research on this group had been done prior to our research. However, the kind of paradigm used to study them did not lead to normative data. A paradigm provides the framework for investigation. It embodies the procedures for doing research and the theoretical model for interpreting observations in relation to accepted facts. Although we may be led to believe that paradigms evolve solely from the weight of empirical observation and logic, sociopolitical context is relevant here too, as the history of language research on African American children illustrates.

Language research had been no exception to the predominant use of a comparative paradigm to study African American children in any domain. They were studied primarily in relationship to other groups with the goal of revealing differences, not similarities. Even when different age groups were included, the studies did not focus on within-group changes in performances across age for the separate participant groups compared. Instead, the goal was to reveal whether group differences persisted across age (e.g. Anastasiow and Hanes 1974). Such comparative studies are especially limiting. As quasi-experiments, they require uniform observation conditions for the groups compared in order to control for extraneous effects. For language research, this requirement was met by giving norm-referenced, standardized tests to all the children in quasi-laboratory settings. However, a linguistically and culturally unbiased protocol cannot be constructed without knowing a lot about the relevant characteristics of each group. In the absence of normative data on African American children, the protocols often used were existing norm-referenced psychometric tests that were standardized on mostly Caucasian speakers of SE. It should not be surprising that African

Americans typically obtain the lower scores. The interpretation of their generally lower scores as a deficit instead of a source of normal variation reflects the view of African Americans as a social pathology in the larger society. Bereiter and Engelmann had this to say about African American children's language:

> Although a lack of verbal learning is the outstanding characteristic of culturally deprived children, the verbal deficiencies reflect a more basic lack of concrete non-verbal learning experiences.   (1966:28)

The use of a comparative paradigm to study the language of African American children departed radically from the language acquisition research on mostly Caucasian children in the same time period (Bloom 1970, Bowerman 1973, Brown 1973, Nelson 1973). The latter research involved intensive study of small groups of three or more children and analyses of longitudinal samples of their spontaneous oral language in natural, low-structured conditions. This approach had been viewed as necessary for understanding development from the child's rather than the adult's perspective. Developmental descriptions were guided by the theoretical claims of Noam Chomsky's influential theory of syntax and counter-Chomskian claims that respected the roles of cognitive and sociocultural factors in achieving linguistic competence. But none of this theoretical orientation was reflected in the language research on African American children. There were no descriptions of their language use in natural settings. Scholars were debating whether AAVE, the English dialect acquired, was even a legitimate language. In effect, there was one paradigm for studying Caucasian children and another one for studying African American children.

The fascination with group differences in the research on African Americans led to a narrowly focused description of their language, namely, one that focused on the small set of surface dialect forms (i.e. grammatical and phonological features) that most often are used to distinguish AAVE and SE forms (Stockman 1986b, Stockman and Vaughn-Cooke 1982a, 1989). This was the case even though the meaning and use of a language were considered the driving forces of acquisition in mainstream research. The emergence of sociolinguistics and the evidence for the rule-governed nature of non-standard English dialects did not usher in a new research thrust. Scholars persisted with the comparative framework and the quasi-experimental methodology it required. The goal simply shifted to determining how African American and Caucasian children differ on language tasks designed to measure proficiency with SE grammatical rules. Traces of the difference paradigm still appeared in the work of the earliest scholars, who in the mid to late 1970s abandoned the comparative group design and focused only on African American children. Seminal developmental studies by Margaret Steffensen, Nona Stokes, Lorraine Cole, Wilhelmina Reveron, and Ceil Kovac (Lucas), as cited in Stockman and Vaughn-Cooke (1982a, 1989), focused on just a small set of grammatical forms that frequently are used to distinguish AAVE and SE.

Consequently, at the time of the 1979 Joiner ruling in Ann Arbor and the initiation of our research project, there still were major gaps in knowledge about the normal language development of African American children, at least those who spoke AAVE. There were no answers to such basic questions as when they acquire their first words, word combinations, complex sentences, and so on, and what the meaning and pragmatic functions of their words and sentences are. Although it was speculated that language differences were at the root of their lower academic achievement, research had not yielded a good picture of the typical communicative skills that these children had when first entering school. The research needs exceeded what could be accomplished with a single study of one or two language patterns. In proposing a research agenda, it was argued that an adequate response to the relative absence of developmental data demanded nothing less than a research initiative of broad scope. It also seemed that the same method used as a starting place for studying young SE speakers – namely, observation of language use in the natural contexts of ordinary social interaction in the home – was an equally valid starting point for studying young AAVE speakers.

In retrospect, it seems clear that by proposing to focus just on African American children with the same kind of methods used to study the language development of Caucasian children, this research was among the earliest to depart radically from the way this minority group had been studied. This paradigmatic shift responded directly to the sociopolitical context in which African Americans were viewed inside and outside of the research community.

The early price of paradigm shift

Encouraged by the success of initial funding and preliminary work, we were unprepared for what happened to us over the next few years. The political tidal wave that had given urgent birth to our study of African American children's language development in 1980 was short-lived. In 1982, we were stunned by the NIE's rejection of our request for another year of funding. The project's goals and methodological framework were no different than the ones funded initially. Two years had been spent gathering what was likely the largest database of natural home samples of speech ever collected on young African American children in the US at the time. Data analysis had begun and the research thrust had received commendation from the scholarly community. Perhaps we had been naive to believe that a research study that produced no quick fixes for the problems that African American children posed for schools would be worthy of sustained support. This kind of research was no longer a priority for a government agency undergoing major organizational revision.

We continued to explore funding from federal and private sources over the next three years with no success. Some reactions to our work reflected deeply entrenched biases about what constitutes good or creative research, irrespective of the problem at hand or the historical context to which it responded. Our research was not viewed as innovative, given its goal of replicating some of the existing language development research. Its normative descriptive goal was not theoretically inspired. The qualitative evidence for behavior was not quantifiable. However, what disturbed us most by the lack of success were the criticisms that seemed peripheral to the rigorous test of new ideas. Some objections to our work stirred suspicions of reviewer bias against our paradigm for studying African American children. The Laboratory of Comparative Human Cognition in San Diego, California, shared this suspicion. Responding to the National Science Foundation's (NSF) rejection of our proposal, the Laboratory commented in its quarterly newsletter on the issue of using minority participants for normative language research:

> In the discussion from both sides of the debate, the preference for publishing and funding was laid out: study Caucasian middle-class children as normative or don't get funded and published, and then you don't get tenure. If you study minorities, study them as minorities. Have a control group of "normals" or evidence from "normals" in the literature for comparison or else don't do basic research; study the problems the minority participants have such that they deviate from the "norm." This logic doesn't even rise to separate but equal; it's outright second-class citizenship!   (October 1983:90)

Some objections to our research reflected just this kind of thinking. Among reviewer comments from several agencies were those that suggested African American children should not be participants in a normative study because it was known that they use language "at a lower level than other children." We were advised to get a control group of normal Caucasian children and do a comparative analysis, the very framework we had rejected. Our research was not really justified because there had already been numerous studies of the language and cognitive abilities of African American children. There were even veiled assertions that we were not qualified to do the proposed research. These were the concerns that led us to take bold, and by some accounts inappropriate, steps to publicly appeal the National Science Foundation's decision to reject a funding request in 1983. Having retreated from the goal of providing a broad systemic description of the participants' language in our database, we sought funding to study their acquisition of a single semantic field, namely, spatial locatives. Reviewer critiques of the proposal were circulated in the scholarly community along with our written response to them. Some respondents were sympathetic to our viewpoint; others understandably viewed us as impatient and naive about the research funding process, arguing that most proposals are not funded the first time. However, our appeal was motivated by issues that could not be fixed by repeated proposal submissions. We could not change who the participants were nor what our credentials were or who we were as African American investigators.

The fruits of change

Subsequent funding from the NSF and other sources enabled data analyses to continue, although not with the broad research program goals with which we began. The early results were neither surprising nor perhaps of much interest to those who all along expected African American children to have language use and developmental patterns that converged with the research findings on other groups of children. Nevertheless, in the face of the deficit theory and the negative attitudes commonly held toward their dialect, it had been necessary to determine empirically whether the claim to their normalcy was fact or fiction. Developmental data on even a few participants would have to be taken into account in future language development studies of this population.

At the same time, this research provided more evidence for the generalizations made about the type of universal patterns children display in early development (Stockman 1986a, 1986b, 1996a, 1996b, 1999). Despite our participants' low socioeconomic status and acquisition of a non-standard English dialect, they were combining words by 17–18 months (Stockman and Vaughn-Cooke 1982a). Their grammatical patterns were purposeful and rule governed. Contrary to the claims of the deficit theory, the children did not live in non-verbal homes. There was a continuous stream of talk in their homes.

As the children got older, they talked more. Their turn-taking responses became longer, phonetically clearer, and grammatically more elaborated (Stockman and Vaughn-Cooke 1982a, 1989, Stockman 1986a, 1986b, 1996a). Their language coded the same kind of basic semantic distinctions (e.g. action, state, location, time, and possession, causality, and so on; Stockman and Vaughn-Cooke 1986), which had been described for middle-class Caucasian children (Bloom 1970, Bloom, Lightbown, and Hood 1975), working-class Caucasian children (Miller 1982), and other African American children growing up in a different US city (Blake 1984). Our participants used talk to accomplish a variety of pragmatic goals that included requests, comments, and so on (Bridgeforth 1986). By 33–36 months, simple elaborated sentences were in place and complex sentences had also emerged (Stockman 1986a, 1996a). Their consonant repertoire included a variety of singleton and clustered consonants in both word-initial (Stockman 2006b) and final (Stockman 2006a) positions. Before age 4 years, their initial consonant inventories and grammatical patterns differed little from SE (Stockman 1986a, 2006b).

At the same time, the individual differences observed in the amount of their talk and use of particular grammatical and semantic patterns reminded us that all African American children are not alike (Stockman and Vaughn-Cooke 1982a, 1986, 1992). Their talk as a group also differed from SE speakers in some ways. For example, they used a particular existential form of the verb *go* in sentences such as *There go the ball; Here go the ball*. These generative constructions were used to refer to static instead of dynamic events, in contrast to SE speakers. We also corroborated the past evidence for the use of well-known AAVE grammatical and phonological forms, e.g. absence of final consonants, copula, and inflectional verbs. However, such linguistic forms were not always absent but reflected the structured variability observed in adult AAVE (see studies of final consonant deletion [Wolfram 1989, Stockman 2006a] and copula verb absence [Kovac (Lucas) 1980, Wyatt 1996] in African American children).

The database also has been used to explore abnormal language development and the clinical use of oral language samples to identify it. One child in the 18–36-month-old database was later targeted for special education and speech/language therapy when enrolled in a Head Start program after we completed data collection. He had exhibited remarkably poorer language than did his African American, age peers in the database. For example, the number and types of words used to refer to locative action events in sentences were reduced (Stockman 1992). The grammatical length and complexity of utterances were reduced relative to his peers as were the number and types of semantic relational categories and pragmatic intentions coded (Stockman 1996a). The concept of a minimal competency core (MCC) emerged from data analysis as a criterion-referenced approach to assessing the normalcy of a child's language at 3 years of age (Stockman 1996a). Cross-validation of the MCC has now been done on samples of children in Wisconsin (Schraeder, Quinn, Stockman, and Miller 1999) and in Michigan and Louisiana (Stockman, Guillory, Boult, and Seibert forthcoming).

Finally the database on AAVE has been used to generate hypotheses of general relevance to development by extending exploration of the database beyond practical issues. Here reference is made to research on African American children's talk about spatial location. This research converged two aspects that had been separately investigated in studies of SE dialects and other languages besides English, namely, the acquisition of the meaning of individual spatial locative words (e.g. *in*, *on*, *under*) and sentence relations (e.g. *it's on the table; put it on the table*). Our study of African American children revealed that in sentences that referred to a change of place, children first used words that coded the source (e.g. *off*, *out*) and path (*up*, *down*) of movement before they used words to express the movement goal (*in*, *on*, *under*) (Stockman and Vaughn-Cooke 1992). Conversely, in sentences referring to the static position of objects, children first used words (*in*, *on*, *under*) that referred to proximal position before they used words such as *out*, *off*, *up*, and *down* to refer to distal position (Stockman 1991). These outcomes, which implicate verb meaning in lexical organization, offer further evidence for the hypothesis (Bloom 1995) that verbs are central to grammatical structure.

Outlook

What was learned from undertaking language development research on African American children ought to be useful beyond the study of this one racial minority group. When obtaining normative research on any group that has not been studied before, four general principles ought to be embraced by researchers who seek normative language data (Stockman 1986b, Stockman and Vaughn-Cooke 1989), as identified below:

(1) The mother-tongue principle should guide the choice of language studied because the first language is a principal medium for cultural transmission and socialization.

(2) The theoretical framework should focus on linguistic competence in terms of the meaning and pragmatic use of words in addition to their surface grammatical and pronunciation forms.

(3) The research should focus on the linguistic patterns that contrast and those that do not contrast with other dialects or languages.

(4) The data gathering methodology should favor an ethnographic orientation which caters to authentic language use as observed in natural spoken situations as opposed to prestructured, standardized tests.

Fortunately a growing number of studies by other investigators exemplify an expanded investigative framework for studying the typical language of African American children. See book-length summaries of research on just this population (Kamhi, Pollock, and Harris 1996, van Keulen, Weddington, and Debose 1998, Craig and Washington 2006). It is accepted now that a comparison group is not needed to study African American children's normal behavior, as has been illustrated by the more recent research programs of Holly Craig and Julie Washington at the University of Michigan and Harry Seymour, Tom Roeper, and Jill deVilliers at the University of Massachusetts. Exposure to the negative biases of norm-referenced standardized tests has increased the appeal of natural speech sample analysis for normative descriptions of language. In addition, a large federally funded grant has led to the creation of a norm-referenced, standardized test that takes AAVE rules into account (Seymour, Roeper, and deVilliers 2003).

Yet in spite of the expanded investigative frameworks now used to study African American children, it is an illusion to think that attitudes have changed enough over the past decade to regard them as a suitable population for doing basic research of broad relevance to development. The Oakland, California, school crisis in 1996 revealed just how negative the public perception of AAVE and its speakers continues to be in the US (see Rickford and Rickford 2000; Vaughn-Cooke, this volume). When studying their language, researchers continue to focus most often on just those linguistic features that distinguish the AAVE and SE dialects. Any research at all is justified by the need to solve some problem that African Americans present for society. The comparative paradigm also flourishes although groups distinguished by social class instead of racial groups are now more often compared, and natural spontaneous speech analysis more often utilized, e.g. Hart and Risley (1995).

Conclusion

It has been argued that science, as product and process of human activity, is not autonomous from social-political influences. The evolution of knowledge will reflect these influences regardless of whether we view them as peripheral or central to the practice of science or its epistemologic status. Acknowledging the social-political context is not meant to denigrate the value of science. Scientific achievements and their proven value to societies are impressive despite the social political context in which science is practiced. Why bother to make the point then?

There is reason to bother because the edification of science has encouraged us to ignore and even deny the relevance of social-political factors in science. Reflections on the social-political context of science in this chapter are intended to remind the reader that in empowering science, we also empower the judgments of fellow human beings. Social-political factors are powerful enough to undermine their search for truth, particularly if they are not paying attention to them, or, worse, do not acknowledge that they exist. Recognizing social-political factors ought to have at least two consequences for the professional socialization of scientists.

First, it ought to encourage them to make explicit what often remains implicit in activity; namely, strategies for coping with social-political pressures in order to survive as scholars. For as O'Hear pointed out,

> one can certainly notice manifestations of closed-mindedness, such as the length of time it took for Fourier or Faraday to gain acceptance for their unfashionable ideas. That they did eventually gain acceptance for them is not in itself a complete vindication of the rationality and openness of the scientific community. There might, after all, have been other potential Fouriers or Faradays who never broke through the barriers put up by the scientific establishment at the time.   (1989:215)

> Second, recognition of social-political influences ought to sustain the search for ways to minimize the undermining effect that they can potentially have on the search for truth. One way to resist domination by self-interested forces within or outside of science itself is to "insist that honesty in experimentation, openness to rival views, and criticism of established views are values honoured in science, and to an extent enshrined in its institutions."   (O'Hear 1989:216)

If one thing has been written in this chapter to inspire more than casual reflection on the social-political aspects of research practices that lead to scientific knowledge, then its goals will have been met.

16 Sociolinguistic variation and the law

RONALD R. BUTTERS

Introduction

During the past two or three decades, the field of language and law has increasingly become the focus of substantial linguistic interest. For some linguists (sometimes working in interdisciplinary concert with law professors), legal language is of interest in its own right. Also, however, linguists have more and more been engaged to use their professional expertise to assist lawyers in preparing and presenting their clients' cases, and by law-enforcement personnel interested in solving crimes and prosecuting criminals. Taken together, research that includes both the linguistic examination of legal language and the law's use of linguistic insights and expertise is generally termed *Linguistics and Law*. A term that is frequently applied more narrowly to the use of linguistics experts in the legal setting – especially in criminal proceedings – is *Forensic Linguistics*.

Sociolinguistics is a sub-discipline that is especially important to scholars working in the general field of linguistics and law. Legal systems in all cultures general hinge crucially upon language, and, as Labov (1988:181–2) notes, the law is essentially a social institution, and sociolinguists thus appear to be especially well qualified to answer legal linguistic questions. As Labov notes, the centrality of empirical data to sociolinguistic research offers more to the law than other linguistic approaches; for example, a

> theory that builds models out of introspective judgments, extracting principles
> that are remote from observation and experiment, . . . is not the kind of theory
> that . . . [generates] evidence that allows . . . judges . . . to decide a case
> with confidence. . . . It is hard to imagine that a concept like subjacency or
> the Empty Category Principle would be used in court to decide a question of
> fact.   (1988:181)

Sociolinguistic variability, broadly conceived, thus has numerous implications for "forensic linguists" who are called upon to give advice about legal-linguistic matters and even testify in court about linguistic evidence.[1]

---

[1] Shuy (2006), a small handbook on forensic linguistic practice, is an excellent starting place for anyone interested in offering legal consulting services. See also Ainsworth (2006) for an article-length survey about the legal reception of forensic linguistics. A number of scholarly organizations

Among the many linguistic questions and problems that arise in the legal setting in the United States (and cultures having similar legal traditions), the following areas are of continuing concern:

- Constitutions, statutes, ordinances, regulations, and contracts are debated, negotiated, and enacted by means of language and are themselves recorded in writing. One of the chief tasks of judges and juries is to interpret the sometimes vague and ambiguous language of such linguistic instruments. The resolution of such questions frequently depends upon historical, social, and regional variation in language.
- In criminal proceedings, law-enforcement officers interrogate suspects and witnesses and frequently write down (or mechanically record) the interrogations, yielding special types of discourse called *interrogation transcripts*, *confessions*, and *witness statements*. These can all also be vague and ambiguous, and they sometimes contain variable markers indicating that the speakers were insincere, tricked, and/or coerced.
- Court proceedings are carried out in one or more spoken and written languages. Sociolinguists are interested in these types of discourse, particularly the power relationships among the participants, and lawyers and judges can learn from sociolinguists about the significant inherent variability in such speech.
- Witnesses are questioned under oath, and the exchanges are written down (and, increasingly, video-taped) by court reporters; judges and juries are sometimes asked to judge the truthfulness of witnesses on the basis of their demeanor when speaking.
- Juries themselves receive spoken (and, sometimes, written) instruction that they are required to use in formulating their decisions; they debate the issues; they report their conclusions in written and spoken language.

Moreover, citizens have certain linguistic rights that are both defined and proscribed by law. In the United States, certain types of freedom of speech and publication are guaranteed by the Constitution. However, legal tradition has allowed these language rights to be limited in numerous ways: threats, sedition, and publication of government secrets are all forbidden by law and/or threat of civil lawsuits, and language plays a central role in defining obscenity, pornography, inciting to riot, perjury, false advertising, justifiable self-defense in response to putative threats and insults, and illegal discrimination in commerce and government treatment of citizens, including the disadvantaging of linguistic minorities. One or more linguistic acts form the substance of every accusation of slander and

welcome the results of research on language and law, including the American Dialect Society, the American Name Society, the Dictionary Society of North America, the International Association of Forensic Linguists, the Law and Society Association, and NWAV.

libel. The interpretation of linguistic evidence can be crucial in determining the difference between seduction and rape. Warnings, printed instructions, and official documents may legally be judged insufficient or difficult to comprehend, and in some cases the law may require certain goods and services to carry a sufficient warning or disclaimer in advertisements and on packaging.

The application of sociolinguistic theory and methodology can also contribute to a better understanding of evidence that is admitted in court. For example, linguistic evidence is central in determining the criminal intent of speakers in surreptitiously recorded conversations in narcotics sales, money-laundering schemes, solicitation for prostitution, and murder-for-hire propositions. What a medical practitioner did or did not say to a patient can form the basis for distinguishing between medical malpractice and sound medical advice. Lawsuits and disciplinary proceedings that have to do with plagiarism most often center upon linguistic evidence, and the descriptions of patented products and processes generally figure prominently in lawsuits involving patent infringement. Legally, one can even own language, through copyrights, patents, and trademarks, and much of the litigation involving trademarks focuses on linguistic issues.

This chapter reports on representative work on linguistics and law that is related in some way to variationist sociolinguistics. I cannot hope here to survey all of the landmark studies; the individual cases and categories of research discussed must be viewed as representative, not exhaustive.[2] Fortunately, I need say nothing about *linguistic profiling*, itself a topic within the language-and-law purview, because it is treated in this volume by John Baugh, a leading expert in that field.

A number of scholars who work on language and law are concerned with the more traditional variationist approaches involving phonology, morphology, and (occasionally) syntax in the context of social, ethnic, and even regional variation of dialects, pidgins, creoles, and languages in contact. However, much of the work in language and law addresses variation within a standard language, especially recent English, and the research often draws considerably from lexicography, semantics, pragmatics and discourse analysis, and even semiotics. Indeed, one of the important contributions of language and law studies to variationist sociolinguistics may well be the emphasis on linguistic subfields that generally are less frequently examined in the mainstream of variationist research. Variationist sociolinguistics will thus be conceived of quite broadly in this chapter.

---

[2] For a more thorough introduction to the field of language and law, the reader should consult general introductory works such as Levi and Walker (1990), Rieber and Stewart (1990), Gibbons (1994, 2003), Cotterill (2002a), and Solan and Tiersma (2005), as well as such more specialized works as: Hirsch (1998), examining the role of women in East African Islamic courts; Labov (1988:160–70), Dumas (1990a), Ploch, Dumas, Gray, McLennan, and Nolt (1993), Butters (2004), and Tiersma (2006), all of which are concerned with empirical issues in intelligibility and effectiveness of such documents as cigarette warning labels, jury instructions, documents informing workers of their contractual rights, and even allegedly prize-winning lottery tickets; Walker (1990) on court reporting; Lucas (2003) on language and the law in deaf communities. See also Finegan (1997).

The law as sociolinguistic data

One of the earliest landmark studies in language and law is William O'Barr's (1982) empirical research on the effects upon juries of variation in witness testimony and lawyers' questioning, with particular emphasis on the interaction of gender and such stylistic variables as grammar and word choice. O'Barr, a cultural anthropologist, employed student actors as witnesses, lawyers, and mock jury members. He based the actors' scripts upon actual trial transcripts that he manipulated to introduce the variables that he wished to test for. Phonological variables were largely excluded.

O'Barr was greatly interested in the effects upon juries, in testimony and attorney questioning, of various sociolinguistic variables. The use of non-standard grammar reduced the credibility of both witnesses and attorneys, as did what O'Barr termed "hypercorrect" style (needlessly complex syntax and recondite word choice). Features of what O'Barr called "Powerless Style" – a term that has had wide usage in linguistic gender studies (together with its antonym, "Powerful Style") – include hesitation forms (*uh, you know, like*), the use of such mitigating forms as *maybe, sir* and *ma'm*, and *I suppose*, and acquiescence to interruption by the other person in each attorney-witness interaction.[3] O'Barr concluded that the use of Powerless Style also tended to reduce witness and attorney credibility, though this category interacted with gender and role in complex ways: in general, the mock juries interpreted a style that was high in the Powerful variables as aggressive, hostile, and impolite, and therefore lacking in credibility. Women, however, were generally seen as hyper-Powerful at a lower level of aggressiveness than men.

O'Barr's methodologies (in particular, his use of actors and legal transcripts as the source of linguistic data), as well as some of his concerns, are largely distinct from the usual practice in variationist sociolinguistics today. His interest in subjective reactions to features of speech relates especially well to the work of Dennis Preston and others in *Perceptual Dialectology* (e.g. Preston and Long 2002). Later studies of the language of small-claims courts (O'Barr and Conley 1990) and rape trials (O'Barr and Conley 1998) considered unscripted data drawn from actual courtroom usage and did not question mock juries. Other important works drawing upon such discourse for data are Berk-Seligson (1990) on courtroom interpreters; Cotterill (2002b) on the O. J. Simpson murder trial; Matoesian (1993, 2001) on rape trials; Philips (1998) on the use of language by judges; Walter (1988) on jury summation; and Stygall (1994) on courtroom-trial language. Like O'Barr (1982), these later studies are often interested in credibility issues

---

[3] The concept of Powerless-versus-Powerful Speech has its roots in the early work on women's language of Lakoff (1975), who hypothesized that the speech of women in American culture is marked by such "powerless" features, as well as a tendency to frequently use intensifiers and highly specific color terms (*mauve, taupe*).

and power relationships, are not centrally concerned with the usual variationist variables, and generally make use of discourse analysis methodologies. Butters (2000) also analyzes courtroom discourse – the pre-trial questioning of jurors, trial examination of witnesses, the comments and verbal rulings of the judge during the trial – but to the somewhat different end of pointing out evidence of racial prejudice in the trial of a Black man accused of the rape and murder of an elderly White woman.

Recent work by Kendall (2006b, based also on 2006a) on pause and silence examines the video-tape of a legal deposition of an expert witness in an American trademark case as discourse data within a variationist sociolinguistic framework.[4] Kendall's work affirms that "pause can carry speaker-generated meaning, but can also be misinterpreted by listeners based on cultural and social differences." Comparing the video-tape with the court reporters' transcripts of the same material, he notes that reporters normally do not indicate pause, a practice that "creates opportunity for misinterpretations"; he argues that "even simple" indications of pause would make the transcripts clearer.

It should be noted that some of the most important theoretical works in the field of language and law that focus upon courtroom language, while perhaps only indirectly related to variationist studies, have important implications for the forensic linguistics discipline as a whole. Especially notable in this respect is the work of two scholars, Lawrence Solan and Peter Tiersma. Solan, in his landmark book, *The language of judges* (1993), finds sharp limits to the efficacy of syntactic and lexicographical arguments in the interpretation of laws and contracts in difficult cases. Still, as Tiersma says, such analysis is in many respects inevitable:

> Judges often engage in various types of linguistic analysis, . . . exhibit[ing] both surprising linguistic acumen and, on the other hand, woeful disregard for how language operates. . . . But when interpreting a text, be it statutory or conversational, a careful linguistic analysis should always be the point of departure.   (1993:283; see also Tiersma 1999, Butters 1993)

Variation as linguistic evidence

This section outlines representative studies and legal proceedings from a number of areas in which linguists, drawing upon sociolinguistic principles, have been especially productive in forensic linguistic applications.

---

[4] Depositions are pre-trial testimony, mostly reserved for civil cases, in which experts and others with knowledge about the case are questioned under oath by the opposing sides to gather information that could bear on trial issues.

Voice identification

In criminal cases in the United States, so-called "ear-witness testimony" – the admissibility of the testimony of witnesses to a crime based on the witnesses' identification of the voice of particular speakers – is traditional. Although there is considerable evidence that such identification may often not be very reliable (Bull and Clifford 1984, Schiller and Köster 1998, Vanags, Carroll, and Perfect 2005), the scientific evidence that calls earwitness testimony into question has not persuaded courts in general to alter the practice of trusting in the powers of ordinary citizens to remember the voices of strangers (as well as friends and acquaintances) that they may have heard only briefly weeks or months before, frequently under stressful conditions – and to be able to distinguish those voices from all others. Legal tradition, it seems, is difficult to turn in a different direction. For example, in a recent case in North Carolina, a defendant was tried for murder largely on the basis of the sworn testimony of a witness – an acquaintance – who had identified the accused on the basis of a voice line-up. Two armed, hooded persons had burst into the witness's house, shot a man to death, and also shot the witness in the leg before fleeing the scene. In the line-up, the witness listened to the defendant and several others speak the same two sentences – "Where's the money, where's the money?" and "We have to kill the other guy, he knows who I am" – from behind a screen, and then reported that one of the voices – that of the defendant – was the one that he had heard utter the exemplar sentences during the commission of the crime. The acoustics were questionable: the shooter's speech, muffled by a ski mask, had been heard through a closed door, and there was reportedly considerable background noise in the room. The wounded witness was distracted by the bullet wound in his leg.[5] There were potentially prejudicial aspects of the circumstances of the voice line-up, in that the witness was predisposed to identify the defendant, whom he knew, as the criminal because he knew that the defendant had a motive to kill the murder victim. However, the voice line-up was considered admissible, and the witness was allowed to testify in court that the defendant was indeed the person who had shot him and the murder victim. (How much the jury members relied upon this evidence is not known: the case ended with a hung jury, and the defendant later pled guilty to a lesser charge of second-degree murder.)

Even when the speaker is unknown to the potential witness, as is usually the case in such crimes as armed robbery, the victim is generally nonetheless allowed to testify as to the nature of the criminal's voice and to state, if the victim feels able, that the defendant's voice and the voice of the crime's perpetrator are one and the same. In such cases, the role of the linguist in the courtroom can at best be to point out to the jury how the scientific knowledge about the reliability of earwitness testimony applies in the particular case at hand. One highly respected

---

[5] There were additional allegations that the witness was, at the time of the shooting, additionally distracted in that he was allegedly watching a pornographic video and masturbating.

group of prominent British scholars, headed by the phonetician John Peter French of York University, make up an independent consulting firm, JP French Associates, that has consulted on over 4,000 legal cases of various kinds involving forensic phonetics and acoustics, and offers "advice on and critiques of the validity of voice identification parades and claims concerning voice recognition by lay-witnesses" (www.jpfrench.com/expert.htm).

In criminal proceedings in which the disputed voice has been recorded (for example, on a telephone-answering machine or by a surreptitious microphone worn by an undercover policeman), attempts have been made to theorize the use of spectrographic analysis – sometimes called "voiceprints" – to uniquely identify individual voices on the basis of phonological characteristics alone. To linguists, the term VOICEPRINT itself – given its morphological and semantic parallels with the term FINGERPRINT – is highly misleading, suggesting a high level of reliability as a unique marker of every individual. Although some law-enforcement practitioners may disagree, the consensus among linguists seem to be that "voiceprinting" methodology is by itself generally inadequate to the task of telling one speaker from all others with the sort of accuracy needed for positive identification purposes in a court of law. One well-respected phonetician has observed that a conservative estimate of the error rate for even the best of "voiceprint" analysis would be one in twenty, a rate much too low to meet the "reasonable doubt" standard of criminal courts:

> There are occasions when one can say that the voice on a particular recording is *probably not* the same as the voice on some other recording, and times when one can say that the voice on the recording *could be* the same as the voice on another. Speaker identification using spectrographic evidence has been used in a number of criminal cases. . . . In my view, it is completely irresponsible to say, as I have heard witnesses testify in court, "The voice on the recording is that of the accused and could be that of no other speaker."   (Ladefoged 1993:211–12)

And even a strong proponent of spectrographic identification (a Federal Bureau of Investigation agent) writes:

> When properly conducted, spectrographic voice identification is a relatively accurate **but not conclusive** examination for comparing a recorded unknown voice sample with a suspect repeating the identical contextual information over the same type of transmission system (e.g., a local telephone line).   (Koenig 1993:1; emphasis mine)

While many law-enforcement bodies have embraced spectrographic identification as a useful investigative tool, American courts have been generally hesitant to accept such evidence to help a jury in determining the facts. In cases where phoneticians are allowed to testify, equally plausible-seeming testimony may frequently be presented on behalf of the other side, so that the value of spectrographic analysis may be less dependent upon science and more upon the demeanor and general convincingness of the experts presenting the evidence (see Baldwin and French [1990], Hollien [1990:207–230], Rose [2003], and Solan and Tiersma [2005:140–48] concerning the issues of linguistic reliability and legal admissibility of spectrographic analysis). In particular, phonological analysis may be helpful in assisting law-enforcement agents narrow down the list of possible suspects. However, sociolinguistic variables of region are generally of greatest importance here. For example, on the basis of analysis of a taunting message that was sent the police, British linguists were able to locate the dialect of the speaker (who was, however, merely pretending to be the real "Yorkshire Ripper") within a few miles of his neighborhood (Ellis 1994, Lewis 1994).

In criminal prosecutions, then, it is probably too high a goal to demonstrate that the accused person – and not one of what might well be hundreds of thousands of other possible suspects – is the perpetrator of the crime. A more readily attainable – and decidedly more modest – forensic linguistic goal is (as Ladefoged suggested, [1993:211–12]) *negative identification*: to demonstrate merely that a suspect's voice and the perpetrator's voice are NOT the same (i.e. that Speaker A's voice is "probably not" what has been recorded as the known voice of the criminal). In such cases, sociolinguistic variables can be especially telling. Two such cases in which sociolinguists assisted in *negative identification* were discussed fairly early in the literature, by Ash (1988) and by Labov (1988); see also Dumas (1990b, 2000).[6]

Ash was asked by attorneys for Richard Carl, the husband of a former retail home-improvement store worker, to examine four brief threatening messages that had been received and recorded by the local police and fire department after Carl's wife had lost her job. The messages warned of a bomb that the caller claimed to have placed in the store where Carl's wife had formerly worked. Earwitnesses familiar with Carl's voice reported to the police their judgments that he was the speaker of the four messages; he was then arrested. Mr. Carl maintained that he had not made the calls.

Ash limited her assessment to ascertaining whether this was a case in which "the criminal and the defendant belong to different speech communities" (1988:26). Ash noted, "When Mr. Carl spoke, it was immediately obvious that his speech followed the pattern of the White Philadelphia vernacular in every detail." Of greatest significance to Ash's analysis was the vowel /aw/, peculiarities of which had already been identified in studies of Philadelphia White vernacular English, because the word *how* was repeated four times in stressed position in

---

[6] Linguists may also be asked to demonstrate that claims that another "expert" are making about the reliability of "voiceprint" evidence are not scientifically sound. I once spent the better part of an afternoon in an East Coast federal prison attempting to convince a defendant who was being held there without bond that the spectrographic evidence that he hoped to rely on was totally useless for identification purposes. Not only was the acoustic quality of the recordings terrible, the alleged speakers were all middle-aged men of Sicilian parentage who had grown up together in the same New Jersey town. The best that I could have done in court would have been to testify that there was no way that the prosecution witnesses could reliably discern who was saying what in the surreptitiously recorded conversations.

the threatening phone calls. Carl fronted the onset of *how* in the manner typical of the speech community in which he had grown up; the person who made the phone calls did not front the onset. Ash noted also that Carl pronounced the vowels in both *on* and *off* the same – "very high and back" – whereas the speaker of the threatening messages pronounced *on* with "the lowest of all the stressed vowels, . . . and it is midway between front and back" (close to the stressed vowel in most American pronunciations of *father*). A final difference had to do with the pronunciation of *gonna*. Carl pronounced the first syllable to rhyme with *bone*; the caller pronounced it to rhyme with *gun*.

Ash concluded that the speaker of the threatening messages was not a member of the Philadelphia White community; Carl definitely was. Therefore, Carl could not have made the call. Ash presented her case in a written report to the trial judge, using schematic spectrograms of the sort familiar to variationists, to illustrate the differences in the vowels of Carl and the criminal phone-caller. Though the judge in the case did not comment directly on Ash's report, he handed down a directed verdict of not guilty after hearing only limited testimony from the earwitnesses who claimed to be able to identify Carl as the person who had made the call. It seems likely that Ash's presentation was useful to the judge in coming to his conclusion.

The case reported by Labov (1988) was similar. Again there was a tape-recorded telephoned threat (that a bomb had been placed on a commercial airliner). Labov writes, "As soon as I played the tapes I was sure that [the accused man] . . . was innocent. He obviously was a New Yorker: every detail of his speech fit the New York pattern. But it was equally clear that the bomb-threat caller was from Eastern New England" (1988:170–71). One difference between Ash's case and Labov's was that the defense attempted to introduce evidence based on spectrographic analysis alone, as analyzed by Peter Ladefoged and one of his students:

> Although Ladefoged opposed the free use of voice-prints [*sic*] to identify voices as the same, he has . . . concluded that voice-print identification . . . can be used to argue that two voices are different. . . . However, there was considerable legal argument on the admissibility and reliability of voice-print identification [by the prosecuting attorneys in this particular trial]. (1988:172)

Labov, however, was allowed to testify as an expert on the phonetics of "dialect diversity." In court he played the telephoned tape and the voiced exemplar, juxtaposing what he had determined were the key features so that the judge could actually hear the difference. Next, he introduced

> the theoretical basis of the argument. . . . The main emphasis was put on the merger of COT and CAUGHT in the Eastern New England area . . . and on the structural difference between dialects that make such a distinction and those that don't. (1988:172–3)

Like Ash, Labov also pointed to other characteristic differences between the accent of the speaker on the bomb-threat tape and the accent of the defendant that marked the speakers as members of different dialect communities. Next, Labov "introduced evidence from American dialectology, to show that the phonological differences between Eastern New England and New York City were established fact" (1988:174). Finally, Labov introduced

> instrumental measurements of the vowel systems of the bomb threat caller and the defendant [i.e. the same type of schematic spectrograms that Ash also used], providing [visual] confirmation of the auditory impressions of the structural analysis.   (1988:175)

In this case, too, the judge found the defendant not guilty, noting in press interviews that the linguistic evidence had been important to him in concluding that there was at least reasonable doubt that the defendant had committed the crime of which he was accused.

It is often suggested that the use of variationist analysis described in these two cases does not allow for the possibility that speakers may disguise their voices when engaging in criminal enterprises, or that they might intentionally alter their normal speech patterns when giving a voice exemplar. Labov was questioned in court about these possibilities in cross-examination and noted (citing Payne 1980) that, as variationist studies have demonstrated, speakers are not consciously aware of many of their most significant linguistic variables, especially those of other speech communities; an ability to mimic another dialect to the extent of controlling all of the relevant variables is usually unlikely. Ash reports on a pilot study that she conducted to test the possibility of disguised voice, concluding that the likelihood was remote (1988:32). Similar results were reported by Butters, Espy, and Altsuler (1993). The likelihood seems small indeed that, in making bomb threats, either Ash's defendant or Labov's could have eradicated features of their native accent that they did not even consciously know that they had, replacing them consistently with subtle features of a speech community that was not their own.

These two cases indicate the utility of testimony based on sociolinguistic analysis of the membership of individuals in larger speech communities, and that expert linguistic testimony that attempts to demonstrate that the voices on two different tapes are not the same person is on far stronger scientific and legal ground than expert linguistic testimony that attempts to conclude that the voices on two or more different recordings were produced by the same person. Finally, the two cases suggest that the schematic spectrograms familiar to sociophoneticians can be used in the course of expert testimony so long as they are presented as supporting documents indicating the characteristics of the individual's speech within the larger framework of speech communities and are not identified as "voiceprints" nor asserted to display phonetic characteristics that would uniquely identify particular individuals.

Ascertaining historical speech community membership: the case
of the Bear Island land claim

Chambers (1990) reports on one of the most inventive and intriguing (if in the end legally unsuccessful) applications of variationist sociolinguistics to a legal problem involving speech-community membership. The case began in a land dispute involving 6,500 square kilometers of land that the Temagami Canadian Indian tribe had occupied as their ancestral home for over 100 years. The government of Ontario wished to develop an all-season resort on the land and brought suit against the Temagami (who asked for compensation for the loss of the land), claiming that the tribe did not have clear title to the land. Chambers writes, "As the defense saw it, the case rested on a fundamental question of obvious interest to social scientists: . . . Where were the Temagamis in 1763?" (1990:24). In that year, a Royal Proclamation had, in essence, conferred territorial rights to all tribes in lands that they then occupied. The government maintained that the Temagamis were not in 1763 occupying the land in question. Basing their conclusions on cultural arguments, anthropologists testified as experts both for and against the Temagamis. Chambers and a colleague, John Nichols, testified (for ten hours) on behalf of the tribe's case, using linguistic data and analysis that Nichols had assembled. Chambers describes the linguistic evidence as follows:

> Of crucial importance to the interpretation of the linguistic facts is an Ojibwa migration from Sault Ste Marie . . . westward to Milles Lacs, Minnesota . . . that is known to have been completed by 1750. . . . The Temagamis . . . were alleged [according to the government's experts] to have migrated, or drifted, eastward from Sault Ste Marie after 1763, perhaps as late as 1830. If this were so, then the Temagami dialect should be more similar to Sault Ste Marie than is the Milles Lacs dialect. The historical migration of the Milles Lacs nation thus provides a touchstone against which one can judge the plausibility of the chronology of the alleged Temagami migration.   (1990:26)

According to Chambers,

> Nichols' linguistic evidence answers the question of the whereabouts of the Temagamis in 1763 beyond a reasonable doubt. The attested migration to Milles Lacs gives a comparison point against which the Temagamis can be dated, and in virtually all cases Sault Ste Marie and Milles Lacs share features with one another but the Temagamis differ. The differences in morphology and in basic lexical items suggest that the Temagami split from the southern groups is ancient.   (1990:27)

One example of the kind of data that Nichols and Chambers reported to the court is the word for "bullet," which is a lexical item obviously introduced by contact with Europeans. Chambers writes:

> If the Temagamis had been in the Sault Ste Marie region at the time of contact, they would almost certainly have adopted the same lexical terms for new cultural items. . . . [But] they have different words. . . . Temagami

moozinii in the northern region and Sault Ste Marie/Milles Lacs *anwi* in the southern region. . . . Similar patterns emerge from 20 other mappings of post-colonial lexical items, including the words for 'bottle', 'button', 'chair', 'horse', 'money', 'pants', 'he reads', 'scissors', and 'sock'.   (1990:27)

Although "the linguistic evidence seems, simply, incontrovertible" (1990:30), the Ontario Supreme Court was not persuaded. Declaring the linguistic evidence "nebulous," the Court ruled against the Temagamis, basing their conclusion simply on the judges' own historical intuition: it was "inconceivable," they wrote, that the British would have granted a large portion of land to Indians in the eighteenth century. Chambers quotes Judge Steele: "At that time, Europeans did not consider them [i.e. the Indians] equal to themselves."[7]

No matter how solid the linguistic evidence may seem to the linguist, it will be useless in court if it does not in the end persuade the non-linguist judge or jury. Chambers was a seasoned veteran of courtroom testimony and a persuasive writer and speaker known for his clarity and charm, yet in this case the strong scientific evidence did not prevail over the gut feelings of the members of the court.

Authorship identification

The literature on the linguistic determination of the author of an unknown text is much older than that on voice identification, and various methods have also been used both in law-enforcement investigation and even in the courts, though the latter have been nearly as skeptical of some of the linguistic methodology in this field as they have been in voice identification. The types of cases fall into roughly two different groups: (1) plagiarism; and (2) anonymous, pseudonymous, and falsely attributed documents and messages.

Plagiarism and copyright violations

One variety of what I am here considering under the general heading of "plagiarism" is more commonly spoken of as copyright violations and arises in a civil court when one author (or other artist) claims that another author has violated the first author's proprietary rights and sues for financial compensation for the injury. Plagiarism per se arises when, for example, a student attempts to pass off the work of a printed source as the student's own in a report. A third is self-plagiarism: when an author sells substantially the same work twice under different names, or when a scholar attempts to make the scholar's list of publications seem more impressive by publishing more or less the same article in different forms in different venues, usually with different titles (Ahmad 2005).

---

[7] A further appeal was available to the Temagamis (to the Supreme Court of Canada), but Chambers reports that in 1986 the tribe settled out of court for $30,000,000, presumably a much smaller sum than they would have received had their case prevailed in the Ontario court.

Expert determination of plagiarism is a subject that has had little history within classical variationist sociolinguistics. Generally speaking, the analyst is faced with two texts, one allegedly derived from the other. The problem is one of deciding: (1) how plausible it is that the author of the alleged text would have constructed the text entirely independently; and/or (2) whether the debt that the "plagiarized" text owes to the parallel text is great enough to be considered plagiarism, even if a connection of some sort is acknowledged. The kind of expertise needed to make such judgments is not necessarily even that of the linguist, let alone the sociolinguist; college-level teachers of English composition, experienced academic deans, and professors in general may be called upon to judge academic plagiarism (including self-plagiarism). Experts in the field of music, film, and publication are more likely to have a larger contribution to make to the copyright-violation issues. At best, a linguist might be employed to point out to the court the similar passages, credentialing himself or herself in a general way as someone attuned to the nuances of language and, as an academic, to issues of student and collegial plagiarism in general. Whether or not the amount and kind of repetition, even if it is not purely the result of chance, is plagiarism is not in itself a linguistic issue. Whether or not the amount and kind of repetition between any two texts is unlikely to be a matter of pure chance may be open to linguistic analysis, though about this issue there is considerable disagreement in authorship studies in general.

As Olsson (2004:109–118) notes, it is possible to create quantificational metrics that create some kind of a measure of the amount of overlap between two or more documents (see also Johnson 1997). Computer programs such as *Copycatch*, a respected investigative device used for detecting academic and other sorts of plagiarism, make use of such metrics (see www.copycatchgold.com/). Olsson quotes Pappas (1998) to the effect that, for example, there are many passages in the sermons of Martin Luther King that duplicate "the earlier work of Jack Boozer." But it is difficult to imagine how one might quantificationally define "overlap" in a way that would be institutionally probative of plagiarism or copyright violation, or how one might use sociolinguistic variables in framing such a definition. Plagiarism and copyright infringement are subject to a host of non-linguistic rules: for example, what may be permitted in a sermon is not necessarily permitted in a novel or academic writing; such practices as PASTICHE and HOMAGE by definition require the repetition of well-known and recognizable passages from famous works; some phrases are so well known that it is considered superfluous to document them; most politicians do not write their own speeches but pay others to do so; etc. Moreover, the reliability of the metric that is selected must be demonstrated empirically.

As is the case with voice identification, the only sure function of the sociolinguist in such cases (beyond the general task of using the insights of a linguist to point out highly similar passages) may well be negative identification: for example, to point out features of the putatively plagiarized source document that could not possibly have been written by the accused plagiarizer because they have their source in a speech community or repertoire unavailable to the accused. How this might be done is discussed in the section that follows.

Anonymous, pseudonymous, and falsely attributed messages

It is easy to see why legal practitioners would want to be able to find a scientific way to determine with certainty the authorship of an anonymous or pseudonymous document – or even have some scientific clues that would help law-enforcement agents narrow down the range of possible authors. Not only do people sometimes steal other people's words, they also sometimes attempt to pass off their own written words as those of somebody else – for example, in forged wills, false suicide notes, and fabricated confessions. Others with criminal intent generate documents with no attribution at all, or with made-up names – for example, in ransom notes, threatening letters, libelous writings, and negotiations to meet in which the invitee is then robbed or murdered (or, in a recent variant, accused of enticement of a minor to commit sexual acts with an adult).[8] In some investigative cases, there is no second text to compare the offending document with. In other cases, there may be exemplar documents known to have been written by two persons, in which case the goal of the investigator is to determine which of the known writers is the author of the disputed document.

Those linguists who have specialized in author identification make use of two approaches, one statistical, one inductive. The statistical methodology has been developed by a number of different scholars in the past fifty or so years, and it is of course generally not usable if there is only one document available for analysis – as was the case, for example, during the murderous career of the infamous California "Unabomber," whose mailed bombs killed and wounded over thirty people over the course of twenty or so years. He generated copious anonymous material, but it was only when his brother, a person with no legal or linguistic training whatever, recognized elements of Unabomber's unique writing style that he was identified and captured.

Those who employ statistical methodologies agree that there are features of grammar, sentence length and structure, and lexis that are unique to a given individual and statistically discoverable. As early as 1964, Mosteller and Wallace used statistical analysis of linguistic forms found in the texts of the eighteenth-century Federalist Papers to conclude that those essays that were in dispute were written by James Madison and not Alexander Hamilton, as Hamilton had claimed. In a recent paper, Fung (2003) "based [a statistical analysis of the *Papers*] on the relative frequencies of only three words. Using the obtained separating hyperplane

---

[8] The website www.perverted-justice.com/ is devoted to the display of transcripts of Instant Messages between adults pretending to be children who are seeking sexual initiation and unwitting adults who have been accused (and usually convicted) of being sexual predators – entirely on the basis of the evidence of the deceptive Instant Messages.

in three dimensions, all of the 12 disputed papers ended up on the Madison side of the separating plane." Any statistical analysis of this sort needs a large quantity of text (hence the difficulty of coming to probative conclusions about ransom notes, which are usually brief). In addition, the more alike the compared documents are in function (say, two letters to the editor of the *New York Times*), the more readily one can argue that measurably significant negative results are valid, whereas the more unlike the compared documents are in function, the more readily one can argue that measurably significant positive results are valid.

Forensic linguists have played roles in numerous cases involving this sort of analysis in authorship disputes. The statistical methodology, however, intersects very little with sociolinguistics and variationist studies as commonly practiced. Some of the notable contributors to and commentators on this aspect of language and law are: Miron, who notes that his statistics-based conclusions were rejected by a court because they were too arcane for the judge and the jury to understand (1990:57); Smith (1994), who critiques the methodology of Morton (1978); and Chaski (1997, 2001, 2005), who argues on her web site (www.linguisticevidence.org/) that

> subjective techniques are not reliable and such testimony has been excluded or severely restricted [by many courts]. But, more importantly, recent validation results for the syntactic analysis method described in Chaski show a 95% accuracy rate at assigning documents to the correct author.

What Chaski refers to as "subjective techniques" are all of the non-statistical methodologies that linguists and others have employed in authorship cases; her 2001 article strongly criticized those alternative, inductive methodologies.[9] Others disagree with her – for example, McMenamin (2001) and Grant and Baker (2001), who argue against ruling out "subjective techniques" and propose an alternative statistical procedure, the use of Principal Component Analysis. As McMenamin puts it, Chaski's "theoretical position . . . views linguistic variation as a feature of linguistic performance, thus missing the point of the inherent variability of language." He, too, finds Principal Component Analysis to be "a promising method for measuring the range of variation needed for authorship identification" (2001:93).[10]

---

[9] Chaski, a respected former tenured university professor who has practiced as an active independent scholar and forensic practitioner for a number of years, offers her services on her website (www.linguisticevidence.org/) with respect to "ransom notes in kidnapping cases, threatening letters, anonymous letters, suicide notes, patent disputes, interrogation/interview statements, missing person, employment disputes, examination fraud, plagiarism, and peer review of reports by linguists, English professors, Communications professors, police and questioned document examiners related to authorship."

[10] See Solan and Tiersma (2005:149–78) for a balanced overview of the inductivist-vesus-statisticianist controversy that is somewhat critical of both sides. Coulthard (2004) presents a succinct and clear summary of the non-statistical techniques as applied to authorship studies in general. Shuy (1998) outlines several characteristics of confessions that in the aggregate distinguish them from other kinds of speech acts and that can be particularly useful in determining if the confession has been coerced, is essentially untrue from the perspective of the confessor, and/or was rehearsed or in some way generated by someone other than the supposed author.

The literature on inductive applications of linguistic methodology to various authorship questions generally makes use of well-known methods of discourse analysis and takes into account the variability inherent in language, but the actual use of what might be recognized as variationist sociolinguistic insights is less frequent. In the interest of space, I will look closely at only one sort of application, which uses the "subjective methods" of discourse analysis in the analysis of criminal confessions and witness statements, using data from a case in which I testified in court.

State of Louisiana v. Wilbert Rideau (Lake Charles, LA, January 15, 2005) was a robbery and homicide case that was first tried in 1961, when the defendant was only twenty years old. Through a series of mistrials – occasioned in large part from overzealous prosecutorial pre-trial publicity apparently related to the fact Rideau was an African American and his victims were White – the case was not finally decided until January 2005. A trial jury then found Rideau guilty of manslaughter, a crime for which the penalty was a fewer number of years than Rideau had already served in Louisiana prisons. He was therefore set free after over forty years of incarceration (during which time, according to the defense attorneys, he had become completely rehabilitated).

The crimes with which Rideau was charged – and which he almost certainly did commit in 1961 – were indeed serious. According to his confession and the witness statements, he had robbed a bank (where he was a frequent customer and hence readily identifiable), abducted three of the bank employees in a car belonging to one of the employees, and then forced them to drive aimlessly about the countryside for several hours, at which point he ordered them from the car and shot them and stabbed one of the abducted women, who later died. Given the apparent pointlessness of the crime and the desultory way in which it was carried out, many in the legal profession believe that an insanity defense would be plausible today, but in the 1960s in a small town in Louisiana in a case involving a young Black male defendant and a middle-aged White female homicide victim, Rideau was charged with capital first-degree murder.

The appeals and retrials went on for over forty years, at which point the witnesses had all died of old age. As was customary in the 1960s, no records of Rideau's original interrogation had been kept (though a video-tape still exists of an inflammatory television interview with Rideau and several of the police officers who arrested him, which was the basis for the courts' overturning of his first murder trial and death-penalty conviction). The prosecution of the final trial thus had to be based entirely on the transcripts of the sworn testimony from the earlier trials, together with the ancient signed confession of Mr. Rideau and the statements of the material witnesses – the two persons who were abducted (but not killed) in the course of the crime.

The defense attorneys viewed the confession and the sworn statements with suspicion. It appeared to them that the witness statements and confession contained passages that suggested the style of the interrogating police officers. For example, the statement of witness Dora McCain begins:

> My name is Dora McCain. I live at 4919 Center Street, Lake Charles, La. I am 30 years of age. I am employed as a teller with the Gulf National Bank of Lake Charles, La. My post is at the Southgate Branch of this institution. [¶] On Thursday, February 16, 1961, I was at my post at the above business.

And the statement of witness Hickman begins:

> My name is Jay H. Hickman. I live at 1716 West Common Street in Lake Charles, La. I am 54 years old. I am employed as Branch Manager and Assistant Cashier at the Gulf National Bank of Lake Charles, La. My post is at the Southgate Branch of this institution. [¶] On Thursday, February 16, 1961, I was at my post at the above business.

These passages clearly suggest a formula, one that could not represent the way that the two witnesses actually gave their statements; at best, it seems to reflect the way that the questioner presented the initial questions, after which the recording police officer fit the answers into a predetermined matrix. More important, some sort of statement matrix seems to have been followed throughout the two interviews. For example, compare the following two passages (I have italicized the identical portions):

> [from Mrs. McCain's typewritten statement:] He then *marched the three of us towards the front of the bank and towards the teller's cages.* When *we reached the west end of the teller's cages, one or more of the telephones started ringing.*
> [from Mr. Hickman's statement:] He *marched the three of us towards the front of the bank and towards the teller's cages.* Just as *we reached the west end of the teller's cages,* near the vault door, *the telephone rang.*

There is not space to give further examples here, but in fact such nearly identical passages (with identical errors, e.g. *teller's cages* instead of *tellers' cages*) abound in the two witness statements (see Butters 2006).

The role of the forensic linguist in testifying about witness statements of such highly similar construction and wording must of course be limited to the sociolinguistic facts. While it seems wildly improbable that two such documents could have been prepared totally independently of each other, only the judge and/or jury can legally conclude just how improbable such a possibility is – and, more important, just how much the putative third voice of the recording police officer undermines the reliability of the document. However, the linguist who is an expert on linguistic variation speaks from within his or her expertise in pointing out for the court the similar passages and commenting on the stylistic valences of some of the choices (e.g. *at my post* is an oddly formal construction for a bank employee to use, though it is perhaps not so odd a phrase for a police officer).

There was less for the sociolinguist to say about Rideau's confession in that there was no second document to compare it to. However, a large number of features of that document indicated the selection of sociolinguistic variables that were unlikely to have been in the command of a youth of Rideau's race and cultural background in the early 1960s. One conspicuous feature is that the confession frequently refers to the female crime victims by their first names, *Julia* and *Dora*, and to Mr. Hickman merely as *Hickman*, without honorifics; this way of speaking would have been taboo for a young Black man in Louisiana in the early 1960s. Also, the confession uses the term *soft drink*, a somewhat unlikely way of referencing "coke" or "soda" for someone of Rideau's background. And, in general, the diction and syntax were not what one would have expected from the youth, as the following examples will suggest (italics added):

> I bought the blue suitcase, *for which* I paid $12.02.
> I told him to call the tellers and *instruct* them to lock the front door.
> I had told Hickman I wanted money, and he *so informed* the tellers.
> *While* Mr. Hickman was *placing* the money in the suitcase, the *tele*phone rang.
> He talked *briefly*, and hung up.
> I had planned to enter the vault and *obtain* the money there.
> We drove on *perhaps* a half mile to a bridge across a *bayou or creek*, when I *ordered* Julia to turn around and we *re-crossed* the bridge and just south of the bridge, where I told her to stop the car, and I *ordered* them all to get out.
> I believed they were all dead, and I intended that they *be* dead.

In later years, Rideau went on to distinguish himself, after considerable self-education, as a writer in a prison newspaper that gained some fame as the years went by. Even so, the somewhat formal style of the confession would have been highly unlikely in the confession of an uneducated young Black man of his generation in the American South. This is a generalization well within the expertise of a sociolinguist with specialization in American English – but somewhat outside the parameters of salience for the ordinary juror or jurist, who might well sense the incongruities of the confession's style, but would not have the technical knowledge to evaluate the relevance and nature of those intuitions.

Trademarks

Trademarks are words and images of which individuals and corporations have limited ownership for purposes in commerce of uniquely identifying products and services offered for sale to the public. Trademarks are of immense use to consumers, who are accustomed to relying on familiar and established brand names as a means of assuring the quality and nature of their purchases. And trademarks are likewise extremely valuable to their owners, who may have invested billions in advertising dollars and product design and quality control in order to insure that the public identifies their brands with a particular level of cost, quality, good faith, and sometimes such intangibles as prestige and glamor.

Because trademarks are so valuable, and given that the law puts strong constraints of various kinds upon the right to own them, trademark owners are in a constant state of vigilance to protect their ownership and prevent competitors from encroaching on their marks in ways that could damage their good name, offer others a free ride, or even lead to the loss of the owners' rights entirely. In trademark litigation, attorneys have long called upon linguists to advise them on key issues.

One source of litigation comes about if two trademarks seem to be so similar that customers are likely to confuse them, as was the case in a recent court action in which the pharmaceutical firm *Aventis* sought to prevent a start-up competitor from using the proposed trademark *Advancis*. The non-linguist will perceive that *Aventis* and *Advancis* have significant similarities and differences without understanding the source and strength of the potential for confusion. I presented linguistic analysis to the court on behalf of Aventis in which I compared the sight, sound, and meaning of the two marks, noting, for example: (1) the high degree of acoustical similarity between the /t/ of *Aventis* and the /s/ of *Advancis* and between the stressed vowels of the two terms; (2) the normal reduction in speech of the initial vowels in both marks to schwa; and (3) in allegro pronunciation of *Advancis*, the potential weakening of the /d/ and possible introduction of a [t] after the /n/. The judge incorporated much of my analysis into her ruling in favor of Aventis (Robinson 2006).

A second source of lawsuits is the claim that a proposed or established trademark is so indistinct from the general product that it names that the use of the questionable mark will be unfair to the competitors, who have a legitimate right to use terms that are necessary in describing their products – especially terms that generically indicate the product itself (e.g. *toothpaste*, *aspirin*). I have consulted with attorneys as to these issues of "descriptiveness" and "genericness" with respect to a number of such terms and phrases, for example *Beanie Baby*, *Whisper Quiet*, *Life's Good*, and *Steakburger*. Shuy also discusses several such examples, most notably the *Mc-* morpheme of *McDonald's* of hamburger fame (2002:95–109), which Shuy found to be generic, though the court disagreed with him in a famous case in which Quality Inns was enjoined from using the term *McSleep* as a trademark for a chain of motels on the grounds that McDonald's rights to *Mc-* would be diluted (see also Lentine and Shuy 1990).

A third source of linguistic disagreement about trademarks lies in the requirement in federal law that bans derogatory, scandalous, or obscene words from serving as trademarks. For example, the Washington Redskins football team has been the subject of zealous legal maneuvers (still unsuccessful after a number of years of litigation) seeking to cancel the *Redskins* trademark on the grounds that some of the litigants found it offensive. In another case, the United States Patent and Trademark Office was the scene of sustained action on the part of the attorneys for a San Francisco women's motorcycle group, Dykes on Bikes; the USPTO at first denied registration of *Dykes on Bikes* on the grounds that *dykes* was thought to be a derogatory term, though in the end this decision was reversed in the face of arguments in the form of affidavits from numerous scholars including lexicographers and other linguists. In both of these cases, I served as a linguistic expert (engaged by attorneys for the Redskins and for Dykes on Bikes), reporting on linguistic evidence relevant to the claims that the terms were unregistrable.

Trademark litigation is one of the most frequent types of legal action in which the expertise of sociolinguists is most welcome – because sociolinguistics depends upon the establishment of linguistic facts that can be studied empirically. Although lexical questions are often upstaged by phonology, morphology, and discourse analysis among sociolinguists, the whole science of dictionary making – lexicography – is grounded in the collection and inductive analysis of the social use of words in the written language of normal speakers of the language. Whether or not a term is merely descriptive – or has become generic – is a matter grounded in the linguistic knowledge and behavior or real people. The linguistic cues by which consumers recognize phonological, morphological, semantic, and even semiotic differences between two trademarks are central to the whole linguistic enterprise. And who better than sociolinguists/lexicographers can explicate the social responses to terms in the realms of obscenity and offensiveness?

Conclusion

When sociolinguists think of forensic linguistics, what may come first to mind is one of the most famous instances of the application of variationist studies to legal questions, one which occurred before the United States District Court, Eastern District of Michigan, Southern Division, in 1979: *Martin Luther King Junior Elementary School Children, et al. v. Ann Arbor School District Board.* The plaintiffs hoped to compel the School Board to take corrective measures to "overcome the barrier . . . to equal participation in the instructional programs" of the Ann Arbor schools imposed by the failure to take into account the disparity between the home language of many of the students, African American Vernacular English, and the more mainstream varieties of American English used as the medium of instruction (Joiner 1979:1). A number of prominent sociolinguists[11] offered their expertise to the court concerning the nature of African American English and the difficulties that this "barrier" presented. Greatly influenced by the linguists' testimony, the judge ordered the School Board to take corrective measures, and within a few months the Ann Arbor School Board offered its "Educational Plan" in response to the judge's orders (1980). A number of linguists have written about what has long been considered a major victory (Labov [1982], the articles in Whiteman [1980] and Smitherman [1981], as well as the more recent evaluations of Ball and Lardner [1997] and Reaser [2004]).

But the *King* decision is but one of many applications of variationist studies to the legal enterprise. As the work cited in this chapter testifies, sociolinguistics and legal studies have both an interesting past and a wide-ranging and promising future.

---

[11] In his published decision (Joiner 1979:4), the presiding judge lists the testifying linguists as Geneva Smitherman, Daniel Fader, Jerrie Scott, William Labov, J. L. Dillard, Gary Simkins, Richard Bailey, Ronald Edmunds, and Kenneth Haskins.

17 Attitudes toward variation and ear-witness testimony[1]

JOHN BAUGH

Introduction

Can the telephone be used as an instrument of racial discrimination? Can a land-lord, or someone selling property, detect a speaker's racial background from the sound of his or her voice over the phone, and then deny that person the opportunity to rent or purchase the property in question? Our experimental results and other anecdotal evidence suggest that the answer is "Yes." Moreover, the courts are ill-equipped to offer adequate legal redress to anyone who falls prey to linguistic profiling at the hands of housing providers or, for that matter, lending institutions and insurance companies.

This paper explores the concepts of linguistic profiling and "ear-witness tes-timony" in cases that call for voice identification, and does so being mindful of research traditions that study language attitudes. Of greatest interest to readers of this volume, linguistic profiling has been shown to have a detrimental impact on our collective quest to advance equal access to fair housing and fair lending. We begin with a review of previous awareness of this problem, including the important role of quantitative and experimental studies of language attitudes, and conclude with some of the legal challenges to discrimination based on language usage, as well as implications for future research.

My research on this topic grew out of personal experience. As a young scholar, I had an opportunity to spend a sabbatical at the Center for Advanced Study in the Behavioral Sciences in Palo Alto, California. Upon moving to Palo Alto, I found that the apartment I had rented didn't fully meet our needs. We had a young family, with one daughter in elementary school, a toddler in diapers, and my wife was expecting our third child.

I began to call around in search of a larger apartment or home, and I had no difficulty whatsoever making appointments. I was shown various homes or

[1] Support for this research has been generously provided by the Ford Foundation and the United States Department of Housing and Urban Development. The research described herein could not have been completed without the timely assistance and hard work completed by H. Samy Alim, Ashlyn Amaral, Charla Larrimore Baugh, Tonkid Chantrasmi, Cerena Sweetland-Gil, and Aaron Welborn, and tremendous legal assistance has been provided by Dawn Smalls. Several members of our national advisory committee are worthy of more formal attribution. I would also like to thank Chris Brancart, Edward Pinder, and Fred Freiberg for helpful suggestions regarding my legal and personal interpretations of ear-witness testimony and linguistic profiling.

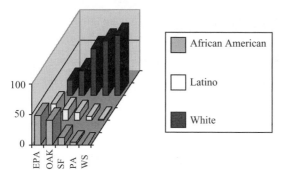

Figure 17.1 *Population distribution for Bay Area communities for three groups: African Americans, Latinos, and Whites*

apartments without incident or fanfare, but in a few instances prospective landlords reacted with visible surprise at my appearance. I suspected that they could not detect that I was African American from the sound of my voice, and once they saw me in person they began to make various excuses for why the dwelling in question was not available. Although I suspected that my race had something to do with these rare declinations, I had no proof.

I spoke with friends about the incidents, and many suggested that I pursue litigation, but I was consumed by other projects and did not want to invest the time and resources that would be necessary to seek relief in the courts. However, I was determined to do something about it. Because of my linguistic heritage, as a child who grew up in inner-city communities in Philadelphia and Los Angeles, I possess the ability to speak different American dialects – namely, African American vernacular English, Chicano (Mexican American) vernacular English, and Standard (mainstream) American English. As a result of this personal linguistic dexterity, I began to conduct controlled experiments of housing discrimination. The results of those experiments are spelled out in thorough detail in Purnell, Idsardi, and Baugh (1999). In short, prospective landlords responded quite differently to my requests for appointments. I would consistently use the phrase, "Hello, I'm calling about the apartment/house you have advertised in the paper."

By holding the phrase constant, linguistic control of the verbal stimuli was constrained to matters of intonation and prosody. I intentionally avoided using different words or grammatical structures for these experiments, which might otherwise introduce incomparable linguistic variables. My earliest studies of housing discrimination were conducted in the San Francisco Bay Area in 1988. The residential composition of five communities is illustrated in Figure 17.1.

East Palo Alto (EPA), Oakland (OAK), San Francisco (SF), Palo Alto (PA), and Woodside (WS) are the communities where I solicited rentals using three different dialects. Figure 17.2 shows the number of confirmed appointments that I received in these neighborhoods. East Palo Alto and Oakland have relatively fewer White residents and are less affluent per capita than San Francisco, Palo Alto, and Woodside.

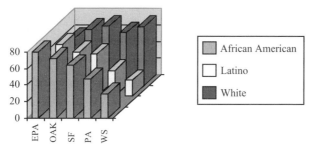

Figure 17.2 *Percentage of rental or purchase appointments that were granted for five Bay Area communities based on three controlled speech renditions: African American, Latino, and White*

The number of appointments that I was granted dropped precipitously in the affluent communities whenever I employed non-standard speech. Although it is impossible to pin down causal inferences from these data regarding the basis for this higher rate of rejection, I took extraordinary care to employ Standard English as the final call. In other words, although my initial calls always used African American English or Chicano English (which were randomly selected), positive replies to requests in Standard English frequently followed prior rejections of the ethnic non-standard dialects.

Linguistic profiling: operational definitions

It is expedient to think of *linguistic profiling* as the auditory equivalent of racial profiling. However, there are noteworthy differences between the two concepts. Racial profiling first came into common currency as a term when evidence of racial bias against Black and Brown motorists in New Jersey captured headlines. Exceedingly high arrest rates for African American and Latino motorists were confirmed in various states, and the phrase "racial profiling" became part of the national nomenclature. Pundits soon coined another racially evocative phrase to describe these motorists' imaginary crime: "Driving while Black" or "Driving while Brown" (DWB).

It is essential to recognize that racial profiling first resulted from the visual identification of non-White drivers, and increased harassment of Black and Brown drivers that grew substantially from America's "War on Drugs." As of this writing, racial profiling remains politically controversial, and some police departments have resisted calls to document the race of motorists who are stopped for traffic violations, lest they leave a trail of empirical evidence either confirming or refuting the practice of racial profiling.

By striking contrast, linguistic profiling is not visual and tends not to be initiated by a person in authority. Rather, linguistic profiling typically results from a discriminatory reaction to a phone call. Frequently these discriminatory responses are racially motivated, but unlike incidents of racial profiling they are not exclusively based on race. For example, we have discovered cases of linguistic profiling where the prejudicial behavior is associated with region.[2] As a reactive form of discrimination, linguistic profiling occurs when a caller seeking goods or services is told that the goods or services in question are not available when, in fact, they are, but the caller is denied access to them based on linguistic stereotypes harbored by the person on the other end.

One of the most publicly visible accusations of linguistic profiling occurred during the 1995 O. J. Simpson murder trial. A witness who had not seen Mr. Simpson in person claimed that he overheard the voice of a Black man yelling, "Hey! Hey! Hey!" at the murder scene. This elicited a forceful response from Mr. Simpson's lead attorney, Johnnie Cochran: "You can't tell by listening to someone if they are Black or White or whatever. I don't think you can tell if they're young. You can tell if it's a child or not, but I resent that entire area. I think it's entirely inappropriate . . . This statement about whether somebody sounds Black or White is racist, and I resent it!" Although Cochran was attempting to free his client, many people agreed with his observation that it is "racist" to draw any racial inference from the sound of someone's voice, particularly if you have not actually seen the person.

In a way, Mr. Cochran was both right and wrong. In many instances, it is difficult to deduce a person's race from their speech, but doing so does not necessarily constitute a racist act – that is, unless the person who hears the voice acts upon their racial deduction in a discriminatory manner. Unlike overt face-to-face discrimination, linguistic profiling is inherently covert because those who knowingly practice it can deny and therefore conceal their bigoted actions.

Although the preceding examples focus on race, we should stress that linguistic profiling is not restricted to race. Speculation about a person's sex, age, or socioeconomic status based upon hearing their voice need not be sexist, ageist, or classist. Such speculation only qualifies as linguistic profiling if it is acted upon in a way that intends to deny goods or services based on assumptions about sex, age, socioeconomic status, etc.

When viewed within the broader context of potential discrimination against women, speakers from a particular region of the country, or speakers of a given sexual orientation, we find that linguistic profiling always includes a three-step process:

(1) a person initiates a telephone call soliciting goods or services;
(2) the recipient of the call draws demographic inference(s) from the caller's voice, sight unseen;
(3) the recipient of the call then denies access to the requested goods or services based on deductions about the caller's voice, in an intentionally deceptive act of (race, sex, age, etc.) discrimination.

[2] Someone who grew up in the South may initiate a call for goods or services over the telephone, and the recipient of the call – who may share the same racial background – may choose to deny otherwise available goods or services based on regional bigotry that exceeds considerations of race.

Although linguistic profiling can be found in various kinds of telephone service encounters, such as ordering a pizza or calling for emergency assistance, it first came to our attention in response to housing discrimination, and the most advanced work on the subject pertains to efforts to eliminate illegal discrimination in housing, lending, and purchasing insurance.

Previous research: linguistic profiling foci

Four publications in particular are worth noting because of their immediate relevance to this discussion:

(1) "Perceptual and phonetic experiments on American English dialect identification," by Purnell et al. (1999);
(2) "Racial identification by speech," by Baugh (2000);
(3) "Use of Black English and racial discrimination in urban housing markets: new methods and findings," by Massey and Lundy (2001);
(4) "Linguistic profiling and the law," by Smalls (2004).

Numerous other studies are relevant to the theoretical and empirical foundations of interdisciplinary studies of linguistic profiling (see Alim 2005, Bobo 2001, Grier 2001, Preston 2000a, Squires 2006, Steele 1992, Wiehl 2002). However, for the sake of illustration and expedience, we will concentrate narrowly on studies that have specifically considered racially targeted housing discrimination based on voice recognition.

Purnell *et al.* (1999) detail four experiments showing that housing discrimination based solely on telephone conversation does occur, dialect identification is possible using just the word *hello,* and phonetic correlates of dialect can be discovered. In one experiment, a series of telephone surveys was conducted requesting housing from the same landlord over a short time period using both standard and non-standard dialects. The results demonstrate that landlords discriminate against prospective tenants based on the sound of their voice during telephone conversations. Another experiment was conducted with untrained subjects to confirm this finding; the untrained listeners identified the dialects significantly better than chance. Corresponding phonetic analyses reveal that phonetic variables potentially distinguish the dialects, yielding discriminatory consequences.

Baugh (2000) begins to explore the legal foundations of linguistic profiling based on a court ruling in which "an overheard voice was that of a particular nationality or race" (*Clifford v. Kentucky*, 1999). This and other cases affirm that lay witnesses routinely "identify a voice as being that of a particular race or nationality, so long as the witness is personally familiar with the general characteristics, accents, or speech patterns of the race or nationality in question, that is, so long as the opinion is 'rationally' based on the perception of the witness" (*Clifford v. Kentucky*, 1999). Baugh (2000) also observes that "many defendants in housing discrimination or insurance redlining cases deny that they can make any determination of the race or ethnicity of prospective home buyers or tenants based on speech during telephone conversations" (2000:363). In this regard, such defendants are woefully out-of-step with the majority of subjects we have evaluated.

Massy and Lundy (2001) proved that "racial discrimination in housing markets need not involve personal contact between agents and renters" (2001:452). They also found that racial discrimination in housing was further "exacerbated by class and gender. Poor Black women, in particular experienced the greatest discrimination" (2001:452). Massey and Lundy systematically document the existence of phone-based racial discrimination in a large eastern metropolitan area.

Smalls (2004) has conducted a comprehensive review of criminal and civil cases where African American voice identification has been central. She also examines basic tenets regarding rules of evidence and the necessary qualifications of lay and expert witnesses to pose new questions about ear-witness testimony (see Conclusion, below). Smalls' evaluation of linguistic profiling and the law covers a combination of civil and criminal trials, with emphasis on employment discrimination, housing discrimination, and criminal law. She observes that the courts have been somewhat capricious in their acceptance or rejection of speech identification testimony, calling particular attention to the admissibility of such evidence based on Rule 701 of the Federal Rules of Evidence, which makes distinctions between "lay" and "expert" witnesses. Briefly, Smalls concludes that witnesses who are familiar with the languages and dialects that are critical to a case involving voice identification must have considerable knowledge and exposure to those dialects to increase the veracity of their claims. Our own findings concur with her observation. For example, we find that someone who was raised in the South is more likely to identify accurately the race and region of other Southerners than someone who has never lived in the South.

Critical limitations of previous lingusitic profiling research

Purnell *et al.* (1991) maintain strict linguistic and experimental control, albeit devoted to one tridialectal subject. However, due to their small sample, their results cannot be generalized. Massey and Lundy (2001) offer the first solution to that limitation by using a larger sample and introducing three linguistic classifications, including "native speakers of Black English Vernacular (BEV), Black Accented English (BAE), and White Middle-Class English (WME)" (2001:456).

The Black English Vernacular dialect is typically associated with highly non-standard usage and is more representative of speech among less well educated African Americans. Black Accented English maintains African American phonology and other pronunciations that are associated with Black speech patterns, but the grammar is closer to that of Standard American English. White Middle-Class English is similar to "broadcast speech," and not necessarily associated with White speech from any particular region.

Massey and Lundy (2001) emphatically demonstrate that the race of the caller significantly influences access to housing. Judge Cooper's ruling (see *Clifford v. Kentucky*, 1999) sets the legal standard, which demands that we fully define people who are "familiar" with "the general characteristics, accents, or speech patterns of

Table 17.1 *General confusion matrices*

| | STIMULI | | | | | | | | |
Response	AAVE	ChE	SAE	"Chance"			"Perfect"		
AAVE	a	b	c	11	11	11	33	0	0
ChE	d	e	f	11	11	11	0	33	0
SAE	g	h	i	11	11	11	0	0	33

NOTE: AAVE = African American Vernacular English; ChE = Chicano English; SAE = Standard American English.

the race or nationality in question." Auditory line-ups could provide an empirical foundation toward the definition Judge Cooper seeks. Prior studies, including our own, have exposed the need to determine the validity of claims by witnesses that they can accurately identify the voices of different groups of speakers, to say nothing of specific individuals.

The present discussion strives to overcome these and other barriers by affirming the extent to which Americans from various walks of life evaluate their fellow Americans on the basis of speech. Our results in turn may have the potential to provide fair housing advocates, and their attorneys, with statistically robust findings that can directly challenge defendants, witnesses, real estate agents, lenders, or others who may use linguistic profiling as a surrogate for racial profiling during telephone conversations.

Upon reflection, we have come to appreciate some flaws in our early formulation of these analyses. For example, we did not closely monitor any call that was not answered by a person; missed calls or calls retrieved by answering machines were overlooked in Purnell *et al.* (1999). However, that shortcoming was rectified in the work of Massey and Lundy (2001).

Another limitation derived from our earliest investigations resulted from restricted linguistic stimuli. At the outset of our experiments, we sought to answer basic questions about accent or dialect perception. The most unexpected linguistic result, which bears directly upon linguistic profiling in housing and lending markets, confirms that many native and non-native speakers of English can accurately detect the racial background of a speaker based on hearing the single word *hello*. This is illustrated in Tables 17.1 and 17.2.

Table 17.1 illustrates two opposing interpretations of general confusion matrices representing hypothetical extremes between dialect evaluations: pure chance, on the one hand, and perfect evaluations, on the other. Listeners are presented with linguistic stimuli from one of three dialects: AAVE, ChE, or SAE. Upon hearing the AAVE dialect, if responses are purely random, the distribution of results is shared equally among all three groups. By contrast, when results are perfect, every listener who hears AAVE, ChE, or SAE accurately identifies each dialect.

Table 17.2 *Confusion matrix and summary statistic by dialect*

| | STIMULI | | | |
Response	AAVE	ChE	SAE	Row Total
AAVE	a 923 (15%)	b 280 (05%)	c 196 (03%)	1,399 (23%)
ChE	d 235 (04%)	e 1,607 (27%)	f 41 (01%)	1,883 (31%)
SAE	g 842 (14%)	h 113 (02%)	i 1,736 (29%)	2,718 (45%)

NOTE: AAVE = African American Vernacular English; ChE = Chicano English; SAE = Standard American English.
$p < .001$; Accuracy Index (AI) $= .72$; percentages = percentage of total for that cell.

Table 17.2 presents experimental results where listeners attempted to identify AAVE, ChE, or SAE based only upon hearing the word *hello*. The evidence strongly suggests that the average listener, being a native speaker of American English, can accurately identify diverse dialects of vernacular speech based on hearing another speaker of American English say *hello*. We chose *hello* in particular because it is the most common greeting used when answering the telephone in the US.

This ability to detect different dialects of American English from very short segments of speech provides the foundation upon which linguistic profiling is based. However, as previously indicated, simply identifying a particular dialect as AAVE, ChE, or some other American English dialect does not constitute a discriminatory act unless someone who purveys goods or services chooses to act on that dialect judgment in a discriminatory way.

Foundational studies of linguistic attitudes

Experimental studies of linguistic attitudes and ethnolinguistic evaluations of linguistic preference have greatly informed our work on linguistic profiling. The seminal studies by Fishman (1968, 1972a, 1972b, 1991) that gave birth to "The Sociology of Language" are particularly inspiring for their corresponding efforts to value heritage languages throughout the world while simultaneously confronting the linguistic foundations of social strife. Likewise, Lambert's (1972) classical matched guise tests toward bilingual attitudes greatly influenced our own experimental methods.

Before returning to the legal implications of our voice discrimination experiments, it is essential that readers of this volume understand more fully the sociolinguistic bases upon which the entire linguistic profiling enterprise rests. As indicated, Lambert's (1972) matched guise tests in Canada not only broke new ground in research on language attitudes in bilingual communities, but also had a tremendous impact on the field of social psychology. The elegance of Lambert's experiment lies in the fact that the judges who evaluated "French" vs. "English" did not know they were hearing the same person speak two different languages.

Lambert's experimental elegance stands as an answer to early calls by leading sociolinguists for comprehensive linguistic analyses – that is to say, socially grounded studies of language in use (Baugh and Sherzer 1984). Hymes' (1974) formulation of "Communicative Competence" within his framework for "The Ethnography of Communication" lends essential cultural texture to Lambert's experimental abstractions. As Hymes has noted on several occasions, any child who utilizes language based purely on his or her "linguistic competence" will surely be a social misfit. It is our communicative competence that informs our day-to-day linguistic behavior and usage, to say little of the opinions that we form of others – opinions which frequently include value judgments about the way other people speak.

Readers of this volume likely want to incorporate specific methods into research and analyses, and therein lies the potential for combining established research procedures with new technologies that will allow us to explore linguistic attitudes and their consequences with greater precision. In much the same manner that quantitative analyses of linguistic variation are carefully tailored to meet the disparate speech communities they study, so too must analyses of linguistic preference and prejudice be accurately contextualized. That is to say, linguistic preferences are relative by nature, and Goffman (1972) reminds us all to situate our research, be it observational or experimental.

In thankful tribute to my mentors, I also want to acknowledge that our current efforts to dissect ear-witness testimony grow substantially from the quantitative foundations of sociolinguistics embodied in the classical AAVE studies pertaining to "The logic of non-standard English" (Labov 1969b) and "Contraction, deletion, and inherent variablity of the English copula" (Labov 1969a) – the research that gave birth to variable rules. Hymes (1974) taught me about important qualitative dimensions of ethnography that quantitative analyses may not detect, and he did so with recognition that quantitative and qualitative analyses could live in harmony, if not be incorporated into a single research paradigm (Baugh 1983).

I know that many linguists (and other scholars) are consumed by theory in its own right, or the evaluation of cognitive linguistic details divorced from any social or cultural consideration. However, the collective studies of language attitudes as they occur in experimental, ethnographic, and/or situated contexts gives rise to potentially powerful social policy diagnostics and other policy instruments that far exceed the legal considerations to which we now turn.

Implications for legal testing of voice discrimination in pursuit of fair housing and fair lending

Purnell *et al.* (1999) and Massey and Lundy (2001) suggest that prospective landlords tend to prefer tenants who are proficient speakers of Standard American

English. These authors were careful to control their experiments based on the race and/or dialect background of each speaker. However, their findings do not imply that negative reactions to Black or Latino speech in housing markets is based on race or speech alone.

Linguistic stereotypes about minority speech patterns evoke a plethora of reactions beyond racial speculation. Massey and Lundy's (2001) study implies that perceptual differences about education and economic status may exceed race, thereby complicating any claim that prospective sellers or landlords dismiss telephone inquiries from minorities based exclusively on race. Such an interpretation excludes the prospect that prospective sellers or landlords may be deducing a caller's sex, education, or socioeconomic status from the sound of their voice. For this and other reasons, it is important for fair housing advocates to support telephone testing with other evidence of discrimination whenever possible.

Most successful legal cases involving voice discrimination have not relied exclusively on telephone testing. Rather, telephone testing was often among the first tests conducted to determine if the prospective landlord or seller had engaged in a systematic pattern of discrimination against an identifiable group. For example, some landlords and sellers routinely use answering machines for the purpose of screening incoming calls. Those who never receive a return call may be unaware of the fact that their voice has triggered linguistic profiling (see Massey and Lundy 2001). Under these circumstances, and many others, additional testing is essential for the purpose of bolstering, and eventually proving, claims of discrimination.

In those instances where testing has exposed unequivocal patterns of discrimination against particular groups seeking housing, landlords usually deny any discriminatory intent, appealing to Johnnie Cochran's logic that one cannot determine a person's race from their speech and that to do so would be racist. When additional testing evidence is available, the veracity of such claims is often weakened in the face of other attempts to exclude the group in question. Attorneys and housing advocates who seek to advance fair housing would do well to consider gathering as much evidence as possible prior to filing charges against a prospective seller or landlord.

Be that as it may, the telephone is typically the first point of human contact when someone is seeking housing, and the inability of the courts to effectively eliminate illegal linguistic profiling as a barrier to housing, lending, insurance, or employment is unfortunate at best, and a glaring injustice at worst.

Conclusion: ear-witness testimony and "auditory line-ups"

Linguistic profiling in its most basic form constitutes "ear-witness testimony," and the legal challenges that face lay witnesses and the judges and attorneys who question them will continue to daunt plaintiffs and defendants from diverse cultural and linguistic backgrounds. Smalls' (2004) analyses confirm that the reliability of witnesses to accurately identify the linguistic background of an individual varies tremendously from person to person, depending upon their own linguistic experience compared to that of the speaker they would presume to identify.

Anyone who has ever heard the voice of a stranger over the phone knows that we speculate about various characteristics (e.g. sex, age, race, education, etc.) of callers we don't recognize. In cases where voice recognition is called for, it would be beneficial to all parties to test the linguistic reliability and veracity of individual witnesses through the use of auditory line-ups.

In much the same manner that eye-witness testimony commonly employs the use of visual line-ups to test the veracity of eye-witnesses, so too should judges and attorneys utilize "auditory line-ups" to test the veracity of "ear-witness testimony." Ironically, and perhaps unfortunately, procedures for conducting visual line-ups are not codified in law. Those who use line-ups to enhance the veracity of eye-witnesses must do so in a way that does not leave them open to accusations of bias. How, then, should we conduct auditory line-ups in ways that are likewise unbiased? Surely, if a suspect's speech is associated with a particular dialect, the auditory line-up should consist of other speakers who share many comparable linguistic characteristics.

Our ongoing research hopes to identify procedures for conducting linguistically unbiased auditory line-ups for every linguistic group in America that can withstand legal scrutiny. At this stage, attorneys and judges would be well advised to draw their own analogy between tests for scrutinizing "eye-witness testimony" and potential tests for "ear-witness testimony."

These needs are nowhere more evident than in the current American housing market, where new immigrants and poorer Americans who lack proficiency in Standard American English seek to procure better housing for themselves and their families. While it is true that many ethnic Americans feel a strong cultural affinity to the communities in which they were raised, others seek to live among more affluent Americans in communities where Standard English predominates. It is our contention that unbiased auditory line-ups in legal cases involving voice identification may promote greater access to fair housing and fair lending for every American citizen who shares in our collective dream of a truly egalitarian nation.

Afterword: Walt Wolfram and the study of sociolinguistic variation

ROGER W. SHUY

I would imagine that the reason I was asked to write the epilogue to this book honoring Walt Wolfram is that I've known him longer, and in many ways better, than most others. Walt is indeed loved by his students and colleagues for his perpetually friendly ways, his unwillingness to surrender evidences of his working-class roots, his overpowering sense of fairness, his long-term efforts to bring about justice, his perpetual sense of humor, and, of course, for his brilliance in linguistics. Although this epilogue focuses on the development of his linguistic accomplishments, it also intends to try to show some endearing personal things about Walt that many may not know. If I am too personal, I beg his forgiveness in advance, but this is the Walt I know.

Our early relationship, soon to become a close friendship, began when he was an undergraduate student at Wheaton College from 1959 to 1963. Walt chose Wheaton over dozens of college offers and scholarships that came to him because of his outstanding athletic career at Philadelphia's Olney High School, where he starred in baseball, basketball, and football and received state-wide recognition and honor for his abilities. At Wheaton he continued with all three sports but he finally focused his athletic attention on football and baseball. Having watched him play basketball at Wheaton during his freshman year, it is not hard to understand why he narrowed down his options. It may be somewhat comforting to the rest of us to know that Walt wasn't always superior in everything.

Some may not know that Walt grew up in a conservative Christian faith, which became so strong for him that he planned to become a missionary. The Wycliffe Bible Translators gave him a summer of intensive linguistic training at their camp in Ecuador after his second year at Wheaton, strengthening his resolve to work with them eventually in Central or South America. As a handsome, affable, athletic undergraduate, Walt could have had his pick of potential Wheaton College girl friends. In fact, I once asked him about this. But he was already committed to his high school sweetheart, Marge, who stayed home, training for mission work at the Philadelphia Bible College. And I learned that once Walt commits, he stays committed. Those who have had the privilege of knowing Marge will immediately understand why.

Since Walt had studied core linguistics (phonetics, phonemics, morphology, syntax) with Wycliffe (which also goes under the name of the Summer Institute of Linguistics), I never got a chance to have Walt as a student in my linguistics courses at Wheaton. However, he was assigned to me as my student assistant, at which time I suspect he learned a few things about American dialects and the history of English, since these were among the other courses I taught, taken mostly by English majors. He helped me organize my classes, grade papers, and once in a while even teach some segment of phonetics and morphology in my core linguistics courses.

Perhaps because I was only a few years older than Walt, he quickly became a family friend. In fact, he was our major baby-sitter for our two small boys. And he was a good one too. Etched in memory are the times he dressed up as a clown for my sons' birthday parties. After football games he would often come to my house and talk to my young sons about the game. They were thrilled with Uncle Walt's description of what happened. They loved him and even though they are now grown men with their own families, they often ask me about Walt. But then it's easy to love Walt Wolfram.

I am also probably one of the very few people in our field who ever knew Walt's parents. My family and I stopped at the Philadelphia home of his parents one time on our way to the New Jersey shore for vacation. I will never forget his rather stern German father, who exemplified the working-class background that Walt proudly never forsook. After a great dinner at his parents' home, I asked Walt for directions to the ocean and learned, for the first time, that his sense of mapping and routing was every bit as bad as my own. I got totally lost more than once. Walt can map the direction of virtually anything linguistic but roadmaps must be an exception to his otherwise great talents.

Even before Walt graduated from Wheaton, he realized that he needed advanced training in linguistics in order to be most useful to Wycliffe. So he enrolled at the Hartford Seminary Foundation, where two of the leading linguists of the day were on the faculty – H.A. Gleason and William Samarin. Since this institution offered doctoral degrees in both religion and linguistics, it seemed ideal for him at the time. One must remember that linguistic study in the sixties was not nearly as widespread as it is today. Virtually all courses at that time were in the mode of structural linguistics and few did this better than programs such as those at Michigan (led by Kenneth Pike), at Hartford, and, by today's standards, at a relatively small number of universities.

I kept in contact with Walt while he studied at Hartford, and when he finished his doctoral coursework, we discussed his possible dissertation topic. As it turns out, he was then in a quandary about whether he really wanted to become a missionary linguist. By 1964, I had left Wheaton for Michigan State University, where I managed to get a research grant from the US Office of Education to conduct a survey of Detroit speech. I had moved from my own specialization in traditional dialectology into the exciting but very new field called sociolinguistics. During the summer of 1966, the Detroit study was to interview and analyze the speech of a stratified random sample of 700 Detroiters of all ages, race, and socioeconomic status. I needed fieldworkers, so I offered one of the positions to Walt and, as it turns out, this was one of the best decisions I ever made. His missionary training was perfect for this work and he was the best fieldworker of the twelve I hired. He lived with my family during that summer, baby-sitting along the way and giving him a chance to renew his clowning skills for my sons.

After we had collected all the data, the next step was to analyze it and write up our report. Again I turned to Walt, since he needed a dissertation topic and here was one right in his lap if he wanted it. He waffled for a while, then decided to take the offer. We spent a happy but vigorous summer in 1967, writing the report for the USOE. Etched in my memory is the sound of Walt singing popular rock songs in an odd falsetto voice while we marched around a conference table, collating the mimeographed pages of our hundred page report on Detroit speech. He lived with my family again during that summer, in exchange for mowing my lawn. In fact, he was part of my family then and, in a perhaps more limited way, still today.

Walt then went back to Hartford for a short while, writing up his dissertation proposal on Detroit speech, but returning regularly to check on the data. By that time I had decided to move from Michigan to Washington, DC, where I became head of the newly formed sociolinguistic research program at the Center for Applied Linguistics (CAL). Taking advantage of his muscular build and cooperative nature, I got him to help drive my U-Haul truckload of furniture and books from Michigan to DC. Again I got to hear many hours of his odd falsetto singing, but we also had a memorable time talking all during the trip, largely about his dissertation plans.

The first thing I needed to do at CAL was to hire new staff for our already funded Ford Foundation projects. I again invited Walt and again he waffled for a while, since that step must have seemed like moving even further away from his goal of becoming a missionary. I felt a bit guilty about this (well, not too guilty) but the idea of his getting paid to do a deeper analysis of the Detroit data that could serve as his dissertation was a very attractive offer. After a period of agonizing, he accepted my offer and joined Ralph Fasold (also a former Wheaton student, then finishing his dissertation at the University of Chicago) and me in Washington.

The three of us made a great team. We worked together, talked together, and even ate our bag lunches together, sitting on benches in Dupont Circle and admiring the young ladies as they walked by. Since our research focused on Black English, we did what linguists usually do when they are learning a new language. We often made our best efforts to speak Vernacular Black English to each other in the office. Little did we know, at least not until later, that our Black secretary was offended by hearing us talk that way. When Addie finally confronted us, we were crestfallen, since we had no idea that she would think we were mocking her. We all learned an important lesson about language attitudes and beliefs from this experience – one that we never forgot.

Walt, Ralph, and I sometimes traveled together to do workshops in various parts of the country, trying to repair the damage done to Black children whose vernacular speech was then considered by many educators as evidence of their severe cognitive deficits. In one such workshop in Mississippi we had some free time to kill before our return flight to DC. Since none of us had ever set foot in Arkansas before, we decided to drive our rental car across a bridge over the Mississippi River to see at least a bit of Arkansas and then drive back. Unfortunately, our mapping skills again failed us. We got terribly lost and I'm not sure to this day that we actually ever crossed into Arkansas. But we had a wonderful time and have laughed about it ever since.

After three years at CAL, funding became scarce and it was time for us to move on to other things. I took a position at Georgetown University to set up a new doctoral program in sociolinguistics. Walt, still harboring some of his missionary instincts, thought he might serve those ends better at Federal City College (eventually renamed the University of the District of Columbia). Walt and I both kept on working at CAL part-time as we took on our new positions. I stayed at CAL only for a few years but Walt lasted much, much longer. His work at UDC and CAL didn't end until he was awarded an endowed chair at North Carolina State University.

Getting a chair at a big university is the greatest hoped-for accomplishment of most academics. I can think of no scholars who deserved this honor more than Walt Wolfram. At North Carolina State, almost immediately he became even more productive than he had been in his already very productive past. There he has had good grad students to work with, along with more time for research, less classroom teaching, and all the perks that come with holding an endowed chair. As his reputation continued to grow, he was given still another great honor – being elected president of the largest and most prestigious linguistic organization in the world, the Linguistic Society of America. I have to admit that tears of pride rolled down my cheeks when I sat in the audience and heard him deliver his presidential address.

One of the things that I admire most about Walt is his ability to stick with the specialization that he has so ably developed rather than flitting from one academic topic to another. Once he committed to study the social and regional variation of American English, he steadfastly and systematically attacked it in all its manifestations, including urban English, Vernacular Black English, Puerto Rican English, Southern English, and Native American English. As noted earlier, once Walt commits, he stays committed. Although he's now senior enough to coast a bit, this prospect isn't likely for Walt. His energy and creativity simply do not permit him to slow his pace.

Another sterling quality in Walt is his ability to survive and prosper throughout the great linguistic theory revolution that began during his graduate study and escalated shortly after. Many linguists with the conventional training of our day were left in limbo. Some left linguistics altogether; others fought a rearguard battle against change. But not Walt, who, as might be expected, did the sensible thing. He retooled with the new theories but at the same time wisely hung on to the best of the older ones. To this day he preserves a strong allegiance to real language as it is actually used while calling on modern theoretical developments in his analyses of language variation. The chapters in this book honoring him reflect his leadership in this approach to the field.

I, along with all of the many friends he has made throughout his career, stand in awe of Walt Wolfram, including all those who contributed to this book. And I am proud to say that I have known and benefited from his abundance of talents, endless energy, and personal charm, almost from the very beginning.

References

Abercrombie, D. 1967. *Elements of general phonetics*. Edinburgh: Edinburgh University Press.

Abu-Jamal, M. 1997. The mother tongue: Black English revisited. *Black Scholar* 27(1): 26–27.

Adams, M., Foorman, B., Lundberg, I., and Beeler, T. 1998. *Phonemic awareness in young children*. Baltimore, MD: Paul Brookes.

Adamson, H.D. 1988. *Variation theory and second language acquisition*. Washington, DC: Georgetown University Press.

Adamson, H.D., and Kovac, C. 1981. Variation theory and second language acquisition. In D. Sankoff and H. Cedergren (eds.), *Variation omnibus*. Edmonton: Linguistic Research. 285–293.

Adamson, H.D., and Regan, V. 1991. The acquisition of community speech norms by Asian immigrants learning English as a second language. *Studies in Second Language Acquisition* 13: 1–22.

Adank, P., Smits, R., and van Hout, R. 2004. A comparison of vowel normalization procedures for language variation research. *Journal of the Acoustical Society of America* 116: 3009–3107.

Adger, C.T., and Schilling-Estes, N. 2003. *African American English: Structure and clinical implications*. Rockville, MD: American Speech-Language-Hearing Association.

Adger, C.T., Snow, C., and Christian, D. (eds.). 2002. *What teachers need to know about language*. Washington, DC, and McHenry, IL: Center for Applied Linguistics and Delta Systems.

Adger, C.T., Wolfram, W., and Detwyler, J. 1993. Confronting dialect minority issues in special education: Reactive and proactive perspectives. In *Third National Research Symposium on Limited English Students' Issues*. Washington, DC: Government Printing Office. 737–762.

Adger, D., and Smith, J. 2005. Variation and the minimalist program. In L. Cornips and K. Corrigan (eds.), *Syntax and variation: Reconciling the biological and the social*. Philadelphia: John Benjamins. 149–178.

Agard, J., and Nichols, G. (eds.). 1994. *A Caribbean dozen: A collection of poems*. London: Walker Books.

Ahmad, K. 2005. Checking up and looking in: Self-plagiarism in science and technology. Plenary lecture, Language and the Law 2005: East Meets West, University of Lodz, September.

Ainsworth, J.E. 2006. Linguistics as a knowledge domain in the law. *Drake Law Review* 54: 651–669.

Alim, H.S. 2005. Critical language awareness in the United States: Revisiting issues and revising pedagogies in a resegregated society. *Educational Researcher* 34: 24–31.

Alim, H.S. 2006. *Roc the mic right: The language of hip hop culture*. London: Routledge.

Allsopp, R. 1996. *Dictionary of Caribbean English usage*. Oxford: Oxford University Press.

Alvarez, L., and Kolker, A. (producers). 1987. *American tongues*. New York: Center for New American Media.

American heritage dictionary of the English language. 2000. 4th edn. Boston: Houghton Mifflin.

American School for the Deaf. 1818. Second Report of the Directors of the Connecticut Asylum for the Education and Instruction of Deaf and Dumb Persons, 5.

American School for the Deaf. n.d. History of Deaf Education in America. www.asd-1817.org/history/history-deafed.html

Anastasiow, N., and Hanes, M. 1974. Cognitive development and the acquisition of language in three subcultural groups. *Developmental Psychology* 10: 703–709.

Ann Arbor School Board. 1980. An educational plan submitted by the Ann Arbor Board of Education in response to the order of July 12, 1979 from the honorable Judge Charles W. Joiner. In *The Ann Arbor decision: Memorandum, opinion and order and the educational plan*. Arlington, VA: Center for Applied Linguistics. 13–22.

Anttila, A. 1997. Deriving variation from grammar. In F. Hinskens, R. van Hout, and W. L. Wetzels (eds.), *Variation, change, and phonological theory*. Amsterdam: John Benjamins. 35–68.

Anttila, A., 2002. Variation in phonological theory. In J. K. Chambers, P. Trudgill, and N. Schilling-Estes (eds.), *The handbook of language variation and change*. Oxford: Blackwell. 206–243.

Anttila, A., and Cho, Y.Y. 1998. Variation and change in Optimality Theory. *Lingua* 104: 31–56.

Ariel, M. 2004. Most. *Language* 80: 658–706.

Arnold, J., Blake, R., Eckert, P., Iwai, M., Mendoza-Denton, N., Morgan, C., Polanyi, L., Solomon, J., and Veatch, T. 1993. Variation and personal/group style. Paper presented at New Ways of Analyzing Variation 22, Ottawa, October.

Ash, S. 1988. Speaker identification in sociolinguistics and criminal law. In K. Ferrara, B. Brown, K. Walters, and J. Baugh (eds.), *Linguistic change and contact. Proceedings of the Sixteenth Annual Conference on New Ways of Analyzing Variation in Language*. Austin: Department of Linguistics, University of Texas. 25–33.

Ash, S., and Myhill, J. 1986. Linguistic correlates of inter-ethnic contact. In D. Sankoff (ed.), *Diversity and diachrony*. Amsterdam: John Benjamins. 33–44.

Bailey, C.-J.N. 1970. Lectal groupings in matrices generated with waves along the temporal parameter. *Working Papers in Linguistics* 2/214.

Bailey, C.-J.N. 1971. Variation and language theory. Unpublished ms.

Bailey, C.-J.N. and Shuy, R. W. (eds.). 1973. *New ways of analyzing variation in English*. Washington, DC: Georgetown University Press.

Bailey, G. 1997. When did southern American English begin? In E. Schneider (ed.), *Englishes around the World, vol. I: General Studies, British Isles, North America*. Amsterdam: John Benjamins. 255–75.

Bailey, G. 2002. Real and apparent time. In J.K. Chambers, P. Trudgill, and N. Schilling-Estes (eds.), *The handbook of language variation and change*. Oxford: Blackwell. 312–332.

Bailey, G., and Maynor, N. 1985. The present tense of be in southern black folk speech. *American Speech* 60: 195–213.

Bailey, G., Maynor, N., and Cukor-Avila, P. 1989. Variation in subject-verb concord in early Modern English. *Language Variation and Change* 1: 285–300.

Bailey, G., Maynor, N., and Cukor-Avila, P. (eds.). 1991. *The emergence of Black English: Text and commentary*. Amsterdam: John Benjamins.

Bailey, G., and Thomas, E. 1998. Some aspects of African-American Vernacular English phonology. In S.S. Mufwene, J. Rickford, J. Baugh, and G. Bailey (eds.), *African American English: Structure, history and use*. London: Routledge. 85–109.

Bailey, G., Wikle, T., and Tillery, J. 1997. The effect of methods on results in dialectology. *English World-Wide* 18: 35–63.

Baker, M.C. 1996. *The polysynthesis parameter.* New York: Oxford University Press.

Baker, M.C. 2002. *The atoms of language.* New York: Oxford University Press.

Bakhtin, M.M. 1935 [1981]. Discourse in the novel. In M.M. Bakhtin, *The dialogic imagination* (ed. M. Holquist, trans. C. Emerson and M. Holquist). Austin: University of Texas Press. 259–422.

Bakhtin, M.M. 1953 [1986a]. The problem of speech genres. In M.M. Bakhtin, *Speech genres and other late essays* (ed. C. Emerson and M. Holquist, trans. V.W. McGee). Austin: University of Texas Press. 60–102.

Bakhtin, M.M. 1970 [1986b]. The problem of the text in linguistics, philology, and the human sciences: An experiment in philosophical analysis. In M.M. Bakhtin, *Speech genres and other late essays* (ed. C. Emerson and M. Holquist, trans. V.W. McGee). Austin: University of Texas Press. 103–131.

Baldwin, J., and French, P. 1990. *Forensic phonetics.* London: Pinter.

Ball, A., and Lardner, T. 1997. Dispositions toward language: Teacher constructs of knowledge and the Ann Arbor Black English case. *College Composition and Communication* 48: 469–485.

Baratz, J.C., and Shuy, R.W. (eds.). 1969. *Teaching Black children to read.* Washington, DC: Center for Applied Linguistics.

Barbiers, S., Cornips, L., and van der Kleij, S. (eds.). 2002. *Syntactic microvariation.* Electronic publication of the Meertens Institute. Amsterdam: Meertens Institute. www.meertens.knaw.nl/projecten/sand//synmic/

Barnes, B. 1989. *About science.* Maldon, MA: Blackwell.

Battison, R. 1980. Signs have parts. In C. Baker and R. Battison (eds.), *Sign language and the Deaf community.* Silver Spring, MD: National Association of the Deaf. 35–51.

Battison, R., Markowicz, H., and Woodward, J. 1975. A good rule of thumb: Variable phonology in American Sign Language. In R.W. Fasold and R.W. Shuy (eds.), *Analyzing variation in language.* Washington, DC: Georgetown University Press. 291–302.

Bauer, L. 2002. Inferring variation and change from public corpora. In J.K. Chambers, P. Trudgill, and N. Schilling-Estes (eds.), *The handbook of language variation and change.* Oxford: Blackwell. 97–114.

Bauer, R.S., Cheung K.-H., and Chung P.-M. 2003. Variation and merger of the rising tones in Hong Kong Cantonese. *Language Variation and Change* 15: 211–225.

Baugh, J. 1983. *Black street speech.* Austin: University of Texas Press.

Baugh, J. 1988. Discourse features for COME in Black English Vernacular. In K. Ferrara, B. Brown, K. Walters, and J. Baugh (eds.), *Linguistic change and contact: Proceedings of the Sixteenth Annual Conference on New Ways of Analyzing Variation.* Austin: Department of Linguistics, University of Texas. 42–49.

Baugh, J. 1998. Linguistics, education and the law: Educational reform for African American language minority students. In S. Mufwene, J. Rickford, G. Bailey, and J. Baugh (eds.), *African American English.* London: Routledge. 282–301.

Baugh, J. 1999a. *Out of the mouths of slaves: African American language and educational malpractice.* Austin: University of Texas Press.

Baugh, J. 1999b. Reading, writing and rap: Lyric shuffle and other motivational strategies to introduce and reinforce literacy. In J. Baugh, *Out of the mouths of slaves: African American language and educational malpractice.* Austin: University of Texas Press. 31–40.

Baugh, J. 2000. Racial identification by speech. *American Speech* 75: 362–363.

Baugh, J., and Sherzer, J. (eds.). 1984. *Language in use: Readings in sociolinguistics.* New York: Prentice Hall.

Bayley, R. 1994a. Consonant cluster reduction in Tejano English. *Language Variation and Change* 6: 303–326.

Bayley, R. 1994b. Interlanguage variation and the quantitative paradigm: Past-tense marking in Chinese-English. In E. Tarone, S.M. Gass, and A. Cohen (eds.), *Research methodology in second-language acquisition*. Hillsdale, NJ: Lawrence Erlbaum. 157–181.

Bayley, R. 1996. Competing constraints on variation in the speech of adult Chinese learners of English. In R. Bayley and D.R. Preston (eds.), *Second language acquisition and linguistic variation*. Amsterdam: John Benjamins. 97–120.

Bayley, R. 2002. The quantitative paradigm. In J.K. Chambers, P. Trudgill, and N. Schilling-Estes (eds.), *The handbook of language variation and change*. Oxford: Blackwell. 117–141.

Bayley, R. 2005. Second language acquisition and sociolinguistic variation. *Intercultural Communication Studies* 14(2): 1–13.

Bayley, R., and Langman, J. 2004. Variation in the group and the individual: Evidence from second language acquisition. *IRAL* 42: 303–319.

Bayley, R., and Preston, D.R. (eds.). 1996. *Second language acquisition and linguistic variation*. Amsterdam: John Benjamins.

Bayley, R., and Regan, V. 2004. Introduction: The acquisition of sociolinguistic competence. *Journal of Sociolinguistics* 8: 323–338.

Baynton, D. 1996. *Forbidden signs: American culture and the campaign against sign language*. Chicago: Chicago University Press.

Bean, J., Cucchiara, M., Eddy, R., Elbow, P., Grego, R., Haswell, R., Irvine, P., Kennedy, E., Kutz, E., Lehner, A., and Matsuda, P. 2003. Should we invite studies to write in home dialects or languages? Complicating the yes/no debate. *Composition Studies* 31: 25–42.

Becker, M. 2000. The acquisition of the English copula. In S.C. Howell, S.A. Fish, and T. Keith-Lucas (eds.), *Proceedings of the 24th Annual Boston University Conference on Language Development, vol. 1*. Somerville, MA: Cascadilla Press. 104–115.

Beckman, M.E., and Hirschberg, J. 1994. The ToBI annotation conventions. Online typescript: www.ling.ohio-state.edu/~tobi/ame_tobi/annotation_conventions.html

Beckman, M.E., Munson, B., and Edwards, J. In press. Vocabulary growth and developmental expansion of types of phonological knowledge. In J. Cole and J.I. Hualde (eds.), *Laboratory Phonology 9*. Berlin: Mouton de Gruyter.

Beebe, L.M. 1977. The influence of the listener on code-switching. *Language Learning* 27: 331–339.

Bell, A. 1984. Language style as audience design. *Language in Society* 13: 145–204.

Bell, A. 1997. The phonetics of fish and chips in New Zealand: Marking national and ethnic identities. *English World-Wide* 18: 243–70.

Bell, A. 2000. Maori and Pakeha English: A case study. In A. Bell and K. Kuiper (eds.), *New Zealand English*. Wellington and Amsterdam: Victoria University Press and John Benjamins. 221–248.

Bell, A. 2001. Back in style: Re-working audience design. In P. Eckert and J.R. Rickford (eds.), *Style and sociolinguistic variation*. New York: Cambridge University Press. 139–169.

Bell, J. 1991. Donegal women as migrant workers in Scotland. *Review of Scottish Culture* 7: 73–80.

Benedicto, E., Abdulkarim, L., Garrett, D., Johnson, V., and Seymour, H. 1998. Overt copulas in African American English speaking children. In A. Greenhill, M. Hughes, H. Littlefield, and H. Walsh (eds.), *Proceedings of the 22th Annual Boston University Conference on Language Development, vol. 1*. Somerville, MA: Cascadilla Press. 50–57.

Benor, S. 2004. Second style acquisition: The linguistic socialization of newly Orthodox Jews. Ph.D. dissertation, Stanford University.

Berdan, R. 1977. Polylectal comprehension and the polylectal grammar. In R.W. Fasold and R.W. Shuy (eds.), *Studies in language variation*. Washington, DC: Georgetown University Press. 12–29.

Bereiter, C., and Engelmann, S. 1966. *Teaching disadvantaged children in the preschool.* Englewood Cliffs, NJ: Prentice-Hall.

Berk-Seligson, S. 1990. *The bilingual courtroom: Court interpreters in the judicial process.* Chicago: University of Chicago Press.

Berlin, I., Ready, J.P., and Rowland, L.S. (eds.). 1982. *The Black military experience.* Cambridge: Cambridge University Press.

Bezooijen, R. van. 2002. Aesthetic evaluation of Dutch: Comparisons across dialects, accents, and languages. In D. Long and D.R. Preston (eds.), *Handbook of perceptual dialectology, vol. 2.* Amsterdam: John Benjamins. 13–30.

Bezooijen, R. van, and van den Berg, R. 1999. Word intelligibility of language varieties in the Netherlands and Flanders under minimal conditions. In R. Kager and R. van Bezooijen (eds.), *Linguistics in the Netherlands 1999.* Amsterdam: John Benjamins. 1–12.

Bezooijen, R. van, and Gooskens, C. 1999. Identification of language varieties: The contribution of different linguistic levels. *Journal of Language and Social Psychology* 18: 31–48.

Bezooijen, R. van, and Ytsma, J. 1999. Accents of Dutch: Personality impression, divergence, and identifiability. *Belgian Journal of Linguistics* 13: 105–129.

Bialystok, E., and Hakuta, K. 1994. *In other words: The science and psychology of second language acquisition.* New York: Basic Books.

Biber, D. 1987. A textual comparison of British and American writing. *American Speech* 62: 99–119.

Biber, D., and Finegan, E. 1989. Drift and evolution in English style: A history of three genres. *Language* 65: 487–517.

Bickerton, D. 1971. Inherent variability and variable rules. *Foundations of Language* 7: 457–492.

Blake, I.K. 1984. Language development in working-class black children: An examination of form, content and use. Ph.D. dissertation, Columbia University.

Bliss, A.J. (ed.). 1979. *Spoken English in Ireland, 1660–1740: Representative texts assembled and analysed.* Dublin: Cademus.

Bloch, B. 1948. A set of postulates for phonemic analysis. *Language* 24: 3–46.

Bloom, L. 1970. *Language development: Form and function in emerging grammars.* Cambridge: MIT Press.

Bloom, L. 1992. Racism in developmental research. *Division 7 Newsletter.* American Psychological Association. 1–2.

Bloom, L. 1995. *The transition from infancy to language: Acquiring the power of expression.* Cambridge: Cambridge University Press.

Bloom, L., Lightbown, P., and Hood, L. 1975. Structure and variation in child language. *Monographs of the Society for Research in Child Development* 40 (serial no. 160).

Bloomfield, L. 1933. *Language.* New York: Holt.

Blyth, C., Jr., Recktenwald, S., and Wang, J. 1990. I'm like, "say what?!": A new quotative in American oral narrative. *American Speech* 65: 215–227.

Boberg, C. 2005. The Canadian shift in Montreal. *Language Variation and Change* 17: 133–154.

Bobo, L. 2001. *Urban inequality.* New York: Russell Sage.

Bock, K., Butterfield, A., Cutler, A., Cutting, J.C., Eberhard, K.M., and Humphreys, K.R. 2006. Number agreement in British and American English: Disagreeing to agree collectively. *Language* 82: 64–113.

Boersma, P., 2003. Stochastic optimality theory. Paper presented at the Linguistic Society of America Annual Meeting, January.

Boersma, P., and Hayes, B. 2001. Empirical tests of the gradual learning algorithm. *Linguistic Inquiry* 32: 45–86.

Boling, B.D. 1994. Features from Irish emigrant letters. Unpublished ms.

Borzone de Manrique, A.M., and Signorini, A. 1983. Segmental duration and rhythm in Spanish. *Journal of Phonetics* 11: 117–128.

Bourgerie. D.S. 1990. A quantitative study of sociolinguistic variation in Cantonese (China). Ph.D. dissertation, Ohio State University.

Bowerman, M. 1973. *Early syntactic development: A cross-linguistic study with special reference to Finnish*. Cambridge: Cambridge University Press.

Bowman, R. 1997, January 13. Ebonics earns a failing grade. *The Washington Times*. C5.

Boyd, H. 1997. Been dere, done dat! *Black Scholar* 27(1): 15–17.

Branson, A. 1996, December 26. Beltway crowd weighs in on Oakland School Board's talk of Black English. *Legis-Slate News Service*. www.legislate.com

Bresnan, J., Dingare, S., and Manning, C. 2001. Soft constraints mirror hard constraints: Voice and person in English and Lummi. In M. Butt and T.H. King (eds.), *Proceedings of the LFG '01 Conference*. Stanford: CSLI. 13–32.

Bridenbaugh, C. 1963. *Myths and realities of the colonial South*. New York: Atheneum.

Bridgeforth, S. 1986. The language functions of three- and four-year-old black children from working-class families. Ph.D. dissertation, Georgetown University.

Britain, D. 1992. Linguistic change in intonation: The use of high rising terminals in New Zealand English. *Language Variation and Change* 4: 77–104.

Browman, C.P., and Goldstein, L. 1990. Tiers in articulatory phonology, with some implications for casual speech. In J. Kingston and M. Beckman (eds.), *Papers in laboratory phonology I: Between the grammar and physics of speech*. Cambridge: Cambridge University Press. 341–376.

Brown, J.R. 2001. *Who rules in science: An opinionated guide to the wars*. Cambridge, MA: Harvard University Press.

Brown, P., and Levinson, S.C. 1987. *Politeness: Some universals in language usage*. Cambridge: Cambridge University Press.

Brown, R. 1973. *A first language: The early stages*. Cambridge, MA: Harvard University Press.

Brown, V. 1991. Evolution of the merger of /ɪ/ and /ɛ/ in Tennessee. *American Speech* 66: 303–315.

Bucholtz, M. 1999a. "Why be normal?" Language and identity practices in a community of nerd girls. *Language in Society* 28: 203–231.

Bucholtz, M. 1999b. You da man: narrating the racial other in the production of white masculinity. *Journal of Sociolinguistics* 3: 443–460.

Bull, R., and Clifford, B.C. 1984. Earwitness recognition accuracy. In G.L. Wells and E.F. Loftus (eds.), *Eyewitness testimony: Psychological perspectives*. Cambridge: Cambridge University Press. 92–123.

Burnett, P. (ed.). 1986. *The Penguin book of Caribbean verse in English*. New York: Viking Penguin.

Butters, R.R. 1982. Editor's note [on "be+like"]. *American Speech* 57: 149.

Butters, R.R. 1987. Linguistic convergence in a North Carolina community. In K.M. Denning, S. Inkelas, F.C. McNair-Knox, and J.R. Rickford (eds.), *Variation in language: NWAV-XV at Stanford*. Stanford, CA: Center for the Study of Language and Information. 52–60.

Butters, R.R. 1990. Current issues in variation theory. Paper presented at the First International Congress of Dialectologists, University of Bamberg, August 2.

Butters, R.R. 1993. If the wages of sin are for death: The semantics and pragmatics of a statutory ambiguity. *American Speech* 68: 83–94.

Butters, R.R. 2000. "What Is about to take place is a murder": Construing the racist subtext in a small-town Virginia courtroom. In P. Griffin, J. Peyton, W. Wolfram, and R. Fasold (eds.), *Language in action: New studies of language and society: Essays in honor of Roger Shuy*. Cresskill, NJ: Hampton Press. 373–399.

Butters, R.R. 2004. How not to strike it rich: Semantics, pragmatics, and semiotics of a Massachusetts lottery ticket. *Applied Linguistics* 25: 466–490.

Butters, R.R. 2006. Linguistic and semiotic evidence in American death penalty cases. Paper presented at the International Summer School in Forensic Linguistic Analysis, Birmingham, England, September 20.

Butters, R.R., Espy, T., and Altsuler, K. 1993. The imitation of dialect for illegal purposes: An empirical study. Paper presented at the Conference on New Ways of Analyzing Variation in English and Other Languages 22, October.

Bybee, J. 2001. *Phonology and language use*. Cambridge: Cambridge University Press.

Bybee, J. 2002. Word frequency and context of use in the lexical diffusion of phonetically conditioned sound change. *Language Variation and Change* 14: 261–290.

Cable News Network. 1997, January 3. *Crossfire – Ebonics debate*.

Carter, P.M. In press. Prosodic variation in SLA: Rhythm in an urban North Carolina Hispanic community. *Penn Working Papers in Linguistics* 11(2).

Cashmore, E. 1996. *Dictionary of race and ethnic relations*, 4th edn. New York: Routledge.

Cassidy, F.G., and Le Page, R.B. (eds.). 1980. *Dictionary of Jamaican English*, 2nd edn. Cambridge: Cambridge University Press.

Cazden, C.B., Cancino, H., Rosansky, E.B., and Schumann, J.H. 1975. *Second language acquisition sequences in children, adolescents, and adults*. Final Report, National Institute of Education (Grant no. NE-6–00–3–0024). ERIC Document: ED 121–115.

Cedergren, H.J. 1973. On the nature of variable constraints. In C.-J.N. Bailey and R.W. Shuy (eds.), *New ways of analyzing variation in English*. Washington, DC: Georgetown University Press. 13–22.

Cedergren, H.J., and Sankoff, D. 1974. Variable rules: Performance as a statistical reflection of competence. *Language* 50: 333–355.

Center for Applied Linguistics. 1980. *The Ann Arbor decision: Memorandum, opinion and order and the Educational Plan*. Arlington, VA: Center for Applied Linguistics.

Chalmers, A. 1982. *What is this thing called science?* Milton Keynes: Open University Press.

Chalmers, A. 1990. *Science and its fabrication*. Minneapolis: University of Minnesota Press.

Chambers, J.K. 1990. Forensic dialectology and the Bear Island land claim. R.W. Rieber and W.A. Stewart (eds.), *The language scientist as expert in the legal setting*. Annals of the New York Academy of Sciences, col. 606. New York: The New York Academy of Sciences. 19–31.

Chambers, J.K. 2002a. Studying language variation: An informal epistemology. In J.K. Chambers, P. Trudgill, and N. Schilling-Estes (eds.), *The handbook of language variation and change*. Oxford: Blackwell. 3–14.

Chambers, J.K. 2002b. *Sociolinguistic theory*, 2nd edn. Oxford: Blackwell.

Chambers, J.K., and Trudgill, P. 1998. *Dialectology*, 2nd edn. Cambridge: Cambridge University Press.

Chambers, J.K., Trudgill, P., and Schilling-Estes, N. (eds.). 2002. *The handbook of language variation and change*. Oxford Blackwell.

Charen, M. 1997, January 2. Is street slang a distinct language? *The Detroit News*. A7.

Charity, A.H. 2005. Dialect variation in school settings among African-American children of low-socioeconomic status. Ph.D. dissertation, University of Pennsylvania.

Charity, A.H., Scarborough, H.S., and Griffin, D.M. 2003. Familiarity with school English in African American children and its relation to early reading achievement. *Child Development* 75: 1340–1356.

Chaski, C.E. 1997. Who wrote it? Steps toward a science of authorship identification. *National Institute of Justice Journal*, September: 15–22.

Chaski, C.E. 2001. Empirical evaluations of language-based author identification techniques. *Forensic Linguistics: The International Journal of Speech, Language, and the Law* 8: 1–65.

Chaski, C.E. 2005. Who's at the keyboard? Authorship attribution in digital evidence investigations. *International Journal of Digital Evidence* 4.1. www.utica.edu/academic/institutes/ecii/ijde/articles.cfm?action= issue&id=11

Chen, M.Y. 1995. Acoustic parameters of nasalized vowels in hearing-impaired and normal-hearing speakers. *Journal of the Acoustical Society of America* 98: 2443–2453.

Chesterman, A. 1991. *On definiteness*. Cambridge: Cambridge University Press.

Childs, B. 2005. Investigating the local construction of identity: Sociophonetic variation in Smoky Mountain African American women's speech. Ph.D. dissertation, University of Georgia.

Childs, B., and Mallinson, C. 2004. African American English in Appalachia: Dialect accommodation and substrate influence. *English World-Wide* 25: 27–50.

Chomsky, N. 1957. *Syntactic structures*. The Hague: Mouton.

Chomsky, N. 1965. *Aspects of the theory of syntax*. Cambridge, MA: MIT Press.

Chomsky, N. 1988. *Language and problems of knowledge: The Managua Lectures*. Cambridge, MA: MIT Press.

Chomsky, N. 1995. *Minimalist Program*. Cambridge, MA: MIT Press.

Chomsky, N., and Halle, M. 1968. *The sound pattern of English*. New York: Harper and Row.

Chronicle of Higher Education. 1996, March 29. More money for science. 40–44.

Clark, B. 2005. On stochastic grammar. *Language* 81: 207–217.

Clark, K., and Holquist, M. 1984. *Mikhail Bakhtin*. Cambridge, MA: Belknap/Harvard University Press.

Clarke, S. 1987. Dialect mixing and linguistic variation in a non-overtly stratified society. In K.M. Denning, S. Inkelas, F.C. McNair-Knox, and J.R. Rickford (eds.), *Variation in language: NWAV-XV at Stanford*. Stanford, CA: Center for the Study of Language and Information. 74–85.

Clarke, S. 1997. On establishing historical relationships between old and new world varieties: Habitual aspect and Newfoundland vernacular English. In E. Schneider (ed.), *Englishes around the World, vol. 1: General studies, British Isles, North America*. Amsterdam: John Benjamins. 277–293.

Clarke, S., Elms, F., and Youssef, A. 1995. The third dialect of English: Some Canadian evidence. *Language Variation and Change* 7: 209–228.

Cleaver, E. 1997, February 4. Ebonics belongs in the streets. *Newsday*. A36.

Clements, G.N., and Keyser, S.J. 1983. *CV phonology: A generative theory of the syllable*. Cambridge, MA: MIT Press.

Clifford v. Kentucky, 7 S.W.3d 371. 1999.

Clopper, C.G., and Pisoni, D.B. 2004a. Homebodies and army brats: Some effects of early linguistic experience and residential history on dialect categorization. *Language Variation and Change* 16: 31–48.

Clopper, C.G., and Pisoni, D.B. 2004b. Some acoustic cues for the perceptual categorization of American English regional dialects. *Journal of Phonetics* 32: 111–140.

Coates, J. (ed.). 1998. *Language and gender: A reader*. Oxford: Blackwell.

Cole, J., Thomas, E.R., Britt, E.R., and Coggshall, E.L. 2005. Intonational distinctiveness of African American English. Paper presented at New Ways of Analyzing Variation 34, New York, October 23.

Coleman, J. 2002. Phonetic representations in the mental lexicon. In J. Durand and B. Laks (eds.), *Phonetics, phonology, and cognition*. Oxford: Oxford University Press. 96–130.

Conference on College Composition and Communication. 1974. *Students' rights to their own dialects*. Urbana, IL: CCC.

Cooley, M. 1995. Sources for the study of 18th century literary dialect. Unpublished ms.

Cooley, M. 1997. An early representation of African American English. In C. Bernstein, T. Nunnally, and R. Sabino (eds.), *Language variety in the South revisited*. Tuscaloosa: University of Alabama Press. 51–58.

Comrie, Bernard. 1981. *Language universals and linguistic typology*. Chicago: University of Chicago Press.

Cornips, L., and Corrigan, K. 2005. Convergence and divergence in grammar. In P. Auer, F. Hinskens, and P. Kerswill (eds.), *Dialect change*. Cambridge: Cambridge University Press. 96–134.

Cosby, B. 1997, January 10. Elements of Igno-Ebonics style. *The Wall Street Journal*.

Cotterill, J. (ed.). 2002a. *Language in the legal process*. Basingstoke: Palgrave MacMillan.

Cotterill, J. 2002b. Language and power in court: A linguistic analysis of the O.J. Simpson trial. Basingstoke: Palgrave MacMillan.

Coulthard, M. 2004. Author identification, idiolect and linguistic uniqueness. *Applied Linguistics* 25: 431–447.

Coupland, N. 2001. Language, situation and the relational self: Theorizing dialect-style in sociolinguisitcs. In P. Eckert and J.R. Rickford (eds.), *Style and sociolinguistic variation*. Cambridge: Cambridge University Press. 185–211.

Coupland, N., Coupland, J., Giles, H., and Henwood, K. 1988. Accommodating the elderly: Invoking and extending a theory. *Language in Society* 17: 1–41.

Cox, F. 1999. Vowel change in Australian English. *Phonetica* 56: 1–27.

Craig, D. 1999. *Teaching language and literacy: Policies and procedures for vernacular situations*. Georgetown, Guyana: Education and Development Services.

Craig, H., and Washington, J.A. 2002. Oral language expression for African American preschoolers and kindergarteners. *Journal of Speech, Language, Hearing Research* 1: 59–70.

Craig, H., and Washington, J.A. 2006. *Malik goes to school: Examining the language skills of African American students from preschool – 5th grade*. Mahwah, NJ: Lawrence Erlbaum.

Craigie, W. 1936. The value of the period dictionaries. *Transactions of the Philological Society* 53–62.

Croneberg, C. 1965. The linguistic community. In W. Stokoe, D. Casterline, and C. Croneberg. *A dictionary of American Sign Language*. Washington, DC: Gallaudet College Press. 297–311.

Crowell, S.C., Kolba, E.D., Stewart, W.A., and Johnson, K.R. 1974. *TALKACROSS: Materials for teaching English as a second dialect*. (Teachers handbook and student activity book.) Montclair, NJ: Caribou Associated.

Cukor-Avila, P. 2002. She say, She go, She be like: Verbs of quotation over time in African American Vernacular English. *American Speech* 77: 3–31.

Curtiss, S. 1977. *Genie: A psycholinguistic study of a modern day wild child*. New York: Academic.

Dahl, Ö. 1985. *Tense and aspect systems*. Oxford: Blackwell.

Danesi, M., and DiPietro, R.J. 1991. *Contrastive analysis for the contemporary second language classroom*. Toronto: OISE Press.

Datcher, M. 1997, January 13. Black English: An issue of pain and pride. *The Athens News*.

Dauer, R.M. 1983. Stress-timing and syllable-timing reanalyzed. *Journal of Phonetics* 11: 51–62.

Davidson, R. 1996, December 31. Jackson shifts stance on Black English effort. *The Washington Post*. A6.

Davis, N.A. (ed.). 2004. *Paston letters and papers of the fifteenth century*. Oxford: Oxford University Press.

Dawson, H. 2005. Morphological variation and change in the Rigveda. Ph.D. dissertation, Ohio State University.

DeGraff, M. 1999. Creolization, language change, and language acquisition: A prolegomenon. In M. DeGraff (ed.), *Language creation and language change: Creolization, diachrony, and development*. Cambridge, MA: MIT Press. 1–46.

Demolin, D. 2001. Some phonetic and phonological observations concerning /ʀ/ in Belgian French. In H. Van de Velde and R. van Hout (eds.), *'r-atics: Sociolinguistic, phonetic and phonological characteristics of /r/*. Brussels: Institut des Langues Vivantes et de Phonétique. 63–73.

DeSantis, S. 1977. Elbow to hand shift in French and American Sign Languages. Paper presented at the Conference on New Ways of Analyzing Variation, Georgetown University, Washington, DC.

Deschaies-Lafontaine, D. 1974. A socio-phonetic study of a Québec French community: Trois-Rivières. Ph.D. dissertation, University College London.

Deterding, D. 2001. The measurement of rhythm: A comparison of Singapore and British English. *Journal of Phonetics* 29: 217–230.

Dewaele, J.M. 2004. Retention or omission of the ne in advanced French interlanguage: The variable effect of extralinguistic factors. *Journal of Sociolinguistics* 8: 333–350.

DeWitt, K. 1996, December 29. Ebonics, language of Richard Nixon. *The New York Times*, sec. 4: 3.

Dickens, M., and Sawyer, G.M. 1952. An experimental comparison of vocal quality among mixed groups of Whites and Negroes. *Southern Speech Journal* 17: 178–185.

Dickerson, L.J. 1975. The learner's interlanguage as a system of variable rules. *TESOL Quarterly* 9: 401–407.

Dillard, J.L. 1972. *Black English: Its history and usage in the United States*. New York: Random House.

Dillard, J.L., Sledd, J., Hamp, E.P., and Hill, A.A. 1979. Joinder and rejoinder. *American Speech* 54: 113–119.

Di Paolo, M. 1992. Hypercorrection in response to the apparent merger of (ɔ) and (ɑ) in Utah English. *Language and Communication* 12: 267–292.

Di Paolo, M., and Faber. A. 1990. Phonation differences and the phonetic content of the tense-lax contrast in Utah English. *Language Variation and Change* 2: 155–204.

Disner, S.F. 1980. Evaluation of vowel normalization procedures. *Journal of the Acoustical Society of America* 67: 253–261.

Dobson, E.J. 1968. *English pronunciation, 1500–1700*. 2 vols. Oxford: Oxford University Press.

Docherty, G.J., and Foulkes, P. 1999. Newcastle upon Tyne and Derby: Instrumental phonetics and variationist studies. In P. Foulkes and G.J. Docherty (eds.), *Urban voices*. London: Arnold. 47–71.

Docherty, G.J., and Foulkes, P. 2001. Variability in (r) production – Instrumental perspectives. In H. Van de Velde and R. van Hout (eds.), *'r-atics: Sociolinguistic, phonetic and phonological characteristics of /r/*. Brussels: Institut des Langues Vivantes et de Phonétique. 173–184.

Dr. Karenga speaks on Ebonics debate. 1997, March 3. *Long Beach Union*. 2–3.

Douglas-Cowie, E., Cowie, R., and Rahilly, J. 1995. The social distribution of intonation patterns in Belfast. In J.W. Lewis (ed.), *Studies in general and English phonetics: Essays in honour of Professor J.D. O'Connor*. London: Routledge. 180–186.

Dumas, B.K. 1990a. Adequacy of cigarette package warnings: An analysis of the adequacy of federally mandated cigarette package warnings. In J.N. Levi and A.G. Walker (eds.), *Language in the judicial process*. New York: Plenum. 309–352.

Dumas, B.K. 1990b. Voice identification in a criminal law case. *American Speech* 65: 341–348.

Dumas, B.K. 2000. Dialect variation and legal process. *American Speech* 75: 267–270.

Duranti, A. 1997. *Linguistic anthropology*. Cambridge: Cambridge University Press.

Ebonics: Hearing before the Subcommittee on Labor, Health and Human Services, and Education, of the Senate Committee on Appropriations, 105th Cong., 1st Sess. 54 (1997) (testimony of Michael Lampkins).

Ebonics: Hearing before the Subcommittee on Labor, Health and Human Services, and Education, of the Senate Committee on Appropriations, 105th Cong., 1st Sess. 68 (1997) (testimony of Orlando Taylor).

Ebonics: Hearing before the Subcommittee on Labor, Health and Human Services, and Education, of the Senate Committee on Appropriations, 105th Cong., 1st Sess. (1997) (testimony of Armstrong Williams).

Eckert, P. 1989a. *Jocks and burnouts: Social categories and identities in the high school*. New York: Teachers College Press.

Eckert, P. 1989b. The whole woman: Sex and gender differences in variation. *Language Variation and Change* 1: 245–267.

Eckert, P. (ed.). 1991. *New ways of analyzing sound change*. New York: Academic.

Eckert, P. 2000. *Linguistic variation as social practice: The linguistic construction of identity in Belten High*. Oxford: Blackwell.

Eckert, P., and McConell-Ginet, S. 1992. Think practically and look locally: Language and gender as community-based practice. *Annual Review of Anthropology* 21: 461–490.

Eckert, P., and Rickford, J.R. (eds.). 2001. *Style and sociolinguistic variation*. New York: Cambridge University Press.

Edwards, W.F. 1981. Two varieties of English in Detroit. In G. Smitherman (ed.), *Black English and the education of black children and youth*. Detroit, MI: Center for Black Studies. 393–408.

Ekman, P. 1985. *Telling lies: Clues to deceit in the marketplace, politics, and marriage*. New York: Norton.

Ellis, M. 1994. Literary dialect as linguistic evidence: Subject-verb concord in nineteenth-century southern literature. *American Speech* 69: 128–144.

Ellis, R. 1985. *Understanding second language acquisition*. Oxford: Oxford University Press.

Ellis, R. 1987. Interlanguage variability in narrative discourse: Style shifting in the use of past tense. *Studies in Second Language Acquisition* 9: 1–20.

Ellis, S. 1994. The Yorkshire ripper inquiry: Part I. *International Journal of Speech, Language and the Law* 1: 197–206.

Emmorey, K. 1999. The confluence of space and language in signed languages. In P. Bloom, M.A. Peterson, L. Nedel, and M. Garrett (eds.), *Language and space*. Cambridge, MA: MIT Press. 171–209.

Emonds, J. 1976. A transformational approach to English syntax. New York: Academic Press.

Erickson, C. 1972. *Invisible immigrants*. Ithaca, NY: Cornell University Press.

Esling, J.H. 1978. The identification of features of voice quality in social groups. *Journal of the International Phonetic Association* 7: 18–23.

Esling, J.H., and Warkentyne, H.J. 1993. Retracting of /æ/ in Vancouver English. In S. Clarke (ed.), *Focus on Canada*. Varieties of English around the World, General Series, 11. Amsterdam: John Benjamins. 229–246.

Evans, M. 1997, January 13. Locally, few favor movement. *Newsday*. A17.

Faber, A. 1992. Articulatory variability, categorical perception, and the inevitability of sound change. In G.W. Davis and G.W. Iverson (eds.), *Explanation in historical linguistics*. Amsterdam: John Benjamins. 59–75.

Faber, A., and Di Paolo, M. 1995. The discriminability of nearly merged sounds. *Language Variation and Change* 7: 35–78.

Fairclough, N. 1989. *Language and power*. London and New York: Longman.

Fairclough, N. 1992. Discourse and social change. Cambridge: Polity Press.

Fant, G. 1966. A note on vocal tract size factors and non-uniform F-pattern scalings. *Speech Transmission Laboratory – Quarterly Progress and Status Report (STL-QPSR)* 4: 22–30.

Fasold, R.W. 1972. *Tense marking in Black English: A linguistic and social analysis*. Washington, DC: Center for Applied Linguistics.

Fasold, R.W. 1973. The concept of "earlier-later": More or less correct. C.-J.N. Bailey and R.W. Shuy (eds.), *New ways of analyzing variation in English*. Washington, DC: Georgetown University Press. 183–197.

Fasold, R.W. 1991. The quiet demise of variables rules. *American Speech* 66: 3–21.

Fasold, R.W., and Schiffrin, D. (eds.). 1989. *Language change and variation*. Philadelphia: John Benjamins.

Fasold, R.W., and Shuy, R.W. (eds.). 1975. *Analyzing variation in language*. Washington, DC: Georgetown University Press.

Fasold, R.W., and Shuy, R.W. (eds.). 1977. *Studies in language variation*. Washington, DC: Georgetown University Press.

Feagin, C. 1979. *Variation and change in Alabama English: A sociolinguistic study of the white community*. Washington, DC: Georgetown University Press.

Feigenbaum, I. 1970. The use of nonstandard in teaching standard. In R.W. Fasold and R. Shuy (eds.), *Teaching Standard English in the inner city*. Washington, DC: Center for Applied Linguistics. 87–104.

Ferguson, C.A. 1959. Diglossia. *Word* 15: 325–340.

Ferrara, K., and Bell, B. 1995. Sociolinguistic variation and discourse function of constructed dialogue introducers: The case of be+like. *American Speech* 70: 265–289.

Feyerabend, P.K. 1975. *Against method*. London: New Left Books.

Finegan, E. 1997. Sociolinguistics and the law. In F. Coulmas (ed.), *Handbook of sociolinguistics*. Oxford: Blackwell. 421–435.

Finegan, E., and Biber, D. 1994. Register and social dialect variation: An integrated approach. In D. Biber and E. Finegan (eds.), *Sociolinguistic perspectives on register*. New York: Oxford University Press. 315–347.

Fischer, D.H. 1989. *Albion's seed: Four British folkways in America*. New York: Oxford University Press.

Fischer, J.L. 1958. Social influences on the choice of a linguistic variant. *Word* 14: 47–56.

Fischer, K. 1992. Educating speakers of Caribbean English creole in the United States. In J. Siegel (ed.), *Pidgins, creoles and nonstandard dialects in education. Occasional Paper* no. 12. Canberra: Applied Linguistics Association of Australia. 99–123.

Fishman, J.A. 1965. Who speaks what language to whom and when. *La Linguistique* 2: 67–88.

Fishman, J.A. (ed.). 1968. *Readings in the sociology of language*. The Hague: Mouton.

Fishman, J.A. 1972a. *Advances the sociology of language*, vol. I. The Hague: Mouton.

Fishman, J.A. 1972b. *Advances in the sociology of language*, vol. II. The Hague: Mouton.

Fishman, J.A. 1991. *Reversing language shift: Theoretical and empirical foundations of assistance to threatened languages*. Clevedon, UK: Multilingual Matters.

Fogel, H., and Ehri, L.C. 2000. Teaching elementary students who speak Black English Vernacular to write in Standard English; Effects of dialect transformation practice. *Contemporary Educational Psychology* 25: 212–235.

Foreman, C.G. 1999. Identification of African-American English dialect from prosodic cues. In N.M. Goss, A. Doran, and A. Coles (eds.), *SALSA VII, Proceedings of the Seventh Annual Symposium About Language and Society*. Austin: Texas Linguistic Forum 43: 57–66.

Foster, M. 1997. Ebonics and all that jazz: Cutting through the politics of linguistics, education, and race. *The Quarterly* 19: 7–12.

Fought, C. 1999. A majority sound change in a minority community: /u/-fronting in Chicano English. *Journal of Sociolinguistics* 3: 5–23.

Fought, C. 2002. Ethnicity. In J.K. Chambers, P. Trudgill, and N. Schillinges-Estes (eds.), *The handbook of language variation and change*. Oxford: Blackwell.

Fought, C., and Fought, J. 2002. Prosodic rhythm patterns in Chicano English. Unpublished ms.

Foulkes, P., and Docherty, G.J. (eds.). 1999. *Urban voices*. London: Arnold.

Foulkes, P., and Docherty, G.J. (2006). The social life of phonetics and phonology. *Journal of Phonetics* 34: 409–438.

Foulkes, P., Docherty, G.J., and Watt, D. 2005. Phonological variation in child-directed speech. *Language* 81: 177–206.

Fourakis, M., and Port, R. 1986. Stop epenthesis in English. *Journal of Phonetics* 14: 197–221.

Franklin, J., and Moss, A., Jr. (1994). *From slavery to freedom: A history of African Americans.* New York: McGraw-Hill.

Frazer, T.C. 1987. Attitudes toward regional pronunciation. *Journal of English Linguistics* 20: 89–100.

Fridland, V. 2000. The Southern shift in Memphis, Tennessee. *Language Variation and Change* 11: 267–285.

Fridland, V. 2003. Network strength and the realization of the Southern vowel shift among African Americans in Memphis, Tennessee. *American Speech* 78: 3–30.

Frishberg, N. 1975. Arbitrariness and iconicity: Historical change in American Sign Language. *Language* 51: 696–719.

Fung, G. 2003. *The disputed Federalist Papers: SVM feature selection via concave minimization.* New York: ACM Press. www.cs.wisc.edu/~gfung/federalist.pdf

Gahl, S., and Garnsey, S.M. 2004. Knowledge of grammar, knowledge of usage: Syntactic probabilities affect pronunciation variation. *Language* 80: 748–775.

Ghafarsamar, R. 2000. Aspects of second language speech: A variationist perspective on second language acquisition. Ph.D. dissertation, University of Ottawa.

Gibbons, J. (ed.). 1994. *Language and the law.* London: Longman.

Gibbons, J. 2003. *Forensic linguistics: An introduction to language in the justice system.* Oxford: Blackwell.

Giles, H., and Powesland, P.F. 1975. *Speech style and social evaluation.* New York: Academic.

Gilles, P., and Peters, J. (eds.). 2004. *Regional variation in intonation.* Tübingen: Max Niemeyer Verlag.

Gilliéron, J., and Edmond, E. 1902–10. *Atlas linguistique de la France.* 13 vols. Paris: Champion.

Godfrey, E., and Tagliamonte, S. 1999. Another piece for the verbal -s story: Evidence from Devon in southwest England. *Language Variation and Change* 11: 87–121.

Godinez, M., Jr. 1984. Chicano English phonology: Norms vs. interference phenomena. In J. Ornstein-Galicia (ed.), *Form and function in Chicano English.* Rowley, MA: Newberry. 42–48.

Goeke, A. 2006. Variation in ASL: Articulator deletion in two-handed signs. Unpublished ms., Gallaudet University.

Goffman, E. 1972. The neglected situation. In P. Giglioli (ed.), *Language in social contexts.* New York: Penguin. 61–66.

Gordon, M.J. 2001. *Small-town values and big-city vowels: A study of the Northern Cities Shift in Michigan.* Publication of the American Dialect Society 84. Durham, NC: Duke University Press.

Grabe, E. 2004. Intonational variation in urban dialects of English spoken in the British Isles. In P. Gilles and J. Peters (eds.), *Regional variation in intonation.* Tübingen: Max Niemeyer Verlag. 9–31.

Grabe, E., Post, B., Nolan, F., and Farrar, K. 2000. Pitch accent realization in four varieties of British English. *Journal of Phonetics* 28: 161–185.

Graham, S. 1992. Most of the participants were Caucasian and middle class. *American Psychologist* 47: 629–639.

Grant, T., and Baker, K. 2001. Identifying reliable, valid markers of authorship: A reply to Chaski. *Forensic Linguistics: The International Journal of Speech, Language, and the Law* 8: 66–79.

Green, L. 1990. Intonational patterns of questions in black English: Some observations. Unpublished ms., University of Massachusetts.

Green, L. 2001. Negative concord and negative inversion in African American English. Unpublished ms., University of Texas at Austin.

Green, L. 2002. *African American English: A linguistic introduction*. Cambridge: Cambridge University Press.

Green, L. 2005. Negation in African American English. Paper presented at the First International Conference on the Linguistics of Contemporary English, University of Edinburgh, Scotland.

Gregg, K. 1990. The variable competence model of second language acquisition, and why it isn't. *Applied Linguistics* 11: 365–383.

Grier, S. 2001. The FTC report on the marketing of violent entertainment to youth: Developing policy tuned research. *Journal of Public Policy and Marketing* 20: 123, 132.

Groer, A., and Gerhart, A. 1997, January 8. Bill Cosby, standing up for the caucus. *The Washington Post*. C3.

Guasti, M.T. 2002. *Language acquisition: The growth of grammar*. Cambridge, MA: MIT Press.

Guenter, J. 2000. Vowels of California English before /r/, /l/, and /n/. Ph.D. dissertation, University of California, Berkeley.

Gumperz, J.J., and Hymes, D. (eds.). 1972. *Directions in sociolinguistics: The ethnography of communication*. New York: Holt, Rinehart, and Winston.

Gussenhoven, C., and van der Vliet, P. 1999. The phonology of tone and intonation in the Dutch dialect of Venlo. *Journal of Linguistics* 35: 99–135.

Gut, U. 2002. Prosodic aspects of Standard Nigerian English. In U. Gut and D. Gibbon (eds.), *Typology of African prosodic systems*. Bielefeld, Germany: Bielefeld Occasional Papers in Typology 1: 167–178.

Gut, U., Urua, E.-A., Adouakou, S., and Gibbon, D. 2002. Rhythm in West African tone languages: A study of Ibibio, Anyi and Ega. In U. Gut and D. Gibbon (eds.), *Typology of African prosodic systems*. Bielefeld, Germany: Bielefeld Occasional Papers in Typology 1: 159–65.

Guy, G.R. 1980. Variation in the group and in the individual: The case of final stop deletion. In W. Labov (ed.), *Locating language in time and space*. New York: Academic. 1–36.

Guy, G.R. 1981. *Linguistic variation in Brazilian Portuguese: Aspects of the phonology, syntax, and language history*. Sydney: Sydney University, Department of Linguistics.

Guy, G.R. 1988. Advanced VARBRUL analysis. In K. Ferrara, B. Brown, K. Walters, and J. Baugh (eds.), *Linguistic change and contact*. Austin: Department of Linguistics, University of Texas at Austin. 124–136.

Guy, G.R. 1991a. Contextual conditioning in variable lexical phonology. *Language Variation and Change* 3: 223–239.

Guy, G.R. 1991b. Explanation in variable phonology: An exponential model of morphological constraints. *Language Variation and Change* 3: 1–22.

Guy, G.R. 1993. The quantitative analysis of linguistic variation. In D.R. Preston (ed.), *American dialect research*. Amsterdam: John Benjamins. 223–249.

Guy, G.R. 1997. Violable is variable: Optimality theory and linguistic variation. *Language Variation and Change* 9: 333–348.

Guy, G.R., and Boberg, C. 1997. The obligatory contour principle and sociolinguistic variation. *Language Variation and Change* 9: 149–164.

Guy, G., Horvath, B., Vonweiler, J., Daisley, E., and Rogers, I. 1986. An intonational change in progress in Australian English. *Language in Society* 15: 22–52.

Haack, S. 2003. *Defending science within reason: Between scientism and cynicism*. Amherst, NY: Prometheus Books.

Habick, T. 1980. Sound change in Farmer City: A sociolinguistic study based on acoustic data. Ph.D. dissertation, University of Illinois at Urbana-Champaign.

Hakuta, K. 1976. A case study of a Japanese child learning English as a second language. *Language Learning* 26: 321–351.

Hall, K., and Bucholtz, M. 1995. *Gender articulated: Language and the socially contructed self*. London: Routledge.

Halliday, M.A.K. 1973. *Explorations in the functions of language*. London: Edward Arnold.

Hammersley, M. 1995. *The politics of social research*. London: Sage.

Hammersley, M., and Atkinson, P. 1995. *Ethnography: Principles and practice*, 2nd edn. New York: Routledge.

Hancock, I.F. 1987. A preliminary classification of the Anglophone Caribbean creoles, with syntactic data from thirty-three representative dialects. In G. Gilbert (ed.), *Pidgin and creole languages: Essays in memory of John E. Reinecke*. Honolulu: University of Hawaii Press. 264–333.

Hanham, A. (ed.). 1975. *The Cely letters, 1472–1488*. London: Early English Text Society.

Harper, M.S., and Walton, A. 2000. Paul Laurence Dunbar (1872–1906). In M.S. Harper and A. Walton (eds.), *The Vintage book of African American Poetry: 200 years of vision, struggle, power, beauty and triumph from 50 outstanding poets*. New York: Vintage. 72–73.

Harris, J. 1996a, December 25. U.S. bilingual education funds ruled out for Ebonics speakers. *The Washington Post*. A2.

Harris, J. 1996b. Issues in recruiting African American participants for research. In A. Kamhi, K. Pollock, and J. Harris (eds.) *Communication development and disorders in African American children: Research, assessment, and intervention*. Baltimore, MD: Brookes Publishers. 19–34.

Harris-Wright, K. 1999. Enhancing bidialectalism in urban African American students. In C.T. Adger, D. Christian, and O. Taylor (eds.), *Making the connection: Language and academic achievement among African American students*. McHenry, IL and Washington, DC: Delta Systems and Center for Applied Linguistics. 53–60.

Hart, B., and Risley, T. 1995. *Meaningful differences*. Baltimore: Brookes Publishers.

Hawkins, S. 2003. Roles and representations of systematic fine phonetic detail in speech understanding. *Journal of Phonetics* 31: 373–405.

Hay, J., and Sudbury, A. 2005. How rhoticity became /r/-sandhi. *Language* 81: 799–823.

Hazen, K. 1998. The birth of a variant: Evidence for a tripartite negative past *be* paradigm. *Language Variation and Change* 10: 221–244.

Hazen, K. 2000a. *Identity and ethnicity in the rural South: A sociolinguistic view through past and present Be*. Publication of the American Dialect Society 83. Durham, NC: Duke University Press.

Hazen, K. 2000b. Subject-verb concord in a post-insular dialect: The gradual persistence of dialect patterning. *Journal of English Linguistics* 28: 127–144.

Hazen, K. 2001. An introductory investigation into bidialectalism. *University of Pennsylvania Working Papers in Linguistics* 7(3): 85–100.

Hazen, K. 2002. Identity and language variation in a rural community. *Language* 78: 240–257.

Heidelberger Forschungsprojekt "Pidgin-Deutsch." 1978. The acquisition of German syntax by foreign migrant workers. In D. Sankoff (ed.), *Linguistic variation: Models and methods*. New York: Academic. 1–22.

Hendrick, R. 1982. Reduced questions and their theoretical implications. *Language* 58: 800–819.

Henry, A. 1995. *Belfast English and standard English: Dialect variation and parameter setting*. New York: Oxford University Press.

Henry, A. 2002. Variation and syntactic theory. In J.K. Chambers, P. Trudgill, and N. Schilling-Estes (eds.), *The handbook of language variation and change*. Oxford: Blackwell. 267–282.

Henry, A., Maclaren, R., Wilson, J., and Finlay, C. 1997. The acquisition of negative concord in non-standard English. In E. Hughes, M. Hughes, and A. Green (eds.), *Proceedings of the 21st Annual Boston University Conference on Language Development*, vol. 1. Somerville, MA: Cascadilla Press. 281–292.

Henton, C.G., and Bladon, R.A.W. 1985. Breathiness in a normal female speaker: Inefficiency versus desirability. *Language and Communication* 5: 221–227.

Henwood, K., and Pidgeon, N. 1993. Qualitative research and psychological theorizing. In M. Hammersley (ed.), *Social research: philosophy, politics and practice*. London: Sage. 14–32.

Heselwood, B., and McChrystal, L. 1999. The effect of age-group and place of L1 acquisition on the realisation of Panjabi stop consonants in Bradford: An acoustic sociophonetic study. *Leeds Working Papers in Linguistics* 7: 49–68.

Heuven, V.J. van, Edelman, L., and van Bezooijen, R. 2002. The pronunciation of /Ei/ by male and female speakers of avant-garde Dutch. In H. Broekhuis and P. Fikkert (eds.), *Linguistics in the Netherlands 2002*. Amsterdam: John Benjamins. 61–72.

Hickey, R. 2003. Corpus Presentor: Software for language analysis with a manual and a corpus of Irish English as sample data. Amsterdam: John Benjamins.

Hill, J.H., and Hill, K.C. 1986. *Speaking Mexicano: Dynamics of syncretic language in central Mexico*. Tucson: University of Arizona Press.

Hillenbrand, J., Cleveland, R.A., and Erickson, R.L. 1994. Acoustic correlates of breathy vocal quality. *Journal of Speech and Hearing Research* 37: 769–778.

Hindle, D.M. 1979. The social and situational conditioning of phonetic variation. Ph.D. dissertation, University of Pennsylvania.

Hirsch, S.F. 1998. *Pronouncing and persevering: Gender and the discourses of disputing in an African Islamic court*. Chicago: University of Chicago Press.

Hitchcock, C. 2004. Contemporary debates in philosophy of science. Malden, MA: Blackwell.

Hoffman, M. 2004a. All for none and none for all: /s/ deletion in the group and the individual. Paper presented at the Conference on New Ways of Analyzing Variation 33, University of Michigan, September 30–October 3.

Hoffman, M. 2004b. Sounding Salvadorean. Phonological variables in the Spanish of Salvadorean youth in Toronto. Ph.D. dissertation, University of Toronto.

Hollien, H. 1990. *The acoustics of crime*. New York: Plenum.

Holmes, J. 1997. Maori and Pakeha English: Some New Zealand social dialect data. *Language in Society* 26: 65–101.

Holquist, M. 1981. Introduction. In M.M. Bakhtin, *The dialogic imagination* (ed. M. Holquist, trans. C. Emerson and M. Holquist). Austin: University of Texas Press. xv–xxxiv.

Holton, S.W. 1984. *Down home and uptown: The representation of black speech in American fiction*. Rutherford, NJ: Fairleigh Dickinson University Press.

Hoopes, R. 1998. A preliminary examination of pinky extension: Suggestions regarding its occurrence, constraints, and function. In C. Lucas (ed.), *Pinky extension and eye gaze: Language use in Deaf communities*. Sociolinguistics in Deaf Communities, vol. 4. Washington, DC: Gallaudet University Press. 3–17.

Hoover, M. 1978. Community attitudes toward black English. *Language in Society* 7: 65–87.

Horvath, B. 1985. *Variation in Australian English*. Cambridge: Cambridge University Press.

Houston, A. 1985. Continuity and change in English morphology: The variable (ING). Ph.D. dissertation, University of Pennsylvania.

Howard, M., Lemée, I., and Regan, V. 2006. The L2 acquisition of a phonological variable: The case of /l/ deletion in French. *Journal of French Language Studies* 16: 1–24.

Huber, M. 2004. Nova Scotian-Sierra Leone connection: New evidence on an early variety of African American Vernacular English in the diaspora. In G. Escure and A. Schwengler (eds.), *Creoles, contact, and language change: Linguistics and social implications*. Amsterdam: John Benjamins. 67–95.

Hudson, A.I., and Holbrook, A. 1981. A study of reading fundamental frequency of young Black adults. *Journal of Speech and Hearing Research* 24: 197–201.

Huebner, T. 1983. *A longitudinal study of the acquisition of English*. Ann Arbor, MI: Karoma.

Hunter, K. 1997, January 17. Ebonics is Black-on-Black crime. *New York Daily News*. 41.

Hutcheson, N. (producer). 2005. Voices of North Carolina. Raleigh: North Carolina Language and Life Project.

Hymes, D. 1972a. Models of the interaction of language and social life. In J.J. Gumperz and D. Hymes (eds.), *Directions in sociolinguistics*. New York: Holt, Rinehart, and Winston. 35–71.

Hymes, D. 1972b. The scope of sociolinguistics. In R.W. Shuy (ed.), *Sociolinguistics: Current trends and prospects*. Washington, DC: Georgetown University Press. 313–333.

Hymes, D. 1974. *Foundations in sociolinguistics*. Philadelphia: University of Pennsylvania Press.

Ihalainen, O. 1994. The dialects of England since 1776. In R. Burchfield (ed.), *Cambridge history of the English language, vol. 5: English in Britain and overseas*. Cambridge: Cambridge University Press. 197–274.

Irish, J.A.G. (ed.). 1995. *Caribbean students in New York. Occasional Paper* no. 1. New York: Caribbean Diaspora Press.

Ito, R., and Preston, D.R. 1998. Identity, discourse, and language variation. *Journal of Language and Social Psychology* 17: 465–483.

Jaberg, K., and Jud, J. 1928–43. *Sprach- und Sachatlas Italiens und der Südschweiz*. 8 vols. Zofingen: Ringier.

Jakendoff, R. 1994. *Patterns in the mind*. New York: Basic Books.

Janson, T. 1983. Sound change in perception and production. *Language* 59: 18–34.

Janson, T., and Schulman, R. 1983. Non-distinctive features and their use. *Journal of Linguistics* 19: 321–336.

Jefferson, M. 1997, January 7. The two faces of Ebonics: Disguise and giveaway. *The New York Times*. C11.

Johnson, A. 1997. Textual kidnapping – A case of plagiarism among three student texts? *Forensic Linguistics: The International Journal of Speech Language and the Law* 4: 210–225.

Johnson, J.W. 1927. *God's trombones: Seven Negro sermons in verse*. New York: Viking Press.

Johnson, J.W. 1933. *Along this way: The autobiography of James Weldon Johnson*. New York: Viking Press.

Johnson, K. 1997. Speech perception without speaker normalization. In K. Johnson and J.W. Mullenix (eds.), *Talker variability in speech processing*. San Diego: Academic. 145–165.

Johnson, K. 2003. *Acoustic and auditory phonetics*, 2nd edn. Oxford: Blackwell.

Johnson, K. In press. Resonance in an exemplar-based lexicon: The emergence of social identity and phonology. *Journal of Phonetics*.

Johnson, K., and Mullenix, J.W. 1997. *Talker variability in speech processing*. San Diego: Academic.

Johnstone, B. 1988. Local color: Orientational detail in midwestern personal narrative. In K. Ferrara, B. Brown, K. Walters, and J. Baugh (eds.), *Linguistic change and contact: Proceedings of the Sixteenth Annual Conference on New Ways of Analyzing Variation*. Austin: Department of Linguistics, University of Texas. 152–159.

Johnstone, B. 2000. *Qualitative methods in sociolinguistics*. New York: Oxford University Press.

Joiner, C.W. 1979. Memorandum opinion and order: Martin Luther King Junior Elementary School Children et al. v. Ann Arbor District School Board. In *The Ann Arbor decision: Memorandum, opinion and order and the Educational Plan*. Arlington, VA: Center for Applied Linguistics. 1–11.

Jones, C.F. 1991. Appendix: Some grammatical characteristics of the Sierra Leone letters. In C. Fyfe (ed.), *"Our children free and happy": Letters from black settlers in Africa in the 1790s*. Edinburgh: Edinburgh University Press. 79–104.

Jones, M., and Tagliamonte, S. 2004. From Somerset to Samaná: Preverbal *Did* in the voyage of English. *Language Variation and Change* 16: 93–126.

Jordan, J. 1985. Nobody mean more to me than you and the future life of Willie Jordan. *On call: Political essays*. Boston: South End. 123–139.

Joseph, B., and Wallace, R. 1992. Socially determined variation in ancient Rome. *Language Variation and Change* 4: 105–119.

Jowett, B. (trans.). 1937. *The dialogues of Plato*. New York: Random House.

Jun, S.-A., and Foreman, C. 1996. Boundary tones and focus realization in African-American intonation. Paper presented at the 3rd Joint Meeting of the Acoustical Society of America and the Acoustical Society of Japan, Honolulu, HI, December 6.

Kamhi, A., Pollock, K., and Harris, J. 1996. *Communication development and disorders in African American children: Research, assessment and intervention*. Baltimore, MD: Paul Brookes.

Kaminskaia, S., and Poire, F. 2004. Comparing intonation of two varieties of French using normalized F_0 values. Paper presented at Interspeech 2004/8th International Conference on Spoken Language Processing, Jeju Island, Korea, October 4–8. www.isca-speech.org/archive/interspeech_2004/i04_1305.html

Kaplan, A. 1984. Philosophy of science in anthropology. *Annual Review of Anthropology* 13, 25–38.

Kautzsch, A. 2002. *The historical evolution of earlier African American English: An empirical comparison of early sources*. Berlin: Mouton de Gruyter.

Kayne, R. 2000. *Parameters and universals*. New York: Oxford.

Keep, J.R. 1857. The mode of learning the sign language. In *Convention of American Instructors of the Deaf, Proceedings*. 133–153.

Kendall, T. 2006a. A sociolinguistic analysis of pause in North Carolina. Paper presented at the Southeastern Conference on Linguistics, Auburn, AL, April 29.

Kendall, T. 2006b. Listening to silence: Interpretation and transcription of pause in deposition. Paper presented at the Second European IAFL Conference on Forensic Linguistics /Language and Law, Barcelona, Spain, September 14–16.

Kiesling, S.F. 1998. Men's identities and sociolinguistic variation: The case of fraternity men. *Journal of Sociolinguistics* 2: 69–99.

Kingston, J., and Diehl, R.L. 1994. Phonetic knowledge. *Language* 70: 419–454.

Kiparsky, P. In press. Where Stochastic OT fails: a discrete model of metrical variation. *BLS 31, Prosodic variation and change*. Berkeley: Berkeley Linguistics Society.

Kloeke, G.G. 1927. De Hollandsche expansie de zestiende en zeventiende eeuw en haar weerspiegeling in de hedendaagsche Nederlandsche dialecten. The Hague: Nijhoff.

Koenig, B.E. 1993. Enhancement of tape-recorded voices to facilitate transcription and aural identification. Legal Language Services. www.legallanguage.com/forensic/Spectrographic.htm

Koerner, K. 1991. Toward a history of modern sociolinguistics. *American Speech* 66: 57–70.

Kolakowski, L. 1993. An overview of positivism. In M. Hammersley (ed.), *Social research: Philosophy, politics and practice*. London: Sage Publications. 1–8.

Kovac (Lucas), C. 1980. *Children's acquisition of variable features*. Ph.D. dissertation, Georgetown University.

Kovac (Lucas), C., and Adamson, H.D. 1981. Variation theory and first language acqusition. In D. Sankoff and H. Cedergren (eds.), *Variation omnibus*. Edmonton: Linguistic Research. 403–410.

Kroch, A. 1989a. Function and grammar in the history of English: Periphrastic *do*. In R.W. Fasold and D. Schiffrin, (eds.), *Language variation and change*. Philadelphia: John Benjamins. 133–172.

Kroch, A. 1989b. Reflexes of grammar in patterns of language change. *Language Variation and Change* 1: 199–244.

Kroch, A. 1994. Morphosyntactic variation. In R. Knippen, L. Melnar, H. Suzuki, and E. Zeinfeld (eds.), *Papers from the 30th Regional Meeting of the Chicago Linguistics Society, vol 2*. Chicago: Chicago University Press. 180–201.

Kuhl, P.K. 1991. Human adults and human infants show a "perceptual magnet effect" for the prototypes of speech categories, monkeys do not. *Perception and Psychophysics* 50: 93–107.

Kuhn, T. 1970. *The structure of scientific revolutions*. Chicago: University of Chicago Press.

Kurath, H. 1949. *Word geography of the eastern United States*. Ann Arbor: University of Michigan Press.

Kurath, H., and McDavid, R.I., Jr. 1961. *The pronunciation of English in the Atlantic states*. Ann Arbor: University of Michigan Press.

Kurath, H. *et al.* 1941. *Linguistic atlas of New England*. Providence: American Council of Learned Societies.

Kypriotaki, L. 1973. A study of dialect: Individual variation and dialect rules. In C.-J.N. Bailey and R.W. Shuy (eds.), *New ways of analyzing variation in English*. Washington, DC: Georgetown University Press. 198–210.

Kytö, M. 1996. *Manual to the diachronic part of the Helsinki Corpus of English Texts*. http://khnt.hit.uib.no/icame/manuals/HC/INDEX.HTM

Kytö, M., and Rissanen, M. 1997. Language analysis and diachronic corpora. In R. Hickey, M. Kytö, I. Lancashire, and M. Rissanen (eds.), *Tracing the trail of time: Proceedings from the Second Diachronic Corpora Workshop, New College, University of Toronto, Toronto, May 1995*. Amsterdam: Rodopi. 9–24.

Laboratory of Comparative Human Cognition at University of California-San Diego. 1983. Paradigms and prejudice. *The Quarterly Newsletter of the Laboratory of Comparative Human Cognition* 5(1): 87–92.

Labov, W. 1963. The social motivation of a sound change. *Word* 19: 273–309.

Labov, W. 1966. *The social stratification of English in New York City*. Washington, DC: Center for Applied Linguistics.

Labov, W. 1969. Contraction, deletion, and inherent variability of the English copula. *Language* 45: 715–762.

Labov, W. 1970. The logic of non-standard English. In J. Alatis (ed.), *Linguistics and the teaching of standard English to speakers of other languages and dialects. Georgetown University Round Table on Languages and Linguistics 1969*. Washington, DC: Georgetown University Press. 1–44.

Labov, W. 1972a. Academic ignorance and Black intelligence. *The Atlantic Monthly* 229: 59–67.

Labov, W. 1972b. *Language in the inner city: Studies in the Black English vernacular*. Philadelphia: University of Pennsylvannia Press.

Labov, W. 1972c. The linguistic consequences of being a lame. In *Language in the inner city*. Philadelphia: University of Pennsylvania Press. 255–292.

Labov, W. 1972d. Negative attraction and negative concord in English grammar. *Language* 48: 773–818.

Labov, W. 1972e. Rules for ritual insults. In T. Kochman (ed.), *Rappin' and stylin' out: Communication in urban Black America*. Urbana-Champaign: University of Illinois Press. 265–314.

Labov, W. 1972f. The social stratification of (r) in New York City department stores. In W. Labov, *Sociolinguistic patterns*. Philadelphia: University of Pennsylvania Press. 43–69.

Labov, W. 1972g. *Sociolinguistic patterns*. Philadelphia: University of Pennsylvania Press.

Labov, W. 1972h. Some principles of linguistic methodology. *Language in Society* 1: 97–120.

Labov, W. 1972i. The study of language in its social context. In W. Labov, *Sociolinguistic patterns*. Philadelphia: University of Pennsylvania Press. 183–259.

Labov, W. 1980. The social origins of sound change. In W. Labov (ed.), *Locating Language in time and space*. New York: Academic. 251–265.

Labov, W. 1982. Objectivity and commitment in linguistic science. *Language in Society* 11: 165–201.

Labov, W. 1984. Field methods of the project on linguistic change and variation. In J. Baugh and J. Sherzer (eds.), *Language in use: Readings in sociolinguistics*. Englewood Cliffs, NJ: Prentice Hall. 28–53.

Labov, W. 1988. The judicial testing of linguistic theory. In D. Tannen (ed.), *Linguistics in context: Connecting observation and understanding*. Norwood, NJ: Ablex. 159–182.

Labov, W. 1989. The child as linguistic historian. *Language Variation and Change* 1: 85–97.

Labov, W. 1990. The intersection of sex and social class in the course of linguistic change. *Language Variation and Change* 2: 205–254.

Labov, W. 1991. The three dialects of English. In P. Eckert (ed.), *New ways of analyzing sound change*. New York: Academic. 1–44.

Labov, W. 1994. *Principles of linguistic change, vol. 1: Internal factors*. Oxford: Blackwell.

Labov, W. 1998. Co-existent systems in African-American English. In S. Mufwene, J.R. Rickford, G. Bailey, and J. Baugh (eds.), *African-American English*. London: Routledge. 110–154.

Labov, W. 2001. *Principles of linguistic change, vol 2: Social factors*. Oxford: Blackwell.

Labov, W., and Ash, S. 1997. Understanding Birmingham. In C. Bernstein, T. Nunnally, and R. Sabino (eds.), *Language variety in the South revisited*. Tuscaloosa: University of Alabama Press. 508–573.

Labov, W., Ash, S., and Boberg, C. 2006. *The atlas of North American English: Phonetics, phonology, and sound change*. New York: Mouton de Gruyter.

Labov, W., Cohen, P., Robbins, C., and Lewis, J. 1968. *A study of non-standard English of Negro and Puerto Rican speakers in New York City*. 2 vols. Philadelphia: US Regional Survey.

Labov, W., Karen, M., and Miller, C. 1991. Near-mergers and the suspension of phonemic contrast. *Language Variation and Change* 3: 33–74.

Labov, W., Yaeger, M., and Steiner, R. 1972. *A quantitative study of sound change in progress*. Philadelphia: U.S. Regional Survey.

Ladefoged, P. 1993. *A course in phonetics*, 3rd edn. New York: Harcourt Brace Jovanovitch.

Lado, L. 1957. *Linguistics across cultures: Applied linguistics for language teachers*. Ann Arbor: University of Michigan Press.

Laffey, J., and Shuy, R.W. (eds.). 1973. *Language differences: Do they interfere?* Newark, DE: International Reading Association.

Lakoff, R. 1975. *Language and woman's place*. New York: Harper and Row.

Lambert, W.E. 1972. *Language, psychology, and culture: Essays*. Ed. by A.S. Dil. Stanford, CA: Stanford University Press.

Lambert, W.E., Hodgsen, R.C., Gardner, R.D., and Fillenbaum, S. 1960. Evaluational reaction to spoken language. *Journal of Abnormal and Social Psychology* 60: 44–51.

Lane, H., Hoffmeister, R., and Bahan, B. 1996. *Journey into the DEAF^WORLD*. San Diego: DawnSign Press.

Langman, J., and Bayley, R. 2002. The acquisition of verbal morphology by Chinese learners of Hungarian. *Language Variation and Change* 14: 55–77.

Lee, M. 2002. A pause for the cause: African American folk sayings in rhyme. Paper presented at the NWAV-31 Preconference on AAVE, Stanford, October.

LeMoine, N. 2001. Language variation and literacy acquisition in African American students. In J.L. Harris, A.G. Kamhi, and K.E. Pollock (eds.), *Literacy in African American communities*. Mahwah, N.J: Erlbaum. 169–194.

LeMoine, N., and the Los Angeles Unified School District. 1999. *English for your success: A language development program for African American children*. Maywood, NJ: Peoples Publishing Group.

Lentine, G., and Shuy, R.W. 1990. *Mc-*: Meaning in the marketplace. *American Speech* 65: 349–366.

Leonard, T.C. 2002. Reflections on rules in science: An invisible-hand perspective. *Journal of Economic Methodology* 9(2): 141–168.

Le Page, R.B. 1968. Problems to be faced in the use of English as a medium of education in four West Indian territories. In J. Fishman, C.A. Ferguson, and J. Das Gupta (eds.), *Language problems of developing nations*. New York: John Wiley. 431–443.

Lerner, R. 1990. Changing organism-context relations as the basic process of development: A developmental contextual perspective. *Developmental Psychology* 27: 27–32.

Levelt, W.J.M. 1989. *Speaking: From interaction to articulation*. Cambridge, MA: MIT Press.

Levi, J.N., and Walker, A.G. (eds.). 1990. *Language in the judicial process*. Law, Society, and Policy, vol. 5. New York: Plenum.

Lewis, J.W. 1994. The Yorkshire Ripper inquiry: Part II. *International Journal of Speech, Language and the Law* 1: 207–216.

Lewis, J.W. 1995. *Studies in general and English phonetics: Essays in honour of Professor J.D. O'Connor*. London: Routledge.

Lewis, N.A. 1996, December 23. Black English isn't a second language, Jackson says. *The New York Times*. B9.

Liddell, S.K., and Johnson, R.E. 1989. American Sign Language: The phonological base. *Sign Language Studies* 64: 195–278.

Lightfoot, D. 1999. Creoles and cues. In M. DeGraff (ed.), *Language creation and language change: Creolization, diachrony, and development*. Cambridge, MA: MIT Press. 431–452.

Linguistic confusion. 1996, December 24. *The New York Times*. A10.

Linguistic Society of America. 1997, January. *LSA resolution on the Oakland "Ebonics" issue*. www.lsadc.org/web2/ebonicsfr.htm

Lippi-Green, R. 1994. Accent, standard language ideology, and discriminatory pretext in the courts. *Language and Society* 23: 163–198.

Lippi-Green, R. 1997. *English with an accent*. New York: Routledge.

Loman, B. 1975. Prosodic patterns in a Negro American dialect. In H. Ringbom, A. Ingberg, R. Norrman, K. Nyholm, R. Westman, and K. Wikberg (eds.), *Style and text: Studies presented to Nils Erik Enkvist*. Stockholm: Språkförlaget Skriptor AB. 219–242.

Low, E.L., and Grabe, E. 1995. Prosodic patterns in Singapore English. In K. Elenius and P. Branderud, (eds.), *Proceedings of The XIIIth International Congress of Phonetic Sciences, vol. 3*. Stockholm: KTH and Stockholm University. 636–639.

Low, E.L., Grabe, E., and Nolan, F. 2000. Quantitative characterizations of speech rhythm: Syllable-timing in Singapore English. *Language and Speech* 43: 377–401.

Lucas, C. 1995. Sociolinguistic variation in ASL: The case of DEAF. In C. Lucas (ed.), *Sociolinguistics in Deaf communities*. Washington, DC: Gallaudet University Press. 3–25.

Lucas, C. (ed.). 2001. *The sociolinguistics of sign languages*. New York: Cambridge University Press.

Lucas, C. (ed.). 2003. *Language and the law in Deaf communities*. Washington, DC: Gallaudet University Press.

Lucas, C., and Bayley, R. 2005. Variation in ASL: The role of grammatical function. *Sign Language Studies* 6: 38–75.

Lucas, C., Bayley, R., and Kelly, A.B. 2005. The sociolinguistics of sign languages. In M.J. Ball (ed.), *Clinical sociolinguistics*. Oxford: Blackwell. 250–264.

Lucas, C., Bayley, R., Rose, M., and Wulf, A. 2002. The impact of variation research on Deaf communities. In D.F. Armstrong, M.A. Karchmer, and J.V. Van Cleve (eds.), *The study of signed languages; Essays in honor of William C. Stokoe*. Washington, DC: Gallaudet University Press. 137–160.

Lucas, C., Bayley, R., and Valli, C. 2001. *Sociolinguistic variation in American Sign Language*. Sociolinguistics in Deaf Communities, vol. 7. Washington, DC: Gallaudet University Press.

Lucas, C., Bayley, R., Valli, C., Rose, M., and Wulf, A. 2001. Sociolinguistic variation. In C. Lucas (ed.), *The sociolinguistics of sign languages*. Cambridge: Cambridge University Press. 61–111.

Lucas, C., and Valli, C. 1992. *Language contact in the American Deaf community*, San Diego: Academic Press.

Macaulay, R.K.S. 1978. Variation and consistency in Glaswegian English. In P. Trudgill (ed.), *Sociolinguistic patterns in British English*. London: Arnold. 105–124.

Macaulay, R.K.S. 2002. Discourse variation. In J.K. Chambers, P. Trudgill, and N. Schilling-Estes (eds.), *The handbook of language variation and change*. Oxford: Blackwell. 283–305.

Maclagan, M.A. 1982. An acoustic study of New Zealand English vowels. *New Zealand Speech Therapists' Journal* 37: 20–26.

Maddahian, E., and Sandamela, A.P. 2000. Academic English mastery program: 1998 evaluation report. Publication #781, Program Evaluation and Research Branch, Research and Evaluation Unit, Los Angeles Unified School District.

Major, R.C. 2004. Gender and sylistic variation in second language phonology. *Language Variation and Change* 16: 169–188.

Mallinson, C. 2006. The dynamic construction of race, class, and gender through linguistic practice among women in a black Appalachian community. Ph.D. dissertation, North Carolina State University.

Mallinson, C., and Childs, B. In press. The language of Black women in the Smoky Mountain region of Appalachia. In M. Picone and C.E. Davies (eds.), *Language variety in the South: Historical and contemporary perspectives*. Tuscaloosa: University of Alabama Press.

Manion, M.L., and Bersani, H.A. 1987. Mental retardation as a western sociological construct: A cross-cultural analysis. *Disability and Society* 2: 231–245.

Mann, E., Ikeda, Y., Mueller, C., Takahashi, A., Tao, K., Humris, E., Li, B., and Chin, D. 1992. Cross-cultural differences in rating hyperactive-disruptive behaviors in children. *American Journal of Psychiatry* 149(11): 1539–1542.

Marsh, J. 1981. Social factors of language use in physician-patient interaction. In D. Sankoff and H. Cedergren (eds.), *Variation omnibus*. Edmonton: Linguistic Research. 545–562.

Martin, S.E. 1992. *Topics in the syntax of nonstandard English*. Ph.D. dissertation, University of Maryland.

Martin, S., and Wolfram, W. 1998. The sentence in African-American Vernacular English. In S. Mufwene, J.R. Rickford, G. Bailey, and J. Baugh (eds.), *African-American English*. London and New York: Routledge. 11–36.

Massey, D.S., and Lundy, G. 2001. Use of Black English and racial discrimination in urban housing markets: New methods and findings. *Urban Affairs Review* 36(4): 452–469.

Mather, J.Y. 1966. Aspects of the linguistic geography of Scotland II: East coast fishing. *Scottish Studies* 10: 129–153.

Mather, J.Y. 1972. Linguistic geography and the traditional drift-net fishery of the Scottish east coast. In M. Wakelin (ed.), *Patterns in the folk speech of the British Isles*. London: Athlone. 7–31.

Matoesian, G.M. 1993. *Reproducing rape: Domination through talk in the courtroom*. Chicago: University of Chicago Press.

Matoesian, G.M. 2001. Law and the language of identity: Discourse in the William Kennedy Smith rape trial. Oxford: Oxford University Press.

McCloskey, J. 1992. Adjunction, selection and embedded verb second. Ms. Santa Cruz: University of California.

McClure, J.D. 1995. The vowels of Scottish English – formants and features. In J.W. Lewis (ed.), *Studies in general and English phonetics: Essays in honour of Professor J.D. O'Connor*. London: Routledge. 367–378.

McDavid, R.I., Jr. 1948. Postvocalic /r/ in South Carolina: A social analysis. *American Speech* 23: 194–203.

McGrory, M. 1996, December 29. The GOP's Newt-bonics. *The Washington Post*. C1.

McGuire, G.L. 2002. The behavior of interdental fricatives in Columbus, Ohio AAVE. Poster presented at the Conference on New Ways of Analyzing Variation 31, Stanford, California, October.

McLemore, C.A. 1991. The pragmatic interpretation of English intonation: Sorority speech. Ph.D. dissertation, University of Texas at Austin.

McMenamin, G.R. 2001. Style markers in authorship studies. *Forensic Linguistics: The International Journal of Speech, Language, and the Law* 8: 93–97.

McNair, E.D. 2005. *Mill villagers and farmers: Dialect and economics in a small southern town*. Publication of the American Dialect Society 90. Durham, NC: Duke University Press.

McWhorter, J. 1997a. Wasting energy on an illusion. *The Black Scholar* 27(1): 9–14.

McWhorter, J. 1997b. Wasting energy on an illusion: Six months later. *The Black Scholar* 27(2): 2–5.

McWhorter, J. 2001. *The word on the street: Debunking the myth of pure Standard English*. New York: Plenum.

Medawar, P.B. 1984. *The limits of science*. New York: Harper and Row.

Meier, T. 1999. The case for Ebonics as part of exemplary teacher preparation. In C.T. Adger, D. Christian, and O. Taylor (eds.), *Making the connection: Language and academic achievement among African American students*. Washington, DC, and McHenry, IL: Center for Applied Linguistics and Delta Systems. 97–114.

Menand, L. 1997, January 13. Johnny be good: Ebonics and the language of cultural separatism. *The New Yorker*. 4–5.

Meurman-Solin, A. 1995. A new tool: The Helsinki Corpus of Older Scots. *ICAME Journal* 19: 49–62.

Meyer, C. 2002. *English corpus linguistics: An introduction*. Cambridge: Cambridge University Press.

Meyerhoff, M. 1994. Sounds pretty ethnic, eh? – A pragmatic particle in New Zealand English. *Language in Society* 23: 367–388.

Mielke, J., Baker, A., and Archangeli, D. 2006. Forever young: Inaudible /r/ allophony resists conventionalization. Paper presented at the annual meeting of the Linguistic Society of America, Albuquerque, January 4.

Millard, A.V. 1994. Furor in the academy: Diversity, cultural relativism, and institutional discrimination. *Graduate Post of Michigan State University* 2(1): 10–12.

Miller, M. 1984. On the perception of rhythm. *Journal of Phonetics* 12: 75–83.

Miller, P. 1982. *Amy, Wendy, and Beth*. Austin: University of Texas Press.

Miller, R. (ed.). 1978. *"Dear Master": Letters from a slave family*. Ithaca, NY: Cornell University Press.

Milloy, C. 1996, December 29. Nothing's funny about Ebonics. *The Washington Post*. B1.

Milroy, J. 1992. *Linguistic variation and change*. Oxford: Blackwell.

Milroy, L. 1987. *Language and social networks*, 2nd edn. Oxford: Blackwell.

Milroy, L., and Gordon, M. 2003. *Sociolinguistics: Method and interpretation*. Oxford: Blackwell.

Milroy, J., and Milroy, L. 1978. Belfast: Change and variation in an urban vernacular. In P. Trudgill (ed.), *Sociolinguistic patterns in British English*. London: Arnold. 19–36.

Miron, M. 1990. Psycholinguistics in the courtroom. In R.W. Rieber and W.A. Stewart (eds.), *The language scientist as expert in the legal setting*. Annals of the New York Academy of Sciences, vol. 606. New York: The New York Academy of Sciences. 55–64.

Mishoe, M., and Montgomery, M. 1994. The pragmatics of multiple modals in North and South Carolina. *American Speech* 69: 3–29.

Montgomery, M. 1989. Exploring the roots of Appalachian English. *English World-Wide* 10: 227–278.

Montgomery, M. 1994. The evolution of verb concord in Scots. In A. Fenton and D. MacDonald (eds.), *Studies in Scots and Gaelic: Proceedings of the Third International Conference on the Languages of Scotland*. Edinburgh: Canongate Academic. 81–95.

Montgomery, M. 1995. The linguistic value of Ulster emigrant letters. *Ulster Folklife* 26: 26–41.

Montgomery, M. 1997a. Making the trans-Atlantic link between varieties of English: the case of plural verbal -s. *Journal of English Linguistics* 25: 122–41.

Montgomery, M. 1997b. A tale of two Georges: the language of Irish Indian traders in colonial North America. In J. Kallen (ed.), *Focus on Ireland*. Amsterdam: John Benjamins. 227–254.

Montgomery, M. 1999. Sierra Leone Settler English: Another exported variety of African American English. *English World-Wide* 20: 1–34.

Montgomery, M. 2000. Isolation as a linguistic construct. *Southern Journal of Linguistics* 1: 25–36.

Montgomery, M. 2001a. British and Irish antecedents. In J. Algeo (ed.), *Cambridge history of the English language, vol. 6: American English*. Cambridge: Cambridge University Press. 86–153.

Montgomery, M. 2001b. Trans-Atlantic connections for variable grammatical features. *University of Pennsylvania Working Papers in Linguistics* 7(3): 205–24.

Montgomery, M. 2003. The history of American English. In D.R. Preston (ed.), *Needed research in American dialects*. Publication of the American Dialect Society 88. Durham, NC: Duke University Press. 1–23.

Montgomery, M. 2004. How the Montgomeries lost the Scots language. In J.D. McClure (ed.), *Doonsin' Emerauds: New Scrieves anent Scots and Gaelic/New Studies in Scots and Gaelic*. Belfast Studies in Language, Culture and Politics 11. Belfast: Clo Ollscoil na Banriona. 43–59.

Montgomery, M. 2005. Seeking the voices of my ancestors: A personal search for the language of the Scotch-Irish. *American Speech* 80: 341–65.

Montgomery, M. 2006. "It'll kill you or cure you, one": The history and function of alternative one. In T.E. Murray and B. Simon (eds.), *Language variation and change in the American midland*. Amsterdam: John Benjamins. 151–161.

Montgomery, M. In press. The crucial century in southern English. In M.D. Picone and C.E. Davies (eds.), *Language variety in the South: Historical and comparative perspectives.* Tuscaloosa: University of Alabama Press.

Montgomery, M., and Eble, C. 2004. Historical perspectives on the pen/pin merger in southern American English. In A. Curzan and K. Emmons (eds.), *Studies in the history of the English language II: Conversations between past and present.* Berlin: Mouton de Gruyter. 429–449.

Montgomery, M., Fuller, J.M., and DeMarse, S. 1993. "The black men has wives and sweet harts [and third person plural -s] jest like the white men": Evidence for verbal -s from written documents on nineteenth-century African American speech. *Language Variation and Change* 5: 335–354.

Montgomery, M., and Hall, J.S. 2004. *Dictionary of Smoky Mountain English.* Knoxville: University of Tennessee Press.

Montgomery, M., and Kirk, J.M. 1996. The origin of the habitual verb be in American Black English: Irish or English or what? *Belfast Working Papers in Linguistics* 11: 308–333.

Montgomery, M., and Nagle, S.J. 1994. Double modals in Scotland and the southern United States: Trans-Atlantic inheritance or independent development? *Folia Linguistica Historica* 14: 91–107.

Moreton, E., and Thomas, E.R. In press. Origins of Canadian raising in voiceless-coda effects: A case study in phonologization. In J. Cole and J.I. Hualde (eds.), *Papers in laboratory phonology 9.*

Morgan, M. In press. *The real hiphop: Battling for knowledge, power and respect in the underground.* Durham, NC: Duke University Press.

Morse, R. 1997, January 3. 1996: E coli, Odwalla, ebola, ebonics. *San Francisco Examiner.* A3.

Morton, A.Q. 1978. *Literary detection: How to prove authorship and fraud in literature.* New York: Scribner.

Mosteller, F., and Wallace, D.L. 1964. *Inference and disputed authorship: The Federalist.* Reading, MA: Addison-Wesley.

Mougeon, R., and Dewaele, J.-M. 2004. Preface. *IRAL* 42(4): 295–301 [Special issue: *Variation in the interlanguage of advanced second language learners*, eds. R. Mougeon and J.-M. Dewaele].

Mougeon, R., and Rehner, K. 2001. Variation in the spoken French of Ontario French immersion students: The case of *juste* vs. *seulement* vs. *rien que. Modern Language Journal* 85: 398–415.

Mougeon, R., Rehner, K., and Nadasdi, T. 2004. The learning of spoken French variation by immersion students from Toronto, Canada. *Journal of Sociolinguistics* 8: 408–432.

Mufwene, S.S. 1996. The founder principle in creole genesis. *Diachronica* 13: 83–134.

Mufwene, S.S. 2001. *The ecology of language evolution.* Cambridge: Cambridge University Press.

Mulkay, M. 1979. *Science and the sociology of knowledge.* London: Allen and Unwin.

Mulrooney, K. 2002. Variation in ASL fingerspelling. In C. Lucas (ed.), *Turn-taking, fingerspelling, and contact in signed languages.* Sociolinguistics in Deaf Communities, vol. 8. Washington, DC: Gallaudet University Press. 3–23.

Munro, M.J., Derwing, T.M., and Flege, J.E. 1999. Canadians in Alabama: A perceptual study of dialect acquisition in adults. *Journal of Phonetics* 27: 385–403.

Murray, S.O. 1998. *American sociolinguistics: Theorists and theory groups.* Amsterdam: John Benjamins.

Myers, S. 2005. Vowel duration and neutralization of vowel length contrasts in Kinyarwanda. *Journal of Phonetics* 33: 427–446.

Myhill, J. 1995. The use of features of present-day AAVE in the ex-slave recordings. *American Speech* 70: 115–147.

Nadasdi, T. 1995. Subject NP doubling, matching, and minority French. *Language Variation and Change* 7: 1–14.

Nagy, N., Blondeau, H., and Auger, J. 2003. Second language acquisition and "real" French: An investigation of subject doubling in the French of Montreal Anglophones. *Language Variation and Change* 15: 73–103.

Nagy, N., and Reynolds, W. 1997. Optimality theory and variable word-final deletion in Faetar. *Language Variation and Change* 9: 37–55.

Napoli, D.J. 1974. Variations on relative clauses in Italian. In R.W. Fasold and R.W. Shuy (eds.), *Studies in language variation*. Washington, DC: Georgetown University Press, 37–50.

National Council of Teachers of English/International Reading Association. 1996. *Standards for the English language arts*. Newark, DE: IRA/NCTE.

National Council of Teachers of English/National Council for the Accreditation of Teacher Education. 2003. *Program standards for the initial preparation of teachers of secondary English language arts*. Urbana, IL: NCTE.

Nelson, K. 1973. Structure and strategy in learning to talk. *Monographs of the Society for Research in Child Development* 38: 1–135.

Nero, S. (ed.). 2006. *Dialects, Englishes, Creoles and education*. Mahwah, NJ: Lawrence Erlbaum.

Neu, H. 1980. Ranking of constraints on -t,d deletion in American English. In W. Labov (ed.), *Locating language in time and space*. New York: Academic. 37–54.

Neuman, W.L. 1997. *Social research methods: Qualitative and quantitative approaches*, 3rd edn. Boston: Allyn and Bacon.

Nevalainen, T. 2000. Gender differences in the evolution of standard English. *Journal of English Linguistics* 28: 38–59.

Nevalainen, T., and Raumolin-Brunberg, H. (eds.). 1996. *Sociolinguistics and language history: Studies based on the Corpus of Early English Correspondence*. Amsterdam: Rodopi.

Niedzielski, N. 1999. The effect of social information on the perception of sociolinguistic variables. *Journal of Language and Social Psychology* 18: 62–85.

Nix, R.A. 1980. *Linguistic variation in the speech of Wilmington, North Carolina*. Ph.D. dissertation, Duke University.

Noyau, C. 1990. The development of means for temporality in the unguided acquisition of L2: Cross-linguistic perspectives. In H.W. Dechert (ed.), *Current trends in second language acquisition*. Clevedon: Multilingual Matters. 143–170.

O'Barr, W.M. 1982. *Linguistic evidence: Language, power, and strategy in the courtroom*. San Diego: Academic Press.

O'Barr, W.M., and Conley, J. 1990. *Rules versus relationships: The ethnography of legal discourse*. Chicago: University of Chicago Press.

O'Barr, W.M., and Conley, J. 1998. *Just words: Law, language, and power*. Chicago: University of Chicago Press.

O'Hear, A. 1989. *An introduction to the philosophy of science*. Oxford: Clarendon Press.

Olson, R. 1982. *Science deified and science defied*. Berkeley: University of California Press.

Olsson, J. 2004. *Forensic linguistics: An introduction to language, crime, and the law*. London: Continuum.

Oreskes, N. 1999. Rejection of continental drift: Theory and method in American earth science. Oxford: Oxford University Press.

Orton, H., Sanderson, S., and Widdowson, J. (eds.). 1978. *The linguistic atlas of England*. London: Croom Helm.

Paolillo, J. 2002. *Analyzing linguistic variation*. Stanford, CA: Center for the Study of Language and Information.

Pappas, P. 2004. *Variation and morphosyntactic change in Greek: From clitics to affixes*. New York: Palgrave Macmillan.

Pappas, T. 1998. *Plagiarism and the cultural war: The writings of Martin Luther King, Jr., and other prominent Americans*. Tampa, FL: Hallberg.

Pater, J., and Coetzee, A. 2005. Lexically specific constraints: Gradience, learnability, and perception. In *Proceedings of the 3rd Seoul International Conference on Phonology*. Seoul: The Phonology-Morphology Circle of Korea. 85–119.

Patrick, P.L. 2002. The speech community. In J.K. Chambers, P. Trudgill, and N. Schilling-Estes (eds.), *The handbook of language variation and change*. Oxford: Blackwell. 573–598.

Paul, H. 1891. *Principles of the history of language*. Trans. from the second edition by H.A. Strong. New York: Longman.

Paulston, B.P., and Tucker, G.R. (eds.). 2003. *Sociolinguistics: The essential readings*. Oxford: Blackwell Publishers.

Payne, A. 1980. Factors controlling the acquisition of the Philadelphia dialect by out-of-state children. In W. Labov (ed.), *Locating language in time and space*. New York: Academic. 143–178.

Pederson, L. *et al.* 1986–92. *Linguistic atlas of the gulf states*. 7 vols. Athens: University of Georgia Press.

Pellowe, J., and Jones, V.M. 1978. On intonational variability in Tyneside speech. In P. Trudgill (ed.), *Sociolinguistic patterns in British English*. London: Arnold. 101–21.

Penfield, J., and Ornstein-Galicia, J.L. 1985. *Chicano English: An ethnic contact dialect*. Amsterdam: John Benjamins.

Petyt, M. 1980. *The study of dialect*. Boulder, CO: Westview.

Philips, S.U. 1998. *Ideology in the language of judges: How judges practice law, politics, and courtroom control*. Oxford: Oxford University Press.

Pica, P., and Rooryck, J. (eds.). 2001. *Linguistic variation yearbook*. Amsterdam: John Benjamins.

Pickford, G.R. 1956. American linguistic geography: A sociological approach. *Word* 12: 211–233.

Pierrehumbert, J. 1994. Knowledge of variation. In Beals *et al.* (eds.), *CLS 30, vol. 2: Parasession on Variation in Linguistic Theory*. Chicago: Chicago Linguistic Society. 232–256.

Pierrehumbert, J. 2003. Probabilistic phonology: Discrimation and robustness. In R. Bod, J. Hay, and S. Jannedy (eds.), *Probabilistic linguistics*. Cambridge, MA: MIT Press. 177–228.

Pike, K.L. 1945. *The intonation of American English*. Ann Arbor: University of Michigan.

Pisoni, D.B. 1997. Some thoughts on "normalization" in speech perception. In K. Johnson and J.W. Mullennix (eds.), *Talker variability in speech processing*. San Diego: Academic Press. 9–32.

Pitiless hoax: Ebonics hinders learning standard English. 1996, December 23. *The San Diego Union-Tribune*. B6.

Plichta, B. 2002. Coarticulatory nasalization and the Northern Cities vowel shift: Is /æ/ really raising? Paper presented at NWAV 31, Stanford University, October 10–13.

Plichta, B. 2006. Interdisciplinary perspectives on the Northern Cities chain shift. Ph.D. dissertation, Michigan State University.

Plichta, B., Preston, D.R., and Rakerd, B. 2005. "Did you say sod or sad?" Speaker cues and hearer identity in vowel perception in an area of ongoing change. Paper presented at Methods XII: 12th International Conference on Methods in Dialectology, Moncton, New Brunswick, August.

Ploch, D.R., Dumas, B.K., Gray, G.B., McLennan, B.J., and Nolt, J.E. 1993. Readability of the law: Forms of law for building legal expert systems. *Jurimetrics Journal* 33: 189–221.

Poplack, S. 1980a. Deletion and disambiguation in Puerto Rican Spanish. *Language* 56: 371–385.

Poplack, S. 1980b. The notion of plural in Puerto Rican Spanish: Competing constraints on /s/ deletion. In W. Labov (ed.), *Locating language in time and space*. New York: Academic. 55–68.

Poplack, S. (ed.). 2000a. *The English history of African-American English*. Oxford: Blackwell.

Poplack, S. 2000b. Introduction. In S. Poplack (ed.), *The English history of African-American English*. Oxford: Blackwell. 1–32.

Poplack, S., and Tagliamonte, S. 1989. There's no tense like the present: Verbal -s inflection in early Black English. *Language Variation and Change* 1: 47–84.

Poplack, S., and Tagliamonte, S. 2001. *African American English in the diaspora*. Oxford: Blackwell.

Port, R.F., and Leary, A.P. 2005. Against formal phonology. *Language* 81: 927–964.

Preston, D.R. 1989. *Sociolinguistics and second language acquisition*. Oxford: Blackwell.

Preston, D.R. 1991a. Sorting out the variables in sociolinguistic theory. *American Speech* 66: 33–56.

Preston, D.R. 1991b. Style, status, and change: Three sociolinguistic axioms. In F. Byrne and T. Huebner (eds.), *Development and structures of creole languages. Essays in honor of Derek Bickerton*. Amsterdam: John Benjamins. 43–59.

Preston, D.R. 1991c. Variable rules and second language acquisition: An integrationist attempt. *PALM (Papers in Applied Linguistics Michigan)* 6: 1–12.

Preston, D.R. 1992. Talking black and talking white: A study in variety imitation. In J.J. Hall, N. Doane, and D. Ringler (eds.), *Old English and new: Studies in language and linguistics in honor of Frederic G. Cassidy*. New York: Garland. 327–355.

Preston, D.R. 1996a. Variationist perspectives on second language acquisition. In R. Bayley and D.R. Preston (eds.), *Second language acquisition and linguistic variation*. Amsterdam: John Benjamins. 1–45.

Preston, D.R. 1996b. Variationist linguistics and second language acquisition. In W.C. Ritchie and T.K. Bhatia (eds.), *Handbook of second language acquisition*. New York: Academic. 229–265.

Preston, D.R. 1996c. Whaddayaknow? The modes of folk linguistic awareness. *Language Awareness* 5: 40–77.

Preston, D.R. 2000a. Some plain facts about Americans and their language. *American Speech* 75: 398–400.

Preston, D.R. 2000b. Three kinds of sociolinguistics and SLA: A psycholinguistic perspective. In B. Swierzbin, F. Morris, M.A. Anderson, C.A. Klee, and E. Tarone (eds.), *Social and cognitive factors in second language acquisition: Selected Proceedings of the 1999 Second Language Research Forum*. Somerville, MA: Cascadilla Press. 3–30.

Preston, D.R. 2001a. Applied linguistics and sociolinguistics. In R. Mesthrie (ed.), *Concise encyclopedia of sociolinguistics*. Oxford: Elsevier. 691–696.

Preston, D.R. 2001b. Style and the psycholinguistics of sociolinguistics: The logical problem of language variation. In P. Eckert and J.R. Rickford (eds.), *Style and sociolinguistic variation*. Cambridge: Cambridge University Press. 279–304.

Preston, D.R. 2002. A variationist perspective on second language acquisition: A psycholinguistic view. In R.B. Kaplan (ed.), *The Oxford handbook of Applied Linguistics*. Oxford: Oxford University Press. 141–159.

Preston, D.R. 2004. Three kinds of sociolinguistics: A psycholinguistic perspective. In C. Fought (ed.), *Sociolinguistic Variation: Critical Reflections*. Oxford: Oxford University Press. 140–158.

Preston, D.R., and Long, D. (eds.). 2002. *Handbook of perceptual dialectology, vol. II*. Amsterdam: John Benjamins.

Purnell, T., Idsardi, W., and Baugh, J. 1999. Perceptual and phonetic experiments on American English dialect identification. *Journal of Language and Social Psychology* 18: 10–30.

Purnell, T., Salmons, J., and Tepeli, D. 2005. German substrate effects in Wisconsin English: Evidence for final fortition. *American Speech* 80: 135–164.

Purnell, T., Tepeli, D., Salmons, J., and Mercer, J. 2005. Structured heterogeneity and change in laryngeal phonetics: Upper Midwestern final obstruents. *Journal of English Linguistics* 33: 307–338.

Quirk, R., Greenbaum, S., Leech, G., and Svartvik, J. 1972. *A grammar of contemporary English*. London: Longman.

Radford, A. 1997. *Syntax*. Cambridge: Cambridge University Press.

Rampton, B. (ed.). 1999. *Styling the other*. Theme issue of *Journal of Sociolinguistics* 3(4).

Ramsey, S.R. 1987. *The languages of China*. Princeton, NJ: Princeton University Press.

Ramus, F., Nespor, M., and Mehler, J. 1999. Correlates of linguistic rhythm in the speech signal. *Cognition* 73: 265–292.

Rand, D., and Sankoff, D. 1990. *GoldVarb: A variable rule application for the Macintosh*. Montreal, PQ: Centre de recherches mathématiques, Université de Montréal.

Raspberry, W. 1996, December 26. To throw in a lot of "bes," or not? *The Washington Post*. A27.

Raumolin-Brunberg, H. 1997. Incorporating sociolinguistic information into a diachronic corpus of English. In R. Hickey *et al.* (eds.), *Tracing the trail of time: Proceedings from the Second Diachronic Corpora Workshop, New College, University of Toronto, Toronto, May 1995*. Amsterdam: Rodopi. 105–119.

Rawick, George. 1972/77/79. *The American slave: A composite autobiography*. Westport, CN: Greenwood.

Reaser, J.L. 2004, October. Revisiting the Ann Arbor decision in film: Wasted decision or educational opportunity? Paper presented at the Conference on New Ways of Analyzing Variation 23, Ann Arbor, Michigan.

Reaser, J.L. 2006. The effect of dialect awareness on adolescent knowledge and attitudes. Ph.D. dissertation, Duke University.

Reaser, J.L., and Wolfram, W. 2006a. *Voices of North Carolina: Language and life from the Atlantic to the Appalachians*. Instructor's manual. Raleigh: North Carolina Language and Life Project.

Reaser, J.L., and Wolfram, W. 2006b. *Voices of North Carolina: Language and life from the Atlantic to the Appalachians: Student workbook*. Raleigh, NC: North Carolina State University.

Regan, V. 1996. Variation in French interlanguage: A longitudinal study of sociolinguistic competence. In R. Bayley and D.R. Preston (eds.), *Second language acquisition and linguistic variation*. Amsterdam: John Benjamins. 177–201.

Rehner, K., Mougeon, R., and Nadasdi. T. 2003. The learning of sociolinguistic variation by advanced French FSL leaners: The case of *nous* versus *on* in immersion French. *Studies in Second Language Acquisition* 25: 127–156.

Reiber, R., and Stewart, W. (eds.). 1990. *The language scientist as expert in the legal setting: Issues in forensic linguistics*. New York: New York Academy of Sciences.

Renzetti, C., and Lee, R. 1993. The problems of researching sensitive topics: An overview and introduction. In *Researching sensitive topics*. London: Sage Publications. 3–13.

Rich, F. 1997, January 8. The Ebonic plague. *The Wall Street Journal*.

Rickford, A.E. 1999. *I can fly: Teaching reading and narratives to African American and other ethnic minority students*. Lanham, MD: University Press of America.

Rickford, A.E., Sweetland, J., and Rickford, J.R. 2004. African American English and other vernaculars in education: A topic-coded bibliography. *Journal of English Linguistics* 32: 230–320.

Rickford, J.R. 1979. Variation in a Creole continuum: Quantitative and implicational approaches. Ph.D. dissertation, University of Pennsylvania.

Rickford, J.R. 1986a. The need for new approaches to social class analysis in linguistics. *Language and Communication* 6: 215–221.

Rickford, J.R. 1986b. Social contact and linguistic diffusion. *Language* 62: 245–290.

Rickford, J.R. 1987. *Dimensions of a creole continuum: History, texts, and linguistic analysis of Guyanese Creole*. Stanford, CA: Stanford University Press.

Rickford, J.R. 1997a. Prior creolization of African American Vernacular English? Sociohistorical and textual evidence from the 17th and 18th centuries. *Journal of Sociolinguistics* 1: 315–336.

Rickford, J.R. 1997b. Unequal partnership: Sociolinguistics and the African American speech community. *Language in Society* 26: 161–197.

Rickford, J.R. 1999. *African American Vernacular English*. Oxford: Blackwell.

Rickford, J.R. 2002. Linguistics, education, and the Ebonics firestorm. In J.E. Alatis, H.E. Hamilton, and A.-H. Tan (eds.), *Linguistics, language and the professions. Georgetown University Round Table on Languages and Linguistics 2000*. Washington, DC: Georgetown University Press. 25–45.

Rickford, J.R. 2006. Down for the count? The creole origins hypothesis of AAVE at the hands of the Ottawa circle, and their supporters. *Journal of Pidgin and Creole Languages* 21: 97–155.

Rickford, J.R., and Handler, J.S. 1994. Textual evidence on the nature of early Barbadian speech. *Journal of Pidgin and Creole Languages* 9: 221–255.

Rickford, J.R., and McNair-Knox, F. 1994. Addressee- and topic-influenced style shift: A quantitative sociolinguistic study. In D. Biber and E. Finegan (eds.), *Sociolinguistic perspectives on register*. Oxford: Oxford University Press. 235–276.

Rickford, J.R., and Rickford, A.E. 1995. Dialect readers revisited. *Linguistics and Education* 7: 107–128.

Rickford, J.R., and Rickford, R.J. 2000. *Spoken soul: The story of Black English*. New York: John Wiley.

Roach, P. 1982. On the distinction between "stress-timed" and "syllable-timed" languages. In D. Crystal (ed.), *Linguistic controversies*. London: Edward Arnold. 73–79.

Roberts, J. 2002. Child language variation. In J.K. Chambers, P. Trudgill, and N. Schilling-Estes (eds.), *The handbook of language variation and change*. Oxford: Blackwell. 333–348.

Robinson, R. 1998. *Defending the spirit: A Black life in America*. New York: Dutton.

Robinson, S., Chief Judge. 2006. Opinion: *Sanofi-Aventis v. Advancis Pharmaceutical*. United States District Court for the District of Delaware, September 26.

Robson, B. 1973. Pan-lectal grammars and adult language change. In C.-J.N. Bailey and R.W. Shuy (eds.), *New ways of analyzing variation in English*. Washington, DC: Georgetown University Press. 164–170.

Roeper, T. 2006. Nodes and features: how the multiple grammar perspective predicts stable and unstable dialects and the order of acquisition. Unpublished ms., University of Massachusetts.

Romaine, S. 1982. *Socio-historical linguistics: Its status and methodology*. Cambridge: Cambridge University Press.

Romaine, S. 1984. On the problem of syntactic variation and pragmatic meaning in sociolinguistic theory. *Folia Linguistica* 18: 409–439.

Romaine, S., and Lange, D. 1991. The use of like as a marker of reported speech and thought: A case of grammaticalization in progress. *American Speech* 66: 227–279.

Ronkin, M., and Karn, H.L. 1999. Mock Ebonics: Linguistic racism in parodies of ebonics on the internet. *Journal of Sociolinguistics* 3: 360–380.

Rose, P. 2003. *Forensic speaker identification*. London: Taylor and Francis.

Ross, J.R. 1973. A fake NP squish. In C.-J.N. Bailey and R.W. Shuy (eds.), *New ways of analyzing variation in English*. Washington, DC: Georgetown University Press. 96–140.

Rowan, C. 1996, December 25. "Ebonics" a false promise of self-esteem. *Chicago Sun-Times*.

Sag, I. 1973. On the state of progress on progressives and statives. In C.-J.N. Bailey and R.W. Shuy (eds.), *New ways of analyzing variation in English*. Washington, DC: Georgetown University Press. 83–96.

Sanchez, F. 1986. *Of*-reduction in black English: A quantitative study. In D. Sankoff (ed.), *Diversity and diachrony*. Amsterdam: John Benjamins. 59–72.

Sanchez, S. 1987. *Under a soprano sky*. Trenton, NJ: Africa World Press.

Sankoff, D. (ed.). 1986. *Diversity and diachrony*. Amsterdam: John Benjamins.

Sankoff, D. 1988a. Sociolinguistics and syntactic variation. In F.J. Newmeyer (ed.), *Linguistics: The Cambridge Survey, vol. 4, Language: The Socio-cultural context*. Cambridge: Cambridge University Press. 140–161.

Sankoff, D. 1988b. Variable rules. In U. Ammon, N. Dittmar, and K.J. Mattheier (eds.), *Sociolinguistics: An international handbook of the science of language and society, vol. 2*. Berlin: Mouton de Gruyter. 984–997.

Sankoff, D., and Cedergren, H. (eds.). 1981. *Variation omnibus*. Edmonton: Linguistic Research Inc.

Sankoff, D., and Labov, W. 1979. On the uses of variable rules. *Language in Society* 8: 189–222.

Sankoff, D., and Rousseau, P. 1979. Categorical contexts and variable rules. In S. Jacobson (ed.), *Papers from the Scandinavian Symposium on Syntactic Variation, Stockholm, May 18–19*. Stockholm: Almqvist and Wiksell. 7–22.

Sankoff, G. 1973. Above and beyond phonology in variable rules. In C.-J.N. Bailey and R.W. Shuy (eds.), *New ways of analyzing variation in English*. Washington, DC: Georgetown University Press. 44–61.

Sankoff, G. 1974. A quantitative paradigm for the study of communicative competence. In R. Bauman and J. Sherzer (eds.), *Explorations in the ethnography of speaking*. Cambridge: Cambridge University Press. 18–49.

Sankoff, G. 1980. A quantitative paradigm for the study of communicative competence. In G. Sankoff (ed.), *The social life of language*. Philadelphia: University of Pennsylvania Press. 47–79.

Santa Ana, O. 1992. Chicano English evidence for the exponential hypothesis: A variable rule pervades lexical phonology. *Language Variation and Change* 4: 275–289.

Sapir, E. 1921. *Language, an introduction to the study of speech*. New York: Harcourt, Brace, and Company.

Saussure, F. de 1916 [1959]. *Cours de linguistique générale*, C. Bally and A. Sechehaye (eds.), trans., with an introduction and notes, by W. Baskin. New York: Philosophical Library.

Saussure, F. 1916 [1972]. *Cours de linguistique générale*. Paris: Payot.

Scarborough, W. 1966. *The Overseer: Plantation management in the old south*. Baton Rouge: Louisiana State University Press.

Schembri, A., Johnston, T., and Goswell, D. 2006. NAME dropping: Location variation in Australian Sign Language. In C. Lucas (ed.), *Multilingualism and sign languages: From the Great Plains to Australia*. Sociolinguistics in Deaf Communities, vol. 12. Washington, DC: Gallaudet University Press. 121–156.

Scherre, M.M. Pereira, and Naro, A. 1991. Marking in discourse: "Birds of a feather." *Language Variation and Change* 3: 23–32.

Schiffrin, D. 1981. Tense variation in narrative. *Language* 57: 45–62.

Schiller, N.O., and Köster, O. 1998. The ability of expert witnesses to identify voices: A comparison between trained and untrained listeners. *Forensic Linguistics* 5: 1–9.

Schilling-Estes, N. 1998. Investigating "self-conscious" speech: The performance register in Ocracoke English. *Language in Society* 27: 53–83.

Schilling-Estes, N. 2001. Variation and discourse: The sociolinguistic interview as a situated speech event. Paper presented at the Conference on New Ways of Analyzing Variation 30, Raleigh, North Carolina, October.

Schilling-Estes, N. 2002. On the nature of insular and post-insular dialects: Innovation, variation, and differentiation. *Journal of Sociolinguistics* 6: 64–85.

Schneider, E.W. 1989. *American earlier Black English*. Tuscaloosa: University of Alabama Press.

Schneider, E.W. 2002. Investigating variation and change in written documents. In J.K. Chambers, P. Trudgill, and N. Schilling-Estes (eds.), *The handbook of language variation and change*. Oxford: Blackwell. 67–89.

Schneider, E.W., and Montgomery, M. 2001. On the trail of early nonstandard grammar: an electronic corpus of southern U.S. antebellum overseers' letters. *American Speech* 79: 388–409.

Schraeder, T., Quinn, M., Stockman, I., and Miller, J. 1999. Authentic assessment as an approach to preschool speech-language screening. *American Journal of Speech-Language Pathology* 8(3): 95–200.

Schumann, J.H. 1978. *The pidginization process: A model for second language acquisition*. Rowley, MA: Newbury House.

Scott, D. 1973. *Uncle time*. Pittsburgh, PA: University of Pittsburgh.

Scott, J. 1998. The serious side of ebonics humor. *Journal of English Linguistics* 26: 137–155.

Searle, J. 1984. *Minds, brains, and science*. Cambridge, MA: Harvard University Press.

Selinker, L. 1972. Interlanguage. *International Review of Applied Linguistics* 10: 219–231.

Selinker, L., and Douglas, D. 1985. Wrestling with "context" in interlanguage theory. *Applied Linguistics* 6: 67–92.

Sells, P., Rickford, J.R., and Wasow, T. 1996. An optimality approach to variation in negative inversion in AAVE. *Natural Language and Linguistic Theory* 14: 591–627.

Seltung, E. 2003. Treppenkonturen im Dresdenrrischen. *Zeitschrift für Germanistische Linguistik* 31: 1–43.

Senate mulls Black English as teaching aid. 1997, January 23. *Yahoo News Reuters Limited*.

SEP handbook, n.d. [ca. 1984]. *Proficiency in Standard English for Speakers of Black language*.

Seymour, H.L., Roeper, T.W., de Villiers, J. 2003. *Diagnostic evaluation of language variation test (DELV)*. San Antonio, TX: Psychological Corporation.

Shanker, A. 1997, January 5. Where we stand: Ebonics. [American Federation of Teachers advertisement.] *The New York Times*.

Shankweiler, D. 1989. How problems of comprehension are related to difficulties in decoding. In D. Shankweiler and I. Liberman (eds.), *Phonology and reading disability: Solving the reading puzzle*. Ann Arbor: University of Michigan Press.

Shrivastav, R., and Sapienza, C. 2003. Objective measures of breathy voice quality obtained using an auditory model. *Journal of the Acoustical Society of America* 114: 2217–2224.

Shuy, R.W. 1990. A brief history of American sociolinguistics, 1949–1989. In F.P. Dinneen and E.F.K. Koerner (eds.), *North American contributions to the history of linguistics*. Amsterdam: Benjamins. 183–209.

Shuy, R.W. 1993. *Language crimes: The use and abuse of language evidence in the courtroom*. Oxford: Blackwell.

Shuy, R.W. 1998. *The language of confession, interrogation, and deception*. Thousand Oaks, CA: Sage.

Shuy, R.W. 2002. *Linguistic battles in trademark disputes*. Basingstoke: Palgrave MacMillan.

Shuy, R.W. 2006. *Linguistics in the courtroom: A practical guide*. Oxford: Oxford University Press.

Shuy, R.W., Wolfram, W., and Riley, W.K. 1968a. *A study of social dialects in Detroit*. Washington, DC: Educational Resources Information Center.

Shuy, R.W., Wolfram, W., and Riley, W.K. 1968b. *Field techniques in an urban language study.* Washington, DC: Center for Applied Linguistics.

Silva, G. de O.e. 1981. Perspective sociolinguistique de la forme *você* a Rio de Janeiro. In D. Sankoff and H. Cedergren (eds.), *Variation omnibus.* Edmonton: Linguistic Research. 481–488.

Simpkins, G.A., Holt, G., and Simpkins, C. 1977. *Bridge: A cross-cultural reading program.* Boston, MA: Houghton-Mifflin.

Singham, M. 2003. The achievement gap: Myths and reality. *Phi Delta Kappan* 84: 586–591.

Singler, J. 1988. The place of variation in the formal expression of inflectional processes: Evidence from Kru Pidgin English. In K. Ferrara, B. Brown, K. Walters, and J. Baugh (eds.), *Linguistic change and contact: Proceedings of the Sixteenth Annual Conference on New Ways of Analyzing Variation.* Austin: Department of Linguistics, University of Texas. 345–353.

Singler, J.V. 1991. Liberian Settler English and the Ex-Slave recordings: A comparative study. In G. Bailey, N. Maynor, and P. Cukor-Avila (eds.), *The emergence of Black English: Text and commentary.* John Benjamins: Amsterdam. 249–274.

Slaate, H. 1981. *Modern science and the human condition.* Washington, DC: University Press of America.

Sledd, J. 1969. Bidialectalism: The linguistics of white supremacy. *English Journal* 58: 1307–1329.

Smalls, D. 2004. Linguistic profiling and the law. *Stanford Law and Policy Review* 15(2): 579–604.

Smith, W. 1994. Computers, statistics, and disputed authorship. In J. Gibbons (ed.), *Language and the law.* London: Longman. 374–413.

Smitherman, G. (ed.). 1981. *Black English and the education of black children and youth.* Detroit: Center for Black Studies, Wayne State University.

Smitherman, G. 1986. *Talkin and tesifyin: The language of Black America.* Detroit: Wayne State University.

Smitherman, G. 1997/1986. Black language and the education of Black children: One mo once. *Black Scholar* 27(1): 28–35.

Smitherman, G. 2000. *Talkin that talk: Language, culture, and education in African America.* New York: Routledge.

Sneider, D. 1996, December 23. Black English in Oakland Schools: Slang or language. *Christian Science Monitor* 1.

Solan, L. 1993. *The language of judges.* Chicago: University of Chicago Press.

Solan, L., and Tiersma, P.M. 2005. *Speaking of crime: The language of criminal justice.* Chicago: University of Chicago Press.

Squires, G.D. 2006. Linguistic profiling: A continuing tradition of discrimination in the home insurance industry? *Urban Affairs Review* 41(3): 400–415.

Steele, C. 1992, April. Race and the schooling of Black Americans. *Atlantic Monthly.*

Stephenson, E.A. 1967. On the interpretation of occasional spellings. *Publication of the American Dialect Society* 48: 33–50.

Steptoe, J. 1997. (compiler and illustrator) 1997. *In Daddy's arms I am tall: African Americans celebrating fathers.* New York: Lee and Low Books.

Stewart, W.A. 1968. Continuity and change in American Negro dialects. *Florida Foreign Language Reporter* 6: 2: 3–4, 14–16, 18.

Stockman, I. 1986a. The development of linguistic norms for non-mainstream populations. *ASHA Reports* 16: 101–110.

Stockman, I. 1986b. Language acquisition in culturally diverse populations: The Black child as a case study. In O. Taylor (ed.), *Nature of communication disorders in culturally and linguistically diverse populations.* San Diego, CA: College Hill Press. 117–155.

Stockman, I. 1991. Lexical biases in dynamic and static locative expressions. Boston University Conference on Language Development, Boston, Massachusetts, October.

Stockman, I. 1992. Another look at semantic relational categories and language impairment. *Journal of Communication Disorders* 25: 175–199.

Stockman, I. 1996a. The promises and pitfalls of language sample analysis as an assessment tool for linguistic minority children. *Language, Speech, and Hearing Services in Schools* 27: 355–366.

Stockman, I. 1996b. Phonological development in African American children. In A. Kamhi, K. Pollock, and J. Harris (eds.), *Communication development and disorders in African American children: Research, assessment and intervention*. Baltimore, MD: Brookes Publishers. 117–153.

Stockman, I. 1999. Semantic development of African American children. In O. Taylor and L. Leonard (eds.), *Language acquisition across North America: Cross-language and cross-linguistic perspectives*. San Diego: Singular Publishing Group. 61–107.

Stockman, I. 2006a. Alveolar bias in the final consonant deletion patterns of African American children. *Language, Speech, and Hearing Services in Schools* 27: 85–95.

Stockman, I. 2006b. Evidence for a minimal competence core of consonant sounds in the speech of African American children: A preliminary study. *Journal of Clinical Linguistics and Phonetics* 20(10): 1–28.

Stockman, I., Guillory, B., Boult, J., and Siebert, M. (Forthcoming). Cross-validation of a minimal competence core for assessing young African American children.

Stockman, I., and Vaughn-Cooke, F. 1982a. A re-examination of research on the language of Black children: The need for a new framework. *Journal of Education* 164: 157–172.

Stockman, I., and Vaughn-Cooke, A.F. (1982b). Semantic categories in the language of working class Black children. In C. Johnson and C. Thew (eds.), *The Proceedings of the Second International Congress for the Study of Child Language*. Washington, DC: University Press of America. 312–327.

Stockman, I., and Vaughn-Cooke, F. 1986. Implications of semantic category research for the language assessment of nonstandard speakers. *Topics in Language and Language Disorders* 6: 15–25.

Stockman, I., and Vaughn-Cooke, F. 1989. Addressing new questions about Black children's language. In R. Fasold and D. Schriffrin (eds.), *Language change and variation*. Amsterdam: John Benjamins. 275–300.

Stockman, I., and Vaughn-Cooke, F. 1992. Lexical elaboration of children's locative action expressions. *Child Development* 63: 1104–1125.

Stokoe, W.C. 1960. *Sign language structure: An outline of visual communication systems of the American Deaf*. Studies in Linguistics: Occasional Paper 8. Buffalo, NY: Linguistics Department, University of Buffalo.

Stokoe, W.C., Casterline, D.C., and Croneberg, C.G. 1965. *A dictionary of American Sign Language on linguistic principles*. Silver Spring, MD: Linstok Press.

Strand, E.A. 1999. Uncovering the role of gender stereotypes in speech perception. *Journal of Language and Social Psychology* 18: 86–99.

Stromswold, K.J. 1990. *Learnability and the acquisition of auxiliaries*. Ph.D. dissertation, Massachusetts Institute of Technology.

Stuart-Smith, J. 1999. Glasgow. In P. Foulkes and G. Docherty (eds.), *Urban voices: Variation and change in British accents*. London: Arnold. 203–222.

Sturtevant, E. 1947. *An introduction to linguistic science*. New Haven: Yale University Press.

Stygall, G. 1994. *Trial language: Differential discourse processing and discursive formation*. Amsterdam: John Benjamins.

Suñer, M. 1988. The role of agreement in clitic doubled constructions. *Natural Language and Linguistic Theory* 6: 391–434.

Supple, M. 1993. Sociolinguistics: The clinical perspective. In M. Leahy and J.L. Kallen (eds.), *International perspectives in speech and language pathology*. Dublin: Trinity College. 24–29.

Sweetland, J. 2006. *Teaching writing in the African American classroom: A sociolinguistic approach*. Ph.D. dissertation, Stanford University.

Syrdal, A.K. 1996. Acoustic variability in spontaneous conversational speech of American English talkers. Paper presented at the International Conference on Spoken Language Processing.

Tagliamonte, S. 1998. *Was/were* variation across the generations: View from the city of York. *Language Variation and Change* 10: 153–191.

Tagliamonte, S. 1999. Back to the roots: what British dialects reveal about North American English. Address at Methods in Dialectology X, St. John's, Newfoundland.

Tagliamonte, S. 2002. Comparative sociolinguistics. In J.K. Chambers, P. Trudgill, and N. Schilling-Estes (eds.), *The handbook of language variation and change*. Oxford: Blackwell. 729–762.

Tagliamonte, S. 2005. *So* who? *Like* how? *Just* what? Discourse markers in the conversations of young Canadians. *Journal of Pragmatics*. (Special issue, guest eds. A.-B. Stenström and K. Aijmer) 37(11): 1896–1915.

Tagliamonte, S. 2006. *Analysing sociolinguistic variation*. Cambridge: Cambridge University Press.

Tagliamonte, S., and D'Arcy, A. 2004. *He's like; She's like*: The quotative system in Canadian youth. *Journal of Sociolinguistics* 8: 493–514.

Tagliamonte, S., and D'Arcy, A. 2007. Frequency and variation in the community grammar: Tracking a new change through the generations. *Language Variation and Change* 19(2): 1–19.

Tagliamonte, S., and Hudson, R. 1999. Be like et al. beyond America: The quotative system in British and Canadian youth. *Journal of Sociolinguistics* 3: 147–172.

Tagliamonte, S., and Smith, J. 1997. Analogical levelling in Samaná English: The case of *was* and *were*. *Journal of English Linguistics* 27: 8–26.

Tagliamonte, S., and Smith, J. 1998. "We *were* all thegither . . . I think we *was* all thegither": *was* regularization in Buckie English. *World Englishes* 17: 105–126.

Tagliamonte, S., and Smith, J. 2000. Old *was*, new ecology: Viewing English through the sociolinguistic filter. In S. Poplack (ed.), *The English history of African-American English*. Oxford: Blackwell. 141–171.

Tagliamonte, S., and Smith, J. 2002. "Either it's not or it isn't": neg/aux contraction in British dialects. *English World-Wide* 23: 251–281.

Tannen, D. 1986. Introducing constructed dialogue in Greek and American conversational and literary narrative. In F. Coulmas (ed.), *Introducing constructed Dialogue in Greek and American conversational and literary narrative*: Direct and indirect speech. Berlin: Mouton de Gruyter. 311–332.

Tarone, E. 1973. Aspects of intonation in Black English. *American Speech* 48: 29–36.

Tarone, E. 1979. Interlanguage as chameleon. *Language Learning* 29: 181–191.

Tarone, E. 1985. Variability in interlanguage use: A study of style-shifting in morphology and syntax. *Language Learning* 35: 373–404.

Tarone, E., and Swain, M. 1995. A sociolinguistic perspective on second language use in immersion classrooms. *Modern Language Journal* 79: 166–178.

Taylor, H.U. 1990. *Standard English, Black English, and bidialectalism: A controversy*. New York: Peter Lang.

Taylor, O. 1969. Social and political involvement of the American Speech and Hearing Association. *ASHA* 11: 216–218.

Thomas, E.R. 2000. Spectral differences in /ai/ offsets conditioned by voicing of the following consonant. *Journal of Phonetics* 28: 1–25.

Thomas, E.R. 2001. *An acoustic analysis of vowel variation in New World English*. Publication of the American Dialect Society 85. Durham, NC: Duke University Press.

Thomas, M. 2002. The specious battle between contrastive analysis and creative construction. Paper presented at the Annual Meeting of the North American Association for the History of the Language Sciences, San Francisco, January 5.

Thomas E.R. 2003. Secrets revealed by Southern vowel shifting. *American Speech* 78: 150–170.

Thomas, E.R., and Bailey, G. 1992. A case of competing mergers and their resolution. *The SECOL Review* 16: 179–200.

Thomas, E.R., and Carter, P.M. 2006. Prosodic rhythm and African American English. *English World-Wide* 27: 331–355.

Thomas, E.R., and Reaser, J. 2004. Delimiting perceptual cues used for the ethnic labeling of African American and European American voices. *Journal of Sociolinguistics* 8: 54–87.

Tiersma, P.M. 1993. The judge as linguist. *Loyola of Los Angeles Law Review* 27(1): 269–83.

Tiersma, P.M. 1999. *Legal language*. Chicago and London: University of Chicago Press.

Tiersma, P.M. 2006. The language of jury instructions. www.languageandlaw.org/ JURYINST.HTM

Titunik, I.R. 1984. Bakhtin &/or Voloshinov &/or Medvedev: Dialogue &/or doubletalk? In B.A. Stolz, I.R. Titunik, and L. Dolezel (eds.), *Language and literary theory*. Ann Arbor: University of Michigan Press. 535–564.

Titunik, I.R. 1986. The Baxtin Problem: Concerning Katerina Clark and Michael Holquist's *Mikhail Bakhtin*. *Slavic and East European Journal* 30: 91–95.

Trudgill, P. 1974. *The social differentiation of English in Norwich*. Cambridge: Cambridge University Press.

Tsitsipis, L.D. 2004. A sociolinguistic application of Bakhtin's authoritative and internally persuasive discourse. *Journal of Sociolinguistics* 8: 569–594.

Tucker, W. 1994. *The science and politics of racial research*. Chicago: University of Illinois Press.

Udofot, I. 2003. Stress and rhythm in the Nigerian accent of English: A preliminary investigation. *English World-Wide* 24: 201–220.

Uritescu, D., Mougeon, R., Rehner, K., and Nadasdi, T. 2004. Acquisition of the internal and external constraints of variable schwa deletion by French Immersion Students. *IRAL* 42: 349–364.

Vanags, T.S., Carroll, M., and Perfect, T.J. 2005. Verbal overshadowing: A sound theory in voice recognition? *Applied Cognitive Psychology* 19: 1127–1144.

Van de Velde, H., and van Hout, R. (eds.). 2001. *r-atics: Sociolinguistic, phonetic and phonological characteristics of /r/*. Brussels: Institut des Langues Vivantes et de Phonétique.

Van Herk, G. 2002. A message from the past: past temporal reference in early African American letters. Ph.D. dissertation, University of Ottawa.

Van Herk, G., and Poplack, S. 2003. Rewriting the past: bare verbs in the Ottawa Repository of Early African American Correspondence. *Journal of Pidgin and Creole Languages* 16: 231–64.

Van Herk, G., and Walker, J.A, 2005. *s* marks the spot? Regional variation and early African American correspondence. *Language Variation and Change* 17: 113–131.

van Keulen, J.E., Weddington, G.T., and Debose, C.E. 1998. *Speech, language learning and the African American child*. Boston: Allyn and Bacon.

Veatch, T.C. 1991. English vowels: Their surface phonology and phonetic implementation in vernacular dialects. Ph.D. dissertation, University of Pennsylvania.

Voloshinov, V.N. 1929 [1973]. *Marxism and the philosophy of language* (trans. L. Matejka and I.R. Titunik). New York and London: Seminar Press.

Walker, A.G. 1990. Language at work in the law: The customs, conventions, and appellate consequences of court reporting. In J.N. Levi and A.G. Walker (eds.), *Language in the judicial process*. Law, Society, and Policy, vol. 5. New York: Plenum. 203–245.

Walter, B. 1988. *The jury summation as speech genre: An ethnographic study of what it means to those who use it.* Amsterdam: John Benjamins.

Walker, J. 1791. *Critical pronouncing dictionary and expository of the English language to which are prefixed, principles of English pronunciation.* London: Robinson.

Walton, J., and Orlikoff, R. 1994. Speaker raace identification from acoustic cues in the vocal signal. *Journal of Speech and Hearing Research* 37: 738–745.

Wardhaugh, R. 1970. The contrastive analysis hypothesis. *TESOL Quarterly* 4: 123–130.

Warren, P. 2005. Patterns of late rising in New Zealand English: Intonational variation or intonation change? *Language Variation and Change* 17: 209–230.

Webster, Y.O. 1992. *The racialization of America.* New York: St. Martin's Press.

Weiner, J., and Labov, W. 1982. Constraints on the agentless passive. *Journal of Linguistics* 19: 29–58.

Weinreich, U., Labov, W., and Herzog, M.I. 1968. Empirical foundations for a theory of language change. In W. Lehmann and Y. Malkiel (eds.), *Directions for historical linguistics.* Austin: University of Texas Press. 95–195.

Weiss, R. 1997, January 6. Among linguists, Black English gets respect. *The Washington Post.* A10.

Wells, J. 1982. *Accents of English.* Cambridge: Cambridge University Press.

Wenk, B.J., and Wiolland, F. 1982. Is French really syllable-timed? *Journal of Phonetics* 10: 193–216.

Wheeler, R., and Swords, R. 2006. *Code-switching: Teaching Standard English in urban classrooms.* Urbana, IL: National Council of Teachers of English.

White, J. 2006. Negative inversion and negative movement in African American English and Southern white English: an existential analysis. M.A. thesis, University of Texas at Austin.

Whiteman, M.F. (ed.). 1980. *Reactions to Ann Arbor: Vernacular Black English and education.* Washington, DC: Center for Applied Linguistics.

Wiehl, L. 2002. "Sounding Black" in the courtroom: Court sanctioned racial stereotyping. *Harvard Blackletter Law Journal* 18: 185–210.

Wiley, B.I. 1980. *Slaves no more: Letters from Liberia, 1833–1869.* Lexington: University Press of Kentucky.

Will, G. 1997, January 2. An example of problem solving. *The San Diego Union-Tribune.* B12.

Williams, P. 1996, December 29. The hidden meaning of Black English. *The New York Times,* sec. 4: 9.

Williams, R. 1975. *Ebonics: The language of Black folk.* St. Louis: Center for Black Studies.

Williams, R. 1997. The Ebonics controversy. *Journal of Black Psychology* 23: 208–214.

Willis, E. 2003. The intonational system of Dominican Spanish: Findings and analysis. Ph.D. dissertation, University of Illinois at Urbana-Champaign.

Wilson, J., and Henry, A. 1998. Parameter setting in a socially realistic linguistics. *Language in Society* 27: 1–21.

Wolfram, W. 1969. *A sociolinguistic study of Detroit Negro speech.* Washington, DC: Center for Applied Linguistics.

Wolfram, W. 1970. Sociolinguistic premises and the nature of nonstandard dialects. *The Speech Teacher* September: 176–186.

Wolfram, W. 1973. On what basis variable rules? In C.-J.N. Bailey and R.W. Shuy (eds.), *New Ways of Analyzing Variation in English.* Washington, DC: Georgetown University Press. 1–12.

Wolfram, W. 1974. *Sociolinguistic aspects of assimilation: Puerto Rican English in New York City.* Washington, DC: Center for Applied Linguistics.

Wolfram, W. 1983. Test interpretation and sociolinguistic differences. *Topics in Language Disorders* 3: 21–24.

Wolfram, W. 1985. Variability in tense marking: A case for the obvious. *Language Learning* 35: 229–253.

Wolfram, W. 1989. Structural variability in phonological development: Final nusals in vernacular Black English. In R.W. Fasold and D. Schiffrin (eds.), *Language change and variation*. Amsterdam: John Benjamins. 301–332.

Wolfram, W. 1991. The linguistic variable: Fact and fantasy. *American Speech* 66: 22–32.

Wolfram, W. 1993. Ethical considerations in language awareness programs. *Issues in Applied Linguistics* 4: 225–255.

Wolfram, W. 1997, January 11. [Challenge to Bill Cosby.] Unpublished letter to *The Wall Street Journal*.

Wolfram, W. 2003. Reexamining the development of African American English: Evidence from isolated communities. *Language* 79: 282–316.

Wolfram, W. 2005a. *African American English*. In M.J. Ball, *Clinical sociolinguistics*. Malden, MA: Blackwell. 87–100.

Wolfram, W. 2005b. Sociolinguistics and speech and language pathology. In U. Ammon, N. Dittmar, K.J. Mattheier, and P. Trudgill (eds.), *Sociolinguistics: An international handbook of the science of language and society*. Berlin: Walter de Gruyter. 1–8.

Wolfram, W., and Adger, C.T. 1993. *Handbook on language differences and speech and language pathology: Baltimore City Public Schools*. Baltimore, MA: Division of Instruction, Department of Support and Special Pupil Services, Baltimore City Public Schools.

Wolfram, W., Adger, C.T., and Christian, D. 1999. *Dialects in schools and communities*. Mahwah, NJ: Lawrence Erlbaum.

Wolfram, W., Carter, P., and Moriello, B. 2004. The emergence of Hispanic English in the American South. *Journal of Sociolinguistics* 8: 339–358.

Wolfram, W., and Christian, D. 1976, *Appalachian speech*. Arlington: Center for Applied Linguistics.

Wolfram, W., and Christian, D. 1989. *Dialects and education: Issues and answers*. Englewood Cliffs, NJ: Prentice-Hall.

Wolfram, W., and Dannenberg, C.J. 1999. Dialect identity in a tri-ethnic context: The case of Lumbee American Indian English. *English World-Wide* 20: 179–216.

Wolfram, W., Dannenberg, C., Knick, S., and Oxendine, L. 2002. *Fine in the World: Lumbee Language in time and place*. Raleigh: Humanities Extension/ Publications, North Carolina State University.

Wolfram, W., and Fasold, R.W. 1969. Toward reading materials for speakers of Black English: Three linguistically appropriate passages. In J.C. Baratz and R.W. Shuy (eds.), *Teaching Black children to read*. Washington, DC: Center for Applied Linguistics. 41–86.

Wolfram, W., and Fasold, R.W. 1974a. Field methods in the study of social dialects. In W. Wolfram and R.W. Fasold, *The study of social dialects in American English*. Englewood Cliffs, NJ: Prentice-Hall. 36–72.

Wolfram, W., and Fasold, R.W. 1974b. *The study of social dialects in American English*. Englewood Cliffs, NJ: Prentice-Hall.

Wolfram, W. and Hatfield, D. 1984. *Tense marking in second language learning: Patterns of spoken and written English in a Vietnamese community*. Washington, DC: Center for Applied Linguistics.

Wolfram, W., Hazen, K., and Ruff Tamburro, J. 1997. Isolation within isolation: A solitary century of African-American Vernacular English. *Journal of Sociolinguistics* 1: 7–38.

Wolfram, W., Hazen, K., and Schilling-Estes, N. 1999. *Dialect change and maintenance on the Outer Banks*. Publication of the American Dialect Society 81. Tuscaloosa: University of Alabama Press.

Wolfram, W., Reaser, J., and Adger, C.T. 2005. Video and curriculum resources for English and social studies. Presentation at the Southeast Conference on Linguistics, Raleigh, NC.

Wolfram, W., and Schilling-Estes, N. 1996a. Dialect change and maintenance in a post-insular island community. In E.W. Schneider (ed.), *Varieties of English around the world: Focus on the USA*. Amsterdam: John Benjamins. 103–148.

Wolfram, W., and Schilling-Estes, N. 1996b. *Linguistics and the Human Capital Initiative*. A Report to the National Science Foundation. Text available on the web at www.cal.org/pubs/LHCI.html.

Wolfram, W., and Schilling-Estes, N. 1997. *Hoi Toide on the Outer Banks: The story of the Ocracoke Brogue*. Chapel Hill: University of North Carolina Press

Wolfram, W., and Schilling-Estes, N. 2004. Remnant dialects in the coastal United States. In R. Hickey (ed.), *Legacies of colonial English: Studies in transported dialects*. Cambridge: Cambridge University Press. 172–202.

Wolfram, W., and Thomas, E.R. 2002. *The development of African American English*. Oxford: Blackwell.

Wolfram, W., and Wolfram, T.D. 1977. How come you asked how come? In R.W. Fasold and R.W. Shuy (eds.), *Studies in language variation*. Washington, DC: Georgetown University Press. 237–254.

Wolfson, N. 1976. Speech events and natural speech: Some implications for sociolinguistic methodology. *Language in Society* 5: 189–209.

Wolfson, N. 1979. The conversational historical present alternation. *Language* 55: 168–182.

Wolfson, N. 1981. Tense-switching in narrative. *Language and Style* 14(3): 226–231.

Woodward, J.C. 1973. Implicational lects on the Deaf diglossic continuum. Ph.D. dissertation, Georgetown University.

Woodward, J.C., and DeSantis, S. 1977. Two to one it happens: Dynamic phonology in two sign languages. *Sign Language Studies* 17: 329–346.

Woodward, J.C., Erting, C., and Oliver, S. 1976. Facing and hand(l)ing variation in American Sign Language. *Sign Language Studies* 10: 43–52.

Wright, L.C. 2001. Third person singular present tense *-s*, *-th*, and zero. *American Speech* 76: 236–258.

Wyatt, T.A. 1996. Acquisition of the African American English copula. In A.G. Kamhi, K.E. Pollock, and J.L. Harris (eds.), *Communication development and disorders in African American children*. Baltimore: Paul H. Brookes Publishing. 95–115.

Yip, M. 1988. The obligatory contour principle and phonological rules: A loss of identity. *Linguistic Inquiry* 19: 65–100.

Young, B.J. 1991. Fannie Lou Hamer: This little light of mine . . . . In D. Abbott (ed.), *Mississippi writers: Reflections of childhood and youth: vol. IV. Drama*. Jackson: University of Mississippi Press. 516–530.

Young, R.F. 1991. *Variation in interlanguage morphology*. New York: Peter Lang.

Young, R.F., and Bayley, R. 1996. VARBRUL analysis for second language acquisition research. In R. Bayley and D.R. Preston (eds.), *Second language acquisition and linguistic variation*. Amsterdam: John Benjamins. 253–306.

Zentella, A.C. 1997. *Growing up bilingual: Puerto Rican children in New York*. Oxford: Blackwell.

Zhang, Q. 2001. Changing economy, changing markets: A sociolinguistic study of Chinese yuppies. Ph.D. dissertation, Stanford University.

Zilles, A.M.S. (ed.). 2005. *Estudos de variação lingüística no Brasil e no Cone Sul*. Porto Alegre: Editora UFRGS.

Zubritskaya, K. 1997. Mechanism of sound change in Optimality Theory. *Language Variation and Change* 9: 121–148.

Index

Abdulkarim, L. 40, 41, 42
Abu-Jamal, M. 257
Academic English Mastery Program, Los Angeles 281
accountability 76, 191, 192–194
Adamson, H. D. 86, 134, 142, 144
Adank, P. 221
Adger, C. T. 26, 237–246, 253
African American children
  communicative skills when entering school 312
  developmental norms 309
  differences from Standard English 314
  language acquisition 297
  language development 315–316
  speech therapy for 298
  study of language development 305–306
    data analysis 307, 312, 313–315
    external social-political factors 307–308
    funding by NIE 308, 312–313
    internal social-political factors 309–312
    methodology 306–307
    objections to 313
    research goals 306
    social-political perspective on 307
  talk about spatial location 315
African American Vernacular English 79–80, 82, 87, 92, 272, 343; *see also* Ebonics
  child language development 33–34, 37, 39, 40, 42, 43
  copula and auxiliary *be* 38, 39, 41, 42, 43, 75–76
  debate about origins of 80, 88, 298
  expletives in negative concord constructions 37
  historical sources of information on 111, 113
  intonation, tone and tone-accent 225
  negative attitudes toward 314, 316
  negative inversion 25–26, 36, 37
  perception of inferiority of 297, 298, 314
  reading and writing proficiency 278, 281, 282
  social-political perspective on a study of 305–315
  systematic and rule-governed nature of 241
  third person singular -*s* 138

value of in narrative texts 284
voice quality features 228
vowel configurations 221
wh-questions 29, 30, 32
yes-no questions 28, 29, 32
Afro-Nova Scotian communities 128, 129
American Appalachian English 36, 86
American English: *see* African American Vernacular English, American Appalachian English, American Indian English, Okracoke English
American Federation of Teachers 269
American Indian English 36
American School for the Deaf 146
American Sign Language 133, 146
  constraints 151, 153
  grammatical functions and variation 155, 156
  phonological variation in 150, 155, 158
  variation in 152–158
American Speech-Language-Hearing Association 242, 243, 272
Anastasiow, N. 310
Angelou, M. 269
Ann Arbor, MI court case 83, 188, 241, 242, 254, 308, 311, 337
anthropology, linguistic 88
Anttila, A. 21, 22, 83
Ariel, M. 87
Ash, S. 294, 325–326, 327
audience 105, 106, 229
Audience Design Framework 105, 106
Auer, P. 225
Auger, J. 143
Australian Sign Language 158
authorship identification 329–335
  inductive methodologies 332, 333
  methodologies 331
  Principal Component Analysis 332
  statistical methodologies 331

Bahan, B. 146
Bailey, C.-J.N. 84
Bailey, G. 123, 176
Baker, K. 332

393